Tourist Guide

MICHELIN®

French Alps

Key

	Sight	Seaside Resort	Winter Sports Resort	Spa
Worth a journey	★★★	☆☆☆	�֎�֎�֎	⚓⚓⚓
Worth a detour	★★	☆☆	�֎�֎	⚓⚓
Interesting	★	☆	✖	⚓

Tourism

⊘ Admission Times and Charges listed at the end of the guide

⊙━▷ Sightseeing route with departure point indicated

🏛⚜🏛⚜ Ecclesiastical building

✡ ◻ Synagogue – Mosque

⌂ Building (with main entrance)

■ Statue, small building

† Wayside cross

◎ Fountain

●━●━● Fortified walls – Tower – Town gate

►► Visit if time permits

AZ B Map co-ordinates locating sights

🛈 Tourist information

✕ ⁘ Castle, historic house – Ruins

∪ ✿ Dam – Factory or power station

☆ ∩ Fort – Cave

🌱 Prehistoric site

▼ Ⓦ Viewing table – View

▲ Miscellaneous sight

Recreation

🏇 Racecourse

⛸ Skating rink

≋ 🏊 Outdoor or indoor swimming pool

⛵ Marina, moorings

⌂ Mountain refuge hut

□━■━■━□ Overhead cable-car

🚂 Tourist or steam railway

🏃 Beginning of waymarked footpath

◆ Outdoor leisure park/centre

🎠 Theme/Amusement park

🐃 Wildlife/Safari park, zoo

✿ Gardens, park, arboretum

🐦 Aviary, bird sanctuary

Additional symbols

═══ ══ Motorway (unclassified)

❶ ❶ Junction: complete, limited

▭▭ Pedestrian zone

ɪ═════ɪ Unsuitable for traffic, street subject to restrictions

▭▭▭ ---- Steps – Footpath

🚆 🚌 Railway – Coach station

□++++++□ Funicular – Rack-railway

━━● Tram – Metro station

Bert (R.)... Main shopping street

✉ ◉ Post office – Telephone centre

⊠ Covered market

⚕ ⚔ Police station (Gendarmerie) – Barracks

△ Swing bridge

∪ ✕ Quarry – Mine

Ⓑ Ⓕ Ferry (river and lake crossings)

🚢 Ferry services: Passengers and cars

🚤 Foot passengers only

③ Access route number common to MICHELIN maps and town plans

Abbreviations

A Agricultural office (Chambre d'agriculture)

C Chamber of commerce (Chambre de commerce)

H Town hall (Hôtel de ville)

J Law courts (Palais de justice)

M Museum (Musée)

P Local authority offices (Préfecture, sous-préfecture)

POL. Police station (Police)

T Theatre (Théâtre)

U University (Université)

Contents

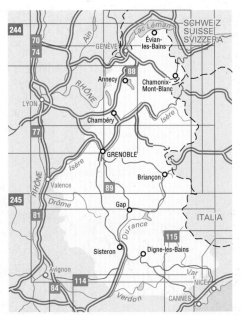

The Michelin maps you will need with this guide are:

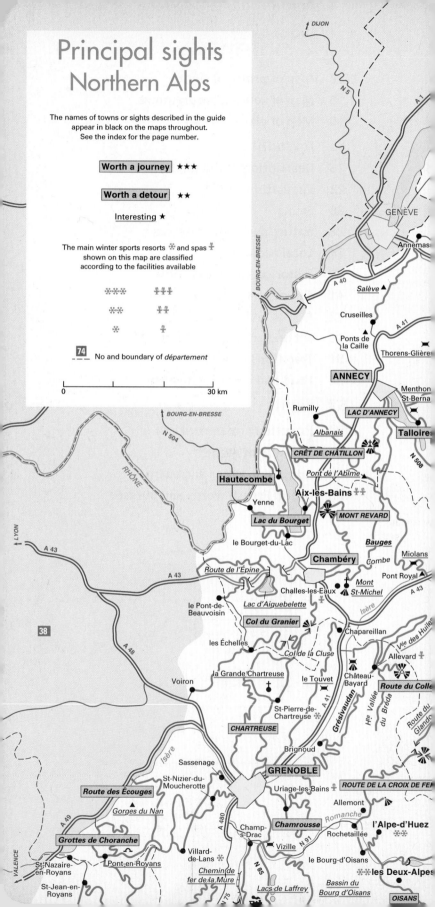

Principal sights
Northern Alps

The names of towns or sights described in the guide appear in black on the maps throughout.
See the index for the page number.

Worth a journey ★★★

Worth a detour ★★

Interesting ★

The main winter sports resorts ✳ and spas ♨ shown on this map are classified according to the facilities available

✳✳✳   ♨♨♨

✳✳   ♨♨

✳   ♨

74 No and boundary of *département*

0 _____ 30 km

DIJON

GENÈVE

Annemas

BOURG-EN-BRESSE

N 5

N 40

A 1

A 40

A 41

Salève ▲

Cruseilles

Ponts de la Caille

Thorens-Glière

ANNECY

Menthon St-Berna

Rumilly

LAC D'ANNECY

Albanais

Talloires

CRÊT DE CHÂTILLON

BOURG-EN-BRESSE

N 504

Hautecombe

Pont de l'Abîme

Yenne

Aix-les-Bains ♨♨

Lac du Bourget

MONT REVARD

N 508

le Bourget-du-Lac

Chambéry

Bauges

Combe

Miolans

Pont Royal ▲

RHÔNE

LYON

A 43

Route de l'Épine

Challes-les-Eaux

Mont ✝ *St-Michel*

Isère

A 43

le Pont-de-Beauvoisin

Lac d'Aiguebelette

Chapareillan

Vée des Huile

Col du Granier

Allevard ♨

les Échelles

Col de la Cluse

Route du Colle

38

A 48

la Grande Chartreuse ✝

le Touvet

Château-Bayard

Voiron

St-Pierre-de-Chartreuse ✳

Grésivaudan

Hte Vallée du Bréda

Route du Glando

CHARTREUSE

Brignoud

Isère

Sassenage

GRENOBLE

St-Nizier-du-Moucherotte

Uriage-les-Bains ♨

ROUTE DE LA CROIX DE FE

Route des Écouges

Allemont

Gorges du Nan

Champs-s'-Drac

Chamrousse ✳

Romanche

l'Alpe-d'Huez ✳✳

Vizille

Rochetaillée

Grottes de Choranche

Villard-de-Lans ✳

N 91

le Bourg-d'Oisans

✳✳**les Deux-Alpes**

St-Nazaire-en-Royans

Pont-en-Royans

Chemin de fer de la Mure

A 49

VALENCE

St-Jean-Royans

A 480

N 85

Lacs de Laffrey

N 75

Bassin du Bourg d'Oisans

OISANS

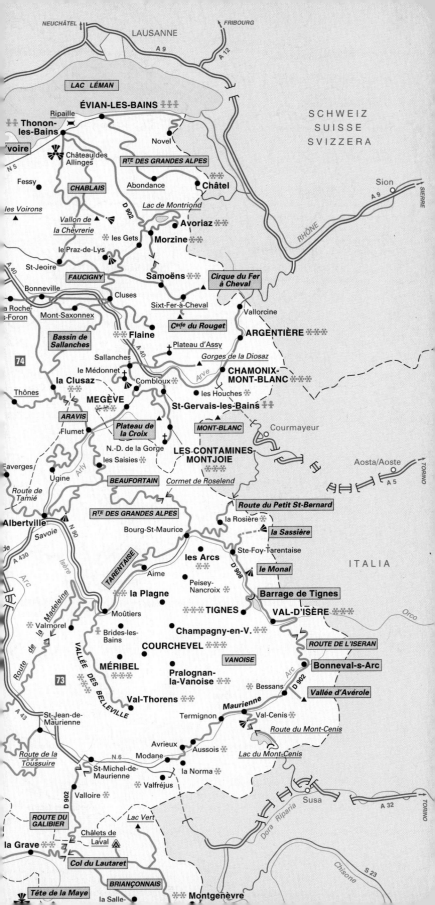

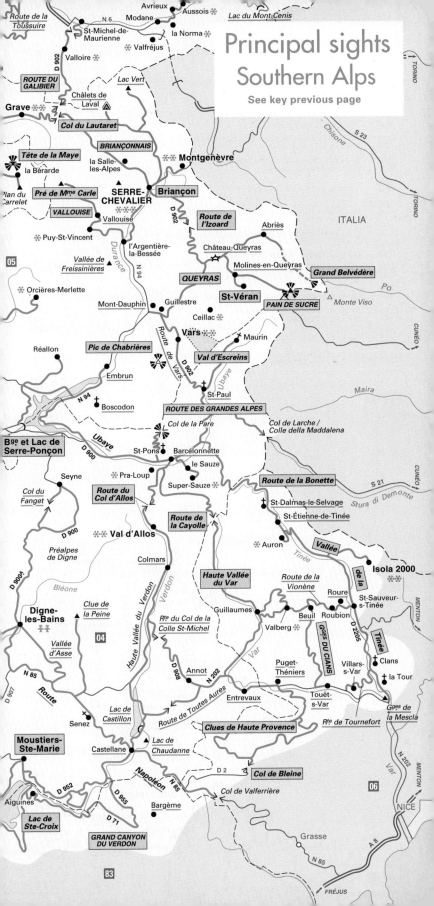

Principal sights
Southern Alps

See key previous page

Route de la Toussuire
N.6
Avrieux
Modane
Aussois ✲
Lac du Mont-Cenis
St-Michel-de-Maurienne
la Norma ✲
Valloire ✲
D 902
✲ Valfréjus
TORINO
Lac Vert
ROUTE DU GALIBIER
Châlets de Laval ⛺
Grave ✲✲
Col du Lautaret
Chisone
S 23
Tête de la Maye ❋
BRIANÇONNAIS
✲✲ Montgenèvre
la Salle-les-Alpes
la Bérarde
TORINO
Plan du Carrelet
Pré de Mᵐᵉ Carle
SERRE-CHEVALIER
Briançon
D 902
ITALIA
VALLOUISE
Vallouise
Route de l'Izoard
Abriès
❋ Puy-St-Vincent
l'Argentière-la-Bessée
Château-Queyras ☆
05
Durance
Vallée de Freissinières
N 94
QUEYRAS
Molines-en-Queyras
Grand Belvédère
Po
❋ Orcières-Merlette
Mont-Dauphin
Guillestre
St-Véran
PAIN DE SUCRE ❋
△ Monte Viso
CUNEO
Réallon
Ceillac ❋
Maira
Pic de Chabrières ❋
Vars ❋✲
Route de Vars
Maurin +
Embrun
Val d'Escreins
D 902
Ubaye
Maira
Boscodon +
ROUTE DES GRANDES ALPES
St-Paul +
Bᵍᵉ et Lac de Serre-Ponçon
Ubaye
D 900
❋ Col de la Pare
Col de Larche / Colle della Maddalena
CUNEO
Seyne
St-Pons +
Barcelonnette
Col du Fanget
le Sauze
Route de la Bonette
S 21
D 900
Route du Col d'Allos
❋ Pra-Loup
Super-Sauze ❋
Stura di Demonte
+ St-Dalmas-le-Selvage
Route de la Cayolle
St-Étienne-de-Tinée
✲✲ Val d'Allos
❋ Auron
Tinée
Vallée
Préalpes de Digne
Colmars
Haute Vallée du Var
Route de la Vionène
Roure
de la
Isola 2000 ✲✲
D 900A
Bléone
Verdon
Guillaumes
Beuil
Roubion
St-Sauveur-s-Tinée
MENTON
Clue de la Peine
Rᵗᵉ du Col de la Colle St-Michel
Valberg
Gᵉˢ DU CIANS
D 2205
Tinée
Digne-les-Bains
04
Haute Vallée du Verdon
Var
Puget-Théniers
Villars-s-Var
Clans +
Vallée d'Asse
Verdon
+ la Tour
N 85
D 907
Route
D 908
Annot
N 202
Entrevaux
Touët-s-Var
Gᵉˢ de la Mescla
Senez +
Lac de Castillon
Route de Toutes Aures
Rᵗᵉ de Tournefort
Var
N 202
Moustiers-Ste-Marie
Castellane
▲ Lac de Chaudanne
Clues de Haute Provence
N 85
MENTON
Aiguines
D 952
Napoléon
N 85
D 2
Col de Bleine
NICE
Lac de Ste-Croix
D 955
Col de Valferrière
Var
N 202
D 71
Bargème
06
A 8
GRAND CANYON DU VERDON
Grasse
83
N 85
FRÉJUS

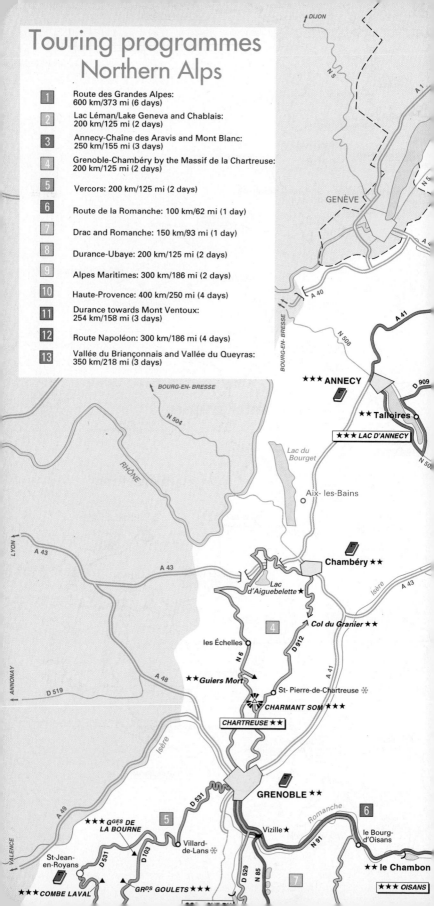

Touring programmes
Northern Alps

1. Route des Grandes Alpes:
600 km/373 mi (6 days)

2. Lac Léman/Lake Geneva and Chablais:
200 km/125 mi (2 days)

3. Annecy-Chaîne des Aravis and Mont Blanc:
250 km/155 mi (3 days)

4. Grenoble-Chambéry by the Massif de la Chartreuse:
200 km/125 mi (2 days)

5. Vercors: 200 km/125 mi (2 days)

6. Route de la Romanche: 100 km/62 mi (1 day)

7. Drac and Romanche: 150 km/93 mi (1 day)

8. Durance-Ubaye: 200 km/125 mi (2 days)

9. Alpes Maritimes: 300 km/186 mi (2 days)

10. Haute-Provence: 400 km/250 mi (4 days)

11. Durance towards Mont Ventoux:
254 km/158 mi (3 days)

12. Route Napoléon: 300 km/186 mi (4 days)

13. Vallée du Briançonnais and Vallée du Queyras:
350 km/218 mi (3 days)

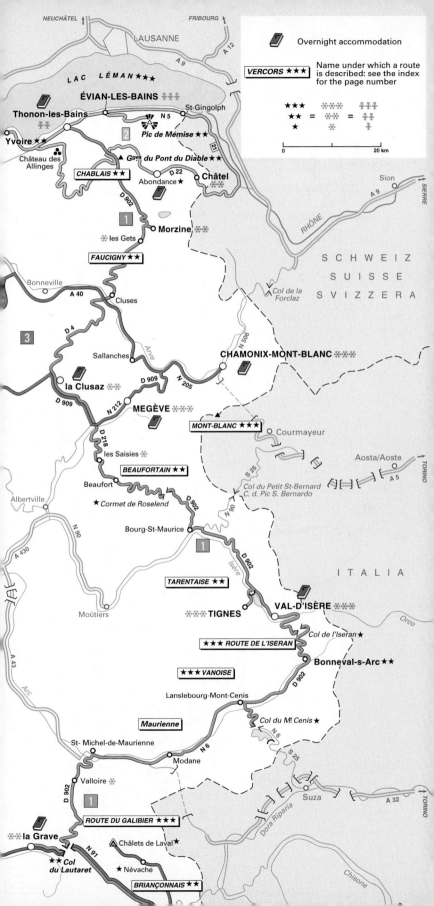

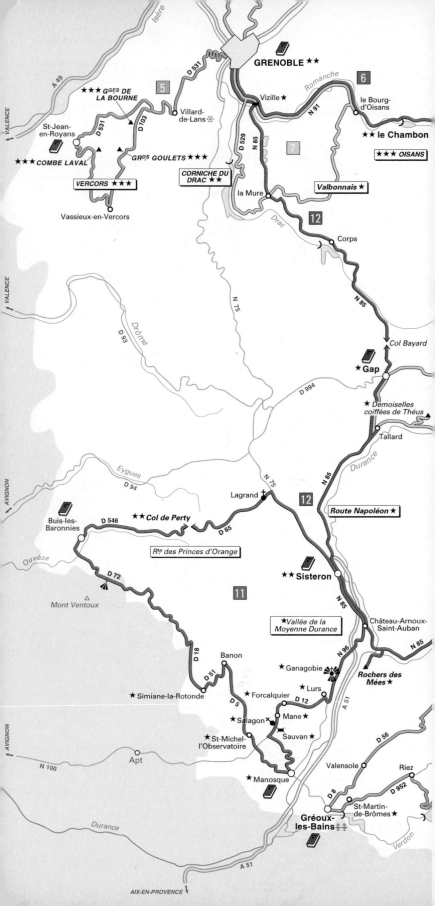

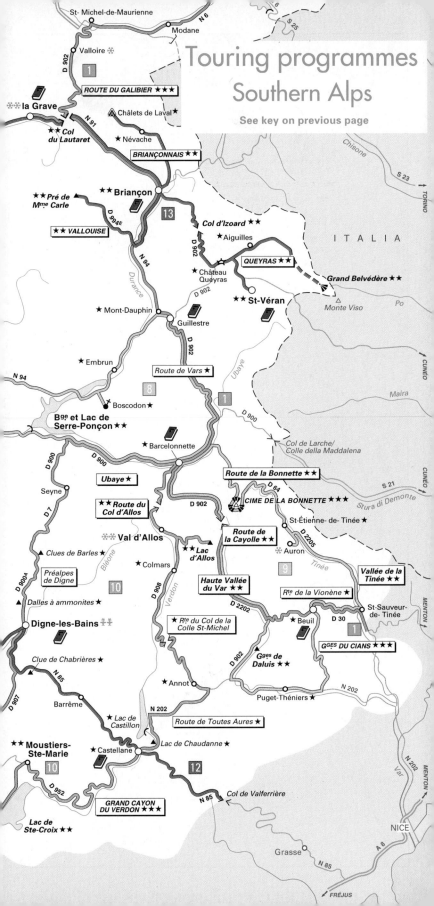

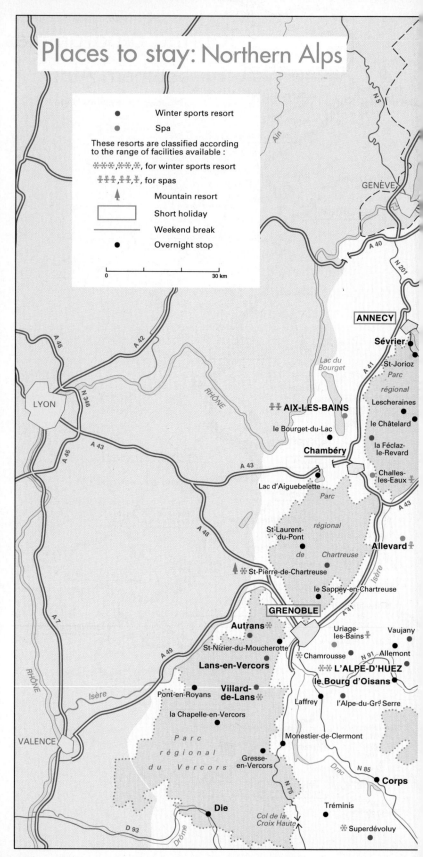

Places to stay: Northern Alps

● Winter sports resort

● Spa

These resorts are classified according to the range of facilities available :

✳✳✳,✳✳,✳, for winter sports resort

‡‡‡,‡‡,‡, for spas

⬆ Mountain resort

▭ Short holiday

— Weekend break

● Overnight stop

0 _____ 30 km

GENÈVE

ANNECY

Sévrier

St-Jorioz

Parc

régional

Lescheraines

le Châtelard

Lac du Bourget

‡‡ AIX-LES-BAINS

le Bourget-du-Lac

la Féclaz-le-Revard

Chambéry

Challes-les-Eaux ‡

LYON

RHÔNE

Lac d'Aiguebelette

Parc

régional

Allevard ‡

St-Laurent-du-Pont

de   Chartreuse

⬆ ✳ St-Pierre-de-Chartreuse

le Sappey-en-Chartreuse

GRENOBLE

Autrans ✳

St-Nizier-du-Moucherotte

Uriage-les-Bains ‡

Vaujany

✳ Chamrousse

Allemont

Lans-en-Vercors

✳✳ L'ALPE-D'HUEZ

le Bourg d'Oisans

Villard-de-Lans ✳

Pont-en-Royans

Laffrey

l'Alpe-du-Gr.ᵈ Serre

la Chapelle-en-Vercors

VALENCE

Isère

Parc

régional

du   Vercors

Monestier-de-Clermont

Gresse-en-Vercors

Corps

RHÔNE

Drac

Die

Tréminis

Col de la Croix Haute

✳ Superdévoluy

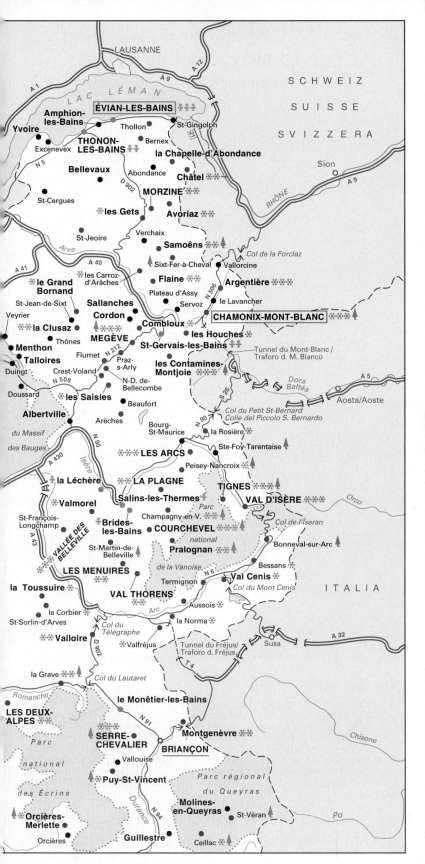

LAUSANNE

SCHWEIZ

SUISSE

SVIZZERA

LAC LÉMAN

ÉVIAN-LES-BAINS

Amphion-les-Bains

Yvoire

Thollon

St-Gingolph

Excenevex

Bernex

THONON-LES-BAINS

Sion

Bellevaux

Abondance

la Chapelle-d'Abondance

RHÔNE

St-Cergues

Châtel ✳✳

MORZINE ✳✳

✳les Gets

Avoriaz ✳✳

St-Joire

Verchaix

Samoëns ✳✳

Col de la Forclaz

✳les Carroz-d'Arâches

Sixt-Fer-à-Cheval

Vallorcine

✳le Grand Bornand

Flaine ✳✳

Argentière ✳✳✳

St-Jean-de-Sixt

Plateau d'Assy

Servoz

le Lavancher

Veyrier

Sallanches

✳✳la Clusaz

Cordon

Thônes

Combloux

CHAMONIX-MONT-BLANC ✳✳✳

Menthon

MEGÈVE

les Houches ✳

Talloires

Flumet

St-Gervais-les-Bains ✳

Duingt

Prazs-s-Arly

les Contamines-Montjoie ✳✳✳

Tunnel du Mont-Blanc / Traforo d. M. Bianco

Crest-Voland

N-D. de-Bellecombe

Doussard

✳les Saisies

Beaufort

Dora Baltéa

A 5

Albertville

Arèches

Aosta/Aoste

du Massif

des Bauges

Bourg-St-Maurice

la Rosière

Col du Petit St-Bernard
Colle del Piccolo S. Bernardo

Ste-Foy-Tarentaise

✳✳✳ LES ARCS

Peisey-Nancroix ✳

Orco

‡la Léchère

✳✳ LA PLAGNE

TIGNES ✳✳✳

✳Valmorel

Salins-les-Thermes

VAL D'ISÈRE ✳✳✳

St-François-Longchamp

Champagny-en-V.

Parc

Col de l'Iseran

‡Brides-les-Bains

Champagny-en-V. ✳✳

COURCHEVEL ✳✳✳

VALLÉE DES BELLEVILLE

St-Martin-de-Belleville

national

Bonneval-sur-Arc

Pralognan ✳✳

la Toussuire ✳

de la Vanoise

Bessans

✳✳ LES MENUIRES

Val Cenis ✳

ITALIA

VAL THORENS

Termignon

Col du Mont Cenis

le Corbier ✳

Arc

Aussois

St-Sorlin-d'Arves

la Norma ✳

A 32

✳✳ Valloire

Col du Télégraphe

✳Valfréjus

Susa

Tunnel du Fréjus/
Traforo d. Fréjus

la Grave ✳✳

Col du Lautaret

Romanche

le Monêtier-les-Bains

Chisone

LES DEUX-ALPES ✳✳

Parc

✳✳✳

SERRE-CHEVALIER

N 91

Montgenèvre ✳✳

national

BRIANÇON

Vallouise

✳Puy-St-Vincent

Parc régional
du Queyras

des Écrins

Molines-en-Queyras

Po

✳Orcières-Merlette

St-Véran

Orcières

Guillestre

Ceillac ✳

11

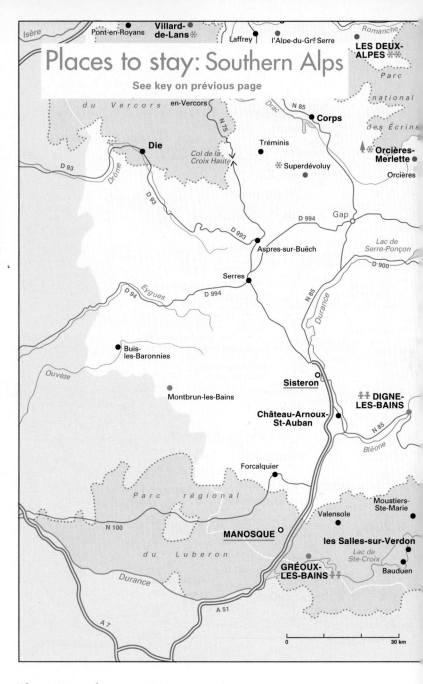

Places to stay: Southern Alps

See key on prévious page

Isère
Pont-en-Royans
Villard-de-Lans ❋
Laffrey
l'Alpe-du-Grd Serre
Romanche
LES DEUX-ALPES ❋❋
Parc
du Vercors
en-Vercors
N 85
Drac
national
N 75
Corps
des Écrins
Die
Col de la Croix Haute
Tréminis
Orcières-Merlette
❋ Superdévoluy
Orcières
D 93
Drôme
D 93
D 994
Gap
D 993
Lac de Serre-Ponçon
Aspres-sur-Buëch
D 900
Serres
Eygues
D 94
D 994
N 85
Durance
Buis-les-Baronnies
Ouvèze
Sisteron
DIGNE-LES-BAINS
Montbrun-les-Bains
Château-Arnoux-St-Auban
N 85
Bléone
Forcalquier
Parc régional
Moustiers-Ste-Marie
Valensole
les Salles-sur-Verdon
N 100
MANOSQUE
Lac de Ste-Croix
Bauduen
du Luberon
GRÉOUX-LES-BAINS
Durance
A 51
A 7
0   30 km

Choosing where to stay

The map above and on the previous pages shows a number of "overnight stops" - largish towns which deserve a visit and which offer many opportunities for accommodation. Évian, Annecy, Chamonix, Grenoble, Briançon, Digne-les-Bains and Manosque are all ideal destinations for a short break on account of their influence, their myriad sights and museums and the important events they stage.

Besides the hotels and camp sites mentioned in the Michelin guides, these places offer other forms of accommodation (furnished rooms, country cottages, board and lodging for live-in residents): apply to the local Tourist Information Centre to ask for a list of possibilities.

Plan ahead! To plan your route, the sights to see, to select a hotel or a restaurant, Internet users can log in at **www.michelin-travel.com.**

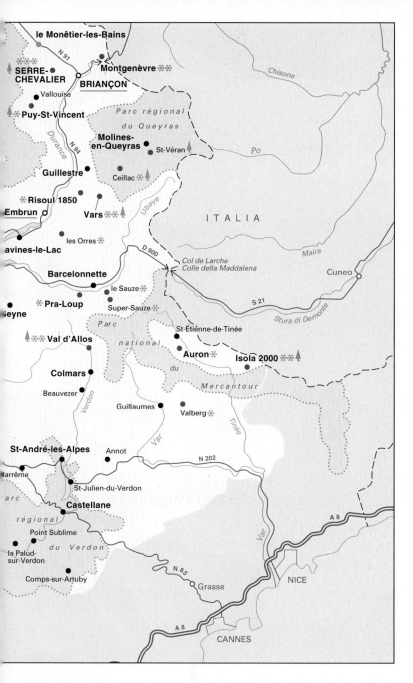

Accommodation

The **Michelin Red Guide** of hotels and restaurants and the **Michelin Guide Camping Caravaning France** are annual publications which give details of a selection of hotels, restaurants and camp sites.

The final listing is based on regular on-the-spot enquiries and visits. Both the hotels and restaurants are classified according to the standard of comfort of their amenities. Establishments which are notable for their setting, their decor, their quiet and secluded location and their warm welcome are indicated by special symbols.

The Michelin Red Guide France also gives the addresses and telephone numbers of the local Tourist Information Centres.

For a pleasant and quiet hotel in a convenient location,
consult the current edition of the **Michelin Red Guide France.**

Combloux

14

Introduction

15

Description of the region

The mountain range of the Alps stretches along a curved line from Nice on the Mediterranean coast to Vienna in Austria, over a distance of 1 200km/750mi. It was formed during the Tertiary Era, at the same time as the Pyrenees, the Carpathians, the Caucasus and the Himalayas.

The French Alps extend from Lake Geneva to the Mediterranean over a distance of 370km/230mi and they are over 200km/125mi wide at their widest point, between the Rhône Valley and the Italian Piedmont. The highest peak, Mont Blanc, rises to 4 807m/15 771ft but the altitude gradually decreases towards the southern part and the range is easily accessible through a series of deep wide valleys.

It is an area full of contrasts from the colourful shores of Lake Geneva to the glaciers of Mont Blanc, the chalk cliffs of Vercors and the dry Mediterranean landscapes of Haute-Provence.

Geologists agree to divide the French Alps into four main areas:
– The **Préalpes**, consisting almost entirely of limestone rocks formed during the Secondary Era, except in the Chablais area.
– The **Alpine trench** *(sillon alpin)*, a depression cut through marl, lying at the foot of the central massifs.
– The **central massifs** *(massifs centraux)*, consisting of very old and extremely hard crystalline rocks. The tectonic upheavals of the Tertiary Era folded the ancient land mass *(see below)*, creating "needles" and high peaks, which are the highest of the whole Alpine range. From north to south, these massifs are: the Mont-Blanc, the Belledone, the Grandes Rousses, the Ecrins and the Mercantour.
– The **intra-Alpine zone**, forming the axis of the Alps. It consists of sedimentary rocks transformed and folded by the violent upheavals which took place in the area. It includes the Vanoise, the Briançonnais and the Queyras as well as the upper valleys of the Tarentaise, the Maurienne and the Ubaye.

FORMATION OF THE ALPS

During the **Primary Era**, which began 600 million years ago, Hercynian mountains, similar to the Vosges, the Massif Central and the Massif Armoricain, appeared where the central massifs now stand. This folding was followed by considerable erosion and, by the end of the Primary Era, the Alps looked like Brittany today. The luxuriant vegetation, stimulated by the hot and humid climate, produced a considerable amount of plant deposits which are at the origin of several coalfields at La Mure and in the Briançonnais.

The **Secondary Era** began approximately 200 million years ago. Following the subsidence of the whole region, a vast marine depression was formed where the high Alps now stand. Deposits of limestone and sand – which were transformed into sandstone when compressed – as well as clay – which under high pressure often flaked into shale – piled up on the old foundation of crystalline rocks. The climate was uniform; forests consisted of pines, oaks, walnut-trees, eucalyptus and palm-trees. Huge reptiles such as dinosaurs roamed the earth and the first birds appeared.

The **Tertiary Era**, which began 65 million years ago, saw the formation of the high range of mountains as we know them. Under pressure from the east, on the Italian side, huge layers began to slide westwards forming the Briançonnais and the Vanoise. During the second half of the Tertiary Era, the old foundation rose in turn to form the Mont-Blanc, Écrins and Mercantour massifs. Various theories have been devised to explain this phenomenon. The concept of moving "plates" describes the earth's crust as consisting of a number of rigid plates moving in relation to one another and causing what is known as "continental drift". Situated at the boundary of the African and European plates, the Alps folded, according to this theory, like putty pressed between one's fingers. Following this tectonic upheaval, the sedimentary deposits left behind during the Secondary Era drifted down the slopes and hit against the edge of the Dauphiné. As a result, the pliable layers of sediments folded, creating the Préalpes. A depression appeared between the crystalline massifs and the Préalpes, which eventually became the Alpine trench through the work of erosion. To this north-south uplifting was added, in the southern part of the Alps, an east-west folding of Pyrenean origin which explains the complicated structure of this particular region. The Tertiary Era also saw the accumulation of sand deposits which were later transformed into sandstone in the Champsaur and Annot areas or into

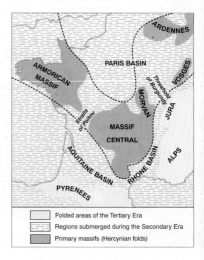

	Folded areas of the Tertiary Era
	Regions submerged during the Secondary Era
	Primary massifs (Hercynian folds)

GEOLOGY OF THE FRENCH ALPS

▨	Limestones of the Préalpes (Cretaceous)
▨	Préalpes of the southern and middle Durance (Jurassic limestones)
▨	Sedimentary strata covering the central massifs
▨	Intra-Alpine zone (crystalline and metamorphic rocks)
▨	Crystalline central massifs
▨	Tertiary conglomerate rocks of the Plateau de Valensole
▨	Flysch (black soils) of the Ubaye and Embrunais districts
▨	Piedmontais schists
▨	Chablais
▨	Sub-Alpine Furrow

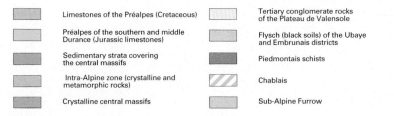

Flysch in the Ubaye Valley. The relatively recent **Quaternary Era** began 2 million years ago. Owing to a general cooling of the earth's atmosphere, there were four successive glacial periods during which the whole region was covered over with a huge mantle of ice. Erosion then worked relentlessly on a complete remodelling of the Alps into the mountain range it is today.

17

LANDSCAPES

They vary considerably according to the different geological structure of each area. It seems therefore logical to adopt the geologists' division of the Alps into four distinct parts preceded by what we might call the Alpine fringe. Listed from west to east and south to north, they are: the Préalpes, the Alpine trench, the central massifs and the intra-Alpine zone.

Alpine fringe

The Albanais, the Geneva area and the Bornes plateau situated on the edge of the northern Alps offer landscapes of green rolling hills dominated by a few moderate mountain ranges such as the **Salève** south of Geneva and the **Mont du Chat** near the Lac du Bourget. The basins left behind by retreating glaciers have been filled in by deep lakes: the Lac d'Aiguebelette and Lac du Bourget.

Préalpes

The northern Préalpes lie just beyond the Alpine fringe along a north-south axis, forming a barrier which rarely rises above 2 000m/6 561ft. They consist of five distinct massifs carved out of limestone (except for the Chablais), separated by the *cluses* of the Arve, Annecy, Chambéry and Grenoble.

Overlooking Lake Geneva and drained by the three Dranses, the **Chablais** is backed by the **Giffre** with its lively winter resorts, Samoëns and Flaine.

The **Bornes** Massif, flanked by the **Chaîne des Aravis** in the east, is drained by several rivers including the Fier; La Clusaz is an important skiing resort.

Further south, the **Bauges** Massif offers pleasant pastoral landscapes where small skiing resorts are developing.

The **Chartreuse** Massif stands like an imposing limestone fortress; features include high cliffs, deep gorges, valleys with pastures and magnificent dense forests on the well-watered slopes.

The **Vercors** is the largest of the Préalpes massifs; within its impressive outer ramparts, this natural citadel offers beautiful forest and pastoral landscapes, as well as striking gorges and popular resorts such as Villard-de-Lans.

The southern Préalpes spread over a vast area along a curved line in a northwest-southeast direction. The Durance Valley divides them into two groups:

West of the river, on the Dauphiné side, is the wild and austere **Dévoluy**, with its cliffs and bare summits below which sheep and cattle graze.

The wooded **Bochaine** marks the transition between north and south whereas the **Diois** and **Baronnies** already offer typical southern landscapes where the Alpine and Pyrenean folds mingle in conflicting directions. To the south, the limestone massif of **Mont Ventoux** stands alone, towering 1 909m/6 263ft above the Avignon Basin.

East of the Durance, the relief becomes more intricate, without any apparent plan; the mountain ranges of the **Préalpes de Digne** and **Préalpes de Castellane** are cut crosswise by deep wild gorges, known as *clues,* guarded by picturesque towns like Sisteron, Digne and Castellane. These areas are the least populated of the Alps region: owing to strict conservation regulations, the slopes have retained their varied vegetation, but the summits are mostly bare.

Préalpes de Digne

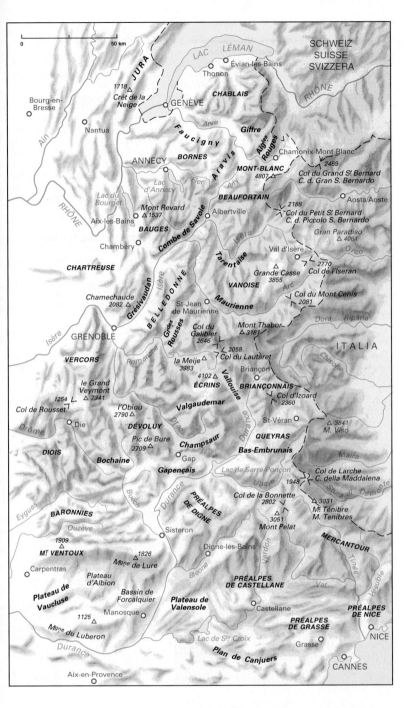

Lying between the Verdon and Var rivers, the **Préalpes de Grasse** rise to an altitude of 1 100m/3 609ft to 1600m/5 250ft.

The **Préalpes de Nice** are deeply cut in a north-south direction by rivers (Var, Tinée, Vésubie) which make their way to the sea through impressive gorges overlooked by villages perched high above the river beds.

Lying between the Préalpes, the **Plateau de Valensole** occupies the former delta of the Durance River filled in by an accumulation of rocks from nearby mountains. These rocks and pebbles, bound together by a natural kind of cement, form a conglomerate which has been carved by erosion into the famous **Pénitents des Mées** *(see Vallée de la Moyenne DURANCE)*.

Further east, there are several limestone plateaux through which streams penetrate and disappear into sink-holes. Spectacular gorges have been carved out by the Verdon and Artuby rivers.

Alpine trench

In the northern Alps, the **Bassin de Sallanches** and the **Val d'Arly** form, together with the depression of the **Combe de Savoie** and **Grésivaudan**, a wide longitudinal plain into which open the upper valley of the Isère River (Tarentaise), the valleys of the Arc (Maurienne) and of the Romanche (Oisans). Owing to the means of communication provided by this internal plain, to the fertile soil which favours rich crops (maize, tobacco, vines) and to the availability of hydroelectric power, the Alpine trench has become one of the most prosperous areas of the whole region.

In the southern Alps, a similar depression cut through marl runs along the foot of the Écrins, Briançonnais and Queyras massifs; the Durance River and its tributaries flow through this relatively flat area partly flooded by the artificial lac de Serre-Ponçon. Some strange rock formations, carved out of ancient moraines, can be seen in this region. They stand like groups of columns and are known as **Demoiselles coiffées** because they are crowned by a piece of hard rock *(see Barrage et lac de SERRE-PONÇON and Demoiselles coiffées de THÉUS)*. Between Sisteron and Manosque, the fertile Durance Valley brings Provence, its typical vegetation and orchards to the heart of the southern Alps.

Central massifs

This central mountain range includes the **Mont-Blanc**, the **Aiguilles-Rouges**, the **Beaufortain**, the **Belledonne**, the **Grandes Rousses**, the **Écrins-Pelvoux** and, in the south, the **Mercantour**. Together, these massifs form the high Alps, consisting of hard crystalline rocks, which were uplifted during the Tertiary Era while their sedimentary cover was removed. Austere and impressive, they are highly appreciated by mountaineers who like to cross the glaciers and climb the needles and snow-capped peaks. The Beaufortain is the only massif to have retained its layers of schist: it offers pleasant pastoral landscapes scattered with wooden chalets. Beautiful lakes have filled in the basins left by the glaciers.

Intra-Alpine zone

Situated between the central massifs and the Italian border, the **Vanoise** Massif and the **Briançonnais-Queyras** also belong to the high Alps but they consist of a mixture of schist and metamorphic crystalline rocks. Valleys are deep and slopes are covered with pastures. Thanks to its mild sunny climate and snow-covered slopes, the Vanoise, which has the Tarentaise and Maurienne as natural boundaries and includes the Parc national de la Vanoise *(see Nature parks and reserves)*, has recently acquired the highest concentration of winter resorts in the French Alps: Val-d'Isère, Tignes, Courchevel, La Plagne, Méribel-les-Allues, les Arcs...

The Briançonnais-Queyras Massif has a more complicated relief due to the diversity of its rock structure: sandstone, limestone and schist carried over from the Italian side as a result of overthrust. Owing to its characteristic southern light, blue skies and generous sun, this area is one of the healthiest in Europe, which explains the rapid development of summer and winter tourism centred 'round high villages such as St-Véran (2 040m/6 693ft).

The **Gap**, **Embrun** and **Ubaye** districts, lying between the high Alps and the Préalpes, offer a mosaic of heights, small basins and wide valleys carved out of layers of "black soil" or flysch (alternate strata of sandstone) in the case of the Ubaye.

ALPINE RELIEF

Tourists, who are not familiar with mountain relief resulting from the action of streams and glaciers, will find below the names of the main Alpine features accompanied by a brief description.

The slow but irresistible action of glaciers, rivers, rain and frost has completely remodelled the Alps over thousands of years into the mountain range it is today.

La Clarée Valley

The action of the glaciers – Around 10 000 years ago, glaciers covered the whole Alpine range and spread over the adjacent flat areas as far as the region of Lyon. Some of these "solid rivers" were huge, reaching thicknesses of 1 100m/3 609ft in the Grésivaudan for instance. They scooped out cirques with steep back walls and dug U-shaped valleys with tributary valleys "hanging" over the main ones.

Alpine glaciers today – Since the beginning of the 20C, Alpine glaciers have been consistently receding because they are not being sufficently renewed and today they only cover an area of 400km²/154sq mi; four fifths of them are in Savoie (Mont-Blanc and La Vanoise), the remainder being inside the Écrins Massif.
The Mer de Glace is a very good example of "valley glacier". Moving downstream, we find in succession a **névé**, an expanse of snow not yet turned into ice, and a **glacial "tongue"** cut by deep crevaces. Level changes are marked by jumbled piles known as **seracs**; accumulations of debris carried down by the glacier are called **lateral moraine** when deposited on the edges, **terminal moraine** when deposited at the extremity and **medial moraine** when deposited between two conjoining glaciers. Alpine glaciers move at a speed of 70m/230ft per year.

Erosion by water – When the ice mantle disappeared, mountain streams and rivers began to smooth out the relief. "Connecting gorges" opened up the "bolts" and joined the floor of a "hanging" valley to that of the main valley. The gorges of the Diosaz and of the Doron de Champagny are good examples of this kind of defile.
There are gorges of another kind, mainly in the Préalpes, which cut across the axis of the folds: they are called **cluses** (transverse valleys). They are often the only means of communication between the mountain and the lower areas, since roads have been boldly carved out of the rock face (Défilé de Pierre-Châtel or the Gorges de Guiers).

STREAMS AND RIVERS

The southern Alps have three distinct river networks: in the centre the Durance and its tributaries, in the east the Var which gathers water streaming down the Alpes Maritimes and in the west the tributaries of the Rhône.
Mediterranean rivers are particularly interesting because they behave like real mountain streams: during the summer, they are reduced to a trickle of water owing to the absence of rain and intensive evaporation. But in spring and autumn, violent rain storms fill up the river beds so suddenly that the flow of foaming water tumbles down at the speed of a galoping horse. The Durance, Verdon, Aigues and Ouvèze rivers are equally capricious. However, the Durance and Verdon have been harnessed through the building of dams (Serre-Ponçon across the Durance, Castillon and Ste-Croix across the Verdon) and canals. The impressive gorges dug by these rivers (Grand Canyon du Verdon, Gorges du Cians) are one of the main attractions of Haute-Provence.

ALPINE CLIMATE

The Alpine range is divided into two distinct climatic regions: the northern Alps which are subjected to oceanic influences and the southern Alps which enjoy a Mediterranean climate. The separation between these two regions follows a line drawn from west to east between the following mountain passes: Col de Rousset, Col de la Croix Haute, Col du Lautaret and Col du Galibier.

J.-P. Chanut/DIAF

Pointe de l'Échelle and Lac Blanc in the Massif de la Vanoise

Rainfall over the **northern Alps** is abundant all year round and temperatures are low. The Préalpes and central massifs get the brunt of the rainy weather. The intra-Alpine zone, protected by these barriers, is drier and sunnier; snow remains on the slopes longer. However, many factors such as altitude, aspect, general direction of the various ranges and valleys, contribute to create a great variety of local climatic conditions.

Altitude – Temperatures fall rapidly as the altitude gets higher (roughly 0.5°C/1°F every 100m/328ft); this phenomenon can be reversed in winter, during periods of settled weather, as cold air which is heavy, slips down the slopes and accumulates in the valleys, whereas, higher up, renewed air is warmer.

Aspect – South-facing slopes, called "**adrets**", enjoy more sunshine than north-facing slopes called "**ubacs**", usually covered with forests and on which snow holds better.

Relief – It has an influence on rainfall and wind direction; rain and snow fall more generously on the first heights in their path and on slopes exposed to the wind. Winds generally blow along wide valleys, particularly during the warm season when, towards midday, warm air rises from the valleys and causes clouds to form round the summits. This is a sign of steady fine weather. Later on in the day, the processus is reversed and a cold mountain breeze blows down the valleys
Heights usually attract storms which are often violent and spectacular.
The climate enjoyed by the **southern Alps** displays typical Mediterranean features: a good deal of sunshine, dry weather, clear skies, the absence of mist or fog, rare yet abundant precipitations and the famous *mistral* wind. In winter there is a fair amount of snow and plenty of fine weather to enjoy it. Spring is characterised by a short rainy spell while the *mistral* blows hard in the southwest. Summer is hot and dry over the whole of Haute-Provence and the air filled with the delicate scent of lavender and thyme. In the autumn, violent storms are succeeded by sunny spells, the air is pure and the light ideal for discovering the beauty of nature.

Vegetation

In mountain areas, the pattern of vegetation is not only influenced by the climate and the type of soil but depends also on aspect and altitude which defines a succession of vertical stages. This staging is modified by man who has done much to alter original landscapes. South-facing slopes *(adrets)*, which offer the best conditions for settlement and agriculture, have been the most subject to deforestation, whereas north-facing slopes *(ubacs)*, often uninhabited, have retained their trees which thrive in the prevailing wetter conditions. This pattern is seen at its best in valleys running east-west.
Farming is usually practised up to an altitude of about 1 500m/5 000ft; above this, there is a belt of conifer forest. From around 2 200m/7 000ft upwards, the trees give way to Alpine pastures with their rich mixture of wild grasses and Alpine flora. Above 3 000m/10 000ft, bare rock prevails, with mosses and lichens clinging to it in places.

TREES

The Alps are famous for their vast forests of conifers, although beeches prevail in the Préalpes up to an altitude of 800m/2 625ft.

Conifers

Fir tree – Old trees have broad crowns with flattened points looking like storks' nests. The bark is greyish; the cones, standing up like candles, break up when ripe and shed their scales. The soft needles are lined up like the teeth of a comb (hence the name *sapin pectiné*) and have a double white line on their inner surface (hence the name *sapin argenté* – silver fir).

Spruce – This tree is the most commonly found on north-facing slopes. It has a pointed, spindle-shaped crest and drooping branches, and its reddish bark becomes deeply fissured with age. It has sharp needles and its hanging cones fall to the ground in one piece when ripe.

Larch – The only conifer in the French Alps to shed its leaves in winter, the larch is commonly found growing on south-facing slopes, particularly in the "Alpes sèches" (dry Alps). The cones are quite small. The delicate light-green foliage casts relatively little shade, thus favouring the growth of grass, one of the attractive features of larch woods.

Forest pine – The many species of pine trees all have needles growing in tufts of two to five encased in scaly sheaths. The cones have hard rough scales. The forest pine, with its tall slender trunk, grows in considerable numbers in the southern Alps, usually on the *adrets* (sunny slopes).

Deciduous trees

The grey-trunk beech prevails in the Préalpes. With its thick boughs it provides shade for many rare plants: Turk's-cap lily, belladonna or deadly nightshade, medicinal speedwell and many more. Among other deciduous trees, there are alders, maples, birches, service trees, willows, laburnums with their lovely clusters of yellow flowers...

Trees of the Maritime Alps

Forest pine

Almond tree

Fir

Spruce

Larch

Cypress

Olive tree

Beech

23

MEDITERRANEAN VEGETATION

Trees and xerophilous plants (adapted to extremely dry conditions) require mild temperatures which do not fall below 4°C/39°F during the coldest month of the year.

Trees – Several varieties of oaks and pines, as well as almond trees and the typically Provençal cypresses and olive trees grow in the southern Alps, either in cultivated areas or scattered on dry rocky moors known as *garrigues*. Such landscapes can be seen in the Durance Valley, on the southern slopes of Mont Ventoux or the Montagne de Lure and in the Baronnies and Diois areas. Further north, above 600-800m/1 968-2 625ft, forests of white oaks, forest pines and beeches prevail, particularly on *ubacs* (north-facing slopes). Such forests often alternate with heaths where gorse, box and lavender grow.

The evergreen **holm oak** has a short thick-set trunk with a wide-spreading dome and fine dark green leaves. It grows on arid calcareous soil at less than 1 000m/328ft. In stunted form, it is a characteristic element of the *garrigues (see below)* in association with all sorts of shrubs and aromatic plants.

The deciduous **downy** or **white oak** (the undersides of the leaves are covered with dense short white hairs) requires more water than the evergreen oak above. It is found in valleys and on the more humid mountain slopes.

The **Aleppo pine**, one of the Mediterranean species of pine trees, has a light, graceful foliage and a trunk covered with grey bark which twists as it grows.

The outline of the dark **cypress**, a coniferous evergreen, marks the Mediterranean landscape with its tapered form pointed towards the sky, while the common **almond tree** delights the eye with its lovely early-spring pink blossoms.

Garrigues – This word is used to describe vast expanses of rocky, limestone moors. Vegetation is sparse, consisting mostly of holm oaks, stunted downy oaks, thistles, gorse and cistus as well as lavender, thyme and rosemary interspersed with short dry grass which provides pasture for flocks of sheep.

Forest fires

The forests of Haute-Provence are particularly exposed to fires, the majority of which are due to carelessness or pyromaniacs. A forest fire has two natural allies: drought and wind.

During the summer months, the dried-up plants of the underbrush, pine needles, resins exuded by leaves and twigs are highly combustible and sometimes catch fire spontaneously. Once a fire has started, it spreads to the pine trees and, if the wind is strong, disaster may follow. Huge walls of flames, sometimes more than 10km/6mi long and 30m/98ft high, spread at a speed of 5-6kph/2-3mph. Fires leave nothing standing except the blackened skeletons of the trees and a thick layer of white ash covering the ground.

Very often the only hope to stop a fire is for the wind to drop or change direction. Little by little, fires have, over the years, altered the balance of the ecosystem: thus, for instance, oak forests are receding and the soil remains barren for a long time.

The numerous means of fighting forest fires do not provide a satisfactory solution to the problem; prevention alone through systematic surveillance, regular clearing of the underbrush, creation of fire-breaks and above all public awareness, particularly that of tourists, can help combat this enemy of nature.

Dial 18 to call the fire brigade (pompiers).

ALPINE FLORA

The name "Alpine" is normally used to describe those plants which grow above the tree line. Because of the short growing season (July and August), these hardy and mostly small species flower early, while the disproportionate development and colouring of the flowers is the result of exposure to intense ultra-violet light. Their resistance to drought is often their main characteristic (woolly leaf surfaces, thick water-retaining leaves).

Remote origins – Most Alpine plants originated elsewhere. Some came from the lower mountains and plains but adapted to the harsher conditions at high altitude (dandelion, centaury); others come from the Mediterranean area (pink and narcissus), from the Arctic (buttercup, white poppy) or even from Asia (edelweiss, primula). The few truly indigenous species (columbine, valerian) managed to survive the Quaternary glaciations.

Suitable sites – Mountain plants do not grow at random: some need an alkaline soil, others prefer an acid soil; some flourish on scree, in a cleft in the rock or in a bog, depending on their particular environmental requirements. Each type of site has its specific plant species or combination of species – always the same – able to thrive in the given conditions.

Alpine flora

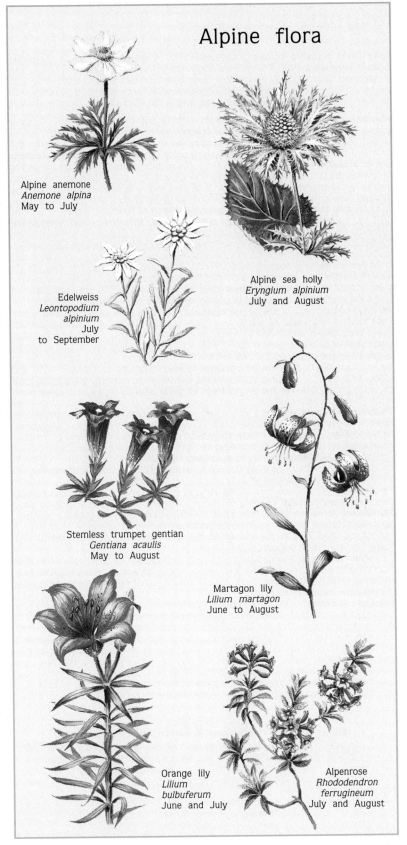

Alpine anemone
Anemone alpina
May to July

Alpine sea holly
Eryngium alpinium
July and August

Edelweiss
*Leontopodium
alpinium*
July
to September

Stemless trumpet gentian
Gentiana acaulis
May to August

Martagon lily
Lilium martagon
June to August

Orange lily
*Lilium
bulbuferum*
June and July

Alpenrose
*Rhododendron
ferrugineum*
July and August

Fauna

Alpine fauna in France includes a limited number of species: fish such as the pollan found in large lakes; birds like the royal eagle, the jackdaw, the snow-partridge as well as mammals which include, apart from those described below, the Alpine shrew and the snow-mouse. Unfortunately, most of these species seem doomed to extinction in the near future except in conservation areas within the nature parks.

Adaptation to a specific environment – Above the tree line, at high altitudes, animals have learnt how to adapt to the special conditions of a harsh environment, in which it is only possible to survive by building up one's defences against the cold, the snow and the lack of food. Some animals are protected against the cold by their thick coat or plumage, others such as the marmot hibernate below ground, solving at the same time the problem of food shortage. The blue hare and the snow-partridge, who are the favourite game of foxes and birds of prey, make themselves inconspicuous by changing colour with the seasons. In winter, large herbivores like the ibex and the chamois make their way down to the forests in search of food and shelter.

Most of these animals live in places only accessible to Alpinists and as they are extremely shy, they run away at the slightest noise.

The **Ibex** is a stocky wild goat with a pair of easily recognisable curved ridged horns which can be more than a metre long; this peaceful animal enjoys basking in the sun. Males sometimes gather in groups of more than 50. When snow begins to fall, they join up with the females who are smaller and shier. The males then fight for the females and the sound of their horns knocking echoes throughout the mountains. The actions undertaken by the Parc national de la Vanoise to protect the species have ensured its survival.

The graceful silhouette of the nimble **chamois** can be seen high up on the steep rocky peaks capped with snow all year round. The "Alpine antelope" has a tough reddish brown coat, thicker and darker in winter, with a black line on its back. Its small head is surmounted by curved slender dark horns. Its thin strong legs and its special hooves explain its extraordinary agility. This extremely strong animal jumps from one rock to the next and climbs the steepest passages. It lives in groups of between three and twenty head, led by a male goat. A chamois can weigh as much as 50kg/110lb (half the weight of an ibex). In summer, it feeds on grass whereas in winter, it goes down to the forest and nibbles at the bark of trees.

The **marmot** is a charming rodent with a yellowish brown coat which lives in colonies. Its behaviour is characteristic: it stands erect on its back legs most of the time. Easily scared, the whole colony disappears in holes in the ground when the prolonged whistle of the look-out sounds the alarm. During the summer, the marmots' bodies store fat and, as soon as it turns cold, these clever animals dig three to four-metre-deep galleries in the mountainside and line them with dry grass. They then lie inside these galleries in small groups and fall into a kind of lethargic sleep which lasts until the return of the fine weather.

The **blue hare** lives in the very high Alpine pastures and it is very difficult to observe owing to its scarcity and above all its ability to change colour with the seasons in order to blend in better with its surroundings. Pure white in winter, it thus becomes greyish in summer.

The reddish brown summer coat of the **stoat** becomes white in winter apart from a thin tuft of black hair at the end of its tail. This small flesh-eating mammal lives among stones or near chalets.

The **Corsican moufflon** is a large wild sheep living in flocks led by the older males. As it is particularly well-adapted to the Mediterranean climate and vegetation, it has been introduced into the Mercantour and Queyras nature parks. Males are easily identified by their thick scroll-shaped horns.

Butterflies and **moths** are plentiful in Haute-Provence: there are more than 1 300 different species in the Alpes-de-Haute-Provence *département* alone and more than 600 species in the area around Digne (there is an exceptionally fine collection in the local museum), among them some 180 butterflies which represent three quarters of the total butterfly population in France. Among the most remarkable species are the swallowtail butterfly, the parnassius and, smaller but also rarer, the Diana and the Proserpina, the Jason, the vanessas and the érèbes (including the scipio presently becoming extinct) which hover over lavender fields. The destruction of the traditional environment and the development of industries in the area are responsible for numerous species becoming extinct every year.

Help protect the environment in nature parks and reserves

– do not pick fruit and flowers (they wither rapidly), do not uproot plants and collect fossils; many species growing inside nature parks are protected: information panels at the entrance of protected areas help visitors to identify them;
– rubbish and empty containers must be taken out of protected areas (take rubbish bags with you);
– do not light fires and, in some areas, smoke; do not throw cigarette ends when they are still alight, since the slightest wind can set fire to pine needles covering the ground.

Alpine fauna

Golden eagle ①

Bearded vulture ②

Ibex

Stoat ③

Lynx ④

Chamois

Black grouse ⑤

Dessins de F. Desbordes ① ② ⑤ ; J. Chevalier ③ ④ : extrait de l'inventaire de la Faune de France. Nathan. MNHN 1992

Nature parks and reserves

Three out of the six French national parks are situated in the Alps region; they are the Parc national de la Vanoise, des Écrins and du Mercantour. There are also five regional parks: the Parc naturel régional du massif des Bauges, de Chartreuse, du Vercors, du Queyras and du Luberon. A sixth is being set up to protect the environment of the Grand Canyon du Verdon. In addition, there are numerous nature reserves of varying sizes.

NATIONAL PARKS

The national parks were created for the protection of natural areas containing a noteworthy environment and the simultaneous development of tourism coupled with an introduction to nature. In order to achieve these seemingly conflicting aims, each national park comprises two distinct zones.

The park itself or **central zone**, which includes an uninhabited area where the protection of the natural environment is achieved through strict regulations: no fishing, no hunting, no picking of plants of any kind, no dogs allowed, no camping, no building...

In the **peripheral zone**, on the other hand, various activities backed up by information and education are programmed, together with the development of agriculture, natural and cultural ressources. There are hotels and suitable social, economic and cultural institutions.

Parc national de la Vanoise

Local map see Massif de la VANOISE. France's first national park, created in 1963 – almost 100 years after the first American national park – includes, within a vast area covering 53 000ha/ 130 963 acres, the whole Massif de la Vanoise, between the upper valleys of the Isère and Arc rivers, thereby prolonging the Parco nazionale del Gran Paradiso on the Italian side to which it is adjacent over a distance of 14km/8.7mi.

Within the park, where the altitude varies from 1 200 to 3 855m/3 937 to 12 648ft (the altitude of the Grande Casse), there are extremely varied geological formations (limestone, schist etc) and numerous interesting species of fauna and flora. One of the aims, which the park shared with the Parco nazionale del Gran Paradiso when it was created, was the protection of the last ibexes still living in the Alps. Between 1963 and 1986, the number of these animals increased from 40 to 1 200, while the number of chamois increased from 400 to 5 200. The ibex was chosen as the first emblem of the park.

The exceptionally rich flora includes more than 1 000 different species, among them arctic varieties such as the buttercup and the catchfly.

The park is ideal for hiking with more than 500km/310mi of hiking trails (GR 5 - GR 55 and footpaths inside the park) as well as 35 mountain shelters, including 19 belonging to the park, so that it is today one of the areas most sought-after by hikers. In addition, five shelters, situated at the entrances to the park, play an informative role and offer a programme of activities.

The local fauna includes 7 000 chamois as well as golden eagles.

More than 50 000 sheep spend the summer in the area. In October, their trek down from the high summer pastures is marked by picturesque fairs in the villages of La Chapelle-en-Valgaudemar and St-Bonnet.

The peripheral zone, which covers an area of 178 000ha/439 838 acres, comprises the upper valleys of the Drac, Romanche, Malsanne, Guisane and Durance rivers where several winter resorts have developed in recent years.

Information and exhibition centres have been set up at the "entrances" to the park and the Maison du parc national des Écrins is situated near the village of Vallouise. In summer, guided tours are organised by the Guides de l'Oisans et du Parc des Écrins.

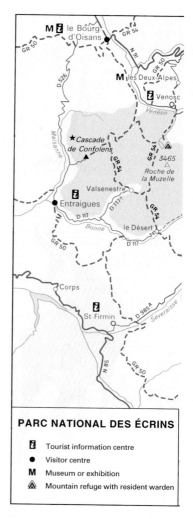

PARC NATIONAL DES ÉCRINS

🛈	Tourist information centre
●	Visitor centre
M	Museum or exhibition
⛺	Mountain refuge with resident warden

In the peripheral zone, covering an area of 145 000ha/358 295 acres, an impressive number of accommodation and sports facilities are available in the Tarentaise and Maurienne regions.

The whole area represents a third of the Savoie *département*.

Parc national des Écrins

Created in 1973, it is France's largest national park, covering an area of 92 000ha/227 332 acres, a third of which are in the Isère *département* and two thirds in the Hautes-Alpes *département*. This high mountain region includes numerous peaks above 3 000m/9 843ft such as la Meije, le Pelvoux, les Bans, l'Olan, les Agneaux and the highest of them all, la Barre des Écrins which reaches 4 102m/13 458ft. Within the park, which was formerly known as the parc domanial du Pelvoux, there are glaciers covering an area of 12 000ha/29 653 acres, such as the glacier Blanc on the north side of the Barre des Écrins, and lakes such as Lac Lauvitel, Lac de Vallon and Lac de l'Eychauda.

The Massif du Pelvoux, situated at the heart of the park, offers marvellous possibilities for mountain-climbing whereas the diverging Vénéon, Valgaudemar and Vallouise valleys are ideal starting-points for hiking. More than 1 000km/621mi of footpaths are available inside the park, including the GR 54 "Tour de l'Oisans" and the GR 50 "Tour du Dauphiné" offering a wider round trip.

Oceanic influences in the north and west and Mediterranean influences in the south are responsible for the extremely varied flora which is a characteristic feature of the Massif des Écrins and includes 1 800 different species of flowering plants such as the lady's slipper, the orange lily, the wormwood, the Alpine columbine and the Alpine sea holly.

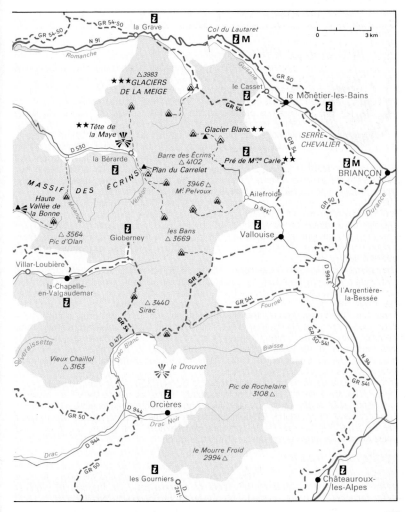

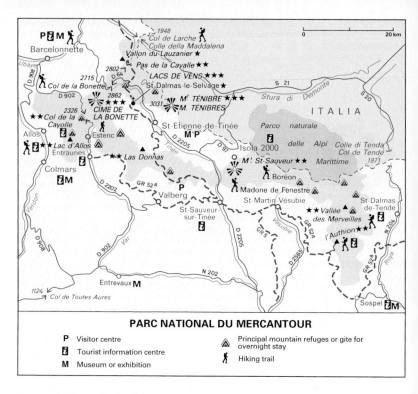

PARC NATIONAL DU MERCANTOUR

P Visitor centre	⚠ Principal mountain refuges or gîte for overnight stay
🛈 Tourist information centre	🚶 Hiking trail
M Museum or exhibition	

Parc national du Mercantour

Created in 1979, this is France's most recent national park; it extends over the Alpes-Maritimes and Alpes-de-Haute-Provence *départements* and covers an area of 68 500ha/169 264 acres. Situated on the French side of the former hunting grounds of the kings of Italy which, in 1861, spread on both sides of the Alpine range, the Parc du Mercantour has, since 1987, been twinned with the Italian nature park Alpe Marittimi (formerly known as the Argentera). Both parks have a 33km/20mi-long common border and work together for the introduction and

progress of animal species which roam over the whole conservation area. Ibexes, for instance, move to their summer quarters in the Mercantour after having spent the winter in the Argentera Massif, whereas moufflons do the reverse.

The altitude of this high mountain region ranges from 500 to 3 143m/1640 to 10 308ft and the park offers beautiful views of cirques, glacial valleys and deep gorges.

The rich flora comprises more than 2 000 species including the **saxifraga florulenta** which was the first emblem of the park. All the levels of vegetation are represented, from the olive tree to the rhododendron and the gentian which, in springtime, offers a splendid display of colours.

The animal population of the park includes 6 300 chamois, some 300 ibexes and 1 250 moufflons, well adapted to the Mediterranean climate. Wooded areas situated at moderate altitudes are inhabited by red deer and roe-deer as well as smaller mammals such as the blue hare, the stoat and the marmot. The most common birds are the black grouse, the snow-partridge and birds of prey such as the short-toed eagle and the golden eagle. The bearded vulture was successfully reintroduced into the area during the summer of 1993 so that there are at present five specimens in the park. Wolves have come back to the region of their own accord for the first time since 1942. They cross over from Italy where this protected species is growing in numbers.

The park has a network of footpaths totalling 600km/373mi, including the GR 5 and the GR 52A, the Mercantour panoramic footpath. There are nature trails with explanatory panels such as the Circuit du lac d'Allos and the Route de la Bonette.

The peripheral zone includes 22 municipalities from the Alpes-Maritimes *département* and six from the Alpes-de-Haute-Provence *département*. The Ubaye, Col d'Allos and Vallée de la Tinée regions are dealt with in this guide.

REGIONAL PARKS

The principles on which the creation of regional parks is based and the goals they are meant to achieve are different from those of national parks. In the case of regional parks, inhabited areas are selected with a view to introduce activities liable to:

– develop the economy (cooperatives, handicraft);
– protect the natural and cultural heritage (museums, architecture...);
– introduce visitors to nature.
Regional nature parks are administered by bodies which include local representatives, landowners, representatives of various associations etc. A charter, drawn up with the assent of the local inhabitants, stipulates the limits of the park and suggests a programme of activities and projects to be realised.

Parc naturel régional du massif des Bauges

Created at the end of 1995, this is the most recent park within the Rhône-Alpes region. Covering an area of 80 000ha/197 680 acres, it includes 57 municipalities spread over the whole territory of the Massif des Bauges; it is limited to the north by the shores of the Lac d'Annecy, to the east by the valley of the Isère River, to the south by the *cluse* (transverse valley) de Chambéry and to the west by the hills of Albanais country. While having a definite geographical unity, the Massif des Bauges consists of small well-defined areas, each marked with the economic and cultural imprint of various religious orders. The regional park ensures the preservation of local traditions and of the architectural heritage in the form of traditional houses *(see Traditional Architecture page 48)* together with the protection and development of the most outstanding natural sites.

The Réserve cynégétique des Bauges (National Game and Wildlife Preserve of the Bauges) is situated in the northern part of the massif, in the upper valley of the Chéran River. It contains more than 1 000 chamois as well as numerous moufflons, roe-deer and black grouse. The rich flora includes most protected species from the Savoie region.

Parc naturel régional de Chartreuse

Local map see Massif de la CHARTREUSE. Inaugurated in 1995, this park, which extends over 63 000ha/155 673 acres, includes 46 municipalities spread over the Savoie and Isère *départements* throughout the whole of the Massif de la Chartreuse.

The climatic conditions of the Massif de la Chartreuse (high rainfall alternating with intense sunshine) are responsible for a great variety of natural environments: cliffs, vast forested areas, damp areas, pastureland. Each environment has its own endemic species: kidney vetch, potentilla and lousewort. Most Alpine mammals are to be found in the park: the lynx is spreading from Switzerland while the forest birdlife is so remarkable that the eagle owl has become the emblem of the park. Other species include the black grouse, the Tengmalm's owl and the pygmy owl, while the golden eagle and the peregrine falcon can be seen near the numerous cliffs.

The cultural heritage of the park bears the strong imprint of the Carthusian monks who have been in the area for 900 years and still possess seven monasteries; they developed some original economic activities (liqueur and metalwork).

Some of the goals of this recent park are to preserve from urban development areas which have a specific biological value, to insure the protection of the land and waterways by means of special river projects such as "Guiers propre" (clean Guiers), and to safeguard the natural heritage of the Chartreuse high plateaux with a view to having them declared nature reserve areas.

Projects in the field of tourism include the marking of five itineraries of cultural hiking tours, the setting up of a "chain of Carthusian heritage" and the development of hiking, free flying and rock-climbing. *(See Practical information: Hiking.)*

Parc naturel régional du Vercors

Local map see Le VERCORS. Created in 1970, the park covers an area of 175 000ha/432 425 acres and includes 62 municipalities situated in the limestone Massif du Vercors and also in the Royans, Trièves and Diois regions.

Several cultural projects have been carried through; they are: the information centre on the prehistoric site of Vassieux, the Royans memorial museum in Rochechinart and the Resistance national site in Vussieux. In the field of environmental preservation, five nature trails have been set up and the high plateaux, overlooked by Mont Aiguille are now protected under the label of nature reserve.

However, the park has realised its greatest achievement in the field of sport. Its has become the paradise of cross-country skiing based in the resorts of Autrans and Villard-de-Lans; the area is criss-crossed with marked trails and cross-country skiing clubs. Several hiking footpaths go through the area, including the GR 91 which crosses the high plateaux and the whole region is sought after by hikers. It is also one of the main potholing areas in France with the national potholing centre based near St-Martin-du-Vercors.

The *maisons du Parc*, which are information centres, provide visitors with details on all leisure and discovery activities organised by the Parc naturel régional du Vercors.

Parc naturel régional du Queyras

Inaugurated in 1977, the park comprises eight municipalities of the Queyras region and part of Vars, Eygliers and Guillestre, covering a total area of 65 000ha/160 615 acres.

The main aims which led to its creation are the protection of various sites (architecture, landscapes) and species, the fitting-out of a permanent exhibition centre (Château-Queyras), the development of outdoor sports, of long-distance footpaths (GR 5 and GR 58 "Tour du Queyras"), of cross-country skiing trails, the setting-up of shelters and laying-out of nature trails such as those linking Ristolas to the Mont Viso belvedere.

One of the animal species which are increasing in numbers is the Corsican moufflon, brought into the park in 1973 and today numbering more than 300 head to the point that it sometimes clashes with indigenous species. The ibex, on the other hand, has recently been reintroduced into the area in a more discreet way.

Sheep and cattle breeding still plays an important economic role together with the revival and development of the craft of woodworking, which forms part of the local cultural heritage: regular exhibitions are held in the Maison de l'Artisanat in Ville-Vieille, in the Espace géologique de Château-Queyras and in Ceillac as part of the permanent exhibition of daily and religious life.

The nature reserve of **Val d'Escreins** *(see VARS)* is included in the park.

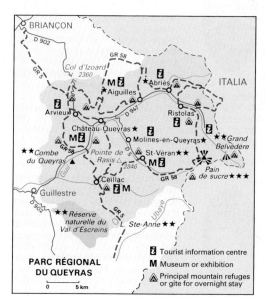

PARC RÉGIONAL DU QUEYRAS

0 — 5 km

🛈 Tourist information centre
M Museum or exhibition
Ⓐ Principal mountain refuges or gite for overnight stay

The reintroduction of the ibex within the Parc naturel régional du Queyras in 1995 was supported by a campaign of information undertaken jointly by the park and the Italian authorities of Val Pellice with the aim of drawing the attention of hikers. Local tourist offices hand out forms on which people can jot down their observations, concerning in particular numbered rings of different colours, which are tied to the animals' ears and represent a reliable means of identification.

Parc naturel régional du Luberon

Created in 1977, the park covers an area of 152 000ha/ 375 592 acres, two thirds of which are situated in the Vaucluse *département* and one third in the Alpes-de-Haute-Provence *département;* it includes 60 municipalities.

Its goals are to protect and improve the environment, to encourage economic development and offer visitors the possibility of discovering traditional Provence.

The *borie* (drystone hut) illustrates the typical local architecture and has become the emblem of the park. *(See Introduction: Traditional Architecture.)*

The limited network of waterways is centred round the lower Durance and Aigue Brun valleys and the Étang de la Bonde.

Birdlife is the most interesting form of animal life inside the park. Among the protected species are: the Bonelli's eagle (a typical Mediterranean bird of prey), the Egyptian vulture, the short-toed eagle (a migrating bird which feeds on reptiles) and the eagle owl. Two mammals symbolize wildlife in Luberon country: the wild boar and the beaver.

The local flora is represented by a few specific species such as the *lauzée* bearing resinous cones at its extremity, the fluffy-leaved cistus and the Etrurian honeysuckle which gives off a particularly strong fragrance. Forested areas are essentially planted with cedars. There is a special trail in the park called the cedar forest botanic trail which offers visitors the possibility of observing typical species of the Luberon region. There are other nature trails in the area of the park described in the Provence guide.

NATURE RESERVES

Nature reserves include areas which are interesting from various points of view: ecosystems containing rare or remarkable animal and plant species; areas of particular interest for their geological formation and for the purpose of speleological studies; stopovers for migrating birds. In Savoie, reserves are mainly adjacent to the Parc national de la Vanoise: Plan du Tuéda (1 112ha/2 748 acres), Hauts de Villeroper (1 114ha/2 753 acres), Tignes-Champagny (999ha/2 469 acres), Val-d'Isère, la Grande Sassière (2 230ha/5 510 acres); in Isère, on the other hand, they are linked to the Parc national des Écrins: Haute Vallée du Vénéon (90ha/222 acres), Haute Vallée du Béranger (85ha/210 acres), or to the Parc national du Vercors: Hauts-Plateaux (16 000ha/39 536 acres).

In the Haute-Savoie region, which has no nature park, several important nature reserves were founded instead; they include information centres and nature trails. Among them are the following: les Aiguilles Rouges (3 279ha/ 8 102 acres), Sixt-Passy (9 200ha/27 733 acres),

les Contamines-Montjoie (5 500ha/13 590 acres) as well as smaller ones such as the marshland near Bout-du-Lac d'Annecy (84.5ha/209 acres), le Delta de la Dranse on the southern shores of Lake Geneva (45ha/111 acres) and le Roc de Chère (68ha/168 acres) on the northern shores of the Lac d'Annecy.

Réserve géologique de Haute-Provence

Founded in 1984, this geological reserve includes 37 municipalities surrounding the town of Digne and covers an area of 145 000ha/358 295 acres.

Based on a novel idea, the reserve, which is the largest in Europe, is situated in a area of geological transition. The reserve lies at the heart of the region occupied by the "Alpine sea" during the Secondary Era, while the land was situated to the south.

Sedimentary deposits were laid during each era. The amount varied considerably but the density was amazing. Plant deposits inform us about the flora of the Primary Era. The Secondary Era, characterised by a rich marine life, retained the skeleton of a large reptile, numerous fossils (ammonites etc) and coral reefs, while the Tertiary Era preserved for us the imprint of birds' feet on the shores of the Alpine sea.

Besides paleontological vestiges, the sites offer a vast panorama of the various changes which marked the folding of the Alpine range: the strata of the transverse valleys for instance (Verdaches, Chabrières and Péroué) are like an open book of local geology.

The nature reserve is in two parts: 18 sites protected for their exceptional scientific value are scattered over the whole area; some of them, provided with information panels, are more accessible to the general public and are described under Préalpes de DIGNE.

It is forbidden to dig up or pick up fossils on these sites.

Nature study tours led by a geologist are organised during the summer either for a day or a week's hiking or riding. *(See Practical Information: Something different...)*

Local economy

For hundreds of years, Alpine economy was based on agriculture and handicraft until the region witnessed two economic revolutions: the first, which happened as a result of the discovery of hydroelectric power, led to the industrialisation and urbanisation of the valleys; the second, which was the rapid development of tourism, led to drastic changes in high mountain landscapes. These two phenomena, however, saved the region from the population drift to the cities, which threatened its future prosperity.

Today, the northern Alps are already a very dynamic region with important towns such as Grenoble and Annecy, whereas the southern Alps are changing at a slower pace and still retain a strong traditional economy with small and medium-sized towns such as Briançon, Sisteron and Digne.

AGRICULTURE

Cattle – In mountainous regions, south-facing slopes are generally devoted to pastures and farming whereas north-facing slopes are covered with forests. In the Alps this pattern has been significantly altered as arable land was gradually turned into pastureland, although cereal farming is developing in the southern Alps. On the other hand, seasonal migrations from the villages to high mountain pastures are being discontinued owing to a shortage of cowherds and cattle are now kept near the villages, which makes it easier to collect and sell dairy produce.

Alpine cattle are famous for their sturdiness and ability to walk, which enables them to adapt to the difficult physical and climatic conditions of their natural environment. In the Préalpes, the predominant breeds originate from Abondance and Villars-de-Lans, whereas in the high mountain areas, the most common breed is known as "Tarine" for the simple reason that it originates from the Tarentaise region.

Montbéliarde   Tarine   Abondance

In many areas, hay making is still done by hand in view of the steepness of the slopes. In the northern massifs, milk is essentially used to make various kinds of cheese in the "fruitières" (cheese cooperatives): *Reblochon* from the Bormes, *Vacherin* from the Bauges, *Beaufort* from the Beaufortain, *Tomme* from Savoie, *Bleu de Sassenage* and *St-Marcellin* from Dauphiné.

Pig farming is developing in cheese-producing areas: by-products from cheese making, especially Reblochon, are used to feed pigs, which explains why most cheese cooperatives keep a lot of pigs as a side line.

Sheep – Sheep farming is one of the main economic activities of the Alpes du Sud and Haute-Provence *départements*. These specialise in the production of lambs fattened quickly and sold when they reach the age of three months. In summer, the resident population is joined by sheep migrating from the lower Provence in search of greener grass. This migration, known as **transhumance**, begins around Midsummer's Day and ends around Michaelmas at the end of September. Unfortunately, it is no longer as picturesque as it used to be when shepherds, donkeys, goats and sheep travelled for days through many villages before reaching the Vercors or the upper valley of the Durance. Nowadays, 200 000 head travel every year by special trucks or trains.

At the end of their journey, the sheep are gathered in flocks numbering between 300 and 4 000 head and taken by shepherds to high pastures rented by the farmers who own the sheep. These pastures can be communal or privately owned and their use is strictly regulated.

Sheep from Haute-Provence do not migrate since they can roam freely on vast areas during the warm season and take shelter in large sheds known as *jas* when winter approaches.

34

Forestry – In recent years, the policy of reafforestation, which is intensive in some areas, has been helped by the restrained use of high pastures and the discontinuation of mowing at high altitude. In fact, forests now cover more than a third of all usable land, and even half in the Préalpes and the northern Alps. They are essentially made up of conifers (fir trees and spruce), and of deciduous trees at low altitude; more than half the forested areas belong to municipalities or private owners. The rest belongs to the state and is administered by the Office national des Forêts (Forestry Commission).

Even though the northern Préalpes boasts some splendid specimens of beeches, which thrive so much in humid countries, forests of conifers predominate as in the rest of the Alpine region. Spruce is the most common conifer of the Salève, Faucigny, Aravis and Bauges areas, whereas fir trees grow most happily in the Chartreuse, Vercors, Beaufortain, Maurienne, and Grésivaudan, as well as in the Diois and Préalpes de Digne; in the high mountain areas of the southern Alps, such as the Briançonnais, Queyras, Embrunais, Ubaye and Mercantour areas, there are mixed forests of fir trees, spruce and larch.

Many Alpine areas owe their prosperity to their forests; some have retained the traditional practice of *"affouage"*, which consists in allotting a certain quantity of wood to each household within the precinct of a given municipality. Forestry development has become easier through the improvement of forest tracks and the use of chain saws as well as towlines when access is particularly difficult. Wood is essentially used as timber or sold to sawmills and paper mills. Quantities are indicated in cubic metres. One cubic metre (35.3 cubic ft) of spruce can be converted into $800m^2$/957sq yd of paper suitable to print 24 000 ordinary newspaper pages.

Whole areas of Haute-Provence have been reafforested since the middle of the 19C and forests, which are now protected, are not used for industrial purposes.

Lavender and lavandin – The delicate scent of lavender is characteristic of Haute-Provence. At the beginning of this century, the picking of the flowers of this wild plant, which grows at an altitude of between 600m/1 968ft and 1 400m/4 593ft on the southern slopes of Mont Ventoux and Montagne de Lure, represented an extra income. Then, when it became necessary to replace cereal crops, lavender was cultivated on the plateaux and high slopes. Well adapted to the climate and calcareous soils of Provence, this plant helped many farmers to survive when they were about to give up. Land, which had not been ploughed for 20 years, was suddenly covered with numerous green shrubs with mauve flowers giving off a delightful fragrance in July.

Later on, Lavandin, a more productive but less fragrant hybrid, was cultivated on the lower slopes and in the valleys between 400m/1 312ft and 700m/2 297ft. Superb fields of lavandin can be spotted on the Plateau de Valensole and along the road from Digne to Gréoux-les-Bains. The harvest takes place from July to September according to the region: most of the picking is now mechanised but the inaccessible or closely planted older fields are still picked by hand. After drying for two to three days, the picked lavender is sent to a distillery equipped with a classic still.

Each complete operation lasts 30min: 1 000kg/2 205lb of picked lavender are needed to produce 5kg/11lb to 10kg/22lb of lavender essence or 25kg/55lb to 40kg/88lb of lavandin essence. Lavender essence is reserved for the perfume and cosmetic industries whereas lavandin essence is used to give a pleasant smell to detergents and cleaning products. Lavender flowers can also be dried and placed in scent bags.

The annual production for the whole of Provence varies from 30t to 40t of lavender essence and from 800t to 900t of lavandin essence.

Olive trees and olive oil – Olive groves traditionally mark the northern boundaries of the Mediterranean region. The production of olive oil, which represents more than two thirds of the national production, comes mainly from the Alpes-de-Haute-Provence and the Luberon area. Following the hard winter of 1956, when almost a quarter of the olive trees growing in the Baronnies area died, olive groves were renewed with more hardy species. There are many varieties and the flavour of the fruit varies accordingly; the type of soil and picking time are also very important. Tradition requires that several varieties should grow in the same olive grove. The harvest begins as early as the end of August, depending on the area. Olives are picked by hand when they are intended to be eaten whole or shaken down into nets with a pole and then sent to the mill. Olives from Nyons *(tanches)* are at present the only ones to have been granted an AOC (Appellation d'Origine Contrôlée) seal of origin. Picked when ripe (black) and preserved in brine, they are a delicacy. *(See ROUTE DES PRINCES D'ORANGE: the box on olive oil.)*

Truffles – The truffle is an edible, subterranean fungus which develops from the mycelium, a network of filaments invisible to the naked eye. They live symbiotically in close association with the root of the downy oak, known in Provence as the white oak. These small stunted oaks are planted in fields called *truffières*. The most productive of these are situated below 500m/1 640ft, but there are a few up to an altitude of 1 000m/3 281ft. The Vaucluse *département* is the main producing area of the Mediterranean region, followed by the Lubéron, Riez and Forcalquier areas as well as the upper valley of the Var River. Truffles, known as the "black gold" of Haute-Provence, are harvested from mid-October to mid-March, when they are ripe and odorous. Pigs are traditionally used to detect the presence of truffles, but they are being replaced by dogs, easier to train and less greedy. Once the animal has spotted a truffle (sometimes buried as deep as 25cm/10in), it is delicately dug up by hand. A white variety of truffle, which is harvested between May and mid-July, mainly in the upper valley of the Var River, is used as a flavouring in cooking.

HYDROELECTRIC POWER AND INDUSTRY

In the French Alps, industries were at first intended to satisfy local needs, but then they undertook to work for the rest of the country and even for the export trade. This led to the development of clock factories in Cluses, of several silk factories, subsidiaries of the textile industries in Lyon, of paper mills in Dauphiné, supplied with wood from the forests of the Chartreuse and the Vercors, of cement factories in the Préalpes, of glove factories in Grenoble and of steel foundries in Ugine.

Hydroelectric power – Known as "houille blanche" (literally white coal), it was the fuel which drove Alpine industry forward.

The cradle of hydroelectric power – During the late 1860s, a factory owner of the Grésivaudan region, called Amable Matussière, who wished to increase the driving power of his mills, called on two engineers, Fredet and **Aristide Bergès**. The latter deserves credit for having harnessed the first 200m/656ft waterfall at Lancey in 1869. At first, the power of the turbines was used mechanically, but by 1870 the invention of the dynamo by Gramme, followed by the building of the first power lines on an industrial scale (the first line dates from 1883), made the new power stations switch to the production of electricity.

Technical development – The Alpine relief lends itself to the production of hydroelectricity: the combination of high mountain ranges and deep valleys creates numerous waterfalls. Engineers began by using waterfalls with a low rate of flow, situated high above the main valleys. They then tapped the main valley rivers, which had a much higher rate of flow, thus creating a concentration of industries along these valleys (valley of the Isère River, known as Tarentaise, valley of the Arc, known as Maurienne, valley of the Romanche).

Today, most of the turbines are connected to alternators, which are in turn linked to the EDF (Électricité de France) network.

The new reservoirs – During the 1950s, engineers conceived "complex projects" embracing whole massifs and involving water storage. The flow of waters, channelled through miles of tunnels and sometimes diverted from the natural river basin, are collected in huge reservoirs like that formed by the Tignes and Roselend dams or ducted into neighbouring, more deeply cleft valleys (Isère-Arc bypass). The rearrangement of the Mont-Cenis basin was completed in 1970 whereas that of the Émosson basin was carried out in 1975, in cooperation with Switzerland.

A new type of equipment was introduced: "energy transfer power stations" fitted with turbines which can release the energy stored by pumping during off-peak hours. The most important power stations of this type are those of Super-Bissorte and Grand-Maison.

In 1991, the production of hydroelectricity in the northern Alps rose to 13.6 billion kWh, which represent a quarter of the total French production.

Different types of dams – There are basically four main types of dams:
– **Gravity dams** withstand water-pressure by their weight alone. They are triangular in section with an almost vertical upstream face and a back sloping at about 50° (Chambon, Bissorte).
– **Arch dams**, graceful and economic in design, have a curved structure with its convex side upstream which transfers the pressure of water laterally to the steep sides of the gorge (Tignes, le Sautet, St-Pierre and Monteynard).
– **Buttressed dams** are used when the width of the dam does not allow the use of an arch; they are a combination of gravity and arch dams (Girotte, Plan d'Amont, Roselend).
– **Riprap dykes** such as la Sassière, Mont-Cenis and Grand-Maison.

Industries stemming from the availability of hydroelectric power – Hydroelectricity was first used in the paper mills of the Grésivaudan region. Today the Lancey mill is equipped with one of the largest paper-making machines in France; there are other mills in Vizille, Pont-de-Claix, Voiron, Domène and Brignoud.

However, **electrometallurgy** and **electrochemistry** were the two industries which benefitted most from the use of hydroelectricity. They settled near the power stations built by the industrialists themselves before the foundation of EDF in 1946. This combination was at the origin of typical Alpine industrial landscapes such as those of the Maurienne, Tarentaise, Grésivaudan and Romanche valleys. However, the cost of transport of raw materials is a real handicap for this mountainous region (7.5t of raw materials are needed to produce 1kg/2.2lb of aluminium). Factories are therefore compelled to turn to more and more complex products, which are rare and expensive, such as certain steel alloys.

Nowadays, electrochemical factories are huge complexes where basic products (chlorate, chlorine and soda) are used to produce detergents, weed-killers and solvents.

The second stage of industrialization – The future belongs to processing industries, which are light and highly specialised industries with hardly any transport problems. They settle in *cluses* (transverse valleys) near large towns such as Grenoble, Annecy and Chambéry. Being located in the outer Alpine area, they are able to communicate more easily with the rest of the country, in particular with the Rhône Valley.

The main assets of the region include its location between France, Italy and Switzerland, plenty of man power and a high proportion of engineers and researchers trained in Grenoble.

Mechanical engineering (Grenoble) and **electrical engineering** have become vital aspects of the industrial landscape of the Alps while the traditional clock industry is still going strong in Annemasse.

Historical table and notes

Events in italics indicate milestones in history

The Celts and the Romans

6-5C BC	The Celts progressively occupy the whole Alpine region; the Allobrogi settle in the area situated between the Rhône and the Isère rivers.
218	Hannibal crosses the Alps in spite of the Alloborgi's attempt to stop him.
125-122	The Romans conquer southern Gaul.
121	The Allobrogi finally acknowledge Roman superiority.
1C	During the reign of Augustus, the whole Alpine region is pacified.
End of AD 2C	The first Christian communities expand in spite of persecutions.
4C	Christianism gets a firm hold on the region and bishoprics are founded.
313	*Proclamation of the edict of Milan, through which Constantine grants religious freedom to the Christians.*
443	Burgundians from the Rhine region settle on the land of the Allobrogi with the permission of the Romans. This land is also called "Sabaudia", the land of fir trees, which later became Savoie.
476	*Fall of the Roman Empire.*

The Franks and the kingdom of Burgundy

534-536	The Franks seize Burgundy and invade Provence.
800	*Charlemagne becomes Emperor of the West.*
8C	Franks and Arabs devastate Provence.
987	*Hugues Capet is crowned King of France.*
10C	Provence becomes part of the kingdom of Burgundy. The Saracens are repelled.
1032	The kingdom of Burgundy is annexed by the Holy Roman Empire. At the same time, the archbishop of Vienne splits his huge territory into two: the future Savoie to the north and the future Dauphiné to the south.

Savoie, Dauphiné and Provence

11-12C	Expansion of the three provinces. The dynasty of the Count of Savoie becomes the guardian of the Alpine passes. The ruler of Dauphiné adopts the title of "Dauphin" and the Count of Provence Raimond Bérenger V inherits the County of Forcalquier which is thereafter united with Provence. Building of abbeys and monasteries throughout the land. St Bruno founds the Carthusian Order and monastery.
1209	*Albigensian Crusade led by Simon de Montfort.*
1268	The Dauphin Guigues VII marries the daughter of the Count of Savoie.
1270	*Death of King St Louis of France, who was married to the daughter of the Count of Provence.*
1337-1453	*Hundred Years War.*
14C	Savoie becomes a powerful feudal state under Amadeus VI, VII and VIII.
1349	Dauphin Humbert II, being in political and financial difficulties, negotiates the sale of Dauphiné to the King of France. It is decided that the heir to the throne of France will, from then on, bear the title of "Dauphin".

C. de Torquat/PIX

Seal of Amadeus VI

37

1416	Savoie becomes a dukedom.
1419	Savoie and Piedmont are united.
1447	Dauphin Louis II (the future King Louis XI) settles on his domains, puts an end to the feudal system and creates the Parliament of Grenoble.

Italian Wars and Wars of Religion

1461-1483	*Louis XI's reign.*
1488	Crusade against Vaudois heretics in the Alpine valleys.
1489-1564	Life of Guillaume Farel, a native of Gap, who preaches the Reformation.
1492	*Christopher Columbus discovers America.*
1494-1559	The Italian Wars reveal the strategic importance of the Dauphiné passes.
1536	François I invades Savoie which remains under French rule for 23 years.
1559	Treaty of Cateau-Cambrésis: Savoie is returned to the Duke of Savoie who transfers his capital from Chambéry to Turin.
1543-1626	Life of Lesdiguières, the protestant governor of Dauphiné, who fights the Duke of Savoie.
1562-1598	Fierce fighting between Catholics and Protestants: Sisteron, Castellane and Seyne are besieged.
1589	*Beginning of Henri IV's reign.*
1598	*End of the Wars of Religion; Edict of Nantes: Protestants obtain the free-dom of worship and guaranteed strongholds.*
17C	Savoie is occupied several times by French troops.
1628	Dauphiné looses all its administrative autonomy.

From Louis XIV to the Revolution

1643-1715	*Louis XIV's reign.*
1685	*Revocation of the Edict of Nantes: Protestants flee the country.*
1692	The Duke of Savoie invades the southern Alps. The king sends Vauban to the area in order to build fortresses and strengthen existing ones (Briançon, Mont-Dauphin, Sisteron, Colmars...).
1707	Invasion of Provence by Prince Eugene of Savoie.
1713	Treaty of Utrecht: Dauphiné and Provence expand; France looses part of the Briançonnais but receives the Ubaye region in compensation.
1736	Jean-Jacques Rousseau settles in Les Charmettes near Chambéry.
1740-1748	War of the Austrian Succession. Eastern Provence is invaded by Aus-trian and Sardinian troops; Savoie is occupied by the Spaniards, France's allies. The treaty of Aix-la-Chapelle ends the war and the Spaniards have to give up Savoie.
1774	*Beginning of the reign of Louis XVI guillotined less than 20 years later.*
1786	Balmat and Paccard are the first Alpinists to climb Mont Blanc.
1788	Preliminary symptoms of the Revolution in Grenoble and Vizille.
1789	*Bastille day signals the start of the French Revolution; départements are created the following year.*
1791	Dauphiné is divided into three *départements*: Isère, Drôme and Hautes-Alpes.
1792	French revolutionary troops occupy Savoie which becomes the "Mont-Blanc *département*".
1793	Creation of the "Alpes-Maritimes *département*" (returned to the king-dom of Sardinia in 1814).

19C

1811	The Route du Mont-Cenis is built by order of Napoleon I
1815	By the treaty of Paris, Savoie is given back to King Victor-Emmanuel I of Sardinia. Napoleon I, returning from exile on Elba, lands in Golfe-Juan on the Mediterranean coast and crosses the southern Alps to Grenoble.
1852	*Napoleon III becomes Emperor of France.*
1858	Napoleon III meets the Italian statesman Cavour in Plombières (Vosges region): they agree that France shall help the King of Sardinia to drive the Austrians out of Italy; in exchange, France is to receive Nice and Savoie.
April 1860	A plebiscite is organised in Savoie: an overwhelming majority vote in favour of the union with France. The new province is divided into two *départements*: Savoie and Haute-Savoie.
1869	Aristide Bergès harnesses the first high waterfall in Lancey thus becoming the "father" of hydroelectric power.
1870	*Proclamation of the Third Republic on 4 September.*
1872	Inauguration of the Fréjus railway tunnel.
End of the 19C	Acceleration of the population drift from the mountainous areas to the towns.

1924	First Winter Olympic Games held in Chamonix.
June 1940	The advancing German army is temporarily halted by the Isère River. Italian attacks are repelled by border garrisons.
1944	Fierce fighting in the Vercors: Dauphiné is one of the main strongholds of the Resistance. One of the underground fighters' most heroic feats takes place on the Plateau des Glières *(see THORENS-GLIÈRES)*.
1945	The Resistance liberates the Ubaye region.
1947	The treaty of Paris alters the Franco-Italian border in favour of France who receives the Vallée Étroite *(see Le BRIANÇONNAIS)*.
1955-1967	Construction of the huge Serre-Ponçon dam.
1962	Signing of the Accords d'Évian (Treaty of Évian, *see ÉVIAN-LES-BAINS*)
1963	Creation of the Parc national de la Vanoise, the first French national park.
1965	Inauguration of the Mont-Blanc road tunnel.
1968	Winter Olympics held in Grenoble.
1980	Inauguration of the Fréjus road tunnel, over 100 years after the opening of the railway tunnel.
1992	16th Winter Olympic Games held in Albertville.
1995	Creation of the Parc naturel régional de Chartreuse.
1996	Creation of the Parc naturel régional du massif des Bauges.

DAUPHINÉ AND PROVENCE: A fluctuating border

Antiquity – The powerful Vocontii, who, before the Roman conquest, dominated the mountainous region situated between the Isère River and the Mont Ventoux, were defeated by the Romans in 121 BC; however, they did not submit. Resistance continued until the reign of Augustus. Victorious in 13 BC, the Emperor determined the boundaries of a new province, the Alpes-Maritimes, east of Narbonensis (from the name of the first Roman colony of Narbonna). The Romans founded several cities such as Die, Sisteron, Briançon, Embrun, Riez etc and country estates *(villae)* and roads. Areas bordering the important road *(via)* which followed the Durance River were quite prosperous. During the last 200 years of the Roman Empire, administrative reorganisation took place. In about AD 400, the region was split between four Roman provinces: the Viennoise to the north and west, the Second Narbonensis to the south and, to the east, the Alpes Maritimes (main town: Embrun) and the Alpes Cottiennes (including the Briançonnais), linked to the Italian diocese. The organisation of the Church was well on the way with the foundation of the bishoprics of Embrun, Digne, Riez, Gap, Die...

Barbarian invasions, which took place during the 5C, completely changed the map of the area. North of the Durance, the Burgundians controlled the Alpine massif; to the south, the Visigoths having invaded Provence, were compelled to let the Ostrogoths have it. Finally, in 534-36; the Franks remained the sole masters of the region.

The Middle Ages – The situation remained confused until the 13C, while Franks and Arabs fought to control Provence which was made a kingdon in 855. Besides Provence, this kingdom, ruled over from 879 onwards by Boson, Charles the Bold's brother-in-law, included the regions of Lyon, Vienne and the Alps. During the course of the next century, it was joined to the vast kingdom of Burgundy, which spread from Basel to the Mediterranean, then became part of the Holy Roman Empire in 1032.

In the 12C, there were three main states: Southern Viennois belonging to the counts of Albon (one of them, Guigues IV, had "Dauphin" as his second name); Provence shared between the counts of Toulouse and the counts of Barcelona; Haute-Provence (with the added Gapençais and Embrunais areas) ruled over by the powerful counts of Forcalquier. In the 14C, apart from the papal possessions, there were only two large states left: Provence belonging to the counts of Anjou and Dauphiné belonging to the **Dauphins**. Between the two, the border remained vague owing to the feudal principal of allegiance. In 1337, King Robert, count of Provence, turned down the proposal made to him by Dauphin Humbert II of buying his estates for the sum of 190 000 florins.

Union with France – Dauphiné was united with the kingdom of France in 1349 and Provence in 1481.

The "transfer" of Dauphiné – **Humbert II** became Dauphin at a very early age. He was ambitious, extravagant, inconsistent and squandered his fortune on religious foundations and offerings; he also founded the Grenoble university, was a patron of the arts and literature and held court like a king. His departure for the crusade left his coffers quite empty so that, upon his return, having lost his wife and son, he decided to abdicate and sell Dauphiné. The king of France, Philippe VI of Valois, seized the opportunity. The contract, which was called "Transport du Dauphiné à la France", was signed in Lyon in 1349 and Humbert II became a Dominican monk.

Provence bequeathed to the King of France – King René's successor, his nephew Charles du Maine, only ruled for a year and in his will bequeathed Provence to his cousin King Louis XI of France. However, the union was only ratified by the Estates of Provence in 1486 during the reign of Charles VIII. The whole of southeast France was thus included in the kingdom, but in the east, the Var River and the Ubaye Valley marked the limits of French territory.

From the 16C to the present day – The provinces gradually lost their autonomy. In 1535, the Edict of Joinville made the administration of Provence more dependent on royal power. In 1539, it was decided that Dauphiné should be governed by the same laws and regulations as the other parts of the kingdom. During the next 200 years, the borders were modified from time to time: in 1513, Dauphiné gained the Gapençais area and, in 1536, François I temporarily occupied Barcelonnette and Savoie. During Louis XIV's reign, Dauphiné which was deemed strategically important as a neighbour of Savoie and Piedmont, was fortified by Vauban. In 1713, following the Treaty of Utrecht, France lost part of the Briançonnais but gained the Barcelonnette and Ubaye valleys.

Dauphiné was one of the cradles of the French Revolution. As early as 1763, the Dauphiné parliament refused to ratify royal edicts considered too harsh on tax matters. In 1788, the promulgation of several edicts intended to curb the parliament's authority led to protests *(see GRENOBLE: "the Day of the Tiles")*. A few days later, the famous Vizille Assembly met *(see VIZILLE)*.

During the Revolution, the division of the national territory into *départements* put an end to Provence and Dauphiné as political entities; papal domains were annexed. Centralisation contributed to unify France who acquired Nice and Savoie in 1860. A century later however, the regions were reborn: to the north, the Rhône-Alpes region including the Drôme (Diois and former Baronnies); to the south, the Provence-Alpes-Côte-d'Azur region comprising the southern Alps and Haute-Provence.

THE HOUSE OF SAVOIE

The House of Savoie was the oldest reigning dynasty in Europe: it began with the feudal lord Humbert "White Hands", who became Count of Savoie in 1034 and ended with the last king of Italy, Humbert II, Victor-Emmanuel III's son, who abdicated in 1946. During nine centuries, the House of Savoie ruled over Savoie when it was a county, then a duchy and it governed Piedmont from 1429 onwards, Sardinia from 1720 and finally produced Italy's monarchs from 1861 to 1946.

How counts became dukes – Their role as "gatekeepers" of the Alps gave the counts and later the dukes of Savoie exceptional power. Owing to its strategic position, Savoie was constantly coveted by its neighbours to the point that its history amounts to a string of successive occupations, each followed by a treaty returning it to its rightful owner.

During the Middle Ages, three of Savoie's rulers, Amadeus VI, VII and VIII, gave the region unprecedented ascendency; their court, held in Chambéry, rivalled in splendour with that of the most important sovereigns of Europe. The most illustrious, Amadeus VIII, was the first to bear the title of Duke of Savoie; he was elected pope at the end of his life under the name of Felix V against the Roman popes Eugene IV and Nicholas V. In the 16C, the Treaty of Cateau-Cambrésis freed Savoie from French domination which had lasted 23 years. Duke Emmanuel-Philibert reorganised his domains and established his capital in Turin instead of Chambéry (less easily accessible to French

monarchs). His wish to expand on the Italian side of the Alps was accomplished during the reign of Victor-Amadeus II, who gained the kingdom of Sicily by the Treaty of Utrecht, then promptly exchanged it for Sardinia and became the king of that region.

Union with France – The people of Savoie were tired of their government which they ironically called "il Buon Governo". Moreover, they were worried by Cavour's anticlerical policy and turned towards France for help. Napoleon III and Cavour met in Plombières in 1858 and decided that, in exchange for France's help against Austrian occupation, Italy would relinquish Nice and Savoie if the populations concerned agreed. This led to the plebiscite of April 1860: by 130 533 yeas against 235 nays, the people of Savoie overwhelmingly agreed to become French.

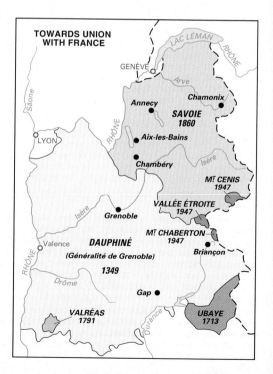

TOWARDS UNION WITH FRANCE

LAC LÉMAN
RHÔNE
GENÈVE
Arve
Saône
Annecy
Chamonix
SAVOIE 1860
RHÔNE
LYON
Aix-les-Bains
Chambéry
Isère
M^T CENIS 1947
VALLÉE ÉTROITE 1947
Isère
Grenoble
M^T CHABERTON 1947
RHÔNE
Valence
DAUPHINÉ
(Généralité de Grenoble) 1349
Briançon
Drôme
Gap
VALRÉAS 1791
Durance
UBAYE 1713

Famous natives of the Alps

SCHOLARS AND WRITERS

Savoie, which has only belonged to France for just over 100 years, was, strangely enough, the cradle of the French language for it was the humanist **Guillaume Fichet** (1433-1478) who set up the first printing press in Paris. Almost two centuries later, in 1606, the first French Academy was founded in Annecy (soon followed by Richelieu's famous Académie Française); one of its founders was **Saint François de Sales** (1567-1622), who inspired religious life in his native Savoie and whose works contributed to the blossoming of the French language.

One of the early prominent figures of the southern Alps was another humanist **Guillaume Farel** (1489-1565), a native of the Gap area, who preached the Reformation with Jean Calvin in Geneva. At the same time, Occitan was the dominant language of the southern Alps as indeed of the whole of southern France and, although its official use was discontinued in the 16C, it continued to be spoken by the people for another three centuries.

During the late 18C and early 19C, the brothers **Joseph** (1753-1821) and **Xavier** (1763-1852) **de Maistre** rejected the ideals of the French Revolution and supported absolute monarchy.

However, the most famous man of letters of the Alpine region was undoubtedly the novelist **Henri Beyle** (1783-1842), a native of Grenoble, better known by his pseudonym **Stendhal**. Besides his masterpieces, *Le Rouge et le Noir* (1830) and *La Chartreuse de Parme* (1839), he wrote numerous studies, including *De l'Amour* (1822), in which he analysed love from a psychological as well as a historical and

Stendhal

V. d'Amboise/PIX

social point of view, and several volumes of autobiography, including *La Vie d'Henry Brulard* in which he depicted his childhood and adolescent years in Grenoble.

The 19C also saw the revival of the Occitan language and of Provençal traditions under the leadership of Frédéric Mistral. One of his disciples, **Paul Arène** (1853-1896), a native of Sisteron, wrote tales and poems both in French and Occitan. Better known was **Jean Giono** (1895-1970), born in Manosque, who celebrated Haute-Provence and its country folk in works such as *Regain* (1930) and *Jean le Bleu* (1932). His contemporary, **Alexandre Arnoux** (1884-1973), also chose Haute-Provence as the setting to most of his works *(Haute-Provence, Rhône, mon fleuve)*.

SOLDIERS AND POLITICIANS

Born in Grésivaudan, **Bayard** (1476-1524), known as *"le chevalier sans peur et sans reproche"* (fearless and above reproach) has gone down in history as the model soldier of his time. He had the honour of knighting King François I after the battle of Marignan in 1515.

François de Bonne de Lesdiguières (1543-1626) led the Huguenots from Dauphiné during the Wars of Religion and was given command of the armed forces of his native region by King Henri IV, which led him to fight against the Duke of Savoie. He was the last Constable of France before Richelieu abolished the title in 1627.

In 1788, two natives of Grenoble, judge **Jean-Joseph Mounier** and barrister **Antoine Barnave**, led the peaceful protest of the Assemblée de Vizille which paved the way for the French Revolution a year later. Another native of Grenoble, **Casimir Perier**, was prime minister of France in 1831-32, during the reign of King Louis-Philippe. His grandson was President of the French Republic in 1894-95.

SCIENTISTS AND INVENTORS

Among her famous sons, Savoie counts the mathematician **Gaspard Monge** (1746-1818), who devised "descriptive geometry" at the age of 19 and later was one of the initiators of the École polytechnique where he taught, and the chemist **Claude Louis Berthollet** (1748-1822), who discovered the whitening properties of chlorine, widely used in the manufacture of linen.

Dauphiné on the other hand prides itself on having had several inventors such as **Vaucanson** (1709-1782), who built automata and partly mechanised the silk industry, and **Xavier Jouvin** (1800-1844), who devised a system of classifying hand sizes and invented a machine for cutting gloves to corresponding sizes.

41

ABC of architecture

Religious architecture

SISTERON – Ground plan of the Église Notre-Dame (12-15C)

The early Romanesque style from northern Italy is characterised by a chancel with three capital apsidal chapels and a single nave. The basilical plan has no transept.

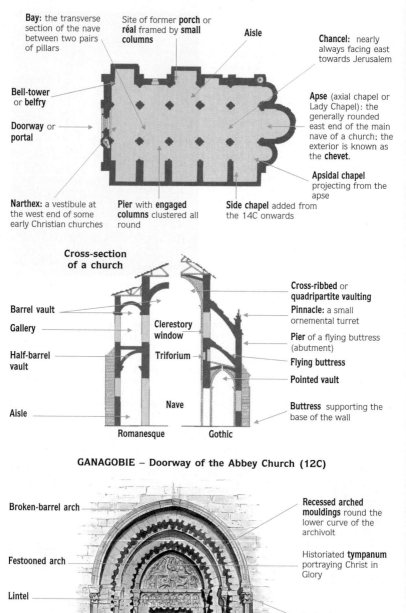

Bay: the transverse section of the nave between two pairs of pillars

Site of former **porch** or **réal** framed by **small columns**

Aisle

Chancel: nearly always facing east towards Jerusalem

Bell-tower or **belfry**

Doorway or **portal**

Apse (axial chapel or Lady Chapel): the generally rounded east end of the main nave of a church; the exterior is known as the **chevet.**

Apsidal chapel projecting from the apse

Narthex: a vestibule at the west end of some early Christian churches

Pier with **engaged columns** clustered all round

Side chapel added from the 14C onwards

Cross-section of a church

Barrel vault

Gallery

Half-barrel vault

Aisle

Clerestory window

Triforium

Nave

Romanesque

Cross-ribbed or **quadripartite vaulting**

Pinnacle: a small ornemental turret

Pier of a flying buttress (abutment)

Flying buttress

Pointed vault

Buttress supporting the base of the wall

Gothic

GANAGOBIE – Doorway of the Abbey Church (12C)

Broken-barrel arch

Festooned arch

Lintel

Twisted column

Recessed arched mouldings round the lower curve of the archivolt

Historiated **tympanum** portraying Christ in Glory

Corinthian capital

Jambs: uprights supporting the archivolt

R. Corbel

EMBRUN – Porch (14C) of the Cathédrale Notre-Dame

This highly ornamented and elegant feature, usually found on the north side of a church, is common in northern Italy.

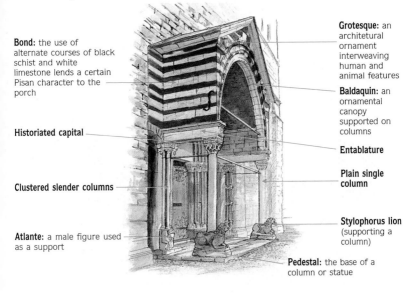

Bond: the use of alternate courses of black schist and white limestone lends a certain Pisan character to the porch

Historiated capital

Clustered slender columns

Atlante: a male figure used as a support

Grotesque: an architetural ornament interweaving human and animal features

Baldaquin: an ornamental canopy supported on columns

Entablature

Plain single column

Stylophorus lion (supporting a column)

Pedestal: the base of a column or statue

EMBRUN – Chancel and crossing of the Cathédrale Notre-Dame (12-13C)

The Romanesque parts (barrel-vaulted aisles and apse) blend harmoniously with the pointed vaulting of the Gothic nave

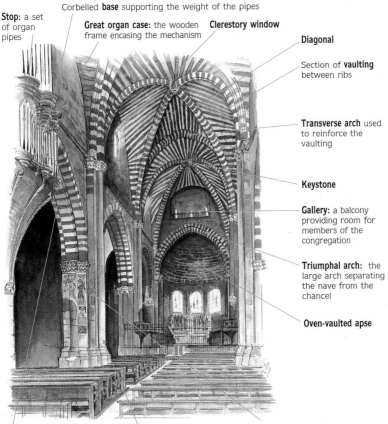

Corbelled **base** supporting the weight of the pipes

Stop: a set of organ pipes

Great organ case: the wooden frame encasing the mechanism

Clerestory window

Diagonal

Section of **vaulting** between ribs

Transverse arch used to reinforce the vaulting

Keystone

Gallery: a balcony providing room for members of the congregation

Triumphal arch: the large arch separating the nave from the chancel

Oven-vaulted apse

Main arch separating the nave from the aisles

Engaged column

Backing **pilaster** against which a column rests

R. Corbel

ARVIEUX – Nave of Renaissance church (16C) with Baroque altarpiece

Cornice: the third or upper part of an entablature resting on a frieze

Attic: the top part of a structure designed to make it more impressive

Altarpiece

Frieze: a decorative band near the top of an interior wall below the cornice

Entablature: it comprises the architrave, the frieze and the cornice.

Corner piece: the wall section situated between the arch and its frame

Coffer: a sunken panel in a vault or ceiling

Pilaster: an engaged rectangular column

Agrafe: an ornamental element in the form of a mascaron placed on the keystone

NÉVACHE – Baroque altarpiece from the Église St-Marcellin-et-St-Antoine (15-17C)

Modillion: a small console supporting a cornice

Crowning piece

Scroll

Armature: a frame of metal bars supporting and protecting a window

Cartouche: an ornamental tablet often inscribed or decorated

Composite capital combining elements from different classical orders

Saddle-bars fixed into the masonry to maintain stained-glass panels in place

Twisted columns decorated with vine branches

Foliated scrolls: a kind of ornamentation depicting foliage

Niche: recess in a wall, usually meant to contain a statue

Altar front

Altar table

Predella: the bottom tier of an altarpiece divided into several panels

R. Corbel

44

GRENOBLE – Façade of the Palais de Justice (16C)

The doorway and chapel of the former palace of the Dauphiné Parliament date from the Late Gothic. The main part of the edifice bearing the Renaissance imprint contrasts with the plainer left-hand extremity which is more recent.

Triangular pediment

Corinthian pilaster

Chimney stack: a structure in which several chimneys are grouped

Table: a flat vertical surface

Mullioned window: a **mullion** is a vertical post dividing a window

Curved pediment

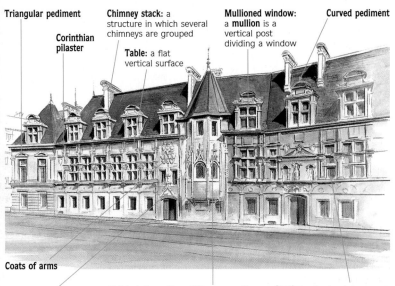

Coats of arms

Basket-handled arch

Pointed decorative **gable** surmounting the doorway and windows

Cornice: a horizontal projection crowning a wall

ST-GEOIRE-EN-VALDAINE – Château de Longpra (18C)

This former fortified castle, turned into a residential castle in the 18C, has very steep roofs well-suited to the hard winters of the Dauphiné region.

Dormer window

Chimney pot

Central block projecting from the rest of the building

Roof clad with **shingles**

Wrought-iron balcony

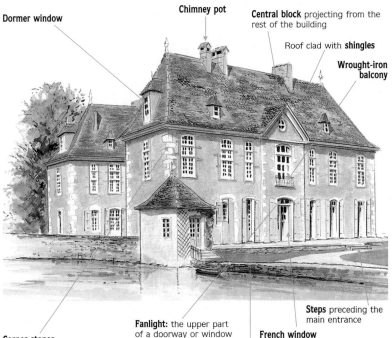

Corner stones

Fanlight: the upper part of a doorway or window

French window

Stone base of the edifice

Steps preceding the main entrance

R. Corbel

Art and architecture in the Alps

RELIGIOUS ART

Churches and chapels

In the north of the region, churches and chapels are small but solidly built on steep slopes or summits where their thick stone walls, pierced by small windows, have been braving the bad weather for centuries, their wide roof structures forming an awning to protect the most exposed façades. In Savoie, churches are surmounted by characteristic steeples swelling out into onion shapes, whereas in Dauphiné, stone spires are topped by pyramids. The names of these humble churches built by thrifty peasants are suggestive: Notre-Dame de-Tout-Secours (Our Lady of All Assistance), Notre-Dame-des-Neiges (Our Lady of the Snowfields)...

In the south, the majority of churches date from the Romanesque period. The main features of the **early Romanesque** style, imported from Italy, are the simple plan, massive appearance and rustic aspect of the buildings. Moderate in size, churches were designed without a transept and with a single nave with narrow openings, surmounted by barrel vaulting or a strong timber frame and ending with an oven-vaulted apse. The best examples of this early style, in which a minimum of decoration was used, are the Église St-Donat, the crypt of Notre-Dame-du-Dromon and of the Prieuré de Vilhosc near Sisteron. The **late Romanesque** style flourished during the 12C and 13C, introducing a new harmony between volumes, openings and curves as well as the general use of more refined building stones. However, in spite of gaining in height, churches retained their rustic look while the influence from Lombard and Piedmont could still be felt, particularly in the Briançonnais, Queyras, Ubaye and Embrun regions. Designed like basilicas, these churches were adorned with baldaquined porches, often supported by squatting lions as in Embrun, Guillestre, St-Véran and La Salle. The slender steeples were surmounted by four-sided pyramids. Exterior ornamentation remained sobre owing to the use of hard limestone, difficult to carve. Interior decoration was also rare, with one exception however, the Monastère de Ganogobie which has a beautifully carved pediment and remarkable mosaics. On the other hand, the stylistic simplicity of the Abbaye de Boscodon bears evidence of the primitive Cistercian influence.

The Romanesque style lasted into the 13C and 14C with the building of the Église Notre-Dame in Forcalquier, of the Église St-Sauveur in Manosque and of the churches in Seyne-les-Alpes and Bayons.

The **Gothic** style had only a limited impact on the region and is best represented by the cathedrals built in Embrun and Forcalquier.

The only worthy example of the **Baroque** architectural style in the southern Alps is the Église Notre-Dame in Briançon, built between 1703 and 1718. However there is a wealth of Baroque ornamentation, such as wreathed columns, carved pulpits, organ cases, altarpieces and recessed statues all richly painted and gilt.

In the north, on the other hand, particularly in Savoie, many churches were built or decorated at the time of the Counter-Reformation (a movement which, during the 16C and 17C, tried to counteract Huguenot austerity with an abundance of ornamentation, concerning mainly altarpieces and pulpits). Artists mostly came from Italy. The best examples of this rich style are Notre-Dame-de-la-Gorge and the church of Champagny-en-Vanoise, whereas, in the Maurienne and Tarentaise areas, Baroque trails *("les Chemins du Baroque")* have been specially designed to enable visitors to discover this unique heritage *(see Practical information)*.

Belfry of Notre-Dame-de-Bellecombe

Murals – Pilgrims and travellers crossing the Alps in the 14C and 15C decorated churches and chapels with bright frescoes in naïve style illustrating scenes from the life of Jesus (Chapelle St-Antoine in Bessans, Chapelle de Puy-Chalvin, Chapelle de Prelles...) and various saints (the most popular being St Christopher, who looks after travellers, St Sebastian, who cures the plague...), as well as many episodes from the Old and New Testaments.

An equally favourite theme was that contrasting the "**virtues**", represented by beautiful young maidens, and the "**vices**", riding various animals, such as pride riding a lion, anger riding a leopard and laziness riding a donkey. The corresponding punishments were depicted with great realism and, for that reason, they have generally disappeared. The most common technique was tempera painting using an emulsion of pigment mixed with egg, glue and casein. In the Alpes-Maritimes region, the name of some of the artists who painted these murals are known, for instance **Canavesio** in St-Étienne-de-Tinée, **Andrea de Cella** in Roure. From the mid 15C to the mid 16C, a Gothic school of painting, based in the Comté de Nice, produced some remarkable pictures and altarpieces such as the altarpiece by **Louis Bréa** which decorates the church of the tiny village of Lieuche.

Crosses and oratories – Discreet and humble, dotted along paths and on the edge of precipices, crosses and oratories represented an art form which expressed the religious fervour of mountain folk and travellers having to face a hostile natural environment. Oratories were originally mere heaps of stones known as *"Montjoie"* but they gradually became larger, were surmounted by crosses and included a recess which sheltered a small statue. Crosses were erected in the most dangerous places, in order to comfort passers-by. The most remarkable of these, which are situated in the Queyras, bear the symbols of Christ's Passion and are known as *"croix de la Passion"*.

CASTLES AND FORTS

Feudal castles – These, or what is left of them, usually draw the visitors' attention because of the sheer beauty of their ruins standing in picturesque surroundings in isolated spots or overlooking ancient villages. Very few of them offer any real architectural interest either through their style or state of preservation. Particularly noteworthy, however, are the château de Simiane and its famous rotunda, dating from the 12C and 13C, the château de Bargème, dating from the 13C, and the château de Montmaur, dating from the 14C. Many castles, such as those of Montbrun-les-Bains and Tallard, were seriously damaged during the Wars of Religion, which were particularly violent in that area. Some castles were entirely rebuilt during the 17C and 18C, while sometimes retaining part of their former structure: such is the case of the castles of Gréoux-les-Bains, Esparron-du-Verdon and Château-Queyras.

Fortifications – Towns had, since Antiquity, been protected by walls which often had to be rebuilt or consolidated during the Middle Ages and even later, until the reign of Louis XIV, owing to constant border conflicts. Embrun has retained a 12C tower and Sisteron still boasts four 14C towers and a citadel dating from the end of the 16C... However, most of the border fortifications were built by Vauban who, from 1693 onwards, endeavoured to "enclose" Haut-Dauphiné.

Sébastien le Prestre de Vauban (1633-1707) took his inspiration from his predecessors, in particular Jean Errard (1554-1610), who is believed to have rebuilt the Sisteron fortifications and wrote a treatise on fortifications published in 1600. Having observed the numerous sieges which took place during his lifetime, Vauban was able to evolve a series of new types of fortifications, well adapted to the local terrain. In his opinion, Dauphiné was not sufficiently well protected by the natural barrier of the Alps which could be crossed at certain times of the year. He therefore studied in great detail the advantages and drawbacks of natural sites such as peaks, passes and valleys in order to choose the best position for his defences.

He protected gun-sites from enemy fire by means of armoured casings, shielded gunners and soldiers, created many obstacles such as fortified gates, broken-line walls etc... The result of his ingenuity can be seen in Briançon, Mont-Dauphin, Château-Queyras, Colmars and Entrevaux, for these fortresses were still being used in the 19C. Vauban was equally aware of the aesthetic aspect of his works and of its importance: he thus made skillful use of local materials (for instance pink marble in Mont-Dauphin), which blend well with the landscape, and from this point of view too, his works were a great success.

Residential castles – They first appeared in the 16C, when former castles were often remodelled and a Renaissance building was added to the existing structure (Allemagne-en-Provence, Château-Arnoux and Tallard).

During the 17C and 18C, castles lost their military aspect, which gave way to comfort and attractive features. There are practically no constructions of this type in the area with the exception of the château de Sauvan, designed by Jean-Baptiste Franque in 1719, which is a real gem. The château de Malijai is another example of the classical style in the region.

Traces from the past – Most ancient villages, especially in the southern Alps, have retained a wealth of details from the main architectural styles of the past: Romanesque vaults, cellars and doorways; Gothic arches and twin openings; Renaissance lintels, carved jambs decorated with acanthus leaves, mullioned windows and elegant wrought iron; 17C pediments and bosses; 19C neo-Classical buildings and various other imitations.

TRADITIONAL ARCHITECTURE
Houses

In the Savoie and Dauphiné mountains, rural dwellings are in harmony with the harsh conditions of the natural environment: isolation, bad weather and intense cold. Houses are therefore stocky with a minimum of openings. A lot of space is set aside for storage: barns for hay and grain (often situated above the house to isolate it from the cold); larders for the storage of cheese and *charcuterie;* wood store.

In areas where snow is abundant, roofs are of prime importance and are always very large, overhanging all round to protect the houses and their immediate surroundings. They are either steep and smooth in order to allow the snow to slide off easily or almost flat in order to allow the snow to form a protective layer against the cold.

Préalpes de Savoie – In the forested areas of the Chablais, Aravis and Bauges mountains, the most traditional type of house is the wooden chalet built on a stone base with an overhanging roof covered with wood or slate and balconies all round. The living quarters for people and animals as well as the storage space are on the ground floor whereas the barn is on the upper floor.

Préalpes du Dauphiné – In the Chartreuse area, large stone-built houses are surrounded by various outbuildings. In the Vercors area, on the contrary, stone-built gabled houses consist of a single large building, two or three storeys high.

Oisans region – In this high mountain area, houses are very rustic in appearance and their rather flat roofs are covered with heavy slabs of schist, known as *lauzes*, although these are now often replaced by slates or corrugated metal.

House from the Maurienne region

Beaufortain, Tarentaise and Maurienne regions – In forested areas, houses have wooden façades and flat roofs covered with wood. Wherever scree-covered slopes predominate, houses are stone built with wooden balconies, few small openings and flat roofs covered with *lauzes*, which retain a thick layer of snow in winter.

Briançonnais and Vallouise regions – This is an area of scattered stone-built houses: the stables are on the lower level underlined by stone arches, the living area, entirely surrounded by wooden balconies, is on the intermediate level and the barn, directly accessible from the rear, on the upper level. The roof is usually covered with slates.

Queyras region – built of stone and wood, the houses of this area are highly original *(see ST-VÉRAN)*. The ground floor, which includes the living area and stables, is stone built and surmounted by several wooden storeys used for drying and storage. The roofs, overhanging on the balconies, are covered with wood or *lauzes*.

House from the Vercors region

Embrunais and Ubaye regions – This area, which marks the transition between the high mountains and Haute-Provence, offers a great architectural variety. Houses are rectangular and stocky, stone built with wooden balconies; the steep four-sided roofs are covered with slates. The interior plan is simple: the kitchen and stables are on the ground floor, the bedroom and threshing-floor above and the barn at the top of the house.

Haute-Provence – Village houses, often built of irregular stones and several storeys high, have a Mediterranean look about them, owing to their rounded tiles covering the roofs and forming under the eaves a decorative frieze known as a *génoise*. Isolated houses, called *granges*, are generally larger, but still fairly high, and surrounded by outbuildings.

Dovecotes and bories

There are many **dovecotes** in the southern Alps, particularly in the Diois, Baronnies and Forcalquier areas: pigeons were a precious source of food and their droppings were used as fertilizer for the kitchen garden. There were two basic styles: some dovecotes formed part of a larger structure including a shed and hen house on the lower level; others were separate buildings raised on pillars. The latter were subject to tax.

The drystone huts known as **bories** are typical of the Forcalquier area. Their use was never clearly defined and could no doubt vary according to the need: sheep pens, tool sheds, shepherds' huts, temporary dwellings. Whether round or square, they only have one opening, the door. They were built of 10-15cm/3.9-5.9in-thick limestone slabs, according to the technique of the false corbelled vaulting.

Much larger than *bories* are the **jas**, similar drystone constructions covered with *lauzes* and used as sheep pens.

Hilltop villages

These hilltop villages and small towns (Sisteron, Forcalquier, Digne) contain an amazing number of dwellings within a relatively small area enclosed by a wall.

Their origin is thought to go back to the 10C Arab invasions. In fact, the inhabitants of the region deliberately chose to build their villages on high ground, between the vineyards (which have now disappeared) and other crops. These villages are situated high above the surrounding countryside.

The steep and twisting streets or lanes are only fit for walking; they are paved or simply stony, interrupted now and then by flights of steps and often spanned by arches. In some cases, the ground floor of the houses consists of rows of arcades which protect passers-by from the sun and rain. Tiny shaded squares are adorned with attractive fountains and sometimes with a belfry surmounted by a wrought-iron campanile. The high, narrow houses huddle together round the church or the castle which dominates them. Seen from above, their bright tiled roofs appear to be tangled in a confused mass. Old studded doors, bronze door knockers and carved lintels draw the visitors' attention to the former residences of the local nobility and wealthy middle class. Very often, these small villages are still enclosed within their walls and one has to enter through a fortified gate.

During the 19C and 20C, villages moved down into the valleys as peasants chose to live in the middle of their land where they built their farmhouses, known as *mas* in Provence. However, places like Montbrun-les-Bains, Lurs, Banon, Bargème, Brantes, Valensole, Auvare, Simiane-la-Rotonde and St-Auban-sur-l'Ouvèze still remind visitors of the old Provençal way of life.

Campaniles

These metal structures, which can either be simple cages containing a bell, or wrought-iron masterpieces, form part of the Provençal landscape. In this part of the world, campaniles were designed to withstand the assaults of the powerful *mistral* better than the traditional limestone spires and today they can be seen on top of church towers, belfries, town gates and other public buildings.

Generations of craftsmen have toiled to produce elaborate wrought-iron works, onion or pyramid-shaped, spherical or cylindrical. Most remarkable are the tower of the Église St-Sauveur in Manosque, the clock tower in Sisteron, the church tower in Mane and that of the Chapelle St-Jean in Forcalquier, not forgetting the lace-like onion-shaped structure surmounting the Soubeyran gate in Manosque.

Manosque St-Sauveur   Quinson   Allemagne-en-Provence

P. Ricou

Sundials

In the southern Alps, from the Briançonnais to the Vallée de la Tinée, numerous buildings, houses, churches and public buildings are decorated with colourful sundials appreciated by amateurs of popular art and photographers alike. Considered as a kind of homage to the sun, so omnipresent in this region, these dials, dating mostly from the 18C and 19C, were the work of travelling artists, very often natives of Piedmont like Jean-François Zarbula who travelled the length and breadth of the region for 40 years making many sundials on his way and decorating them with colourful exotic birds. The sundial makers had to be familiar not only with gnomonic science (the art of setting up a dial) but also with the art of fresco painting. **Decorations** are often naïve yet charming, dials being set within a round, square or oval frame and surrounded by motifs depicting aspects of nature such as flowers, birds, the sky, the sun or the moon. The most elaborate of these sundials include some Baroque features: *trompe-l'œil* decoration, fake marble, scrolls, shells, foliage, fake pilasters.

Mottos are equally interesting; often written in Latin, sometimes in French, they express the passing of time: "Passers-by, remember as you go past that everything passes as I pass" (Villard-St-Pancrace); or death: "All the hours wound, the last one kills"; or the sun: "Without the sun I am nothing, but you, without God, are powerless" (Val-des-Prés). These mottos, which often make an attempt at moralizing, remind men that they must make good use of their time.

Briançonnais façades

CONTEMPORARY ARCHITECTURE

During the past few years, the economic expansion of the Alps, the rapid development of the towns, the birth and growth of winter sports resorts have created a real need for public and residential buildings. Today, owing to the number and quality of these contemporary architectural projects, the Alps rank as one of the most prominent French regions in this field.

Churches – The first modern art edifice built in the Alps was the Église-Notre-Dame-de-Toute-Grâce on the Plateau d'Assy. Its completion in 1950 marked a turning point. Designed by **Novarina** who erected many buildings in the Alps, it had no revolutionary feature but, for the first time in the history of contemporary religious art, great artists were commissioned to decorate the church. Numerous other churches and chapels were built after this one: in Annecy, Aix-les-Bains, Grenoble, l'Alpe-d'Huez...

Public buildings – Between 1964 and 1970, Grenoble was turned into a vast building site in preparation for the Winter Olympic Games. At the same time, an extensive programme of research into the technical and aesthetic aspects of modern architecture was launched.
Urbanisation was not so systematic in other Alpine cities; however, there were some modern achievements such as the sports complex in Chamonix, the Maison des Arts et Loisirs (Arts and Entertainment Building) in Thonon, the Palais de Justice (Law Courts) in Annecy, the Maison de la Culture (Cultural Centre) in Chambéry, the Dôme in Albertville and the Grenoble Museum.

Winter sports resorts – Newly created resorts tended to combine the general trends of contemporary urban architecture with the pursuit of comfort and organised entertainment. Some of these creations are highly original: for instance Avoriaz with its strange rock-like buildings, La Plagne with its triple pyramid etc...

Traditions and folklore

In spite of harsh living conditions, the Alps have always been densely populated, with a well-structured social life following the rhythm of the seasons and strongly attached to its traditions, each valley having its own customs, dialect and costume.

TRADITIONAL LIFE

Traditional life in the Alps was regulated in two ways: by the main events of life (birth, marriage and death) and by the impact of the seasons on the environment.

Birth – The first thing a mother did after the birth of her child was to go to church to express her gratitude to God. Children were christened very soon after being born.

Marriage – Many rituals were linked to marriage: in some areas, young maidens prayed the local saint to provide a husband for them, elsewhere they made a clay figure of the ideal partner. There were also all kinds of symbolic customs before a wedding: in the Embrunais area, the young man would offer his fiancée some jewellery on the Sunday preceding the ceremony. In the Hautes-Alpes region, a young man who married someone from another village had to cross a symbolic barrier (ribbon, decorated log etc) on the day of the wedding, whereas a young maiden in the same situation had to offer drinks to the young men of her village in order to make amends for not having chosen one of them. After the wedding, the locals played a variety of tricks on the young couple throughout the wedding night.

Funerals – When a death occurred, the whole village would take turns in watching over the body while members of local brotherhoods sang the De profundis and Miserere. A funeral banquet inevitably took place after the funeral. In high mountain areas, it was impossible to bury the dead in winter because the ground was frozen, so the bodies were kept covered with snow, on the roof of houses, until the thaw came.

The seasons – In the Alps, the year was divided in two: summertime during which people worked in the fields, looked after the animals, and wintertime, when all outdoor activity ceased.

Summer was a particularly busy time because the haymaking and harvesting season was short. Bread was made once a year by the whole village, the large loaves having to last a whole year. Cattle and sheep farming were the main source of wealth; the herds were taken from the stables to the summer pastures where they were looked after on a private or collective basis.

In winter, village folk usually stayed at home and lived on what had been stored during the summer: wood for heating, bread, dry vegetables, smoked meat, charcuterie and cheese for human consumption. Men would repair their tools and make furniture and other objects such as toys, while women were busy at their spinning-wheels. Many men however left their homes to wander from region to region, selling Alpine plants and herbs, sweeping chimneys, or finding temporary employment in the valleys as masons and builders. Some were even wandering schoolmasters hired by villages. Many left the mountains for good and settled in the towns. Today, those who remained find winter employment in the numerous sports resorts.

COSTUMES

A shawl, an embroidered bodice and belt, and an apron brightened up the long black skirt women wore, and still do, on festive occasions. Headdresses were extremely varied and consisted of a lace or linen bonnet decorated with ribbons and worn under a felt or straw hat. Most remarkable of all was the **frontière**: worn by women from the Tarentaise area, it was richly adorned with gold and silver braid and had three points framing the face like a helmet. Gold belts and necklaces were the most popular pieces of jewellery.

Men's costumes were simpler, consisting of a loosely fitting jacket of dark ordinary cloth, a pair of black trousers, a white shirt with a touch of lace around the collar, a black tie and wide woollen belt, not forgetting a large felt hat.

G. Biollay/DIAF

Frontière

LEGENDS

The devil of Bessans – However clever he may have been, the devil was ridiculed by a native of Bessans who sold his soul to him in exchange for supernatural powers. As death drew close, the man went to see the pope in Rome and asked for his pardon. He obtained it on the condition that he would hear mass in three towns at a great distance from one another. He therefore used the powers he still had to get from one place to the next in a flash. Since then, the men of Bessans have been carving devils.

St John's fingers – In the 6C, St Thècle, a native of Valloire, dreamt that she saw St John the Baptist blessing Christ with three fingers as he baptised him. The saint's search for those three fingers ended in Alexandria on the grave of St John where they suddenly appeared. She took them back to her local diocese, a town which was later called St-Jean-de-Maurienne, where the relic is still kept.

The seven wonders of Dauphiné – These seven wonders, which are the pride of the people of Dauphiné, are either sites or monuments steeped in mystery and strange myths: **Mont Aiguille,** known as the mount Olympus of Dauphiné, is a kind of "table mountain" dominating the Vercors, believed by local people to be inhabited by angels and supernatural animals until someone climbed it a long time ago. Fairies were thought to live in the **Grottes de Sassenage,** near Grenoble but it was the devil who haunted the "fontaine ardente" near the Col de l'Arzelier. Between Grenoble and St-Nizier, a ruined keep still bears the name of "**Tour sans venin**" because, according to the legend, no snake can get near it since the lord of the castle brought back some magic earth from the crusades. The remaining wonders include the remarkable **Pont de Claix,** built by Lesdiguières, the **Grottes de la Balme** and the **Pierre Percée,** a rock shaped like an arch.

Ancient beliefs from Haute-Provence – Legend has it that fairies live in the rocks overlooking Moustiers-Ste-Marie. On the other hand, the people of Arvieux *(see Le QUEYRAS)* were, for a long time, divided into two groups: the "gens du Renom", who were thought to have made a deal with the devil, and the "gens de la Belle", who invented all sorts of rituals to protect themselves from the former, marriage between the two groups being, of course, strictly forbidden.

FESTIVALS

Paganism and religion were often associated with the numerous traditional feasts and religious fervour was mixed with superstition. Nowadays, however, these events have become merry folk festivals.

Feasts and processions – They are an important feature of village life. Each village celebrates its own patron saint as well as various events linked with work in the fields, not forgetting pilgrimages which are still popular. The religious side of these festivals consists of a procession followed by mass or a benediction. Non-religious events also form part of the festivities, among them the Provençal *bravade*, which is a kind of mock attack organised by the local youth, or the sword dance, which takes place in Pont-de-Cervières every year on 16 August. Entrevaux has its feast on Midsummer's Day, when the hero of the day, St John, is carried to the chapelle St-Jean-du-Désert, 12km/7.5mi out of town and back.

Wedding chest from Queyras

HANDICRAFT
Woodwork

The densely forested Alps have, for centuries, produced enough wood to keep local craftsmen busy during the long winter evening gatherings, thus maintaining a strong wood-carving tradition which blossomed between the 17C and 19C, particularly in the Maurienne and Queyras areas.

These regions have retained some splendid samples of this popular art including furniture and other objects — made by the local farmers out of larch or walnut wood.

Wood-carving in Maurienne — The Maurienne region was famous for its carved religious furnishings and objects: pulpits, altars, statues. Bessans was well known as early as the 17C for the skill of its craftsmen. One of them, Étienne Vincendet, who lived in the 19C, was the first craftsman to carve the famous "devils" whose tradition has survived to this day.

Chests and toys from Queyras — Wedding chests are an ancient speciality of the Queyras region. Carved out of larch with chisels and gouges, they are made up of four panels and a lid. Inside, there is often a small compartment meant for silverware and precious objects. The best samples of these chests have remarkable carvings on their front panels. Geometric motifs (rosettes) were first drawn with the help of a pair of compasses, whereas other motifs (interlacing, palmette, hearts, foliage and arabesques) were copied from Gothic motifs or inspired by the Renaissance style and leather objects from Cordoba. The wood was carved with a knife; this took a very long time. Some chests bear a mark indicating when it was made and by whom.

The people from Queyras made numerous other pieces of furniture which testify to their considerable woodworking skills: dressers, chairs, salt-boxes, cots, kneading-troughs/cupboards as well as a wealth of objects for daily use such as spinning-wheels, lace hoops, bread seals (which enabled housewives to distinguish her own bread baked in the communal oven), butter-boards, and boxes of all shapes and sizes.

Traditional toys, which used to be so popular, have practically disappeared except in La Chalp where, in 1919, a Swiss vicar had the good idea of encouraging the local production of wooden toys in order to slow down the drift from the land to the towns. Small characters, animals and pieces of dolls' furniture are cut out of thin planks of wood and then assembled and painted by hand in the craftsmen's homes.

Provençal furniture — In Haute-Provence, furniture is mainly made of walnut and more or less decorated according to the prosperity of the area. In addition to chests, tables and beds, there are combined wardrobes and sideboards, credences and kneading-troughs. A wardrobe cum sideboard has two double doors separated by two drawers. This massive piece of furniture is sometimes decorated with foliage, grotesque and diamond motifs. A credence is a kind of cupboard with two drawers, sometimes with an added crockery shelf. The kneading-trough or bread box was the most common piece of furniture; often placed on top of a low cupboard, it was used to store food.

Moustiers earthenware

Manufacturing technique — The word *faïence*, which means earthenware in French, comes from the name of an Italian town, Faenza, already renowned for its earthenware production before the 15C.

There are several manufacturing stages. A kind of paste made of a mixture of clay, sand and chalk is moulded into shape then dried and fired in an oven at a temperature of about 1 000°C/1 832°F. This "terracotta", which is hard and porous, is then dipped into tin oxide, forming an enamel, and slightly fired again. The artist then paints his motifs on the object, using metal oxide colours. Another high temperature (850°C/1 562°F to 950°C/1 742°F) firing session follows. With this method, the choice of colours used is limited to those able to withstand such high temperatures. There is, however, another method, which allows the use of a wider choice of colours: the earthenware object is fired before being painted; the artist then applies the colours mixed with certain chemicals which act as a fixative, then the object is fired a second time at a lower temperature of around 400°C/752°F.

Earthenware decoration through the ages — Clay, water and wood found in the vicinity of Moustiers account for the earthenware tradition of that village. However, the turning-point came in the 17C, when a monk brought back from Italy the secret process of earthenware making.

There are four main types of earthenware:
– the blue monochrome earthenware (1680-1730), influenced by the Nevers and Rouen traditions.
– the Bérain decoration (early 18C) named after the artist who introduced new motifs.
– the refined polychrome decoration imported from Spain in 1738.
– the "petit feu" (low temperature) decoration (late 18C), with bright colours.

"Santons"

They are the symbol of Provençal handicraft. These small earthenware characters intended to represent the villagers of Bethlehem at the time of Christ's birth are, in fact, typical Provençal villagers dressed in regional costume and bringing back to life 19C village trades. There is a famous annual fair *(foire aux santons)* in the village of **Champtercier**, near Digne.

Food and drink in the Alps

Alpine cuisine owes more to the quality and freshness of local produce than to the complexity of its recipes: cheese from the rich Alpine pastures, fish from the lakes and rivers, mushrooms from the forests, crayfish from the mountain streams, game (thrush patés from Provence are delicious!), potatoes, fruit etc form the basis of most Alpine dishes, served with wine from Savoie or Provence. As for Provençal cuisine, its main characteristic is the generous use of garlic and olive oil, the latter replacing butter so liberally used in the north.

REGIONAL PRODUCE

Fish – Fish from the lakes and mountain streams are a must in any gastronomic menu: arctic char, pike and trout are prepared in many different ways: meunière (dipped in flour and slowly fried in butter), poached, in butter sauce, braised...

Meat – Beef from Dauphiné is particularly famous; it is delicious served *en daube* (stewed) with herbs from Provence. Lamb from the Sisteron area is said to be more tender and savoury than anywhere else and there is a whole range of charcuterie available, such as ham cured with herbs and spices from the Mont Ventoux region. Rabbit is appreciated by gourmets, particularly **lapin en cabessol**, stuffed and cooked in a white wine sauce.

Cheeses – Made from cow's, ewe's or goat's milk, cheeses vary a great deal according to the manufacturing process. Alpine pastures of the Beaufortain and Tarentaise areas pro- duce one of the tastiest kinds of Gruyère: **Beaufort**, whereas **Reblochon**, an Alpine farm- house cheese, is a speciality of the Aravis. Among the rich choice of *"tommes"* – the name means "cheese" in Savoyard dialect – available in the northern Alps, **"Tomme de Savoie"** is the best known. The small **Saint-Marcellin** is the most popular cheese of the lower Dau- phiné area. Originally made from pure goat's milk, it is now processed from mixed goat's and cow's milk. **Bleu de Sassenage** includes ewe's milk as well. Several regional dishes are based on these tasty cheeses, one of the most famous being the **fondue savoyarde**, which successfully combines Gruyère cheese with the local dry white wine.

In the southern Alps, **Picodon** from the Diois area is a sharp goats' cheese matured for at least three months whereas **Banon** is a rustic, strong-tasting cheese from the Montagne de Lure.

Herbs – Either growing wild or cultivated on sunny slopes, herbs are essential ingredients of Alpine cuisine, especially in Haute-Provence. The general term *"herbes de Provence"* includes **savory** used in the making of goat's and ewe's milk cheeses, **thyme** used to flavour vegetables and grilled meat or fish, **basil, sage, wild thyme, rosemary** (which helps the digestion), **tarragon, juniper berries** (used in the preparation of game dishes), **marjoram** and **fennel**. The secret of tasty cooking lies in the subtle combination of these herbs.

SPECIALITIES AND RECIPES

Gratins – The universally known **gratin dauphinois** is a delicious mixture of sliced potatoes, eggs and milk; **gratin savoyard**, topped with Tomme de Savoie is a similar dish in which milk is replaced by broth. Few people know, however, that there are numerous other kinds of gratins made with pumpkin, courgette, spinach, beans, millet and crayfish tails, the latter being an outstanding delicacy.

Tarte au Beaufort – This tart is filled with fresh cream mixed with Beaufort cheese and served hot.

Toasts savoyards – This delicious snack is made from creamy Reblochon mixed with peeled walnuts and spread on toasted rye bread.

Tartiflette – Cut a whole Reblochon cheese in thin slices. In a flat dish, arrange alternate layers of sliced potatoes and Reblochon; add chopped garlic, herbs, salt and pepper. Cook in the oven for 30min, adding fresh cream 5min before the time is up. Serve with smoked charcuterie and a dry white wine from Savoie.

Tourte de veau – This pie from the Ubaye region is filled with pieces of shoulder of veal marinated in onion and garlic and covered with bone jelly. It can be eaten hot or cold.

Raïoles – These "ravioli" from Haute-Provence are stuffed with a paste made from dried walnuts and saffron and served with spinach and pumpkin.

Aïoli – This is a mayonnaise made with olive oil and flavoured with crushed garlic, intended to be served with hors-d'œuvre, poached fish and various other dishes.

Fougasse – This kind of flat bread dough cooked in olive oil and topped with crushed anchovies is served with hors-d'œuvre. It is sold in most baker's shops in Haute-Pro- vence.

Desserts – In Savoie, strawberries, raspberries and bilberries are used to make delicious tarts; **gâteau de Savoie**, on the other hand, is a light sponge cake unlike the rich **walnut cake** from the Grenoble region.

Fruit is abundant in the southern Alps, particularly in the Durance Valley. It is used to make a traditional tart, known as *tourte*.

Thirteen desserts – Traditionally served for Christmas, in honour of Christ and the twelve apostles, these desserts include raisins, dried figs, several kinds of nuts, apples, pears, nougat (made from honey), prunes stuffed with marzipan, melons and dry cakes flavoured with orange blossom.

Pompe à huile – This large "fougasse" *(see above)* was traditionally served on Christmas Eve with liqueur wine.

Lou Pasteloun – A stodgy pie made with walnuts and sugar, a speciality of Haute-Provence.

WINES AND LIQUEURS

Vines have been growing in Savoie since Roman times and wine-growing is today one of the most dynamic activities of the region; this is a remarkable feat, considering the drawbacks of the local climate. In fact vines grow in areas enjoying a microclimate (south-facing slopes up to an altitude of 500m/1 640ft, shores of lakes) and where the soil is well drained and stony (moraines). There are several types of local vines; one of these, the **Mondeuse**, with its delicate strawberry, blackcurrant and bilberry bouquet, produces one of the best red wines of the region, which matures very well. According to a local saying, "September makes the wine" for this month is generally mild, sunny and dry. The area produces light dry white wines, which must be drunk while they are still young.

White wines from **Seyssel** and **Crépy** (on the shores of Lake Geneva), both A.O.C. (Appellation d'Origine Contrôlée, guaranteeing the quality) are fruity and go well with fish; they are at their best when they are between two and four years old.

The label "**Vins de Savoie**" includes several wines from the Massif des Bauges: dry white wines, extra dry sparkling white wines, as well as red wines.

The label "**Roussette de Savoie**" concerns light dry white wines with a fruity taste.

The wine production of Haute-Provence has considerably declined and there are now fewer quality wines. However, two A.O.C. *(see above)* wines are among the most palatable: **Côtes du Ventoux** from the Bédoin area *(see Michelin Green Guide Provence)* and **Côte du Lubéron**, from the mountainous area of the Luberon *(see Michelin Green Guide Provence)*. On the southern border of Haute-Provence, there are some excellent rosé wines whereas, to the north of the region, the famous **Clairette de Die** is one of the great French sparkling wines, made from a mixture of *clairette* and muscat grapes by the same method as Champagne.

Among the liqueurs produced in the northern and southern Alps, **Chartreuse**, known as the "elixir of life" is undoubtedly the most famous; its formula, dating from the 16C, includes the essence of 130 different plants to which are added alcohol distilled from wine and honey.

Others include gentian liqueur, marc brandy from Savoie, "Origan du Comtat" from the Ventoux area and above all **absinthe** based on wormwood, a medicinal plant well known in the Alps. The success of the liqueur, which goes back to the 19C, is principally due to its digestive and tonic properties (it is said to cure mountain sickness). White, green or brown depending on the ingredients used, the liqueur is between 30° and 40° proof. In order that it may retain its green colour, the bottles used are protected from daylight by a casing. Local distillers each have their own recipe; however, they generally abide by the "rule of forty": 40 sprigs of wormwood are left to macerate for 40 days in one litre of marc brandy to which are added 40 lumps of sugar. The bottle is exposed to daylight every day for 40min.

A. Le Toquin/EXPLORER

Chartreuse Distillery, Voiron

Palais de l'Isle, Annecy

Sights

ABONDANCE ★

Population 1 251
Michelin map 89 fold 2 or 244 fold 9
Local map see Le CHABLAIS

The massive buildings of the Abbaye d'Abondance bear witness to the past vitality of one of the most important monasteries in the Alps. The village, which developed in the Val d'Abondance *(see Le CHABLAIS)* below the abbey, is a winter sports centre as well as a pleasant summer and health resort producing an excellent cheese similar to Tomme de Savoie.

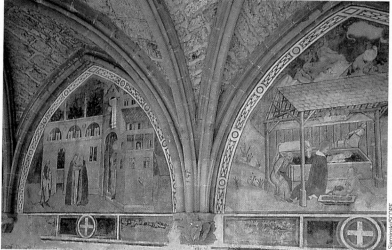

Frescoes in the abbey cloisters

★ABBEY *1hr*

During the Middle Ages, the Abbaye d'Abondance had a major religious and cultural impact on the northern Alps under the rule of the Augustinian order. A branch of the Cistercian order took over in 1607 and remained there until 1761.

Cloisters ⊘ – There are only two galleries left, dating from the 14C. The Porte de la Vierge (the Virgin Mary's door), which gave access to the church, is richly decorated, although badly damaged, with a Virgin and Child on the tympanum and graceful statues on either side. The remaining keystones are carved with the signs of the Zodiac.

★★Frescoes – Surprisingly fresh, sometimes naïve, the frescoes decorating the cloisters depict scenes from the life of Christ and of the Virgin Mary, believed to have been painted by Giacomo Jacquerio from Piedmont between 1410 and 1420. The Wedding at Cana is particularly remarkable with a wealth of details on daily life in Savoie in the 15C.

Church ⊘ – The five bays of the 13C nave and the aisles were destroyed by successive fires. Two bays were rebuilt in the 19C, the remainder of the church is original. The chancel paintings by Vicario date from 1846. Note the fine 15C abbot's seat.

Museum of Religious Art ⊘ – Part of the abbey buildings house an important collection of religious vestments, paintings, statues, silver and gold plate, 15C manuscripts... The chapter house has been reconstructed.

EXCURSION

Les Plagnes – *5.5km/3.4mi southeast. Cross the Dranse d'Abondance and turn left before a saw-mill towards Charmy-l'Adroit and Les Plagnes.*
The road reveals the bottom of the valley dotted with large chalets and dominated by the Pic de la Corne and the Roc de Tavaneuse.
Beyond a hamlet called Sur-la-Ravine, it dips into the forested upper Malève Valley and reaches Les Plagnes de Charmy, within sight of the Pointe de Chavache, in front of a lake framed by wooded slopes *(beware of felled trees rolling down the slopes).*

ABRIÈS ★

Population 297
Michelin map 77 fold 19 or 244 fold 43
Local map see Le QUEYRAS

Situated at the confluence of the Guil and the Bouchet, this village is, depending on the season, the starting point of excursions, hikes, climbing or cross-country skiing expeditions. In winter-time, the Télésiège de Jilly (Jilly chair-lift) completed by several ski-lifts attracts crowds of skiing enthusiasts.

A calvary including 14 Stations of the Cross overlooks the village to the west. The **church** is surmounted by a steeple with an octagonal spire; the sundial bears the inscription: "It is later than you think".

Trail of the inscribed stones – This interesting trail, lined with inscribed stones illustrating the history of Abriès, is complemented with a brochure published by the Parc naturel régional du Queyras, available at the tourist office.

The hamlets of Valpreveyre – **Valpreveyre** can be reached by following the Bouchet mountain stream and turning right at Le Roux *(6km/3.7mi)*; the road is rough but offers beautiful views of neighbouring peaks and goes past authentic old hamlets.

HIKES

★Walk to La Colette de Jilly Alt 2 467m/8 094ft

Take the Jilly chair-lift ⊙ on the way out of Abriès towards Ristolas. From the station (2 150m/7 054ft), a path (with red and white markings of trail GR 58) climbs steeply to La Colette de Jilly *(45min)* then on to the Jilly Peak (2 467m/8 094ft), offering **panoramic views★** of the Tête du Pelvas, Bric Bouchet, Grand Queyron, Ségure and Fond de Peynin.

★★Hiking round the Bric Bouchet (2 997m/9 833ft) via Italy

About 8 hr; one night in the Lago Verde (Italy) mountain refuge.

Marked itinerary with possible alternatives from Abriès or Valpreveyre. Here are two of them: the shorter and more demanding one leads to the border pass of Valpreveyre with close views of the Bric Bouchet; then on to the Lago Verde refuge where the two alternatives meet. The longer one offers better views of the various landscapes from Valpreveyre through the hamlet of Le Roux to the border pass of **Abriès** or **St-Martin** (2 657m/8 717ft) during an easy 4hr walk. Superb **view★★** of the **Val Germanisca** (Italy) and the Bric Bouchet Summit. The Largo Verde refuge (2 583m/8 474ft) is an hour further on, along the well-marked path. The **Grand Queyron Peak** (3 060m/10 039ft) stands out to the north. From the refuge, **Prali** and its ethnological museum can be reached in 2hr 30min. There is a way back from Prali through the Col de la Croix or the Col d'Urine *(see below)* over two or three days. *Information about these itineraries is available from the tourist offices of Aiguilles and Abriès.*

★★Col de la Croix and Col d'Urinevia Ciabot del Pra (Italy)

Two days' walk and a night spent in the Jervis refuge.
From La Monta, a 2 hr walk to the Col de la Croix; follow path GR 58; note the old border stone with a fleur de lys on the French side. The Jervis refuge is a 1hr 30min walk further on; the footpath goes down to Ciabot del Pra *(food available in season at the inn and Jervis refuge).* Continue northwards to reach the **Col d'Urine** in about 3 hr. The imposing **Tête du Pelvas** (2 929m/9 610ft) towers over the pass and the small valley which prolongs it to the west and leads to the valley of Valpreveyre *(2 hr walk from the pass).* Trail GR 58B takes you back to Abriès in 30min.

MOUNTAIN BIKE TOURS

The most interesting itineraries start with the section Abriès-La Monta and diverge beyond that point. There is a one-day excursion to the Col de la Croix (2 298m/7 539ft) and a longer and more fascinating one to the Val Pellice and the **Barbara-Lowrie refuge** (1 753m/5 751ft) with an impressive climb to the Col du Baracun (2 380m/7 808ft) before the final descent towards the refuge.

*The chapter on **Practical information** at the end of the guide lists :*
– local or national organisations providing additional information;
– events of interest to the tourist
– admission times and charges.

Population 24 683
Michelin map 89 fold 15 or 244 fold 18
Local map see Lac du BOURGET

Aix-les-Bains lies at the foot of Mont Revard, on the eastern shore of the Lac du Bourget. This well-known spa, which specialises in the treatment of rheumatism and respiratory ailments, is also one of the best-appointed tourist centres in the Alps, with lively streets, splendid palace hotels near the baths and attractive lake shores.

Taking the waters: a fashionable pastime – The remains of the Roman baths can only give a rough idea of their former splendour (24 different kinds of marble were used to decorate them). The Romans excelled in the art of hydropathy and the baths were at once a social club, a casino and a fitness club. The name of the town comes from *Aquae Gratianae*, "the waters of Emperor Gratian".

During the Middle Ages, the baths were severely neglected. Taking the waters became fashionable again in the 16C but the first real establishment dating from the 18C was only equipped with showers. The treatment offered became more sophisticated in the 19C with the introduction of the steam bath and shower-massage which is still the great speciality of the spa.

In 1816, Aix-les-Bains was the setting of one of the most famous love stories in literature, between the Romantic French poet, **Alphonse de Lamartine**, and Julie Charles who died a year later and inspired the moving lines of *Le Lac*.

THE SPA TOWN

The life of the spa town is concentrated round the baths, the municipal park with its vast open-air theatre, the Palais de Savoie and the new casino, as well as along the lake with its beach and marinas. The rue de Genève, rue du Casino and adjacent streets form the shopping centre of the town.

Treatment – The baths, which are open all year round, are supplied by two hot springs, the sulphur spring and the alum spring. There are four specialised pools for the treatment of rheumatism. Cold water from the St-Simon spring is used for drinking.

To the south, the **Établissement thermal de Marlioz** (Marlioz baths) (AX), situated in a peaceful shaded park, treats disorders of the respiratory system. Several crowned heads of Europe, including Queen Victoria, have, in the past, benefited from this treatment.

The splendour of Aix-les-Bains at the turn of the century

The expansion of the spa town, which began in 1860, reached its peak during the Belle Époque. Luxury hotels were built in order to attract the aristocracy and the crowned heads of Europe: the "Victoria", for instance, welcomed Queen Victoria on three separate occasions, whereas the Splendide and the Excelsior counted among their guests a maharajah from India, the emperor of Brazil and Empress Sissi of Austria. Most of the buildings in the spa town were designed by an architect from Lyon, **Jules Pin the Elder** (1850-1934), whose masterpiece was undoubtedly the Château de la Roche du Roi.

After the Second World War, most of these magnificent hotels could not adapt to the new type of clientele and had to close down for economic reasons; some of them were turned into apartments.

Visitors strolling through the town and its immediate surroundings will be able to admire the façades of some of the prestigious symbols of a bygone era: the **Splendide**, the **Royal** and the **Excelsior**, rue Georges I (CZ), the **Bernascon** (AX) and the **Château de la Roche du Roi** on the way to the Établissement thermal de Marlioz.

SIGHTS

★**Musée Faure** ⊙ (CY) – In 1942, Dr Faure bequeathed to the town a rare collection of paintings and sculptures including a large number of works by the Impressionists and their predecessors, Corot, Jonkind and Boudin. Note in particular *Mauve Dancers* by Degas, the *Seine in Argenteuil* by Sisley, *Ferryboat in Bonnières* by Cézanne and works by Vuillard and Pissarro.

The collection of sculptures is also rich in works by Carpeaux and Rodin, including a series of bronze, marble and terracotta sculptures forming part of his project entitled *The Doorway to Hell*, inspired by Dante's *Divine Comedy*. The last floor houses furniture and objects recreating Lamartine's surroundings in the Perrier boarding-house, which is no longer there.

Thermes nationaux ⊘ (**CZ**) – Inaugurated in 1864, the baths were enlarged by the addition of the Nouveaux Thermes in 1934, modernised in 1972, which can be visited. A vast room in the basement contains the **Roman remains** of a *caldarium* (hot bath) and of a circular pool. A 98m/322ft-long gallery gives access to the **caves** where one of the sulphur springs can be seen.

Arc de Campanus (**CZ B**) – Erected by a member of the "Pompeia" family, this arch stood 9m/30ft high in the centre of the Roman town.

AIX-LES-BAINS

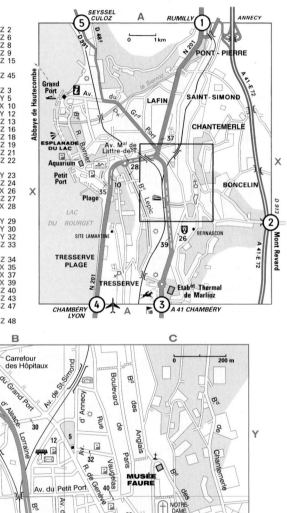

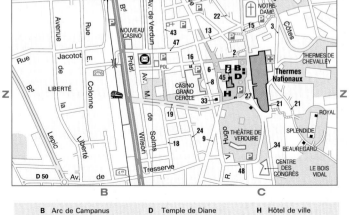

| B | Arc de Campanus | D | Temple de Diane | H | Hôtel de ville |

Hôtel de ville (CZ H) – This former castle conveys a Savoyard look to the spa district. The elegant **staircase★** was built during the early Renaissance period, with stones from the Roman monuments.

Temple de Diane (CZ D) – This remarkable rectangular Roman monument houses the Museum of Archeology.

Musée d'Archéologie et de Préhistoire ⊙ **(CZ)** – *Access through the Tourist Information Centre.* Stone fragments, ceramics, glassware and coins dating from the Gallo-Roman period. Remarkable male bust, probably of a Roman emperor.

★THE LAKE SHORES (AX) *1hr*

Follow avenue du Grand-Port to leave Aix by ⑤ *on the town plan.*

Grand Port – **Boat trips** ⊙ to Le Bourget-du-Lac, the Abbaye de Hautecombe and the Rhône leave from this pier.

Follow boulevard Robert-Barrier to the left.

★**Esplanade du bord du lac** – This vast open space (10ha/25 acres) is equipped with children's games and is suitable for picnics. A shaded alleyway skirting the Lac du Bourget calls for pleasant walks within sight of the Hautecombe abbey and the steep slopes of the Dent du Chat.

Petit Port – This is a fishing port and a marina. An **aquarium** ⊙, containing fresh water species in their natural environment, is housed in the centre of hydrobiological studies. The **beach** is just beyond.

EXCURSIONS

★★**Lac du Bourget** – *See Lac du BOURGET.*

★★**Abbaye royale de Hautecombe** – A regular ferry service *(see boats trips above)* links the Grand-Port and the abbey which can also be reached by driving round the lake *(see Lac du BOURGET: Round tour of the lake).*

★★**Circuit de la Chambotte** – *36km/22.4mi - about 2hr 30min. Leave Aix by* ① *on the town plan and N 201. Turn left at La Biolle along D 991^B; turn left in St-Germain and left again at La Chambotte past a small chapel.*

★★**View from the Restaurant de la Chambotte** – Splendid **view** over the Lac du Bourget and the mountains lining its shores; in the distance, one can see the Allevard, Grande-Chartreuse and southern Jura massifs.

Return to La Chambotte and follow D 991^B to Chaudieu.

This road offers good bird's-eye views of the northern extremity of the lake and of the Marais de Chautagne (Chautagne marshland).

From Chaudieu, return to Aix by the lakeside road described under Lac du BOURGET.

★★**Mont Revard** – *See Les BAUGES: Mont Revard.*

L'ALBANAIS ★

Michelin map 89 fold 15 or 244 fold 18

The Albanais depression, situated between the Lac du Bourget and the Lac d'Annecy and framed by the Gros Foug, Revard and Semnoz mountains, is a rich agricultural region, once specialized in tobacco-growing, which not only connects Aix-les-Bains and Annecy, but also gives access to the Jura mountain range via Bellegarde and to Switzerland via Geneva.

ROUND TOUR *40km/25mi – allow half a day*

Rumilly – This former stronghold at the confluence of two mountain streams is the capital of the Albanais region, a lively market town and industrial centre. The old town, nestling round the "Halle aux blés" (corn exchange, rebuilt in 1869), includes a few interesting 16C and 17C buildings, in particular round **place de l'Hôtel-de-Ville** with its graceful fountain. Also worth visiting are the **Église Ste-Agathe** with its Tuscan-style façade and the 13C **Chapelle Notre-Dame-de-l'Aumône** ⊙ on the bank of the Chéran.

The **Musée de l'Albanais** ⊙ *(avenue Gantin)*, housed in a former tobacco factory, deals with local history from the 17C onwards.

Leave Rumilly by D 3 going south.

★**Alby-sur-Chéran** – This picturesque village was an important shoemaking centre housing no fewer than 200 craftsmen in the 19C. The charming triangular **place du Trophée★**, situated in the old part of Alby, is surrounded by medieval arcaded workshops, which have been tastefully restored. The **Musée de la Cordonnerie** ⊙, located inside the town hall, is devoted to the shoemaking industry. The Église Notre-Dame-de-Plainpalais (1954) has a remarkable stained-glass wall.

Place du Trophée in Alby-sur-Chéran

Canoe trips through the Gorges du Chéran to Rumilly offer stunning views of the area enhanced by the luxuriant vegetation.

Leave Alby by D 3 towards Le Châtelard.

The road offers fine views of the Chéran. Beyond Cusy, where the itinerary bears left, the Bauges Massif bars the horizon to the south. Another left turn leads to the **Pont de l'Abîme** *(see Les BAUGES)* which spans the Chéran, 94m/308ft above the river bed in a spectacular **setting★** including, to the northeast, the imposing rocky peaks of the **Tours St-Jacques.**

It is possible to drive on to the Vallon de Bellevaux along D 911 (see Les BAUGES). Alternatively, drive north to Gruffy after crossing the Chéran.

Musée de la Nature (Gruffy) – *Guevin farm as you enter the village.* The museum gives a good idea of traditional life in Savoie by means of the reconstruction of a 19C farm, a mountain chalet and the cheese-making process.

Continue towards Viuz-la-Chiésaz; the dark silhouette of the **Crêt de Châtillon★★★** (1 699m/5 574ft), the highest peak of the Semnoz Mountain, towers over the village. Roads D 141, D 241 and D 41 lead to the summit *(see Lac d'ANNECY, excursion [3]).*

Drive west along D 38 to Marcellaz-Albanais.

Marcellaz-Albanais – *Go through the village towards Rumilly and turn right.*

Musée "l'Art de l'enfance **"** – This is a real treasure cave for children with magic lanterns, optical illusions, games and ancient toys.

★VAL DU FIER *42km/26mi – allow 2 hr*

Leave Rumilly by D 31 across the Pont Édouard-André towards Lornay. Note, on the right, a group of old houses clinging to the forested bank of the Néphaz.

At first, the road follows the Fier, then crosses it before reaching the hilltop village of Clermont.

Château de Clermont – Built straight onto the rock at the end of the 16C, this palace in Italian Renaissance style consists of three 2-storey wings, an imposing gateway and two square towers.

Return to St-André along D 31 and turn right.

★**Val du Fier** – This is a typical transverse valley hidden under greenery, seen at its best in the late-afternoon light. The road goes through several narrow passages including two tunnels. Just before the last tunnel, a path on the left leads to a gate barring the entrance to the **Voie romaine du Val du Fier** (Val du Fier Roman way), part of the road which, in the 1C AD, linked the Albanais region and the Rhône Valley.

Return to Rumilly via Val-de-Fier and Vallières.

From Vallières it is possible to make an interesting detour to **Vaulx** *(follow D 14 to Hauteville and D 3 to Vaulx)* in order to stroll through the **Jardins secrets** , a pleasant succession of small gardens in a wooded setting, with fountains, pergolas and patios.

ALBERTVILLE

Population 17 411
Michelin map 89 fold 15 or 244 fold 19 and 20
Local map see Le BEAUFORTAIN

Lying at the entrance of the Arly Valley, Albertville is the converging point of several scenic roads leading to the Beaufortain and Tarentaise areas. The old town of Conflans, perched on a rocky spur overlooking the confluence of the Isère and Arly rivers, is well worth visiting.

OLYMPIC CITY

In 1992, Albertville hosted the opening and closing ceremonies of the 16th Winter Olympic Games while events took place in nearby resorts. It was the third time since 1924 that the Games were held in the French Alps.

Olympic venues – The venue where the opening and closing ceremonies were staged is now a sports and leisure park where major events are held.
The **Halle olympique** (Olympic stadium) is a training centre for the French ice-hockey team as well as a public ice-skating rink and a venue for the European Ice-skating Championship.
The **Anneau de vitesse** (Speed rink) has become a sports stadium hosting regional competitions.
The **Maison des 16^{es} Jeux olympiques** ⊘ (16th Olympic Games Centre) houses an exhibition devoted to the 1992 Olympic Games with audio-visual support.

Le Dôme – Designed by Jean-Jacques Moisseau, this new cultural centre stands on place de l'Europe and comprises a theatre, a multimedia reference library and a cinema with a panoramic screen.

★CONFLANS *allow 45min*

Drive north across the pont des Adoubes and up the montée Adolphe-Hugues; leave the car in the car park on the right; continue on foot as indicated below.

Château Manuel de Locatel ⊘ – This 16C castle, recently restored, overlooks the new town of Albertville. Note the 17C ceiling painted by an Italian artist.

Porte de Savoie – Before going through the gate, admire the lovely **view★** of the edifice dominated by the slender Tour Ramus and of the charming 18C fountain.

Rue Gabriel-Pérouse – This is the former "Grande-Rue" (High Street), lined with medieval workshops still occupied by craftsmen.

Turn left to go up to the church.

Conflans

64

Church – This hall-church is in authentic 18C style; the nave, which consists of four bays, is prolonged by a chancel with a flat east end. The carved **pulpit**, dating from 1718, is remarkable; note also the baptismal font and the retable over the high altar.

Return to rue Gabriel-Pérouse, which leads to the Grande Place.

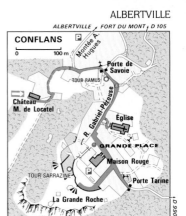

ALBERTVILLE, FORT DU MONT, D 105
CONFLANS

★**Grande Place** – A lovely 18C fountain decorates the centre of this picturesque square, lined on one side with a 14C brick building, known as **Maison Rouge** ⊙, which houses the municipal **museum**: reconstruction of Savoyard homes, local religious statues, regional furniture, traditional tools, weapons, documents etc.

La Grande Roche – This terraced area shaded by ancient lime trees, overlooks the confluence of the rivers Isère and Arly, offering fine views of the Combe de Savoie depression with the rocky peaks of the Chartreuse Massif in the distance.

Walk as far as the 14C **Porte Tarine** before returning to the car park.

EXCURSION

★★**Fort du Mont** *29km/18mi – about 1hr 30min*

From the Porte de Savoie in Conflans, drive along D 105.

The road climbs continuously, soon offering a panoramic view of the Doron and Arly valleys with the pyramid-like Mont Charvin in the distance, to the north.

Higher up, a wide bend forms a good **belvedere** over the Basse-Tarentaise Valley which narrows between Feissons and Aigueblanche.

Continue past the Fort du Mont to the second hairpin bend (*two chalets stand nearby* – alt 1 120m/3 675ft) with fine **views**★★ of pastures in the foreground and, beyond, of the Combe de Savoie through which flows the River Isère.

Return by the forest road on the left towards Molliessoulaz and admire the splendid view of Mont Blanc. From Molliessoulaz, a path leads down into the Doron Valley and joins up with D 925 which takes you back to Albertville.

ALLEVARD ✝

Population 2 558
Michelin map 89 fold 17 or 244 fold 29
Local maps see p 66 and Le GRÉSIVAUDAN

Allevard, lying in the green Bréda Valley, at an altitude of 475m/1 558ft, is the starting point of numerous excursions.

It is also a popular spa resort for the treatment of respiratory complaints.

The jagged ridges of the Allevard Massif (highest peak: Puy Gris, 2 908m/9 541ft), which are covered with snow for the greatest part of the year, convey a genuine Alpine atmosphere to the whole area.

The vast forests of conifers covering the lower slopes from 1 500m/4 921ft are the main attraction of mountain resorts of the upper Bréda Valley such as Le Curtillard.

The **Chaîne de Belledonne**, which forms part of the central massifs *(see Introduction: Formation of the Alps)*, overlooks the Isère Valley from Allevard to the Croix de Chamrousse towering above Grenoble. Its highest point is the Rocher Blanc (2 928m/9 606ft) and it only includes two small glaciers.

EXCURSIONS

★★① **Route du Collet** *10km/6.2mi – about 30min – local map see p 66*

Leave Allevard by D 525ᴬ to Fond-de-France. Turn left after 1.4km/0.9mi on D 109 to Le Collet.

Climbing in a series of hairpin bends, the road affords successive glimpses of Allevard and its immediate surroundings, of the Veyton and Gleyzin valleys separated by the Pic de Gleyzin and finally of the upper Bréda Valley. As the road reaches the winter sports resort of **Le Collet d'Allevard** (1 450m/4 757ft), it reveals a vast panoramic view embracing the Vercors, Chartreuse and Bauges massifs as well as the Grésivaudan, Chambéry and Combe de Savoie depressions. The view is even better 3km/1.9mi further on, from the summit of **Grand Collet** (1 920m/6 299ft), which can be reached by chair-lift.

ALLEVARD

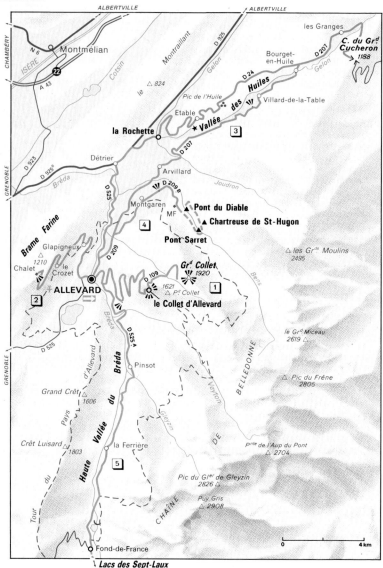

★ ② **Route de Brame Farine** *12km/7.5mi – about 45min – local map above*
Leave Allevard by avenue Louaraz. The road surface is poor beyond Le Crozet.

The winding road offers fine views of the Allevard basin and, from left to right, on the Bauges heights, Vallée des Huiles, Allevard Massif and Belledonne range.
Turn back on reaching the Chalet de Brame-Farine (alt about 1 200m/3 937ft).

★ ③ **Vallée des Huiles**
50km/31mi round tour – about 2hr 30min – local map above
Leave Allevard by D 525 north then bear right on D 925 towards Albertville.

La Rochette – The cardboard factories of this industrial town and tourist centre are among the largest in Europe.
Drive east towards Étable for 1km/0.6mi and turn right.

The road climbs through the upper Gelon Valley, known as the Vallée des Huiles, along the cultivated slope of the valley which contrasts with the forested slope opposite. Upstream from Étable stands the solitary Pic de l'Huile which gave its name to the whole valley.

At Les Granges, turn right towards the Col du Grand-Cucheron. Return to Bourget-en-Huile and turn left along D 207.

After crossing the Gelon, the road winds along the forested slope of the valley. Just beyond Villard there is a fine view of the basin of La Rochette and the lower Bréda Valley leading to the Grésivaudan. Woods give way to pastures dotted with walnuts and chestnuts as one approaches the lovely village of Arvillard.

Return to Allevard along D 209.

④ Chartreuse de St-Hugon

8.5km/5.3mi, then 1hr return on foot – local map see opposite

Leave Allevard by D 525 north, turn right onto D 209 then right again after the bridge across the Buisson.

The road offers panoramic views of the Combe de Savoie and Massif des Bauges before following the Bens Valley.

After 6.5km/4mi, ignore D 109 on your right and park the car near the St-Hugon forest lodge; continue on foot along the forest track for 1.5km/0.9mi then left onto a path leading down to Pont Sarret (boots may be needed).

Pont Sarret – This bridge spans the Bens in a pleasant forest setting with the foaming torrent below.

Cross the bridge and follow the path on the opposite bank of the Bens.

Chartreuse de St-Hugon ⊙ – Nothing remains of the Carthusian monastery founded in the 12C except a 17C building with a Gothic-style pediment surmounted by a wrought-iron fan light, now occupied by a Buddhist centre, the most important of its kind in Europe; the Dalai Lama visited it several times.

Continue along the path and bear left at the fork.

Pont du Diable – This 200-year-old bridge over the Bens used to mark the border between France and Piedmont *(see engraved stone).*

Cross the bridge to rejoin the road and return to the lodge on the right.

⑤ Haute Vallée du Bréda *17km/10.6mi – about 30min – local map see opposite*

Follow D 525ᴬ to Fond-de-France.

This excursion through restful landscapes is popular with tourists taking the waters in Allevard. **Fond-de-France** (alt 1 089m/3 573ft) is the ideal starting-point for mountain hikes.

★★**Hike to the Lacs des Sept-Laux** – *Leave the car in Fond-de-France in front of the Sept-Laux hotel. This trip is suitable for experienced hikers: 3hr 45min climb; 1 150m/3 773ft difference in altitude; it is advisable to wear mountain boots.*
The major part of the itinerary goes through woodland *(follow the yellow and then yellow and red markings)*. At the halfway mark, take the less demanding Sentier des deux ruisseaux track. Beyond the Lac Noir *(2hr 30min walk)*, the hike is easier and quite pleasant, as the path skirts several **glacial lakes**, **Lac Carré**, **Lac de la Motte**, **Lac de Cottepens** and **Lac du Cos**★★. Walk along the Lac de Cottepens towards the Col des Sept-Laux; bear left where you see yellow, white and red markings on a rock. The path leads through pastureland and rocks up to a mound overlooking the small Lac Blanc and affording a stunning **view**★★★ of the Sept-Laux, of the Eau d'Olle Valley and of numerous peaks and ridges all around.

MICHELIN GREEN GUIDES
Art and Architecture
History
Geography
Ancient monuments
Scenic routes
Touring programmes
Plans of towns and buildings
A selection of guides for holidays at home and abroad.

Route du col d'ALLOS ★★

Michelin map 81 fold 8 or 245 folds 9 and 22

This road, linking the Barcelonnette depression with the upper Verdon Valley, gives access to the Var Valley and, beyond, to Nice via the Col de la Colle St-Michel.

FROM BARCELONNETTE TO COLMARS *44km – about 2hr*

The Col d'Allos is blocked by snow from November to May.

★**Barcelonnette** – *See BARCELONNETTE.*

Leaving Barcelonnette and the Ubaye Valley, the road climbs above the wild forested Gorges du Bachelard *(see Route de la CAYOLLE).*

After the bridge across the Fau, road D 908 makes a detour via the Vallon des Agneliers, overlooked by the ridge of the Grande Séolane (alt 2 909m/9 544ft), before affording once more bird's-eye views of the deep Gorges du Bachelard.

La Foux d'Allos and Col d'Allos

★★**Col d'Allos** – Alt 2 240m/7349ft. From the platform of the refuge situated just below the pass *(viewing table)*, there is a fine **view**★ of Barcelonnette to the north, of the Pain de Sucre and Chapeau de Gendarme to the northeast and of the Grand Cheval de Bois to the east. The Grande Séolane and the skiing area of La Foux d'Allos can be seen from the pass itself.

The road continues down to the pastures where the Verdon takes its source.

★★**La Foux d'Allos** – *See VAL D'ALLOS.*

The road, cut through black schist, winds from one gorge to another between La Foux d'Allos and Allos.

Allos – *See VAL D'ALLOS.*

As one approaches Colmars, the road affords a lovely view of the fortified town.

★**Colmars** – *See COLMARS.*

L'ALPE-D'HUEZ ✳✳

Michelin map 77 fold 6 or 244 fold 40
Local map see Bassin du BOURG-D'OISANS

L'Alpe-d'Huez, lying at an altitude of 1 860m/6 102ft, more than 1 000m/3 281ft above the Bourg-d'Oisans Valley, is one of the most attractive winter sports resorts in the French Alps. In summer, l'Alpe-d'Huez is the starting-point of fascinating **hikes** and mountaineering expeditions in the Massif des Grandes Rousses.

THE RESORT

The twisting road leading to L'Alpe-d'Huez, with its 21 numbered hairpin bends, provides one of the most famous climbs of the Tour de France cycle race. The resort comprises numerous large chalet-style hotels close to the swimming-pool and the summer pastures.

Skiing area – L'Alpe-d'Huez is the most important ski resort in Dauphiné. Although its skiing area is not so extensive as that of other resorts in the Tarentaise region, it has developed considerably and there are now more than 100 Alpine ski runs including 10 black pistes. The spectacular course of some of these attracts daring skiers. The main attraction of L'Alpe-d'Huez is that it is linked with nearby resorts: Villard-Reculas, Auris-en-Oisans, Oz-en-Oisans and Vaujany. In July, the **Sarennes glacier** provides a thrilling black piste when snow cover is adequate.

Centre Notre-Dame-des-Neiges – The modern rotunda-like building (1970), surmounted by a spiral roof, houses a meeting centre and a crypt which serves as a parish church and a concert venue ⊙; the organ is particularly noteworthy.

Musée d'Huez et de l'Oisans ⊙ – *Route de la Poste*. This municipal museum displays objects discovered since 1977 on the **Brandes** archeological site (near the airfield). The remains of a 13C-14C silver mine were unearthed. There are also exhibits concerning traditional life in the Oisans area, local fauna and flora.

★**Route de Villars-Reculas** – *4km/2.5mi along D 211ᴮ – local map see Bassin du BOURG-D'OISANS*. This steep road offers bird's-eye views of the Bassin du Bourg-d'Oisans below.

HIKES

★★★**Pic du Lac Blanc** ⊙ – *Access is by means of two successive gondola runs followed by a cable-car run.*

Lac Blanc – During the second run, the lake can be seen in a stony depression.

★★**Dôme des Petites Rousses** – This peak can be reached from the Lac Blanc *(1hr return)*.

★★★**Pic du Lac Blanc** – Alt 3 323m/10 902ft. As you come out of the cable-car *(viewing table)*, there is a sweeping **view**, from left to right, of Les Deux-Alpes, Lac Lauvitel, Mont Ventoux (in the distance), L'Alpe-d'Huez (below), Le Taillefer, as well as the Belledonne and Chartreuse massifs. Go to the main platform and climb on to a mound *(viewing table)*. The **panoramic view** is even wider, with Pic Bayle in the foreground and, in the distance, the heights of the Maurienne and the peaks of the Vanoise and Écrins massifs.

★**La Grande Sure** ⊙ **(or Le Signal)** – Alt 2 114m/6 936ft. *Access by the Grande Sure chair-lift in winter and on foot (1hr 50min return) in summer*. Extensive **views** of the Grandes Rousses range, L'Oisans region, Le Taillefer and the Belledonne range.

★**Lac Besson** – *6.5km/4mi by the road leading to Col de Poutran in the north*. The road winds through pastures, reaches Col de Poutran and L'Alpe-d'Huez basin and, beyond, a high plateau dotted with glacial lakes. From Lac Besson, the most picturesque of these lakes, it is possible to climb on foot up to a ridge which reveals **Lac Noir** below in wild surroundings. A path *(30min return)* goes round the lake, offering more impressive views.

To plan a special itinerary:
– consult the Map of touring programmes which indicates the recommended routes, the tourist regions, the principal towns and main sights.
– read the descriptions in the Sights section which include Excursions from the main tourist centres.

Michelin Maps *nos 70, 74, 77, 81, 84, 88, 89, 243, 244 and 245 indicate scenic routes, interesting sights, viewpoints, rivers, forests...*

ANNECY★★★

Conurbation 122 622
Michelin map 89 fold 14 or 244 folds 18 and 19
Local maps see Lac d'ANNECY and Massif des ARAVIS

Annecy lies on the shores of the Lac d'Annecy, water and mountains blending admirably to form one of the most remarkable landscapes in the French Alps. The town is continually developing and its economic importance increases with the growth of its industrial potential (manufacture of ball bearings and skiing equipment). The Paccard bell-foundry, where the famous "Savoyarde" bell (19t) of the Sacré Cœur Basilica in Montmartre was cast, still exports to all parts of the world from Sévrier, 5km/3mi out of town *(see Lac d'ANNECY)*. In addition, there is a nuclear physics research centre in Annecy-le-Vieux.

This industrial and scientific expansion was achieved with proper care for the beauty of the site and supported by various town planning projects designed to improve living conditions in the old town without altering its character (Ste-Claire district), to extend the modern town (law courts, Centre Bonlieu, new railway station, Impérial conference centre and ATRIA business centre) and to improve the lake shores as well as certain monuments (east end of the Église St-Maurice).

The shores of the lake and Old Annecy are the main tourist attraction. There is a fine overall view from the height crowned by the castle and overlooking the town.

HISTORICAL NOTES

Beginnings – The site was occupied as far back as prehistoric times (a lake settlement stood where the harbour is now situated). The town, which owes its name to a Roman villa, Villa Aniciaca, developed round its castle from the 12C onwards under the name of Annecy-le-Neuf, to distinguish it from the neighbouring Gallo-Roman city of Annecy-le-Vieux. It became important in the 16C when it replaced Geneva as the regional capital.

Humanist and spiritual father – The outstanding religious and literary figure of Annecy is **François de Sales** (1567-1622). Born in the nearby Château de Sales *(see THORENS-GLIÈRES)*, he studied law before being ordained in Annecy. He preached against Calvinism and was soon famous all over France. He later became a bishop and, in 1607, 30 years before the foundation of the Académie française by Richelieu, he was the co-founder of the **Académie florimontane**, a literary institution devoted to work for the public good, influence opinion and spread the cult of beauty; it was housed in the home of one of the founders, at 18 rue Ste-Claire. The academy still exists and meets regularly.

In 1608, François de Sales published his *Introduction à la Vie Dévote* (Introduction to a Life of Piety) which met with great success and was translated into many languages. Forty editions were sold in the author's lifetime. Having perceived the usefulness of a congregation devoted to the poor and the sick, he met Jeanne de Chantal, the ancestor of Madame de Sévigné, who later founded the first Convent of the Visitation of the Virgin. François de Sales was canonised in 1665 and **Jeanne de Chantal** in 1767. Their relics are kept in the basilica of the Visitation.

Jean-Jacques the proselyte (1728) – At the age of 16, **Jean-Jacques Rousseau**, ill-treated by his employer, fled from his native town, Geneva, to Annecy; there he was dazzled by **Madame de Warens** who had been asked to convert him to Catholicism. Her task was easy for he was "sure that a religion preached by such a missionary could not fail to lead him to Paradise". Readers of the *Confessions* can see the place where they met in the Ancien palais épiscopal.

★★LES BORDS DU LAC *1hr*

Leave the car in the car park of Centre Bonlieu or place de l'Hôtel-de-ville.

Centre Bonlieu (**EY**) – This cultural centre, designed in 1981 by Novarina, houses the Maison du Tourisme, the library, the theatre and several shops.

Avenue d'Albigny (**EFXY**) – This royal avenue, lined with hundred-year-old plane trees, crosses the common where the townspeople used to take a stroll. The concrete and glass law courts (1978), built by Novarina, stand to the left.

Walk across the Champ de Mars to the viewing table by the lake.

There is an extensive **view★** of the Grand Lac framed by mountains, with Mont Veyrier and Crêt du Maure in the foreground.

Return to the town along the lake shore.

Pont des Amours (**FY**) – The bridge spans the Canal du Vassé, offering lovely views of the shaded canal one way, dotted with small crafts, and of the wooded Île des Cygnes the other way.

★**Jardins de l'Europe** (**FY**) – These gardens, which used to form an island, were joined to the town and laid as an arboretum with a variety of species from Europe, America and Asia including several huge sequoias and a ginkgo biloba, also called "maidenhair tree". From the harbour along the Thiou, there are interesting views of the massive castle.

Walk to place de l'Hôtel-de-ville and continue on foot through Old Annecy.

USEFUL TIPS

Where to have a drink and relax? – Rue Ste-Claire and rue Royale are the centre of the Annecy nightlife. Connoisseurs will appreciate the "Griffith's" (rue de la Porte) and the "Milton Club" (rue Ste-Claire) for their wide choice of beers; on the other hand, visitors looking for a change of scenery are bound to like the pre-1940s decor of the "Café Cuit" or the opulence of the "Pub Cheltenham". There is themed entertainment at the "Captain Pub" (rue du Pont-Morens) which mixes amazing beer cocktails. The Compagnie des bateaux d'Annecy (Annecy boat trips) organises dinner-show cruises aboard the "Libellule", ☎ 04 50 51 08 40.

In Sévrier, the "Dinecittà" restaurant stages themed shows renewed every year in a cinema setting.

Where to end the evening in music – The "Pop Plage", 30 avenue d'Albigny, is a discotheque suitable for all ages *(open during the season only)*. Other establishments suggest themed evenings; information is available from the tourist office or in the local press; or you could try your luck at the **Casino**, 32 avenue d'Albigny.

Specialities – Many shops, in particular rue Ste-Claire and rue Royale, sell sweets with tantalising names: "le roseau du lac" (black chocolate filled with coffee cream), la Cloche d'Annecy and la Savoyarde, named after the famous bell (chocolate filled with praline and hazelnut-flavoured cream). Ravey's (3 rue de la République) has mouth-watering displays.

The numerous specialities of Savoyard cuisine can be enjoyed in traditional surroundings along the narrow streets of the old town, in particular rue Ste-Claire (local cheese at no 12). There are attractive cheese stands at the market held on Tuesdays in rue Ste-Claire.

Books about the area and guide books are on sale at the "Fnac", rue Sommeiller, as well as in the Grandchamp and "L'Imaginaire" bookshops.

Sport – For a beginner's course in canyoning or rock-climbing, contact the **Bureau des Guides**, Centre Bonlieu, ☎ 04 50 45 00 33. The Club nautique de Doussard (☎ 04 50 44 81 45) offers a choice of water sports as does the Ski club nautique in Sévrier. The Col de la Forclaz is the favourite haunt of paragliders (first flight from the "Chalet du Mini-golf" in Montmin).

Rental of sports equipment – "Locasport", 37 avenue de Loverchy, in Annecy and "Ogier Sports" in La Clusaz.

Bathing in the lake – Many beaches *(free or with admission charge)* line the shores of the lake: "Plage d'Albigny" *(admission charge)*, "Plage des Marquisats" and "Plage du Petit Port" *(free)* in Annecy.

★★OLD ANNECY *1hr 30min – see plan p 72*

The old part of town has been largely pedestrianised and renovated during the past decades. Note the arcaded houses and Italian-style wells. A colourful market *(wide choice of regional cheeses)*, held on Tuesday, Friday and Sunday mornings, brings life to rue de la République and rue Ste-Claire.

Start from place de l'Hôtel-de-ville and walk across quai Chappuis.

Église St-Maurice (EY **B**) – The church was built in the 15C with a large overhanging roof in typical regional style. Inside, the vast Gothic nave is flanked with side chapels built by aristocratic families or guilds, whose arms and emblems are displayed. Note in particular a 16C fresco near the pulpit and, in the chancel, a fine **Deposition★** by Pourbus the Elder and a remarkable **mural painting** in grisaille dating from 1458.

Walk towards the river past the Église St-François.

Église St-François (EY) – St François de Sales and St Jeanne de Chantal were originally buried in this former 17C monastery church with a Baroque façade, now the parish church of the Italian community.

Cross the bridge over the Thiou River, which is the natural outlet of the lake.

Pont sur le Thiou (EY **N**) – The picturesque **Palais de l'Isle** standing in the middle of the river offers the most famous **view★** of Old Annecy *(see photograph p 57)*.

Continue along rue Perrière.

Rue Perrière (EY **75**) – The houses are built over a row of arcades.

Turn right, then right again and cross the Thiou once more.

From the bridge, enjoy a lovely view of the houses lining the river bank. The entrance of the Palais de l'Isle is on the right.

★**Palais de l'Isle** ⊘ (**EY M²**) – This monument is the emblem of the town. Built on an island in the 12C, the edifice was used in turn as the Count of Geneva's residence, the mint, the law courts and a fearsome prison, which it remained until 1870, resuming that role for a time during the Second World War.
It now houses the **Musée de l'histoire d'Annecy**, illustrating the town's prestigious past and the history of Savoie; the cells, kitchen and prison can be visited.
Turn left along quai de l'Isle, cross the pont Morens and turn right.

★**Rue Ste-Claire** (**DY 91**) – The high street of Old Annecy is lined with arcaded houses. The 16C mansion at **no 18** is associated with the foundation of the Académie florimontane and the bishopric of St François de Sales.
On the corner of rue de la République stands a former convent known as the "**Manufacture**" because a spinning mill was set up there in 1805. The whole area has been tastefully renovated and pedestrianised (the lively placette Ste-Claire and place Volland contrast with the peaceful quai des Clarisses).
Turn back at the porte Ste-Claire and walk along rue de la République to rue Jean-Jacques-Rousseau.

Ancien palais épiscopal (**DY**) – It was built in 1784, on the site of Madame de Warens's house; a bust of Rousseau stands in the courtyard. St François de Sales wrote his famous *Introduction à la Vie Dévote* (Introduction to a Life of Piety) in the 16C **Maison Lambert** (**EY D**), at no 15 rue Jean-Jacques-Rousseau *(see p 70)*.

Cathédrale St-Pierre (**EY**) – Built in the 16C with a Renaissance façade and a Gothic interior, it became the cathedral of Bishop François de Sales; Jean-Jacques Rousseau sang in the choir and played the flute in the cathedral.
Turn left into rue Filaterie lined with imposing arcades.

Continuing past the Église Notre-Dame-de-Liesse with its tower which leans slightly, one reaches rue du Pâquier, also lined with arcades: the 17C Hôtel de Sales, decorated with sculptures illustrating the Seasons, is at no 12.
Turn right into quai E-Chappuis to return to place de l'Hôtel-de-ville.

ANNECY

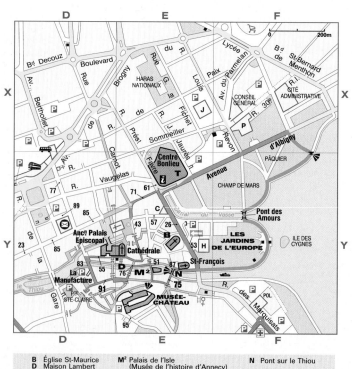

B Église St-Maurice
D Maison Lambert
M² Palais de l'Isle (Musée de l'histoire d'Annecy)
N Pont sur le Thiou

Annecy on the shores of Lac d'Annecy

★MUSÉE-CHÂTEAU D'ANNECY ⊙ (EY)

*Access by car via chemin de la Tour la Reine, or on foot, up the castle ramp or the steep
hill starting to rise from rue Ste-Claire.*

This former residence of the junior branch of the House of Savoie, dating from the
12C to the 16C, was damaged by fire several times, abandoned, then used as a
garrison before being restored with the help of public funds.

To the right of the entrance stands the massive 12C **Tour la Reine**, with 4m/13ft-
thick walls; this is the oldest part of the castle. From the centre of the courtyard,
one faces the austere living quarters of the **Logis Vieux** (14C-15C), with its stair
turret and deep well; to the left is the early Renaissance façade of the **Logis Nemours**
(16C) and to the right the late 16C **Logis Neuf**, which housed the garrison of the
castle. At the end of the courtyard are the recently restored 15C **Logis** and **Tour
Perrière**, which house the **Observatoire régional des lacs alpins** ⊙, illustrating the various
aspects of mountain lakes including the effects of pollution on the fauna and
displaying archeological finds. In the **Salle des fresques**, on the top level, fragments of
15C murals give a good idea of what the medieval castle was like.

From the terrace, there is a good overall view of Old Annecy and of the modern
town beyond.

The Logis Vieux and the Logis Nemours house an interesting **regional museum** on
three floors linked by a spiral staircase. Note the remarkable fireplaces facing each
other in the vast kitchen, the splendid guardroom with its rows of columns and the
great hall. There are collections of contemporary art, carved glass and popular art
(pottery, earthenware, glassware, furniture etc).

ADDITIONAL SIGHTS

Conservatoire d'Art et d'Histoire de la Haute-Savoie ⊙ – This art museum,
situated just south of the castle, is housed in a fine 17C building in Sardinian style.
The collections include numerous paintings and engravings depicting landscapes of
Haute-Savoie, as well as 18C and 19C paintings.

Basilique de la Visitation ⊙ – The church of the Couvent de la Visitation stands
on the slopes of Crêt du Maure, affording a vast open vista of Annecy and the
western Préalpes. The richly decorated interior of the 1930 building, with its
grey-marble pillars, attracts many pilgrims, particularly for the feast-day of St
François on 24 January and in August. The relics of St François de Sales and St
Jeanne de Chantal are displayed at the end of the aisles; the stained-glass windows
illustrate the life of the patron saints of Annecy as does the small **museum** adjoining
the church on the right. The church has a peal of 38 bells.

Revival of the ecosystem of the Lac d'Annecy

In spite of the many mountain streams which flow into it, the fairly shallow lake (30-45m/98-148ft deep) had, by the end of the 1960s, lost most of its bird population as pollution from hotels along the shores and from motor boats had upset its fragile ecosystem. The local municipalities clubbed together to build an impressive network of underwater drainpipes leading to an ultra-modern filtering plant.

This action, combined with collective awareness of the dangers of pollution, led to the lake waters becoming pure again. Chars and trouts have come back and swans are nesting in the reeds once more.

The **Réserve naturelle du Bout du Lac**, situated at the western end of the lake, shelters local species: reptiles, ducks, swans and beavers.

Basilique St-Joseph-des-Fins ⊙ – Designed by the Benedictine architect Dom Bellot just before the Second World War, this church is plain outside with a few regional features such as its onion-shaped steeple and large steep roof. By contrast, there is a wealth of interior decoration illustrating many teachings from the Bible (chancel, high altar, stained glass, baptistery, triumphal arch). Note the lovely 15C Virgin Mary in a side chapel and the 15C Christ in the baptistery.

Parc de l'Impérial – The park, situated at the eastern end of avenue d'Albigny and covering an area of 2ha/5 acres shaded by beautiful trees, includes an aviary, a sports centre and a former hotel turned into a conference centre.

★★★**Lake cruises** ⊙ – The Compagnie des bateaux d'Annecy organises various trips on the lake aboard their launches with stops in several ports: Veyrier, Menthon, Duingt, St-Jorioz and Sévrier. The *Libellule*, a panoramic boat with a capacity of 600 passengers, proposes lunch-cruise and dinner-show formulae; departure from the pier along the Thiou (**FY**) in Annecy.

EXCURSION

★★Gorges du Fier and Château de Montrottier

20km/12.4mi. About 2hr 30min. Leave Annecy by N 508; 3km further on, beyond the motorway underpass, turn left on D 14.
Turn left again past the Église de Lovagny along D 64 and drive down a steep hill.

★★**Gorges du Fier** ⊙ – Visitors can walk along galleries clinging to the straight walls of the gorge while the sunlight plays through the foliage forming an arched roof over the narrow passage. Beyond the exit and a cluster of beeches, there is a belvedere on a rocky promontory, which affords a good view of the "Mer de Rochers" (sea of rocks), an impressive heap of boulders piled on one another.

Drive back to D 116 junction and turn left then right up the path leading to the Château de Montrottier.

★**Château de Montrottier** ⊙ – The castle stands on an isolated mound between the Fier and its former bed, known as the "Grande Fosse". Built between the 13C and the 16C, it is a fine specimen of Savoyard military architecture; a 36m/118ft-tall round keep towers over it.

G Sommer/EXPLORER

Gorges du Fier

The castle houses important **collections**★ bequeathed in 1916 by the former owner to the Académie florimontane: weaponry, earthenware, porcelain, ceramics, ivory from the Far East, antique furniture, statuettes and four 16C bronze reliefs by Peter and Hans Vischer from Nuremberg.

In fine weather, it is worth climbing (86 steps) up to the crenellated walk at the top of the castle for a panoramic view of nearby peaks with Mont Blanc in the distance.

Go back to D 116 and turn right towards Corbier.

The road runs along the cliff for a short while then rapidly leads down to the river and crosses it. After a steep climb through a small wood, one is rewarded by a magnificent view of the castle and the valley below.

In Corbier, take D 16 to the left towards Annecy.

Lac d'ANNECY ★★★

Michelin map 89 fold 14 or 244 folds 18 and 19 – Local map see p 78

The Lac d'Annecy is the jewel of the Savoie region. The snow-capped peaks of La Tournette (2 351m/7 713ft), the pointed needles of the Dents de Lanfon or the elegant curves of the Montagne d'Entrevernes towering above its deep blue waters form one of the most attractive Alpine landscapes, discovered barely 100 years ago by artists and writers. A tour of the lake by boat or car enables one to appreciate the full beauty of this impressive lake setting.

The lake – The picturesque vistas afforded by the lake are largely due to its twisting contour. It consists of two depressions originally separated at the straits overlooked by Duingt Castle. Smaller (2 800ha/6 919 acres) and less deep (40m/131ft on average) than the Lac du Bourget it is supplied by several streams and a powerful underwater spring, the Boubioz, located 250m offshore from La Puya. The main outlet of the lake is the Thiou which flows into the Fier.

The steep wooded slopes of the Petit Lac in the south offer a more austere aspect than the more accessible shores of the Grand Lac in the north, dotted with villages and hamlets surrounded by vineyards and clusters of trees. Pollan is often found on local menus but gourmets prefer arctic char, trout, perch, carp etc.

★★THE WEST SHORE

① From Annecy to Faverges

38km/23.6mi – about 1hr 30min – Local map see p 78

This itinerary through the Parc régional des Bauges offers lovely views of the lake, of the heights of La Tournette and of the jagged peaks of the Dents de Lanfon. *A cycle track runs above, along the same route.*

★★★**Annecy** – *See ANNECY.*

Leave Annecy by N 508.

The road skirts the promontory of La Puya, offering good views of Mont Veyrier in the foreground.

Sévrier – This resort lies on the very edge of the lake, overlooked by the church occupying a prominent position.

Écomusée du costume savoyard ⊘ – Opposite the church, housed in the former girls' school. Reconstructions of scenes of traditional life in Savoie help to appreciate the amazing variety of costumes between the 18C and the 20C. The skills of needlework are explained.

★**Musée de la Cloche** ⊘ – *N 508, on the way out of Sévrier.*
The museum, created by the **Paccard Bell-foundry**, explains the manufacturing process and retraces the history of this ancient craft through a collection of bells dating from the 14C to the 19C; other exhibits include tuning forks, which were of prime importance in the making of peals. The "Savoyarde" now in the Sacré Cœur Basilica and the "Jeanne d'Arc" in Rouen Cathedral were cast in Annecy.

★**Duingt** – Situated at the narrowest part of the lake which marks the separation between the Grand Lac and Petit Lac, this pleasant summer resort has retained its rustic Savoyard character. The **castle** *(not open to the public)* has been keeping watch on the straits from a tiny wooded island since the 11C; like the Château d'Héré just south of Duingt, it once belonged to the De Sales family and was restored in the 17C and 19C. Further on, the road skirts the steep and more austere shores of the Petit Lac.

At Doussard, follow the road leading through the Combe d'Ire for 6km/3.7mi.

★**Combe d'Ire** – This deep wooded furrow overlooked by the Montagne de Charbon, through which runs a tumultuous stream, used to be one of the wildest and most mysterious Alpine valleys; the last bear was killed in 1893. It is now part of the **Réserve cynégétique des Bauges** (Les Bauges game preserve), rich in chamois, roe-deer, black grouse, rock-partridge, marmots and moufflons.

Rejoin N 508 and turn right to Faverges.

The road goes through the marshy valley of the River Eau Morte, offering closer views of the Bauges Massif and the jagged crest of its highest peak, l'Arcalod (2 217m/7 274ft).

Faverges – *See below.*

★★★**ROUTE DE LA FORCLAZ**

2 **From Faverges to Annecy**

49km/30.4mi – about 1hr 45min – local map see p 78

The road climbs up to the Col de la Forclaz through the fine Alpine valley of Montmin beneath the escarpments of La Tournette. Beyond the pass, the drive down to Menthon and Annecy leads through pleasant agricultural landscapes.

Faverges – Situated at an important crossroads, between the Chaîne des Aravis and Massif des Bauges, this large village is overlooked by the 13C round keep of its castle; traditional industries include prefabricated wooden chalets,

Lac d'Annecy and Duingt castle

mechanical engineering, household appliances and luxury goods.

Grotte and Cascade de Seythenex ⊙ – *2km/1.2mi south of Faverges then right; path signposted "grottes de Seythenex".*
Several footbridges lead to the top of the waterfall which drops 30m/98ft through a narrow crack into a picturesque wooded vale. It is possible to walk along the former underground river bed testifying to the power of water erosion. An exhibition shows how craftsmen use water power in their workshops (sawmill, oil-mill...).

Return to Faverges and drive north along D 12.

Viuz – This hamlet is within sight of the snow-capped summit of Mont-Blanc. Next to the church and its 12C Romanesque apse, a small **Musée archéologique** ⊙ houses a collection of Gallo-Roman objects found locally, including a remarkable cauldron of the 3C AD, an amber necklace and numerous Roman coins.

Continue on D 282 to Vesonne.

The climb from Vesonne to Montmin reveals panoramic views of the Massif des Bauges to the south, including some of its highest summits, the Belle Étoile, Dent de Cons, Sambuy and Arcalod, and of La Tournette to the north.

Montmin – Set in pastoral surroundings, this attractive resort is the ideal starting-point of mountain expeditions, such as the ascent of La Tournette.

From Le Villard, the road climbs to the Col de la Forclaz through pastures and picturesque hamlets.

★★**Col de la Forclaz** – Alt 1 157m/3 796ft. From the belvedere on the left, there is a bird's-eye view of the Lac d'Annecy: note the shallow bank just off Duingt, occupied by lake-dwellings in prehistoric times: it casts a yellowish shadow on the deep blue waters of the lake.

Follow a path on the right, which goes up to a small café, known as La Pricaz, then turn left to reach the belvedere (15min return).

Fine panoramic view of the summits of the Bauges Massif.

The steep drop from the Col de la Forclaz to Rovagny reveals more beautiful views of the Bauges, the Semnoz, the curve of the Grand Lac and Annecy nestling on its shores. Further on, the Ermitage de St-Germain overlooks a narrow wooded valley.

★**Ermitage de St-Germain** – *From D 42, 15min return up a steep footpath starting on the left of the first tunnel (on the way down).*

JL. Gallo/MICHELIN

This is a centre of local pilgrimage *(particularly on Whit Monday)*; otherwise, the place is a charming retreat. According to tradition, St Germain, the first abbot of the Abbaye de Talloires, retired to a grotto in the small escarpment overlooking the road. The splendid **landscape** formed by the chapel and its ancient lime tree with the Talloires bay, the Duingt straits and the Bauges mountain range in the background also attracted St François de Sales *(see ANNECY)* who planned to retire here.

There is a wider **panorama** of the Grand Lac and the surrounding mountains from the **Belvédère de la Vierge★** *(15min return along a steep footpath skirting the cemetery)*. Go back to the tunnel entrance and start walking along the second path on the left: the view of the Talloires bay *(see TALLOIRES)* is magnificent.

Beyond the tunnel, there are more stunning views of Annecy and the Grand Lac.

Past the junction with the direct road to Annecy, D 909ᴬ, the Château de Menthon comes into view, higher up on the right.

★**Menthon-St-Bernard** – This is a pleasant family resort on the shores of the Lac d'Annecy. The **Château de Menthon** ⊙★ *(2km/1.2mi climb by D 969 starting from the church)* was the birthplace of St Bernard de Menthon, who founded the Grand St-Bernard hospice; the present castle, dating from the 13C and 15C, is crowned with turrets and offers a beautiful **view★** of the lake from the terrace.

The **Roc de Chère★** *(2hr return on foot)*, a wooded promontory separating Menthon-St-Bernard and Talloires, shelters a **nature reserve** covering 68ha/168 acres with interesting species of Mediterranean and boreal flora. The **view** extends across the Petit Lac to La Tournette and the Bauges mountain range, with Duingt castle in the foreground.

Veyrier – There is a lovely view of the Grand Lac from the garden behind the town hall.

★★**Mont Veyrier** – *1km/0.6mi, then 5hr return on foot. Leave Veyrier by the Route du Mont Veyrier, turn left into the Route de la Combe. Leave the car at the end of the road and follow the Sentier du Col des Contrebandiers which leads to the summit.* From the Mont Baron viewing table, there is a bird's-eye **view** of the Lac d'Annecy, framed by mountains on all sides. In fine weather, the view extends southeast to the glaciers of the Vanoise Massif and northeast as far as Lake Geneva.

From Chavoire onwards, the road widens, affording a good overall view of Annecy overlooked by the Basilique de la Visitation and the castle.

★★★**Annecy** – *See ANNECY.*

Lac d'ANNECY

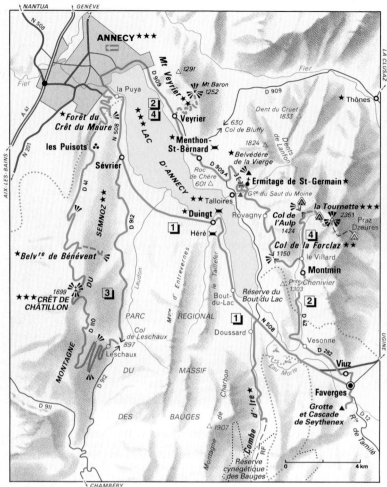

★★ LE SEMNOZ

③ Round tour from Annecy

52km/32mi – about 2hr – local map see above

Le Semnoz is a picturesque wooded ridge stretching from Crêt du Maure, a forested area ideal for walking, to Crêt de Châtillon, its highest peak.

The road leading to the summit can be blocked by snow from November to May, but it is usually cleared by Whitsun.

★★★ **Annecy** – See ANNECY.

Leave Annecy by D 41 towards Crêt de Châtillon. The road rises quickly.

★ **Forêt du Crêt du Maure** – This vast wooded area, which is, to a large extent, the result of 19C reafforestation, is crisscrossed by footpaths leading to numerous belvederes and includes a few pens for marmots, deer, roe-deer and reindeer along D 41. The Chalet Super-Panorama offers one of the loveliest **views**★★ of the lake *(from the Semnoz road, follow a path which starts at the second hairpin bend after entering the forest, by a reservoir).*

Les Puisots – The old hamlet, burnt down in 1944 (memorial), was replaced by the chalets of a *centre aéré* (outdoor centre) for children and a public park.

The road goes through the forest, offering a few glimpses of the Albanais depression.

Follow the forest road leading to the Belvédère de Bénévent. Leave the car in a bend on the left and follow a footpath on the right.

★ **Belvédère de Bénévent** – View of La Tournette and Duingt straits.

Return to D 41.

The landscape changes to stony pastures dotted with blue gentians in early summer. The climb becomes more pronounced and, after a right bend, a vast mountain panorama opens out in front of your eyes.

★★**Crêt de Châtillon** – *15min return on foot. Leave the car at the end of the road and walk up through pastureland to the summit where a tall cross and a viewing table stand.*
The **panoramic view** embraces some of the most famous summits of the western Alps: Haut-Faucigny, Mont-Blanc, Vanoise, Écrins, Aiguilles d'Arves, Viso...
The road goes down to the Col de Leschaux through a forest of resinous trees and continues in a series of hairpin bends along the steep slopes of Semnoz, offering fine views of the surrounding mountains.
From the Col de Leschaux, return to Annecy by D 912 and N 508 via Sévrier (see Les BAUGES ①).

★★★BELVÉDÈRE DE LA TOURNETTE

④ **Round tour from Annecy** Hike from the Chalet de l'Aulp

35km/22mi – allow 2hr – local map see p 78
Leave Annecy by ③ on the town plan, follow D 909 to Menthon-St-Bernard then D 42 towards the Col de la Forclaz.

Route du Col de l'Aulp – *3.5km/2.2mi from Le Villard* – This forest road goes past Le Villard then climbs between steep wooded slopes, revealing the chalk cliffs of La Tournette on the right. The road gives way to a track which leads to the Col de l'Aulp (1 424m/4 672ft) just below La Tournette: from the mound situated behind the chalet, there is a lovely **view** of part of the Lac d'Annecy.

From the Chalet de l'Aulp to the Refuge de la Tournette – *2hr return on foot; difference in height 350m/1 148ft. You will need a good pair of binoculars to look at ibexes roaming around.*
A marked path rises to the east of the pass then skirts the limestone cliffs overlooking the Cirque du Casset. From the viewing table near the Refuge de la Tournette (alt 1 774m/5 820ft), there is a splendid **panorama**★★ of the western shore of the lake overlooked by the Semnoz. Climbing to the summit of La Tournette requires a solid experience of hiking through rocky terrain; however, no special equipment is necessary as there are handrails and ladders along the way. One of the finest **panoramas**★★★ of the northern Alps unfolds from the summit (alt 2 351m/7 713ft).

ANNOT★

Population 1 053
Michelin map 81 fold 18 or 245 fold 23

This small town, lying on the banks of the River Vaire, 700m/2 297ft above sea level, is the oldest settlement in the valley, having retained to this day its Alpine and Provençal characteristics. Annot is surrounded by picturesque rocks, known as **grès d'Annot**. These sandstone formations, which were sculpted by erosion into strange shapes and natural arches, offer interesting walks around the town.

★OLD TOWN

The old town looks quaint with its steep twisting lanes, its arcades, its arched alleyways and its leaning houses. For a good overall view, walk along rue Basse then **Grande-Rue** leading through a fortified gate to the church. On the way, note the 16C-18C carved doorways and the **Maison des Arcades**, a fine 17C mansion.
The Romanesque **church** has an unusual raised east end designed as a defensive tower, a lovely Renaissance steeple, as well as a 17C aisle and adjoining chapel. Walk under a gateway into rue des Vallasses where there is a wash-house opposite the Tour du Peintre (Artist's Tower). Rue Notre-Dame on the left leads back to Grande-Rue.

ADDITIONAL SIGHTS

Cours – This typical Provençal avenue, lined with splendid old plane trees, is the centre of activity. The old **cutwater bridge** across the Vaire dates back to Roman times. Follow the river to the **Chapelle de Vérimande**, a busy place of pilgrimage.

Croix tréflée – This strange 13C Romanesque cross can be seen on the left of the road, on the way out of town towards Nice.

Chapelle Notre-Dame de Vers-la-Ville – *20min return on foot. From the Cours, follow the street to the right of the fountain then the chemin de Vers-la-Ville.* This path is lined with the Stations of the Cross. The 12C chapel is surrounded by rocks piled on one another, lending to a good overall view of the village and its mountain setting.

★LES GRÈS D'ANNOT

These rock formations are the paradise of amateur and professional climbers alike. Others will be content to take a leisurely walk to the **Rochers de la gare** along a trail marked "chemin des grès" and to watch the climbers' progress. The vegetation seems to bind the rocks together and sometimes literally come out of the blocks which have been given appropriate names: the camel, the stem, the zodiac, the face, the king's bedroom... It is worth walking as far as the Arches de Portettes.

Massif des ARAVIS★★

Michelin map 89 folds 4, 5, 14 and 15 or 244 folds 8, 9, 19 and 20
Local map see p 81

The natural boundaries of the Massif des Aravis, which forms part of the western Préalpes, are the Lac d'Annecy basin, the valleys of the Arly and Arve rivers and the Bornes depression.

A strong backbone – Two powerful streams, the Fier and the Borne cut through the massif by way of some long and narrow gorges such as the **Défilé de Dingy** (Fier), the **Défilé des Étroits** and **Gorge des Éveaux** (Borne). Between the Fier and the Borne, the **Parmelan** (alt 1 832m/6 010ft), which stretches its tall cliffs across the Annecy landscape, is the favourite goal of mountain hikers. The area was chosen by the Resistance unit of the "Maquis des Glières" *(see THORENS-GLIÈRES)* for its impressive natural defences.

The rocky **Chaîne du Bargy** and **Massif de Jallouvre** bar the horizon to the north and the **Chaîne des Aravis** stretches its mighty barrier between the Val d'Arly and Vallée de Thônes (highest peak: Pointe Percée at 2 752m/9 029ft), prolonged to the north by the **Chaîne du Reposoir**.

Reblochon country – The Vallée de Thônes, lying at the heart of the Aravis region, is Reblochon country: after maturing in the high Alpine pastures, this strong creamy cheese is sold in the market towns of Thônes and Grand-Bornand.

★★ROUTE DE LA CLUSAZ

1 From Annecy to La Clusaz

41km/25.5mi – about 1hr – local map see opposite

The road rises above the lake then goes through the wooded valleys of the Fier and Nom rivers, beneath the towering cliffs of the Parmelan Massif.

★★★**Annecy** – *See ANNECY.*
Leave Annecy by D 909.

At first the wide road follows the contour of the lake, revealing the Semnoz and Entrevernes mountains on the opposite shore.

Veyrier – *See Lac d'ANNECY.*

Between Veyrier and Col de Bluffy, there are open views of the Grand Lac and, in the distance, of the Sambuy and Charbon mountains *(stop the car by a disused bend)*. Further up, the Château de Menthon comes into view beneath the Dents de Lanfon.

★**Château de Menthon** – *2km from Col de Bluffy. See Lac d'ANNECY, 2.*

From Col de Bluffy to the bridge at Alex, the road leads down into the Fier Valley and through the Défilé de Dingy. Further upstream, one can see the **Cascade de Morette** (waterfall) on the opposite slope.

Cimetière des Glières – The cemetery, situated on the right of the road, contains the graves of 105 Resistance fighters of the Plateau des Glières *(see THORENS-GLIÈRES)*. An inscription relates the different stages of the operation.

The **Musée de la Résistance** ⊙ in Haute-Savoie, housed in a reconstructed 18C chalet on the

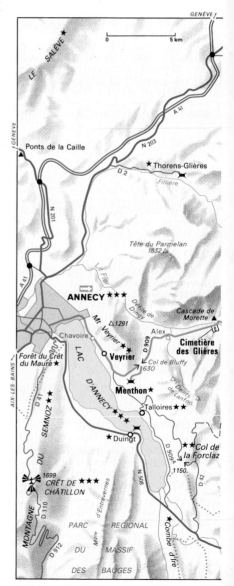

right of the cemetery, illustrates in detail the successive episodes of the fierce fighting that took place on the plateau. In addition, there is a memorial to those deported during the Second World War.

★**Thônes** – See THÔNES.

Drive south on D 12 then take the first left (D 16).

The road follows the **Vallée de Manigod**★★, the name given to the upper valley of the Fier.
The slopes are planted with fir trees alternating with orchards and dotted with old chalets.

Les clefs – The church built on a wooded height overlooking the Fier forms a charming picture beneath the steep cliffs of La Tournette.
The road rises further still, to Col de la Croix-Fry.

Col de la Croix-Fry – The pass is equipped with ski-lifts. The vast **panorama**★ includes the whole Aravis range. On the way down, the transverse valleys of La Clusaz (River Nom) and Les Étroits (River Borne) appear successively.

D 909 leads to La Clusaz.

✳✳**La Clusaz** – See La CLUSAZ.

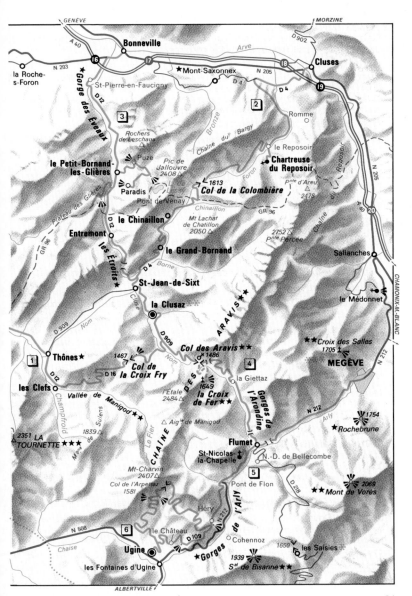

★ROUTE DE LA COLOMBIÈRE

② From La Clusaz to Cluses

40km/25mi – about 1hr 30min – local map see p 81

Linking the Thônes and Arve valleys, this route offers a succession of contrasting landscapes from the austere upper valley of the Chinaillon River to the delightful Vallée du Reposoir beyond the Col de la Colombière *(blocked by snow from the end of November to May)*.

✳✳**La Clusaz** – *See La CLUSAZ.*

North of La Clusaz, the road follows the wooded valley of the River Nom.

St-Jean-de-Sixt – This peaceful resort lies on the edge of the Nom and Borne valleys, at the heart of the Aravis Massif.

Turn right along D 4 towards Le Grand-Bornand.

✳**Le Grand-Bornand** – The pleasant, sunny home town of Reblochon cheese *(market on Wednesdays)*, is also a winter sports resort, with an annexe at Le Chinaillon *(6km/3.7mi higher up)*, and the starting point of fine excursions to Pointe Percée via Le Bouchet.

The road continues up to Pont de Venay, past Le Chinaillon, in a series of hairpin bends offering fine **views** of La Tournette and the high peaks of the Aravis range.

Le Chinaillon – The ski resort nestles round the old village, close to the ski slopes of Mont Lachat de Châtillon.

Beyond Pont de Venay, the landscape becomes wilder as the rocky escarpments of the Jallouvre Massif replace the Alpine pastures.

Col de la Colombière – Alt 1 618m/5 308ft. The view extends to the northeast towards the limestone heights of the Faucigny, Les Dents Blanches and Les Avoudrues. On the way down to Le Reposoir, the green summits and rocky peaks of the Chaîne du Reposoir come into view and the roofs of the Chartreuse du Reposoir can be seen in the foreground, below the village.

From Le Reposoir, take a narrow road to the Chartreuse.

Chartreuse du Reposoir – This monastery, in typical Carthusian style, was founded in 1151 and restored in the 17C. Abandoned by the order of St Bruno in 1904, it is now a Carmelite monastery.

From Le Reposoir to Cluses, the road overlooks the wooded gorge of the Foron before reaching the orchards of the Arve Valley and Cluses.

Cluses – *See Le FAUCIGNY, Route des Gets.*

★VALLÉE DU BORNE

③ From La Clusaz to Bonneville

40km/25mi – about 1hr 15min – local map see p 81

This pleasant itinerary follows the Borne Valley through two picturesque gorges.

St-Jean-de-Sixt – *See above.*

★**Défilé des Étroits** – The River Borne cut crosswise through the limestone range to form this narrow gorge which the road follows beneath impressive cliffs.

Entremont – As the valley widens, the village comes into view amid lush meadows. In the church, remodelled several times, there is an interesting **treasury** ⊙, in particular a gilt wood reliquary dating from the 12C.

The road continues through a pleasant pastoral landscape with the Jallouvre Massif looming in the distance (highest peak, 2 408m/7 900ft).

Le Petit-Bornand-les-Glières – This small summer resort, set in restful surroundings, is the ideal starting point of pleasant excursions to the Plateau des Glières *(2km/1.2mi south of the village, a forest road leads to the plateau)*.

Take the signposted road to the left of the town hall.

★**Route de Paradis** – The breathtaking climb up the steep slopes of the Jallouvre offers bird's-eye views of the lower and upper Borne Valley *(for the best views, stop at Puze and again at a crossroads, 2.5km/1.5mi further on)*.

The road ends at the Paradis ski centre with stunning **views**★ of the Rochers de Leschaux and the funnel-shaped chasm below.

Return to Petit-Bornand and continue on D 12 towards Bonneville.

★**Gorge des Éveaux** – The road follows the Borne through another transverse valley which narrows down considerably, the stream running below at the bottom of the gorge.

The road crosses the Borne in St-Pierre-en-Faucigny and reaches the River Arve in Bonneville.

Bonneville – *See Le FAUCIGNY, Route de Mont-Saxonnex.*

★★ROUTE DES ARAVIS

4 **From La Clusaz to Flumet**
19km/11.8mi – about 1hr – local map see p 81

This is one of the best known itineraries in the Savoie Alps, its greatest attraction being the view of Mont Blanc from Col des Aravis, particularly late in the afternoon *(the pass can be obstructed by snow from December to April).*

✻✻**La Clusaz** – *See La CLUSAZ.*
The road climbs to the pass in a succession of hairpin bends, beneath the escarpments of L'Étale. Mont Blanc suddenly appears as one reaches the pass.

★★**Col des Aravis** – Alt 1 498m/4 915ft. A small chapel dedicated to St Ann stands amid pastures overlooked by the impressive cliffs of L'Étale. The **view** finally extends over the whole Massif du Mont-Blanc, from Aiguille Verte in the north to Mont Tondu in the south, with Tête du Torraz in the foreground. The slopes are covered with wild violets and gentians in May and with alpenroses in early summer.

Col des Aravis

★★**La Croix de Fer** – *2hr return on foot. Follow the path (chemin du Chalet du Curé) starting from the restaurant and leading to the Croix de Fer.*
The **panorama** is even more grandiose here than from the pass, extending beyond Mont Blanc south to the Vanoise glaciers.

Gorges de l'Arondine – On the way down from the pass, the road goes through deeply cut gorges, where slate used to be extracted at the beginning of the century.

Flumet – This large village, situated at the confluence of the Arly and Arondine rivers and at the intersection of the Val d'Arly, Col des Saisies and Col des Aravis roads, is very busy in season. It is a pleasant summer resort offering walks through forested areas on the road to Notre-Dame-de-Bellecombe. It is also a lively winter resort linked to the nearby village of **St-Nicolas-la-Chapelle**.
The **bridge** which spans the Arly 60m/197ft above the river bed opens the way to the picturesque village of Notre-Dame-de-Bellecombe.

★GORGES DE L'ARLY

5 **From Megève to Fontaines-d'Ugine**
28km/17.4mi – about 1hr 30min – local map see p 81

Most of the traffic on its way to Mont Blanc or on its way back follows N 212 which runs along the Arly Valley.
The use of chains is recommended from mid-December to the end of February.

✻✻✻**Megève** – *See MEGÈVE.*
Leave Megève by ② on the town plan towards Annecy.

Massif des ARAVIS

From Megève to Flumet, the Arly Valley offers open landscapes in spite of being framed with forests; looking up-river, one can still see Mont Blanc, whereas down-river, the pyramidal Mont Charvin stands isolated. Shortly before Flumet, the road passes under overhanging rocks.

Flumet – *See p 83.*

Soon after Flumet, the onion-shaped steeple and chalets of St-Nicolas-la-Chapelle form an idyllic picture.

At Pont de Flon, take D 109 on the right.

The road rises quickly towards Le Château, offering, beyond Héry, some fine bird's-eye views of the wooded Gorges de l'Arly. Just before the road reaches Le Château, a tiny rock spur *(parking facilities)* forms a **belvedere★** over the Ugine basin and its smoking factories with the snow-capped peaks of the Allevard Massif in the distance.

Ugine – The old village nestling round its church overlooks the industrial centre of **Fontaines-d'Ugine**. The Ugine Aciers steelworks is one of the most important industries in the area.

The **Musée d'Arts et Traditions Populaires du Val d'Arly** ⊙ displays collections of regional costumes and furniture, craftsmen's workshops and tools etc in a fortified 13C building, the Château de Crest-Cherel.

★ROUTE DES MONTAGNES D'UGINE

6 From Ugine to the Col de l'Arpettaz

27km/16.8mi round tour – about 1hr 30min – local map see p 81

Ugine – *See above.*

Take D 109 on the east side of the church and drive north for 500m/0.3mi, then turn left onto the road signposted Col de l'Arpettaz.

The road winds upwards within sight of Mont Charvin, goes through a spruce forest and finally reaches a barren rocky area.

From the **Col de l'Arpettaz** (alt 1 581m/5 187ft), which affords a view of the summit of Mont Blanc, the road runs along the top of a ridge overlooking a series of coombs. At La Lierre *(ski-lift)*, take a narrow rough road to the right which goes steeply down offering splendid **views★** of the Arly Valley, with Signal de Bisanne and the village of Cohennoz on the other side of the river.

The road joins D 109 south of Héry.

It is also possible to drive from Fontaines-d'Ugine to Villard-sur-Doron and Signal de Bisanne (see Le BEAUFORTAIN).

Les ARCS★★

Michelin map 89 fold 4 or 244 fold 21
Local map see Massif de la VANOISE

This resort, which is one of the most important ski centres in the Alps, includes Arc 1600, Arc 1800 and Arc 2000. In addition, Arc 1800 is linked by ski runs in winter and by road in summer to Vallandry and **Peisey-Nancroix** *(see PEISEY-NANCROIX)*, situated in a forested area on the edge of the Parc national de la Vanoise.

Les Arcs is also famous for its **Kilomètre Lancé** (speed-skiing) competitions carried out with special equipment. The track, which has a 77% gradient, was used for the 1992 Winter Olympic Games, when the record speed of 229.299kph/142.5mph was reached.

THE RESORTS

The three resorts are modern and functional but their architectural style blends reasonably well with the landscape owing to the extensive use of wood.

Arc 1600 (or Arc Pierre Blanche) – Access is by the "**Arc-en-ciel**" ⊙ Funicular; starting point behind the station. This resort is reputed for its traditional family atmosphere. There is a lovely **view★** of Bourg-St-Maurice, Le Beaufortain and Mont Blanc.

Arc 1800 – South of Arc 1600; this resort occupies a fine position overlooking the Isère Valley and offering **panoramic views★** of the Beaufortain, Mont-Blanc and Bellecôte massifs as well as the Haute Tarentaise Valley.

Arc 2000 – More recent and remote than the other two, this high-mountain resort, lying just beneath the Aiguille Rouge, attracts advanced skiers.

Skiing area – It is on the whole not so vast as that of Les Trois Vallées *(see Massif de la VANOISE)* but extremely varied. The ski slopes of Arc 1600 and Arc 1800 offer few difficult passages except in the Deux Têtes area. Skiing above Arc 2000, on the other hand, is more than satisfying for advanced skiers: the Dou de l'Homme chair-lift, Grand Col ski-lift and Aiguille Rouge cable-car give access to 10 black runs technically very demanding.

HIKES

The beautiful panoramas more than make up for the unattractive aspect of the skiing area in summer.

★★★**Aiguille Rouge** ⊘ – Alt 3 227m/10 587ft. *From the main square in Arc 2000, a path leads to the Dou de l'Homme chair-lift, followed by the Aiguille Rouge cable-car. Go to the viewing table. Mountain boots and sun glasses are recommended.*
Enjoy the stunning close-up view of Mont Pourri and, further away, of the Sommet de Bellecôte and Les Trois Vallées. One can spot in the distance the Belledonne and Lauzière ranges as well as the Aravis Massif to the west, the Mont-Blanc Massif to the north and the summits marking the Italian and Swiss borders to the east.
Take the cable-car back to the chair-lift, but instead of taking the latter, go down on foot to the lovely **Lac Marlou** *(beware of avalanches).*

★★**Télécabine le Transarc** ⊘ – *Access from Arc 1800.*
The gondola passes over the Col du Grand Renard and reaches the foot of the Aiguille Grive at an altitude of 2 600m/8 530ft. There are good views of the Aiguille Rouge, Mont Pourri, Grande Motte de Tignes and the impressive ridge of Bellecôte, as well as Mont Blanc and Beaufortain to the north.
Numerous possibilities of hikes of varying levels of difficulty. Some itineraries are described below.

★★★**Aiguille Grive** – Alt 2 732m/8 963ft. *Experienced hikers, who do not suffer from vertigo, can reach the summit in about 30min up very steep slopes. The ascent should only be attempted in dry weather.*
From the viewing table, there is a stunning **view**★★★ of the Vanoise Massif.

★★**Refuge du Mont Pourri** – *Round tour on the edge of the Parc de la Vanoise, via Col de la Chal, Mont Pourri mountain refuge and Lac des Moutons (3hr).*
It is also possible to take a trip to the Aiguille Rouge from the highest point reached by the Transarc.

★**Télésiège de la Cachette** ⊘ – Alt 2 160m/7 087ft. *Access from Arc 1600.*
Fine views of the Isère Valley, Bourg-St-Maurice and Mont Blanc.

★★**Hike to l'Arpette** – From the top of the chair-lift, go right to join a path which climbs alongside L'Arpette chair-lift and leads to Col des Frettes. Once there, take a path to the left which leads to l'Arpette (alt 2 413m/7 917ft), a hang-gliding and paragliding take-off point. Splendid **views**★★ of La Plagne, Les Arcs and the main peaks of the Haute Tarentaise.

ARGENTIÈRE ✳✳✳

Michelin map 89 fold 4 or 244 fold 21 – 8km/5mi north of Chamonix
Local map see Massif du MONT-BLANC

Argentière is the highest (1 252m/4 108ft) resort in the Chamonix Valley; with its annexes of Montroc-le-Planet and Le Tour, it forms an excellent holiday and mountaineering centre offering a wide choice of expeditions to the Massif du Mont-Blanc and Massif des Aiguilles Rouges. The relatively gentle slopes of the upper Arve Valley, with its fringe of larch woods, provide pleasant walks and encourage the practice of winter sports.
The Argentière Glacier is hardly visible from the village: note, however, the morainal debris forming a bulge round the rock surface once covered by the tip end of the glacier and, higher up, the vertical walls of the U-shaped valley which the glacier used to fill completely.

THE RESORT

Skiing area – The **Grands-Montets** ski slopes are among the finest and most famous in Europe. Argentière is a real paradise for experienced skiers: most of the runs, are not packed, yet they are popular because of their length, their gradient, the quality of the snow and the splendid landscapes. The Point de Vue black run, which starts from the Aiguille des Grands-Montets and stretches over 5.2km/3.2mi, is an exceptional downhill run offering unforgettable views of the Argentière Glacier, Aiguille Verte and Aiguille du Chardonnet. The Chamois run along the Combe de la Pendant is also worth mentioning. These runs are only suitable for experienced skiers. Others will find easier runs along the Bochard and Marmottons chair-lifts. As for hikers, a special trail linking the Plan Joran and Pendant plateaux is at their sole disposal.

HIKES

★★Aiguille des Grands-Montets Alt 3 295m/10 810ft

Access by the Lognan and Grands-Montets cable-cars ⊙. About 2hr 30min return. From the last platform, climb to the viewing table (120 fairly steep steps).
The **panorama**★★★ is breathtaking. The view extends to the Argentière Glacier over which tower the Aiguille du Chardonnet and Aiguille d'Argentière to the north, Mont Dolent to the east, Aiguille Verte and Les Drus to the south, with the Aiguille du Midi, Mont Blanc and Dôme du Goûter further away. Slightly to the west, there is a fine view of the Chamonix Valley as far as Les Houches with the Aravis range in the distance.

★Hikes to the Col de Balme

Le Tour – *3km/1.8mi northeast of Argentière.* This pleasant village lies just below the Tour Glacier which, in summer, reveals many crumbling seracs *(for general information on glaciers see Introduction: Alpine relief).* The resort is the starting point of easy hikes to the Col de Balme during the fine season and, in winter, the skiing area is ideal for beginners and intermediate skiers owing to its gentle slopes, the quality of its snow and the amount of sunshine.

★★Col de Balme – Alt 2 204m/7 231ft. *Access all year round by the Col de Balme Gondola ⊙. Allow 10min to walk from the lift to the pass.*
The **view**★★ extends northeast to the Swiss Alps and southwest to the Chamonix Valley surrounded by the Aiguille Verte, Mont Blanc and the Aiguilles Rouges massif. Food and drinks are available in several places. At the beginning of July, when the herds go up to the high pastures, there are lively festivities including bull or rather cowfighting!

★Aiguillette des Posettes – Alt 2 201m/7 221ft. *Hiking enthusiasts can prolong the excursion to the Col de Balme by coming down via the Tour du Mont-Blanc – Col des Posettes alternative, then climbing alongside the Aiguillette ski-lift. From the top of the ski-lift, there is a 10min ascent to the summit.*
Fine **view** of the Col de Balme, the Aiguille du Tour and glacier of the same name, Argentière and Grands-Montets, the Aiguille Verte, Aiguilles Rouges and Émosson dam.

★★RÉSERVE NATURELLE DES AIGUILLES ROUGES

3km/1.8mi north of Argentière on N 506
This nature reserve, situated between Argentière and Vallorcine and covering an area of 3 300ha/8 155 acres at an altitude of 1 200m/3 937ft to 2 995m/9 826ft, offers a selection of high-mountain landscapes within sight of the magnificent Massif du Mont-Blanc.
The **Chalet d'accueil** (Information Centre) ⊙, situated at the Col des Montets (alt 1 471m/4 826ft), presents exhibitions, slide shows and video films about the fauna, flora and geology of the cristalline massifs.

Argentière Glacier

An **ecological discovery trail**, which follows the old stagecoach route from Chamonix to Martigny, enables nature lovers to discover the remarkable diversity of high-altitude flora and fauna *(guide for sale at the chalet)* over a distance of 2km/1.2mi. The nature reserve is inhabited by ibexes, chamois, blue hares and black salamanders. More than 500 species of plants have been identified.

The itinerary is split into some 15 numbered sections which specify the different ecosystems: peat bogs, alder plantations, avalanche corridors, screes... In addition, there are beautiful views of the Tour and Argentière glaciers.

A legend among mountain guides – Armand Charlet (1900-1975), a native of Argentière, was held to be the king of mountain guides until the early 1960s. He set a record, which has never been equalled, by climbing the Aiguille Verte (4 121m/13 520ft) more than a hundred times.

L'ARGENTIÈRE-LA-BESSÉE
Population 2 312
Michelin map 77 fold 18 or 244 fold 42
Local map see Le BRIANÇONNAIS

This industrial centre, which owes its name to ancient silver-lead mines, lies at the confluence of the Gyronde and Durance rivers. In summer, it is a good base for the practice of sports such as canyoning and rock-climbing.

L'ARGENTIÈRE-ÉGLISE

The old district of L'Argentière-Église, 2km/1.2mi from N 94, has retained its rustic character. Arriving from Briançon, turn right, cross the Durance then turn left towards the industrial zone and drive beyond the railway line.

Chapelle St-Jean ⊘ – This chapel, one of the few Romanesque buildings (12C) in the Hautes-Alpes region, was founded by the Knights Hospitallers, established along the road to Italy. Note the carved capitals.

Musée des mines d'argent ⊘ – This museum retraces the evolution of silver mining which used to be the most important economic activity of the valley. The Château St-Jean comprises the main house (municipal library; note the rocaille ornamentation in one of the rooms), a farmhouse (Silver Mine Museum housed in three vaulted rooms) and an 18C chapel.

Church ⊘ – It dates from the 15C; the exterior is decorated with murals (1516) depicting the vices and the virtues; the door is adorned with a splendid 16C wrought-iron bolt representing a chimera's head.

EXCURSION

★Vallon du Fournel

Leave L'Argentière on D 423 up the narrow valley of the Fournel (access not allowed in winter). Walking shoes recommended.
Drive up to l'Eychaillon from where there is a fine view of the Gorges du Fournel and the ruins of the medieval castle. Leave the car and walk down the miners' path to the bottom of the gorge. Silver mining had its heyday in the 19C, when up to 500 miners were employed. The mines closed down in 1908.

Anciennes mines d'argent ⊘ – Archeological finds have revealed mining activity in the area going back to the 11C.

Réserve biologique des Deslioures ⊘ – One of the aims of this nature reserve, which forms part of the Parc national des Écrins, is the preservation of **Alpine sea holly**.

INTRODUCTION TO MOUTAINEERING ACTIVITIES

★**Via ferrata des Vigneaux** – *Situated at the end of the village of Vigneaux, on D 4 to Prelles; rock-climbing enthusiasts are advised to refer to the Practical information chapter at the end of the guide.* This is the most popular "via ferrata" in the Briançonnais region; it is less crowded in the early morning or late afternoon. There are two courses to choose from.

Canyon du Fournel – *Follow D 423 towards the silver mines. The canyoning course is situated up-river from the rock-climbing school (leave the car there).* The canyon is fully equipped and the site is one of the most popular among those wishing to be introduced to canyoning. However, those who wish to do the course unaccompanied when the water level is low, are advised to ask about meteorological conditions at the guides' office in Argentière.

★★**LA VALLOUISE** *Drive from L'Argentière-la-Bessée to Ailefroide; 38km/ 23.6mi. See La VALLOUISE.*

★**BELVÉDÈRE DU PELVOUX** *See Le BRIANÇONNAIS* ⑥.

AURON ✳

This former hamlet, occupying a fine position on top of a sunny plateau at an altitude of 1 608m/5 276ft, with Las Donnas towering above at 2 474m/8 117ft, is a lively summer resort and winter sports centre.

The village is named after a 6C bishop of Gap, called Aurigius, who became a saint: according to legend, he was being chased by highway robbers on his way back from Rome when his horse saved him by jumping in one single leap from the Tinée River to Auron 500m/1 640ft above.

THE RESORT

Skiing area – Auron is the favourite ski resort of the inhabitants of Nice; it combines fine ski slopes with constant sunshine and a sufficient supply of snow thanks to adequate snow-cannon equipment. Experienced skiers appreciate the Colombier and La Plaque red runs or the Olympique and Dôme black runs. Intermediate skiers find the Chalvet and Gaudissart areas more manageable. There are also numerous possibilities of sledge rides.

Chapelle St-Érige ⊘ – This Romanesque chapel has a square tower with diamond fret and a single nave with a double apse covered with a larch framework carved with notched motifs. The rich

J Guillard/SCOPE

The martyrdom of St Denis in the Chapelle St-Érige in Auron

decoration★ painted in tempera dates from 1451.

The vaulting of the right hand apse illustrates Christ in glory within a mandorla surrounded by the emblems of the four evangelists. Below are depicted six episodes of the life of St Érige. The left hand apse relates the story of St Denis. Between the two apses, a recess surmounted by a canopy is covered with paintings illustrating the life of Mary Magdalene clad with long golden hair.

On the left hand wall, a huge St Christopher holds Jesus as a child.

From outside, there is a fine **view★** of the mountains all round.

★★Las Donnas – A cable-car ⊘ in two sections takes visitors up to 2 256m/7 402ft in 7min, close to the summit of Las Donnas. Panoramic **view** of the upper Tinée Valley and summits on the Franco-Italian border.

AUSSOIS ✳

Population 501
Michelin map 77 fold 8 or 244 fold 32
Local map see La MAURIENNE

Set in **fine surroundings★** at an altitude of 1 500m/4 921ft, beneath the towering summits of Rateau d'Aussois and Dent Parrachée, Aussois enjoys a remarkable amount of sunshine.

THE RESORT

The 17C church still has its original rood beam and Gothic font instead of a stoup. The charming old village overlooking the Arc Valley lies on the doorstep of the Parc national de la Vanoise *(see Introduction)*; in summer, it offers numerous possibilities of hikes and mountain-bike tours.

Skiing area – The south-facing skiing area, which reaches an altitude of 2 750m/9 022ft and has reliable equipment, is popular with intermediate skiers and family parties. Snow conditions on the slopes situated above 2 000m/6 562ft are usually good until April. For cross-country skiers, there are 35km/21.7mi of tracks available between Aussois and Sardières.

WALKS AND HIKES

★Télésiège le Grand Jeu – The chair-lift reaches 2 150m/7 054ft. Views across the Arc Valley towards the summits of Longe-Côte, Aiguille de Scolette, Pointe de la Norma with Mont Thabor in the distance. Climb alongside the Eterlou chair-lift for more panoramic views: Rateau d'Aussois, artificial lakes of Plan d'Amont and Plan d'Aval. From there, the Plan Sec mountain refuge is accessible in dry weather. In winter it is possible to reach the foot of Dent Parrachée by the Bellecôte chair-lift: **views★★** of the Haute-Maurienne's northern slopes, with Grande Ruine and Meije to the southwest.

★★Walk to Fond d'Aussois – *6km/3.7mi uphill drive from the Maison d'Aussois. The itinerary leads to the Plan d'Aval dam, then the Plan d'Amont dam where you leave the car and continue on foot (3hr 30min return).*
The footpath skirts the lake shore then leads to the Fond d'Aussois refuge. View of the glacial cirque beneath Dent Parrachée.

★★★Hike to the Col d'Aussois – *Access from the Fond d'Aussois refuge – 4hr return. Difference in altitude: 700m/2 297ft – Should only be attempted in dry weather and not before the end of July. Mountain boots are a must.*
For superb views all round, experienced hikers can climb to the **Pointe de l'Observatoire** (3 015m/9 892ft).

AVORIAZ★★

Michelin map 89 fold 3 or 244 fold 10 – 14km/8.7mi east of Morzine
Local map see Le FAUCIGNY
Accessible by cable-car from a station 4.5km/2.8mi from Morzine

Avoriaz is a modern resort situated at an altitude of 1 800m/5 906ft. Its original and uniform architectural style blends well with the surroundings, its buildings, clad with wood, looking like huge rocks. Private motor vehicles are banned from the centre and replaced by sledges.

Avoriaz

THE RESORT

Skiing area – Avoriaz enjoys excellent snow conditions and a favourable position at the heart of the vast **Portes du Soleil ★★ Skiing Area**, which includes 12 French and Swiss winter resorts between Lake Geneva and Mont Blanc with an impressive total of 650km/404mi of ski slopes. However, in order to take full advantage of the area, it is necessary for the snow to be plentiful at low altitudes (all the resorts, except Avoriaz, are barely above 1 000m/3 281ft).
The Avoriaz ski slopes are ideal for intermediate skiing; the ski runs leading to Les Lindarets offer pleasant skiing through the forest. Advanced skiers can take the La Combe chair-lift which gives access to four black runs, including La Combe-du-Machon. There are also ski-lifts to the Châtel and Morzine areas and, in Switzerland, to the resorts of Champéry and Les Crosets.

The **Festival du film de demain** (Tomorrow's Film Festival) following the Festival du fantastique (Supernatural Film Festival) created in 1973, takes place every year in January and attracts enthusiasts from all over the world.

★**Télésiège du Choucas** ⊘ – *From the top of the chair-lift, go to Pas de Chavanette on the left (arrival point of two ski-lifts).* View of the Swiss Alps and Avoriaz.

EXCURSION

In summer, it is well worth exploring the surrounding area along D 338 to Morzine. After 1km/0.6mi, the **Chapelle d'Avoriaz**, designed by Novarina, appears on the right and there is a fine view of the Lac d'Avoriaz. The road then overlooks the Vallon des Ardoisières with the snow-capped Hautforts Summit (2 466m/8 090ft) in the distance.

After running for a while along a ledge covered with pastures and dotted in summer with colourful pansies and gentians, the road reaches the resort of Super-Morzine (view of Mont Blanc) then runs down towards Morzine.

BARCELONNETTE★

Population 2 976
Michelin map 81 fold 8 or 245 fold 9 – Local map see opposite

Barcelonnette lies at the heart of the Ubaye Valley amid orchards and lush meadows. This Mediterranean little town is one of the administrative centres of the Alpes-de-Haute-Provence *département* (county).

Public figures born in Barcelonnette include **JA Manuel** (1775-1827), a member of parliament during the reign of Charles X (1824-1830) who was thrown out of the House for having criticized the King's policy, and **Paul Reynaud** (1878-1966), who resigned as prime minister of France in 1940 and was replaced by Marshall Pétain. Sent to prison, he was deported to Germany in 1942 but was able to resume his political career at the end of the war.

The "Barcelonnettes" in Mexico

It all started in Jausiers *(9km/5.6mi northeast of Barcelonnette)* in 1805, when two brothers, Jacques and Marc-Antoine Arnaud decided to leave the family business and try their luck in America. In Mexico, Marc-Antoine opened a fabric store known as "El cajon de ropas de las Siete Puertas" (a craft centre in Barcelonnette now bears the same name). The success of the business was such that by 1893 there were more than 100 fabric stores in Mexico owned by natives of the Ubaye region. Some tried their hand at other businesses (paper, breweries and finance, including the London and Mexico Bank which was empowered to print money!).

The 1910 Mexican revolution followed by the First World War put an end to the flow of emigrants which, however, started again in 1930 and finally stopped in 1950. Most of the emigrants were country folk who, except for the Arnaud brothers, eventually returned to their native country and built sumptuous villas to mark their success in the New World.

A troubled past – Founded in 1231 by the count of Barcelona and Provence, under the name of Barcelone, the town, and the Ubaye region with it, first belonged to the House of Savoie then to France in 1713, when it was exchanged for part of Dauphiné under the Treaty of Utrecht. Soon afterwards, the townspeople asked to join the Parlement de Provence and the town took the name of Barcelonnette.

SIGHTS

Place Manuel – This vast open space at the heart of the grid-like former *bastide* (walled town in southern France), is surrounded by colourful buildings and pavement cafés full of holiday-makers. Note the **fountain** with a medallion of JA Manuel by David d'Angers and the **Tour Cardinalis** (15C), the former bell-tower of a Dominican convent which once stood here.

"Mexican" villas – Set amid spacious parks, these opulent houses built between 1880 and 1930 testify to the spectacular success of their owners. Architectural styles vary considerably and denote various influences, Italian, "Tyrolian", Baroque, but certainly not Mexican. There are two fine examples along avenue des Trois-Frères-Arnaud and avenue Antoine-Signoret and several along avenue de la Libération. One of the last to be built was the Villa Bleue (1931), avenue Porfirio-Diaz, which is decorated with an impressive monochrome stained glass depicting the owner's Mexican textile factories.

Villa la Sapinière – Housed in one of the most splendid Mexican villas, the **Musée de la Vallée** ⊙ illustrates the history of the Ubaye Valley: Iron-Age burial rites, the charter of the town dating from 1231, an 18C map showing the chequered layout of the town, various objects connected with agriculture and handicraft in the 19C. The first floor is devoted to the "Mexicans" with costumes and reconstructions of the Barcelonnettes' life in Mexico.

During the season, the ground floor houses the **Maison du Parc national du Mercantour** ⊙ where information about guided **themed hikes** ⊙ is available.

Cemetery – Situated at the end of allée des Rosiers, it houses a fascinating array of funeral monuments erected by the emigrants after their return: temples, mausoleums, chapels in stone and Carrara marble were, for the most part, the work of Italian artists.

EXCURSIONS

St-Pons – *2km/1.2mi northwest.* The interesting church, which formed part of a Benedictine monastery, has retained some Romanesque features (west doorway, chancel and apse). The two doorways are remarkable: their arching is decorated with mouldings and supported by columns with a frieze at the top. Note in particular the naïve style of the frieze on the 12C **west doorway**. The 15C **south doorway**★ is more richly decorated although the style remains naïve; the themes illustrated are all connected with death since this door used to give access to the cemetery.

★**Col de la Pare via the Riou Bourdoux vale** – *From the Dalis parking, 2hr there on foot, 1hr back – difference in altitude: 800m/2 625ft.*

From Barcelonnette, follow D 900 towards Gap then turn right onto D 609 to La Frâche. Leaving the access road to La Frâche on your left, cross the Riou Bourdoux and continue along the forest road.

The unpredictable character of the Riou Bourdoux led to the construction, during the late 19C, of some of the most important dams in Europe at that time. Stop by the Treou forest lodge and walk to the mountain stream to get a good **view** of the 1880 dam which contributed to minimize the devastating effects of the floods and retain the alluvial deposits.

Continue along the forest road to the parking of the Dalis forest lodge. The path on the right, signposted "Col de la Pare" leads to a mountain stream and an abandoned village. Take the path on the left to the gîte GTA de la Pare (45min).

The trail goes through a forest of larch and pine trees; beyond the cottage, a path goes up to an altitude of 2 000m/6 562ft, above which there is no vegetation, and continues along the scree-covered slopes to Col de la Pare (2 655m/8 711ft), overlooked by the Grande Épervière (2 884m/9 462ft), with the impressive Grand Bérard (3 048m/10 000ft) further away to the north. There is a fine **view**★ of the Barcelonnette basin and of the surrounding mountains. The fauna in this area is protected so that discreet and patient visitors may be rewarded with the sight of mouflons frisking about.

WINTER SPORTS RESORTS

※**Le Sauze and Super-Sauze** – *4km/2.4mi southeast.* Situated at an altitude of 1 380m/4 528ft, Le Sauze is one of the oldest winter sports resorts in the Alps (dating from the 1930s), linked to the recent Super-Sauze (alt 1 700m/5 577ft) by road (6km/3.6mi) and **cable-car** ⊙. There is a wide choice of summer hikes and mountain expeditions to the nearby Chapeau de Gendarme and Pain de Sucre.

The two resorts are well known for their family atmosphere, their generous sunshine and the low gradient of their slopes, offering numerous possibilities of cross-country skiing. Artistic and acrobatic skiing are also a speciality.

The **Col de Fours** (2 314m/7 592ft), accessible via the **Télésiège de la Rente** and a short walk, offers a panoramic **view**★ of Barcelonnette and the surrounding area. On the other side of the pass, the path joins up with the road leading to Col de la Cayolle (*see Route de la CAYOLLE*).

From the parking de la Raquette in Super-Sauze (*4hr 30min return*), a marked path follows the ski runs then goes through the woods to a stream (*where hikers are advised to fill up with water*). The path continues alongside the stream before heading due west to a ridge. Follow the ridge towards the southwest then go round a rock spur and join up with another trail. Continue south towards **Chapeau de Gendarme**★★ and take the right-hand fork to Col de Gyp and to the summit (2 685m/8 809ft) which affords a splendid **view**★★ of the Barcelonnette basin and the Gorges du Bachelard.

※**Pra-Loup** – *8.5km/5.3mi southwest. See PRA-LOUP.*

BARGÈME★

Population 86
Michelin map 84 fold 7, 114 fold 10 or 245 fold 35

Situated in beautiful surroundings, a few miles northeast of Comps-sur-Artuby, this hilltop village is the highest municipality of the Var *département* (1 097m/3 599ft). The church, the ruined walls and the towers of the castle can be seen from afar. In the last few years, the village has regained its old-world charm through a programme of extensive restoration work.

THE VILLAGE

Motor vehicles are banned from the village.

Walk through the "Porte de garde", one of the two 14C fortified gates still standing. The narrow streets, linked by alleyways and arched passages, are lined with old houses brightened up by colourful hollyhocks.

Church ⊙ – The stone-built 11C Romanesque church has an oven-vaulted apse. Note in particular the **Retable de Saint-Sébastien**★ (altarpiece) in carved wood and, near the altar, a Primitive painting in naïve style.

Castle – *Restoration work in progress.* Dating from the 13C, it comprised four round towers, a square keep and a main courtyard. Although the edifice is in ruins, its plan is revealed by the remaining stairs, chimneys and windows.
From the castle, the **view**★ extends to the Malay and Lachens mountains and, beyond, to the Préalpes de Grasse, Canjuers Plateau and Maures Massif.

Chapelle Notre-Dame-des-Sept-Douleurs – This small edifice, facing the castle, in typical local style with its awning and wooden railings, was built to make amends for a murder committed during the Wars of Religion.

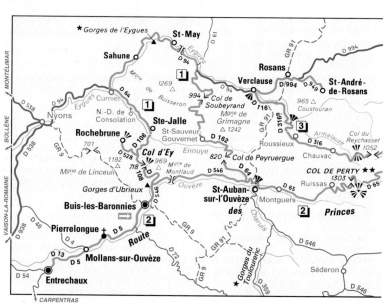

Les BARONNIES ★

Michelin map 81 folds 3 to 5 or 245 folds 4, 5, 6, 17, 18 and 19

This relatively low range (1 757m/5 764ft) of the Préalpes du Sud stretches from west to east, its limestone ridges being separated by the upper valleys of the Eygues and Ouvèze rivers. Mountain streams gully the slopes, sculpting a landscape of barren mud-slides, characteristic of the area.

Rivers have dug deeply into the soft limestone and their narrow valleys are natural channels of communication along which villages have settled, often clinging to the steep slopes, overlooking vineyards, olive groves and orchards down in the valley.

Fields of lavender and lavandin *(see Introduction)* supply many distilleries operating on a family basis and 80% of the French production of lime tea comes from this area. Cattle-farming is progressing thanks to the increasing number of cultivated meadows but sheep and goats still graze on natural pastures.

★BUIS-LES-BARONNIES AREA

① Round tour from Buis-les-Baronnies

97km/60mi – about 3hr

Buis-les-Baronnies – *See BUIS-LES-BARONNIES.*
From Buis-les-Baronnies drive northeast along D 546.

The road follows the Ouvèze amid olive groves and goes through the **Gorges d'Ubrieux**.

Turn left onto D 108 and drive up to Col d'Ey.

Olive trees, pines and broom grow on south-facing slopes. Fine views of the Ouvèze Valley and Mont Ventoux.

Col d'Ey – Alt 718m/2 356ft. From the pass, flanked by Montagne de Montlaud to the east and Montagne de Linceuil to the west, the view extends to the Ennuye Valley and Montagne de Buisseron.

Take D 528 left to Rochebrune.

Rochebrune – The village stretches over a rock spur; its only street leads to a round tower (all that remains of the 13C castle) and to the 12C church remodelled in the 15C. Fine **view** of the Ennuye Valley.

Return to D 108 and turn left.

Ste-Jalle – The **old town** has retained part of its walls and two of its gates. One of these is surmounted by the Chapelle des Pénitents (17C). The **castle** consists of a massive square keep (12C-13C), a round tower with Renaissance windows and living quarters (17C-18C) looking more like a large house.

The size of its bell-tower spoils the otherwise fine proportions of the 12C Romanesque church of **Notre-Dame-de-Beauver**. The unusual carved **doorway** has a tympanum depicting a rooster and three figures of a farmer, a lord and a troubadour representing the different social classes. A large transept separates the barrel-vaulted nave from the three semicircular apsidal chapels. The oven-vaulted axial chapel is decorated with very simple arcading.

Follow the Ennuye River along D 64 then turn right onto D 94 after Curnier.

The road runs through the pleasant valley of the Eygues River, planted with vines, peach, cherry and olive trees.

Sahune – The old village lies on the left bank of the Eygues. Beyond Sahune, the road makes its way through the deep **Gorges de l'Eygues★**; note the regular layers of the rock-face and the foaming waterfall on the left.

St-May – This village is perched on a promontory overlooking the gorge. Beyond St-May, the Eygues flows between brightly coloured limestone cliffs.

Turn right onto D 162.

The road rises through orchards to **Col de Soubeyrand** (alt 994m/3 261ft) set among fir trees. On the way down from the pass, firs give way to oaks and the view extends to Mont Ventoux. *Go through St-Sauveur-Gouvernet and turn left onto D 64, then right onto D 546.*

ROUTE DES PRINCES D'ORANGE

② From Entrechaux to Eyguians

78km/48.5mi – about 3hr

See ROUTE DES PRINCES D'ORANGE.

ORPIERRE AND ROSANS COUNTRY

③ From Orpierre to St-André-de-Rosans
40km/25mi – about 2hr

Orpierre – This small mountain village lies at the bottom of the Céans Valley. From its past as the seat of a barony belonging to the prince of Orange, it has retained some fine Renaissance doorways along the **Grand-Rue** and the narrow passages, known as *"drailles"*, linking its picturesque old streets.

The paradise of rock-climbers – The cliffs overlooking the village offer rock-climbing enthusiasts many opportunities to practise their favourite sport (level 5 to 6a). There are numerous marked and suitably equipped itineraries (Quiquillon, Falaise de Quatre heures, Cascade de Belleric) to choose from for anyone wanting to learn the technique of rock-climbing in the safest conditions *(See Practical information)*.

From Orpierre, drive west along D 30 then turn right onto D 130.

The road follows the St-Cyrice Valley, then goes through a forest as it climbs to Col du Reychasset; beyond the pass, there is a fine **view** of the Armalauze Valley.

Take D 316 on the left, then D 316ᴮ through Roussieux and D 116 to Verclause.

Good **views** of the pyramid-shaped Coustouran summit (965m/3 166ft).

Verclause – The old fortified village spreads the ruins of its castle and chapel on top of a promontory offering a lovely **view**★ of the Eygues Valley.

St-André-de-Rosans – One of the most important Cluniac monasteries in Haute-Provence, founded here in the 10C, disappeared during the Wars of Religion, leaving behind the ruins of a vast 12C **church**, including the walls of the nave and an apsidal chapel with traces of a rich decoration inspired by Antique art.

Les BAUGES ★

Michelin map 89 folds 15 and 16 or 244 fold 18

The Massif des Bauges stands like a powerful citadel between the Annecy and Chambéry valleys. In spite of its impressive outer defences (Dent du Nivolet towering above Chambéry, Mont-Revard above Aix-les-Bains and Montagne du Charbon above the Lac d'Annecy), the centre of the range, through which flows the Chéran, offers gently modelled Alpine landscapes and forested slopes.

The **Réserve nationale des Bauges**, created in 1950, stretches over 5 500ha/13 591 acres and is home to 600 chamois and 300 moufflons; the conservation programme of the area was completed in 1995 by the creation of the **Parc naturel régional du massif des Bauges** *(see Introduction: Nature parks and reserves)*.

Traditional economic activities such as steelworks and manufactures of wooden crockery disappeared at the turn of the century thus starting a wave of emigration. Today, tourism has given a new lease of life to the region and led to the creation of the modern resort of **Aillon-le-Jeune** and well-equipped skiing areas, in particular at La Féclaz.

① From Chambéry to Annecy
68km/42.3mi – about 2hr – local map see opposite

★★★**Chambéry** – *See CHAMBÉRY.*

From Chambéry take N 6 towards Albertville then, at the intersection of N 512 and N 6, turn onto D 11 towards "Curienne".

Beyond Leysse, there is a clear view of the Chambéry Valley and the Combe de Savoie-Grésivaudan meeting at right angles with the jagged silhouette of the Allevard Massif in the background.

From Le Boyat, follow the lane to Montmerlet. Continue on foot (45min return).

★**Mont-St-Michel** – *See CHAMBÉRY: Excursions.*

From Le Boyat to Col des Prés, the view extends north to Mont de Margeriaz and south to the Chambéry Basin overlooked by Mont Granier. The pastures around **Col des Prés** (alt 1 135m/3 724ft) are dotted with a profusion of buttercups and daffodils.

Aillon-le-Jeune – Situated at the relatively low altitude of 1 000m/3 281ft, this winter sports resort spreads its chalets all over the valley.

The road then follows the Aillon Valley with the grass-covered Grand Colombier (2 043m/6 703ft) and the more arid Dent de Rossanaz (1 891m/6 204ft) on the right. Beyond Le Cimeteret, the **Lescheraines** basin comes into view: Le Châtelard village *(see below)* lies on the opposite bank of the Chéran backed by the Charbon Massif with the Pécloz summit (2 197m/7 208ft) in the distance.

Pont du Diable – *Follow the road to Col de Leschaux for 600m/656yd; leave the car near two chalets facing each other and follow the marked path on the right; it goes round a private house to reach the wood and the bridge (15min return on foot).*

A small bridge spans the foaming Bellecombe mountain stream. This place is the main starting point of hikes in the area.

Between **Col de Leschaux** and Sévrier, there are fine **vistas**★ of the "Grand lac" d'Annecy, overlooked by the Château de Menthon and framed by Mont Veyrier, Dents de Lanfon and La Tournette, and lower down, of the picturesque Roc de Chère facing the Château de Duingt at the narrowest part of the lake.

Sévrier – *See Lac d'ANNECY.*

2km/1.2mi before reaching Annecy, the road comes close to the lake as it goes round La Puya promontory.

★★**Annecy** – *See ANNECY.*

② From the Pont de l'Abîme to the Pont Royal

60km/37.3mi – about 3hr – local map see below

★**Pont de l'Abîme** – The bridge spans the gorge through which flows the Chéran, 94m/103yd above the river bed in a spectacular **setting**★.

From Pont de l'Abîme to La Charniaz, D 911 follows the narrow Chéran Valley, affording views of the Montagne du Charbon and then, just before La Charniaz, of the summits enclosing the upper Chéran Valley. The road then goes through the Lescheraines depression, where several routes intersect.

Le Châtelard – The village lies on either side of a wooded ridge once crowned by a castle, which separates the wide and open Lescheraines Basin from the more austere upper Chéran Valley. The administrative centre of the Parc naturel régional du massif des Bauges is here.

Beyond Le Châtelard, landscapes are definitely more Alpine with the impressive silhouette of the Dent de Pleuven (1 771m/5 810ft) towering over the valley and Arcalod (2 217m/7 274ft) looming in the distance.

On reaching École, turn onto the Route de Jarsy at the church then follow the forest road through the Vallon de Bellevaux.

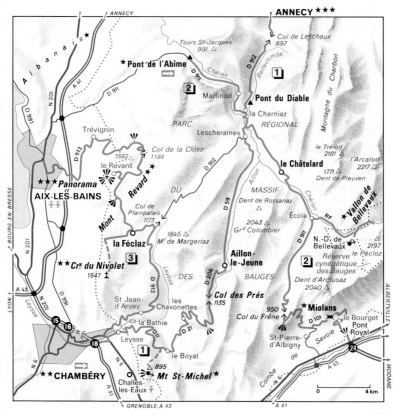

Les BAUGES

★**Vallon de Bellevaux** – Turn right immediately after a bridge over the Chéran and continue to follow the stream through its wooded upper valley, one of the narrowest in the Alps.

Turn back at the end of the road.

Chapelle Notre-Dame de Bellevaux – On the way back, leave the car on the parking of the Office National des Forêts then take the narrow path on the left to a plantation of young trees. A small oratory marks the place where the Bellevaux monastery once stood. Further up, in a clearing, stands the **Chapelle Notre-Dame de Bellevaux**, known as the Sainte Fontaine, a place of fervent pilgrimage *(Whit Monday)*. There is a refreshing spring nearby.

From **Col du Frêne** and on the way down to St-Pierre-d'Albigny there are splendid **vistas★** of the Combe de Savoie through which flows the Isère River, with close-up views of the Dent d'Arclusaz and, in the distance, from north to south, the Beaufortain Massif, Maurienne Valley, Belledonne range and Grésivaudan depression.

★**Château de Miolans** ⊘ – The castle occupies a commanding **position★★** on an isolated rock spur overlooking the Combe de Savoie; it is one of the finest examples of medieval military architecture in the Savoie region. When the dukes of Savoie inherited the castle, they turned it into a state prison (1559-1792).

Go to the parking, 100m/110yd out of Miolans village; allow 1hr.

Fine panoramic **view★** extending to the Chartreuse and Belledonne ranges.
The square **keep**, flanked by four turrets, is the most characteristic part of the castle. From the top of the **Tour St-Pierre**, there is an even more breathtaking view★★ which includes Mont Blanc. In the garden, narrow steps lead down to the **oubliettes**; equally interesting is the **Souterrain de défense★**, a kind of underground watchpath with loopholes covering the access ramp to the castle.

Narrow twisting lanes link the Château de Miolans to the Pont Royal.

★★ ③ Mont Revard

From Chambéry to Aix-les-Bains
48km/30mi – about 2hr – local map see p 95

★★**Chambéry** – *See CHAMBÉRY.*

From Chambéry take D 912 and follow the signposting "Massif des Bauges".

The road climbs rapidly beneath the cliffs of Mont Peney and Dent du Nivolet, surmounted by a monumental cross (lit up at night), past the Château de La Bathie. Look back towards the Chambéry basin and the massive silhouette of Mont Granier. From St-Jean-d'Arvey to Plainpalais, the upper valley of the Leysse unfolds beneath the road; straight ahead are the escarpments of Mont de Margeriaz.

La Féclaz – This important centre of cross-country skiing is popular with the inhabitants of Lyon and Chambéry.
There is an interesting hike to the **Croix du Nivolet** *(2hr return on foot; park the car at the start of the chair-lift);* follow the yellow-marked footpath *(no 2)* to the Chalet du Sire and continue through the woods. From the top, there is a superb **view★★** of the Lac du Bourget and of the mountain ranges as far as Mont Blanc.

The wooded area between La Féclaz and Le Revard is rich in undergrowths and clearings. Once out of the forest, the road skirts the edge of the cliff affording magnificent bird's-eye **views★★** of the Lac du Bourget and the town of Aix-les-Bains.

★★**Mont Revard** – Alt 1 537m/5 043ft. Drive along the road to Le Revard until you reach the former cable-car station. The **panorama★★★** is splendid: to the west, there is an aerial view of the Lac du Bourget, the Dent du Chat, the Rhône like a shiny ribbon in the distance and Aix-les-Bains in the foreground; to the east, there is a fine vista of Mont Blanc behind a series of forested heights.
Beyond Col de la Cluse, the **view★** embraces the whole verdant Albanais depression and the heights of southern Jura in the distance. Further down, the Lac du Bourget comes into view.
Pleasant rural landscapes unfold between Trévignin and Aix-les-Bains *(reached by D 913).*

‡‡ **Aix-les-Bains** – *See AIX-LES-BAINS.*

Many campsites have shops, bars, restaurants and laundries;
they may also have games rooms, tennis courts, miniature golf courses,
playgrounds, swimming pools...
Consult the current edition of the Michelin Camping Caravaning France.

Le BEAUFORTAIN★★

Bound by the Val d'Arly, Val Montjoie and Tarentaise, the Beaufortain forms part of the central massifs *(see Introduction: Landscapes)* in the same way as the Massif du Mont-Blanc but barely rises to 3 000m/9 843ft (Aiguille du Grand Fond: alt 2 889m/9 478ft) and displays neither glaciers nor peaks with sharp outlines, apart from the Pierre Menta monolith.

On the other hand, the Beaufortain offers visitors an unbroken belt of forest (lower Doron Valley) and pastoral landscapes likely to appeal to amateurs of medium-height mountains.

The Beaufortain is the grazing area of "Tarine" cows whose milk is used to make Beaufort cheese. Cattle-farmers often own several farms and the sight of so many wooden chalets scattered over south-facing slopes gives the impression that the mountain is densely populated.

The smooth curves of the slopes favour long ski runs and several winter sports resorts have developed in the area, namely Arèches, Les Saisies, Val-Joly and Queige-Molliessoulaz.

Searching for water power – The Beaufortain region is a fully tapped source of water power. The **Lac de la Girotte** *(2hr 30min return on foot from the Belleville power station to the end of the road running through the Hauteluce Valley)* was the first reservoir to be tapped (1923). The lake then helped to regulate the supply of water to seven power stations along the Dorinet and Doron rivers until its capacity was doubled following the building of a dam. An additional supply of water from the Tré-la-Tête glacier compensated for the seasonal shortage of water. It was channelled to the lake via a tunnel beneath the glacier.

The building of the Roselend dam was an even more daring technical achievement. Its supply of water comes along 40km/25mi of tunnels from the Doron Valley and from tributaries of the Isère River. The water then drops from a height of 1 200m/3 937ft to the Bathie power station in the Basse-Tarentaise region. The production of electricity totals 982 million kWh. There are additional reservoirs at St-Guérin and La Gittaz nearby.

★★ROUTE DU CORMET DE ROSELEND

① From Albertville to Bourg-St-Maurice
94km/58.4mi – about 3hr

Albertville – See ALBERTVILLE.

From Albertville drive east on D 925 towards Beaufort and Bourg-St-Maurice.

D 925 climbs above the confluence of the Arly and Doron rivers, with views of the Ugine Basin and the imposing silhouette of Mont Charvin, then follows the densely forested Doron Valley.

In Villard-sur-Doron, take the road signposted Signal de Bisanne (13km/8mi).

★★**Signal de Bisanne** – The twisting road overlooks the Doron Valley. From the top (1 939m/6 362ft), the splendid **panorama** extends all around to the Combe de Savoie, the Aravis Mountains, the Beaufortain and Mont-Blanc massifs.

Access is also possible from Les Saisies.

Return to Villard.

Between Villard and Beaufort, the valley widens below the impressive mass of the Montagne d'Outray, guarded by the ruined tower of the **Château de Beaufort**. The V-shaped gorge known as Défilé d'Entreroches can be seen beyond Beaufort.

Beaufort – This village has given its name to the region and to a tasty cheese *(see Introduction: Food and drink in the Alps)*. The old district of Beaufort stands tightly clustered on the south bank of the river. The **church** offers a typical example of Savoyard decoration, with its rood beam, altars in carved gilt wood and a remarkable pulpit dating from 1722.

Park the car 1km/0.6mi beyond Beaufort, near the first bridge over the Doron.

Défilé d'Entreroches – The tumultuous stream has dug some fine pot-holes.

Return to Beaufort and take D 218 to Arèches.

Arèches – Surrounded by gentle slopes ideal for skiing, Arèches is today one of the most typical winter resorts of the Beaufortain region.

Boudin

★**Boudin** – From the road leading to the St-Guérin dam, there is a fine overall view of this characteristic Alpine village with its large chalets rising in tiers.

Barrage de Roselend – The buttressed dam rests against a natural arch obstructing the gorge of the Doron River. The **artificial lake★** and its austere surroundings come into view on the way down from Col du Pré. Past a belvedere, the road follows the top of the dam then skirts the edge of the lake which flooded the village of Roselend (the chapel is a copy of the old church) and begins its final climb. The view extends westwards to Mont Mirantin and Grand Mont (2 687m/8 816ft), two of the best-known summits of the Beaufortain.

★**Cormet de Roselend** – This depression, stretching over several kilometres, links the Roselend and Chapieux valleys at an altitude of more than 1 900m/6 234ft, in a landscape of remote treeless pastures, dotted with rocks and a few rustic shelters. From the small mound on the right, surmounted by a cross, there is a wide **view★** of the surrounding summits towering over the Chapieux Valley, including the Aiguille du Grand Fond (2 889m/9 478ft), the highest of them all.

The drive down from Cormet offers a glimpse of the Aiguille des Glaciers (3 816m/12 520ft), the most southern peak of the Mont-Blanc Massif. Road D 902 continues past Les Chapieux village towards Bourg-St-Maurice.

Two mountain streams meet in the **Vallée des Chapieux★**. Beyond Bonneval, the road follows the forested valley of the Versoyen until it reaches a rock spur crowned with a ruined tower. There are fine views of the Haute-Tarentaise just before the road veers to the right towards Bourg-St-Maurice.

Bourg-St-Maurice – *See BOURG-ST-MAURICE.*

★ROUTE DES SAISIES

② **From Flumet to Beaufort**
41km/25.5mi – about 1hr 30min – local map see opposite

Flumet – *See Massif des ARAVIS: Route des Aravis.*

The road starts climbing through a forest of fir trees; view of the Aiguille Verte and Mont Blanc just before the last hairpin bend.

Notre-Dame-de-Bellecombe – This is the most popular of the Val d'Arly skiing resorts.

Turn right onto D 71 (liable to be blocked by snow from late November to April).

Beaufort cheese

It takes 10l/2.2g of milk from cows of the Tarine and Abondance breeds, processed through 10 different stages, to make 1kg/2.2lb of cheese. Copper vats with a capacity of 4 000l of milk can produce eight rounds of Beaufort.

The first stage is called **emprésurage**, during which rennet is added to the heated milk; the curd is then allowed to harden and the cheese is continually heated and mixed. During the fourth stage, it is poured into moulds known as **cloches de soutirage** from which rounds of cheese later emerge pressed between wooden hoops and covered with linen. **Pressage** and **retournement** give the cheese a denser and firmer aspect. **Saumurage** comes next, causing the crust to form. The long maturing process can then start: during six months, the 40kg/88lb rounds of cheese are salted, rubbed with linen and turned over twice a week in damp cellars kept at a constant temperature of 10°C/50°F.

Crest-Voland – This typical Savoyard village is a peaceful summer and winter resort; linked by ski-lifts to the nearby resort of Les Saisies under the name of **Espace Cristal**, it offers a wide choice of skiing, including cross-country skiing. It is well known to advanced skiers for its treacherous black run nicknamed the "kamikaze run". There are numerous possibilities of summer hiking, in particular to Le Cernix, Cohennoz or Les Saisies, and of travelling on snowshoes through the surrounding snowfields in winter.

Return to Notre-Dame-de-Bellecombe.

The next part of the journey to Col des Saisies offers wide vistas of the Aravis mountains extending to Pointe Percée, their highest peak (2 752m/9 029ft).

Les Saisies – This winter sports resort was founded in 1963 near the **Col des Saisies** (alt 1 633m/5 358ft) on land belonging to nearby villages in characteristic pastoral surroundings. All the cross-country skiing events of the 1992 Winter Olympics took place in Les Saisies which is today the main Alpine centre for that sport. It is also the home town of **Frank Piccard** who became Olympic champion twice in Calgary in 1988.

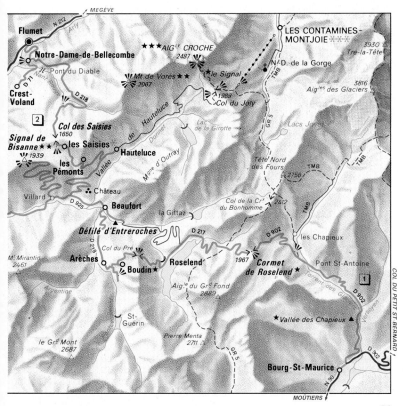

99

From the pass and from **Les Pémonts** village, there are wide **views★** of the Beaufortain mountains.
The road then runs along the green **Vallée de Hauteluce.**

Hauteluce – This sunny summer and winter resort offers visitors the lovely picture of its graceful onion-shaped steeple in the foreground and Mont Blanc in the distance, seen through the Col du Joly in the upper part of the valley.
The **Écomusée** ⊙, situated at the heart of the village, organises exhibitions on traditional life and development projects concerning the Beaufortain region.
Before reaching Beaufort, note the tower of the ruined castle perched on a wooded height.

Beaufort – *See p 97.*

La vallée des BELLEVILLE ✳✳✳

Michelin map 77 folds 7 and 8 or 244 fold 31
Local map see Massif de la VANOISE

This huge area covering 23 000ha/56 835 acres (Bella Villa means large estate) lies between the Tarentaise and the Maurienne on the western edge of the Massif de la Vanoise. St-Martin-de-Belleville became an important tourist centre with the creation of the Les Ménuires (1964) and Val-Thorens (1972) resorts. Its vast and splendid **skiing area** forms the main part of **Les Trois Vallées**✳✳✳ *(see Massif de la VANOISE).* Besides its 120 marked ski runs, the valley has retained large sites in their natural state, which make it one of the most attractive areas in Europe for off-piste skiing.
In summer, the valley is ideal for **walking** and **hiking** (180km/112mi of footpaths and trails) and not yet overcrowded. Furthermore, the wealth of traditional villages in the area and the 36 churches and chapels, most of them Baroque, cannot fail to attract visitors who appreciate the cultural aspect of tourism. **Circuits sur les chemins du Baroque** (Along Baroque trails, *see Practical information*) are organised to help visitors who wish to discover the historic heritage of the valley.

VILLAGES OF THE LOWER VALLEY

The deep valley is dotted with clumps of deciduous trees.

St-Jean-de-Belleville – Rebuilt after a major fire, the village has retained a richly decorated church (Baroque altarpiece by Todescoz and imposing altarpiece over the high altar in early Empire style, beginning of the 19C). From St-Jean, there is an interesting detour through the **Nant Brun Valley**.

St-Martin-de-Belleville – Alt 1 400m/4 593ft. This charming old village has some gentle sunny slopes linked by chair-lift to those of Meribel and Les Ménuires. In summer there are numerous possibilities of hikes in the surrounding area as well as concerts in the churches.

Église St-Martin – This stocky building, surmounted by a Lombard-style steeple, is characteristic of 17C-18C hall-churches. It contains a remarkable **altarpiece★** by Todescoz as well as a profusion of decoration where gold (symbolizing prayer) and red (symbolizing Christ's blood) predominate.

Chapelle Notre-Dame-de-Vie – *1km/0.6mi south, along the road to Les Ménuires.* This 17C edifice, crowned with a cupola and surmounted by a slender steeple, is an important place of pilgrimage (15 August and first Sunday in September) set in pastoral surroundings. The high altar **retable★**, dedicated to the Virgin Mary, was carved in arolla pine by JM Molino; the paintings decorating the cupola are the work of Nicolas Oudéard's School.

★**Salins-les-Thermes via D 96** – *Narrow road safe in summer and dry weather only.* This itinerary offers picturesque views of the villages.

WINTER SPORTS RESORTS OF THE UPPER VALLEY

Beyond the Chapelle Notre-Dame-de-Vie, the slopes become smooth and moderately steep; Les Ménuires can be seen in the distance, with Pointe de la Masse and Cime de Caron *(both accessible by cable-car)* towering over the resort.

✳✳Les Ménuires

This modern resort consists of seven units stretching over 2km/1.2mi at an altitude varying between 1 780m/5 840ft and 1 950m/6 365ft. The two main sites (La Croisette and Les Bruyères) are functional and pleasant at the same time; the skiing area is nearby and there is a large shopping centre.

Skiing area – Enjoying a fair amount of sunshine, Les Ménuires is appreciated by advanced skiers for its demanding ski runs (Les Pylônes, la Dame Blanche and le Rocher Noir). The off-piste area is easily accessible and skiing facilities are extended over the whole skiing area of Les Trois Vallées. There are some 30km/18.6mi of cross-country skiing tracks, particularly fine between Le Bettaix and Le Châtelard.

In winter, guided excursions are available for ski-trekking enthusiasts and, in summer, a wide choice of activities is on the menu.

★★**Mont de la Chambre** – Alt 2 850m/9 350ft. From La Croisette, take the gondola then walk up to the summit only a few minutes away. The fine panorama includes Mont Blanc, the Vallée de Méribel, the Val-Thorens and Vanoise glaciers. It is possible to walk back to Les Ménuires *(2hr)*.

★★Val-Thorens

In winter, the car-free village has parking available outside with shuttle services to the centre. The highest ski resort in Europe, set in magnificent surroundings, is overlooked by the Aiguille de Péclet (3 561m/11 683ft) and bounded by three glaciers marking the limits of the Parc national de la Vanoise. The barren landscape does not entice hikers but attracts rock-climbers instead.

Skiing area – Situated between 1 800m/5 905ft and 3 300m/10 827ft and covered with snow from November to May, Val-Thorens is the skiers' paradise: snowfields all round, high mountain atmosphere, breathtaking views of Mont Blanc, La Vanoise and Les Écrins, famous ski runs including la Combe de Caron and access in 20min to the skiing areas of Mont de la Chambre and Mont Vallon de Méribel. Inaugurated in 1996, the Orelle Gondola takes skiers from the Maurienne Valley up to the Val-Thorens skiing area in 20min. In July, several pistes are available on the Glacier de Péclet.

There is a wide choice of après-ski activities in a complex extending over 9 000m²/10 764sq yd. Childcare facilities include the Village d'Enfants-Académie des Neiges, created and run by the ski champion Marielle Goitschel *(see VAL D'ISÈRE)* who shares her love of the mountains with the children.

★★★**Cime de Caron** – Alt 3 198m/10 492ft. *Access by the Caïrn and Caron gondolas followed by the Caron cable-car ⊘ (minimum 2hr return).*
The summit can then be reached in 5min. The extraordinary **panorama**★★★ unfolding from the viewing table embraces practically the whole of the French Alps, in particular the imposing summits of the **Mont-Blanc, Vanoise, Queyras** and **Écrins** massifs to the northeast and south, the **Belledonne** and **Aravis** ranges to the west and northwest with the Jura mountains on the horizon.

★**Glacier de Péclet** – *Access by Funitel ⊘ (twin-cable cable-car).* Close-up view of the glacier and Cime de Caron. Advanced skiers can, in summer and autumn, take the 3 300 chair-lift to the summit *(caution is advisable at the summit!)* from which there is a splendid **panorama**★★★ of the Mont-Blanc and Vanoise massifs.

HIKES

A map of the local footpaths is available from the tourist office. The various summits in the surrounding area can all be spotted from the Cime de Caron and Pointe de la Masse viewing tables.
There are pleasant walks for inexperienced hikers to **Lac du Lou** *(2hr 30min return from Les Bruyères)* and **Hameau de la Gitte**★ *(1hr 45min return from Villaranger).* The following hikes are suitable for experienced hikers.

★★★**La Croix-Jean-Claude** – *4hr 30min. Difference in height: about 600m/1 968ft. Just before Béranger, take a path on the right to the hamlet of Les Dogettes; turn right towards two small mountains (Les Fleurettes); continue to the spring and beyond to the ridge separating the Belleville and Allues valleys; turn left to Croix Jean-Claude and Dos de Crêt Voland (2 092m/6 864ft).*
Magnificent **view**★★ of the Belleville villages, Méribel, La Vanoise, La Plagne and Mont Blanc. The path reaches Roc de la Lune *(signposted Col de la Lune)*. The walk down to Béranger offers fine views of the villages.

★★★**Crève-Tête** – Alt 2 342m/7 684ft. *Take a small road starting in a bend preceding Fontaine-le-Puits; it leads to Col de la Coche and to the dam of the same name (alt 1 400m/4 593ft). A rough road on the left leads directly to Pas de Pierre Larron. If you do not wish to take it, park your car at the end of the dam and walk along the Darbellaz path to Pas de Pierre Larron in 1hr 30min.*
From **Pas de Pierre Larron**, the **view**★ extends to the valley of the Isère River and Mont-Blanc. Go to the refuge on the left. A steeper and more demanding path leads to the summit *(2hr)* offering superb **views**★★★ *(see VALMOREL).*

La vallée des BELLEVILLE

Le Châtelard and Vallée des Encombres

★★**Pointe de la Masse and tour of the lakes** – *Take the gondola to La Masse. From the first section, allow 5hr for the whole itinerary. Less experienced hikers are advised to skip the ascent of La Masse (in this case allow 3hr 30min). The tour includes Lac Longet, Pointe de la Masse, Lac Noir, Lac Crintallia and Le Teurre.*
From the viewing table at the top of La Masse (2 804m/9 200ft), there is a splendid **panorama★★** of Les Écrins, Les Grandes Rousses, the Belledonne range, Mont Blanc, La Vanoise and the Vallée des Encombres immediately below.

Vallée des Encombres – The village of **Le Châtelard**, near St-Martin, lies at the entrance to this secluded 14km-long valley. Tourist facilities have been kept to a minimum in order to preserve the exceptionally rich fauna which includes 250 ibexes and 400 chamois. There are fine guided hikes *(ask at Les Ménuires)* to the **Petit Col des Encombres★★** (alt 2 342m/7 684ft) and the **Grand Perron des Encombres★★★** (alt 2 825m/9 268ft) offering impressive views of the Maurienne Valley and Écrins Massif.

BESSANS ✳

Population 273
Michelin map 77 fold 9 or 244 fold 33 – Local map see La MAURIENNE

Bessans lies in a small valley enclosed by high summits, at the heart of the traditional Maurienne region. Some of the land belonging to the municipality forms part of the Parc national de la Vanoise *(see Introduction: Nature parks and reserves)*.
The village has retained its ancient traditions (the local costume is still worn on festive occasions) and woodcarving, which has been a speciality of the area since Renaissance times, is now exclusively devoted to the production of the famous **diables de Bessans** *(see Introduction: Traditions and folklore)*.

Skiing area – The resort has more than 80km/49.7mi of cross-country tracks. Its superb snow coverage at a moderate altitude of 1 700m/5 577ft offers fine ski-treks during the greatest part of the season.

SIGHTS

Church ⊙ – It contains many 17C statues and an altarpiece by Clappier, one of the famous sculptors from Bessans. There is also a very expressive Crucifixion and a remarkable Ecce Homo.

Chapelle St-Antoine ⊙ – *Access through the cemetery, opposite the side door of the church.* Although still used for services, the chapel is now a museum.
Built in the 14C and restored in the 19C, the edifice is decorated outside with murals in poor condition, depicting the virtues and the vices. Inside, the **paintings★**, dating from the 15C, illustrate the life of Jesus Christ. The chapel also contains statues carved by local sculptors between the 17C and the 19C including several representations of Christ at the time of the Passion and St Anthony with his bell (hermits used bells in the past to frighten evil spirits away). The Renaissance coffered ceiling, decorated with stars, dates from 1526.

★★VALLÉE D'AVÉROLE

At the time of the Renaissance, Italian artists came through this valley, dotted with chapels and pastoral villages, characteristic of the Haute-Maurienne (La Goula, Vincendières, Avérole). Visitors must leave their car in the parking located 500m/0.3mi before Vincendières and continue on foot to Avérole *(45min return)*: view of the Pointe de Charbonnel (south) and the Albaron (north).

★★**Refuge d'Avérole** – Alt 2 210m/7 250ft. *Easy hike from Avérole (2hr 15min return); difference in altitude: 200m/656ft.*
Beautiful mountain setting with glaciers, waterfalls and the Bessanese summit (3 592m/11 785ft) in the foreground.

BEUIL★

Population 330
Michelin map 115 fold 4, 81 fold 9 or 245 fold 24

This picturesque village clinging to a steep south-facing slope of the upper valley of the Cians River overlooked by Mont Mounier (2 817m/9 242ft) is a pleasant winter sports resort and a peaceful summer resort.

The Grimaldi dynasty – From the 14C to the 17C, Beuil belonged to the powerful **Grimaldi** family in perpetual conflict with the dukes of Savoie, who never hesitated to make use of treachery to achieve their ends. In 1617, the last comte de Beuil, Annibal Grimaldi, secured the protection of King Louis XIII of France; however, the latter soon forgot his promise when he signed a truce with the duke of Savoie. Annibal Grimaldi took refuge in his fortress but the duke once again used treachery to get the better of his enemy.

SIGHTS

Church – Rebuilt in the 17C, it has retained a 15C Romanesque bell-tower and some fine **paintings:** on the right there is an Adoration of the Magi from the Veronese School and, further along, fragments of an altarpiece and a predella. The high-altar retable in Primitive style has 16 panels and, on the left, there is a predella illustrating Christ coming out of his grave as well as the panel of an altarpiece depicting St Catherine of Sienna.

Chapelle des Pénitents Blancs ⊘ – This Renaissance chapel was built with stones from the Grimaldi castle. The façade decorated in *trompe-l'œil* was recently re-stored by Guy Ceppa.

EXCURSION

★**From Beuil to Guillaumes**
20km/12.4mi west along D 28 – about 45min.

This road links the Gorges du Cians *(see Gorges du CIANS)* and the upper valley of the Var River *(see Haute vallée du VAR)* over the Valberg Pass.

✳**Valberg** – See VALBERG.
On the way down from the Col de Valberg to Guillaumes, the road offers a succession of picturesque **views**. There is a striking contrast between the forested north-facing slope and the cultivated south-facing slope (vineyards, orchards, wheat).

Guillaumes – *See Haute vallée du VAR.*

Le BOCHAINE

Michelin map 77 fold 15, 81 fold 5 or 245 fold 6

This depression of the Préalpes du Sud is an important communications link between north and south through the upper valley of the Buëch which opens the way to the main Alpine winter route *(N 75)* and to the railway line from Grenoble to Marseille via the Col de la Croix Haute.
The area enjoys a Mediterranean climate, although pastures and fir forests still predominate as far south as St-Julien-en-Beauchêne.

VALLÉE DU BUËCH

From Lus-la-Croix-Haute to Serres
32km/20mi – about 1hr 30min

Lus-la-Croix-Haute – Lying at the centre of a wide Alpine basin through which flows the Buëch, at an altitude of 1 030m/3 379ft, Lus-la-Croix-Haute is the highest resort of the Bochaine area.
From the Grande-Place in Lus, drive east along D 505.

★**Vallon de la Jarjatte** – The road follows the upper valley of the Buëch, with forested slopes on either side.

On approaching the ski resort of La Jarjatte, there are impressive **views**★★ of the indented silhouettes of Les Aiguilles framed by Vachères (2 400m/7 874ft) and Tête de Garnesier (2 368m/8 769ft). The head of the valley forms a cirque in a setting of dark escarpments towering over a dense fir forest.

Return to N 75.

The road follows each bank of the Buëch in turn. The wide riverbed is overlooked by the jagged peaks of the Diois, known as "*serres*"; the wooded slopes of the Montagne Durbonas can be seen on the left as the road reaches the village of **St-Julien-en-Beauchêne**.

Beyond St-Julien, the landscape becomes more arid, deep gullies run down the mountain slopes, with a few pines and oaks dotted about; rocky peaks are now and then surmounted by ruined castles such as the 12C fortress of La Rochette.

Aspres-sur-Buëch – This lively town lies at the intersection of N 75 and D 993/ D 994 linking Die and Gap, in a picturesque mountain setting (good overall **view** from the mound crowned with a war memorial).

The **church** has an interesting Romanesque doorway bearing statues of Christ between Mary and St John the Baptist (unfortunately mutilated).

Beyond Pont de la Barque, at the confluence of the Buëch and Petit Buëch, a narrowing of the valley hides the village of Serres.

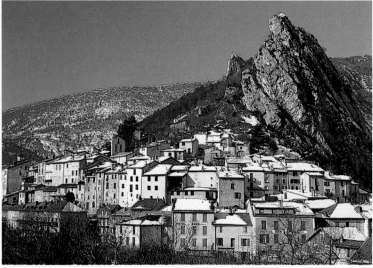

Serres

Serres – The picturesque old village clings to a pointed rock above the Buëch River. In 1576 it became the property of the **Duc de Lesdiguières** and a refuge for Huguenots (Protestants) at the time of the Wars of Religion, only interrupted during the reign of Henri IV. In 1633 Richelieu ordered the destruction of the citadel and the Huguenots either converted to Catholicism or went into exile.

The old town is very attractive with its narrow lanes and covered passageways. From the arcaded square, walk up to the old high street where the **town hall** stands Lesdiguières' former residence (17C porch and fine 16C vaulting inside). *Turn back and walk eastwards along the high street, now* **rue Henri-Peuzin**. Note on the right the belfry surmounted by a campanile and several carved doorways along the street, in particular **no 56**. The Romanesque **church** was remodelled in the 14C; the south side is the most interesting with its six **funerary recesses** and two beautifully carved doors. Opposite the church, a passageway leads to the former Jewish quarter and back to the square.

Route des cadrans solaires

This tour through the valleys of the Buëch region leads to the discovery of an interesting collection of sundials showing the diversity of local pictorial art during the 18C and 19C. In **St-Julien-en-Beauchêne**, the Durbon forest lodge (a former Carthusian monastery) is decorated with two 18C sundials. In **Aspres-sur-Buëch**, a contemporary sundial, made according to traditional techniques, adorns the town hall. At **Col de Cabre**, near La Beaume, a sundial has been carved in the rock at the western exit of the tunnel. The primary school in **Serres** also has its sundial, showing the sun's trajectory and the position of the equinox *(see Practical information)*.

LE PETIT BUËCH

Veynes – Owing to its position on the main Gap-Die route, this former stronghold suffered much at the hands of the Huguenots and the duke of Savoie's troups. From 1894 onwards, it gradually became a major railway junction with lines to Grenoble, Marseille, Briançon and Valence as well as an industrial centre. Today, this role is no longer as important and the town has turned to tourism instead; it is the ideal starting point of hikes and pony-treks in the south Buëch region and the Base nautique des Isles (water sports park) provides plenty of summer activities.

Hikes

★**Pic d'Oule** – Alt 1 608m/5 276ft. *Ascent 3hr; difference in altitude 800m/2 625ft.* Cross the Pont de la Morelle spanning the Petit Buëch just south of Veynes, follow the path leading to several farms and over a small stream; continue through a fine forest of maples and beeches to Col d'Oule then follow the ridge to the summit which affords a splendid **panorama**★★ of the Val d'Oze below and the Bure Massif to the north.

★**Montagne de Céüse** – This tabular mountain offers interesting hikes from different starting points.
From Veynes: take D 20 on the right towards Châteauneuf d'Oze then turn left at the intersection onto the forest road leading to Col des Guérins.
Footpath GR 94 skirts the east side of the isolated mountain to reach Manteyer on the northeast slope.
From the Céüse 2000 resort: take the track which starts opposite Hôtel Gaillard, climb up to a ledge then follow the steep course of the Marseillais ski-lift to the top. Go up towards the Torrent chair-lift until you reach a signpost. A path leads to the Pic de Céüse which reveals a splendid **view**★★ of the Massif de Bure and Massif des Écrins to the north and of the Ubaye to the east. It is possible to return via the west side, skirting the top of the rock-climbing course, going down through the Vallon d'Aiguibelle and then following the signs.

★★**Pic de Bure** – *See MONTMAUR.*

Route de la BONETTE★★

Michelin map 81 folds 8 and 9 or 245 folds 10, 23 and 24

This road stretches from the Ubaye Valley to Nice via the Vallée de la Tinée over a distance of some 150km/93mi. Several military constructions along the route are a reminder of its long-standing strategic importance. The present road, built in 1963-64, goes through part of the Parc national du Mercantour and over the Col de la Bonette, which makes it the highest road in France.

★★★CIME DE LA BONETTE

From Barcelonnette to St-Étienne-de-Tinée
64km/40mi – about 3hr

The twisting road is blocked by snow from November to the end of June.

★**Barcelonnette** – *See BARCELONNETTE.*
From Barcelonnette, follow D 900 towards Italy.

Jausiers – *See L'UBAYE: BARCELONNETTE BASIN.*
Coming out of Jausiers, turn right towards Nice.

The road climbs towards **Le Restefond** in a series of hairpin bends offering lovely views of the Ubaye Valley. Between the Casernes de Restefond, a complex fortified by Maginot in 1931, and St-Étienne-de-Tinée, 18 special viewing tables set along the road, explain the main features of the landscape.
The road continues to climb past the **Col de la Bonette** (2 715m/8 907ft) to an altitude of 2 802m/9 193ft before skirting round the foot of Cime de la Bonette. It is one of the highest altitudes reached by a European road.

★★★**Cime de la Bonette** – Alt 2 862m/9 390ft. *From the highest point of the road, 30min return on foot. Viewing table.* The breathtaking **panorama** embraces most of the mountain ranges of the southern Alps: the Queyras (Font Sancte), the Viso and Ubaye (Brec de Chambeyron and Tête de Moïse) to the north, the Pelvoux to the northwest; then the upper Verdon (Grande Séolane and Mont Pelat) and the southern Alps to the west, the Préalpes de Digne to the south and the Corborant and Argentera to the east. A special viewing table explains the formation of the Alps.

View of Pas de la Cavale from Col des Fourches

On its way down, the road reaches the ruins of **Camp des Fourches**, a large encampment occupied until the end of the Second World War by a battalion of *chasseurs alpins* (mountain troops). From there, a path leads in 5min to the Col des Fourches which affords a superb **view★** of the vast cirque of Salso Moreno, close to the Italian border *(viewing table with explanations on local geology)*.

Hikes

★★Hike to Pas de la Cavale – *See ST-ÉTIENNE-DE-TINÉE.*

★★★Hike to Lacs de Vens – *See ST-ÉTIENNE-DE-TINÉE.*

Three kilometres (1.8mi) beyond Le Pra, one can see the Vens waterfall on the left. As the road runs down into the valley, the short grass of the high pastures gives way to a larch forest.

At Pont-Haut, turn right onto D 63 to St-Dalmas.

★St-Dalmas-le-Selvage – *See ST-DALMAS-LE-SELVAGE.*

Return to D 2205 and turn right to St-Étienne-de-Tinée.

The road follows a stream through an impressive gorge.

★St-Étienne-de-Tinée – *See ST-ÉTIENNE-DE-TINÉE.*

BONNEVAL-SUR-ARC★★

Population 216
Michelin map 74 fold 19 or 244 fold 33
Local maps see Route de l'ISERAN and La MAURIENNE

Situated beneath the Col de l'Iseran, in the imposing cirque where the Arc has its source, the highest municipality of the Maurienne region has retained the charming character of its old village. In summer, it is an excursion centre offering many itineraries within the Parc national de la Vanoise as well as a mountaineering centre organising fascinating expeditions to the border massifs of La Levanna, La Ciamarella and l'Albaron.

★OLD VILLAGE

Bonneval has made a point of preserving the character of its old streets and houses by burying electric and telephone cables and banning individual television aerials and satellite dishes as well as cars which are kept outside the village.

Visitors can therefore walk safely and undisturbed through the narrow streets lined with stone houses covered with rust-coloured *lauzes* (slabs of schist) and adorned with wooden balconies where dry cow-dung, still used as fuel, is sometimes stored. At the heart of the village, a large old chalet, known as **La Grande Maison**, houses a butcher's and a baker's.

On the way out of the village, past the 17C church, there is a **fromagerie** ⊙ (cheese dairy) where local cheeses are made, including Beaufort, Emmental, Tomme and Mont Séti.

Skiing area – Most of the tourist facilities can be found in the hamlet of Tralenta, 500m/0.3mi from the village. There are 10 ski-lifts for a skiing area of moderate size but of good quality. Winter sports are practised here from December to May between 1 800m/5 905ft and 3 000m/9 843ft on some of the best snow in the French Alps. Beginners and intermediate skiers enjoy the Moulinet ski-lift, close to the Vallonet glacier. Advanced skiers on the other hand take the 3 000 ski-lift to the foot of **Pointe d'Andagne** from where there is a magnificent **view**★★ of the Haute-Maurienne (Bessans below, Pointe de Ronce on the left and the rocky ridges of the Vanoise on the right) with the Meije and Aiguilles d'Arves in the background. In summer, skiers make for the **Glacier du Grand Pissaillas**, which can be reached from Col de l'Iseran *(see VAL D'ISÈRE)*.

L'Écot – This hamlet, which lies in imposing and austere surroundings, more than 2 000m/6 562ft up, has retained its old stone houses and 12C Chapelle Ste-Marguerite. Once extremely remote, it is today a favourite tourist destination.

Bonneval-sur-Arc

107

HIKES

Bonneval is the ideal starting point of **walks** and **hikes** through the Parc national de la Vanoise and the conservation area of **Les Évettes** which offers hikers 120km/74.6mi of waymarked footpaths. It is also a mountaineering centre organising highly interesting expeditions to the border massifs of La Levanna, La Ciamarella and l'Albaron.

★**Refuge du Criou** – Alt 2 050m/6 727ft. *Access: in winter by the Vallonet chair-lift, in summer on foot in 30min.* View of the seracs of the Glacier du Vallonet and Glacier des Sources de l'Arc and of the Col de l'Iseran road.

★★**Le Carro refuge** – Alt 2 760m/9 055ft. *From L'Écot, 3hr 15min on the way up (steep climb); 2hr on the way down. It is also possible to take the scenic path from Pont de l'Oulietta (alt 2 480m/8 136ft) on the Col de l'Iseran road; this itinerary is easy, long but extremely rewarding.*

Views★★ of l'Albaron and of the glaciers of Les Sources de l'Arc, Les Évettes and Le Vallonet. From the refuge, one can admire the Lac Noir and the Lac Blanc.

★★**Les Évettes refuge** – Alt 2 615m/8 579ft. *From L'Écot, 1hr 45min on the way up, 1hr on the way down.* The steep climb affords views of L'Écot and Bonneval. From the refuge, the **panorama**★★ is splendid: the Glacier des Évettes and L'Albaron are reflected in the still waters of the Lacs des Pareis. The Glacier du Grand Méan and Glacier du Mulinet can be seen beyond the refuge. It is possible to make a detour to the **Cascade de la Reculaz**★ *(1hr return).* When you reach the waterfall, cross the little bridge and go to the left past the waterfall. The view is quite impressive *(unsuitable for persons liable to feel dizzy).*

★**Walk to the Chalets de la Duis** – *From L'Écot: 2hr return. Very easy walk.* Family outing along a broad path in an idyllic setting of green pastures overlooked by fine glaciers.

During the course of a mountain hike or between two downhills, take a pause and taste some diots (finely chopped spicy sausage meat inside a gut casing).
There are different kinds of these delicacies, but the most common are diots in white wine. In the Bonneval Valley, try the pormoniers (with cabbage) or the diots d'anivier, often home-made.

Abbaye de BOSCODON ★

Michelin map 81 fold 7 or 245 fold 9

The golden colour of the stone buildings stands out against a background of pastures, forests and mountains.
Founded in 1130, this abbey soon prospered and was the most important monastery in the southern Alps during the Middle Ages. In 1408, it became affiliated to the Benedictine order. It was burnt down in 1585 by Lesdiguières and his Huguenot troops. However, during the period from 1601 to 1769, the buildings were renovated and the abbey enjoyed a new lease of life. The archbishop of Embrun then dissolved the religious community and the buildings later became public property; they were sold and used as farm buildings until 1972 when the Association des amis de Boscodon acquired them. Since then, teams of young people have worked hard to restore the abbey and a community of Dominican sisters lives there permanently.

TOUR ⊙ 30min

The abbey church and the monks' wing have been restored but the lay community and officers' buildings are still undergoing restoration work.

★**Abbey church** – The recently restored east end is remarkable; inside, one is overwhelmed by the architectural simplicity of this single-nave edifice and the amount of light pouring through its semicircular-arched windows. The door of the sacristy on the right leads to the abbot's chapel beneath which there is a funeral chapel belonging to an older edifice.

Monks' wing – The chapter hall, completely restored, is used as a reception and exhibition area. The former warming-room and refectory (17C) are used as an information centre.

Officers' wing – *Visitors' reception area.*

Lay community wing – *Excavations in progress.*

**FORÊT DE BOSCODON

The forest, which formed part of the estate of the abbey and extends over 850ha/2 100 acres, is famous for its beautiful specimens of larch and fir trees.

From the abbey, take the forest road (surfaced) leading to Fontaine de l'ours.

This fine open space at the heart of the forest owes its name to the spring harnessed by the monks and protected by stone vaulting.

Belvédère du torrent du Colombier – Upstream, there are some fine views of the funnel hollowed out of the mountainside. Downstream, one can see the Serre-Ponçon Lake and the Durance Valley.

Drive on to the Belvédère de Bragousse.

Belvédère de Bragousse – The gullied cirque forms a striking landscape enhanced by the beautiful colour of the soil; chamois can be seen (with binoculars) roaming around in the upper part of the cirque. The mountain stream, subject to sudden summer flooding, has been tamed by a series of dams; the first of these can be seen from the belvedere.

Drive another 500m/0.3mi to reach Fontaine de l'ours; park the car at the end of the road.

Le BOURG-D'OISANS

Population 2 911
Michelin map 77 fold 6 or 244 fold 40
Local maps see Bassin du BOURG-D'OISANS and L'OISANS

Le Bourg-d'Oisans ("Le Bourg" for short) is the modest capital of the Oisans region and one of the most successful tourist resorts in Dauphiné. Fairs, markets and numerous shops ensure that it remains lively all year round.
Some local names testify that, during the Middge Ages, a group of Sarracens colonised the area.

SIGHTS

*★**Musée des Minéraux et de la Faune des Alpes** ⊘ – Housed in one of the aisles of the church, the museum displays a permanent collection of minerals particularly rich in quartz as well as excellent temporary exhibitions. Alpine fauna is also represented: animals (eagle, jackdaw, blue hare...) are exhibited in their natural environment. The paleontology section has a collection of fossils dating back to the time of the Alpine geological upheavals.

Belvedere – *45min return on foot along the shaded alleyway beyond the church.* From the platform built at the highest point of the walk, there is a fairly clear view of the Bassin du Bourg-d'Oisans, of the Grandes Rousses mountain range and of the first peaks rising south of the Vénéon River.

*★**Cascade de Sarennes** – *1km/0.6mi to the northeast, then 15min return on foot. Leave Le Bourg on the road to Briançon; 800m/0.5mi further on, turn left onto D 211 towards L'Alpe-d'Huez and park the car just before the bridge over the Sarennes; continue on foot along the path on the right.* The triple waterfall of this tributary of the Romanche is very impressive in springtime.

Bassin du BOURG-D'OISANS ★

Michelin map 77 fold 6 or 244 fold 40
Local maps see p 111 and L'OISANS

The Bassin du Bourg-d'Oisans, situated at the intersection of several valleys and surrounded by dark escarpments, forms a well-cultivated enclosed plain. The road to L'Alpe-d'Huez provides a good initiation to mountain landscapes and the smaller cliff roads offer one of the best selections of breathtaking itineraries in the Alps.

CORNICHES DU BASSIN D'OISANS

1 From Le Bourg-d'Oisans to L'Alpe-d'Huez

14km/8.7mi – about 30min – local map see p 111

From Bourg-d'Oisans, follow the Briançon road then turn left to L'Alpe-d'Huez.

The road climbs in a series of hairpin bends, affording lovely vistas of the Romanche and Vénéon valleys and, in the distance, the Rochail Massif and Villard-Notre-Dame glacier. Just before the old village of **Huez**, there is a good view of the remote upper Sarennes Valley. As the road reaches L'Alpe-d'Huez, the Meije suddenly appears above the vast white-capped Mont de Lans glacier.

✳✳**L'Alpe-d'Huez** – *See L'ALPE-D'HUEZ.*

② From Le Bourg-d'Oisans to the Valbonnais

29km/18mi – about 1hr – local map see opposite

This interesting itinerary links the Bourg-d'Oisans basin and the Valbonnais via the Col d'Ornon, following the course of the Lignarre and the Malsanne rivers.

From Bourg-d'Oisans take N 91 towards Grenoble. Turn left at La Paute onto D 526.

★**Gorges de la Lignarre** – The river has dug its way through schist (slate used to be quarried here). From Le Rivier, there is a fine view of the Belledonne and Grandes Rousses ranges to the north.

Col d'Ornon – Alt 1 367m/4 485ft. The pass crosses a barren stony landscape. The road follows the narrow valley of the tumultuous Malsanne River.

At Le Périer, turn left towards the Cascade de Confolens. Leave the car at the entrance to the Parc national des Écrins and continue on foot (2hr return).

★**Cascade de Confolens** – The path on the left leads to the 70m/230ft-high waterfall, set in lovely surroundings.

On the way down to Entraigues, there are fine **views**★ of L'Aiguille to the south-west, across the River Drac.

Entraigues – *See Le VALBONNAIS.*

★③ From Le Bourg-d'Oisans to the Refuge de Taillefer and Lac Fourchu

14km/8.7mi drive then 3hr on foot – difference in altitude: 800m/2 625ft – local map see opposite

From Bourg d'Oisans take N 91 to Grenoble; at La Paute turn left onto D 526 (see drive ② above). At Pont-des-Oulles, turn right to Ornon and La Grenonière.

Beyond the Parc des Écrins information panel *(on a bend)*, the road is unsurfaced *(parking)*. Continue on this road for 200m/219yd and take a path on the right which leads to La Basse-Montagne.

From La Basse-Montagne, allow 2hr for experienced hikers. Leave the stream on your left and follow the path (red markings) through the woods. After 1hr, the path, meandering through pastures, reaches the Taillefer refuge.

From the ledge (2 000m/6 562ft), there is a fine view of the Taillefer Massif and the Lignarre Valley, whereas behind the building you can see L'Alpe-d'Huez and Les Grandes Rousses Massif.

Continue westwards to reach the Lac Fourchu in 45min along an easier path.

In spring and summer, the peaceful shores of the lake (2 060m/6 759ft) are dotted with wild flowers, rhododendron bushes, clusters of houseleek and columbine. There is a succession of small lakes lower down.

It is possible to go straight back via the Lac de la Vache and La Basse-Montagne.

★★PETITES ROUTES DES "VILLAGES-TERRASSES"

These itineraries leading to villages perched on heights overlooking the Bassin du Bourg-d'Oisans follow narrow cliff roads where vehicles can only pass one another at specified points. They are not recommended to inexperienced motorists apart from drive ⑧.

★★ ④ **Route de Villard-Notre-Dame** – *From Le Bourg-d'Oisans, 9km/5.6mi – about 1hr – local map see p 111. The road has a 10% gradient and must be avoided during or after a rainy period; nasty ramp at the start.*
This cliff road offers fine views of some wild mountain landscapes and of a remote but picturesque village at the end.
The best view is on a bend, 8km/5mi from Bourg-d'Oisans, and embraces the lower Vénéon Valley with the Aiguille du Plat-de-la-Selle in the distance and a succession of waterfalls in the foreground.

★★ ⑤ **Route d'Auris** – *From La Garde (on the way to L'Alpe-d'Huez), 8km – about 45min – local map see opposite. Follow D 211ᴬ towards Le Freney.*
This itinerary is interesting for its bird's-eye views of the Bassin du Bourg-d'Oisans (sheer drop of some 500m/1 640ft).

★ ⑥ **Route de Villard-Reymond** – *Local map see opposite. From Le Bourg-d'Oisans, drive north along N 91, turn left onto D 526 to Pont-des-Oulles then left onto D 210 for 8km/5mi.*
The road runs up-river along a tributary of the Lignarre.

Villard-Reymond – This hamlet, lying in lovely surroundings, is now a health resort. Walk to the Cross at Col de Saulude *(15min return)* and admire the **view**★ of the village of Auris, of L'Alpe-d'Huez and the Belledonne range.

★★**Prégentil** – *1hr 30min return on foot from Villard-Reymond (northwest).* From the summit (alt 1 938m/6 358ft), there is a sweeping view of the high mountains surrounding the Bassin du Bourg-d'Oisans.

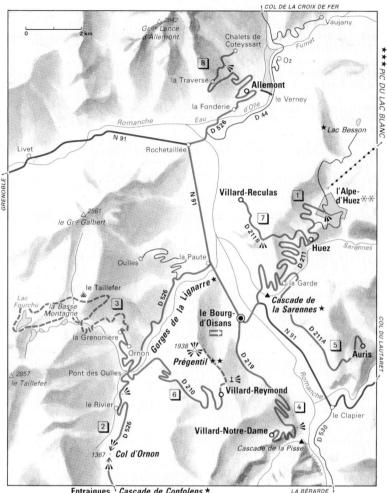

★ 7 **Route de Villard-Reculas** – *From Huez, 4km/12.4mi – See L'ALPE-D'HUEZ.*

★ 8 **Route de la Traverse d'Allemont** – *Local map see above. From Le Bourg-d'Oisans, take N 91 towards Grenoble, turn right onto D 526 to La Fonderie d'Allemont. From there, 6.5km/4mi – about 30min. Take D 43 to Allemont, turn left onto Route de la Traverse; shortly before this hamlet, turn right onto a forest road; after having driven 6km/3.7mi, leave the car beyond a bend (parking); go down 100m/109yd along the path which starts from the bend.*

From that point, there is a splendid **view**★ on the northern well-cultivated part of the Bassin du Bourg-d'Oisans and of the surrounding mountains.

Return to the car and drive for another 200m/219yd.

On the right, there is a **panorama**★★ of Le Bessey village and Dôme des Petites Rousses opposite as well as Col de la Croix-de-Fer and Lac Noir, with the Belledonne and Taillefer massifs barring the horizon to the north and south.

Drive on for another 300m/328yd.

There is a clear view of Les Grandes Rousses and La Combe d'Olle.

A Map of touring programmes
is given at the beginning of the guide.
To plan a special tour
use the preceding Map of principal sights.

Enclosed within its impressive mountain setting, the Lac du Bourget has been the most famous French lake ever since the Romantic poets, headed by Lamartine, celebrated the changing colour of its waters and the wild beauty of its steep shores.

Some facts – The Lac du Bourget is the largest (4 500ha/11 120 acres) – with the exception of five vast expanses of water lying just inland from the Atlantic Ocean and the Mediterranean – and the deepest (145m/476ft) natural lake in France. Unlike the Lac d'Annecy, it has never been seen to freeze in winter. Windstorms can be extremely violent. Like Lake Geneva, it abounds in fish and is continually being cleaned-up.

The lake used to extend northwards to the Grand Colombier Mountain and was supplied directly by the Rhône. Today, it is separated from the river by the Chautagne marsh; it is however still linked to the Rhône by the 3km/1.8mi-long Savières canal. This outlet sometimes works the other way: in spring, when the snow melts, or in autumn, during the rainy season, the Rhône overflows into the lake.

La Chambotte offers the most impressive view of the lake.

★★ROUND TOUR OF THE LAKE

1 Starting from Aix-les-Bains 87km/54mi – about 3hr 30min

The road overlooking the western shore of the lake clings to the steep slopes of Mont du Chat and Mont de la Charvaz, offering superb vistas.

On the east side, the road runs close to the lake at the foot of the cliffs of Mont de Corsuet, revealing the changing moods of the lake.

Aix-les-Bains – *See AIX-LES-BAINS.*

Leave Aix by ④ on the town plan, N 201 towards Chambéry.

The road, skirting the foot of Tresserve hill, a sought-after residential area, follows the low-lying shore, quite busy until Terre-Nue.

Le Bourget-du-Lac – *See p 114.*

Continue along N 504; at the second intersection signposted Bourdeau, turn left onto D 914 signposted Abbaye de Hautecombe.

The road rises above the lake towards Col du Chat; from the second hairpin bend, there is a fine **panorama★** of the Chambéry depression separating the Bauges (Mont Revard) and the Chartreuse (Mont Granier) massifs, with the indented Massif d'Allevard in the distance.

Chapelle Notre-Dame de l'Étoile – *15min return on foot. The signposted path starts on a bend of D 914.* From the platform in front of the church, there is a fine overall **view★★** of the lake and its frame of mountains: Grand Colombier, Semnoz, Mont Revard... The road runs along a ledge and the lake ceases to be visible.

Bifurcation d'Ontex – From this intersection, there is a view of Hautecombe abbey.

The road goes down towards the north end of the lake, where the Château de Châtillon stands on a wooded promontory; on the opposite shore, the Restaurant de la Chambotte occupies a prominent position.

Turn right onto D 18 to the Abbaye de Hautecombe.

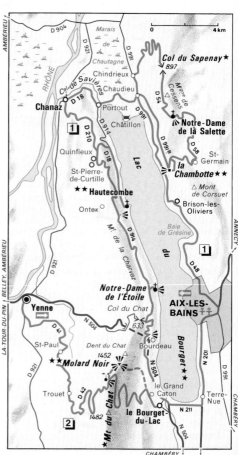

Abbaye royale de Hautecombe

★**Abbaye royale de Hautecombe** – The abbey stands on a promontory jutting out into the lake. It is the burial place of many members of the House of Savoie including **Beatrix de Savoie** whose ambitions for her four daughters were more than fulfilled when three of them became queens (of England, France and the Two-Sicilies) and the fourth one, empress of Germany. The last king of Italy, **Umberto II**, was buried in Hautecombe in 1983.

During the 19C, the **church** ⊙ was entirely restored in neo-Gothic style by artists from Piedmont, which explains the profusion of ornamentation. The 16C former doorway, situated on the left-hand side, is in striking contrast with the highly decorated façade. The interior is also profusely adorned: there are paintings by Gonin and Vacca over the vaulting as well as 300 statues in marble, stone or gilt wood and low-relief sculptures decorating the funeral monuments of the princes of Savoie. Some statues, carved out of Carrara marble, are remarkable, in particular a **Pietà**★ by Benoît Cacciatori.

Near the landing stage, the **grange batelière** (water barn), built by Cistercian monks in the 12C, was designed to store goods reaching the abbey by boat; the barrel-vaulted lower part comprises a wet dock and a dry dock.

Return to D 914 as far as Quinfieux and take D 210 to the left towards Chanaz.

Chanaz – Situated on the banks of the Canal de Savières, a once busy commercial route, this lively old border town found a new lease of life when the canal was opened to pleasure boats. There is an interesting oil-mill still producing walnut oil.

From Chanaz, drive along D 18 towards Aix-les-Bains.

The road crosses the Canal de Savières linking the lake to the River Rhône then runs through marshland to Chaudieu.

Turn left onto D 991 then right at Chindrieux towards Col de Sapenay.

The narrow twisting road affords lovely views of the Lac du Bourget, the Abbaye de Hautecombe and the Dent du Chat summit, with the Rhône Valley to the north, guarded by the impressive Grand Colombier.

★**Col du Sapenay** – Alt 897m/2 943ft. The road goes through a mountain landscape of fir trees and pastures.

Chapelle Notre-Dame de la Salette – From this high point in the Montagne de Cessens, the **view**★ extends over the Albanais depression to the east.

At St-Germain, turn onto D 991ᴮ, then turn left in La Chambotte past a small chapel.

★★**View from the Restaurant de la Chambotte** – See AIX-LES-BAINS: Excursions.

Beyond La Chambotte, the road goes down to Chaudieu, offering fine views of the Lac du Bourget.

In Chaudieu, turn left onto D 991.

From then on, the road skirts the edge of the lake; good views of the Dent du Chat and the Abbaye de Hautecombe on the opposite shore. Just beyond **Brison-les-Oliviers**, a fishing village with a strong wine-growing tradition, the road runs close to the shores of the lovely Baie de Grésine and on to Aix-les-Bains.

‡‡ **Aix-les-Bains** – See AIX-LES-BAINS.

ROUTE DU MONT DU CHAT

② From Yenne to Le Bourget-du-Lac

34km/21mi – about 1hr 30min

Yenne – The small capital of the Bugey Savoyard region occupies a favourable position at the entrance of the Défilé de Pierre Châtel, through which the Rhône forces its way out of the Alps.

The west doorway of the 12C-15C **church** has retained some fine Romanesque capitals; inside, the stalls, dating from the 15C, are delicately carved with Flamboyant motifs. The sacristy contains a fine Christian tombstone from the 6C.

The town centre offers pleasant walks through its streets lined with old houses.

From Yenne take D 41 (which branches off D 921 to the left); from St-Paul continue south on D 41 past Trouet then turn left onto D 42 to the Lac du Bourget.

***Mont du Chat** – A television relay pylon (alt 1 504m/4 934ft) stands some 50m/55yd south of the pass. Fine **view** of Aix-les-Bains and the lake from the platform below (1 470m/4 823ft).

****Molard Noir** – *1hr return on foot from Mont du Chat.* Follow the ridge to the north, through the woods; from the clifftop on the west side, a good stretch of the Rhône Valley can be seen from the Défilé de Pierre Châtel north to the Grand Colombier. The top of Molard Noir (alt 1 452m/4 764ft, viewing tables) offers a vast **panorama** of Mont Revard and, beyond, of Aiguilles de Chamonix, Mont Blanc, La Vanoise, Belledonne and Mont Granier.

On the east side, the road meanders through the woods.

Continue on D 42 to Le Bourget-du-Lac.

Le Bourget-du-Lac – This lakeside town, once linked by steam ships to Lyon via the canal de Savières and the Rhône, is now an expanding holiday resort with a harbour and a beach along the Lac du Bourget.

Built on an ancient religious site, the **church** ⊘ was remodelled in the 15C and partly rebuilt in the 19C. Inside, the **frieze** running round the walls of the apse is a 13C masterpiece. Note also the fine tombstone hanging on the wall of the south aisle and the 15C font.

The **Château-Prieuré** ⊘, adjacent to the church, was built in the 11C then remodelled in the 13C and 15C. The tour includes the refectory, the kitchen, the chapel from which a staircase leads to an oratory opening on to the chancel of the church, and the library with its ceiling lined with Cordoba leather. The 15C cloisters consist of two superposed galleries. The attractive gardens are decorated with fountains and yew trees trimmed to look like chess pieces.

BOURG-ST-MAURICE

Population 6 056
Michelin map 89 fold 5 or 244 fold 21
Local maps see Le BEAUFORTAIN and Massif de la VANOISE

Bourg-St-Maurice is situated at the heart of the Haute-Tarentaise region and occupies a commanding position at the intersection of the upper Isère Valley, the Chapieux Valley and the road leading to Italy via the Col du Petit-St-Bernard.

For this reason, "Le Bourg", as the locals call it, is the ideal starting point of driving tours in the area.

The **"Fête des Edelweiss"** *(see Calendar of events)*, which takes place in July, is an international folk festival showing off the picturesque costumes of the Tarentaise and Aosta valleys.

In winter, ski enthusiasts can enjoy the sophisticated equipment of the fine resort of Les Arcs, whereas, in summer, white-water sports are extremely popular and numerous canoeing competitions take place on the Isère River.

SIGHT

Musée des minéraux et faune de l'Alpe ⊘ – *Avenue du Général-Leclerc.* Fine crystals in their natural setting.

EXCURSIONS

Chapelle de Vulmix ⊘ – *4km/2.5mi south.* This simple chapel, restored in the 17C, contains splendid 15C frescoes depicting the life of St Grat, known as the protector of crops; the legend begins on the south wall.

Hauteville-Gondon – *4km/2.5mi from Bourg-St-Maurice, drive along D 90 towards Aime then follow D 220.*

Musée du Costume ⊙ – Housed in the former presbytery, this museum illustrates the diversity of local costumes during the 19C and early 20C and displays specimens of the *frontière (see Introduction: Traditions and folklore)*, a headdress which became the symbol of Savoie.

Église St-Martin – Built in the 17C, the church is richly decorated in Baroque style: several 18C altarpieces including the fine polychrome retable over the high altar framing an illustration of St Martin's legend.

Les Arcs – *Take N 90 from the northeast exit of Bourg-St-Maurice and turn right almost immediately onto D 119. Arc 1600: 12km/7.5mi (or funicular during the season), Arc 1800: 15km/9.3mi, Arc 2000: 26km/16.2mi (see Les ARCS).*

★★Route du Petit-St-Bernard

31km/19.3mi – about 1hr 45min – local map see Massif de la VANOISE

This former international trade and military route today has a major tourist appeal as part of the famous "Tour du Mont-Blanc". The road leading to the pass on the French side has a 5% gradient as it climbs above the Isère Valley from 904m/2 966ft (at Seez) to 2 188m/7 178ft.

The pass is usually blocked by snow from the end of October to the end of May.
From Bourg-St-Maurice, take N 90 towards Val d'Isère and Italy.

Séez – This ancient village, situated along the main Roman way linking Milan and Lyon, became prosperous in the 19C through its woollen-cloth industry. This activity has recently picked up again after a long period of decline. The Baroque **Église St-Pierre** contains a splendid altarpiece by Fodéré, a local artist, and the 15C recumbent figure of a knight in armour to the left of the entrance.

Bear left as you leave Seez.

The road climbs in a series of impressive hairpin bends with Mont Pouri towering above to the south, offering views of the Moyenne-Tarentaise to the southeast, and then of the upper Isère valley towards the snow-capped peaks round Val d'Isère.

La Rosière – This pleasant resort situated at an altitude of 1 850m/6 070ft overlooks the Tarentaise from a superb commanding position.
Its ski slopes offer good snow coverage and plenty of sunshine within a vast international skiing area linked to the Italian resort of La Thuile. The Roc Noir, Traversette and Belvédère summits, the ski runs of San Bernardo and La Tour, afford splendid **views★★** of Mont Blanc.
In summer, La Rosière is a peaceful holiday resort offering a wide choice of excursions. There are kennels breeding the famous St-Bernard dogs nearby.

★Col du Petit-St-Bernard – Fierce fighting during the Second World War caused great damage to the hospice believed to have been founded by **St Bernard de Menthon** (923-1008) whose statue stands in front of the buildings. The institution provided shelter for travellers facing terrible snow storms. Further on stands the Colonne de Joux, originally surmounted by a statue of Jupiter (Jovis) which was replaced by a statue of the saint carved at the end of the 19C.

Jardin botanique La Chanousia – This recently relaid botanical garden contains about 1 000 species of Alpine plants.

★★★Lancebranlette – *4hr return on foot by a mountain path often in poor condition at the beginning of summer. Mountain boots are recommended. Detailed information is available at the Chalet de Lancebranlette.*
From the chalet, climb the northwest slope of the pass towards an indented crest on the left. An isolated building halfway up the slope is a useful landmark to aim for. Once you reach a vast cirque in a landscape of screes and pastures, keep going left to join the path which winds all the way up to the summit (2 928m/9 606ft). Vast **panorama** including the Italian side of Mont Blanc *(viewing table)*.

Every year
the Michelin Red Guide France
revises the town plans which show
– through routes, by-passes, new streets,
– new roads, one-way systems, car parks
– the exact location of hotels, restaurants, public buildings...
this up-to-date information makes town driving less stressful.

BRIANÇON ★★

Population 11 038
Michelin maps 77 fold 18, 189 fold 9 or 244 folds 42 and 43
Local map see Le BRIANÇONNAIS

Europe's highest town (1 321m/4 334ft) occupies a strategic position at the intersection of the Guisane, Durance, Cerveyrette and Clarée valleys, close to the Montgenèvre Pass leading to Italy. This explains the number of strongholds surrounding the town. The old fortified town or **Ville Haute**, surrounded by a ring of forts planned by Vauban, Louis XIV's military engineer, has retained its steep narrow streets; below the fortifications lies the new town, known as **Ste-Catherine**, with its shops, station and barracks of *chasseurs alpins* (mountain troops). The district of **Briançon-Forville**, situated west of the old town has been a health resort since the 1930s.

Briançon, which has had a military skiing school since 1904, forms part of the winter sports complex of **Serre-Chevalier** *(see SERRE-CHEVALIER)* and is close to the **Montgenèvre** *(see MONTGENÈVRE)* ski resort.

The capital of Briançonnais – According to the **Grande Charte** granted to them in 1343 and later confirmed by the kings of France, 52 municipalities of the Briançonnais region, situated on either side of the border with Italy, formed a kind of free state

Aerial view of Briançon

116

with Briançon as their capital; one of their privileges was to fix and levy their own taxes. Thirty-two of these municipalities became Italian under the Treaty of Utrecht signed in 1713.

A military town – The rock, which towers over the Durance, was fortified in turn by the Celts and the Romans and again during the Middle Ages. The fortifications were strengthened in 1590 by the Huguenot commander Lesdiguières and a second wall was erected in 1690. However, after a fire destroyed most of the town in 1692, Louis XIV asked Vauban to rebuild the fortifications as war had broken out between France and Savoie. Vauban undertook the building of a ring of forts which was completed almost 200 years later. After Napoleon's defeat at Waterloo in 1815, Briançon was besieged by allied forces but held on until peace was signed under the Treaty of Paris several months later.

★★VILLE HAUTE *1hr 30min – Parking on the Champ de Mars*

The walled city is accessible through four gates: Porte Pignerol to the north, Porte d'Embrun to the southwest, Porte de la Durance to the east and Porte Dauphine recently opened to ease the flow of traffic.

It is divided into four districts by the intersection of Grand-Rue and rue Porte-Méane prolonged by rue du Pont d'Asfeld: Quartier du Temple grouped round the Collégiale Notre-Dame, Quartier Mercerie with the Place d'Armes in its centre, which was the commercial and administrative district, the residential district of the Grand Caire to the northeast and Quartier de Roche which included the various monasteries (Récollets, Pénitents...). Two steep streets running through the town, known as *gargouilles*, have a fast-flowing stream in their middle.

Porte Pignerol – As was usual in the 18C, the gate comprises several separate defences. The outer gate, rebuilt in the 19C, bears a mention of the 1815 siege. The guardhouse, known as "d'Artagnan" (**R**), houses temporary **exhibitions** ⊙ in summer. Next come the drawbridge, a gate reinforced by a portcullis and another gate decorated with a splendid frontispiece. A vaulted passage gives access to the walled town. Exhibitions devoted to "Three hundred years of military architecture" are held in the building adjacent to the Porte Pignerol.

★**Viewing table** – It offers a good view of the three tiers of fortifications matching the terrain, of the modern town below, of the Fort des Salettes to the north with Croix de Toulouse above it, of the mountains framing the Briançon Basin and of the Montgenèvre Pass to the east.

Collégiale Notre-Dame – Built during the early 18C, this imposing edifice has a remarkable façade flanked by two high towers decorated with sundials. The left-hand one, dating from 1719, is in Baroque style; it is one of the finest painted sundials in the Alps. The stone lions placed in front of the doorway belonged to a church demolished in 1692. Inside, the nave is vast and the transept crossing is surmounted by an octagonal dome on pendentives. The church is richly decorated: stalls and pulpit in carved walnut, many 17C and 18C pictures, 18C organ case.

Standing next to the Collégiale, the 18C **Ancien hôtel de ville** (**B**) contains the Grande Charte granted to the town in 1343, *(see p 116).*

Petite Gargouille: rue du Commandant-Carlhan (**7**) **and rue de la Mercerie** (**20**) – Narrower and lined with fewer shops than the Grande Gargouille, this street has retained some austere façades and picturesque steps leading to doors decorated with wrought iron.

Porte d'Embrun – Viewed from here, Vauban's fortifications are particularly impressive as they show how this engineer of genius made up for the sloping terrain.

The Grande Gargouille starts from place du Médecin-Général-Blanchard.

★**Grande Gargouille or Grand-Rue** – This is the main shopping street of the walled town, very lively in summer on either side of its fast-flowing middle stream. Going up the street, note the Fontaine Persens on your left and the beautiful doorway of no 64, dating from 1714. A street to the right leads to the former Cordelier monastery (now the town hall) and to its **church** ⊙ (**N**); the imposing façade is decorated with Lombard arcading and there are 15C murals over the barrel-vaulting of the chapel situated on the left of the chancel.

Place d'Armes (**3**) – Its brightly coloured façades and pavement cafés convey a southern atmosphere to this former market square linking the Grande Gargouille and Petite Gargouille; it is decorated with two **sundials**. The left-hand one, painted in the 18C on the façade of the former prison, bears the simple inscription "Life slips by like a shadow", whereas the right-hand one, which adorns the lawcourts, dating from the 19C, bears the more elaborate inscription "From sunrise to sunset, this fleeting shadow rules simultaneously over the work of Themis (the goddess of justice) and of Mars (the god of war)".

Continue up the Grande Gargouille.

The **Fontaine François I**, named after the French king who made a present to the town of the elephants' heads decorating the fountain, stands under an archway on a street corner. The **Maison Jean Prat** (**D**), at no 37 across the street, has a fine Renaissance front decorated with masks and statues (St John the Evangelist with two angels). La **Maison des Têtes** (**E**) at no 13 was decorated at the turn of the century with figures in regional costume representing the owner's family.

Retrace your steps and turn left in rue du Pont-d'Asfeld.

It leads to the "religious" district. The **Chapelle des Récollets** ⊙ (**F**) houses art exhibitions in summer; a little further on stands the **Chapelle des Pénitents** (**K**) with its fine restored steeple. The street ends at the **Porte de la Durance**.

From the terrace, there is a beautiful **view** of the River Durance and Pont d'Asfeld below.

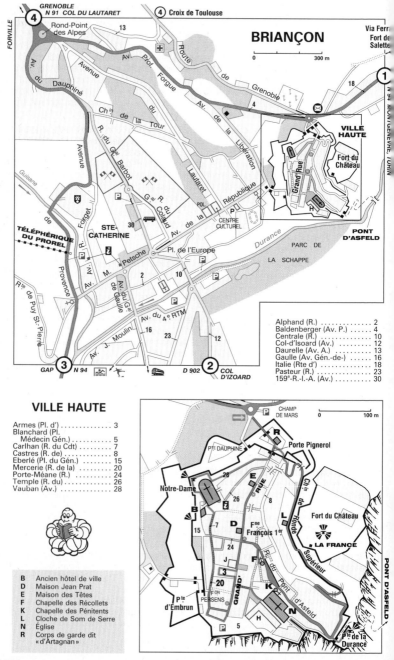

BRIANÇON

VILLE HAUTE

B Ancien hôtel de ville
D Maison Jean Prat
E Maison des Têtes
F Chapelle des Récollets
K Chapelle des Pénitents
L Cloche de Som de Serre
N Église
R Corps de garde dit
   « d'Artagnan »

★**Pont d'Asfeld** – This single-arched bridge spanning the Durance 56m/184ft above the river bed was built in 1729-31 by military engineers headed by Asfeld, Vauban's successor, in order to link the town with the Fort des Trois Têtes.

Continue along the chemin de ronde supérieur (upper watchpath).

Chemin de ronde supérieur – It overlooks the roofs of the walled city with the towers of the Collégiale Notre-Dame rising above and skirts the **Fort du Château** ⊙ in front of which stands a 9m/30ft-high statue of "**France**"★ by Bourdelle. On the left, a small spire houses the **Som de Serre bell** (**L**), used in the past to sound the alarm.

Continue to the Porte Pignerol.

EXCURSIONS

★Fort des Salettes ⊙

From the Champ de Mars, 45min return on foot along the chemin des Salettes.

Designed by Vauban, the fort was built after his death in 1708 and remodelled during the 19C. It was intended to guard the access to Briançon from Montgenèvre and Italy. Its small keep standing in the middle of a courtyard is surrounded by bastions linked to it by underground passages.

From the platform in front of the fort, there is an interesting **view**★ of the walled town and its ring of forts.

★★Croix de Toulouse 8.5km/5.3mi – about 1hr

Leave Briançon by ④ on the town plan and turn left onto D 232^T towards Croix de Toulouse. The narrow road rises through pine trees in a series of hairpin bends. Carry on along the unsurfaced part and leave the car near a blockhouse. It is also possible to reach Croix de Toulouse on foot *(2hr return)* from the Fort des Salettes. A well-marked path runs along the cliffside offering fine views.

Croix de Toulouse (alt 1 962m/6 437ft) is a rock spur situated at the extremity of a ridge separating the Guisane and Clarée valleys and towering over Briançon. From the viewing table, the view extends on one side to the walled town, with its ring of forts and the Durance Valley in the distance, and embraces on the other side the whole Guisane Valley up to the Col du Lautaret.

Via ferrata – *The path leading to the foot of the cliff starts between two cafés opposite the Champ de Mars parking (15min walk). The course ends just east of Croix de Toulouse and it is possible to go back along the chemin des Salettes.*

★★Téléphérique du Prorel ⊙

Start from the cable-car station in the Ste-Catherine district. The journey is in two sections and it is possible to do part of the journey or take a one-way ticket only. Be prepared to face strong winds blowing continuously at the top.

On the way up, there are superb views of the summit (2 566m/8 419ft). There are numerous possibilities of fine walks to the surrounding heights offering magnificent **panoramic views**★★. You can go back down towards Chantemerle or Puy-St-Pierre (via the Chapelle Notre-Dame-des-Neiges).

Chapelle Notre-Dame-des-Neiges – Alt 2 292m/7 520ft. *15min on foot; marked path.* This small chapel decorated with ex-votos can be reached from the cable-car station; it offers a fine view of the Serre-Chevalier Valley.

It is possible to return to Briançon along the marked path running through the high pastures (about 2hr 30min).

Round tour via Puy-St-André and Puy-St-Pierre

15km/9.3mi – about 1hr

From Briançon, drive southwest towards Puy-St-Pierre.

The small road rises quickly above the Durance Valley. Beyond the village of **Puy-St-André**, it affords interesting **views** of the Massif de la Condamine and Les Écrins.

Puy-Chalvin – The 16C **Chapelle Ste-Lucie** ⊙ standing at the heart of this hamlet is covered with murals inside and outside. The front is decorated with panels, separated by interlaced motifs, illustrating scenes from the Passion and representing various saints. Inside, the paintings in naïve style depict scenes from the life of Christ.

Return to Puy-St-André and drive to Puy-St-Pierre along D 335.

Puy-St-Pierre – Almost completely destroyed during the Second World War, this hamlet has retained a church standing on the edge of a cliff and offering a splendid **panorama**★★ of Briançon and the Durance Valley. At night, the lit-up church can be seen clearly from the Ste-Catherine district in Briançon.

Continue along D 335 then D 35 to return to Briançon.

Le BRIANÇONNAIS★★

Michelin map 77 folds 7, 8 and 18, 189 folds 8 and 9 or 244 folds 42 and 43
Local map see opposite

The geography of the Briançonnais is marked by striking contrasts which Vauban described in the following terms: "The area includes mountains reaching for the sky and valleys sinking to incredible depths". In the centre of the area lies Briançon at the intersection of four valleys (Guisane, Clarée, Durance and Cerveyrette). During the Middle Ages, the communities of these valleys formed a kind of federation under the terms of the Grande Charte *(see BRIANÇON)*. The large stone-built houses, decorated with arcades and columns, testify to the fact that the inhabitants were relatively well off. The region is well known for its southern mountain climate, clear skies, unmistakable light and good snow coverage which encouraged the early development of important ski resorts such as Montgenèvre and Serre-Chevalier.

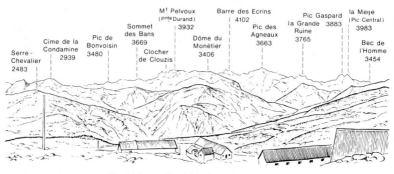

The high massifs visible from the Col de Granon

★VALLÉE DE LA GUISANE

This wide valley, linking the Haute-Durance and Romanche valleys, has acquired a high reputation for the practice of cross-country skiing, ski-trekking and on-piste skiing within the Serre-Chevalier winter sports complex.

① From the Col du Lautaret to Briançon

28km/17.4mi – about 45min – local map see opposite

★★**Col du Lautaret** – *See L'OISANS: VALLÉE DE LA ROMANCHE and SERRE-CHEVA-LIER: HIKES.*

The imposing mass of the Meije glaciers comes into view soon after the Col du Lautaret. The road goes through a wide valley, relatively arid except for the larch forest covering the north-facing slope *(ubac)*. On the way down from the pass, road N 91 skirts the barren slopes of **Grand Galibier** (alt 3 229m/10 594ft). The Grand Pic de Rochebrune can be seen in the distance, down the valley, beyond Briançon. The valley then widens and villages begin to appear.

Le Casset – The elegant steeple rises above the steep roofs of this hamlet lying at the foot of the Glacier du Casset. An Information Centre of the Parc national des Écrins is open in summer *(See SERRE-CHEVALIER: HIKES).*

★**Le Monêtier-les-Bains** – *See SERRE-CHEVALIER.*
In Villeneuve, turn left onto the road leading to La Salle-les-Alpes.

La Salle-les-Alpes – *See SERRE-CHEVALIER.*

★★★**Serre-Chevalier** – *See SERRE-CHEVALIER.*
In Chantemerle, take D 234ᵀ up to the Col de Granon.

The road climbs up the arid slopes overlooking the left bank of the River Guisane, offering broad views of the Briançonnais Mountains and Écrins Massif.

★★**Col de Granon** – Leave the car beyond the barracks and climb to a viewing table on the right: from there, the **panorama** *(see above)* unfolds in front of your eyes.
Go back along D 234ᵀ and rejoin N 91 via the old village of St-Chaffrey.

★★**Briançon** – *See BRIANÇON.*

★★VALLÉE DE LA CLARÉE

This picturesque valley owes its name to the clear waters of the mountain stream running through it. Its slopes being unsuitable for ski-lifts, it has retained its lovely villages, its hamlets, its houses covered with larch shingles and decorated with sundials and its churches adorned with fine murals.
Landscapes change considerably as one drives up the long and narrow valley, fresh and pleasantly wooded at first, then more open and also more densely populated beyond Plampinet, when it suddenly veers to the left. The upper part again becomes narrower as the Clarée comes cascading down among woods of larch trees against the austere landscape formed by a vast glacial cirque crowned by Mont Thabor.

② From Briançon to Chalets de Laval

30km/18.6mi – about 2hr – local map see below

★★**Briançon** – *See BRIANÇON – tour of the town: 1hr 30min*
Leave Briançon by ① on the town plan, N 94 towards Montgenèvre.

The road overlooks the narrow valley of the River Durance and the Pont d'Asfeld with the Chalvet summit towering above the Clarée Valley.

In La Vachette, bear left along D 994ᴳ, which goes up the Clarée Valley.

Shortly beyond La Vachette, the road reaches the confluence of the rivers Durance and Clarée. The mighty river of the southern Alps looks very disappointing compared to its tributary, the Clarée, which the road follows from that point.

Val-des-Prés – Lovely village with typical houses resting on an arcaded base. The **church** has an imposing square bell-tower with two tiers of Romanesque arcading and a large portico in characteristic regional style.

The road follows the Clarée among pine trees through one of the most attractive parts of the valley.

Plampinet – Situated at the top of the village, the **Église St-Sébastien** ⊙ is a solid building, characteristic of mountain architecture, decorated with a fine sundial. The richly decorated interior comes as a surprise. The **murals★**, dating from 1530, which are probably the work of an artist from Piedmont, are remarkable for their lively details and warm colours (ochre, dark red and brown).

Note in particular 19 scenes depicting the Passion in the bay preceding the chancel and an illustration of the Annunciation on the arch separating the nave and the chancel.

The **Chapelle Notre-Dame-des-Grâces** ⊙ has also retained a set of 16C **murals★**, slightly older than those of the church, illustrating the Virtues and the Vices. Kneeling women symbolising the virtues are placed above the seven capital sins mounted on various animals. Other paintings have recently been discovered opposite the entrance.

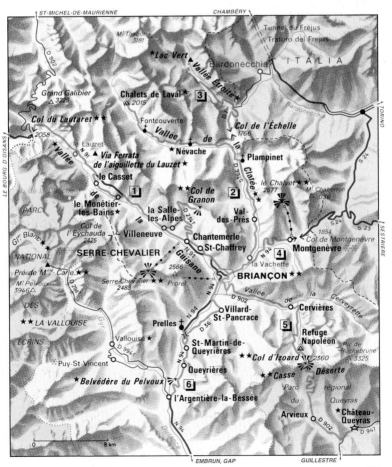

The valley becomes more open beyond Plampinet. The road leading to the Vallée Étroite *(see below)* starts on the right between Plampinet and Névache.

★**Névache** – The **church** ⊙ of the "Ville haute" was built in 1490 following a vow made by Charles VIII during a pilgrimage in Notre-Dame-d'Embrun. The site chosen was that of the castle. The 11C tower was retained as the base of the steeple. A representation of the Annunciation decorates the tympanum of the west doorway, in green and pink marble. The **wooden doors** are beautifully **carved** with scenes of the Deposition and interlaced Gothic motifs. There is a similar doorway on the south side.

Inside, there is a fine Baroque altarpiece in gilt larch wood decorated with 15 statues. The presbytery houses a small **Musée d'art religieux** ⊙ displaying religious objects and larch statues dating from the 17C and 18C.

The **treasury**, exhibited in the cell of the former castle, includes an 11C copper pyx inlaid with enamel.

The gallery dates from the 16C.

Beyond Névache, the road crosses an area of high pastures brightened up by several cascading streams and a carpet of wild flowers in early summer.

Along the way, note the picturesque shingle roofs of the Chalets de Fontcouverte and its lovely **chapel**. The Cascade de Fontcouverte is nearby.

★**Chalets de Laval** – The road ends here (alt 2 015m/6 611ft). This is the starting point of several mountain excursions such as the ascent of Mont Thabor.

★VALLÉE ÉTROITE

★③ Itinerary via the Col de l'Échelle

From Vallée de la Clarée – 17km/10.6mi – about 2hr – local map see p 121

The road leading to the Vallée Étroite, which goes over to the Italian side, is open from mid-June to mid-November exclusively to private cars.

Between Plampinet and Névache, turn right onto D 1 towards Col de l'Échelle.

Col de l'Échelle – Alt 1 766m/5 794ft. This is the lowest border pass in the western Alps. On the Italian side, the road goes down steeply towards the Bardonecchia Valley, with views of the Vallée Étroite and Mont Thabor.

★**Vallée Étroite** – This valley, which was Italian territory between 1713 (Treaty of Utrecht) and 1947, still retains its signposting in Italian, although it now forms part of the municipality of Névache, the largest in the Hautes-Alpes *département*. It is similar to the Vallée de la Clarée but on a smaller scale and offers a landscape of larch trees growing among scree-covered slopes.

★**Lac Vert** – *1hr return on foot. Leave the car at the CAF refuge and continue along the road until you reach the signpost "lago verde". Follow the path.* The small lake suddenly appears framed by larch trees; its colour is due to the profusion of green algae that it contains and its clear icy water.

Lac Vert

ROUTE DE MONTGENÈVRE

④ From Briançon to Montgenèvre
12km/7.5mi – about 30min – local map see p 121

★★**Briançon** – *See BRIANÇON – tour of the town: 1hr 30min.*
Leave Briançon by ① on the town plan, N 94.
The road overlooks the deep valley of the River Durance. Leaving on the right the road which follows the Clarée Valley, it rises rapidly, offering glimpses of the Briançon Basin and the Clarée Valley. As Montgenèvre gets nearer, pine trees give way to a forest of larches.

☀☀**Montgenèvre** – *See MONTGENÈVRE.*

★★ROUTE DE L'IZOARD

⑤ From Briançon to Château-Queyras
See Route de l'IZOARD – local map see p 121

HAUTE DURANCE

⑥ From Briançon to l'Argentière-la-Bessée
17km/10.6mi – about 1hr – local map see p 121

★★**Briançon** – *See BRIANÇON – tour of the town: 1hr 30min.*
Leave Briançon by ③ on the town plan, N 94, then turn right and cross the Durance towards Villard-St-Pancrace.

Villard-St-Pancrace – Note the fine houses in typical Briançonnais style. The 15C **church** has two beautiful south doorways with triple arching resting on slender columns. The artist's signature (1542 J Ristolani) can be seen on the left-hand jamb of the right-hand doorway. A sundial bears the Latin inscription: "They (the hours) all wound, the last one kills".
Next to the church stands the 17C **Chapelle des Pénitents** ⊘ and on a hilltop the **Chapelle St-Pancrace** ⊘, which contains 15C murals.
Drive through the old village of Villard-St-Pancrace and continue along D 36 to rejoin N 94.

Prelles – The **Chapelle St-Jacques** ⊘, situated in the high street, has retained some 15C **murals★**; in the oven-vaulted chancel, there is a Christ in Glory inside a mandorla with the 12 apostles lined up beneath. The arch separating the nave and the chancel is decorated with an illustration of the Annunciation. Scenes depicting the life of pilgrims on their way to Santiago de Compostela can be seen on the left-hand wall of the nave.
Rejoin N 94 and drive south.
Between Prelles and Queyrières, the road clings to the cliffside above the gorge through which flows the River Durance.

St-Martin-de-Queyrières – The church standing on the roadside has a high steeple, typical of the Embrun region, and two doorways.

Queyrières – This village, backing onto a rock, is characteristic of the Briançonnais area.

★**Belvédère du Pelvoux** – A viewing table placed near the road helps to locate the main summits of the Écrins Massif, which can be seen through the depression of the lower Vallouise.

L'Argentière-la-Bessée – *See L'ARGENTIÈRE-LA-BESSÉE.*

BUIS-LES-BARONNIES

Population 2 030
Michelin map 81 fold 3 or 245 folds 17 and 18
Local map see Les BARONNIES

Buis-les-Baronnies lies on the banks of the River Ouvèze, where the valley opens out beyond the Gorges d'Ubrieux *(see ROUTE DES PRINCES D'ORANGE)*.
Sheltered by the heights of the Baronnies, the town enjoys a mild climate which favours the growth of olive, apricot, cherry and almond trees as well as lavender. The area also produces *herbes de Provence* (aromatic herbs) and lime tea; a lively international **fair★** held in Buis-les-Baronnies, along the Ouvèze, on the first Wednesday in July, brings together some 80% of the French production.

OLD TOWN *1hr*

Esplanade – This alleyway, shaded by plane trees, runs along the Ouvèze, where the town walls once stood; it is a typical Provençal *cours* (avenue), particularly lively on market days *(Wednesday mornings)*.

Place du Marché – This "square", looking more like a wide street, is lined with slightly pointed stone arcades dating from the 15C.

Rue de la Conche – The shopping street has retained a few fine doorways.

Turn left into rue de la Commune.

Former Dominican monastery – The recently restored 16C building has been turned into holiday accommodation. Note the staircase and the cloisters.

Walk past a gate on the left and through a vaulted passageway called rue de la Cour-du-Roi-Dauphin.

Church ⊘ – Burnt down during the Wars of Religion and rebuilt in the 17C, it contains wood carvings and stalls from the former Dominican church.

Walk along the left side of the church.

Former Ursuline convent – Founded in the 17C, it is now a cultural centre. The only original feature left is the fine Renaissance doorway of the chapel.

Maison des Arômes ⊘ – *Rue de l'Église.* This medieval building houses a collection of aromatic and medicinal plants from the Baronnies area: lime tea, lavender, saxifrage etc.

Walk past the east end of the church to avenue Aristide-Briand and return to the Esplanade then go to the embankment on the right bank of the river.

The **Tour de Saffre** (12C) is the only part of the town walls left.

EXCURSION

From Buis-les-Baronnies to Montbrun-les-Bains
27km – allow 2hr

Leave Buis-les-Baronnies on D 5 then turn left onto D 72.

The road follows the wild valley of the River Derbous.

Take D 526 on the left.

Clue de Plaisians – The road goes through a narrow gorge beneath overhanging cliffs. Good view of Mont Ventoux beyond the village of Plaisians.

Return to D 72 and turn left.

Col de Fontaube – Alt 635m/2 083ft. There is a fine view downstream of the rocky Derbous Valley, which becomes less arid as one continues upstream.

Brantes – This picturesque village clinging to the northern slope of the Toulourenc Valley, at the foot of Mont Ventoux, is well worth a visit. Beyond the fortified gate at the top of the village, lie the small 18C Chapelle des Pénitents Blancs (temporary exhibitions), part of a Renaissance manor house and the richly decorated fortified church.

On the way up to **Col des Aires** along D 41, there are lovely **views**★ of Brantes and its grandiose **setting**★, the Toulourenc Valley and the north side of Mont Ventoux.

Reilhanette – Built on a height overlooking the Toulourenc Valley, this picturesque village is topped by the ruins of its castle.

★**Montbrun-les-Bains** – *See MONTBRUN-LES-BAINS.*

Michelin Maps (scale 1: 200 000) which are revised regularly, indicate:
– *golf courses, sports stadiums, racecourses, swimming pools, beaches, airfields,*
– *scenic routes, public and long-distance footpaths, viewpoints,*
– *forest parks, interesting sights…*

*The perfect complement to the **Michelin Green Guides** for planning holidays and leisure time.*

*Keep current **Michelin Maps** in the car at all times.*

Ponts de la CAILLE ✢

Michelin map 89 fold 14 or 244 fold 18 – 4km south of Cruseilles

The two very different bridges spanning side by side the gorge of the Usses, 150m/492ft above the river bed, form a fascinating **picture**★.

The **Pont Charles-Albert**, a suspended bridge commissioned in 1838 by Charles-Albert de Sardaigne, is no longer in use.

The **modern bridge**, inaugurated in 1928, consists of a single arch with a 138m/453ft span, one of the largest concrete (non-reinforced) arches of its kind.

> **Detour to Bains de la Caille** – *6km/3.7mi drive. Take D 227 on the left, 600m/0.4mi north of the bridges.* In Féchy, turn left again onto a charming road winding its way through pastures and orchards to the bottom of the gorge, which it reaches after Goths. The road ends at "Bains de la Caille" *(private property):* at that point, the two bridges are exactly overhead.

CASTELLANE ★

Population 1 349
Michelin map 81 fold 18, 114 fold 10 or 245 fold 35
Local maps see Lacs de CASTILLON ET CHAUDANNE
and Grand Canyon du VERDON

This tourist centre, located at the intersection of the Route Napoléon and Route du Haut-Verdon, close to the famous canyon, lies at the foot of a 184m/604ft-high limestone cliff in one of the most striking **settings**★ of the Haute-Provence region. At first, an ancient fort occupied the top of the cliff; then a town was built in the valley below and surrounded with fortifications in the 14C.

Castellane

CASTELLANE

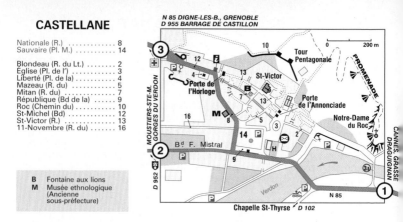

B   Fontaine aux lions
M   Musée ethnologique
      (Ancienne
      sous-préfecture)

SIGHTS

Place Marcel-Sauvaire (14) – This central square decorated with arcades and a fountain is lined with hotels, cafés, shops and administrative buildings.
In the rue Nationale nearby, no 34, which welcomed Napoleon on his way back from Elba in 1815, houses the small **Ethnological Museum** ⊘ (**M**).

Fortifications – Several sections of the walls built in 1359 are still standing: the **Tour Pentagonale** and two complete gates, the **Tour de l'Horloge** surmounted by a wrought iron campanile (near the Tourist Information Centre) and the **Porte de l'Annonciade**. There is a good overall view of the walls and the Tour Pentagonale from the chemin du Roc.

Old town – Situated north of place Marcel-Sauvaire, the old town includes some picturesque twisting lanes and a lovely **Fontaine aux lions (B)** along rue du Mitan.

Église St-Victor ⊘ – This 12C Romanesque church has a remarkable Lombard steeple with embossed angle stones (originally part of the walls) and wide openings with rounded arches. Inside, the quadripartite vaulting and the oven-vaulted apse are characteristic of the transition between the Romanesque and Gothic styles. The walnut decoration of the chancel and the baldaquin surmounting the high altar date from the 18C.

WALK

Chapelle Notre-Dame-du-Roc – *1hr return on foot.* Pleasant **walk**★ offering a fine overall view of Castellane nestling at the foot of its rock.
A path starting behind the church joins up with a wider one; turn right. This path, lined with the Stations of the Cross, rises rapidly over the roofs of the town and the machicolated Tour Pentagonale. Some ruined walls on the left are all that remain of the feudal village.
The chapel, surmounted by a tall statue of the Virgin Mary, dates from 1703; it stands on top of the cliff, 180m/590ft above the bed of the River Verdon and is a popular place of pilgrimage (note the large number of ex-votos).
From the terrace, the **view**★★ extends to the town, the 17C bridge spanning the river, the Castellane Basin surrounded by mountains and the beginning of the Gorges du Verdon.

EXCURSIONS

★**Chapelle St-Thyrse** – *7km/4.3mi south on D 102 towards Robion; beware of the narrowness of the access road.*
The picturesque road rises from the gorge to the plateau where the recently restored 12C Romanesque **chapel** stands in a remarkable **setting**★. The interior is decorated with blind arcading in the oven-vaulted apse and along the north and west walls of the nave.
The 3-tiered steeple is characteristic of early Romanesque style.

★★★**Grand Canyon du Verdon** – *See Grand Canyon du VERDON.*

★**Lacs de Castillon et Chaudanne** – *See Lacs de CASTILLON ET CHAUDANNE.*

"Explorers" of the Verdon Canyon

After several unsuccessful attempts, two local teams headed by a hydrologist, EA Martel, successfully canoed through the famous canyon (a total of 21km/13mi from Rougon) in 1905, after encountering many difficulties. They did it again the following year, but did not manage to reduce their journey time.

Lacs de CASTILLON ET CHAUDANNE ★

Michelin map 81 fold 18 or 245 fold 22

The Castillon and Chaudanne dams across the Verdon created two artificial lakes at the heart of a beautiful mountain setting.

The harnessing of the Verdon – The work undertaken on the River Durance was continued on its tributary, the Verdon, which was harnessed by the building of five dams in the space of 30 years. The first one built was the Barrage de Castillon, completed in 1947 and followed by the Barrage de Chaudanne. The last three were built at Gréoux *(see GRÉOUX-LES-BAINS)*, at Quinson and Ste-Croix *(see Lac de STE-CROIX)*. They provide the Provence region with an invaluable supply of water.

★TOUR OF THE LAKES (starting from Castellane)

47km/29.2mi – allow 3hr

★**Castellane** – *See CASTELLANE.*

Leave Castellane by ③ on the town plan and turn right onto D 955.

On the way up to Col de la Blache, there is a view of the Castellane Basin dotted with typical Provençal country houses.

At Col de la Blache, turn left onto D 402 towards Blaron.

The climb through the arid countryside offers fine views of the Lac de Castillon.

★**Panorama from Blaron** – *Leave the car at the entrance to Blaron village and continue along the footpath (15min return). From the promontory, there is a magnificent* **view** *of the Lac de Castillon, its tiny island and St-Julien-du-Verdon.*

Return to D 955 on the edge of the lake.

Barrage de Castillon – Stop by the belvedere to get a good view of the site: explanatory panels about the dam and the harnessing of the Verdon. This elegant arch dam is only 26m/85ft thick at the base. It is 200m/218yd long across the top and 100m/328ft high. The hydroelectric power station has the capacity to produce 77 million kWh.

The road runs across the dam then follows the left shore of the lake. A road on the right leads to the Col de Toutes Aures *(see Route de TOUTES AURES)*.

St-Julien-du-Verdon – The major part of the area surrounding St-Julien was drowned and the village is now on the edge of the lake (water sports centre).

Go back along the same road and turn left onto D 102 towards Demandoix.

The road rises in a series of hairpin bends. At Croix de la Mission, there is a fine **view**★★ of the Lac de Castillon. On the way down towards the Lac de Chaudanne, there are bird's-eye **views**★★ of this dark green mountain lake.

Barrage de Chaudanne ⊙ – This arch dam (total height 70m/230ft, length across the top 95m/104yd) is built across a gorge of the Verdon downstream from the Barrage de Castillon. The power station can produce 67 million kWh.

Return to Castellane along N 85.

---

*Find the best routes in town using the plans in the **Michelin Red Guide France** which indicate:*
– through routes, by-passes, new streets, one-way systems, car parks...
All the necessary information, revised annually.

Route de la CAYOLLE★★

Michelin map 81 folds 8 and 9 or 245 folds 10 and 23

This section of the Route des Grandes Alpes, linking the Ubaye and upper valley of the River Var, reveals deep gorges and wide panoramas.

FROM BARCELONNETTE TO ENTRAUNES

45km/28mi – about 1hr 30min

The Col de la Cayolle is usually blocked by snow from November to June.

★**Barcelonnette** – *See BARCELONNETTE.*
Between Barcelonnette and the pass, the narrow road runs along the bottom of the Gorges du Bachelard.

★**Gorges du Bachelard** – All the tributaries of this mountain stream have dug their way deeply through the forested area.
Road D 902 follows the Bachelard round the Mont Pelat Massif (alt 3 051m/10 010ft) almost to its source.

★★**Col de la Cayolle** – Alt 2 326m/7 631ft. The wide panorama extends south through the Var Valley to the Préalpes de Grasse in the distance. South of the pass, the road goes down into the upper valley of the River Var to Entraunes.

Entraunes – *See Haute vallée du VAR.*

HIKES

★★**Pas du Lausson and Col de la Petite Cayolle** – *4hr return on foot. Difference in altitude: 350m/1 148ft. Allow one day in order to derive full enjoyment from the beautiful landscapes.*
From the parking at Col de la Cayolle, walk towards Pas du Lausson; lovely views of the Val d'Entraunes. Just before reaching the ridge, admire the exceptionally rich flora. From the summit, there is a remarkable **panorama**★★, in particular towards the east and the Lac du Lausson. From the edge of the plateau, it is possible to get a good view of the **Lac d'Allos** and its surroundings *(see VAL D'ALLOS)*.
Go up, on the right, to **Lac des Garets**; view of the Sommet des Garets and Mont Pelat. After skirting the lake towards the right, one eventually reaches the Col de la Petite Cayolle (2 642m/8 668ft). In clear weather, the view extends to Mont Viso.
Go down on the right to return to the Col de la Cayolle.

CEILLAC ✳

Population 289
Michelin map 77 folds 18 and 19 or 245 fold 10
Local map see Le QUEYRAS

Situated at an altitude of 1 650m/5 413ft, at the confluence of two mountain streams, this lovely village has managed to retain its traditional character and, at the same time, to become one of the most attractive winter sports resorts of the Hautes-Alpes *département*, adapting its lifestyle and activities to the seasons.

THE RESORT

The Alpine **skiing area** is not extensive but has several good points in its favour: beautiful surroundings, fair snow coverage (owing to the altitude, a north-facing aspect and a good upkeep of the slopes), a reasonable gradient (800m/2 625ft) and variety. The skiing area, ideal for beginners and experienced skiers alike, appeals to anyone preferring the quality of the environment to the quality and number of facilities. There are interesting possibilities of ski-trekking towards the Col Girardin and the Cristillan Valley.
The more extensive cross-country skiing area offers 50km of good quality tracks.

In summer, the resort is the ideal starting point of hikes along GR 5 and GR 58 and a centre of rock-climbing, mountain biking, paragliding, angling and riding.

Église St-Sébastien ⊘ – The church is surmounted by an unusual 16C bell-tower housing six bells under a tiled louvre. Inside, the chancel is decorated with 16C murals with, in the centre, Christ in red inside a mandorla.
The **Chapelle des Pénitents** ⊘, adjacent to the church, is now a museum of religious art containing statues, altarpieces, sacred receptacles, paintings etc.

HIKES

Dogs must always be kept on a leash for the protection of cattle and wildlife.

★Vallon du Mélezet – *It is possible to drive upstream for 5km/3mi.* This picturesque valley, dotted with tastefully restored hamlets, has forested slopes rising above 2 000m/6 562ft and a waterfall known as **Cascade de la Pisse**.

★★Lac Ste-Anne – Alt 2 415m/7 923ft. *Park the car at the end of the Vallon du Mélezet road (1 967m/6 453ft). 2hr 15min return on foot.* Pleasant hike through a fine larch forest and across pastures. The deep bluegreen waters of the Lac Ste-Anne are held by a moraine deposited by a former glacier. The reflection of Pic de la Font Sancte adds to the beauty of the landscape. A small chapel stands by the lake (pilgrimage on 26 July).

Église St-Sébastien

★★Col Girardin – Alt 2 700m/8 858ft. *From the Lac Ste-Anne, 1hr 45min return by a narrow footpath, vertiginous in parts. Mountain boots recommended.*
The ascent of this pass situated on the border of the Parc naturel régional du Queyras and of the upper Ubaye Valley, is rewarded by a wide **panorama★★**.

EXCURSION

★Vallée de Ceillac down to Maison du Roy

9km/5.6mi – about 1hr

The road follows the Cristillan Valley; deep and narrow at first, it becomes wider and framed by vast arid slopes. The elegant 14C-15C **Église Ste-Cécile** stands isolated: its tympanum is decorated with a painting representing a Pietà.

Maison du Roy – *See Le QUEYRAS: Combe du Queyras.*

Le CHABLAIS★★

Michelin map 89 folds 2, 3 and 13 or 244 folds 8, 9 and 10
Local map see p 131

The Chablais, extending between Lake Geneva and the Giffre Valley, is the largest massif in the Préalpes. In spite of its complex geological structure, it has some imposing summits such as the Dent d'Oche and its twin peak the Château d'Oche.

Three-tiered area – The massif comprises three distinct areas.
The **Bas-Chablais** is a relatively low hilly area bordering the southern shores of Lake Geneva (Lac Léman in French), where woods of chestnut trees alternate with vineyards. The spa town of Évian-les-Bains is the lively centre of this Savoyard Riviera.
The **Pays Gavot**, situated inland from Évian, is a plateau limited to the south by the Dranse d'Abondance Valley and overlooked in the east by the cliffs of the Pic de Mémise. This open countryside, where woods and pastures predominate, is popular with hikers.
The **Haut-Chablais** (highest point: les Hautforts, alt 2 464m/8 083ft), centred round Morzine, is an area of pastures and forests. Three rivers have cut their way through it: the Dranse d'Abondance, Dranse de Morzine and Brevon, all of which are tributaries of the Dranse de Savoie flowing into Lake Geneva. This is the grazing area of the Abondance cows reputed for the quality of their milk.

Cow bells

GORGES DE LA DRANSE

① From Thonon to Morzine

33km/20.5mi – allow 1hr 45min – local map see opposite

The road follows the Dranse de Savoie Valley through a succession of narrow sections and small basins.

‡‡ **Thonon-les-Bains** – *See THONON-LES-BAINS.*
Leave Thonon by ② on the town plan, D 902 towards Cluses.

From Thonon to Bioge, the road follows the wooded Gorges of the Dranse where impressive red and ochre cliffs tower over the tumultuous stream.

★★**Gorges du Pont du Diable** ⊘ – *200 steps.* Enormous rocks, coloured in ochre, grey, green and blue by various deposits and eroded into all kinds of shapes, a luxuriant vegetation, vertical walls of smooth rock up to 60m/197ft high, all contribute to make this visit a fascinating one; landslides have occurred in places, forming huge piles of boulders and a spectacular natural bridge known as the Pont du Diable.

Stop further on by the Jotty dam and the Église de la Baume, perched on a height. Beyond the Défilé de Tines (tunnel) are the ruins of Notre-Dame d'Aulps.

Abbaye Notre-Dame d'Aulps – The ruins of the 12C-13C church are the only remaining part of this Cistercian abbey. The pilgrimage dedicated to St Guérin, a former abbot, now takes place in the neo-Gothic church of St-Jean-d'Aulps.

★★**Morzine** – *See MORZINE.*

ROUTE DES TROIS COLS

② From St-Jeoire to Thonon *55km/34.2mi – about 2hr*

This varied itinerary through green valleys linked by three mountain passes offers glimpses of Lake Geneva.
From St-Jeoire, drive north along D 26.

Between St-Jeoire and Onnion, the road affords views of the Giffre Valley and, in the distance, of the northern part of the Aravis range.

Gorges du Risse – The Risse flows through a densely forested gorge before joining the Giffre. Further upstream, near Mégevette, the valley offers a landscape of rolling pastures replaced by forests in its upper part leading to the Col de Jambaz.
At the pass, turn right towards Bellevaux then right again along D 236.

★**Vallon de la Chèvrerie** – The upper Brevon Valley, guarded by the narrow pass of La Clusaz, was the secluded site chosen for the **Chartreuse de Vallon** dedicated to St Bruno in the 12C and abandoned in 1619; two small chapels stand on either side of a lake formed by a landslide in 1943. The road ends at La Chèvrerie, beneath a cirque over which the Roc d'Enfer towers at 2 244m/7 362ft.

Go back to the Col de Jambaz, turn left and almost immediately right onto D 32.

Between the Col de Jambaz and the Col de Terramont, the road leaves the Risse Valley, briefly enters the Lullin Valley then the Vallon de Terramont. Further on, towards the Col du Cou, the road reveals the peaceful landscapes of the Vallée Verte framed by forested heights, including Les Voirons, Mont d'Hirmentaz and Mont Forchat (the latter bearing a white statue of St François de Sales).

★**Col de Cou** – Alt 1 116m/3 661ft. Beyond the forested pass, there is a **view**★ of Lake Geneva with the Jura mountain range in the distance.

During the drive down from the pass (16km/10mi), the road offers glimpses through the trees of the lake, of the Yvoire promontory, of Les Voirons and of the Jura mountains.

Further down, there are lovely **views**★ of the pleasant Bas-Chablais countryside overlooked by the ruins of the Château des Allinges.

In Mâcheron, turn left towards the Château des Allinges.

Château des Allinges – *See THONON-LES-BAINS.*

Road D 12 leads to Thonon.

⧓⧓ **Thonon-les-Bains** – *See THONON-LES-BAINS.*

★★ROUTE DES FALAISES DE MEILLERIE

③ From Évian to Novel

23km/14.3mi – about 1hr – local map see below

This itinerary takes you into the free zone *(see Practical information).*

⧓⧓⧓**Évian-les-Bains** – *See ÉVIAN-LES-BAINS.*

Leave Évian by ① on the town plan, along the lake shore.

The road is lined with imposing properties and passes beneath a gallery linking the Château de Blonay (16C-19C) to the shore. Beyond Lugrin, the road skirts the foot of the Meillerie cliffs within sight of Montreux on the Swiss shore of the lake, overlooked by the Rochers de Naye.

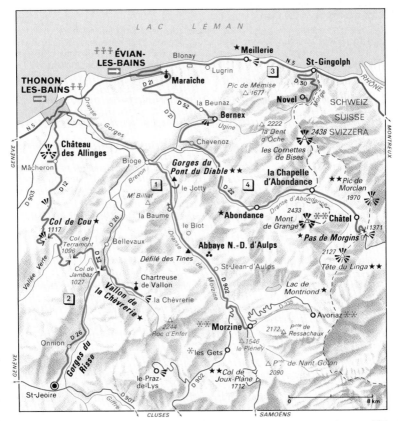

★**Meillerie** – This fishing village, where Rousseau staged some of the action of his *Nouvelle Héloïse*, nestles around its church (13C steeple) in a charming **setting**★ backed by the most impressive cliffs along Lake Geneva.

At the east end of the village, take the ramp down to the quayside where fishermen's nets are drying.

Beyond Meillerie, the view extends over the eastern part of the lake and the surrounding summits (Tour d'Aï).

St-Gingolph – This amusing border village has two sets of public monuments apart from the church and the cemetery situated on the French side.

In the 18C, St-Gingolph was held as one of the most important Swiss towns and young men wishing to enroll in the Swiss regiments of Louis XV's royal guard claimed to be from the Swiss part of the town.

Follow D 30 to Novel.

Novel – Splendid views of Lake Geneva. The village church has a typical Alpine bell-tower.

★ROUTE D'ABONDANCE

④ From Évian to Pas de Morgins

47km/29.2mi – about 2hr – local map see p 131

Before reaching Pas de Morgins, it is necessary to go through French customs in Vonnes (declare your intention to remain on French territory).

‡‡‡**Évian-les-Bains** – *See ÉVIAN-LES-BAINS.*

Leave Évian by ② on the town plan, D 21 towards Thollon.

Chapelle de Maraîche – This small chapel overlooking the lake has a graceful steeple surmounted by a campanile (16C).

Between Évian and St-Paul, road D 21 goes through vineyards and offers fine glimpses of the lake and of the Swiss shore where Lausanne shows like a light patch.

Between La Beunaz and Chevenoz, the itinerary makes a detour through the Ugine Valley over which tower the jagged peaks of Mont César and the Dent d'Oche.

Bernex – This holiday resort and small mountaineering centre is the starting point of the ascent of the Dent d'Oche (alt 2 222m/7 290ft).

From Vacheresse onwards, D 22 follows the deep wooded valley of the Dranse d'Abondance which opens up beyond Abondance. There are quite a few sawmills and chalets in typical local style with large roofs covered with light grey slates, gables marked with a cross and balconies with openwork wooden balustrades.

★**Abondance** – *See ABONDANCE.*

La Chapelle-d'Abondance – This is a charming family resort where typical regional houses, with wooden façades and carved openwork balustrades, are reminiscent of Swiss chalets across the border. The 18C church, decorated in Baroque style, has an elegant onion-shaped steeple.

The resort's ski-lifts give access to the Swiss resort of Torgon and to the whole Portes du Soleil skiing area. Every year in January, a cross-country skiing race over a distance of 35km/21.7mi starts here; there are fine cross-country tracks towards Châtel and Abondance as well as opportunities for snowshoeing, rambling along the Dranse and climbing to the top of the nearby summits.

Les Cornettes de Bises – *Allow 3hr. It is advisable to carry identity papers since the itinerary skirts the Swiss border.* From the village centre, walk north to Chalets de Chevenne then continue to climb alongside the stream to the Col de Vernaz on the Swiss border. Follow the ridge to Chalets de La Callaz, then start the last climb to the summit (alt 2 432m/7 979ft). The splendid **panorama**★★★ extends over the whole lake and the Alps from Mont Blanc to the Bernese Oberland.

Mont de Grange – *Allow 3hr 30min.* Cross the Dranse and walk south along the path leading to Chalets du Follière. The Alpine flora is particularly varied and chamois can be seen on the rocks high above the valley. The ascent starts at the end of the Chemine coomb; from the summit (alt 2 433m/7 982ft) there is a striking **view**★★ of the Val d'Abondance and the shores of Lake Geneva.

Beyond La Chapelle-d'Abondance, the peaks, pastures and forests of the vast Châtel Basin offer some of the best landscapes in the Haut-Chablais.

★★**Châtel** – The highest (1 235m/4 052ft) and one of the most attractive resorts of the Chablais region is camped on the south-facing slopes of the Dranse, covered with green pastures in striking contrast with the forested slopes of the Mont de Grange opposite. It became an important winter sports centre when Super-Châtel (1 647m/5 404ft) was created.

The **skiing area** extends over the Morclan and Linga massifs, linked by shuttle service, and forms part of the **Portes du Soleil** ✲ ✲ skiing area which offers 650km of pistes. The Linga area is particularly suitable for experienced skiers (Renards black piste) and is linked to the Avoriaz pistes via the Col de Bassachaux.

In summer, Châtel offers fine opportunities for drives as well as hikes (300km/186mi of footpaths link the 12 Portes du Soleil resorts).

★★**Pic de Morclan** – *Access by the Super-Châtel gondola* ⊙ *up to an altitude of 1 650m/5 413ft. The summit is reached on foot; allow 1hr 30min return.* From the summit (alt 1 970m/6 463ft) the **panorama** includes the Cornettes de Bises and Mont de Grange to the west and the Diablerets and jagged Dents du Midi on the Swiss side. It is possible to walk along the ridge to the Pointe des Ombrieux or to the Swiss **Lac du Goleit** *(from the La Conche cable-car station).*

★★**Tête du Linga** – Alt 2 127m/6 978ft. *Skiers have access by the Linga 1 cable-car and Linga 2 chair-lift. On arrival, go to the top of the Combes chair-lift and climb to the summit in a few minutes.* Splendid panorama of Morgins below, overlooked by the Dents du Midi.

★**Pas de Morgins** – Alt 1 371m/4 4981ft. The small lake lying at the heart of this forested area forms a picturesque landscape with the jagged heights of the Dents du Midi (Swiss Alps) in the background.

MICHELIN GUIDES

The Red Guides (hotels and restaurants)
Benelux – Deutschland – España Portugal – Europe – France – Great Britain and Ireland – Italia – Switzerland

The Green Guides (fine art, historical monuments, scenic routes)
Austria – Belgium – Berlin – Brussels – California – Canada – Chicago – England: the West Country – France – Florida – Germany – Great Britain – Greece – Ireland – Italy – London – Mexico –
Netherlands – New England – New York City – Paris – Portugal – Quebec – Rome – San Francisco - Scandinavia Finland – Scotland – Spain – Switzerland – Tuscany – Venice – Vienna – Wales – Washington
...and the collection of regional guides for France.

CHAMBÉRY ★★★

Population 54 120
Michelin map 89 fold 16 or 244 fold 29
Local maps see Les BAUGES, Massif de la CHARTREUSE and Route de l'ÉPINE

Chambéry was until the 16C the capital of the sovereign state of Savoie. The town developed in the narrowest part of the depression lying between the Bauges and Chartreuse massifs, close to the three main natural parks in the Alps: Parc national de la Vanoise, Parc naturel régional de Chartreuse and Parc naturel régional du massif des Bauges. In spite of having no striking monument, the capital of the counts and dukes of Savoie has retained a certain aristocratic elegance.

Chambéry is today the administrative centre of the Savoie *département* as well as a commercial city and an important junction. The well-restored old town has regained its past splendour with a hint at modernism in the *trompe-l'œil* paintings decorating some of the walls (in particular those of the covered market), and in the new house of culture (Espace André-Malraux), designed by the Swiss architect Mario Botta.

The capital of Savoie – Chambéry became the capital of the counts of Savoie in 1232. At that time, it was only a large village defended by a fortress. The expansion of the town is due to the prosperity of the House of Savoie and to the efforts of the **three Amédées**.

Amédée VI (Count of Savoie, 1343-1383), the "Green Count" – His nickname comes from the colours he wore when taking part in tournaments. He was a brave knight and a clever statesman, extending his domains towards Switzerland and Italy and taking part in a crusade against the Turks.

Amédée VII (Count of Savoie, 1383-1391), the "Red Count" – The fact that his armour was always covered with blood during the course of a battle accounts for his nickname. He acquired fame fighting the English side by side with the king of France, Charles VI and united the Comté de Nice with his Comté de Savoie.

Amédée VIII (Duke of Savoie, 1391-1434), the "Duke-pope" – He was made duke by the emperor of the Holy Roman Empire and acquired the Geneva and Piedmont provinces. In 1434, at the height of his fame, he abdicated and retired to the castle-monastery of Ripaille. He played the role of anti-pope for 10 years during the Great Schism before returning to his monastery as a simple monk.

After the three Amédées, Savoie went into decline until its prestige and influence were restored by Emmanuel-Philibert who made Turin the capital of Savoie, Chambéry remaining the seat of Justice of the duchy.

USEFUL TIPS

Transport – An electric minibus drives round the town's pedestrian areas. The itinerary is marked on the ground with yellow circles.

Markets – Tuesday and Saturday mornings on the place de Genève; Thursday on the place des Combes.

Where to have a drink in pleasant surroundings – Beer drinkers will love the wide choice available at the Transat (29 place Monge), the Café de l'Horloge (place St-Léger) and the Café du Théâtre (place du Théâtre), whereas the attraction of the rum bar Le Corsaire (avenue des Ducs de Savoie) lies in its youthful atmosphere and exotic setting.

Cyber cafés – Surfers on the Internet can indulge in their pastime while eating at the Café Curial (carré Curial) or drinking at the Coliseum (place d'Italie).

Wish to prolong the evening? – Aix-les-Bains offers many discotheques in original settings: La Péniche (barge), Le Bassamba (castle setting).

Specialities – Local cuisine includes typical invigorating Savoyard dishes such as those on the menu of the Savoyard Restaurant (25 place Monge) and freshwater-fish dishes such as those served at Les Belles Rives in Aiguebelette-le-Lac or L'Auberge du Pont-Rouge (avenue du Grand-Pont) and Le Cochelet (route du Bord du Lac) in Aix-les-Bains.

Confectionery – Chocolate truffles are renowned; in Chambéry they are made with fresh cream (instead of butter). Caramel sweets known as "mazet" are also delicious. There are several excellent confectioners including Mazet, 2 place Porte-Reine; Berland, 28 place St-Léger and the Chocolaterie Royale, 2 rue Albert I.

Drinks – "Chambérysette" is a dry vermouth flavoured with Alpine strawberries whereas the "Vermouth de Chambéry", going back to 1821, is made by macerating many herbs in dry white wine; "Bonal", on the other hand, is a tonic aperitif made with grape juice and gentian roots.

Handicraft – Opinel is a brand of knives of worldwide renown, produced in the vicinity of Chambéry by a dynasty of Savoyard craftsmen. A piece of jewellery in the shape of a cross is another example of local handicraft.

Leisure parks – The Parc du Buisson Rond offering many sporting activities; the Clos Savoiroux, on the Colline du Lémenc, and the sports trail of the Colline des Monts.

★★OLD TOWN *4hr walk including a tour of the castle*

A **small train** ⊙ takes tourists round the pedestrianised historic centre during the summer season. Many blind walls are decorated with impressive *trompe-l'œil* paintings by local artists.
Start from the Fontaine des Éléphants and follow the itinerary marked on the plan.

Fontaine des Éléphants (B F) – Chambéry's most famous monument was erected in 1838 to celebrate **Général Comte de Boigne** (1751-1830), a great benefactor of the town. The elephants are a reminder that he spent some time in India and returned with a fortune.
Follow the boulevard du Théâtre.

Théâtre Charles-Dullin (B T) – Rebuilt following a fire which seriously damaged it in the 19C, the theatre has retained the original stage curtain painted by Louis de Vacca in 1824, depicting "Orpheus's visit to the Underworld"; it is named after the famous actor-director from Savoie.
Continue along the boulevard du Théâtre to the Musée savoisien.

★Musée savoisien ⊙ **(B M¹)** – This museum is housed in a former Franciscan monastery, later used as the archbishop's residence; the 13C, 15C and 17C buildings, surrounding vast cloisters, contain an important collection of prehistoric and Gallo-Roman exhibits on the ground floor. The upstairs galleries are devoted to religious (mainly medieval) art and coins from Savoie. A fine collection of Primitive Savoyard paintings is being restored. There is also a set of non-religious late-13C murals. The ethnographical section displays a fine collection of objects illustrating traditional crafts, agriculture, daily life and popular art. The role played by the Savoie region during the Second World War is also explained.
Continue along rue Ducis, turn right into rue de la Croix-d'Or and right again into the passage Métropole leading to the cathedral.

★Cathédrale métropolitaine ⊙ **(St-François-de-Sales) (B)** – Known as "Métropole", the former church of the Franciscan monastery founded in the 13C, dates from the 15C and the 16C, when the Franciscan order was at its height. It became a *cathédrale métropolitaine* (archiepiscopal) in 1817. The late-15C west front is remarkable with its Flamboyant-Gothic decoration and early-17C wooden doors. The interior is surprisingly vast and the single vaulting over the aisle and side chapel is noteworthy; it was intended to compensate for the instability of the terrain. In 1835, the church was decorated in *trompe-l'œil* by Vicario who used the neo-Gothic style in fashion at the time.
The base of the 13C steeple houses the cathedral **treasury** ⊙: note in particular an ivory **diptych★** from the 10C, a 13C enamel pyx, a carved-wood representation of the Nativity and a 15C Flemish painting.
Walk back to rue de la Croix-d'Or.

Rue de la Croix-d'Or (B) – This street, lined with old mansions, was the most aristocratic avenue in Chambéry. The Hôtel de Châteauneuf at no 18 was built by an ironmaster in the 17C (remarkable **wrought-iron work★** in the courtyard). The **Hôtel des Marches et de Bellegarde** at no 13 opposite, has a lovely late-18C façade (Napoleon and Pope Pius VII both stayed there). Walk along the driveway to admire the staircase.

★Place St-Léger (B) – This vast oblong area was rebuilt and pedestrianised at the end of the 1970s: it was paved with pink porphyry, adorned with fountains and lampposts and its façades were restored and painted in warm colours; lined with numerous pavement cafés, it is the ideal place for a pause.

Rue Basse-du-Château (A 4) – Picturesque footbridge-gallery and old workshops. The street leads to the castle.

Place du Château (A 10) – Overlooked by the castle, the square is framed by the fine 18C **Hôtel de Montfalcon**, an Italian-style palace, and the 17C **Hôtel Favre de Marnix**. A statue of the de Maistre brothers *(see Introduction: Famous natives of the Alps)* stands in the centre.

★Château ⊙ **(A)** – This former residence of the counts and dukes of Savoie was rebuilt in the 14C-15C and partly destroyed by fire in the 18C when the building now housing the Préfecture was erected.
Follow the ramp which passes beneath the former Porterie (lodge) and leads to the courtyard surrounded by the Sainte-Chapelle and the Préfecture.

From the place du Château, there is a good overall view of the oldest part of the castle: the Tour du Carrefour on the left above a terrace, the former Chambre des Comptes in the centre, the east end of the Sainte-Chapelle on the right, the Tour Trésorerie next to it and the massive **Tour Demi-Ronde (K)** at the back.

Tour Trésorerie – 14C. Local history and family tree of the House of Savoie.

The Château in Chambéry

Salles basses – 14C. A monumental staircase leads to these barrel-vaulted rooms with 3m/10ft-thick walls, used as a chapel and a crypt and later as an arsenal.

★ **Sainte-Chapelle** (**A B**) – The east end of the 15C Flamboyant-Gothic chapel is surrounded by a watchpath. The Baroque façade dates from the 17C. The edifice was named Sainte-Chapelle when the Holy Shroud was deposited inside in 1502 (later transferred to Turin; a replica is exhibited).

Numerous historic weddings were celebrated inside, including that of Lamartine and his English wife, Miss Birch. The 16C stained-glass windows are remarkable. There are traces of *trompe-l'œil* frescoes (1836) by the Piedmontese artist Vicario. The large tapestry showing the arms of Savoyard towns was made to celebrate the union of Savoie and France.

A **peal of 70 bells** ⊘, made by the Paccard bell-foundry in Sévrier *(see Lac d'ANNECY)*, was placed inside the Tour Yolande in 1993.

Near the Tour Demi-Ronde, go down the steps leading to place Maché.

Go through the 15C Flamboyant archway of the **Portail St-Dominique** (**A E**), part of a Dominican monastery re-erected here in 1892.

From place Maché, start back towards the castle and turn left into rue Juiverie.

Rue Juiverie (**A**) – Bankers and money changers used to live in this street, recently pedestrianised. Look inside the courtyard of no 60.

Continue along the narrow rue de Lans leading to the place de l'Hôtel-de-ville.

Walk along the covered passage on the right (nos 5 and 6 place de l'Hôtel-de-ville), one of the many **"allées"** in the old town.

Rue de Boigne (**B**) – Designed by Général de Boigne, this street is lined with porticoes as is customary across the Alps, its orderly yet lively atmosphere makes it one of the town's most characteristic streets. It leads back to the Fontaine des Éléphants.

QUARTIER CURIAL (B)

Most of the buildings in this important military district, dating from the Napoleonic period, were restored when the army left in the 1970s.

Carré Curial – *The courtyard is freely accessible.* These former barracks, built in 1802 and modelled on the Hôtel des Invalides in Paris, have retained their original plan and have been refitted to house shops and offices.

Espace André-Malraux – Designed by Mario Botta, this house of culture containing a 900-seat theatre, audio-visual rooms and exhibition areas, stands next to the Carré Curial.

Centre de congrès "le Manège" – The former riding school of the Sard *carabinieri* is a harmonious blend of traditional military architecture and modern design. A transparent peristyle has been added.

Médiathèque Jean-Jacques-Rousseau – Designed by Aurelio Galfetti (1970), the building is crowned by a panoramic glass roof.

ADDITIONAL SIGHTS

Musée des Beaux-Arts ⊘ (A M²) – Temporary exhibitions are held on the ground floor, in the vaulted room where the people of Chambéry voted for the union with France, and on the first floor.

The second floor is devoted to Italian painting: works by Primitive Sienese artists (altarpiece by Bartolo di Fredi), Renaissance paintings (Portrait of a Man, attributed to Paolo Uccello) and works from the 17C and the 18C (Florentine and Neapolitan Schools in particular). The 19C is represented by two major trends, neo-classicism and realism. Still-life painting, Northern schools and regional painting are also represented.

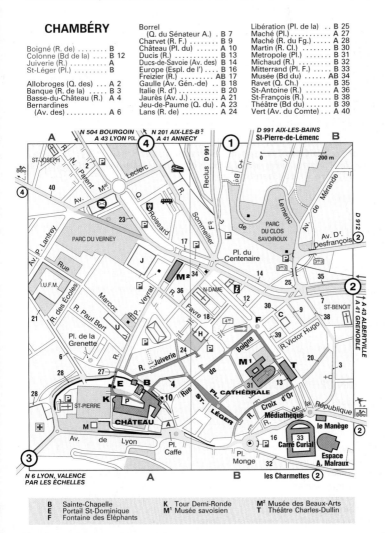

Église St-Pierre-de-Lémenc ⊘ **(B)** – The church stands on the site of an ancient Roman settlement; the priory to which it belonged was one of the liveliest religious centres in medieval times.

★**Crypt** – The Carolingian **baptistery**★ with its columns surmounted by plain capitals is a touching reminder of early Christianism. The chancel of the crypt was built in the 15C as a base for the Gothic church above. It contains a Deposition of the same period, mutilated during the Revolution.

EXCURSIONS

Les Charmettes ⊘ – *2km/1.2mi south. Leave Chambéry along rue Michaud (B 32). At the first major junction out of town, follow D 4 then drive straight on along the narrow surfaced alleyway leading to Les Charmettes. Stop by the former chapel below the house.*
Madame de Warens's country house, which Rousseau described in his *Confessions*, now belongs to the town of Chambéry. The careful restoration has preserved the 18C furnishings: on the ground floor, the dining room has a *trompe-l'œil* decoration and the music room recalls Rousseau's musical career. On the first floor are the rooms occupied by Rousseau and Madame de Warens preceded by an oratory.
The terraced garden overlooks the Chambéry Valley with Dent du Nivolet in the distance. It contains a collection of plants commonly used in the 18C.

✦**Challes-les-Eaux** – *6km/3.6mi southeast. From Chambéry, drive east along avenue Dr-Desfrançois, N 512, which veers southeast and joins N 6.*
This little spa town specialises in the treatment of gynecological and respiratory diseases. The spring waters are cold and contain a high proportion of sulphur.
The casino and the baths, in late-19C style, are pleasantly situated in a shaded park, east of N 6. The former 17C castle is now a hotel.

★**Mont St-Michel** – *9.5km/6mi east, then 1hr return on foot. Drive 1km south of Challes along N 6, turn left then left again onto D 21; at the Boyat junction, turn left then left again towards Montmerlet; leave the car near the hamlet (parking) and take the footpath on the right.*
There is a choice of several itineraries; as you go into the wood, the footpath on the right leads to the Chapelle du Mont St-Michel. Note the variety of tree species according to the aspect of the slopes. From the top, there is a bird's-eye **view** of the Chambéry depression, of the town and of Challes below, with the snow-capped peaks of the Belledonne range in the distance. The Lac du Bourget is partly visible to the northwest, with Mont du Chat towering above.

In his Confessions (Books V and VI), Jean-Jacques Rousseau states that his 10-year stay in Chambéry left him some of his best memories: "If there is a single little town in the world where one can lead a gentle life in pleasant company, it must be Chambéry".

MICHELIN GREEN GUIDES

Architecture
Fine Art
Ancient monuments
History
Geography
Picturesque scenery
Scenic routes
Touring programmes
Places to stay
Plans of towns and buildings
A collection of regional guides for France.

CHAMONIX-MONT-BLANC✳✳✳

Population 9 701
Michelin map 89 fold 4 or 244 fold 21
Local map see Massif du MONT-BLANC

Chamonix is the French mountaineering capital thanks to its Compagnie des guides and it also attracts many hikers who appreciate its 310km/192mi of footpaths. However, the resort mainly owes its popularity to the numerous viewpoints which offer some of the best and most spectacular landscapes in the Alps.

Since the first Winter Olympic Games were held here in 1924, Chamonix has become an important well-equipped ski resort.

The development of the resort has been helped since 1965 by the direct link to the Val d'Aoste and to Courmayeur provided by the Mont-Blanc tunnel *(see Massif du MONT-BLANC)*.

Today, the Chamonix valley looks like a built-up area, offering a mixture of architectural styles and incessant traffic going through during the high season. Its main attraction lies in its magnificent landscapes, lively atmosphere, numerous opportunities for practising sports and cultural events (Semaines musicales du Mont-Blanc). Lovers of peace and nature are advised to avoid school holidays.

Equipment – In summer, all the traditional sports are available (swimming, tennis, golf). Several cable-cars and the Montenvers railway fill up with one-day excursionists and mountaineers anxious to reach their base camp quickly.

The Chamonix Valley is well-equipped all round: the sunny skiing areas of La Flégère and Le Brévent are within easy reach, the Aiguille du Midi cable-car makes summer skiing possible in the Vallée Blanche and the Grands-Montets cable-car above Argentière gives access to some of the best snowfields in Europe. The town is now in the process of modernizing all the lift systems (7 cable-cars, 6 gondolas, 16 chair-lifts) in the valley, of doubling their number and of developing sports and leisure facilities.

Moreover, Chamonix offers ice-skaters first-class equipment with two artificial ice rinks, including a covered one which can be used in summer, and a speed rink.

The Gaillands rock-face is used for the training of rock-climbers.

The Compagnie des Guides

Founded in 1821 in order to try and control the access to Mont Blanc, it originally comprised 34 guides, all natives of Chamonix. At the time, the person in charge was chosen by the Sard government. In 1995, 150 guides listed in the Compagnie's books took care of an average of 10 000 clients a year. The most popular excursions offered by the guides are the TMB (Tour of Mont Blanc with overnight stops in refuges) and the ascent of Mont Blanc in small groups (10hr hard-going trek). In winter, skiing down the Vallée Blanche with a guide is an unforgettable memory for any experienced skier. Charges for the various excursions are available at the Compagnie's offices in Chamonix (☎ 04 50 53 00 88), in Argentière, in Les Houches and in Servoz.

Every summer, the "fête des guides", which takes place on 15 August, gathers mountain lovers for a charitable cause.

THE RESORT

Rue du Dr-Paccard extended by rue Joseph Vallot is the town's main artery. The short rue de l'Église, perpendicular to it, leads to the church at the heart of the old town and to the **Maison de la Montagne** (**AX**) which houses the offices of the Compagnie des Guides. In the opposite direction, avenue Michel-Croz leads, past the **statue** of Docteur Michel Gabriel Paccard (**AX B**) *(see Massif du MONT-BLANC)*, to the station and the recent districts of Chamonix lying on the left bank of the Arve.

The controversial concrete buildings of the Bouchet sports centre and of the place du Mont-Blanc stand on this side of the river.

A **bronze sculpture** (**AY D**) by Salmson, depicting the naturalist Horace Bénédict de Saussure and the mountain guide Balmat admiring Mont Blanc *(see Massif du MONT-BLANC)*, decorates the widened Pont de Cour.

Musée Alpin ⊙ (**AX M**) – The Association des Amis du Vieux Chamonix (Friends of Old Chamonix Association) is in charge of this museum housed in the former Chamonix-Palace, which illustrates the history of the Chamonix Valley, daily life in the 19C, the conquest of Alpine summits, scientific experiments on Mont Blanc and the beginnings of skiing in the valley.

Mer de Glace from Montenvers

There are documents and photographs of famous ascents, old mountaineering equipment, costumes, regional tools as well as 18C and 19C prints and old posters of the valley. Slide shows liven up the visit of the museum. There is also a fine collection of rock crystals.

The last room contains some 30 paintings about mountains by Gabriel Loppé (1825-1913).

The Chamonix Valley can undoubtedly boast the most remarkable **skiing area** in Haute-Savoie for it offers some of the finest runs to be found anywhere, combining length, gradient and unsurpassed mountain scenery.

In order to make the most of this incomparable skiing area, without encountering long queues at the lifts, it is advisable to avoid school holidays and weekends.

The skiing area spreads over several massifs linked by shuttle services: Le Brévent and Aiguille du Midi to Chamonix, La Flégère to Les Praz, Les Grands-Montets to Argentière and La Balme to Le Tour. Snow cover is usually excellent above 1 900m/6 234ft (on the second section of each massif) but is often insufficient to allow skiers to ski right down to the bottom of the valley (return by cable-car is provided for).

Experienced skiers favour such runs as the **Charles Bozon**, the Combe de la Charlanon and Col Cornu (Brévent area), the Pylônes and Pic Janvier (Flégère area) and above all the second section of **Grands-Montets**★★★ *(see ARGENTIÈRE).*

Off-piste itineraries, to be ventured only with a guide, are exceptional, in particular the famous **Vallée Blanche**★★★ (20km/12.4mi downhill run with a 2 800m/9 186ft drop from Aiguille du Midi).

Inexperienced skiers feel particularly at ease in the Balme area, where slopes are moderate and snow plentiful. There are also some fairly easy runs in Planpraz and La Flégère. Note that the **Mont-Blanc Skipass** covers 13 resorts in the Mont-Blanc area (including Megève, Les Contamines, St-Gervais...) and the Chamskipass gives access to all the ski-lifts in the Chamonix-Mont-Blanc area.

In summer, the Aiguille du Midi cable-car enables enthusiasts to ski down the glacial valley known as the Vallée Blanche. Cross-country skiing is practised between Chamonix and Argentière, at the bottom of the valley.

JL Gallo/MICHELIN

EXCURSIONS
Viewpoints accessible by cable-car

★★★**Aiguille du Midi** ⊘ – *2hr return minimum by cable-car* (**AY**).
The Aiguille du Midi cable-car, suspended part of the time 500m/1 640ft above ground, and the daring gondola which prolongs it towards the Col du Géant, together form the most spine-chilling attraction in the French Alps.

BEFORE LEAVING

– Take warm clothing with you as the weather is unpredictable at high altitude;
– Even when going on easy hikes, wear mountain boots and sun glasses;
– Several cable-car rides imply a sudden change in altitude; do not rush to the summits: one ought to be able to hold a conversation whilst climbing;
– The less daring will find that midway cable-car stations offer interesting viewpoints;
– Food and drink are available at the Planpraz and Brévent stations and there are restaurants at the Aiguille du Midi, Brévent and La Flégère top stations;
– Dogs are not usually allowed, particularly when the itinerary goes through a nature reserve;
Advice concerning excursions to the **Aiguille du Midi** and the **Vallée Blanche**:
– During peak periods, departure times are fixed and passengers are given a numbered boarding card: it is imperative to abide by these regulations.
– On arrival at the Piton Nord, it is advisable to go over the footbridge in order to gain access to the Piton Central and Mont-Blanc terrace which ought to be seen first. The Piton Nord can be visited before returning to Chamonix. Access to the Helbronner gondola is via the Vallée Blanche gallery, on the left after the footbridge. The ice tunnel is reserved for suitably equipped mountaineers.

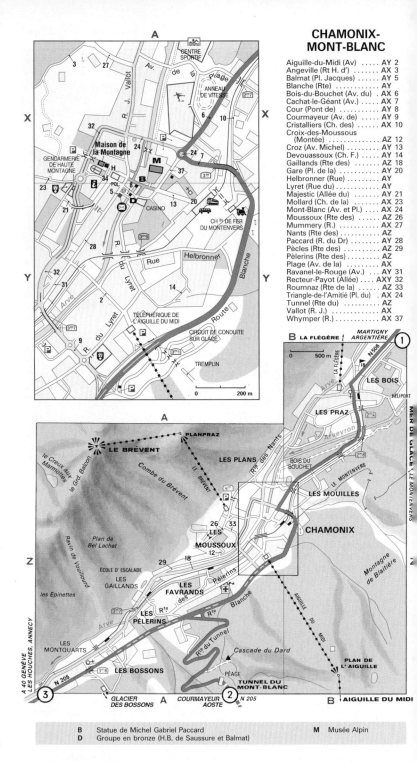

CHAMONIX-MONT-BLANC

Aiguille-du-Midi (Av) ..... AY 2
Angeville (Rt H. d') ...... AX 3
Balmat (Pl. Jacques) ...... AY 5
Blanche (Rte) .... AY
Bois-du-Bouchet (Av. du) . AX 6
Cachat-le-Géant (Av.) ..... AX 7
Cour (Pont de) .... AY 8
Courmayeur (Av. de) ..... AY 9
Cristalliers (Ch. des) ..... AX 10
Croix-des-Moussous
   (Montée) .... AZ 12
Croz (Av. Michel) .... AY 13
Devouassoux (Ch. F.) ..... AY 14
Gaillands (Rte des) .... AZ 18
Gare (Pl. de la) .... AY 20
Helbronner (Rue) .... AY
Lyret (Rue du) .... AY
Majestic (Allée du) .... AY 21
Mollard (Ch. de la) ...... AX 23
Mont-Blanc (Av. et Pl.) ... AX 24
Moussoux (Rte des) ...... AZ 26
Mummery (R.) .... AX 27
Nants (Rte des) .... AZ
Paccard (R. du Dr) .... AY 28
Pècles (Rte des) .... AZ 29
Pèlerins (Rte des) .... AZ
Plage (Rte de la) .... AX
Ravanel-le-Rouge (Av.) .. AY 31
Recteur-Payot (Allée) .... AXY 32
Roumnaz (Rte de la) ...... AZ 33
Triangle-de-l'Amitié (Pl. du) . AX 24
Tunnel (Rte du) .... AZ
Vallot (R. J.) .... AX
Whymper (R.) .... AX 37

B	Statue de Michel Gabriel Paccard	M	Musée Alpin
D	Groupe en bronze (H.B. de Saussure et Balmat)		

★★ **Plan de l'Aiguille (BZ)** – Alt 2 310m/7 579ft. This midway stop, situated at the foot of the jagged Aiguilles de Chamonix, is the starting-point of easy walks. Good view of the upper parts of the Mont-Blanc Massif.

★★★ **Aiguille du Midi** – *Piton Nord:* alt 3 800m/12 467ft. The upper station is separated from the highest point – Piton Central – by an abyss spanned by a footbridge.
From the viewing platform, there is a bird's-eye **view** of the Chamonix Valley 2 800m/9 186ft below. The indented Aiguilles de Chamonix appear slightly below and the most remarkable peaks to be seen are the Aiguille Verte, Grandes Jorasses and Aiguille du Géant overlooking the snowfields of the Col du Géant.

Piton Central (accessible by lift ⊘): alt 3 842m/12 605ft. There is a totally clear **view** of the snow-capped peaks of Mont Blanc and of the dark rock face of the "aiguilles". Mont Rose and Mont Cervin can be seen in the distance.

Before returning to the cable-car, venture through the galleries dug at the base of the Piton Nord: one of them leads to a platform facing Mont Blanc; the other – used by skiers intending to ski down the **Vallée Blanche** ⊘ – to the gondola station *(Aiguille du Midi to Pointe Helbronner, see Massif du MONT-BLANC).*

★★**Le Brévent** ⊘ (**AZ**) – Alt 2 526m/8 287ft. *1hr 30min return by gondola to Planpraz and then cable-car.*

★★**Planpraz** – Alt 2 062m/6 765ft. This relay station offers a splendid view of the Aiguilles de Chamonix.

★★**Le Brévent** – From the summit *(viewing table),* the **panorama** extends over the whole French side of the Mont-Blanc Massif, including the Aiguille du Midi and the Chamonix Valley. Facing them are the high peaks of the Haut-Faucigny, Fiz and Aravis ranges.

★**La Flégère** ⊘ – Alt1 894m/6 168ft. *Access by cable-car, starting from Les Praz* (**BZ**). From the viewing table, there is an impressive **view** of the Aiguille Verte and the Grandes Jorasses summits barring the Mer de Glace depression.

A gondola service links La Flégère and **l'Index** ⊘ (alt 2 385m/7 825ft), from the top of which the **view** embraces the whole Mont-Blanc Massif from Aiguille du Tour to Aiguille du Goûter.

★★Mer de Glace via the Montenvers ⊘

Lowest altitude of the glacier: 1 700m/5 577ft. *1hr 30min return including a 45min journey by rack-railway .*

From the upper station at the top of **Montenvers** (alt 1 913m/6 276ft), famous **panorama★★★** comprising the **Mer de Glace**, two impressive "needles", **Aiguille du Dru** and **Aiguille Verte** with the **Grandes Jorasses** in the background. *Viewing table in front of the Hôtel du Montenvers.*

An annexe of the **Musée alpin** ⊘, housed in the former Hôtel du Montenvers (1840), contains documents relating to the Mer de Glace and the Montenvers rack-railway.

It is possible to visit an **ice cave** ⊘ freshly dug every year through the Mer de Glace. A gondola ⊘ leads to it from the Montenvers Upper Station. In summer, access is also possible along a footpath starting on the right of the station, which also leads to the **Rock-crystal Gallery** ⊘ lower down on the right.

Hikers with high-mountain experience can make their way up the Mer de Glace along the Balcon de la Mer de Glace *via ferrata (information available from the Guides de Chamonix Office).*

Digging the ice cave
The site of the cave changes every year. The glacier moves at a faster pace in the middle (90m/98.4yd per year) than on the sides (45m/49.2yd per year) so that the main chamber moves forward more quickly than the entrance tunnel. When the glacier slips over a rock, the surface cracks open and crevaces split the ice to a great depth, whereas when the glacier goes over a depression, crevaces tend to close up again. It is for this reason that the cave is always dug where the ice covers a depression.

★★★Across the Mont-Blanc Massif

1 day return – see Massif du MONT-BLANC.

The Montenvers rack-railway

This picturesque train, which enables non-specialists to experience the feel of high mountains and glaciers, gets its name from the viewpoint at the end of the line. On this 5km/3mi-long line, there is a drop of 870m/2 854ft between the upper and lower stations.

The service ran in summer from 1908 onwards; the train was pulled by a Swiss steam engine and negotiated slopes with a 20% gradient with the help of a rack; the ascent lasted approximately 1 hr at an average speed of 6kph/3.7mph. Since 1993, the line has been modernised (protection against avalanche) and more powerful engines are now used, so that the service runs all year round and trains have a top speed of 20kph/12.4mph.

Walks and hikes

There are numerous possibilities for hikers along 200km/125mi of marked footpaths. The "Carte des Promenades d'été en montagne" published by the tourist office in Chamonix suggests a wide choice of itineraries of all levels of difficulty. *Ascents, reserved for specialists and requiring special equipment as well as the presence of qualified guides, are not dealt with in this guidebook.*

★★★**Short tour of Mont Blanc** – *4-day round tour – see Massif du MONT-BLANC.*

★★**Lac Blanc** – *Alt 2 352m/7 717ft. From Les Praz, take the cable-car to La Flégère then the gondola to Index. 1hr 15min on foot to the lake. Walk back directly to La Flégère in 1hr. Mountain boots essential (for crossing névés and walking along the stony path).*
Sweeping view from left to right of the Tour Glacier, Aiguille du Chardonnet, Aiguille d'Argentière and glacier of the same name, Grands-Montets, Aiguille Verte, Mer de Glace, Grandes Jorasses, Aiguille du Géant, Aiguille du Midi, Mont Blanc... Lovely shimmering colours of the lake waters (towards the end of July).

★★**Walk from La Flégère to Planpraz** – *Take a bus to Les Praz, then the cable-car to La Flégère. From there, about 2hr on foot to Planpraz. Take the gondola back to Chamonix.*
This easy pleasant walk forms the central part of the Grand Balcon Sud itinerary linking the Col des Montets and Les Houches. The footpath, lined with alpenrose, offers uninterrupted views of the Mont-Blanc Massif.

★**Hike from Plan de l'Aiguille to Montenvers** – *about 2hr 15min on foot.*
Overall views of the valley, from Les Houches to Argentière, and Aiguilles Rouges in particular. Towards the end, take the path on the left leading to the Mer de Glace.

CHAMPAGNY-EN-VANOISE★★

Michelin map 74 fold 18 or 244 folds 31 and 32

This unpretentious village, situated at an altitude of 1 250m/4 101ft, beneath the impressive **Grand Bec** (3 403m/11 165ft) and opposite Courchevel, has retained its traditional character in spite of its recent expansion as a tourist resort.

THE RESORT

The pleasant and sunny **skiing area** is linked to that of **La Plagne** by gondola and chair-lift. The Borselliers and Rossa ski-lifts lead to ideal runs for beginners and intermediate skiers. When snow cover is adequate, the **Mont de la Guerre red run**, with its 1 250m/4 101ft drop, offers splendid views of the Courchevel and Pralognan snowfields. Owing to its beautiful surroundings, Champagny-le-Haut is a fine centre of cross-country skiing although not sunny enough at the beginning of winter.

In summer, Champigny is an ideal **base for hikes** *(ask for the footpath information sheets published by the tourist office)*. In the area around La Plagne, there are excursions to Mont Jovet, La Grande Rochette and Col de la Chiaupe *(from there, access by gondola to the Bellecôte Glacier)*. However, the finest itineraries go through the Parc national de la Vanoise, above Champagny-le-Haut.

Church ⊙ – Erected at the top of a mound in 1250 and rebuilt in 1648, the church contains a remarkable **altarpiece**★ dedicated to the Virgin Mary, by Clérant, a sculptor from Chambéry (1710). The altar front is in similar style.

★**Télécabine de Champagny** ⊙ – Alt 1 968m/6 457ft. The gondola journey reveals the Courchevel skiing area overlooked by La Saulire and Aiguille du Fruit with, in the background, the Péclet, Polset and Grand-bec peaks and the Vanoise glaciers. From the upper station, skiers or hikers, according to the season, can reach the terrace of the restaurant at the top of the Borselliers ski-lift (alt 2 109m/6 919ft, viewing table). The **view**★ extends to the Grande Casse, Aiguille de l'Épena, Grande Glière, Pointe de Méribel summits and to the area of Les Trois Vallées.

★★**Champagny-le-Haut** – The narrow road, sometimes literally hewn out of the rock, overlooks the Gorges de Champagny and leads into the austere basin of Champagny-le-Haut. Note the **Cascade** de la Chiserette on the left, just before the village of the same name. Beyond Chiserette, there is a view of the Grande Motte Glacier with the Grande Casse Peak on the right. The Porte du parc du bois refuge houses an information centre about the Vanoise Massif and is the starting point of a **sentier-découverte** (discovery trail) dotted with information panels explaining the various features of the landscape *(1hr 30min walk on flat ground)*.
The road ends at Laisonnay-d'en-Bas (1 559m/5 115ft). From there, various trails lead to **Col du Palet**★★ *(7hr 30min return, see TIGNES)*, **Col de la Grassaz** *(7hr return)* and **Col du Plan Séry** *(5hr 30min return)*. Hikers, who need to be in top physical condition for these long excursions, are rewarded with magnificent views of the Grand Bec, Grande Motte and Grande Casse summits.

Le CHAMPSAUR ★

Michelin map 77 folds 16 and 17, 89 fold 20, 244 folds 40 and 41
or 245 folds 7 and 8

The Champsaur is the area surrounding the upper Drac Valley up-river from Corps. Lying at altitudes often higher than 1 000m/3 281ft – similar to those of the Chamonix Valley – this region offers rural landscapes of a kind quite unknown in the northern Alps. Between St-Bonnet-en-Champsaur and the confluence of the rivers Séveraisse and Drac, the lower Champsaur is a connecting link along the Route Napoléon *(see ROUTE NAPOLÉON)*. This warm valley, which was dug deep through thick layers of schist, bears many crops (Champsaur means "yellow field"), mainly cereals, on the right bank of the river, whereas the left bank is covered with pastures shared by cattle and sheep. The local cheese is called Tomme du Champsaur.

The upper Champsaur, drier and less wooded, has a more mountainous appearance, particularly upstream from the confluence of the Drac Noir and Drac Blanc.

The valley links up with the Gapençais via the Col Bayard and Col de Manse and with the Dévoluy via the Col du Noyer (impressive bird's-eye views, *see Le DÉVOLUY*).

Several winter sports resorts have developed in the Champsaur area: Orcières-Merlette, Ancelle, St-Michel-de-Chaillol, St-Léger-les-Mélèzes and Laye.

1 FROM COL DE MANSE TO ORCIÈRES

66km/41mi – about 2hr 30min

Col de Manse – It links the Gap Basin and Drac Valley in a landscape of high pastures. Refuge Napoléon *(see ROUTE NAPOLÉON)*.

Follow D 13 towards Ancelle.

The road offers a pleasant drive through pastures, with lovely glimpses of the upper Drac Valley, and then through larch woods down to the bottom of the valley.

In Pont-du-Fossé, turn right onto D 944 then turn left in Pont-de-Corbière.

★★**Vallée du Drac Blanc** – This valley, also known as the Drac de Champoléon valley, is remarkably wild and desolate. The mountain stream is well-known for its sudden floods such as that of 1928 which carried away the entire village of Les Auberts.

★**Walk to the Pré de la Chaumette refuge** – *3hr return via Tour du Vieux Chaillol GR trail. Difference in altitude: 320m/1 050ft. Start from the parking at the end of the road, near Les Auberts bridge. Follow the footpath starting just before the second bridge. This very pleasant walk is suitable for everyone.* The path follows the valley planted with beeches and larches, beneath wild cliffs and waterfalls, before reaching Pré de la Chaumette where the refuge is located.

It is possible to return to the parking via the path on the other bank.

Between Corbières and Orcières, the road follows the Drac Noir Valley; the north-facing slope is densely forested with dark firs and lighter larches. The landscape is more mountainous in appearance.

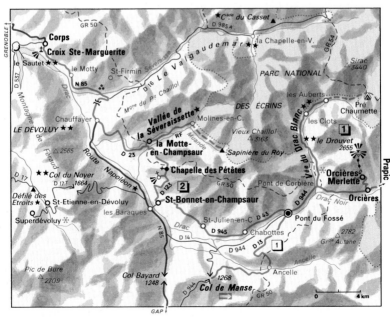

145

Orcières – This south-facing village is the starting point of pleasant forest walks. On the way out towards Prapic, note how the houses in Montcheny are decorated with "pétètes", shaped like heads, typical of the Champsaur.

*Orcières-Merlette** – *5km/3mi from Orcières. See ORCIÈRES-MERLETTE.*

Prapic – This hamlet, situated at the bottom of the valley in a splendid mountain setting, has retained its heritage of traditional houses; a small **museum** ⊙ contains a reconstructed interior (furniture, clothes, tools, newspapers etc). There are numerous opportunities for drives and walks.

Poet's grave – *1hr return; easy walk.* This walk through a lovely dale leads to a rock beneath which is the grave of a local poet, Joseph Reymond.

Chapelle de la Saulce – *2hr return; easy walk.* This rural walk starts with a trail which climbs onto the Charnière Plateau, along the right bank of the Drac Noir. At the oratory, turn left and cross the plateau to reach the chapel.

② FROM PONT-DU-FOSSÉ TO CORPS

60km/37.3mi – about 2hr

Between Pont-du-Fossé and St-Bonnet *(via D 43, D 945 and D 215)*, the road follows the Drac which meanders along its stony bed.

St-Bonnet-en-Champsaur – This small town which, in 1543, was the birthplace of the Duc de Lesdiguières, has retained its medieval appearance and narrow streets. A few art craftsmen have settled in the town. There is a 16C covered market in place Grenette.

From St-Bonnet, follow D 23 towards Bénévent, turn right then left at the signpost "Cimetière".

A small road leads to a chapel surrounded by its cemetery and to the Trois Croix viewpoint offering a wide panorama of the St-Bonnet Valley overlooked by the Dévoluy.

Continue until you reach l'Auberie.

Chapelle des Pétètes – The name of this chapel means "dolls'chapel". The façade has lots of small recesses sheltering naïve statuettes carved by a shepherd between 1730 and 1741. Inside, the leather-covered altar comes from the chapel of Lesdiguières' former castle.

La Motte-en-Champsaur – Picturesque village with fine stone houses covered with tile shingles.

Take the forest road leading to Molines-en-Champsaur along the Séveraissette.

★**Vallée de la Séveraissette** – The road follows the green narrow valley to the tiny village of Molines at the entrance of the Parc national des Écrins. Possible hike to the Sapinière du Roy *(2hr 30min return).*

Return to La Motte-en-Champsaur and turn right to Chauffayer and N 85.

Between Chauffayer and Le Motty, the Route Napoléon makes a detour into the lower Séveraisse Valley guarded by the ruined Château de St-Firmin *(D 16 on the right goes up the valley).* In the distance looms the pyramid-shaped **Pic d'Olan** (alt 3 564m/11 693ft).

Beyond Le Motty, there are bird's-eye views of the artificial Lac du Sautet, which blends well with its mountain setting.

Croix-Ste-Marguerite – Lovely view of the Lac du Sautet and Obiou Summit.

Corps – *See Barrage et Lac du SAUTET.*

Massif de CHAMROUSSE★★

Michelin map 77 fold 5 or 244 folds 39 and 40

The summits of the Chamrousse Massif, which are the last important heights at the southwest extremity of the Belledonne range, are the favourite haunt of skiers from Grenoble. The area has been so extensively equipped with access roads, a large-capacity cable-car to the Croix de Chamrousse viewpoint and a winter sports resort that it has become a sought-after tourist centre in summer as well as in winter.

In the valley below, the spa town of Uriage and the nearby village of St-Martin are pleasant holiday resorts.

TOUR STARTING FROM URIAGE *39km/24.2mi – about 2hr*

✛ **Uriage-les-Bains** – This spa resort lies in a green, sheltered valley, at the foot of the Belledonne mountain range. The baths, the casino, hotels and villas are scattered over a 200ha/494-acre park. The isotonic waters, containing sodium chloride and sulphur, are used in the treatment of skin diseases, chronic rheumatism as well as ear, nose and throat complaints.

Road D 111 climbs through the **Forêt de Prémol**★ (deciduous trees, gradually replaced by firs and spruce). In spite of the abundant vegetation, it is possible to catch glimpses of the Vercors and Chartreuse massifs.

Ancienne chartreuse de Prémol – The only remaining building of this former Carthusian monastery has been turned into a forest lodge. The vast clearing is the ideal place for a pause. Beyond the Col Luitel, the road continues to climb in a series of hairpin bends, reaching its highest point at the Highways Department chalet where the snowploughs are kept and which controls the various means of access to Roche-Béranger.

★**Réserve naturelle du Luitel** – *See GRENOBLE: Excursions.*

※**Chamrousse** – This vast winter sports complex overlooking the Grenoble Basin includes the Recoin de Chamrousse (alt 1 650m/5 413ft) and Roche-Béranger (alt 1 750m/5 741ft) resorts.

★★**Croix de Chamrousse** ⊙ – Alt 2 257m/7 405ft. *45min return including a 10min cable-car ride.* The upper cable-car station, close to a television relay, is only a few steps away from the base of the cross, a splendid viewpoint affording a vast **panorama** *(viewing panels):* the Drac Valley, Grenoble Basin and Grésivaudan depression over which tower the Chartreuse and Bauges Massifs. In fine weather, the view extends as far as the Cévennes range.

Road D 111 continues beyond Chamrousse on its way down through the Saint-Martin forest, offering **glimpses★** of the densely populated Uriage coomb, the Vercors Massif and Grenoble.

St-Martin-d'Uriage – The spa town of Uriage developed below this old village. The road then goes down into the valley past the 13C-14C castle which once belonged to the Bayard family and reaches **Uriage**.

Massif de la CHARTREUSE★★

Michelin map 74 fold 15, 77 folds 4 and 5 or 244 folds 28 and 29
Local map see p 149

The Grande Chartreuse is a famous monastery; it is also the well-defined mountain range known simply as the Chartreuse, where the monks of the order of St Bruno have built their retreat.

In 1995, this homogenous massif was included in the **Parc naturel régional de Chartreuse** *(see Introduction: Nature parks and reserves)* and a dozen or so sites have been granted added protection. In addition, a nature reserve covering 4 300ha/10 625 acres is being created to preserve the rich natural environment.

From a geological point of view, the Chartreuse Massif contains three of the most extensive networks of underground galleries and caves in the Alps: L'Alpe (nearly 30 access points for a 50km/31mi network), Dent de Crolles (60km/37.3mi network, well known by potholers) and Granier. A great many bones of prehistoric bears, recently discovered in a cave, have given this site a new scientific value.

This Préalpes range comprises striking limestone summits, splendid forests displaying a variety of species, harmonious slopes covered with pastures as well as the impressive gorges of the two Guiers rivers.

A geological wonder – Cretaceous limestone was the basic ingredient of the geological formation of the Chartreuse Massif; 200-300m/656-984ft thick on average, it folded and split alternately. Tall cliffs cut through its thickness show thin layers of marl forming horizontal grassy outcrops suspended above vertical drops.

★★★COL DE PORTE AND ROUTE DU DÉSERT

① From Grenoble to St-Laurent-du-Pont

50km/31mi – about 4hr – local map see p 149

Beyond the Col de Porte, the itinerary follows the "Route du Désert" *(beware of timber-carrying trucks).*

★★**Grenoble** – *See GRENOBLE.*

Leave Grenoble by ① on the town plan.

The road climbs in hairpin bends along the slopes of Mont St-Eynard (alt 1 379m/4 524ft), offering bird's-eye views of the Grésivaudan depression and Grenoble with remarkable **vistas★★** of the Belledonne range, the Taillefer, Thabor and Obiou summits as well as part of the Vercors. Mont Blanc is also visible.

Le Sappey-en-Chartreuse – This high altitude resort nestles in a sunny basin with forested slopes, overlooked by the imposing Chamechaude Peak.
From Sappey to Col de Porte, the road follows the Sappey and Sarcenas valleys with the indented Casque de Néron in the background.

Col de Porte – This important pass is overlooked by the tilted limestone shelf of Chamechaude, looking like a huge lectern.

At Col de Porte, take D 57⁰ on the right towards Charmant Som.

★★★Charmant Som – The road rises steeply *(14% maximum)* through a forest scarred with rocky ridges, which becomes thinner before giving way to pastures. Stop on the edge of the Charmant Som Plateau (alt 1 654m/5 427ft) and take a look at the **panorama** *(see p 150 and 151).*

Leave the car at the Bergeries and continue on foot. *(1hr return).* From the summit (alt 1 867m/6 125ft), there is an interesting **panorama**. Walk to the edge of the escarpment in order to get an overall view of the **setting★** of the Grande Chartreuse monastery.

Return to the Col de Porte.

The road meanders through the woods and across clearings, offering closer views of the extremity of the Chamechaude shelf.

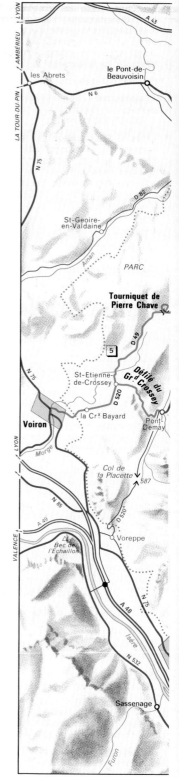

※**St-Pierre-de-Chartreuse** – *See ST-PIERRE-DE-CHARTREUSE.*

Turn back and follow the "Route du Désert" (D 520⁸, to St-Laurent-du-Pont).

★★**Belvédère des Sangles** – *4km/2.4mi on foot from the Valombré bridge. See ST-PIERRE-DE-CHARTREUSE.*

Porte de l'Enclos – The valley seems completely enclosed by high cliffs. This was the upstream entrance of the "Désert" and the beginning of the wooded **Gorges du Guiers Mort★★** overlooked by long limestone ridges. This is the famous "**Route du Désert**" which, in the 16C, bordered the grounds of the Carthusian monastery. The area was celebrated by Chateaubriand, Lamartine and Dumas.

At the St-Pierre bridge, take the road on the right to La Correrie (one way only).

La Correrie – This was an important annexe of the famous Grande Chartreuse monastery. It houses the **Musée Cartusien★** ⊘ which illustrates the history of the Carthusian order and the monks' daily life by means of an audiovisual show and reconstructions of the cloisters and cells.

Couvent de la Grande Chartreuse – Founded in 1084, this monastery was destroyed and rebuilt many times; the present buildings date from 1676 and cannot be visited as it is still the mother house of the Carthusian order. The famous distillery is now in Voiron *(see p 152).*

Return to the Route du Désert.

The road goes downhill through three successive tunnels; note the strange limestone needle, known as **Pic de l'Œillette**, standing 40m/131ft high on the roadside.

Pont St-Bruno – This imposing structure has a single arch spanning the Guiers Mort 42m/138ft above the riverbed.

Leave the car on the left bank and walk down (15min return) to the old bridge once used by the Carthusian monks.

The mountain stream disappears into potholes and flows under a boulder stuck in the gorge and forming a natural bridge *(viewpoint; keep a close watch on children).*

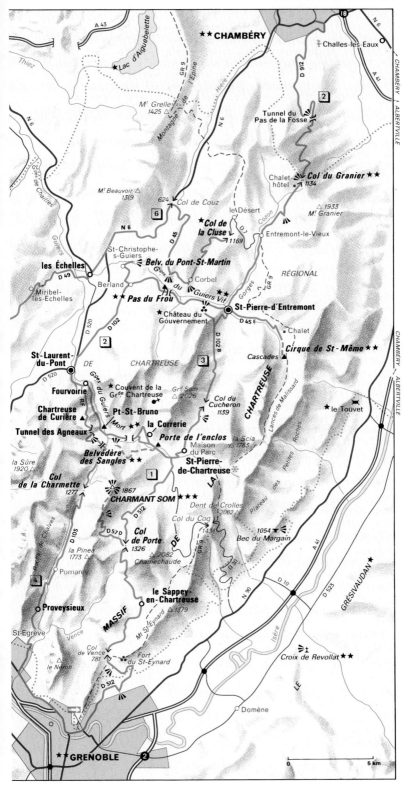

The numbers ① – ② etc indicate the main routes into and out of town.
They are the same on town plans and on **Michelin Maps**

> ### The Carthusian order
>
> In 1084, the bishop of Grenoble had a vision warning him of the arrival of seven travellers who wished to lead a solitary life. He took them to the "Désert" de Chartreuse where **St Bruno** founded the order of the same name. In the 12C, one of his successors laid down the Carthusian rule which has never been altered since. The order developed and included up to 200 monasteries at the time of the Renaissance. Today their number is reduced to just 17 throughout the world plus five convents of Carthusian nuns.
>
> Carthusian monks and nuns lead a solitary life, praying and working. Their cells open onto the cloisters. They meet only three times a day in church, share the Sunday meal and take a walk together through the woods once a week.

Fourvoirie – This place name *(forata via)* is a reminder that, at the beginning of the 16C, the Carthusian monks rough-hewed a passage through the rock which later became a road. Guarded by a fortified gate (now gone), it marked the downstream entrance of the Grande Chartreuse estate.

St-Laurent-du-Pont – This lively tourist centre was formerly know as St-Laurent-du-Désert.

★★GORGES DU GUIERS VIF AND COL DU GRANIER

② From St-Laurent-du-Pont to Chambéry

54km/33.6mi – allow 2hr – local map see p 149

St-Laurent-du-Pont – *See above.*

Leave St-Laurent via Le Révol and follow D 102.

The road rises to a ledge occupied by the village of Berland.

Take a small road to the north.

Belvédère du Pont-St-Martin – *5min return on foot.* Beyond St-Christophe-sur-Guiers, just before the bridge over road D 46, a path on the right follows the left bank of the Guiers Vif and leads to a viewpoint 30m/98ft above the stream, which affords a lovely view of the gorge.

It is possible to come back along the footpath which crosses the old bridge.

Between Berland and St-Pierre-d'Entremont, the road follows the impressive **Gorges du Guiers Vif★★** with some spectacular narrow sections.

★★**Pas du Frou** – This overhang, clinging to the 150m/492ft-high cliff, is the most spectacular section of road in the Chartreuse. "Frou" means awful, frightening in local dialect *(viewpoint).*

St-Pierre-d'Entremont – 459 villagers live in the Isère *département* and 295 in Savoie. From an administrative point of view, there are two villages separated by the stream which used to mark the border between France and Savoie.

It is the starting point of pleasant walks, in particular to the **Château du Gouvernement★** *(3km/1.8mi. Walk south towards Col du Cucheron, turn right just before a bridge onto D 102^B then right again 1.5km/0.9mi further on).* The ruins of the castle stand on a grassy height which offers a lovely **view★** over St-Pierre-d'Entremont and the surrounding area.

Continue along D 45^E to the Cirque de St-Même chalet.

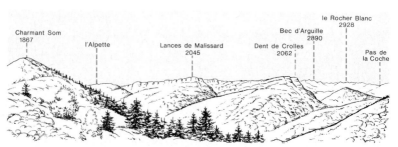

Panorama from the road leading to

★★**Cirque de St-Même** – The Guiers Vif springs out of a limestone cliff rising to 400m/1 312ft and forms two splendid waterfalls.

Return to St-Pierre-d'Entremont and drive north on D 912.

The road follows the Gorges d'Entremont, hardly wide enough at times for the road and the Cozon mountain stream.

Between Entremont-le-Vieux and the Col du Granier, there are closer views of the imposing barrier formed by Mont Granier.

★★**Col du Granier** – Alt 1 134m/3 729ft. This pass, over which tower the impressive cliffs of Mont Granier (alt 1 933m/6 342ft), opens the way to the Chartreuse Massif from Chambéry.

In 1248, a massive landslide buried many villages, killing 5 000 people and forming a huge pile of rocks at the foot of the mountain. Today, the **Abymes de Myans** is an area covered with vines and dotted with small lakes.

From the chalet-style hotel, there are open **vistas★★** of the Combe de Savoie, the Bauges Massif, Belledonne range and Mont Blanc in the distance.

On the way down from the pass, there is a **sweeping view★★** of the Chambéry depression and Lac du Bourget from the exit of the Pas de la Fosse tunnel.

★★**Chambéry** – *See CHAMBÉRY.*

★COL DU CUCHERON

③ From St-Pierre-d'Entremont to St-Pierre-de-Chartreuse

12km/7.5mi – about 45min – local map see p 149

This pleasant shortcut along the Chambéry-Grenoble route enables one to avoid the Gorges du Guiers and discover picturesque landscapes typical of the Préalpes.

★★COL DE LA CHARMETTE

④ From St-Laurent-du-Pont to Grenoble

30km/18.6mi – allow 2hr – local map see p 149

The tricky forest road leading to the Col de la Charmette, built between 1866 and 1876, and D 105, which prolongs it, run almost continually underwood. Several sections, clinging to the cliffside, offer superb bird's-eye views of the Gorges du Guiers Mort.

St-Laurent-du-Pont – *See opposite*

From St-Laurent drive south along the Col de Porte road; 1km/0.6mi further on, take the forest road on the right to Col de la Charmette.

Chartreuse de Curière – This 13C Carthusian monastery, lying in a remote clearing, was occupied until the Revolution. Recently restored and extended, it is once more inhabited by monks and nuns.

Tunnel des Agneaux – Leave the car at the tunnel exit to get a good view of the Gorges du Guiers Mort which suddenly become narrower upstream from the St-Bruno bridge. Further up, the road clings to the cliffside, high above the valley. On the left, the **view★★** embraces the wooded Gorges du Guiers Mort overlooked by the tilted ridges of the Grand Som. The road then follows the Ténaison mountain stream to Col de la Charmette.

Col de la Charmette – Alt 1 277m/4 190ft. The pass owes its name to the nearby woods. The chalet-style hotel is the starting point of hikes to the Charmant Som and Grande Sûre massifs. The road goes down rapidly, revealing the indented silhouette of Le Néron and, across the River Isère, the extremity of the Vercors range overlooked by Le Moucherotte Peak.

Proveysieux – The village and its isolated church clinging to the steep slopes form a charming picture which has inspired artists from Grenoble. The road goes down into the Isère Valley and N 75 on the left leads to Grenoble.

★★**Grenoble** – *See GRENOBLE.*

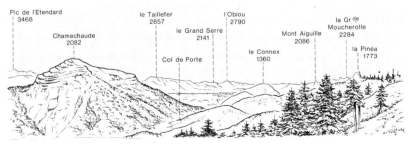

Charmant Son (spot height 1 654m/5 497ft)

Mont Granier in the Chartreuse Massif

★ROUTE DE MIRIBEL

5 From Voiron to Les Échelles

27km/16.8mi – allow 1hr 15min – local map see p 149

Voiron – This busy trading centre is situated on the edge of the Chartreuse Massif; the output of its ski industry represents 65% of the total French production of competition skis.

★**Chartreuse cellars** ⊘ – *Boulevard Edgar-Kofler.* The formula of the elixir of life was given to the Carthusian monks in 1605; from this elixir (71° proof), which is still made today, they later created the Chartreuse Verte (55° proof), the Chartreuse Jaune (40° proof), a Génépi (absinthe, 40° proof), the Eau de Noix des Pères Chartreux (23° proof) and fruit liqueurs (21° proof): raspberry, bilberry, wild blackberry and blackcurrant. The distilling and maturing take place in Voiron as a visit of the cellars reveals, but the selection and preparation involving 130 different plants remain a secret. There are exhibitions and slide shows as well as a video made by the monks themselves, about the various stages needed to produce the famous **Chartreuse** liqueur.

From Voiron, drive east along D 520 towards St-Laurent-du-Pont.

The road offers views of the first heights of the Vercors Massif, in particular the Bec de l'Échaillon promontory, marking the entrance of the Grenoble Valley.

Continue on D 520 past St-Étienne-de-Crossey.

Défilé du Grand Crossey – This wooded transverse valley, hemmed in by high limestone cliffs opens out just below the steep slopes of La Sûre to form an imposing setting particularly striking at sunset.

Turn back in Pont-Demay then turn right in front of the church in St-Étienne-de-Crossey. D 49 leads to Miribel.

Tourniquet de Pierre Chave – In order to come out of a dead-end valley, the road makes a loop, passing successively under and over the same bridge before arriving on top of the ledge dotted with the hamlets of Miribel-les-Échelles. There are fine views of the western part of the Chartreuse Massif: Mont Beauvoir, Col de Couz, Gorges du Guiers Vif, Grand Som, Gorges du Guiers Mort and La Sûre.

Continue along D 49 to Les Échelles.

Les Échelles – This lively tourist centre, situated in Savoie, is twinned with Entre-Deux-Guiers lying across the Guiers Vif in the Isère *département*. The mountain stream joins the Guiers Mort downstream from Les Échelles to form the River Guiers which flows through the impressive wooded Gorges de Chailles.

Grottes des Échelles – *4km/2.4mi along N 6 towards Chambéry. Leave the car at the exit of the Échelles tunnel.* The two caves have historic connections with the **Route royale Sarde**. The gorge separating them is a caved-in natural tunnel which used to be the only through way between the Couz Valley and the Échelles Basin. The steepness of the Roman way was eased in medieval times by a succession of steps (hence the name Échelles), which were levelled in the 17C to allow vehicles through (monument near the lower cave). Napoleon had the tunnel dug; it was completed in 1813.

The **tour of the caves** ⊙ starts from the inn situated on N 6 at the eastern exit *(on the Chambéry side)* of the tunnel. The **upper cave** consists of a corridor spliting into two; the left-hand gallery leads to several chambers linked by narrow strangely eroded corridors. A 220m/240yd-long footbridge clinging to the rock face runs along halfway up the lower cave known as **Grand Goulet★**. From the south exit, there is a lovely **view★** of Chartreuse Valley overlooked by the Grand Som and La Sûre summits.

★COL DE LA CLUSE

⑥ From Les Échelles to Col de la Cluse

21km/13mi – about 2hr – local map see p 149.

Drive along N 6 to Chambéry, past the entrance of the caves (see above), then turn right at Col de Couz and follow D 45.

The road overlooks the Gorges du Guiers Vif, opposite the famous Pas du Frou. Just before Corbel, there is a clear view of the more open Guiers Vif Valley. Corbel marks the entrance of a rural vale, hemmed in by fine escarpments.
Col de la Cluse (alt 1 169m/3 835ft), overlooking the sunny Entremont Valley, is the ideal place for a pause.

It is possible to return to Les Échelles via Le Désert, Entremont-le-Vieux and St-Pierre-d'Entremont.

CHÂTEAU-QUEYRAS ★

Michelin map 77 fold 19, 189 fold 10 or 244 fold 43
Local maps see Le BRIANÇONNAIS and Le QUEYRAS

The village nestles beneath the fortress crowning a rocky knoll left behind by a glacier, which almost completely blocks the entrance of the Guil Valley leaving only a small gap for the road to slip through. This is the most characteristic **scenery★** of the Queyras area. Château-Queyras has linked up with other villages in the valley to form the municipality of Château-Ville-Vieille.

Leave the car on the right, just before climbing to the fort, or on the open space near the river.

★**Fort Queyras** ⊙ – Fortifications crowning the hill since medieval times were extended and improved by Vauban in 1692 and occupied by a garrison until 1967. Beyond the drawbridge, a marked path leads past casemates and bastions to the machicolated 14C keep where exhibitions are held. Note the picturesque bartizan of the eastern bastion and go to the ravelin to get the best overall view of the fort.

★**Espace géologique** ⊙ – *Leave the car on the open space near the river then walk back towards the village and go through the porch.*

The glacial "bolt" of Château-Queyras

The geological centre, housed in the crypt of the village church, illustrates the formation of the Alps through interactive displays presented in a chronological order, starting with *(left as you go in)* the erosion of the Hercynian massifs (300 to 250 million years ago), followed by a build-up of marine deposits during the Secondary Era (230 million years ago) and a long period of submarine volcanic activity producing various types of rock. The formation of the Alps 60 million years ago resulted from the collision of the European and African tectonic plates. There is a fine collection of metamorphic rocks on display, including marble from the Guillestre area. It is also possible to get the smell of algae and plankton going back 170 million years, preserved in mud in the Arvieux area *(see Le QUEYRAS)*. There are exhibits from the former asbestos mine in Vallon Péas, closed in 1957, and from the copper mine in St-Véran also closed in the 1950s.

EXCURSION

★**Sommet Bucher** *11km/6.8mi south – about 1hr return*

The narrow road *(in very bad condition)*, shaded by larches and pines, rises in a series of hairpin bends, offering fine glimpses of Château-Queyras and the Guil Valley. From the end of the road, climb to the viewing tables, situated on either side of a military building. The beautiful panorama includes Mont Viso and St-Véran village, framed by the Pic de Châteaurenard, Pointe de Toillies and Sommet de Razis, with Pic de la Font Sancte to the south, Pelvoux-Écrins Massif to the west and Grand Pic de Rochebrune to the north.

Gorges du CIANS ★★★

Michelin map 81 fold 19, 115 folds 4 and 14 or 245 fold 24

The Gorges du Cians, a tributary of the River Var, are among the most beautiful gorges in the Alps region. In order to negotiate a drop of 1 600m/5 249ft over a distance of only 25km/15.5mi, the Cians has hewn its way through a narrow gorge between superb sheer cliffs which vary in appearance according to the terrain, the lower gorge being cut through limestone and the upper gorge through red schist.

FROM TOUËT-SUR-VAR TO BUEIL *38km/23.6mi – about 2hr*

★**Touët-sur-Var** – Tall and narrow houses, backing onto the rocky slope, line the partly covered streets of this picturesque village overlooking the Var Valley. Nearly all the houses have a south-facing galleried loft, known as the *soleilloir*, used for drying figs. The recently restored 17C parish **church** is decorated with numerous paintings and altarpieces. It is curiously built over an arch spanning a mountain stream which is visible through a small opening in the floor of the nave.

From the upper part of the village, there is a fine view of the valley below.

From Touët, drive west along N 202 and turn right onto D 28.

★★**Gorges inférieures du Cians** – Water oozes from every crack in the spiky rock face. The road makes its way through the tortuous gorge.

Turn right onto D 128, which rises sharply; caution is recommended.

Lieuche – Black schist forms the impressive **setting★** of this tiny mountain village.

The unassuming **church** ⊘ houses the **Retable de l'Annonciation★**, one of Louis Bréa's earliest works, set in carved and gilt wood panelling (17C). The central panel illustrates the Annunciation against a mountain landscape, with a Crucifixion above, and the predella depicts Christ surrounded by the apostles.

Detail of the altarpiece in Lieuche depicting St Christopher and St John the Baptist

From the church terrace, there is an overall **view**★ of the Gorges du Cians, overlooked by the Dôme de Barrot, and part of the Var Valley.

Return to D 28, turn right then 1km/0.6mi further on left onto D 228.

The road climbs above the Cians Valley, revealing an impressive landscape.

Rigaud – This hilltop village overlooking the Cians Valley nestles below the ruins of its medieval fortress in a very attractive **setting**★; there is a fine panoramic view from a spot near place de la Mairie.
The fortified parish **church**, decorated in Baroque style, houses several 17C paintings including a Deposition over the high altar, a panelled naïve painting dating from 1626 *(on the left)* and a Virgin with Child.

Return to D 28 and turn left.

★★★**Gorges supérieures du Cians** – At the entrance of the gorge, 1.6km/1mi beyond Pra-d'Astier, the road overlooks the confluence of the Cians and the Pierlas, 100m/328ft above water level, and rises progressively following the mountain stream which drops down to the valley in a series of steps. The steep bright-red rocky slopes, alternately jagged and smooth, contrast with the dark green scanty vegetation. The narrowest passages, known as the Petite Clue and the Grande Clue, where the road has been hewn out of the rock, are the most picturesque. A tunnel by-passes the Grande Clue which can only be seen on foot *(park before the tunnel)*.
Beuil in its striking **setting**★ suddenly appears on a bend.

★**Beuil** – *See BEUIL.*

CLUES DE HAUTE-PROVENCE★★

Michelin map 81 fold 19, 114 fold 12, 115 folds 13 and 14 or 245 folds 23, 24, 36 and 37

Rivers flowing south of Puget-Théniers have cut their way deeply across the mountains, forming several *clues* (transverse valleys) typical of this region.

★★CLUE DU RIOLAN

① From Puget-Théniers to Roquesteron
23km/14.3mi – about 1hr

★**Puget-Théniers** – *See PUGET-THÉNIERS.*
Cross the River Var and follow D 2211ᴬ.

The road rises in wide hairpin bends above Puget-Théniers to the Col de St-Raphaël.

La Penne – A square keep overlooks the village clinging to a rocky ridge.
At Pont des Miolans, take D 17 on the left towards Sigale.

★★**Clue du Riolan** – This is an impressive gap cut across the mountain range by a tributary of the Esteron. The overhanging road offers a fine **view** of the gorge and the mountain.

Sigale – The village stands in a picturesque **setting**★ on top of an escarpment overlooking the confluence of the Riolan and the Esteron, above terraced orchards. This former stronghold has retained two fortified gates, several Gothic houses and a 16C fountain. The 19C clock tower crowning an isolated rock is surmounted by a wrought-iron campanile.

Notre-Dame d'Entrevignes – This 12C **chapel** ⊘, situated on the right-hand side of the road, was rebuilt in the 15C and decorated in the 16C with murals illustrating the life of the Virgin Mary.

Roquesteron – There are houses on both banks of the River Esteron which marked the border between France and Savoie until 1860, when Savoie became part of France. This is the reason why there are two municipalities, Roquesteron in the north and Roquesteron-Grasse in the south, where the 12C Romanesque **church** stands on top of the rocky knoll.

★★CLUE D'AIGLUN

② From Roquesteron to Col de Bleine 33km/20.5mi – about 1hr

Roquesteron – *See above.*
Between the D 17 junction and Le Mas, the road is very uneven and narrow: passing other vehicles is often tricky and it is recommended to drive cautiously.

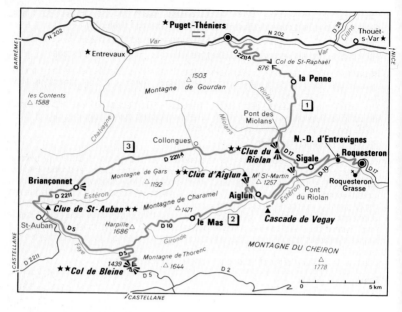

Beyond Notre-Dame d'Entrevignes, follow D 10 on the left.

The bridge over the Riolan offers a lovely **view★** of the gorge and the splendid emerald-green stream flowing among rocks and disappearing into potholes.

Cascade de Végay – It consists of a succession of fine waterfalls.

Aiglun – This picturesque hilltop village celebrated by Frédéric Mistral, clings to the steep slope of the gorge overlooked by the Cheiron Mountain.

★★**Clue d'Aiglun** – The road, which crosses the Esteron as it comes out of the gorge, offers a striking view of the most secluded *clue* in the area: only a few metres/yards wide, between 200-400m/656-1 312ft deep and 2km/1.2mi long, it looks like a gully separating the Charamel and St-Martin mountains.

Le Mas – This village, built on the edge of a beak-shaped limestone spur, has a 13C Romanesque **church**.

The road meanders along the hillside then D 5 *(on the left)* climbs up forested slopes to Col de Bleine.

★★**Col de Bleine** – Alt 1 439m/4 721ft. Magnificent **view** of the deep Faye Valley, the Harpille Peak (alt 1 686m/5 532ft), the ridge of the Charamel Mountain and the Grandes Alpes du Sud in the distance.

★★CLUE DE ST-AUBAN

③ From Col de Bleine to Pont des Miolans
36km/22.4mi – about 1hr

★★**Col de Bleine** – *See Clue d'Aiglun.*

5km/3.6mi beyond the pass, keep left on D 5 which runs along the Faye and joins D 2211.

★★**Clue de St-Auban** – The Esteron, a tributary of the River Var, goes through this impressive gorge with vertical sides hollowed out in places and forming huge caves; the river bed is scattered with boulders marked by deep potholes.

Briançonnet – This tiny village lies in a strange setting, beneath a huge rock. The houses were built with stones from an earlier Roman settlement as the inscriptions set in their walls testify. There is a wide **view★** of the Alpine summits from the cemetery adjacent to the east end of the church.

Beyond Briançonnet, the **view** embraces the Montagne de Gars and the Montagne de Charamel on either side of the River Esteron. Soon after Collongues, the Clue d'Aiglun can be seen on the right; further on, the Clue de Riolan appears like a deep gash in the landscape. From Pont des Miolans, it is possible to return to Puget-Théniers along D 2211ᴬ.

La CLUSAZ ✳✳

Population 1 845
Michelin map 89 fold 14 or 244 fold 19
Local map see Massif des ARAVIS

The most important resort in the Aravis Massif owes its name to the deep gorge or *clue* through which flows the Nom, situated downstream from the village.

The village nestles round the large church with its onion-shaped bell-tower, in an attractive setting of fir woods and gently rolling pastures. The heights of the Aravis mountains rear on the horizon like interlocking scales (Balme, Grandcrêt, Paccaly) and their regularly indented crests stretch towards Pointe Percée.

Skiing area – Winter sports have been practised in La Clusaz since the 1920s and today amateurs of all forms of skiing appreciate the considerable differences in height of the resort's four massifs. The Manigod and Étale massifs offer several runs for intermediate skiers as well as a wide choice of facilities. The Aiguille Massif on the other hand offers advanced skiers a black run (La Vraille) and several red runs. Speed-record trial and acrobatic ski jumping are also available.

Cross-country skiers have at their disposal 70km/43.5mi of tracks, including 12 loops.

The skiing area is linked to that of the Grand-Bornand, both areas having a common skipass under the name of "Aravis".

La Clusaz

EXCURSIONS

✳✳**Vallée de Manigod** – *See Massif des ARAVIS: Route de la Clusaz.*

✳**Vallon des Confins** – *5.5km/3.4mi.* Turn left in the wide bend on the way out of La Clusaz towards the Col des Aravis and follow the Fernuy road which runs along the bottom of the valley then rises rapidly to the Col des Confins, a depression hollowed out by glacial erosion and lying just below the escarpments of the Aravis mountains. Continue along this road beyond the chapel in order to get a clearer view of the Vallon du Bouchet.

*Constantly revised **Michelin Maps** at a scale of 1:200 000
provide much useful information:*
– *latest motorway developments and changes;*
– *vital data (width, alignment, camber, surface) of motorways or tracks*
– *the location of emergency telephones.*
*Keep current **Michelin Maps** in the car at all times.*

Route du col de la COLLE ST-MICHEL ★

Michelin map 81 folds 8 and 18 or 245 folds 22 and 23

This road, linking the upper Verdon Valley and the Var Valley, leads to Entrevaux and from there to Nice and the Côte d'Azur.

FROM COLMARS TO ENTREVAUX *59km/36.7mi – about 2hr*

★**Colmars** – *See COLMARS.*

Leave Colmars south along D 908.

The road goes past the attractive summer resort of Villars-Colmars.

Beauvezer – *See Haute vallée du VERDON.*

The road runs along the bottom of the Verdon Valley, partly forested and partly covered with pastures. Beyond Pont de Villaron, it rises above the river towards St-Michel-Peyresq, clinging to rocky slopes and going through barren ravines.

Col de la Colle St-Michel – Alt 1 431m/4 695ft. The pass offers a soothing landscape of green pastures. In winter, it is a cross-country skiing centre with tuition and 50km/31mi of tracks available.

Beyond the pass, turn left onto D 32 towards Peyresq.

Peyresq – This old shepherds' village, lying in a very picturesque **setting**★ overlooking the source of the Vaïre, which was restored by a group of Belgian students to house an international cultural and artistic university centre, has retained a 15C mansion and a 13C Romanesque church.

Return to D 908.

On the way down, there is a marked contrast between the forested slopes and the barren limestone layer overlooking the valley dotted with picturesque villages; the Digne-Nice railway line shows off civil engineering skills.

★**Méailles** – This hilltop village is built on a limestone ridge overlooking the left bank of the Vaïre. The small church has Gothic features and contains an interesting altarpiece depicting *The Virgin and Child* (early 16C) as well as several 17C paintings.

Grotte de Méailles – *From Méailles, drive towards La Combe and park the car in the first major bend on the right. Wear non-slip shoes and carry several torches. Allow 4hr return for a short exploration of the cave entrance.*

From the parking area, a well-marked path leads north across a ravine then rises in a landscape of scrub dotted with cairns. The two entrances of the cave are situated beyond the ridge, about 10m/11yd apart. The main gallery slopes gently down 150m/164yd to a stream and a vast chamber partitioned by numerous concretions. There are other chambers further on.

The incline of the cave follows that of the geological layers, thus offering potholers the rare opportunity to progress without using the karstic network. Potholing enthusiasts, conscious of the risks and taking the necessary precautions, will enjoy exploring this cave without special equipment. Visitors are asked not to break stalactites or frighten bats.

Le Fugeret – The village lies in a green depression on the left bank of the Vaïre. Note the charming 18C humpback bridge spanning the stream with its single 14m/46ft arch. The slopes of the valley offer a landscape of scattered sandstone rocks, clumps of walnut, chestnut and pine trees as well as lavender fields.

★**Annot** – *See ANNOT.*

Between Annot and Les Scaffarels, the road runs through strange rock formations known as the Grès d'Annot *(see ANNOT).*

Turn onto N 202.

The road follows the River Coulomp to its confluence with the Var and goes past the Pont de la Reine-Jeanne, a medieval humpback bridge.

★**Entrevaux** – *See ENTREVAUX.*

*The annual **Michelin Red Guide France**
revises its selection of establishments which*

 – *serve carefully prepared meals at a reasonable cost,*
 – *include service on the bill or in the price of each dish,*
 – *offer a menu of simple but good food at a modest price,*
 – *provide free parking.*

It is well worth buying the current edition.

COLMARS ★

Population 367
Michelin map 81 fold 8 or 245 fold 22

The splendid wooded mountain setting of this small walled town, guarded by two forts, makes it a pleasant summer resort (alt 1 250m/4 101ft) on the edge of the Parc national du Mercantour and a cross-country skiing centre in winter.

From the hill of Mars to Vauban's stronghold – The town gets its name from a temple built on a hill to celebrate the Roman god, Mars *(collis Martis)*.
The fortified town developed at the foot of the hill and acquired strategic importance when, in the 14C, it became a border town between France and Savoie. In 1528, François I strengthened the walls by adding small square towers which can still be seen today in spite of repeated fires. In 1690, war was declared between France and Savoie and Colmars was besieged but not taken. Plans drawn by Vauban, Louis XIV's military engineer, led to the construction of the forts linked to the town by caponiers (covered passages) and to the fortification of the town gates.

Colmars

SIGHTS

★**Old town** – Once through the Porte de Savoie or the Porte de France, visitors will appreciate the southern atmosphere pervading the city, as they wander through the narrow streets linked by tiny squares adorned with fountains.
The 16C-17C **church** ⊘, built in Gothic style with Romanesque features, has only one side aisle whose wall forms part of the town walls. The side porch is by Mathieu Danvers (1530). There is a fine Baroque altarpiece in a **chapel** near the town hall.

Fort de Savoie ⊘ – Built in 1693-95 at the same time as the Fort de France, this fort comprises two successive enclosures; inside the second one, there are four vaulted rooms which used to house the garrison and where exhibitions are now held. Stairs lead to a round tower and to the vast fencing room; note the remarkable timber roof structure.

WALK TO CASCADE DE LA LANCE

40min return. Follow the road which starts opposite the church.

A pleasant path leads through pine woods to the foot of a cliff then slips through a narrow gorge to reach the waterfall noisily splashing on the rock face.

The length of time given in this guide
*– for **touring** allows time to enjoy the views and the scenery*
*– for **sightseeing** is the average time required for a visit.*

COMBE DE SAVOIE

Michelin map 89 folds 8, 18 and 19 or 244 folds 18 and 19

Combe de Savoie is the name given to the northern section of the "sillon alpin" (Alpine trench) which includes the Isère Valley between Albertville and the Chambéry depression. Unlike the Grésivaudan which prolongs it to the south, it is an area exclusively devoted to agriculture. Villages, occupying sunny positions at the foot of the Bauges mountains between Montmélian and Mercury, are either lost among orchards or surrounded by fields of maize and tobacco or by famous vineyards – this is the main wine-growing area in Savoie.

VIEWPOINTS

The best overall view of the Combe de Savoie can be enjoyed from the Rocher de Montmélian. Moreover, the roads leading to the Fort du Mont, Col du Frêne and Col de Tamié offer bird's-eye views of the depression. The most impressive sight in the area is the "eyrie" at Miolans.

Montmélian – This ancient, rapidly expanding little city surrounds the Montmélian rocky knoll, on which once stood one of the most powerful strongholds in Europe. The top of the rock (accessible by a ramp signposted "le fort"), clear of any fortification since the fort was dismantled in 1706 on the orders of Louis XIV, is now occupied by a platform decorated with flowers which offers a lovely **panorama★** of the Isère Valley and of the Alps as far as Mont Blanc. Another rock to the northwest has been nicknamed "la Savoyarde" because its silhouette suggests a woman's head wearing the regional headdress (see Introduction: Traditions and folklore).

COMBLOUX ✳

Population 1 716
Michelin map 74 fold 8 or 244 fold 20

This summer and winter resort, famous for its mild climate, has retained its traditional farms and old-world charm.

THE RESORT

Skiing area – The resort specialises in family entertainment and skiing without risk. The skiing area is linked to that of Jaillet (Megève) by numerous ski-lifts. Cross-country skiers can enjoy three separate loops totalling 15km/9.3mi. Five snow-cannon ensure adequate snow cover.

The **church**, which has an elegant onion-shaped bell-tower, is characteristic of Alpine churches built during the 18C; the elaborate retable decorating the high-altar dates from the same period.

★THE SETTING

There is a beautiful **panoramic view★★★** of the Mont-Blanc Massif, seen here from an ideal distance. Follow the road to Haut-Combloux for 3km/1.8mi (parking) to reach the viewing table (see also Bassin de SALLANCHES).

Les CONTAMINES-MONTJOIE ✳ ✳ ✳

Population 994
Michelin map 74 fold 8 or 244 fold 21
Local map see Massif du MONT-BLANC

Situated at an altitude of 1 164m/3 819ft, at the foot of Mont Joly and the snow-capped Dômes de Miage, Les Contamines is one of the most pleasant and restful holiday resorts in the Mont-Blanc Massif.

THE RESORT

Skiing area – The resort, created in the 1930s, is surrounded by a well-equipped skiing area with good snow cover. It aims to attract families looking for moderately difficult ski runs and beautiful scenery such as that of Les Contamines just beneath Mont Blanc. The skiing area is linked to that of Mont d'Arbois.
Cross-country skiers can enjoy 30km/18mi of tracks.

In summer, the resort is an exceptionally fine **hiking and mountaineering centre**. Major ascents usually start from the Hôtellerie de Tré-la-Tête (4hr 30min return from Cugnon), built just below the glacier which feeds the Lac de la Girotte. Hikers will encounter some of the most attractive footpaths in the Alps.
In addition, the village offers visitors the opportunity to take part in various sports and cultural activities and to enjoy the **Base de loisirs du Pontet**, a leisure park surrounding a small lake. The 18C church has an attractive painted façade and a large overhanging roof.

View of Les Contamines-Montjoie beneath the snow-capped Dômes de Miage

HIKES

★★Val Montjoie cliff road – *See Massif du MONT-BLANC.*

★Le Signal ⊘ – Alt 1 850m/6 070ft. *Accessible via La Gorge and Le Signal gondolas.* Splendid view of the Dômes de Miage and Tré-la-Tête Massif as well as of the Chaîne des Fiz further north.

★★Walk to Col du Joly – Alt 1 989m/6 526ft. *30min easy climb from Le Signal.* Superb panorama of the Mont-Blanc Massif, the Hauteluce Valley and Lac de la Girotte with the Aravis mountains further away to the northwest.

★★★Hike to the Aiguille Croche – Alt 2 487m/8 159ft. *1hr 30min on foot from Col du Joly. As the path is very steep, mountain boots are recommended.* One's efforts are rewarded by a wide and most beautiful **panorama★★★**, one of the finest in the Alps, which encompasses, in a clockwise direction, the Aiguilles de Chamonix, Aiguille Verte, Aiguille du Midi, Aiguille de Bionassay, Mont Blanc, Mont Pourri, the Grande Motte and Grande Casse Glaciers, Pierra Menta, Les Écrins, Meije, the Mont de Lans and Étendard glaciers, the vast Aravis Range, Megève and its mountain airport...

★★★From Aiguille Croche to Mont Joly along the crest path – *Experienced hikers, using a map and leaving early in the morning to make the ascent of the Aiguille Croche, will be able to carry on to Mont Joly (about 2hr).*

The path, which is narrow but does not often run along the cliff edge, unfolds a succession of splendid views. From Mont Joly *(viewing table, for details see MEGÈVE)*, allow another 2hr to return to Les Contamines. Turn round towards Tête de la Combaz and take the path on the left which leads rapidly down to the bottom of the valley. Turn right in Colombaz onto the surfaced road then left 200m/218yd further on. The path leads to L'Étape from where a gondola takes you down to La Gorge. It is also possible to go back on foot.

★★★ **Short tour of Mont-Blanc** – *4-day round tour – see Massif du MONT-BLANC.*

★ **Lacs Jovet** – Alt 2 174m/7 133ft. *Difference in height: about 1 000m/3 281ft. 5hr on foot return from Notre-Dame de la Gorge.*

This well-marked itinerary, which forms part of the Round Tour of Mont Blanc, goes through the Réserve naturelle des Contamines. Splendid light reflections on the lakes surrounded by Mont Jovet, Mont Tondu, Col du Bonhomme and Aiguilles de la Pennaz.

COURCHEVEL ★★★

Michelin map 89 fold 9 or 244 fold 31
Local map see Massif de la VANOISE

Courchevel is undoubtedly one of the major and most prestigious winter sports resorts in the world. Founded in 1946 by the Conseil général de la Savoie (regional council), it played a leading role in the development of the **Trois Vallées** ★★★ complex *(see Massif de la VANOISE)*. Émile Allais, who was the downhill world champion in 1937, was the first to introduce the idea of maintaining and packing down ski runs in French resorts. Après-ski activities are just as exciting: art exhibitions, classical and jazz concerts, impressive number of luxury shops, sports centres, fitness clubs, famous night-clubs... However, Courchevel also owes its reputation to the quality of its hotels and gastronomic restaurants, unrivalled in mountain areas.

In summer, Courchevel changes radically and becomes a peaceful resort offering numerous activities.

THE RESORTS

Skiing area – Today, the maintainance and development of the Courchevel skiing area is still considered as an example to follow. Snow cover is guaranteed from early December to May, owing to the north-facing aspect of the slopes and an impressive array of more than 500 snow-cannon. The other strong point of the resort is its ski school which employs 480 instructors and ranks first in Europe. There are excellent runs for beginners along the lower sections of the Courchevel 1850 ski-lifts (Verdon, Jardin Alpin). Advanced skiers prefer the great Saulire corridor and the Courchevel 1350 area. As for cross-country skiers, they appreciate the elaborate network of loops linked to the Méribel network.

There are four resorts situated at altitudes ranging from 1 300m/4 265ft to 1 850m/6 070ft on the slopes of the Vallée de St-Bon, among pastures and wooded areas, in a vast open landscape framed by impressive mountains.

Le Praz – Alt 1 300m/4 265ft. The 90m/295ft and 120m/394ft ski jumps used during the 1992 Olympic Games are close to the old village. A picturesque 7km/4.3mi-long forest road leads to the recent resort of La Tania and to Méribel.

Courchevel 1550 – Family resort situated on a promontory next to a pinnacled chapel and near woodlands.

Moriond or Courchevel 1650 – Sunny resort where urban-style architecture contrasts with traditional chalets.

Courchevel 1850 – With its elaborate ski-lift system, Courchevel 1850 is the main resort of the complex as well as the liveliest and the most sought after. There is a wide open view of Mont Jovet, Sommet de Bellecôte and Grand-Bec Peaks.

There are luxury hotels and chalets and a moountain airport where sightseeing flights over the Olympic sites and Mont Blanc are available.

VIEWPOINTS ACCESSIBLE BY GONDOLA

★★★ **La Saulire** ⊙ – *Access from Courchevel 1850 by the Verdon gondola and La Saulire cable-car.* The well-equipped summit *(1 cable-car, 3 gondolas and 3 chair-lifts)* links the Courchevel and Méribel valleys and is the starting point of a dozen famous runs. Non-skiers can take a gondola to Méribel or Mottaret and a cable-car to Courchevel.

From the top platform (alt 2 690m/8 825ft), the view embraces the Aiguille du Fruit (alt 3 050m/10 007ft) in the foreground, the Vanoise Massif and glaciers further away, the Péclet-Polset Massif to the south, the Sommet de Bellecôte and Mont Pourri to the north with Mont Blanc on the horizon.

The upper terrace of the Pierre Plates Restaurant *(viewing table)*, close to the Méribel gondola station, offers a bird's-eye view of the Allues Valley with, in the distance, the northern part of the Écrins Massif (Mont-de-Lans Glacier and Meije) the Grandes Rousses Massif and the Belledonne range.

Sommet de la Saulire (television relay) – Alt 2 738m/8 983ft. *1hr return on foot.* This excursion is recommended in summer to tourists familiar with mountain conditions and not likely to feel dizzy. The summit can be reached from the cable-car station, along a wide, 300m/328yd-long path and then a shorter steep lane. Splendid panorama including the Meije, Les Écrins and the Vanoise.

★★Télécabine des Chenus ⊘ – *Access from Courchevel 1850.* From the upper gondola station, view of the Rocher de la Loze and, further away, of Croix de Verdon, La Saulire, Aiguille du Fruit and the Vanoise. Skiers can reach **Col de la Loze★★** (alt 2 305m/7 562ft) for a fine view of the Allues Valley.

★Mont Bel-Air ⊘ – Alt 2 050m/6 726ft. *Access from Courchevel 1650 by the Ariondaz gondola.* Fine overall view of the Saint-Bon Valley, of the Sommet de Bellecôte, La Grande Casse with Mont Blanc in the distance. It is possible to return to Courchevel on foot in winter as well as in summer.

HIKES

Courchevel is an ideal **hiking centre**. A map of the area's network of footpaths is available from the tourist office.

★★Petit Mont Blanc – Alt 2 677m/8 783ft. *Allow 3hr 30min on the way up and 2hr 15min on the way down. Start from Le Belvédère (Courchevel 1650) or from the top of Mont Bel-Air.*
Walk across the Vallée des Avals then up to the summit via Col de Saulces. Very fine **panorama** of the Pralognan Valley framed by the Grande Casse, the Vanoise Glaciers and Pointe de l'Échelle.

★★Lacs Merlet – Alt 2 449m/8 035ft. *Ascent: 2hr; start from the Mont Bel-air.* The path runs alongside two ski-lifts in succession before entering the Parc de la Vanoise. The position of the lakes at the foot of the Aiguille du Fruit forms a splendid **setting★★**. Go to the upper lake, the deepest of the Vanoise lakes (30m/98ft) and walk along the right-hand shore to the end. The Vanoise glaciers and Aiguille du Rateau are reflected in the waters often partly iced over.

★Via ferrata de la Croix de Verdon – *Access by the Verdon gondola and the Saulire cable-car.* This is a remarkable viewpoint (alt 2739m/8 986ft), fitted with safety cables and ladder rungs, for the amateur of big thrills *(see Practical information)*.

Walk to La Rosière – *Access by car along an unsurfaced forest road starting between Courchevel 1650 and Le Belvédère.*
Lovely little lake overlooked by the Dent de Villard. Nature trail introducing a few rare species (columbine, lady's slipper). Continue along the waterfall path.

Y Bontoux

Lacs Merlet

Route de la CROIX DE FER ★★★

Michelin map 77 folds 6 and 7 or 244 folds 29 and 30

This itinerary, which splits into two halfway through, links the Romanche Valley, known as L'Oisans, and the Arc Valley, also called La Maurienne. The first alternative, which follows the Glandon Valley to its confluence with the Arc, is more direct; the second, leading to St-Jean-de-Maurienne via the Col de la Croix de Fer, is more varied with some spectacular sections (Défilé de Maupas and Gorges de l'Arvan). It is possible to make a round tour of some of the great Alpine passes (**Circuit des Grands Cols★★★**) by prolonging this itinerary with two more described in this guide: St-Michel-de-Maurienne to Col du Lautaret *(see Route du GALIBIER)* and Col du Lautaret to Le Bourg-d'Oisans *(see L'OISANS: Vallée de la Romanche)*. This is one of the finest drives through the Alps *(see also ROUTE DES GRANDES ALPES)*.

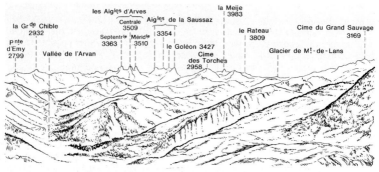

Panorama from the Col de la Croix de Fer, facing east

★★FROM ROCHETAILLÉE TO THE COMBE D'OLLE

45km – about 1hr 30min

The road is blocked by snow from November to May between Le Rivier d'Allemond and the Combe d'Olle.

Between Rochetaillée and Le Verney, the road follows the green lower Olle Valley, known as the *Jardin de l'Oisans*.

Drive along the left bank of the artificial lake and follow signposts to Hydrelec.

As you cross the narrow Flumet Valley, you will get a glimpse of the Cascade de la Fare with the Grandes Rousses Summits in the background.

★**Hydrelec** ⊙ – The Grand'Maison power station and Oz factory are not open to the public. Leave the car in the visitors' parking area at the entrance of the power station and walk down the path on the right to Hydrelec.

The tour starts with a video about the production and storage of electric power. The reconstructions and equipment displayed on two levels illustrate the history of hydroelectric power.

On the ground floor there is a model of the famous piece of machinery which brought water to the Versailles fountains. Further on, the invention of the dynamo and of the transformer are shown to lead to the production of electricity for domestic purposes. **Aristide Bergès** *(see GRENOBLE: Excursions)*, known as the "father of hydroelecticity", inaugurated a new era which led to the creation of turbines; several types of these are on display, different dams are surveyed and a striking model of the Grand'Maison Dam gives an insight into their complexity. In the basement, there is a historical survey of the instruments used to measure and control electric power including cutouts, switchboards, turbines, generators...

Return to D 526 and follow D 43ᴬ on the right towards Vaujany.

★**Vaujany** – This south-facing village lies in a lovely **setting★** on the slopes of the Rissiou, facing the Grandes Rousses. From the end of the village, there is a splendid view of the **Cascade de la Fare★** and its spectacular 1 000m/3 281ft drop.
Vaujany is linked by cable-car to the Dôme des Rousses (2 805m/9 203ft), via the Alpettes Station. From there, it is possible to reach l'Alpe-d'Huez (1 860m/6 102ft).

A road, starting near the cemetery, leads to the Collet de Vaujany.

★★**Collet de Vaujany** – Extended view of the west side of the Grandes Rousses, with the Pic de l'Étendard and Lac Blanc.

Return to Le Verney and turn right into D 526.

The road rises above the stream and crosses many tributaries coming down from the Belledonne mountains. The valley becomes narrower and densely forested.

★**Défilé de Maupas** – Beyond Le Rivier-d'Allemond, the road makes it way through this deep gorge cluttered with fallen rocks. One of the mountain streams rushing down from the Sept-Laux Massif forms a beautiful waterfall, the Cascade des Sept-Laux, which can be seen from the road.

★★**Combe d'Olle** – This pasture-covered valley running between huge hilltops was the site chosen by EDF (the French Electricity Board) for the **Barrage de Grand'Maison** on the Eau d'Olle: the dam, its 220ha/544-acre lake and its power stations are linked by a 7km/4.2mi gallery to the lower reservoir (75ha/185 acres) and to the Verney dam power station in order to insure a production of electricity of a mixed type known as "energy transfer" *(see Introduction: Hydroelectric power and industry)*.
From the dam, there are glimpses of the Cimes de la Cochette up a ravine through which a stream rushes down from the Grandes Rousses Massif. Further upstream, a series of waterfalls draws attention to the opposite slope.

★ROUTE DU GLANDON *22km/13.7mi – allow 1hr*

This is the most direct route from Le Bourg-d'Oisans or Vizille to the Arc Valley. Prolonged beyond La Chambre by the Col de la Madeleine Road *(see Route de la MADELEINE)*, it forms one of the sections of the Grenoble-Moûtiers itinerary.
Bear left along D 927 after the Combe d'Olle. The road is blocked by snow upstream from St-Colomban-des-Villards from November to early June.
The road follows the Glandon Valley (or Vallée des Villards) all the way.

★**Col du Glandon** – Alt 1 924m/6 312ft. *250m/273yd from the Chalet-Hôtel du Glandon.* The pass offers a splendid **vista** of Mont Blanc through the Col de la Madeleine to the northeast; the snow-capped peaks of the Grandes Rousses overlooking the Eau d'Olle Valley, can be seen to the south. The upper Glandon Valley affords austere landscapes of meagre pastures and rocky slopes brightened up by clumps of red alpenrose in early summer.
Beyond Léchet, the slopes are covered with fir trees and the valley gradually looses its Alpine character, in spite of the summits towering above the Col de la Madeleine, which can be seen in the distance.

★★★FROM THE COMBE D'OLLE TO ST-JEAN-DE-MAURIENNE
51km/31.7mi – allow 2hr 30min

This is the longer alternative itinerary leading from the Eau d'Olle Valley to the Arc Valley.
Beyond the Combe d'Olle, keep to the right along D 926. The road is blocked by snow between the Combe d'Olle and St-Sorlin-d'Arves from November to May.

★★**Col de la Croix de Fer** – Alt 2 068m/6 785ft. *15min return on foot.* Climb onto the rocky knoll bearing a commemorative pyramid, south of the pass and turn towards the east for a fine **view** of the Aiguilles d'Arves.
The rocky peaks of the Sept-Laux and Allevard massifs line up above the opposite slope (Aiguilles de l'Argentière and Bec d'Arguille).

★★★**Hike to the Étendard Refuge** – *Allow 3hr 15min return on foot from the pass.* After climbing for 1hr 50min, one suddenly discovers the refuge lower down on the shores of Lake Bramant, overlooked by the Pic de l'Étendard (3 464m/11 365ft). The Belledonne range, stretching across the horizon to the west, is particularly spectacular at sunset and there is a magnificent **view**★★ of the Vanoise Massif to the northeast with the Mont-Blanc Massif in the distance.
The refuge can be reached in 10min. Experienced hikers can walk to the foot of the **St-Sorlin** Glacier, beyond lakes Bramant, Blanc and Tournant *(allow 1 day)*.
Between the Col de la Croix de Fer and St-Sorlin, the road offers open views of the upper Arvan Valley, with its vast sloping pastures dotted with hamlets against a background of high peaks and glaciers (Massif des Grandes Rousses).

St-Sorlin d'Arves – New buildings connected with the nearby skiing area somewhat spoil the traditional character of this village.
The road follows the River Arvan.
In Malcrozet, turn left onto D 80 which climbs towards St-Jean-d'Arves.

St-Jean-d'Arves – The church cemetery outside the village overlooks the upper Arvan Valley, offering an extended **view**★ of the Grandes Rousses Massif, including the ice-capped Pic de l'Étendard and the escarpments of the Cimes de la Cochette. About 2km/1.2mi beyond St-Jean-d'Arves, as you go into a bend, note the narrow Entraigues Valley on the right and further on, as you come out of the tunnel, admire the lovely **picture**★ formed by the hamlet of Montrond with the Aiguilles d'Arves in the background. The road also offers impressive glimpses of the **Gorges de l'Arvan**★ deeply cut through schist.
The road joins D 926 just before a tunnel; turn left.

Col de la Croix de Fer and Aiguilles de l'Argentière

★**Combe Genin** – The late-afternoon light plays on the schist lining the sides of this imposing scree-covered corridor.

Turn back along D 926 to Belleville and take D 80 on the left.

The road crosses the Arvan and climbs above the tree line to the village of Le Mollard with views of the lower Arvan Valley and Combe Genin.

★**Col du Mollard** – Numerous chalets. There are very attractive **views**★ of the Aiguilles d'Arves and Vanoise summits from the highest point of the road (alt 1 683m/5 522ft).

As you drive west out of Albiez-le-Vieux, the thrilling descent into the Arvan Valley begins, offering breathtaking bird's-eye views. The journey down is less impressive beyond Gevoudaz as the road makes its way to St-Jean-de-Maurienne.

St-Jean-de-Maurienne – *See ST-JEAN-DE-MAURIENNE.*

For a quiet place to stay
Consult the annual Michelin Red Guide France (hotels and restaurants)
and the Michelin Guide Camping Caravaning France
which offer a choice of pleasant hotels and quiet campsites
in convenient locations.

Les DEUX-ALPES ✲✲

Michelin map 77 fold 6 or 244 fold 41

Situated at the heart of the Oisans region, the twin resorts of L'Alpe-de-Mont-de-Lans and L'Alpe-de-Venosc, known as "Les Deux-Alpes", spread their modern residential buildings on a vast saddle covered with pastures, which connects the Romanche and Vénéon valleys at an altitude of 1 600m/5 249ft.

THE RESORT

Skiing area – Popular with young sports enthusiasts, Les Deux-Alpes offer a sought-after skiing area extending along the slopes on either side of the resort. Competent skiers aim for the steep first section and the Tête Moute Summit. Less experienced skiers prefer the gentle slopes, the excellent snow and magnificent panoramas of the Mont-de-Lans Glacier, the largest European glacier suitable for skiing: equipped with a dozen ski-lifts, it offers many green and blue runs between 2 800m/9 186ft and 3 568m/11 706ft, the highest altitude of any French pisted run. This enables skiers of a moderate level of competency to experience the thrill of a 2 000m/6 562ft difference in height on the way back to the resort. The Girose Glacier, belonging to the skiing area of La Grave *(see La GRAVE)*, is easily accessible *(by tracked vehicle in winter)* from the Dôme de la Lauze Summit; together they form one of the largest **summer skiing** areas *(mid-June to early September)*.

Although skiing is the main activity in all seasons, Les Deux-Alpes offer in addition a wide choice of other sports: ice-skating, swimming in an open-air heated pool, paragliding... Those who prefer walking can go to the old village of **Venosc** *(see L'OISANS: Route de la Bérarde)*, to the La Fée Refuge and to Le Sapey.

Chapelle St-Benoît ⊘ – This modern chapel, traditionally built in undressed stone, contains a few original sculptures including the Stations of the Cross.

VIEWPOINTS

✲✲✲**Glacier du Mont-de-Lans** ⊘ – *2hr return to the Dôme du Puy Salié and half a day to the Dôme de Lauze. Climbing boots, sunglasses and binoculars recommended.*
Access by the Jandri Express cable-car from the resort centre, near the tourist office. There is a cable-car change at 2 600m/8 530ft; the next one takes you up to 3 200m/10 499ft. Fine **view** of the Vercors and Oisans areas.
A tilted lift and rack-railway then lead to the Dôme du Puy Salié (3 421m/11 224ft). Magnificent **view**✲✲ of the Écrins Massif. Go to the ski-lift arrival point to get a panoramic view of the Vercors, Belledonne Range, Grandes Rousses Massif (L'Alpe-d'Huez resort and Pic du Lac Blanc), Mont-Blanc Massif, the indented Aiguilles d'Arves and the Vanoise. Mont Ventoux can also be seen in fine weather conditions.
Skiers can take the ski-lift to La Lauze and admire the splendid **panorama**✲✲✲ of the Rateau Summit, the Écrins and Soreiller massifs and, further away to the northeast, of the Péclet, Grande Casse and Mont Pourri summits.

Grotte de glace ⊘ – Several caves, dug through thick ice, are decorated with ice sculptures representing a slate-quarry worker, a pedlar, the crystals room... Non skiers can also reach the Dôme de la Lauze by tracked minibus. This excursion, known as **Croisière Blanche**✲ is unique in France.

✲**Croisière Blanche** ⊘ – *It is advisable to get bookings from the tourist office during the season. Departure from the cable-car station.* Visitors on foot can reach the **Dôme de la Lauze** by tracked minibus. This excursion offers a unique experience in a high-mountain environment.

✲**Belvédère des Cimes** – Alt 2 100m/6 890ft. *Access via the Cimes chair-lift; departure: as you go into the resort, on the Mont-de-Lans side.*
This viewpoint, situated on the northeast slope of Pied Moutet, offers a fine view of the Romanche Valley and Bourg-d'Oisans Basin.

✲**Belvédère de la Croix** – From the cross standing on top of a grassy knoll situated behind the UCPA chalet, at the end of the resort on the Alpe-de-Venosc side, one looks down a sheer drop to the bottom of the Vénéon Valley with jackdaws whirling above. The pointed Aiguille de Venosc stands across the river and the Roche de la Muzelle (alt 3 459m/11 348ft), with its characteristic suspended glacier, towers above the whole landscape.

Except when otherwise stated,
all recommended town tours are intended as walks.

Le DÉVOLUY★★

Michelin map 77 folds 15 and 16 or 244 fold 40 and 245 fold 7

This massif, which forms part of the southern Préalpes, offers desolate and sometimes magnificent landscapes. Barren limestone escarpments back against the highest peak, the Obiou, and surround a central depression through which flow the Ribière and the Béoux. The Dévoluy is riddled with sink-holes known as **"chourums"**, also called "scialets" in the Vercors Massif, which are sometimes filled with ice (Chourum Martin, south of St-Disdier). Roads going across the Dévoluy, particularly the Col du Noyer road, run through treeless landscapes, devoid of fertile soil and streams, scorched by the sun and overlooked by jagged peaks with scree-covered slopes. These mountains look most impressive in the late-afternoon light when the sun shines its golden rays on the bare rock.

★ROUND TOUR VIA COL DU FESTRE AND COL DU NOYER

Starting from Corps *81km/50.3mi – about 3hr 30min*

Corps – *See Barrage et lac du SAUTET.*
From Corps, drive west along D 537.

Once out of the pleasant Drac Valley, the road winds its way through desolate mountain landscapes.

★★**Barrage du Sautet** – *See Barrage et lac du SAUTET.*
Continue along D 537 past the dam.

One may catch a glimpse of the imposing Obiou Summit to the west, towering above the Trièves and the Drac Valley.

Just before Pellafol, there is a lovely view on the left of the village of Ambel perched on a rocky spur.

★**Défilé de la Souloise** – The road runs between splendid limestone escarpments.

St-Disdier – The silhouette of a 13C isolated church can be seen on the slopes overlooking the village to the east.

Col du Festre – Àlt 1 441m/4 728ft. The pass lies below the desolate heights of the Montagne d'Aurouze. The road then runs down towards Montmaur along the Béaux Valley *(see MONTMAUR).*
Turn back and take D 17 on the right.

★**Col de Rioupes** – This pass offers splendid **views** of a vast ring of barren mountains: Crêtes des Aiguilles, Grand-Ferrand, Obiou and Montagne de Féraud separated by the Col du Noyer from the Montagne d'Aurouze riddled with potholes.

★**Défilé des Étroits** – Stop the car between the two bridges which D 17 crosses. The road overlooks the River Souloise which has carved a 40-60m/131-197ft deep passage (only 2m/7ft wide in parts) through the rock.
The Souloise Valley suddenly widens as the road reaches St-Étienne-en-Dévoluy.

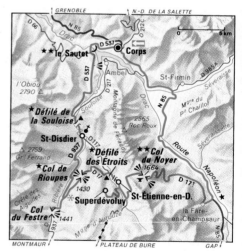

St-Étienne-en-Dévoluy – *See SUPERDÉVOLUY.*

✳**Superdévoluy** – *See SUPERDÉVOLUY.*

★★**Col du Noyer** – *The pass is closed from early November to mid-May.* Both sides of the pass (alt 1 664m/5 459ft – *viewing table 100m/109yd southwest of the former Refuge Napoléon*), offer beautiful contrasting **landscapes**: the barren ridges of the Dévoluy on one side and, on the other, the broad Drac Valley (Bas-Champsaur) chequered with various crops and framed by the heights of the Vieux-Chaillol Massif and the Gapençais mountains, with the high summits and glaciers of the Écrins Massif in the distance.

The road running down towards the River Drac is a test on one's driving skills, particularly for the first 5km/3km. It reaches La Fare-en-Champsaur and the Route Napoléon (N 85) which leads back to Corps.

DIE ★

Population 4 230
Michelin map 77 folds 13 and 14 or 244 fold 38
Local map see Le DIOIS

Lying in one of the most pleasant parts of the Drôme Valley, overlooked by the shiny escarpments of the Glandasse range, south of the Vercors Massif, Die had, by the 2C AD, become an important Gallo-Roman city on the main route from Milan to Vienne. Many visitors were attracted by the cult of Cybele, the mother of the gods, involving the sacrifice of a bull and a ram, as the sacrificial altars exhibited in the museum testify.

During the 3C AD, Die was surrounded by walls and became a Christian city in which bishops played an important role, granting the town its first charter in 1217.

In the 16C, the Reformation had a major impact on Die whose churches were all destroyed, but Louis XIV later reinstated the bishopric.

Today, Die is a small administrative and commercial centre, its main production being the "**Clairette de Die**", a sweet sparkling white wine, made from Clairette and Muscat, two famous types of vine.

SIGHTS

Ramparts – The 3C enclosure, stretching over 2km/1.2mi, is still visible on the northeast side of town. It is possible to walk alongside the 3m/10ft-thick walls, originally strengthened by towers, from the tourist office to the Porte St-Marcel. Gallo-Roman objects found on location are now exhibited in the museum.

Porte St-Marcel – The vaulting of this Roman arch is decorated with interlacing and rosettes; the friezes illustrate chariot racing, dancing and prosperity symbolized by fruit.

Hôtel de ville – The building housing the town hall and the law courts is the former bishop's palace, which has retained the 11C **Chapelle St-Nicolas** ⊙. It is paved with a remarkable 12C **mosaic★** representing the universe, with the North Star in the centre, surrounded by the four rivers of the Garden of Eden, and the cardinal points in the corners. The walls of the chapel are decorated with medieval frescoes and 18C hand-painted wallpaper.

Cathedral – The massive bell-tower is surmounted by a wrought-iron campanile. The south wall and Romanesque porch-tower belonged to the original 12C-13C church. Note the capitals of the doorways, which illustrate biblical scenes and supernatural fighting scenes. Partly destroyed during the Wars of Religion, this church was rebuilt and refurbished in the 17C; particularly noteworthy are the pulpit, the woodwork decorating the chancel, the stalls and the high altar.

Also worth seeing is the Renaissance façade of the Maison de Diane de Poitiers (1499-1566), in rue St-Vincent, next to the cathedral, and the Jesuit chapel now a Protestant church.

Museum ⊙ – Housed in a late-18C mansion, this museum contains interesting local archeological collections, particularly rich in Gallo-Roman exhibits: sacrificial altars, a 4C Christian sarcophagus etc. One room is devoted to popular art and customs and another one to Romanesque sculptures from the cathedral.

EXCURSIONS

Abbaye de Valcroissant ⊙ – *After 6km/3.7mi along D 93 to Sisteron, take the road on the left.* The road goes upstream through a gorge and reaches a cirque below the cliffs of the Vercors Massif. In 1188, Cistercian monks founded an abbey in this remote place. The church and refectory can only be seen from the outside.

Pontaix – *10km/6.2mi west along D 93 towards Crest.*
This old wine-growing village, backing onto a knoll crowned by a 13C castle, forms the most attractive picture of the middle Drôme Valley. The castle keep stands 70m/230ft above the river. The Protestant church contains 15C and 17C paintings.

Le Claps – *20km/12.4mi southeast along D 93, just beyond Luc-en-Diois.* This pile of rocks is the result of a huge landslide which occurred in the 15C. It formed two natural dams and two lakes which have now dried up. The pile of rocks nearer the railway viaduct is the most impressive. Higher up, at a place known as the "**Saut de la Drôme**", the river rushes through a small artificial tunnel and splashes onto the rocks; it is worth stopping when the river is in spate.

DIGNE-LES-BAINS ‡‡

Population 16 087
Michelin map 81 fold 17 or 245 fold 21
Local maps see Préalpes de DIGNE and ROUTE NAPOLÉON

Situated along the Route Napoléon, on the banks of the River Bléone, in a beautiful mountain setting, Digne is a sought-after spa resort and tourist centre.

This important Gallo-Roman city and medieval bishopric is today the main administrative town of the Alpes-de-Haute-Provence *département*, as well as a lively commercial town, which centralises the regional production of fruit and lavender.

A procession of flower-covered floats takes place every year in August and a lavender fair is held in September.

The wide boulevard Gassendi, shaded by plane trees, and the place Charles-de-Gaulle are the liveliest part of town. An international sculpture exhibition organised in Digne between 1983 and 1991 revealed several major talents; prize-winning works in Carrara marble decorate roundabouts, squares and public gardens; note in particular a very realistic "hand" on the right of the town hall. *A list of the works displayed is available at the tourist office.*

Famous personalities – Pierre Gassendi (1592-1655) was a philosopher, mathematician, astronomer and physicist, a great admirer of Galileo, who pioneered the study of astronomical phenomena through a telescope.

The engineer **Alphonse Beau de Rochas** (1815-1893) worked on a telegraphic link between France and England in the 1850s and later suggested the construction of a metallic tunnel under the Channel.

The explorer and writer **Alexandra David-Neel** (1868-1969), who, in 1924, was the first European woman to enter the capital of Tibet disguised as a native, settled in Digne in 1927 and bequeathed her house and her collections to the town.

Réserve géologique de Haute-Provence – Digne is at the heart of a vast conservation area, particularly interesting from a geological point of view. The **Centre de Géologie**, situated in Digne, administers the reserve.

THE SPA TOWN

The town's waters have been famous since Antiquity, but the spa activities had dwindled over the centuries until, in 1975, the municipality took over the running of the baths; a new building was inaugurated in 1982 and the number of people taking the waters has been consistently growing ever since.

The **baths** are situated 3km/1.8mi southeast of the town. The waters, springing from the St-Pancrace Cliff at a temperature of 42°C/107.6°F, are sulphureous, calcareous, slightly radioactive and recommended for the treatment of rheumatism and respiratory ailments.

SIGHTS

Old town – A network of twisting lanes and stairs surrounds the mound crowned by the Cathédrale St-Jérôme with its characteristic campanile. It is possible to reach the cathedral by walking up the picturesque Montée St-Charles which starts on the right of rue de l'Hubac. Pedestrian shopping streets at the foot of the mound have been renovated and the buildings painted in pleasant pastel colours.

★Musée de Digne (B M¹) ⊘ –
Founded in 1889 and housed in the former almshouse, it is both a natural history and fine art museum.

A large collection of 19C scientific instruments is displayed in the entrance hall, as a reminder of the town's vocation for astronomical studies. Among the most remarkable exhibits are the **astronomical clock** which tells both the solar and legal times and gives useful geographical information. It was patented in 1865 after 22 years of research and adjustment.

The natural history collections include minerals, shells, local fossils and butterflies.

The first level displays works by 19C Provençal artists: Martin, Mayan, Guindon, Ponson, Nardi, water-colours by Paul Martin, the founder of the museum...

Musée de Digne

The Virgin with a missal by C Maratta

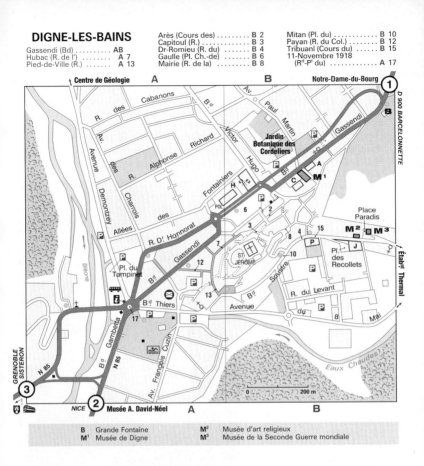

DIGNE-LES-BAINS

Gassendi (Bd) . . . . AB
Hubac (R. de l') . . . . A 7
Pied-de-Ville (R.) . . . . . . A 13

Arès (Cours des) . . . . B 2
Capitoul (R.) . . . . B 3
Dr-Romieu (R. du) . . . . . . B 4
Gaulle (Pl. Ch.-de) . . . . B 6
Mairie (R. de la) . . . . B 8

Mitan (Pl. du) . . . . B 10
Payan (R. du Col.) . . . . B 12
Tribuanl (Cours du) . . . . . . B 15
11-Novembre 1918
(Rd-Pt du) . . . . A 17

B Grande Fontaine
M¹ Musée de Digne

M² Musée d'art religieux
M³ Musée de la Seconde Guerre mondiale

The stock of older works is rich in Italian paintings: the major work is the *Virgin with a Missal* by the 17C Roman artist, **Carlo Maratta**. The Venitian School is represented by *The Allegory of Vice and Virtue* by **Francesco Ruschi**. The Flemish and Dutch Schools are illustrated by two portraits by **Franz Pourbus** (1569-1622) and **Van Ravesteyn**. In addition, there is a small but fine collection of Italian and French drawings and wash-drawings.

On the third floor, southern Alpine society is illustrated by the reconstruction of a street lined with workshops: the hairdresser's, the hatter's, the cobbler's, the photographer's and above all the goldsmith's.

In the basement, a couple of rooms house an important collection of archeological finds from the neolithic, Gallo-Roman and medieval periods.

Musée d'art religieux (B M²) ⊘ – This museum, housed in the Chapelle des Pénitents, displays a regional collection of religious *objets d'art*, presents temporary exhibitions on religious art and shows video films on various subjects.

Musée de la Seconde Guerre mondiale (B M³) ⊘ – This small museum, situated on place Paradis, is appropriately housed in a former civil defence shelter; exhibits include documents and objects from the period of the Second World War showing the strategic importance of Digne and the damages suffered by the town.

Jardin botanique des Cordeliers (B) ⊘ – This is a medieval-style garden laid in the grounds of a former Cordelier monastery with medicinal plants, herbs and a vegetable patch.

Grande Fontaine (B B) – The 19C fountain situated at the end of boulevard Gassendi consists of two Doric porticoes perpendicular to one another and limestone concretions covered with moss.

Ancienne cathédrale Notre-Dame-du-Bourg ⊘ – *Access by ① on the town plan.* This vast Provençal Romanesque church, built of blue schist between 1200 and 1330, has an elegant Lombard doorway surmounted by a large rose-window and preceded by crouching lions.

The vaulting of the imposing nave is slightly pointed; the lower-vaulted chancel ends with a square east end. There is a faded 14C mural on the inside of the west front, depicting the Trinity, and large **painted medalions** in other parts of the church. The nave **murals**, dating from the 15C and 16C, illustrate the Last Judgement, the Garden of Eden, Hell, the Virtues and the Vices.

Excavations in the lower part of the bell-tower, have revealed traces of the vast original church, dating from the 5C AD.

Crypt – The visit starts with the original 5C edifice; in the chancel, note the marble altar which was returned to its original place. The 5C mosaic and the east end can be seen from a high platform. Next comes the burial area and the north wall where the construction of the Romanesque cathedral is explained. Note the beautiful capitals of the bell-tower, which is older than the present building.

This cathedral was used as a model for other edifices in the region *(see SEYNE)*.

Fondation Alexandra-David-Neel ⊙ – *Access by ② on the town plan. Along the road to Nice, past the Total petrol station.*

In 1927, Alexandra David-Neel fell under the charm of the Alpes-de-Haute-Provence region; she bought a house in Digne which she called Samten-Dzong (the fortress of meditation). She lived in it between her long travels throughout Asia and filled it with the souvenirs she brought back; she wrote many books about her unique experiences and bequeathed her house and collections to the town of Digne.

In 1924, she spent months disguised as a Tibetan beggar, her face blackened with soot, in order to cross the Himalayas and reach Tibet and its capital Lhasa, the Forbidden City. On her return, Alexandra David-Neel wrote her most famous book, *Voyage d'une Parisienne à Lhassa* (A Parisian's trip to Lhasa).

Fondation A David-Neel, Digne-les-Bains

Alexandra David-Neel

Centre de Géologie ⊙ – *Follow avenue Demontzey and quai St-Benoît, cross the River Bléone and turn left immediately after the bridge; follow the signs to the parking area. The centre is accessible on foot by the marked path offering fine views of Digne.*

Note the frescoes decorating the façade of the building housing the Centre de Géologie. The edifice is built on tufa, due to the presence of a petrifying waterfall; strange limestone concretions can be seen along the path linking the parking to the centre.

This is the heart of the **Réserve géologique de Haute-Provence** *(see Introduction: Nature parks and reserves)*; open to researchers as well as to the general public, the centre gathers all the information available on the region's geology and its laboratories offer researchers various means of investigation. The information is relayed to the public by the Musée de Géologie and through guided tours of several sites within the reserve's boundaries.

Musée de Géologie ⊙ – Three rooms are devoted to the geological history of the region. Sedimentation and fossilization of the Secondary and Tertiary eras are explained with the help of a video presentation. There are also reconstructions of sections of the seabed with casts of fossils which can subsequently be seen *in situ* throughout the reserve. The most impressive is a 4.5m/15ft-long ichtyosaurus *(see Préalpes de DIGNE)*. Another room shows samples of plants 300 million years old. The aquarium contains the last living fossils: nautilus, limulus...

EXCURSIONS

★**Courbons** – *Leave Digne by ③ on the town plan towards Sisteron and turn right before the railway station.*

The narrow twisting road rises rapidly through orchards of almond trees and offers clear **views**★ of the Digne Basin framed by barren mountains and dotted with drystone sheds and walls. Irrigation canals are also a reminder of traditional agricultural practices. The village clings to a rocky spur; the lovely 14C church stands near the cemetery, shaded by cypresses. From there, is to be had a fine overall **view**★.

Television relay – *8km. Leave Digne as for Courbons, drive for 4km/2.4mi and turn right. Follow the indications posted at the beginning of the road.*
The road climbs above the Bléone Valley, affording fine **views**. A small cedar forest gives way to scrubland brightened with flowers which is in turn replaced by silent and desolate heights. From the relay (1 166m/3 825ft), there is an extended **view**★ of the Préalpes de Digne to the north and of the mountains overlooking Grasse and Nice to the east, as well as bird's-eye views of Digne and the Bléone Valley.

★**St-Michel-de-Cousson** – *11km/6.8mi. Leave Digne towards the baths, along D 20 leading to Entrages.*
As one drives through the baths complex, the ruins of the Roman baths can be seen below on the right; the road then continues towards the Col de Corobin across a typical landscape of parallel ravines dug by erosion through black marl. Turn right onto D 120 towards **Entrages**, a charming village overlooking the Eaux-Chaudes Valley. Go through the village and park the car in front of the heavily restored 17C church. A signpost marks the beginning of the path leading to the Cousson's twin summits *(2hr easy walk; turn left at Pas d'Entrages);* from the top of the ridge, there is a lovely view of Entrages.
The **Chapelle Saint-Michel-de-Cousson** stands on top of the cliff overlooking the Asse Valley. Covered with *lauzes* (slabs of schist), it is plainly decorated apart from the fragment of a Merovingian sarcophagus placed above the doorway.
Gassendi made numerous astronomical observations from the barren summit.
A pilgrimage takes place every year on Whit Monday. There is a splendid overall **view**★ of the Asse Valley, of the Clue de Chabrières to the south and of the Bléone Valley further west.
It is possible to continue along the path to the main Cousson Summit (1 516m/4 974ft); walk round to the left of it to return to Pas d'Entrages.

Préalpes de DIGNE

Michelin map 81 folds 7 and 17 or 245 folds 8, 9 and 21

The Provençal Préalpes de Digne, lying between the Durance and Verdon rivers, are the least populated and most desolate mountains in the Alps region. Gradually left bare as a result of erosion, they were replanted with Austrian pines, larches and forest pines which help to retain the soil they grow on. There are, however, some pastures and cultivated basins. Mountain streams have cut deep through the limestone ridges, creating remote *clues* (gorges) which testify to the amazingly complex geology of the southern Préalpes.

Vallée de la Robine at the heart of the Préalpes de Digne

★VALLÉE DU BÈS

⬛ Round tour starting from Digne *95km/59mi*

This round tour *(3hr on foot excluding visits)* offers visitors the opportunity to discover several listed sites within the Réserve géologique de Haute-Provence, situated along the road which goes up the Bléone and Bès valleys from Digne to Barles *(see also Vallée de l'Asse de Clumanc)*.

‡‡ **Digne-les-Bains** – *See DIGNE-LES-BAINS.*
Drive north out of Digne-les-Bains along D 900ᴬ.

★**Dalle à ammonites géantes** – Situated 1km/0.6mi from Digne, on the left of the road, this tilted black-limestone slab bears the imprint of 1 553 ammonites, some of them huge, which lived here 200 million years ago.

★**Musée de site de l'ichtyosaure** – *After driving 7km/4.3mi north of Digne along D 900ᴬ, turn left towards La Robine. Park the car at the end of the village, past the school. Continue on foot to a fountain on the right, which bears the logo of the fossil. It is the starting point of a path marked by signposts bearing a sketch of the fossil. Access: 1hr on foot; walking shoes essential.*
The path crosses the mountain stream then turns left by a wood; walk past the barrier that bars access to motor vehicles. The path rises along the hillside and offers lovely views of La Robine and the **landscape of ravines**, known as *robines*, surrounding the village. Turn right by the panel marked "Propriété privée" and follow the path down to a stream. The path eventually reaches the site where the fossil lies under glass protection.
Ichtyosaurus, a 4.5m/15ft-long reptile, swam in the sea which covered the whole region 180 million years ago. Its fossilized skeleton, in remarkable condition, has been left *in situ* under glass protection. A frescoe shows the natural environment of this contemporary of the dinosaurs.

Site du "Vélodrome" – *8km/5mi from the intersection of D 900ᴬ and D 103. Leave the car before the bridge over D 900ᴬ. Follow the path signposted "Serre d'Esclangon". About 2hr on foot.*
The itinerary goes across an area where the reddish soil contrasts with the black pines growing on it. Keep going left until you reach the first height and proceed towards the ruins of the village of Esclangon; turn right and aim for the Serre d'Esclangon Summit. The panorama unfolding to the west reveals one of the finest geological phenomena in the Alps, known as the "**Vélodrome**"★. This huge fan-shaped natural feature is the result, over a period of 16 million years, of the folding of layers of sandstone and conglomerate rocks within a basin subjected to intense compression from the surrounding mountains. Constant erosion gradually dug the Bès Valley and gave the landscape its present appearance.

Empreintes de pattes d'oiseaux – *10km/6.2mi from Digne-les-Bains; the site is signposted and it is possible to park on the left-hand side of D 900ᴬ.* Twenty million years ago, the sea had not yet retreated from the area and birds resembling plovers pecked away at what they could find in the damp sand of the beach. Their footprints are clearly visible in several places and a cast with an explanatory panel is exhibited at the roadside.
Various other geological imprints *(signposted and accompanied by explanatory panels)*, which can be seen on the way to Barles, illustrate the exceptional geological diversity of the region. Note, on the left, the fossilized **imprint of water current** in the sand.

★**Clues de Barles** – The road narrowly gets through these two gorges alongside the mountain stream. The second gorge is the most impressive: a rocky knoll, obstructing the valley at the end of an extremely narrow passage, outlines its deeply indented silhouette against the sky.
The **plant imprints** visible further on are the oldest evidence of what life was like 300 million years ago, when the region enjoyed a tropical climate.

Clue de Verdaches – It is covered with a rich green vegetation.

★**Col de Maure** – Alt 1 346m/4 416ft. The pass links the valleys of the Blanche and Bès rivers. In summer, these tributaries of the River Durance are reduced to a mere trickle and the arid appearance of their valleys is striking.
The small resort of **Grand Puy**, close to the pass, in a setting of larch woods and pastures, is a winter annexe of Seyne, situated lower down in the valley.

Seyne – *See SEYNE.*
From Seyne, drive south along D 7.
The road goes through a green valley then a small forested massif before reaching the pass.

★**Col du Fanget** – Alt 1 459m/4 787ft. There is a fine **view** to the north with the Blanche Valley in the foreground, flanked on the right by the Dormillouse Summit (2 505m/8 219ft) and Montagne de la Blanche, with the Parpaillon Massif and Gapençais mountains in the distance.
The narrow road joins D 900ᴬ near the Clue de Verdaches.

VALLÉE D'ASSE

② From Digne to Barrême
32km along D 20 and N 85 – 1hr

From Digne, drive along D 20 towards Entrages (see DIGNE-LES-BAINS: Excursions).
On the left, there is an ancient farm with a dovecote on either side, where Napoleon is
said to have stopped for a meal on his way back from Elba. Further on, the road runs
through the Cousson forest then climbs over the Col de Corobin to join N 85 leading
southeast to Barrême.

Barrême is situated at the confluence of the three small Asse valleys: the Asse de
Moriez (east), Asse de Blieux (southeast) and Asse de Clumanc (north) valleys.
Downstream from Barrême, the river is simply called Asse as it flows towards the
impressive **Clues de Chabrières★** *(see ROUTE NAPOLÉON).*

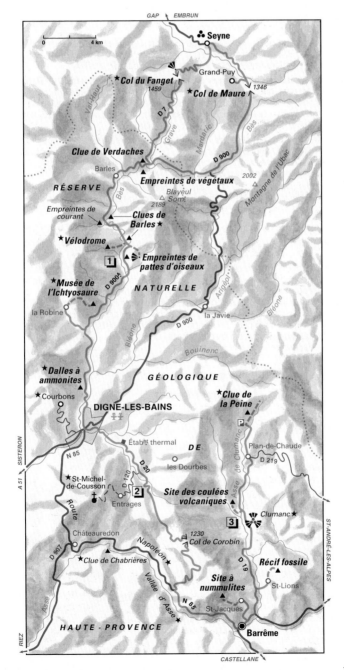

③ Vallée de l'Asse de Clumanc
18km/11.2mi along D 19

The road closely follows the Asse de Clumanc River from Barrême to Plan-de-Chaude. The valley contains a wealth of fossil-bearing layers which provide an invaluable insight into successive geological upheavals. The sites are listed and marked with explanatory panels.

Site à nummulites de St-Jacques – A path leads in 10min to a site close to the village of St-Jacques, where 40-million-year-old nummulite fossils can be seen in limestone strata.

Récif fossile de St-Lions – *Walking shoes recommended.* A path leads underwood in 30min to a site consisting of a coral reef which used to rest on shingles in this shallow part of the Alpine sea 35 million years ago. Sea urchins and oysters are recognisable in the strata; they were subsequently covered with clay and died.

Clumanc – The village spreads its houses covered with *lauzes* along the mountain stream. The Romanesque Église Notre-Dame houses an interesting tabernacle in gilt wood.

A path starting north of the village leads in 10min to the **panorama★** of the castle ruins. The hillside illustrates a period in the formation of the Alps with a mixture of marl and conglomerate rocks, successively folded and eroded.

Site des coulées volcaniques – *Drive to the intersection with D 219, leave the car in the car park before the post office and follow the marked footpath for 15min.* This is the only evidence of volcanic activity in the area: following a volcanic eruption which occurred 35 million years ago, lava and ashes settled at the bottom of the Alpine sea and were carried to this place.

★Clue de la Peine – *Leave the car in the parking area near some houses. Follow the path signposted "Clue de la Peine" for 20min.* The stream has cut vertically through layers of limestone deposited during the Secondary Era, which folded 60 million years later during the formation of the Alps.

Follow the same itinerary to return to Barrême or turn left at Plan-de-Chaude on D 219 to Notre-Dame-d'Entraigues, Lambruisse and St-André-des-Alpes.

Le DIOIS ★

Michelin map 77 folds 13, 14 and 15 or 244 folds 37, 38 and 39
and 245 folds 5 and 6 – Local map see below

Situated south of the Vercors Massif, the Diois is a pleasant area of coombs and plateaux with the wide valley of the River Drôme in its centre. It is an area of vineyards producing the famous Clairette de Die, of orchards, of lavender fields and of meagre pastures where goats and lambs peacefully graze.

Small towns, their squares shaded by plane trees and their houses decorated with pink and white oleander in typical Provençal style, offer tourists a welcome break between two breathtaking excursions through such impressive landscapes as the Cirque d'Archiane.

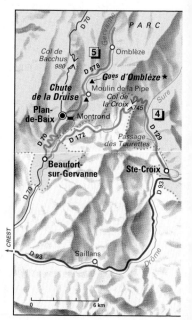

★ROUTE DU COL DE ROUSSET

① From Col de Rousset to Die
22km/13.7mi – 1hr – local map see opposite

This route leading from the Vercors to the Diois region illustrates the striking contrast which exists between the northern and southern Alps.

★★Col de Rousset – Alt 1 254m/4 114ft. The pass marks the climatic boundary between the northern and southern Alps so that one drives out of the tunnel to be suddenly confronted with a complete change of scenery, having left the green undulating landscapes of Vercors to enter the arid depression of the Die Basin, typical of southern areas. The road offers bird's-eye **views** of this depression, which fully reveal the harshness of the **landscape★★**. There are a number of ski runs along the slopes of the Beurre Mountain, near the pass *(chair-lift)*.

The road winds down to the Comane Valley in a series of wide hairpin bends beneath the jagged Rochers de Chironne, with the white cliffs of the Montagne de Glandasse in the distance.

Chamaloc – The mellow-stone houses, roofed with curved tiles, contribute to the Provençal appearance of the village. Between Chamaloc and Die, the **Ferme de Baise** has been turned into the Maison du Parc naturel régional du Vercors and offers visitors an interesting nature trail.

★**Die** – See DIE.

★★ROUTE DE MENÉE

② From Die to Col de Menée
45km/28mi – about 2hr – local map see below

The pass is usually blocked by snow from December to March.

★**Die** – See DIE.

From Die, follow D 93 towards Gap.

The road runs through the Die Basin, among vineyards overlooked by the limestone cliffs of the Glandasse Mountain.

In Pont-de-Quart, turn left onto D 539.

Châtillon-en-Diois – The village has retained its medieval character. An intricate network of streets, narrow lanes and covered passages, known as *viols* in local dialect, surrounds place Reviron overlooked by the clock tower. Cool fountains, flowers, and tiled roofs brighten the grey-limestone buildings.

Turn left into D 120 towards Col de Menée. In Menée, take D 224 to Archiane.

★★**Cirque d'Archiane** – The upper end of the Archiane Valley is barred by escarpments forming a splendid amphitheatre split into two by a huge promontory known as the "Jardin du Roi". The area is ideal for mountaineering and hiking to the high plateaux of the Vercors Massif *(GR 93)*.

Beyond Les Nonières, the road rises in a succession of hairpin bends: the barren landscape, dotted with clusters of lavender and overlooked by the impressive Rocher de Combau, gradually gives way to pine woods and pastures.

★**Col de Menée** – The road goes through a tunnel (alt 1 402m/4 600ft), beneath the pass (alt 1 457m/4 780ft). From the southern end of the tunnel, the view extends to the Montagne de Glandasse on the horizon, whereas from the northern end, there is a fine **panorama** of the isolated Mont Aiguille.

★ROUTE DE GRIMONE

③ From Châtillon-en-Diois to Lus-la-Croix-Haute
32km/20mi – about 1hr – local map see below

Châtillon-en-Diois – See Route de Menée above.
Leave Châtillon-en-Diois along D 539.

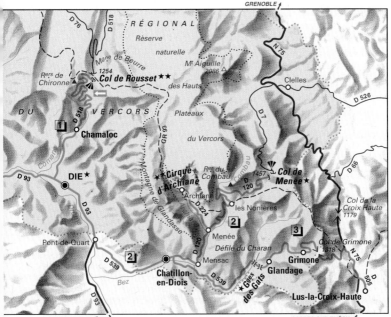

★**Gorges des Gats** – Prior to the building of the road in 1865, several fords had to be crossed in order to go up this extremely narrow gorge (a few metres/yards only in places) with more than 100m/328ft-high cliffs on either side. Further on, four tunnels negotiate the **Défilé du Charan**.

Glandage – A group of young people has given a new lease of life to this more or less abandoned village.
Beyond Glandage, the southern vegetation gives way to oaks and Austrian pines.

Grimone – The closely grouped houses of this hamlet have large steep roofs, well adapted to high altitude.
Beyond the **Col de Grimone** (alt 1 318m/4 324ft), the view extends southeast to the Montagne de Garnesier and Crête des Aiguilles.
Drive south on N 75.

Lus-la-Croix-Haute – *See Le BOCHAINE.*

ROUTE DU COL DE LA CROIX

④ From Die to Plan-de-Baix

37km/23mi – 1hr – local map see p 177

★**Die** – *See DIE.*
From Die, take D 93 towards Crest then turn right onto D 129 to Ste-Croix.

Ste-Croix – Built on a narrow ridge between the rivers Drôme and Sure, the village is overlooked by 13C ruins. The church is divided into two parts to accommodate both Catholic and Protestant services.
Turn left onto D 172.
The narrow twisting road leads through oak and pine woods to the **Col de la Croix** (alt 745m/2 444ft) then down the Sépie Valley to Beaufort-sur-Gervanne.

Beaufort-sur-Gervanne – The way into Beaufort offers a spectacular view which includes what remains of the fortifications now turned into a pleasant walk. The recently rebuilt church has retained an arcaded bell-tower.
Follow D 70 to Plan-de-Baix.

Plan-de-Baix – Built on a hillside, the village is overlooked by limestone cliffs (Rochers du Vellan). The 12C church has retained its dome on squinches.
The 13C-14C **Château de Montrond**, remodelled many times, towers over the Gervanne Valley.
From Plan-de-Baix, it is possible to drive north to Léoncel and the Col de la Bataille via the Col de Bacchus *(see Le VERCORS: Route du Col de la Bataille)*.

★GORGES D'OMBLÈZE

⑤ Excursion from Plan-de-Baix

9.5km/6mi – about 1hr 30min – local map see p 177

Plan-de-Baix – *See Route du col de la Croix.*
At first D 578 follows the deep Gervanne Valley, high above the river-bed, then it runs down the slopes, planted with box trees and pines, towards the entrance of the gorge guarded by a towering rock.

Chute de la Druise – Turn right in Le Moulin-la-Pipe towards Ansage and drive for 1km/0.6mi *(parking area)*. A marked path leads to the top of the waterfall; from there, another steep and stony path leads down to the bottom *(1hr return on foot; wear strong walking shoes and beware of frequently falling rocks)*.
The Gorges d'Omblèze, lined by impressive limestone cliffs, start beyond Le Moulin-la-Pipe. The Cascades de la Pissoire fall by the roadside; one of these waterfalls often dries up in summer. Now and then, there are glimpses of the Col de la Bataille to the north.

Vallée de la Moyenne DURANCE ★

Michelin map 81 folds 5, 6, 15 and 16, 114 fold 5 or 245 folds 20 and 33
Local map see p 180

The River Durance, which is the last main tributary of the Rhône as it makes its way to the sea, takes its source near Briançon and flows along a 324km/201mi course before joining the Rhône. It is the most unpredictable major river of the southern Alps which, for a long time, defied all attempts to harness it but is today one of the great economic assets of the region.

South of Sisteron, the Durance enters the Mediterranean Basin; the gradient of the river bed is less steep, the valley widens and the river flows between stony banks; its rate of flow is regulated by dams built along its course or that of its tributaries.

The Durance

Frédéric Mistral, the famous Provençal poet, used to say: "The Mistral (a strong wind blowing down the Rhône Valley), Parliament and the Durance are the curse of Provence". This unruly river which, in the middle and lower part of its valley, has a 1km/0.6mi-wide bed, used to be a real threat for local people.

Since the 1960s, the flow of the river has been diverted through a complex network of canals for the purpose of irrigation, urban water supply and production of hydroelectricity. In addition, new ecosystems have been able to flourish in the river bed, for instance wooded areas favourable to the development of animal life including beavers.

---

① FROM SISTERON TO MANOSQUE

74km/46mi – about 3hr – local map see p 180

★★**Sisteron** – See SISTERON.

Leave Sisteron by ② on the town plan and drive along N 85.

The road follows the Durance harnessed by the Salignac Dam, makes its way between the river and the steep edge of the Montagne de Lure and skirts the Lac de l'Escale Dam as it reaches Château-Arnoux.

Château-Arnoux-Saint-Auban – The national gliding centre is nearby and the Festival de jazz des Alpes-de-Haute-Provence takes place in the town. The square 16C **castle**, flanked by round and square towers, is now the town hall.

2km/1.2mi further on, along N 96, turn right along the road signposted "route touristique de St-Jean, aire de pique-nique. Vue panoramique".

★**Belvédère de la chapelle St-Jean** – *15min return on foot. Leave the car at the top of the hill (parking area near the chapel) and climb along the footpath to a vewing table near a pylone.*
There is a fine panoramic view from west to east of the Montagne de Lure, the Durance Valley, Sisteron, the Lac de l'Escale Dam and the Rochers des Mées.

Return to N 96 and continue south.

The "Pénitents des Mées"

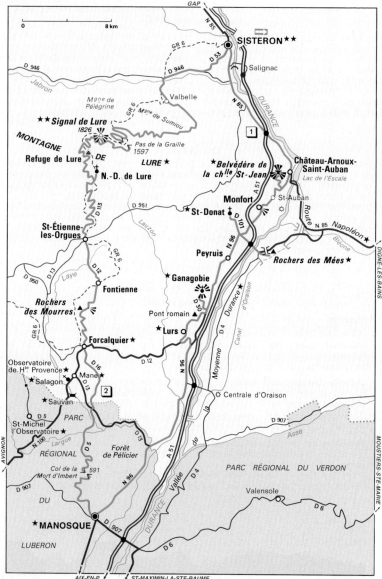

Montfort – This hilltop village overlooking the Durance is extremely picturesque with its stepped streets, lined with charming old houses, climbing up to the 16C castle; there is a fine view of the Durance Valley and Valensole Plateau.

2km/1.2mi further on, turn right onto D 101.

The road follows a wooded vale towards St-Donat.

★**Église St-Donat** – Built in the 11C on the site where St Donat, the religious recluse, had settled in the 6C, the church is one of the rare specimens of early Romanesque style in Provence *(restoration work in progress)*.
Note its harmonious proportions in spite of its extreme simplicity. The large nave is separated from the narrow aisles by rounded arches resting on massive round pillars. This vast basilica was intended to contain a great number of pilgrims.

Rejoin N 96 and cross it to take D 4^A across the River Durance.

★**Rochers des Mées** – These 100m/328ft-high conglomerate rocks, towering over the village of Les Mées and eroded into strange shapes, are known as the "**Pénitents des Mées**". According to **legend**, a group of monks had fallen in love with some beautiful Arab girls whom a local lord had brought back from a campaign against the Sarracens. St Donat punished the monks for their sinful lust by changing them into stones as they walked in procession along the Durance.

★**Walk to the top of the Pénitents** – *3hr on foot. Start from the camp site situated beyond Notre-Dame de la Salette on D 101. Leave the car on the roadside.*
Go down to the bottom of the valley and cross the low wall of the second reservoir to reach the north bank. From there, a path, marked in green, meanders up *(keep to the right)* to the Forêt des Pénitents rich in Mediterranean vegetation (holm oak, Aleppo pine, rock rose, pistachio). As you reach the pass (alt 600m/1968ft), walk 91m/100yd to the left for striking views of the "Pénitents". Return to the pass and go down to the rocky ridge and the foot of the "Pénitents" *(a few steep sections)*. Continue left along the path *(facing the Durance Valley)* until you reach a surfaced road which skirts the old aqueduct and leads to the village of Les Mées.
Turn left and follow D 101. Return to N 96 and drive towards Manosque.

Peyruis – The old part of the village, once guarded by a drawbridge, is still standing. The 16C church has a six-sided bell-tower, built in tufa, with gargoyles in the shape of a lion's head.

Turn right onto D 30 6km/3.7mi beyond Peyruis.

★**Monastère de Ganagobie** – *See Monastère de GANAGOBIE.*

Return to N 96 but turn towards Lurs just before joining it.

The road follows an ancient Roman way and crosses the Buès over a single-arched **Roman bridge** dating from the 2C AD.

★**Lurs** – This village occupies a remarkable **position★** on top of a rocky spur overlooking the Durance and the area around Forcalquier. Once a medieval strong-hold belonging to the bishops of Forcalquier, it was gradually deserted and became derelict until it was "revived" by a group of graphic designers and is today the summer rendezvous of the printing profession through the **Rencontres internationales de Lure** and the capital of graphic arts.
Go through the clock gate surmounted by a campanile, past the church with its interesting wall-tower and along the winding streets lined with corbelled houses; there are traces of the old fortifications. Note the rustic open-air theatre, the restored **priory**, now a cultural centre, and the bishops' castle. Walk round the latter along the **Promenade des Évêques**, lined with 15 oratories dating from 1864, to the Chapelle Notre-Dame-de-Vie offering fine **views** of the Durance and Préalpes de Digne on one side, of the Montagne de Lure and Forcalquier Basin on the other.

A small road south of the village leads to N 96 and to Manosque.

Across the Durance, a canal diverts the flow of the Bléone and Durance rivers to the Oraison power station. Beyond the confluence of the Asse and the Durance, the road leaves the edge of the river to reach Manosque.

★**Manosque** – *See MANOSQUE.*

2 # FROM MANOSQUE TO SISTERON
(across the Montagne de Lure)
87km/54mi – about 2hr 30min – local map see p 180

From Manosque, drive north along D 5 via the Col de la Mort d'Imbert which offers lovely views of Manosque and its surroundings. Turn right onto D 16 *(for the section Forcalquier-Sisteron, see FORCALQUIER: Excursion).*

EMBRUN ★

Population 5 793
Michelin map 77 folds 17 and 18 or 245 fold 9
Local map see Barrage et lac de SERRE-PONÇON

Embrun is picturesquely perched on a rocky ledge, 80m/262ft above the River Durance and the Serre-Ponçon Lake. Its church, the finest in Dauphiné, testifies to its past influence as a religious centre.
Today, the town is a pleasant summer resort offering a wide choice of water sports on the lake as well as canoeing on the Durance and hiking in the surrounding area. In winter, it is a centre of cross-country and Alpine skiing practised on the slopes of Les Orres and near the mountain village of Crévoux.

Religious centre – During the Roman occupation, Embrun was an important town on the way from Briançon to Arles. It later became the main religious centre of the Alpes-Maritimes region and was incorporated into the Holy Roman Empire, the arch-bishops of Embrun being granted temporal power over the whole region.
From the 14C onwards, the pilgrimage to Notre-Dame-du-Réal attracted large crowds. The rank of canon conferred on King Louis XI during his visit was passed on to all his successors and is now bestowed on the elected French president.
Owing to its geographical position, Embrun was invaded many times: by the Sarracens, by the Huguenots during the Wars of Religion, by the duke of Savoie. It lost its importance as a religious centre soon after the Revolution.

★CATHÉDRALE NOTRE-DAME-DU-RÉAL *45min*

"Réal" is a distortion of "royal". The edifice was built during the transition period from the Romanesque style to the Gothic style (late 12C, early 13C). Its originality lies in the alternate use of black schist and white limestone. The steeple was rebuilt in the 19C, taking the 14C steeple as a model *(see Introduction: Art and architecture)*.

★**Portail "le Réal"** – This is a remarkable example of Lombard art. The arch of the doorway is supported by pink-marble columns; the front ones stand on two squatting lions. At the back, two slender columns on either side rest on telamones; a small figure, held between the two left-hand ones, is said to be the dean of the cathedral chapter who refused to pay the workers.

Pilgrims prayed in front of The Adoration of the Magi which used to decorate the tympanum; the painting is now reproduced as a mosaic inside the cathedral.

Interior ⊘ – The Byzantine influence explains the absence of a transept. The chancel, in pure Romanesque style, was once covered with frescoes. The Gothic nave, surmounted with quadripartite vaulting, is flanked by Romanesque aisles.

The stained glass of the rose window over the southwest doorway dates from the 15C; the late-15C organ is one of the oldest in France. Opposite, above the altar, there is a 16C picture depicting the Entombment of Christ. Note, in the right-hand aisle, the Adoration of the Magi mosaic and the 9C christening font.

★**Treasury** ⊘ – It was one of the richest in France before being plundered in the 16C by the duke of Lesdiguières' Protestant troops. However, it still contains an important collection of religious ornaments, paintings, holy receptacles, monstrances, the Embrun Missal and 14C illuminated antiphonaries.

ADDITIONAL SIGHTS

Place de l'Archevêché – The Belvédère du Roc *(viewing tables)* offers a fine view of the Durance Valley and Morgon Mountain.

The cathedral chapter held meetings in the 13C **Maison des Chanonges** ⊘. It is one of the rare examples of medieval domestic architecture in the area.

Tour Brune ⊘ – This 12C tower is the former keep of the episcopal castle; it now houses a **Musée du Paysage**, devoted to the Parc national des Écrins. There is a fine view from the terrace *(viewing table)*.

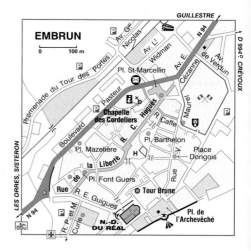

Rue de la Liberté and rue Clovis-Hugues – The town's shopping district is very lively in summer.

Note the fountain on place Font Guers adorned with the arms of France, Dauphiné and the cathedral chapter. Further along rue de la Liberté, at no 6, there is a beautiful wooden doorway in Renaissance style, surmounted by a lion carved in the round. Continue along rue Clovis-Hugues and admire the 12C carved façade between no 29 and no 31. Further on, a beautiful 16C fountain decorates place St-Marcellin and there are interesting 14C corbelled houses along rue Caffe.

Chapelles des Cordeliers ⊘ – *It houses the tourist office.* The side chapels of the former Franciscan church have survived; they are decorated with recently restored 15C and 16C murals★, some of them believed to be the work of Giacomo Jaquerio and his assistants.

EXCURSIONS

✳Les Orres

16km/10mi southeast. Leave Embrun along N 94 towards Gap, drive for 2km/1.2mi and turn left onto D 40.

The twisting road follows the Eyssalette Valley and affords lovely views of the northern part of the Serre-Ponçon Lake.

Turn left onto D 39 leading to St-Sauveur.

St-Sauveur – The bell-tower of the 15C church is surmounted by a spire and pyramidions; the west doorway has a pointed archivolt.

Return to D 40 via Les Gaillards and turn left.

Les Orres – This winter resort (alt 1 600m/5 249ft), created in 1970, developed rapidly to form, with its annexes of Le Pramouton (Alpine skiing) and Champs-Lacas (cross-country skiing), one of the main winter sports resorts of the southern Alps, offering a wide choice of activities: snowmobile, paragliding, snowboarding... There are also numerous summer activities to choose from, including swimming, tennis, trap-shooting, riding and aerial sports.

★**Prelongis and Fontaine chair-lifts** – Alt 2 408m/7 900ft. Fine views of the ski slopes running through a larch and pine forest below the Boussolenc Peak. From the top the view embraces part of the Serre-Ponçon Lake and the Embrun area.

Crévoux

13km/8mi. From Embrun, drive east (the road starts in front of a factory) via Coin.
The road crosses the Durance and rises above the wild Crévoux Valley. The small mountain village of Crévoux appears to be enclosed by the slopes of the Méale Mountain and the rocky wall of the St-André Peak, streaming with cascades.

For a quiet place to stay
*Consult the annual **Michelin Red Guide France** which offers a selection*
of pleasant and quiet hotels in a convenient location.

ENTREVAUX ★

Population 785
Michelin map 81 fold 19, 115 fold 13 or 245 fold 23

Entrevaux lies on the north bank of the River Var, beneath a strange rocky spur crowned by the citadel, in a **setting**★★ which is characteristic of the upper Var Valley. Founded in the 11C, the town was granted its charter in 1542 by King François I. In 1690, when war broke out between France and Savoie, Vauban, Louis XIV's military engineer, linked the castle and the town, built the bastions, the fortified gates and erected a wall round the town. Today, Entrevaux has retained its 17C appearance.

The most famous culinary speciality of Entrevaux is "la Secca d'Entrevaux", thin slices of dried beef sprinkled with olive oil and lemon.

★WALLED TOWN *30min*

Ramparts – The drawbridge of the Porte Royale, flanked by two round towers, leads into the town. The guardsroom situated beneath the archway houses the tourist office from where it is possible to get to the watchpath linking the three fortified gates: Porte de France, Porte Royale and Porte d'Italie.

Medieval gardens – Situated by the old watchpath, these gardens contain exotic and medicinal plants, culinary herbs, vegetables and fruit.

Old town – Three main streets: Haute rue, Basse rue and rue du Marché go through the town, linked by a network of cool and dark alleyways. Most of the houses date from the 17C and the 18C.

Cathedral ⊙ – Entrevaux was a bishopric from the 12C to the 1789 Revolution. The present church was built between 1610 and 1627 and subsequently incorporated into the ramparts.
The **interior**★ contains a wealth of classical and Baroque decoration. The gilt altarpiece of the high altar has a beautiful 17C painting in its centre, depicting the *Assumption of the Virgin Mary* by Mimault. On either side, note the 17C stalls carved by local craftsmen. On the left-hand wall hangs a *Deposition* believed to be by Jouvenet and, opposite, another *Deposition* by Philippe de Champaigne is said to be a gift from Louis XIV. To the left of the entrance, the retable of St John the Baptist, the patron saint of Entrevaux, and the silver bust of the saint are also noteworthy *(see Introduction: Festivals).*
The 1717 organ by Jean Eustache was recently restored.
The vestry contains some lovely 15C and 17C church furniture and splendid 17C silk robes.

Musée de la Moto ⊙ – *Rue Sénéquier.* This small museum houses an interesting collection of motorcycles, all of them in working order, going back to 1901.

The walled town and citadel of Entrevaux

J Guillard/SCOPE

CITADEL ⊘ 1hr

Perched 135m/443ft above the town, the castle is accessible via a ramp following a zigzag course and strengthened by about 20 fortified gates. The ramp rises from the magazine to the entrance of the castle defended by a redoubt with a draw-bridge dating from 1693.

The castle buildings are being restored, but it is worth going round for the remarkable **views**★ of the Var Valley and the roofs of Entrevaux.

ADDITIONAL SIGHTS

Moulin à huile et à farine ⊘ – *Near place Moreau, outside the walled town.* The flow of the River Chalvagne used to drive the oil and flour mills; one of them still produces oil.

★**Viewpoint** – *As you come out of the parking area situated on the opposite bank of the Var, follow the road signposted "Col du Buis".* It rises rapidly and affords fine **views**★ of the walled town, the citadel and the remarkable setting of Entrevaux.

Route de l'ÉPINE ★

Michelin map 74 folds 14 and 15 or 244 folds 17 and 18 – west of Chambéry

The small limestone range, which the road described below crosses, separates the Chambéry and Lac du Bourget depressions from the green hills of the Bugey savoyard area. Geologically, it is an extension of the southern Jura mountains.

LAC D'AIGUEBELETTE

① From Chambéry to Pont-de-Beauvoisin via the Col de l'Épine
47km/29.2mi – 2hr

Roads between Chambéry and the Lac d'Aiguebelette are busy on Sundays during the fine season. The Col de l'Épine is blocked by snow from November to April.

Leave Chambéry by ③ on the town plan along N 6, then turn right onto D 916.

Between St-Sulpice and the pass, the road offers glimpses of Mont Revard with its cable-car station, and of Dent du Nivolet surmounted by a huge cross; beneath them lie Aix-les-Bains, its lake and the Chambéry conurbation; the last bend before the pass makes a good viewpoint.

On the other hand, the drive down from the pass towards Chambéry affords fine views of Mont Granier with the indented Allevard Massif behind it and the snow-capped Lauzière range on the horizon.

Col de l'Épine – Alt 987m/3 238ft. The pass may get its name from a thorn, believed to be from Christ's crown of thorns, which was venerated in Nances Castle nearby. Beyond the pass, the cliff road offers bird's-eye views of the Lac d'Aiguebelette overlooked by the sparsely forested escarpments of Mont Grelle, with the Chartreuse summits in the background and the Vercors cliffs still further away. The Bas-Dauphiné plateaux can be seen to the west.

The road skirts the western shore of the lake before reaching St-Alban-de-Montbel.

★**Lac d'Aiguebelette** – The lake is easily accessible from Lyon via the Lyon-Chambéry motorway. This attractive triangular expanse of water dotted with two islets (a chapel stands on one of them), covers an area of 550ha/1 359 acres; its unpolluted waters are 71m/233ft deep in parts. The steep and forested eastern shore contrasts with the more accessible western and southern shores where leisure activities are concentrated: fishing, swimming, boating and pedalo rides. Marked footpaths offer interesting hikes in the surrounding area.

It is also possible to make a round tour of the lake along a picturesque winding road *(17km/10.6mi)*.

Road D 37 leaves D 921E to the right and rises to a cultivated plateau; beyond Ayn, D 36 climbs over the Col du Blanchet then suddenly runs steeply down to Vérel-de-Montbel and through fields of maize and tobacco towards Le Pont-de-Beauvoisin, with the Sûre, Charmant Som and Grand Som summits on the horizon.

Le Pont-de-Beauvoisin – Situated on the banks of the Guiers, which marks the border between the Savoie and Isère *départements*, this small town is at the centre of an important tobacco-growing area, its other main economic activity being the manufacture of furniture. From the border **bridge** spanning the Guiers, there is a pleasant view of the river lined with fine old houses over which towers the steeple of the "Église des Carmes".

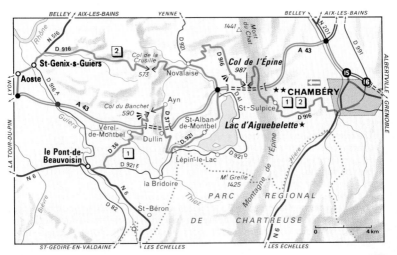

It is worth making a detour to **St-Geoire-en-Valdaine** *(14km/8.7mi to the south along D 82)* to see the 12C-15C church, which contains a set of magnificent Renaissance **stalls★**, and the **Château de Longpra** ⊙ *(see Introduction: ABC of architecture)*, the 18C residence of a former member of the Grenoble Parliament, with a remarkable interior decoration, in particular the chapel and the dining room.

★LE BUGEY SAVOYARD

② From Chambéry to Aoste

50km/31mi – about 2hr (excluding a tour of the museum)
From Chambéry to Novalaise, the itinerary is the same as that of drive ①.

Beyond Novalaise, D 16 winds along the mountainside to the Col de la Crusille (alt 573m/1 880ft) then follows the valley of a small tributary of the Rhône down to **St-Genix-sur-Guiers**. This former border town is now a lively tourist centre close to the vital Lyon-Chambéry motorway.

Drive 3km/1.9mi southwest along N 516.

Aoste – This busy market town with a thriving food-processing industry was, in Roman times, an independent town *(vicus)* controlling the traffic between the main city of Vienne *(south of Lyon)* to Italy via the Petit-St-Bernard Pass. Aoste, named after Emperor Augustus, owed its importance to its production of pottery and ceramics, some of which have been found as far away as Germany and the British Isles.

Musée archéologique ⊙ – Recently reorganised, the museum illustrates life in Aoste under the Roman occupation. Note in particular a **"crossroads altar"** surmounted by a roof with four recesses intended for the deities of travelling. Social life in the Gallo-Roman city is also clearly explained: religious rituals (the goddess of Abundance is particularly attractive), domestic life (reconstruction of a kitchen), crafts (model of potters' workshops and rich collection of **ceramics★**).

Walk south across N 516 towards the old-age pensioners' home; a remarkably well-preserved **pottery kiln** can be seen *in situ*, under a concrete awning and behind glass, about 10m/11yd left of the entrance.

The A 43 motorway takes you back to Chambéry.

ÉVIAN-LES-BAINS ‡‡‡

Population 6 895
Michelin map 89 fold 4 or 244 fold 9 – local map see Le CHABLAIS

Poetically known as the "pearl of Lake Geneva", Évian is remarkably well situated between the lake and the foothills of the Préalpes du Chablais. This famous spa town is also a lakeside and climatic resort, and, during the "season", a centre of fashionable entertainment whose influence extends all round the lake.

Opulent public buildings, palace-hotels nestling amid greenery are characteristic of this international holiday resort where taking the waters is not the main preoccupation.

The **Accords d'Évian** (Évian Treaty), acknowledging Algerian independence, were signed here on 18 March 1962.

THE SPA TOWN

The medicinal properties of Évian water were only discovered in 1789 when a gentleman from Auvergne realised it was dissolving the stones he was suffering from. However, Évian remained a small fortified town until 1865 when the lakeside promenade was built, partly over the water, thanks to Baron de Blonay who bequeathed his castle (situated where the casino now stands) to the town. The attractive promenade is backed by the **Établissement thermal** (the baths, **B F**), the **Villa Lumière** (**B H**), now the town hall, and the **Casino** (**B**), three remarkable examples of spa-resort architecture of the late 19C and early 20C.

The new baths (**C K**) are situated in the **Parc thermal** (**C**). The pump room, designed by Novarina (who is also responsible for the Palais des Congrès), was erected in 1956 and the Espace Thermal in 1983. This edifice is partly built below ground in order to preserve the appearance of the park.

Beyond the harbour where yachts find a mooring and where the ships of the lake shuttle come along the quayside, the **Jardin anglais** (**C**) offers good views of the Swiss shore (the best viewpoint is near the small beacon). A new marina has been created further east. At the other end of the town, there is an ultra-modern water-sports centre. The narrow and long rue Nationale, which has been pedestrianised is the town's main shopping street. Large hotels are scattered inland on the lower slopes of Gavot country.

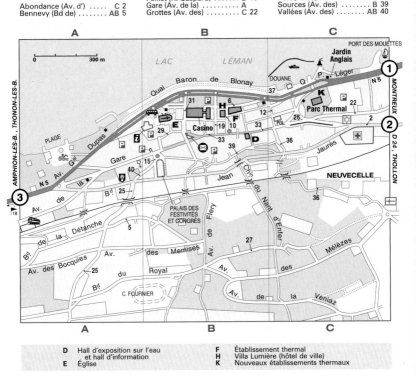

D	Hall d'exposition sur l'eau et hall d'information	
E	Église	
F	Établissement thermal	
H	Villa Lumière (hôtel de ville)	
K	Nouveaux établissements thermaux	

Every year in May, Évian holds the **Rencontres musicales**, an international music festival including a quartet competition *(every other year)* which helps young musicians to become famous.

Not far from Évian, **Amphion-les-Bains** was the first spa resort of the Chablais region, which became fashionable as early as the 17C, when the dukes of Savoie regularly took the waters.

The treatment – The baths are open from 1 February to the end of November. Évian water, filtered by sand of glacial origin, is cold (11.6°C/52.8°F) and low in minerals. It is used for drinking, for bathing or showering, in the treatment of kidney trouble, digestive complaints and other disorders which respond to hydrotherapy. Bottled Évian water is one of the main French mineral waters.

SIGHTS

Exhibition and Information Centre about Évian water ⊘ (**B D**) – The centre is housed in the former pump room (1905) of the **Cachat spring**, an Art-Nouveau building surmounted by a cupola. The spring is named after its owner who improved the installations in 1824.

Church (**B E**) – This church is characteristic of early Gothic style in Savoie (end of 13C); it was remodelled and restored for the last time in 1865; however, it has retained some of its original capitals and a wooden sculpture carved in low relief, dating from 1493, in the side chapel on the right of the chancel.

Monument de la comtesse de Noailles – *Leave Évian by ③ on the town plan, along N 5.* This small rotunda stands at the bottom of a narrow garden, which once belonged to the famous poetess.

Bottling factory ⊘ – This modern bottling factory, set up in Amphion-les-Bains, produces an average of 5 million litres of water per day, which makes it rank first among producers of mineral water.

Fontaines musicales (new marina known as "Les Mouettes") – These fountains, situated on the edge of the lake, perform a ballet to well-known classical music.

Évian and Lake Geneva

★★★LAC LÉMAN (Lake Geneva)

Lac Léman, which covers an area of 58 000ha/143 324 acres and reaches depths of 310m/1 017ft, is 13 times larger than the Lac du Bourget. Shaped like a crescent, it is 72km/44.7mi long and 13km/8mi wide at its widest point; the narrower part between Geneva and Yvoire is known as the Petit lac (small lake), the more open part as the Grand lac (large lake). A natural phenomenon, known as the **"bataillère"** can be observed from the heights overlooking Montreux on the Swiss side and Meillerie on the French side: the muddy waters of the Rhône flowing into the lake seem to be completely absorbed by the lake whereas, in fact, part of the river flow remains at a depth of 20m/66ft until the autumn.

The areas bordering the lake enjoy a microclimate: autumn in the Chablais can be glorious, in spite of frequent mist.

★★★**Boat trips** ⊘ – The ships of the Compagnie générale de navigation link the French and Swiss shores across the lake. From Évian, it is also possible to make a round tour of the lake, to cross over to Lausanne-Ouchy and to go on night excursions *(see Admission times and charges)*.

EXCURSION

Pic de Mémise *15km/9.3mi – 1hr 30min – local map see Le CHABLAIS.*

Leave Évian by ② *on the town plan.*

Road D 24 rises through a landscape of orchards. Two wide hairpin bends offer fine glimpses of the lake through the woods and give access to Thollon lying beneath the cliffs of the Pic de Mémise.

Thollon – This resort, which consists of several hamlets overlooking Lake Geneva stretched out 600m/1 968ft below, has become an annexe of Évian, both in summer owing to its fine situation and in winter because of the proximity of the Mémise ski slopes.

★★**Pic de Mémise** – Alt 1 677m/5 502ft. *30min return on foot.* The gondola brings visitors up to 1 596m/5 236ft on top of the Mémise cliffs. From there it is possible to reach the cross erected at the highest point and enjoy the **panorama** of the lake and of the Swiss shore from Nyon to Montreux, with the Jura mountains, Vaudois hills and Rochers de Naye in the background.

Winds blowing over Lake Geneva

The western part of the lake is particularly exposed to winds blowing from the Jura and Alps mountains. The locals give different names to different winds:
- The *bise*, a northeasterly wind, blows from Switzerland in winter for periods of up to three consecutive days;
- The *séchard*, an easterly wind blowing along the shore, is appreciated by sailing enthusiasts;
- The *joran*, a northwesterly wind blowing from the Swiss Jura mountains, brings spectacular storms which create waves several metres/yards high and stops as quickly as it starts;
- The west wind, which brings rain, is simply called *vent* (wind).

Michelin maps are revised regularly; *never travel with an out-of-date map.*

Le FAUCIGNY★★

Michelin map 89 folds 2, 3 and 13 or 244 folds 8, 9 and 10
Local map see p 191

This region, which, until the 14C, was a bone of contention between the Dauphins (rulers of Dauphiné) and the counts of Savoie, gets its name from Faucigny castle whose ruins still stand on a rocky spur overlooking the Arve Valley between Bonneville and Contamine-sur-Arve. The most interesting area from a touristic point of view, includes the Arve Valley from Bonneville to Sallanches and the valley of the River Giffre, a tributary of the Arve which leads to the heart of the Faucigny limestone heights.

High limestone Alps of the Faucigny area – On the French side of the Alps, this is the area which has the highest summits: huge limestone ridges and sharp peaks, which are the favourite training ground of moutaineers and rock-climbers.

The main tourist attraction is the impressive cirque known as the Fer à Cheval and for motorists, the snow-capped silhouette of **Mont Buet** (alt 3 099m/10 167ft) is a familiar landmark as they drive through the Arve and Giffre valleys.

The **Col d'Anterne** (alt 2 264m/7 428ft) offers experienced hikers the possibility of getting from the Sixt Valley to the Sallanches Basin or Chamonix Valley across the Fiz mountains *(Footpath GR 5)*.

Vallée de l'Arve – The Arve takes its source on the slopes of the Col de Balme, in the upper Chamonix Valley, then runs along the foot of the Mont-Blanc Massif, through the Sallanches Basin, the Magland Cluse and the Faucigny Plain, and eventually flows into the Rhône in Geneva. This Alpine valley became an international line of communication following the opening of the Mont-Blanc tunnel.

Le FAUCIGNY

★ROUTE DES GETS

① From Morzine to Cluses *43km/26.7mi – about 1hr – local map see opposite*

The Route des Grandes Alpes, D 902-N 202, links the Dranse de Morzine Valley to the Giffre and Arve valleys.

❋❋**Morzine** – *See MORZINE.*

From Morzine, drive west along D 28 then take D 902 towards Les Gets.

The road affords views of the Roc d'Enfer (alt 2 244m/7 362ft), one of the most rugged Chablais summits.

❋**Les Gets** – This peaceful summer holiday village is also a ski resort sought-after for the quality of its equipment and its children's facilities, and linked to the Franco-Swiss Portes du Soleil complex, which includes 12 resorts. There are six loops for a total of 20km/12.4mi of cross-country skiing tracks.

Housed in a 16C building, the **Musée de la Musique Mécanique** ⊙ contains an interesting collection of instruments used to reproduce music: barrel organs, music boxes, player-pianos, gramophones, orchestrinas, hurdy-gurdies...as well as automata and animated scenes. There are also reconstructions of various environments connected with music: music room, fairground, 1900-style bistro etc.

★★**Mont Chéry** ⊙ – Alt 1 827m/5 994ft. *10min gondola and chair-lift ride or 2.5km/1.5mi by road to Col de l'Encrenaz then 1hr 30min return on foot.* A vast **panorama** of the limestone Faucigny Mountains.

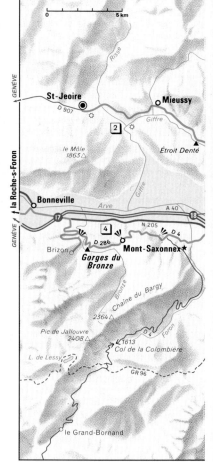

The road winds its way through the woods along the narrow Arpettaz and Foron valleys.

Turn right at Pont des Gets onto D 328.

The road rises above the Foron then veers to the left to reach the vast Praz-de-Lys Basin covered with pastures. From the last bend, there is a wide **panorama**★ embracing from left to right the Dents du Midi, Tour Sallière, Avoudrues, Mont Buet and Chaîne du Reposoir, with Mont Blanc in the distance. The peaceful mountain village of **Praz-de-Lys** is overlooked by the Marcelly Peak (alt 2 000m/6 562ft), crowned by a monumental cross and accessible to experienced hikers *(3hr return on foot).*

Return to D 902 and drive towards Taninges.

The heights of the Chaîne du Reposoir and Chaîne du Bargy line up on the horizon. Beyond Avonnex, there is an overall **view**★ of Taninges and of the Giffre Valley.

Taninges – This large village, which has partly retained its traditional character, is a good starting point for summer walks.

Beyond Châtillon-sur-Cluses, the mountain setting of the small industrial town of Cluses can be fully appreciated.

Cluses – The town nestles at the entrance of an important *cluse* (transverse valley) through which the Arve flows. It is the main French centre of the small metal-parts industry, spread around the Arve Valley, and of the clock-making industry, an old tradition imported from Germany in the 18C.

The **Musée de l'Horlogerie et du Décolletage (Espace Carpano et Pons)** ⊙, which illustrates the technical evolution of time-measuring instruments, includes exhibits such as watches from Louis XIV's time, one of Voltaire's desk clocks, watch mechanisms, chronometers and various clocks.

The 15C and 17C **church** ⊙ contains a monumental 16C stoup surmounted by a stone cross as well as an 18C calvary in the chancel and several painted statues of the same period in the nave.

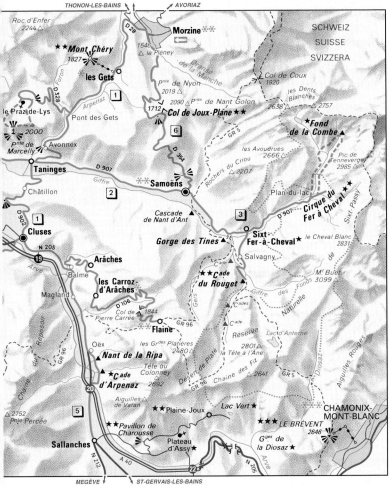

The **road leading to Romme**★ *(11km/6.8mi from Cluses on D 119)* starts from the roundabout opposite the tourist office. Drive towards Scionzier and cross the Pont de l'Europe; D 119 begins after the second roundabout, offering views of the impressive *cluse* of the River Arve between Cluses and Magland, with its frame of mountain peaks. The village of **Romme** overlooks the green Vallée du Reposoir over which tower the rocky ridges of the Bargy and Jallouvre mountains, contrasting with the grass-covered Pointe d'Almet and the surrounding pastureland.

It is possible to return to Cluses via the Chartreuse du Reposoir and the Foron Gorge.

VALLÉE DU GIFFRE

② From St-Jeoire to Samoëns
24km/15mi – about 45min – local map see above

St-Jeoire – Pleasant holiday resort at the heart of a wooded valley.

Road D 907 overlooks the confluence of the rivers Giffre and Risse then goes through a wooded gorge to reach the Mieussy Basin within sight of the snow-capped Mont Buet.

Mieussy – This village is one of the finest sights along the way. The onion-shaped steeple of the **church** ⊙ rises into the sky, enhancing the delightful landscape with its many hues of green.

The Étroit Denté, a short gorge cut through an obstruction of glacial origin, opens into the middle valley of the River Giffre, which widens beyond Taninges.

Taninges – *See Route des Gets above.*

The view embraces the huge escarpments of the Rochers du Criou towering over Samoëns and flanked by the Avoudrues Massif, while Mont Buet can be seen in the distance.

❊❊**Samoëns** – *See SAMOËNS.*

★ ③ CIRQUE DU FER À CHEVAL

13km/8mi from Samoëns – about 45min – local map see p 191

✳ ✳ Samoëns – *See SAMOËNS.*

From Samoëns, drive southeast towards Sixt-Fer-à-Cheval.

The Nant d'Ant Waterfall can be seen across the River Giffre as the valley narrows.

Gorge des Tines – Leave the car in the parking area situated just before the stone quarry and walk to the footbridge on the right from which there is a clear view of the narrow crack and the foaming stream.

★**Sixt-Fer-à-Cheval** – Situated at the confluence of the two upper arms of the Giffre, Giffre Haut and Giffre Bas, Sixt nestles round its former abbey (now a hotel), founded in 1144 by one of the lords of the Faucigny region. The village is a centre of excursion and rock-climbing as well as a ski resort.

Standing in an old square shaded by a lime tree, the **church** has retained its 13C nave. An inscription tells how Jacques Balmat, who was the first mountaineer to climb Mont Blanc, died in the mountains surrounding Sixt while prospecting for gold. The Sixt-Passy Nature Reserve covers three quarters of the borough of Sixt (9 200ha/22 734 acres). The **Maison de la réserve naturelle** ⊘, situated at the heart of the village, illustrates the history of Sixt and above all the natural environment: fauna, flora and geology of the local limestone mountains with their network of underground rivers.

In order to reach the **Cascade du Rouget ★★**, 5km/3mi south of Sixt, cross the bridge over the Giffre and follow the surfaced road past Salvagny to the waterfall; other waterfalls (Cascades de la Pleureuse, de la Sauffa and de Sales) situated further upstream can be reached on foot.

Beyond Sixt, the road is dotted with oratories and calvaries and, from Nambride onwards, it affords views of the Cirque du Fer à Cheval, with the pyramid-shaped Pic de Tenneverge behind.

★★**Cirque du Fer à Cheval** – The final loop in the road offers a splendid panorama of the cirque and its waterfalls. The **Chalet de la réserve** ⊘ is an information centre about high-altitude fauna and flora. The cirque is an amphitheatre formed by limestone escarpments, between 500-700m/1 640-2 297ft high; in June, more than 30 waterfalls streaming down the rock face create an incessant background noise.

★**Fond de la Combe** – *1hr 30min return on foot.* The marked path starts from the loop in the road, 50m/55yd from the bar at Plan du Lac.

The path ends near the place where the Giffre takes its source, below the Ruan and Prazon glaciers.

★ROUTE DE MONT-SAXONNEX

④ From La Roche-sur-Foron to Cluses

36km/22.4mi – about 1hr 30min – local map see p 191

La Roche-sur-Foron – *See La ROCHE-SUR-FORON.*
Drive east along N 203.

Bonneville – The former capital of the Faucigny region is today an administrative centre, situated at a tourist-road junction and at the confluence of the rivers Borne and Arve. A column, standing at the entrance of the bridge across the Arve, commemorates the harnessing of this mighty stream in the early 19C, following the initiative of Charles-Félix de Sardaigne.

From Bonneville, drive east along N 205; after crossing the motorway, turn right towards Mont-Saxonnex then right again to Brizon. Leave the car near a sharp bend to the right.

★**Point de vue de Brizon** – From the viewpoint on the side of the road, there is a bird's-eye view of the Gorges du Bronze with the Môle summits and Pointe de Marcelly in the distance across the Arve Valley.

Return to the Mont-Saxonnex road.

Gorges du Bronze – Leave the car 100m/109yd beyond the first of four hairpin bends and climb onto a rock overlooking the deep wooded ravine.

★**Mont-Saxonnex** – This summer resort, popular for its high position overlooking the Arve Valley *(more than 500m/1 640ft above the river bed)*, includes two main villages: **Le Bourgeal** nestling below the church and **Pincru** at the beginning of the Gorges du Bronze. Leave the car in front of the church and walk round the east end for a bird's-eye **view ★★** of the confluence of the Arve and Giffre valleys flanked by the Môle and Pointe de Marcelly in the foreground and surrounded from left to right by the Salève, Roc d'Enfer, Dents du Midi, Avoudrues, Mont Buet and Aiguille Verte summits.

The road then runs through a wooded area and joins D 4 before reaching Cluses.

Cluses – *See Route des Gets above.*

CLUSE DE L'ARVE

⑤ From Cluses to Sallanches *64km/40mi – about 2hr – local map see p 191*

Cluses – *See Route des Gets above.*

From Cluses, drive south along N 205 towards Chamonix.

The road follows the narrow passage between the Chaîne du Reposoir (Pointe d'Areu on the west bank) and the Chaîne des Fiz (Croix de Fer, Tête du Colonney, Aiguilles de Varan on the east bank) through which the Arve flows; the narrowest part lies between Cluses and Magland where the A 40 motorway and N 205 run alongside of the railway line.

At Balme, turn left onto D 6 towards Arâches.

The road clings to the cliffside; a sudden widening makes it possible to stop the car *(beware of falling rocks)* and admire the long corridor through which the Arve makes its way from Sallanches to Cluses, with Mont Joly barring the horizon.

Arâches – Small ski resort in a pleasant wooded setting.

Les Carroz-d'Arâches – Ski resort situated on the edge of a plateau overlooking the Cluse de l'Arve; 2km/1.2mi further on, there is a clear view of the nearby summits of La Croix de Fer and Les Grandes Platières, with the narrow valley below. The road rises to 1 843m/6 047ft then goes down towards Flaine nestling inside a small basin.

✳ ✳**Flaine** – *See FLAINE.*

Return to N 205 and turn left towards Sallanches.

The road offers views of Mont Joly, up-river beyond Sallanches, and glimpses of the Pointe Percée, the highest point of the Aravis range, to the right.

In Oëx, take a small road on the left.

Nant de la Ripa – The road leads to a bridge affording an amazing view of the lower course of the Ripa, entirely remodelled by 26 small dams looking like so many steps.

★**Cascade d'Arpenaz** – Impressive 200m/656ft-high waterfall, gushing from a curiously stratified channel in the rock.

Turn right in Luzier to return to N 205.

On the way to Sallanches, the imposing Mont-Blanc Massif comes into view.

Sallanches – *See SALLANCHES.*

★★COL DE JOUX PLANE

⑥ From Morzine to Samoëns *20km/12.4mi – about 1hr – local map see p 191*

See MORZINE: Excursions.

The length of time given in this guide
– for touring allows time to enjoy the views and the scenery
– for sightseeing is the average time required for a visit.

FESSY

Population 485
Michelin map 89 fold 12 or 244 fold 8

This charming village, situated at the heart of the Chablais region, just below the Col de Cou, has an interesting arts and crafts museum.

★**Musée d'Art et de Folklore régional** – This private museum, housed in a large old house, contains some 15 000 traditional objects and 1 200 pieces of pottery, displayed in reconstructed workshops and interiors: the joiner's, the clog-maker's (which contains a curious **bench** decorated with a devil, a lion and a wild boar), the living room and bedroom of a farm and the only room of a high-pasture chalet in which all the furniture can be folded or taken apart in order to be carried on the back of a mule.

Toys, masks, games, musical instruments, tools…contribute to make this reconstruction of traditional life in the past even more realistic. The museum also contains a remarkable collection of sigillated tiles.

Metal sculptures representing animals are displayed in the adjacent garden.

FLAINE ✳ ✳

Michelin map 74 fold 8 or 244 fold 20
Local map see Le FAUCIGNY

This attractive modern resort lies in a secluded mountain valley, situated between the rivers Arve and Giffre, at an altitude of 1 600m/5 249ft. The remoteness of the place made it possible for the resort to be planned along modernist architectural lines, justified the building of an important network of ski-lifts and encouraged original initiatives in the field of leisure activities.

THE RESORT

Skiing area – The resort makes use of a vast area, known as "Le Grand Massif", linked to the resorts of Carroz, Morillon, Samoëns and Sixt *(area pass)*. In addition, a remarkable 13km run links Flaine to the latter. Some of the resort's equipments are reserved for snowboarding enthusiasts.

In summer and winter time, life in the car-free resort concentrates round the Forum, decorated with a polychrome geometric sculpture by Vasarely. Not far from there stands a painted sculpture entitled *Woman's Head*, which is the monumental version (12m/39ft) of an 80cm/32in model made by Picasso in 1957. The concrete architecture, denoting a definite homogeneity, is the work of Marcel Breuer, a former member of the Bauhaus School, who contributed to the UNESCO building in Paris and to the Whitney Museum of American Art in New York.

The **Téléphérique des Grandes Platières** ⊘ gives access to the **Désert de Platé** *(see Bassin de SALLANCHES)*, overlooked by the Mont-Blanc Massif, from the Aiguille Verte to the Aiguille de Bionnassay.

FORCALQUIER ★

Population 3 993
Michelin map 81 fold 15 or 245 fold 19
Local maps see Vallée de la Moyenne DURANCE and Pays de FORCALQUIER

This small Provençal city lies at the heart of a low area of rolling hills bordered by the Montagne de Lure, the River Durance and the Luberon. The town, picturesquely built in the shape of an amphitheatre, surrounds a hill once crowned by a citadel. In the Middle Ages, Forcalquier was the capital of a county of Haute-Provence.

A powerful county – At the end of the 11C, the fortified town of Forcalquier became the capital of a county founded by a branch of the Comtes de Provence's dynasty and extending along the Durance from Manosque north to Sisteron, Gap and Embrun. The bishopric of Sisteron was split into two and the church of Forcalquier became a "co-cathedral", a unique precedent in the history of the Church. The Comté of Forcalquier and the Comté of Provence were united at the end of the 12C, under the leadership of **Raimond Bérenger V**, and were eventually bequeathed to the French crown in 1481.

Forcalquier today – Forcalquier is a thriving agricultural and industrial centre and a lively little town where one of the most important markets in the area takes place on Mondays. It is also a busy tourist centre and the starting point of several excursions. In addition, concerts of classical music and local-craft fairs are held every summer *(see Practical information: Calendar of events)*.

SIGHTS

Église Notre-Dame – This former "co-cathedral" offers an interesting contrast between the Romanesque character of its massive rectangular tower and the slender appearance of its steeple crowned by a lantern. The elegant Gothic doorway, surmounted by a rose window, leads to a lofty nave with a roof of broken-barrel vaulting, in typical Provençal Romanesque style. The transept and the chancel built before 1217 are the oldest examples of Gothic style in southern France. The aisles were added in the 17C. The magnificent organ also dates from the 17C.

Couvent des Cordeliers ⊘ – Franciscan friars, known as Cordeliers because they wore a knotted cord round the waist, settled in Forcalquier in 1236, probably at the invitation of Raimond Bérenger V. Their monastery, one of the first of its kind in Provence, was occupied until the 18C. The badly damaged 13C and 14C buildings were remarkably well restored in the 1960s.

Tour – The cloister was at the centre of the monastery. Several funeral recesses on the southwest and southeast sides were used as graves for the lords of Forcalquier. Note the graceful twin windows framing a Romanesque door on the side of the chapter house. Part of the buildings can be visited: the library with its original ceiling, the scriptorium, the oratory (15C Virgin Mary with Child) and the refectory divided into three rooms.

Porte des Cordeliers – As you come out of the monastery, note the gate with its two pointed arches decorated with a torus: this is all that remains of the town's fortifications.

Old county town – Go through the gate into the old town: the narrow streets lined with tall houses were intended as a protection against the *mistral*, a powerful Provençal wind. Walk along rue des Cordeliers leading to rue Passère and rue Béranger then across place du Palais to Grande-Rue. A lovely 16C **Renaissance fountain**, in the shape of a pyramid crowned by St Michael slaying the dragon, decorates place St-Michel. Rue Mercière leads to place du Bourguet at the heart of the city.

Terrasse Notre-Dame-de-Provence – Rue St-Mary

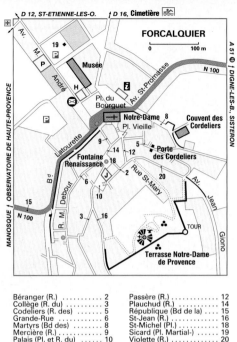

leads up to the site of the citadel where very little remains of the counts of Forcalquier's castle; below are the ruins of a tower which belonged to St Mary's church, the town's first cathedral. Note the set of bells which is played with fists *(concert on Sundays at 11.30am).*

An octagonal chapel dedicated to Notre-Dame-de-Provence stands at the top where the splendid **panorama★** embraces the Forcalquier Basin and the surrounding mountains *(viewing table;)* there is a bird's-eye view of the town just below.

★**Cemetery** – Leave the town centre north along D 16 and turn left 200m/218yd further on. A superb central staircase leads to the lower part of the cemetery with its striking clipped yew trees.

Museum ⊘ – Housed in a former 17C convent, the museum contains utensils and regional decorative objects (old tools, antique furniture, earthenware from Moustiers, Apt and Mane), a fine collection of coins and local archeological finds.

EXCURSION

★**Montagne de Lure** – This impressive ridge, which prolongs Mont Ventoux eastwards over a distance of some 30km/19mi, is austere and practically uninhabited; as the altitude rises, holm oaks, scrubland, lavender fields and cedar trees gradually give way to pastures which release a strong scent of aromatic plants. The northern slopes are more densely forested with firs near the summits, replaced by beeches, larches, oaks and black Austrian pines lower down.

The arid landscapes of the Montagne de Lure were extensively described by the Provençal writer Jean Giono, a native of Manosque *(see Introduction: Famous natives of the Alps).*

From Forcalquier to Sisteron

64km/39.8mi – about 2hr – local map see Vallée de la Moyenne DURANCE

The road is closed from 15 November to 31 May between Refuge de Lure and Jas des Bailles.

★**Forcalquier** – See FORCALQUIER.

Leave Forcalquier along D 12, northwest of the town plan.

The road winds across scrubland, on the lower slopes of the Montagne de Lure.

Rochers des Mourres – These rock formations, eroded into strange shapes, stand on either side of the road.

On the way to Fontienne, the view extends to the Durance Valley on the right.

Fontienne – The small Romanesque chapel of this tiny village, perched on an escarpment, has a belfry-wall with twin-openings; the castle goes back to the 13C.

St-Étienne-les-Orgues – This village marks the gateway of the Montagne de Lure. Its past prosperity was based on the production of numerous remedies based on aromatic and medicinal plants, which were sold by pedlars as far away as the

Montagne de Lure

Auvergne and Bourgogne regions. The 16C houses have mullioned windows and archivolts over the doorways. The **church** ⊘ has a polygonal chancel and the round towers of the 13C **castle** date from the 18C.

As D 113 rises, the slopes become densely forested. Just beyond the Oratoire St-Joseph, a stony road on the right leads to Notre-Dame de Lure.

Notre-Dame de Lure ⊘ – The monks of Boscodon Abbey built a modest monastery here in 1165. The only large barrel-vaulted room remaining is located beneath the small hermitage, a more recent edifice. The abbey church, which became a pilgrims' chapel, has now recovered its original appearance through extensive restoration work.

The trees in front of the chapel are several centuries old.

Return to D 113 and continue upwards.

Refuge de Lure – This small ski centre equipped with a few ski-lifts offers a wide **view**. A memorial to the 17C Belgian astronomer, Wendelin, who set up the first observatory in France, stands on the roadside, 1.5km/0.9mi further on.

Continue for another 3.5km/2.2mi and leave the car on the platform of the tele-communications relay. Access is restricted in winter; enquire in St-Étienne-les-Orgues.

★★**Signal de Lure** – The mountain's highest summit (1 826m/5 991ft) offers a vast **panorama** of Mont Viso, Mont Pelvoux, the Vercors Massif, the Cévennes range, Mont Ventoux and sometimes the Mediterranean coast.

Beyond Pas de la Graille, the road goes down through a splendid beech forest to the Jabron Valley overlooked by the steep slopes of the Montagne de Lure.

Follow the river along D 946 and turn left onto D 53 towards Sisteron.

★★**Sisteron** – See SISTERON.

Pays de FORCALQUIER

Michelin map 81 fold 15 or 245 fold 19

This rich rural area, in striking contrast with the austere surrounding plateaux and Montagne de Lure, is dotted with charming hilltop villages, which are best seen arriving from the east or south since they shelter from the north-blowing mistral.

FROM FORCALQUIER TO BANON 77km – about 3hr

★**Forcalquier** – See FORCALQUIER.

From Forcalquier, follow N 100 towards Manosque.

★**Mane** – See MANE.

Turn onto D 13 then left 4.5km/2.8mi further on towards St-Maime.

St-Maime – A few ruins and the castle chapel overlooking the village are the only remains of the Comtes de Provence's castle in which the four daughters of Raimond Bérenger V were brought up the traditional way *(see FORCALQUIER)*.

Return to D 13 and cross it to reach Dauphin.

Dauphin – Built on another hilltop facing St-Maime, Dauphin has retained part of its 14C fortifications, its medieval streets and its keep, crowned by a balustrade and a statue of the Virgin Mary; from the top there is a wide open **view** of the surrounding area.

Follow D 5 and cross N 100.

★**St-Michel-l'Observatoire** – *See ST-MICHEL-L'OBSERVATOIRE.*

Follow D 105 south.

Chapelle St-Paul – *See ST-MICHEL-L'OBSERVATOIRE.*

Turn right onto D 205.

Lincel – This village, which nestles in a fold, has retained a small Romanesque church and a castle with a few 16C features.

Cross N 100, continue along D 105 then turn right onto D 907 and left towards Montfuron.

Montfuron – Fine restored **windmill** ⊘. From the village, **view** of the heights of Haute-Provence to the northeast and of the Ste-Victoire Mountain to the south-west.

Return to D 907 and turn left; drive across N 100 and follow D 14.

Reillanne – This village is built on the side of a hill crowned by the 18C Chapelle St-Denis, which replaced the castle; avenue Long-Barri leads past the Portail des Forges (all that remains of the castle) to the viewing table: panoramic **view** of the old village, of the Ste-Victoire to the south and Luberon to the west.

Continue along D 14 and make a detour to Vachères.

Vachères – This old hilltop village acquired fame when the statue of a Gallo-Roman warrior, now in the Calvet Museum in Avignon, was discovered nearby.

Musée communal ⊘ – Housed in the village school, the museum contains archeological finds going back to prehistoric times, including flint axes and a copy of the famous **Vachères warrior**, as well as fossils discovered locally.

From Notre-Dame de Bellevue on D 14, take a small road in the direction of Oppedette.

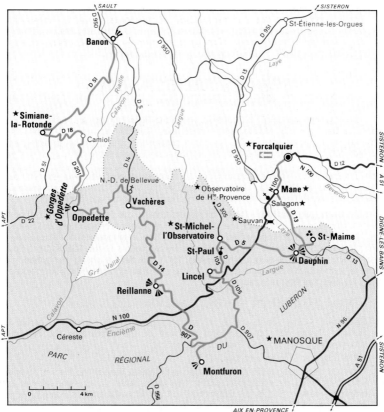

Oppedette – This tastefully restored hamlet overlooks the Gorges d'Oppedette, 2.5km/1.5mi long and 120m/394ft deep in places, through which flows the Calavon. There is a fine **view★** from the viewpoint near the cemetery; a marked path, starting beneath the viewpoint, leads to the bottom of the gorge.

★**Gorges d'Oppedette** – *About 3hr on foot from the viewpoint marked by a metal balustrade. Handrails guide visitors through difficult places. It is not advisable to go on this hike after a storm or when the weather is uncertain. There is no water available on the way. Hikers need a good sense of balance.*
Follow the yellow markings; after three handrail-assisted sections, it is possible to return to the village along the blue-marked path on the left or to carry on down along the yellow-marked path on the right to the bottom of the gorge dotted with pools (known as *gours*) and potholes. The caves in the cliffsides can be spotted at intervals. Beware of slippery surfaces as you go round the numerous *gours*. The path then runs beneath the bridge carrying the road and climbs up to the end of the gorge. Beyond the bridge, follow the yellow-marked path on the left leading to the GR footpath, which offers fine views of the gorge. Return to the viewpoint along the surfaced road.
Continue along D 201 and turn left onto D 18.

★**Simiane-la-Rotonde** – This is one of the loveliest hilltop villages in Haute-Provence: perched on the edge of the Plateau d'Albion, it overlooks vast fields of mauve lavender. Above the tall houses stands the Rotonde, which is all that remains of the castle of the Simiane family.
The **Rotonde★** ⊘ is the late-12C castle keep: the glacis is the only part visible from the outside, but the interior is on two floors; on the upper level, there are 12 recesses in Rayonnant Gothic style, separated by pilasters with carved capitals, and below, 12 ribs supporting a cupola with central oculus. A festival of ancient music takes place in summer.
The houses lining the steep village streets have retained 17C and 18C carved doors; the **church** dates from the 16C and there is a fine **view** of the Forcalquier region from the covered **market**.
Continue along D 51 to Banon.

Banon – A 14C fortified gate and the restored medieval hospital can be seen at the top of the old village, which overlooks the new one; from the east end of the church there is a pleasant **view** of the tiled roofs backed by the Montagne de Lure. A tasty goats' cheese wrapped in chestnut leaves has been named after Banon.

Tradition required that a great amount of chestnuts should be eaten on All Souls' Day; this custom had a double purpose: to secure admission to heaven for a number of souls proportionate to the number of chestnuts eaten and to prevent the dead from pulling the living by the feet!

Vallée de FREISSINIÈRES ★

Michelin map 77 fold 18 or 244 fold 42

This small valley, "hanging" 200m/656ft above the River Durance and hidden behind a rocky barrier typical of Mediterranean landscapes, is in fact an Alpine U-shaped valley scoured by a glacier, with a flat floor and contrasting sides: the south-facing *adret* dotted with houses and crops and the north-facing *ubac* covered with larch and pine woods.
The municipality of Freissinières includes 13 hamlets which reflect the importance of sheep-farming in the area: sheep are kept in the vaulted basement of traditional houses, the upper floors being used as living quarters and for storing hay.

Refuge from persecution – Owing to its remoteness, the valley became a refuge for renegades or dissidents during the long period of religious persecution. Followers of the Waldensian sect, who settled here and in the neighbouring Vallouise *(see La VALLOUISE)* as early as the 13C, were joined by Huguenots in the 16C and the Col de Freissinières became a busy route. In the 19C, **Félix Neff**, a young clergyman from Geneva, came to the area and founded a teachers' training-college in Dourmillouse in order to help the local population.

FROM ST-CRÉPIN TO PALLON 7.5km/4.6mi – about 1hr

St-Crépin – This village stands on top of a pink-marble rock spur barring the Durance Valley. Note the beautiful doorway of the **church** and the bell-tower surmounted by a spire and four corner pinnacles.
Cross the River Durance and follow D 38.
The road rises along a stony slope dotted with juniper bushes and tufts of lavender. Low stone walls are a reminder of the days when these slopes were covered with crops; the view embraces the Guillestre Basin and Mont-Dauphin standing on top of its promontory.

★**Gouffre de Gourfouran** – *30min return on foot. Access is difficult and caution is recommended. Leave the car 500m/547yd beyond the hamlet of Le Chambon. Follow the path to a pile of stones. From there, walk across the fields to a rocky promontory overlooking the chasm and the Durance Valley.* The River Biaisse, which flows through the Freissinières Valley, joins the Durance Valley via a 100m/328ft-deep gorge with sheer sides of a striking reddish colour.

★**FROM PALLON TO DOURMILLOUSE** *18km/11.2mi – about 2hr*

Between Pallon and Freissinières, D 238 follows the Biaisse along the valley floor, through cultivated fields.
In Freissinières, take the road which climbs up the south-facing slope.
From Les Roberts, there is an overall view of the valley blocked by the rocky knoll of Pallon.
Return to D 238 and follow it to the end of the valley.

★**Dourmillouse** – *1hr 30min return on foot.* The path leads to a group of houses, some of which are inhabited in summer. Note the small Protestant church and the restored water-mill *(the path continues to the Col de Freissinières).*

HIKES

★**Sentier des alpages** – *5hr, no major difficulty; a car is needed to go back. Water is available on the way. Departure: "Champs-Queyras", just before the hamlet of Les Aujards (alt 1 568m/5 144ft). Arrival: Dourmillouse (accommodation available).*
This long hike on the south-facing slope makes use of the old footpaths, linking the high-pasture hamlets and overlooking the Fressinières Valley and the River Biaisse. The path climbs to Les Garcines then crosses several streams just above the tree line. Beyond Les Allibrands, the path overlooks the chalets at La Got before reaching Dourmillouse. You are likely to see samples of the rich local fauna: chamois, marmots, falcons, black redstarts and if you are lucky golden eagles. The itinerary also offers the opportunity of observing the results of the geological upheavals in the area: spectacular folds of sandstone alternating with black schist can clearly be seen from Les Allibrands on the opposite slope.

Grotte des Vaudois and Via ferrata de Freissinières – *Leave the car in the parking area at the entrance of Les Roberts. 1hr on foot along a stony steep path.*
In the 15C, this cave was the refuge of followers of the Waldensian sect, pursued by members of the Inquisition.
The Via ferrata de Freissinières, the oldest in France, is well equipped and safe for beginners, in spite of some vertiginous sections; the course offers aerial views which should delight amateurs of heights *(see Practical information: rock-climbing).*

Route du GALIBIER ★★★

Michelin map 77 fold 7 or 244 folds 31 and 42

This road, one of the most famous in the French Alps, linking the Maurienne (the Arc Valley, *see La MAURIENNE*) and the Briançonnais *(see Le BRIANÇONNAIS)*, offers the possibility of driving through an austere and totally unspoilt high-mountain area. The panorama unfolding from the Col du Galibier is one of the finest in France, particularly in the early morning or late afternoon.
The itinerary starts with a steep climb from the Arc Valley to the "hanging" valley of the Valloirette, a tributary of the Arc. As the road continues to rise, the landscape begins to look bleak then utterly grim. The Écrins Massif comes into view beyond the Col du Galibier.

FROM ST-MICHEL-DE-MAURIENNE TO THE COL DU LAUTARET

41km/25.5mi – about 3hr. The Col du Galibier is blocked by snow from October to late May (sometimes until July).
The road rising to the Col du Télégraphe affords views of the escarpments of Croix des Têtes towering over the narrow basin of St-Michel-de-Maurienne, with the Grand Perron des Encombres (alt 2 825m/9 268ft) behind it and, in the distance, the Péclet-Polset glaciers.

★**Col du Télégraphe** – Alt 1 566m/5 138ft. There is a parking area. Climb to the top of the rocky knoll, on the north side, to get a bird's-eye **view** of the Arc Valley. Between the pass and Valloire, the road overlooks the Valloirette rushing through steep gorges towards the River Arc.

✳**Valloire** – Conveniently situated between the Parc national de la Vanoise and the Parc national des Écrins, Valloire is the main tourist centre of the Maurienne region. It lies at the foot of the Rocher St-Pierre, which partly blocks the Valloirette Valley, and marks the transition between two typical Alpine landscapes: down-river, a wooded coomb and, up-river, a desolate corridor of pastureland with scree-covered slopes.

Valloire is a well-equipped ski resort with a variety of slopes as well as a traditional village nestling round its Baroque church. Every year in January, an international ice-carving competition adds an artistic touch to the entertainment programme offered by this pleasant family resort.

Skiing area – There is a choice of red and black runs for experienced skiers in the Colérieux, Grandes Drozes and Plan Palais areas. An impressive number of snow-cannon insure adequate snow cover in all weather conditions. In addition, there are 40km/25mi of cross-country skiing tracks and the skiing area is linked to that of Valmenier *(area pass available)*.

Dating mainly from the 17C, the **church** ⊙ is one of the most richly decorated sanctuaries in the Savoie region; note in particular the gilt-wood retable over the high altar and the statue of St Thècle *(see Introduction: Traditions and folklore)*. The calvary above the vestry door, dating from 1609, is believed to be a copy of Albrecht Dürer's *Christ*.

Beyond Valloire, there are clear views of the barren Grand Galibier Summit. As the road rises from Plan Lachat to the pass, it offers superb views of the Valloirette Valley in the distance.

★★★**Col du Galibier** – The road no longer goes through a tunnel but over the pass (alt 2 646m/8 681ft) which is the highest point of the Route des Grandes Alpes after the Col de l'Iseran (alt 2 770m/9 088ft). *Leave the car and walk up (15min return) to the viewing table* (alt 2 704m/8 871ft); nearby is an old boundary stone marking the border between France and Savoie. The splendid **panoramic view** includes the Aiguilles d'Arves and Mont Thabor to the north and the glaciers and snow-capped peaks of the Écrins Massif to the south.

The pass is traditionally included in the Tour de France itinerary.

★★★**Hike to the Pic Blanc-du-Galibier** – Alt 2 955m/9 695ft. *This 3hr hike is only suitable for experienced hikers. Difference in height: 400m; mountain boots recommended.*

Leave the car at the southern exit of the old tunnel and follow the marked path across the fields, aiming for a round summit on the left which it is advisable to climb on its left side *(steep climb)*: remarkable **panorama**★★ of the Meije and Mont Thabor. *People inclined to feel dizzy are advised to turn back here.*

The itinerary continues along a path following the mountain ridge *(dangerous in wet conditions)*. The ascent to the summit of the Pic Blanc-du-Galibier is very steep but well worth it for the exceptional **panorama**★★★: Pic des Trois Évêchés and Aiguilles d'Arves in the foreground, Mont Thabor and the snow-capped peaks of the Vanoise to the northeast, Mont Blanc and the Grandes Jorasses further away.

On the way back, follow a narrow path on the left leading to the viewing table near the pass then bear right to return to the parking area.

Between the Col du Galibier and the Col du Lautaret, the road offers successive glimpses of the Barre des Écrins and the Guisane Valley towards Briançon. As it comes out of a bend immediately above the Col du Lautaret, it affords a marvellous **view**★★★ of La Meije and of the glacial cirque of L'Homme.

★★**Col du Lautaret** – See L'OISANS.

Monastère de GANAGOBIE★

Michelin map 81 folds 15 and 16 or 245 fold 20
Local map see Vallée de la Moyenne DURANCE

The monastery stands on a remarkable site, on top of the Ganagobie Plateau.

Plateau de Ganagobie – Towering 350m/1 148ft above the Durance Valley, the plateau is planted with pines and holm oaks mixed with broom and lavender.

The presence of megaliths shows that it was already inhabited in Prehistoric times. From its medieval past, it has retained several ruins and above all the monastery.

Caves in the slopes of the plateau were often used as hideouts in the past, particularly during the last war.

Viewpoints – The **Allée des Moines** leads from the left of the church to the edge of the plateau offering an aerial **view**★★ of the Durance Valley, the Valensole Plateau and the Préalpes de Digne, with the high Alpine mountains in the distance.

In the opposite direction, the **Allée de Forcalquier** leads to the western edge of the plateau; from this point, the **view**★ extends to the Forcalquier Basin, and the Montagne de Lure.

Cluniac priory – The present monastery was built in the 12C by monks of the Cluniac order who worked the land until the 16C when the buildings were practically abandoned; they were restored in the 17C. Following the 1789 Revolution, the church was saved just in time by the local people who decided to use it as their parish church. Today, the church and the monastery buildings, which are partly used by Benedictine monks, are being restored.

TOUR ⊘ 30min

Church – The decoration of the doorway is noteworthy. The pointed arches are separated by stone festoons which also surround the door; on the tympanum, a formal Christ in Glory contrasts with the freer representations of the adoring angels. The twelve apostles decorate the lintel.

The single nave, covered with broken barrel vault-ing, is prolonged by a dou-

Mosaic from Ganagobie showing St George slaying the dragon

ble transept and an oven-vaulted central apse. The carved ornamentation is extremely plain since the church was decorated with frescoes (only a few traces remain) as well as polychrome **mosaics★★** in the chancel and transept, which date from the mid 12C and denote a strong Byzantine influence (numerous mythical animals); note in particular, in the left apse, a knight on horseback chasing monsters and, in the south transept, St George slaying the dragon.

GAP★

Population 33 438
Michelin map 77 fold 16, 81 fold 6 or 245 fold 7

The liveliest commercial town of the southern Alps lies in a basin, at the heart of wooded farmland and at the intersection of two major roads, the Route Napoléon (Grasse to Grenoble) and D 994 (Valence to Briançon).

There are few architectural traces of Gap's ancient past as the town was destroyed on several occasions, in particular during the Wars of Religion and in 1692 during the war between France and Savoie. However, Gap has retained the general plan of a medieval city with its narrow twisting lanes, now turned into pedestrian streets offering a pleasant stroll.

The main administrative town of the Hautes-Alpes *département* is also a cathedral town and the headquarters of the Parc national des Écrins. As a tourist centre, it takes advantage of its situation near the Serre-Ponçon Lake, the cross-country skiing area of Col Bayard and ski resorts such as Orcières-Merlette.

SIGHTS

★**Musée départemental** ⊘ – Situated inside the public gardens of La Pépinière, this museum houses fine archeological collections and antique earthenware.

The major exhibit is the **mausoleum of François de Bonne, duc de Lesdiguières★**, carved during his lifetime by Jacob Richier (1585-1640), who also sculpted a low relief of the duke on horseback *(in the Château de Vizille, see VIZILLE)* as well as a bust of him now in the Musée de Grenoble. The alabaster figure of Lesdiguières in full armour lies on top of the mausoleum carved out of black and white marble from the Champsaur area.

In the basement, there are some remarkable pieces of **jewellery★** dating from the late Bronze Age found in the area.

A whole floor is devoted to fine collections of ceramics, mainly from Moustiers.

The display of local ethnography illustrates traditional daily life in the Queyras region from the 17C onwards, with carved furniture and beautifully decorated objects. The third level houses an important collection of European painting from the 14C to the 19C. Another room is devoted to Alpine fauna.

Cathedral – The present edifice, built at the end of the 19C in neo-Romanesque style with neo-Gothic vaulting, is surmounted by a 77m/253ft-tall spire. The use of white, red and grey stone from the area is reminiscent of Embrun's cathedral.

Town hall – It has retained a fine 18C façade bearing the arms of the town.

Domaine de Charance – *On the edge of town as you drive out along D 994 towards Veynes.*

Traditional spinning wheel from Queyras

F.X.Emery/Musée Départemental, Gap

This vast estate, which once belonged to the bishops of Gap, covers an area of 220ha/544 acres. The magnificent house is the headquarters of the Parc national des Écrins and of the Conservatoire botanique national alpin. The park's information centre and the exhibition rooms of the botanical conservatory are open to the public. There are guided tours of the estate, footpaths round the lake and a panoramic view of Gap.

EXCURSIONS

★Round tour via Pelleautier 21km/13mi – about 1hr

From Gap, drive west along D 994.

★**Gap Basin viewing table** – *1.5km/0.9mi, above a sharp bend to the right.*

Wide **view★** of the Gap Basin, extending to the summits along the Italian border (Brec de Chambeyron) in the east and to the mountains lying south of the Écrins Massif (Vieux Chaillol, Sirac) in the north.

At La Freissinouse, turn left onto D 47 then right beyond the railway line onto D 19 past an artificial lake. Turn left to Pelleautier 2km/1.2mi further on.

Beyond Pelleautier, there is a fine view of the Gap Basin and the Durance Valley.

Continue along D 47 then take N 85 back to Gap.

Notre-Dame du Laus 23km – about 1hr

From Gap, drive south towards Valserres then turn left onto D 11 and left again onto D 211. The hamlet of Laus has been a place of pilgrimage since 1664 when a young shepherdess called **Benoîte Rencurel** (1647-1718) had visions of the Virgin Mary.

*Find the best routes in town using the plans in the **Michelin Red Guide France** which indicate:*

– through routes, by-passes, new streets, one-way systems, car parks…

All the necessary information, revised annually.

La GRAVE ✳✳

Michelin map 77 fold 7 or 244 fold 41 – Local map see L'OISANS

La Grave, which is the main ski resort in Dauphiné, is remarkably **well situated**★★ in the shadow of the Meije *(see L'OISANS)*, one of the most impressive summits of the Écrins Massif and undoubtedly the most famous as far as mountaineers and tourists are concerned, for its peaks and glaciers offer spectacular views, particularly from the Oratoire du Chazelet. Beside the Meije, there are, in the immediate vicinity of La Grave, no fewer than 50 summits reaching heights ranging from 3 000m/9 843ft to 4 000m/13 123ft.

In spite of their tourist appeal, La Grave and its picturesque hamlets have avoided property developers and remained a small family resort with traditional houses.

THE RESORT

Skiing area – In spite of having only a few ski-lifts and ski runs, the skiing area is nevertheless impressive owing to the difference in height (2 150m/7 054ft) between the Dôme de Lauze and La Grave.

Alpine skiing takes place on the slopes of the Meije and, in a more modest way, round Le Chazelet and the Col du Lautaret. There are also 30km/18.6mi of cross-country skiing tracks near Villar d'Arène, on the edge of the Parc national des Écrins. Finally there are numerous possibilities of ski touring *(enquire at the Compagnie des Guides de l'Oisans)*.

The cable-car leads to two powder runs (Les Vallons de la Meije and Chancel) offering splendid views and the finest snow from late January to mid-May. This high-mountain area, which can be compared to the Chamonix Valley, is only suitable for competent skiers.

Runs on the Girose Glacier, above the cable-car's upper station, are accessible in winter and summer to less advanced skiers.

Church ⊙ – Surrounded by a small cemetery, this charming 12C Romanesque church, with its Lombard-style silhouette, low bell-tower and oven-vaulted apse, blends well into the splendid setting of the resort. Note the 15C font inside.

Next to it stands the 17C **Chapelle des Pénitents** ⊙ with frescoes all over the ceiling.

HIKES

There is a wide choice of **excursions** at moderate or high altitude. In summer, you need at least four days to explore the surrounding area; the main hiking itineraries lead to the **Plateau d'Emparis** *(starting from Le Chazelet)*, to the **Col d'Arsine** *(starting from Pied du Col)* and to the **Lac du Goléon** *(accessible from Valfroide)*.

In addition, La Grave is the ideal starting point of drives along the Romanche Valley, to the Col du Lautaret and Col du Galibier and to the resorts of Les Deux-Alpes and Serre-Chevalier.

In winter, various forms of skiing take place in the surrounding area *(see Skiing area)*.

View of the Meije Summit from the Oratoire du Chazelet

D Hée/MICHELIN

La GRAVE

★★★**Téléphérique des glaciers de la Meije** ⊘ – *Allow one day in order to explore all the possibilities of the site (1hr 10min return by cable-car).*
The ride is in two sections: the first section leads to the Peyron d'Amont Plateau (alt 2 400m/7 874ft), the second to the Col des Ruillans (alt 3 200m/10 499ft) on the northwest slopes of the Rateau Summit, offering on the way superb views of the Meije, Rateau and Girose glaciers. The view from the upper station includes the Aiguilles d'Arves due north, Mont Thabor to the northeast with the Vanoise summits in the distance and Mont Blanc further still, the Grandes Rousses and Belledonne mountains to the northwest.
From the Col des Ruillans, the **Grotte de glace** ⊘ is easily accessible; this ice cave is decorated with many ice carvings.
Several mountain restaurants offer superb panoramas as well as food.
From the Peyron d'Amont Station lower down, it is possible to explore the area for half a day or a whole day along marked hiking trails *(ask for maps at the tourist office in La Grave).*
The **Trifides and La Lauze Ski-lifts** offer exceptional **views**★★★ at an altitude of 3 550m/11 647ft, extending as far as the Grand Combin in the Swiss Alps.

Starting from Le Chazelet

★★★**Oratoire du Chazelet** – *6km/3.7mi along D 33 branching off from N 91 to the Col du Lautaret at the exit of the first tunnel.* The road goes through the village of **Les Terrasses** with its picturesque church. From the isolated Oratoire du Chazelet, there is a splendid **view** of the Meije Massif *(viewing table higher up, alt 1 834m/6 017ft).* Continue towards the village famous for its balconied houses. On the way down to the valley, it is possible to stop near the **Chapelle de Ventelon**, which offers another view of the Meije.

★★★**Hike to the Lac Lérié and Lac Noir** – *3hr return. Difference in height: 700m/2 297ft. Leave the car at the entrance of Le Chazelet.* Go towards the ski-lifts at the other end of the village, cross the small bridge and follow footpath GR 54. The Emparis Plateau is reached after climbing for 1hr. The itinerary becomes easy and offers clear views of the Meije. Another hour's walk leads to the spot with height marked 2 300m/7 546ft; turn left of the signpost towards the Lac Lérié. Splendid **view** of the Lautaret road, the Rateau Summit and the vast Girose and Mont-de-Lans glaciers (summer skiing area of La Grave and Les Deux-Alpes). Skirt the lake and admire the reflection of the mountains in the water as well as the striking view of the Romanche Valley.
Continue to the right towards the Lac Noir lying in a desolate landscape brightened up by edelweiss and gentians.

Ice caves – Dug through the thickness of the ice, these caves offer visitors the opportunity of going inside glaciers and appreciating the skill of ice-carvers, known as "grottus"; there are ice caves in Chamonix (Mer de Glace), in Les Deux-Alpes, in La Grave and in L'Alpe-d'Huez.

GRENOBLE ★★★

Conurbation 400 141
Michelin map 77 fold 5 or 244 fold 28
Local maps see Massif de la CHARTREUSE, Le GRÉSIVAUDAN and Le VERCORS

Situated at the confluence of the deep valley of the rivers Drac and Isère, Grenoble is a thriving modern city as well as the economic, cultural and touristic capital of the French Alps. Apart from Innsbruck, it is the only important town located at the heart of the Alpine range and completely surrounded by mountains.

The **site★★★** of Grenoble is exceptional: to the north, it is enclosed by the sheer cliffs of the Néron and St-Eynard summits, on the edge of the Chartreuse Massif, to the west by the mighty escarpments of the Vercors and the Moucherotte Peak, and to the east by the dark summits of the Belledonne range.

Grenoble is famous for the quality of the walnuts used by local confectioners, which are produced in the lower Isère Valley, between Thullis and St-Marcellin *(see PONT-EN-ROYANS)*.

HISTORICAL NOTES

Origins – The town, founded by the Gauls at the confluence of the rivers Drac and Isère, was fortified by the Romans and given the name of **Gratianopolis** (after Emperor Gratianus) which, in time, became Grenoble. During the Middle Ages, the town was repeatedly flooded by the River Drac, particularly in 1219 when the only bridge and most of the houses were destroyed.

"Dauphins" – The region belonging to the counts of Albon was named Dauphiné after Count Guigues IV whose second name was "Dauphin". **Humbert II**, the last "Dauphin", sold Dauphiné to the king of France in 1349 and the title was thereafter conferred on the heir to the French throne.

Overall view of Grenoble from the Bastille

GRENOBLE

Vaucanson (1709-1782) – This native of Grenoble made life-size automata (musicians, chess-players, a swimming duck and even the asp which killed Cleopatra!) and became one of the most famous characters of his time.

The "Journée des Tuiles" (Day of the Tiles) – On the eve of the French Revolution, regional parliaments were closed down by Louis XVI. The people of Grenoble rebelled against the royal decree, climbed onto the roofs of the buildings and threw tiles at the troops sent to subdue them.

Industrialization – In the 19C, Grenoble became a prosperous industrial city. Glove-making was the town's speciality whereas, in the surrounding area, there were coal mines and cement factories. Later on, paper mills, water-power, electrometallurgy and electrochemistry increased the town's prosperity with the contribution of industries related to winter sports (ski-lifts). Today, one quarter of the Alps' urban population lives in Grenoble.

Grenoble today – The lively **place Grenette** (EY) and rue Félix-Poulat, the pedestrian streets of the old town, the many parks and flower-gardens, the tree-lined avenues and wide boulevards confer to Grenoble the "feel of a real town and not that of a large village" as Stendhal once said. There is a new international trade centre, **Europole**, near the railway station. The **University**, founded in 1339 by Humbert II, includes highly specialised institutes of Alpine geography and geology and a centre of nuclear studies. The **Synchrotron**, a particle accelerator with a circumference of 850m/930yd standing near the Lyon-Grenoble motorway, symbolizes the dynamic approach of Alpine scientific research.

USEFUL TIPS

Information and public transport – Two weekly publications "Le Petit Bulletin" and "Affiches de Grenoble" list all the shows throughout the region; some local radios broadcast useful information: Radio Brume 90.8 (cultural news) and Radio France Isère 102.8.
The city's transport company, TAG, sells a pass, called **Visitag**, allowing unlimited travel for 1, 2 or 3 days (☎ 04 76 20 66 66); this is available at the tramway station of the main railway station, at the Maison du tourisme and at the Grand-Place shopping arcade.
Books about the region and guide books with local maps are available at the Librairie Arthaud (23 Grande Rue), where a vast choice of books on the Alps are displayed on 4 floors and where exhibitions are held. There is a FNAC (books, CDs, videos, hi-fi etc) nearby in the Centre des 3 Dauphins.

Where to have a drink – The "Palais de la Bière" (4 place Victor-Hugo) has the widest choice of beer in town; the "Scénario" (5 rue Palanka) also has an interesting choice of beers; dart players love the Irish atmosphere of the "Shan-non Pub" (14 rue Fantin-Latour) whereas memories of Stendhal still linger over "La Table Ronde" (7 place St-André), the city's oldest café (1740) and the Library for the original cocktails served at the Happy Hour. The "Brasserie du téléphé-rique", situated near the Bastille, offers customers the possibility to relax in front of a superb panorama *(evenings until midnight in summer)*. Fans of the Internet will be able to "navigate" at the Cybernet Café, 3 rue Bayard.

Music by night – The "Café des Arts" (36 rue St-Laurent) offers classical music while you eat; two music bars, "Couleur Café" (8 rue Chenoise) and "Dorémi" (56 quai Perrière), are definitely in. The "Cargo" stages good-quality theatre performances and the "Soupe aux Choux" (7 route de Lyon) has regular jazz sessions.

Where to hire sports equipment – Mountain bikes can be hired from "Moun-tain Bike Diffusion" (6 quai de France) and mountaineering equipment from "Clavel Sports" (54 cours Jean-Jaurès), where advice in also available. Mountain-eering enthusiasts can train at the Parc sportif de l'Île d'Amour (on the way out of town to the north).

Bureau des Guides de Grenoble – 14 rue de la République, BP 227, 38019 Grenoble cedex, ☎ 04 76 72 26 64.

★★★MUSÉE DE GRENOBLE ⊙ (FY)

The new Museum of Fine Arts, inaugurated in 1994, is located along the River Isère, at the heart of the old town. Its architecture is remarkably plain and lighting can be modified according to the works exhibited. Large windows offer a good view of the monumental sculptures outside, of the adjacent park, of the town and of the mountains in the background.
This is one of the most prestigious French regional museums: its collections of paintings from the 16C to the 20C include a particularly rich collection of modern and contemporary art, which is exceptional even by European standards.

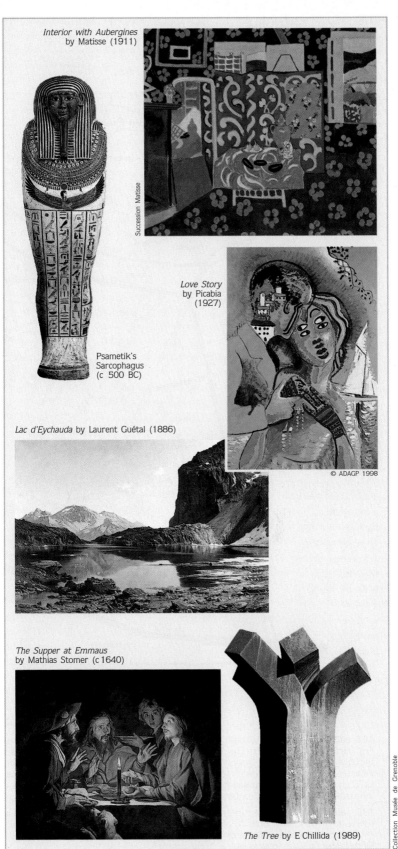

Interior with Aubergines by Matisse (1911)

Succession Matisse

Love Story by Picabia (1927)

© ADAGP 1998

Psametik's Sarcophagus (c 500 BC)

Lac d'Eychauda by Laurent Guétal (1886)

The Supper at Emmaus by Mathias Stomer (c 1640)

The Tree by E Chillida (1989)

Collection Musée de Grenoble

207

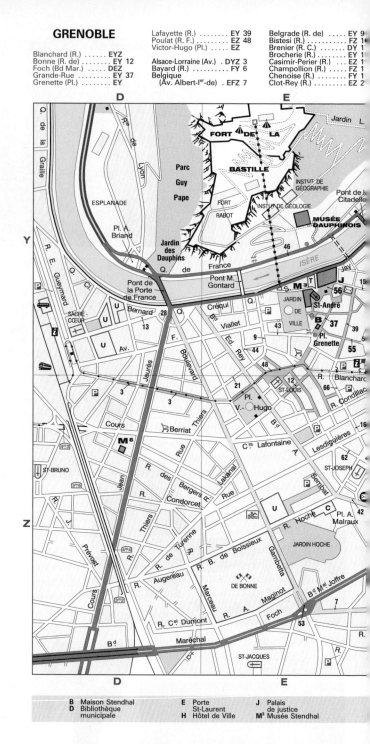

GRENOBLE

16C and 17C painting – Italian painting is represented by Tintoretto, Veronese, Fra Bartolomeo and **Vasari** (*The Holy Family*, in typical Mannerist style). **Rubens**'s Baroque painting of *Pope Gregory surrounded by Saints* dominates Flemish painting whereas the French and Spanish Schools are represented by **Philippe de Champaigne**, La Tour, Le Lorrain and **Zurbarán** (several paintings forming an altarpiece once in the monastery of Jerez de la Frontera).

19C painting – It extends from **neo-Classicism** to **Impressionism** and **Symbolism** and is represented by Ingres, Boudin, Monet, Sisley, Corot, Théodore Rousseau, Gauguin *(Portrait of Madeleine Bernard)* as well as by artists from Grenoble such as **Fantin-Latour** (still life known as the *"Engagement"*).

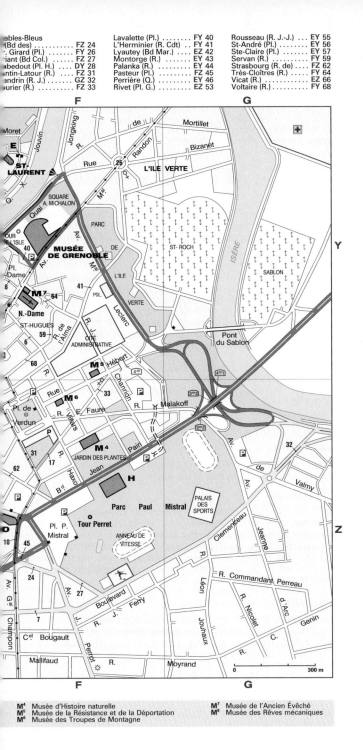

M⁴ Musée d'Histoire naturelle
M⁵ Musée de la Résistance et de la Déportation
M⁶ Musée des Troupes de Montagne
M⁷ Musée de l'Ancien Évêché
M⁸ Musée des Rêves mécaniques

20C modern art – Donations and bequests have considerably enriched the museum so that most schools are represented by the most famous artists. **Fauvism** is illustrated by Signac, Vlaminck, Van Dongen and above all **Matisse** (*Interior with aubergins*, 1911); the **Cubist School** is headed by Braque and **Dadaïsm** is reflected in the works of Picabia *(Idyll)*, Grosz and Ernst. The Paris School is represented by **Chagall** *(Cattle dealers)* and **Modigliani** *(Woman with a white collar)*. There are important works by **Picasso** *(Woman reading)*, **Léger** *(Dancing)*, Chirico *(The Couple)*. Klee, Miró, Kandinsky lead to **Abstract Art** with later representatives such as Taeuber and Domela *(Relief no 12A)*...

Striking contrasts in style highlight outstanding features throughout the visit.

Contemporary art – All the main trends from 1945 onwards, from **Lyrical Abstract Art** to **New Realism** and **Support-Surface** through **Pop Art** and **Minimalism**, are illustrated by major artists such as Dubuffet, Vasarely, Hartung, Atlan, Brauner *(Woman with a bird)*, Wesselman, Boltanski *(Monument)*, Raysse, Judd etc.

Antiquities – *In the basement.* The extremely rich collection of **Egyptian antiquities** includes several royal stelae, brightly decorated coffins and refined funeral masks. The medieval **Tour de l'Isle**, incorporated into the new museum, houses more than 3 000 drawings including several masterpieces such as a 15C *St Jerome* from northern Italy.

★★PANORAMA FROM THE FORT DE LA BASTILLE (EY) *1hr*

The fort is accessible by cable-car ⊙ or by car; car park next to the lower station.
From the rocky promontory situated on the left as you come out of the upper station, the **view★★** embraces the town, the confluence of the Isère and Drac Rivers and the transverse section of the Isère Valley framed by the Néron (right) and Moucherotte (left) Summits.

Go up to the terrace above the restaurant.

Information panels help visitors to detail the **panorama★★** of mountains unfolding all round: Belledonne, Taillefer, Obiou, Vercors (Grand Veymont and Moucherotte) and even Mont Blanc, which can be seen through the Grésivaudan depression. There is a fine bird's-eye view of Grenoble overlooked by the high-rise tower blocks of the **Ile Verte** (**FGY**). Two marked paths lead back to town: one goes through the **Parc Guy-Pape** and Jardin des Dauphins *(about 1hr 30min, see Additional sights)*, the other follows the **Circuit Léon-Moret** which ends at the Porte St-Laurent near the Église St-Laurent.
From the cable-car station, it is possible to walk towards the heights of Mont Jalla *(1hr)* for an even better panoramic view.
Other marked paths including GTA 2, go through the Bastille area *(specialised topographical guidebooks are available)*.

OLD TOWN (EFY) *1hr*

Start from place Grenette.

Place Grenette – This lively square lined with shops is one of the favourite haunts of the locals who like to stroll and stop at the pavement cafés.

The magic of electricity
On the night of 19 June 1889, the people of Grenoble witnessed a technical wonder: the place Grenette, the lively centre of the Alpine capital, lit by SIX lamps set inside the lampposts surrounding the garden, was shining as if it were daylight and it remained brightly lit until 1am! That night, the inhabitants were convinced of the magical properties of electricity, which however encountered the hostility of the companies providing gas-lighting to the city.

Walk along the Grande Rue.

Grande Rue (**EY 37**) – This former Roman way is lined with fine old houses; no 20, facing a Renaissance mansion, is the **Maison Stendhal** ⊙ (**B**): exhibitions are held in the second-floor flat where Stendhal spent part of his childhood.
The **rue J.-J.-Rousseau** (**EY 55**) starts almost opposite; no 14 was Stendhal's birthplace *(not open to the public)*.
Return to the Grande Rue.

Several famous natives of Grenoble were born or lived along this street.

Place St-André (**EY 56**) – In the centre stands a statue of Bayard *(see Introduction: Famous natives of the Alps)*.

★**Palais de Justice** ⊙ (**J**) – *See Introduction: ABC of architecture.* This former palace of the Dauphiné parliament is the finest building in Grenoble; the left wing is in Flamboyant-Gothic style and the right wing in early-Renaissance style. Inside, note the interesting **wood panelling★** and ceilings.

Église St-André – The 13C chapel has a bell-tower surmounted by an octagonal spire; Bayard's funeral monument (17C) is in the north transept.

Walk round St-André to place d'Agier and go into the Jardin de ville.

Musée Stendhal ⊙ (**M³**) – Housed in the **Hôtel de Lesdiguières** (late 16C to 18C), which was the town hall until 1967, the museum contains a collection of illustrations relating to the writer and his background *(see Practical information: Themed itineraries)*.

NOTRE-DAME DISTRICT (FY)

Excavations carried out under the cathedral square have revealed the foundations of the Gallo-Roman walls surrounding Gratianopolis and important paleo-
Christian remains; metal markers embedded in the paving of the square follow
the outline of the walls. Standing with your back to the cathedral, you will
notice a solitary tower: it is all that remains of the episcopal buildings which
stood here during the Middle Ages and included three churches: the Cathédrale
Notre-Dame, the adjacent Église St-Hugues and the baptistery (destroyed in
medieval times).

Cathédrale Notre-Dame – Remodelled many times and recently restored to its
original aspect, the cathedral has retained some pre-Romanesque features such as
the five adjacent naves and the base of the bell-tower. Note the 15C carved-stone
ciborium in the chancel.

Musée de l'Ancien évêché – Patrimoines de l'Isère ⊙ (**M⁷**) – Situated at the
heart of the town's historic centre, this interactive museum is housed in the former
bishops' palace; it offers an account of the regional heritage through a number of
prestigious collections. In the basement, visitors can see *in situ* one of the oldest
paleo-Christian baptisteries.

ST-LAURENT DISTRICT (EFY)

Situated on the right bank of the River Isère this old district, flanked by the Porte
de France and the Porte St-Laurent, is undergoing restoration work.

★**Musée Dauphinois** ⊙ – *Access on foot: walk across the footbridge of the Citadelle
and take the steps on the left leading to the museum. Access by car: along the quai
Perrière and rue Maurice-Gignoux.*
This museum of regional art and traditions is housed in a former 17C convent built
on the hillside in lovely surroundings. The tour takes visitors round the cloister, the
chapter house and the beautiful Baroque **chapel**★. The monochrome murals highlighted with gold, by Toussaint Largeot, illustrate the life of St François de Sales.

Note also the remarkable
Baroque altarpiece.
Chamber music concerts
take place regu-
larly.
The main rooms, devoted
to regional heritage, display a rich collection of
furniture and traditional
tools. Long-term themed
exhibitions illustrate various aspects of life in the
mountains.

★★**Église-musée St-Lau-
rent** ⊙ – This building, one
of the few of its kind in
France, is particularly interesting owing to the extensive excavations which
brought to light the numerous additions and alter-
ations made to it. The **St-
Oyand Crypt**★, located beneath the east end of the
present church, was built in
the 6C-7C on the site of a
pagan necropolis *(excava-
tion work in progress)*. This
early-medieval oratory is
richly adorned with Roman
and Merovingian decorative
motifs skilfully blended
with Carolingian elements.

F Pattou/Musée Dauphinois, Grenoble

Église St-Laurent

The church is entered through the Romanesque porch surmounted by a bell-tower;
from the gallery overlooking the nave, there is a fascinating overall view of the
different architectural styles.
The paintings and decoration of the chancel date from the beginning of the
20C.
The 17C **Porte St-Laurent** (**FY E**) stands near the church, next to some fortifications.

ADDITIONAL SIGHTS

★**Musée de la Résistance et de la Déportation** ⊘ (**FY M⁵**) – This ultra-modern museum recreates original settings and sounds and explains the motives of members of the Resistance and the sacrifices entailed by their action. The intense activity of the local Resistance movements is illustrated by several reconstructions; the German occupation is shown in relation to collaboration and deportation. Note the three authentic doors of the former Gestapo prison in Grenoble, covered with graffiti drawn by members of the Resistance. The importance of the military action of the Resistance movements (highlighted by a huge relief map) and their preparatory work for the liberation of France are also shown. One room is devoted to the "Monaco" meeting which led to the fusion of the various movements.

Musée des Troupes de montagne ⊘ (**FZ M⁶**) – The museum illustrates the role played by mountain troops in various conflicts, in particular the Second World War, when their finest regiment, the *chasseurs alpins*, became known as the "Blue Devils"; they were responsible for the promotion of skiing, for improving communications and for insuring the safety of the local population.

Hôtel de ville (**FZ H**) – Designed by Novarina, it is split in the middle by a vast square **patio**★ decorated with a granite fountain surmounted by an abstract bronze sculpture by Hadju and surrounded by a marble mosaic by Gianferrari. Several official rooms open onto the patio.

Parc Paul-Mistral (**FGZ**) – This green open space is the setting of the new town hall and of the sports complex. The **Tour Perret**, named after its architect, is an 85m/279ft-high concrete needle built for the 1925 water-power exhibition.

Jardin des Dauphins and Parc Guy-Pape (**DY**) – The lower entrance is situated on the square where the Porte de France stands.

The "grey gold" of Grenoble

In the 19C, the Grenoble region was the birthplace of the French cement industry based on research carried out by Louis Vicat (1786-1861), who was looking for the lost secret of Roman cement. Important calcareous deposits, which could supply the raw material, prompted the creation of many factories (the first one dates from 1853). At the height of its production, natural cement from Dauphiné was exported to New-York and South America. The recession, which occurred at the end of the 19C owing to harsh competition, transport costs and equipment becoming outdated, was temporarily offset by new interest in artificial slow-setting cement (known as "Portland").

From this golden age of cement, Grenoble has retained several architectural and decorative elements including:

– the **"Casamaure"** (in St-Martin-le-Vinoux); this neo-Moorish villa offers a profusion of Moorish arches and moucharabies (for a visit of the building, call 04 76 47 13 50);

– the Chapelle Notre-Dame-Réconciliatrice (rue Joseph-Chaurion), also in neo-Moorish style; the Tour Perret (1925) and the picturesque urinals dotted along the avenues of the Alpine metropolis.

These gardens, laid on uneven ground and criss-crossed by winding lanes, offer striking views of the overhanging cliffs of the Rabot. In the lower part, there is a statue of **Philis de la Charce** (1645-1703), a local heroine who fought off the duke of Savoie's mercenaries.

Musée des Rêves mécaniques ⊘ (**DZ M⁸**) – Hidden at the end of a narrow street, this museum houses a rich collection of automata and music boxes.

Bibliothèque municipale (**FZ D**) – Manuscripts from the Grande Chartreuse Monastery and most of Stendhal's works are among its priceless possessions.

Musée d'Histoire naturelle ⊘ (**FZ M⁴**) – The museum which dates from the 18C is being modernized. The Salle des Eaux Vives on the ground floor contains several aquariums. Exceptionally fine collection of minerals and fossils.

Musée Hébert ⊘ – *Northeast of the Musée de Grenoble, along avenue Randon. Entrance in chemin Hébert.* A vast French-style park is the setting of the former home of the painter Ernest Hébert (1817-1908), a native of Dauphiné, and of the museum devoted to his works.

Maison de la Culture – *South of the Parc Paul-Mistral along avenue Perrot then right into avenue de Chamrousse.* Contrasting shapes and colours confer a certain originality to this cultural centre built in 1968.

Centre national d'art contemporain ⊘ – *West of the town centre along cours Berriat (no 155).* Exhibitions of contemporary art are held inside a former industrial building, known as **Le Magasin**, designed in 1900 by the Eiffel Group.

EXCURSIONS

★**Réserve naturelle du Luitel** ⊙ – *From Grenoble drive east towards Uriage-les-Bains then follow D 111 towards Chamrousse and turn right onto the forest road signposted "Col du Luitel". The road skirts the lake before reaching the beginning of the nature trails. Parking near the Information Centre.*
This nature reserve, the oldest in France, covers 18ha/44 acres of peatbog, a unique ecosystem which developed in a depression of glacial origin.
Marked footpaths and platforms on duckboards enable visitors to observe peatbog vegetation. The "lawns" on the lake shores are in fact carpets of moss floating on water. Pine trees take root in the peat but as soon as they reach a height of 3m/10ft they topple over into the lake. The flora includes rare species such as carnivorous plants (sundew, bladderwort, butterwort) and orchids.

Musée de la houille blanche ⊙ – *16km/10mi. From Grenoble, follow D 523 towards Domène. In Lancey, turn right at the lights towards La Combe-de-Lancey and the paper-mills.* The museum is located on the site of the first chute built by **Aristide Bergès** between 1869 and 1875 above the Lancey paper-mills. He invented the term "houille blanche" to draw a comparison with coal which was then the main source of power *(see Introduction: Hydroelectric power)*. The museum illustrates Aristide Bergès's career *(his house, situated on the left of the entrance, is not open to the public)* and the history of water power in the 19C.

GRÉOUX-LES-BAINS‡‡

Population 1 718
Michelin map 81 fold 15, 114 folds 5 and 6 or 245 fold 33

The water of this spa resort was already famous in Roman times, as a stela, excavated last century shows; dating from AD 176, it was dedicated to the nymphs of Gréoux. Rediscovered centuries later, the resort became very popular during the 19C.

THE SPA CENTRE

The baths were bought by the Compagnie française du thermalisme in 1962 and an ultra-modern spa centre was built beneath the park in 1968. It is situated east of the town, along D 952.
Today, the thriving resort, which is sought after for its fine setting and sunny climate, has even more hotels, luxury accommodation and shops as well as a wider choice of leisure activities.

The hot Spring – Gréoux has only one spring which releases 2.5 million l/575 000g of hot (37°C/98.6°F), sulphurous water used for the treatment of rheumatism, arthritis and respiratory complaints.

SIGHTS

Old village – It nestles at the foot of the castle. The restored church has a Romanesque nave and a square Gothic east end; the aisles and side chapels were added in the 16C and 17C.

Castle – The former stronghold of the Knight Templars *(restoration work in progress)* overlooking the village has retained its massive square keep in the northwest corner. Several festivals are staged in the courtyard *(see Calendar of events)*. Wide **view** of the valley from the upper platform.

Troglodytic baths – A pool dating from the 1C AD, found near the spa centre, shows the importance of the Gallo-Roman baths.

Crèche de Haute-Provence ⊙ – *36 avenue des Alpes.* Miniature village displaying some 300 *santons* illustrating daily life in the region at the turn of the century.

EXCURSIONS

Lac du barrage de Gréoux – *10km/6.2mi – about 30min. Drive south out of Gréoux, cross the Verdon River and follow the road to the left, signposted "Notre-Dame-des-Œufs".* It rises through the forest to the top of a hill, affording a beautiful **view**★ of the artificial lake and, across the water, of the Château des Castellane near Esparron-de-Verdon. The road ends at the lakeside.

Plateau de Valensole – *89km/55.3mi – about 5hr – see Plateau de VALENSOLE.*

Allemagne-en-Provence – *12km/7.5mi northeast along D 952.* A fine Renaissance **castle** ⊙ stands beside the River Colostre. During the Wars of Religion, the castle was besieged and the baron of Castellane, who had rallied behind the duke of Lesdiguières, was killed as he was about to celebrate his victory over the Catholics. His son was later killed in a dual in which he had been tied to his opponent by the left arm. The crenellated 12C keep was remodelled in the 16C and mullioned windows, surmounted by carved gables, were opened. The great hall, in Renaissance style, has a monumental fireplace decorated with gypsum carvings and framed by two mythological characters: Hercules and Minerva. Note the fine spiral staircase linking the medieval and Renaissance wings.

Le GRÉSIVAUDAN ★

This part of the Isère Valley, deeply eroded by glaciers, is the most impressive section of the Alpine trench *(see Introduction: Landscapes)*. The atmosphere is stifling in summer, yet this sheltered depression is the Alps' richest agricultural area; in the 19C, the region pioneered the development of water power for industrial use *(see GRENOBLE: Excursions)*.

J.-L. Carmet/EXPLORER

Bayard knights François I

Bayard's youth – Born in the Château de Bayard, near Pontcharra, in 1476, Pierre Terrail belonged to a long line of famous soldiers. As a child, he was only interested in riding and soldiering and soon became more skilled than his tutors. The king of France, Charles VIII, brought him to his court and, at the age of 16, Bayard took part in his first tournament, defeating one of the finest jousters in the kingdom. From then on, Bayard's military career amounted to a succession of daring feats and King François I made him lieutenant-general of Dauphiné in 1515. He died on the battlefield in 1524.

★★ 1 **Route des Petites Roches** *68km/42.3mi – about 2hr 30min – local map see opposite*

This itinerary which runs along the Plateau des Petites Roches, beneath the impressive Chartreuse Massif, offers constant views of the Belledonne range across the River Isère.

★★**Grenoble** – *See GRENOBLE.*

From Grenoble, drive along N 90 towards Chambéry.

In Les Eymes, D 30 starts climbing to the Plateau des Petites Roches, a wide ledge covered with pastures, sheltering beneath the escarpments of the Chartreuse. Mont Blanc can be seen in the distance, to the northeast.

Turn left off D 30, 1km/0.6mi before St-Pancrasse, towards the Col du Coq.

Col du Coq – The road winds along the slopes of the Dent de Crolles offering lovely views of the Isère Valley before reaching the pass (alt 1 434m/4 705ft).

Return to D 30.

St-Pancrasse – The village lies on the very edge of the plateau, beneath the Dent de Crolles.

★★**Bec du Margain** – *From D 30, 30min return on foot. Leave the car 150m/164yd past the football ground and follow the path to the right through a wood.* Walk along the edge of the escarpment to the viewing table situated 800m/2 625ft above the Isère Valley: superb **view** of the Vercors, Belledonne, Grandes Rousses, Sept-Laux, Bauges and Mont-Blanc massifs.

St-Hilaire-Du-Touvet – This small health and ski resort is also an important gliding centre (paragliding and hang-gliding). It is linked to Montfort on N 90 by the steepest **rack-railway** ★ ⊙ in Europe, which negotiates a 65% gradient (83% at one point, inside a tunnel) over a distance of 1.5km/0.9mi. From the upper station, there is a striking **view** ★ of the Grand Pic de Belledonne across the valley. The road continues at the same average altitude of 900m/2 953ft then goes down towards St-Georges and La Palud. From there, it is possible to drive to Chambéry across the Col du Granier.

In La Palud, D 285 turns to the right towards Chapareillan.

Chapareillan – The village lies just south of the former border between Dauphiné and Savoie.

★ 2 **From Brignoud to Pontcharra** *47km/29mi – about 2hr – local map see opposite*

This itinerary explores the slopes of the Belledonne range on the left bank of the River Isère. The road rises from Brignoud to Laval past the Château du Mas.

Laval – Lovely village with overhanging roofs and a charming manor, the Château de la Martellière. In the **church** ⊘, there is a 15C mural depicting the Virgin Mary protecting the congregation.

Between Prabert and the Col des Ayes, there is a fine overall view of the Chartreuse Massif, including Dent de Crolles and Chamechaude.

Theys – The village, which has retained many old houses, nestles in a green basin.

⚜ **Allevard** – *See ALLEVARD.*

Between Allevard and Pontcharra, D 9 goes round the heights of Brame Farine *(see ALLEVARD: Excursions)* and offers a close **view★** of the lower Gelon Valley.
Lower down, the road overlooks the vast intersection of the Chambéry depression, the Grésivaudan and the Combe de Savoie.

From Pontcharra, follow a small road on the right to Château-Bayard.

Château-Bayard – *The road starts climbing from a tree-shaded square and goes past Pontcharra's schools; at the end of the climb, turn right then immediately left. Leave the car in the car park on the left of the buildings.*

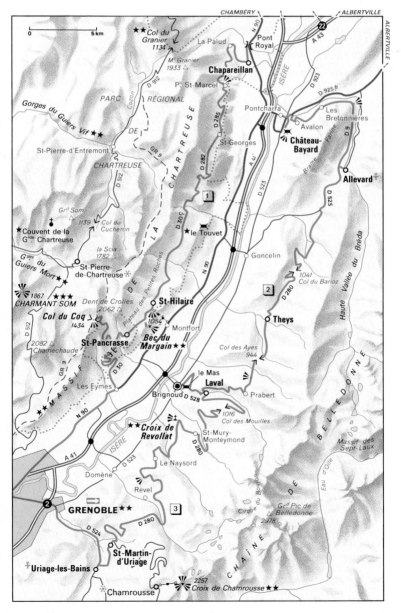

The doorway situated between the farm buildings and the former gatehouse *(now private property)* gives access to the terrace and the **Musée Bayard** ⊙ housed in a 15C square building with mullioned windows, which is all that remains of the castle where the "Knight without fear and above reproach" was born. The museum contains a few documents and an audiovisual presentation of his life and heroic military career.

Impressive **panorama★** of the Grésivaudan and of the Chartreuse, Belledonne and Bauges massifs.

③ From Brignoud to Grenoble

62km/38.5mi – about 2hr 30min – local map see p 215

The Cirque du Boulon and its many waterfalls towers over D 280 winding its way to Croix de Revollat.

★★**Croix de Revollat** – *50m/55yd to the right of D 280.* The main interest of the itinerary lies in the panorama which unfolds from this viewpoint: the Grésivaudan below and, across the river, the Plateau des Petites Roches overlooked by the Chartreuse; the Vercors Massif to the left and the Bauges Massif to the right.

The road continues through a forest offering bird's-eye views of Grenoble then goes down towards **St-Martin-d'Uriage** and **Uriage-les-Bains** *(see Massif de CHAMROUSSE).*

In Uriage, turn right onto D 524 to Grenoble.

★★**Grenoble** – *See GRENOBLE.*

GUILLESTRE

Population 1 999
Michelin map 77 fold 18 or 245 fold 9 – Local map see Le QUEYRAS

Situated on the edge of the Queyras region, this thriving market town is an overnight stop along the Route des Grandes Alpes between the Col d'Izoard and the Col de Vars. Very little remains of the medieval fortifications. Place Albert and its monumental fountain mark the town centre.

The Parc régional du Queyras has its headquarters here and the town is the starting point of many hiking itineraries which explore the surrounding area. *(Details available at the tourist office.)*

Church ⊙ – Built in the 16C, the church has a similar porch or **"real"★** to that of Embrun, supported by four columns; two of them, in pink marble, rest on a base formed by squatting lions carved in limestone from the Briançon area. The doors are decorated with Renaissance panels.

HIKES

Pain de sucre – *1hr 30min. Orange markings to begin with. Walk from the tourist office to the Gendarmerie then towards La Font-d'Eygliers via the Simoust district. Leave the road before the left-hand bend and follow the path on the right, heading due east to the Gorges du Guil. Walk to the right of the Pain de sucre; a path leads to the summit (viewing table). Fine* **view★** *of the Gorges du Guil and of the fortifications of Mont-Dauphin.*

Return to Guillestre along the path skirting the canal.

★**Mont-Dauphin** – *2hr on foot along an itinerary marked in orange. From Guillestre, follow D 902 towards Briançon until you reach the Chapelles district. Walk across the Plateau de la Chalp and take a footbridge across the Guil.*

The itinerary, leading to the Porte d'Embrun at the entrance of the fort, makes it possible to admire the natural defences of Mont-Dauphin from a different angle *(see MONT-DAUPHIN).*

How to tell the age of a male moufflon

When the animal is perfectly still, look at his horns; their growth stops in wintertime and a ring appears. It is therefore easy to count the number of sections separated by rings, from the extremity to the base. In the case of older males, the extremity of the horns may be worn and the rings not clearly visible.

The age of a female is more difficult to tell: it is proportionate to the size of her white facial patch.

EXCURSIONS

✴Risoul 1850 – *14km/8.7mi along D 186.*

The winding road offers panoramic views of Mont-Dauphin and its exceptional site. The resort has a speed-skiing piste and snow-making equipment. The skiing area, shared with Vars *(see VARS)*, known as the **Domaine de la Forêt Blanche**, is one of the largest in the southern Alps, with a total of 160km/99.4mi of piste.

An unsurfaced road leads to the Col de Chérine and to the **Belvédère de l'Homme de Pierre** (alt 2 374m/7 789ft). From the viewing table, there is a superb **panorama★★** extending north to the Vanoise Massif, south to Mont Ventoux and southwest to the Serre-Ponçon Lake.

★Mont-Dauphin – *See MONT-DAUPHIN.*

Les HOUCHES ✴

Population 1 766
Michelin map 89 fold 4 or 244 fold 21 – Local map see Massif du MONT-BLANC

Les Houches spreads its houses across the widest and sunniest part of the Chamonix Valley, beneath the Aiguille du Goûter and in view of the monumental **Statue du Christ-Roi** erected on the wooded slopes of the Aiguillette du Brévent. The setting is less impressive than that of Chamonix and Les Houches is content in being a pleasant family resort.

THE RESORT

Skiing area – The resort, which has retained its mountain village atmosphere, offers skiers a wide range of difficulties in the Lachat, Bellevue and Prarion areas. The famous "green run" (black in fact!), brilliantly skied by Émile Allais in 1937, requires a high level of skiing skill. The skiing area is linked to that of the main neighbouring resorts.

There are, in addition, some 30km/18.6mi of cross-country skiing tracks.

VIEWPOINTS

★★Le Prarion ⊘ – *Alt 1 967m/6 453ft. 30min return (to the viewing table) including a 20min cable-car ride.* From the viewing table (alt 1 860m/6 102ft), standing next to the Hôtel du Prarion, there is an extended **view** of the Mont-Blanc Massif. In order to enjoy the **full panorama★★★**, it is recommended to climb *(about 1hr return on foot)* to the summit of Le Prarion *(indicated).*

★★Bellevue ⊘ – *Alt 1 812m/5 945ft. 1hr return including a 15min cable-car ride. It is possible to continue up to the Nid d'Aigle (Glacier de Bionnassay) and go back down via St-Gervais on board the Tramway du Mont-Blanc (study the timetable and see ST-GERVAIS and Admission times and charges).*

★★Parc du Balcon de Merlet ⊘ – *6km/3.7mi – 10min return on foot. From Les Houches Station, drive 3km/1.8mi along the mountain road to Coupeau and turn right onto the forest road (partly surfaced) towards the Parc de Merlet (3km/1.8mi). Leave the car and continue on foot (300m/328yd).*
The Balcon de Merlet is a promontory covered with pastures, occupying a prime position opposite Mont Blanc. The park shelters a typical mountain fauna (deer, moufflons, chamois, llamas, ibexes, marmots) roaming freely over a steep wooded area covering 20ha/49 acres. From the terrace of the restaurant, or from the chapel (alt 1 534m/5 033ft), there is a superb close-up **view★★** of the Mont-Blanc Massif.

MICHELIN GREEN GUIDES

Art and Architecture
History
Geography
Ancient monuments
Scenic routes
Touring programmes
Plans of towns and buildings
A selection of guides for holidays at home and abroad.

Route de l'ISERAN ★★★

Michelin map 74 fold 19 or 244 folds 32 and 33

This road, which goes over the Col de l'Iseran, was built in 1936 to link the Tarentaise and Maurienne valleys. It climbs to the highest point (2 770m/9 088ft) of the Route des Grandes Alpes. In the whole of the French Alps, only the Route de la Bonette in the southern Alps reaches a higher point (2 802m/9 193ft). This itinerary goes through austere landscapes characteristic of high-mountain areas.

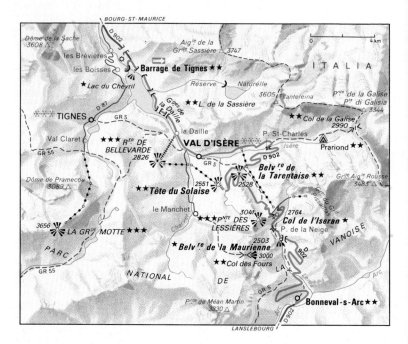

FROM THE BARRAGE DE TIGNES TO BONNEVAL-SUR-ARC *32km/20mi – about 1hr 30min*

The Col de l'Iseran is usually blocked by snow from early November to early July. It is recommended to drive along this road from Val d'Isère to Bonneval.

★★**Barrage de Tignes** – *See TIGNES: Excursions.*

The construction of D 902 running from the Barrage de Tignes to Val d'Isère involved the building of eight tunnels (one of them is 459m/502yd long) and three avalanche barriers. The road therefore offers intermittent views of the Vanoise Massif to the south and of Mont Pourri down-river.

The Gorges de la Daille open the way into the Val-d'Isère Basin.

★★★**Val d'Isère** – *See VAL D'ISÈRE.*

From Val d'Isère to the Pont St-Charles, the road continues along the Isère Valley which becomes more and more desolate, barred up-river by the Pointe de la Galise. Beyond Le Fornet, there are stunning views of the Grande Motte at the heart of the Vanoise Massif and of the Tsanteleina Summit on the Italian border.

The road enters the Parc national de la Vanoise at the Pont St-Charles.
There is a parking area for 150 cars just before the bridge.

The road then rises along the southern slopes of the valley offering views of the Val-d'Isère Basin with the snow-capped Dôme de la Sache in the background and Mont Pourri just behind it. There are glimpses of the artificial Lac de Tignes through the Gorges de la Daille.

★★**Tête du Solaise** – Alt 2 551m/8 369ft. *1hr 30min on foot return along a path providing a pleasant mountain hike; the summit can also be reached by cable-car from Val d'Isère (see VAL D'ISÈRE).*
The **panorama** is similar to that which can be admired from the Belvédère de la Tarentaise *(see below)* but there is a clearer view down the Isère Valley towards Tignes and its dam.

★★**Belvédère de la Tarentaise** – Alt 2 528m/8 294. *15min return on foot. Park the car as you come out of the bend.* From the viewing table, the view extends all round from Val d'Isère, the Lac de Tignes and the Pointe des Lessières in the foreground to the Vanoise Massif, Mont Pourri and Grande Sassière further out.

★**Col de l'Iseran** – Alt 2 770m/9 088ft. The harshness of the landscape is impressive. The snow cover remains throughout the summer on the Tarentaise side of the pass. The Chapelle Notre-Dame-de-l'Iseran was built in a sheltered spot in 1939. L'Albaron Summit comes into view on the Maurienne side of the pass.

★★★**Pointe des Lessières** – Alt 3 041m/9 977ft. *From the Col de l'Iseran, 2hr 30min return on foot along a steep mountain path which can be dangerous for inexperienced hikers (vertiginous handrail-assisted sections towards the top). Mountain boots with non-slip soles are essential. The path starts behind the Chalet-hôtel de l'Iseran.*

This hike must only be attempted in clear weather; it offers an almost unique opportunity of climbing over 3 000m/9 843ft. The view from the summit is ample reward for one's efforts: the Vanoise Massif, Mont Pourri, the Italian side of Mont Blanc and the border range between La Grande Sassière and l'Albaron.

The road continues across the Parc national de la Vanoise, offering views of the barren cirque of the upper Lenta Valley beneath the Grand Pissaillas Glacier *(ski-lifts for summer skiing)*.

★**Belvédère de la Maurienne** – Alt 2 503m/8 212ft. View of the Haute-Maurienne, the Ciamarella and Albaron summits, the Pointe de Charbonnel along the Italian border. Beyond the Pont de la Neige, the "hanging" Lenta Valley offers a landscape of high pastures backed by the snow-capped Albaron. Lower down, the road overlooks the austere upper Arc Valley which forms the setting of the village of Bonneval. The Albaron is flanked on the left by a vast area of glaciers and on the right by the pyramid of the Pointe de Charbonnel and dome of the Pointe de Ronce.

★**Bonneval-sur-Arc** – *See BONNEVAL-SUR-ARC.*

ISOLA 2000 ✻ ✻

Michelin map 81 folds 9, 10 and 20, 115 folds 4 and 5 or 245 folds 24 and 25

Isola 2000, built in 1972 in a beautiful mountain setting, close to the Italian border, is the nearest Alpine ski resort to the Côte-d'Azur-Region.

In summer, Isola 2000 is the ideal **starting point of hikes** for the nearby Parc national du Mercantour and Parc naturel de l'Argentera on the Italian side or for the mountain lakes surrounding the resort; numerous chamois roam around the area which used to be part of the Italian royal hunting grounds and has retained a network of well-marked paths *(map available from the tourist office)*.

THE RESORT

It owes its popularity to its sunny climate and to its good-quality snow cover, partly due to the high altitude.

Skiing area – It is situated at an altitude ranging from 1 800m/5 906ft to 2 600m/8 539ft and extends towards the Vallon de Chastillon. Snow cover is frequently exceptional considering the southern latitude of Isola 2000, less than 100km/62mi from Nice. The ski runs are varied enough to satisfy the most demanding skiers (Génisserie and Le Méné black runs) and the less experienced (blue runs starting from Les Marmottes). Adequate snow-making equipment makes up for the eventual lack of snow. Other possibilities: ice-driving and sleigh rides.

Isola 2000

HIKES

★**Tête de Pélévos** ⊘ – Alt 2 455m/8 054ft. *Take the Pélévos cable-car.* From the upper station (alt 2 320m/7 612ft), follow a path on the right, which climbs towards the Marmottes lifts. Bear left at the second lift and go to the summit offering a fine **panorama**★ of the skiing area, the Lombarde and Malinvern summits.

★★**Lacs de Terre Rouge** – *Difference in height: about 650m/2 133ft. Allow 4hr return.* Start from the restaurant called "La Bergerie" at the end of the resort and climb to the Hôtel Diva. From there, a marked path leads to the lakes lying at the foot of the Cime de Tavels and Mont Malinvern. Continue up to the **Baisse de Druos**★★ (alt 2 628m/8 622ft) which offers a fine view of the Argentera Nature Park on the Italian side and of Mont St-Sauveur and Mont Mounier on the French side.

★★**Mont St-Sauveur** – Alt 2 711m/8 894ft. *Allow 2hr on the way up and 1hr 30min on the way down. Difference in height: about 400m/1 312ft.* Go up to the Marmottes 2 drag-lift *(see Tête de Pélévos above)* and continue to the Col Valette. From there, take a narrow path *(marked with wooden signpost)* which runs along the mountainside towards Mont St-Sauveur *(caution is required at the beginning as the path is rather stony).* Turn left at marker 89 and follow the short path running along the crest of the mountain. Extended **panorama**★★ from the summit including the Isola skiing area in the foreground as well as a large area of the Parc national du Mercantour and, clockwise, the Gorges de Valabrès, the Valberg skiing area, Mont Mounier, Auron, Mont Viso and the snow-capped Pelvoux.

Col de la Lombarde – Alt 2 350m/7 710ft. *5km/3mi north of Isola 2000. Follow the narrow road which prolongs D 97 north of Isola 2000 and leads to the Italian border. It is possible to reach the pass on foot (3hr return on foot by following the easy marked path beyond the Belvédère Chair-lift.* The pass is framed on the right by the Lombarde Peak and on the left by the Lausetta Ridge, which provides fine walks or mountain-bike hikes. Lovely overall **view** of the Isola 2000 cirque, overlooked by the Tête Mercière, and of the deeper valley on the Italian side.

EXCURSIONS

★★**Santuario di Santa Anna (Italy)** – *12km/7.5mi. 45min drive and 45min walk return. Have your identity papers on you.*
From the Col de la Lombarde, the road runs through a splendid rocky landscape, skirts Lake Orgials and goes down through larch woods. In a bend, turn left towards Santa Anna. As you reach the sanctuary, turn left and continue to the end of the surfaced road. **View**★ of the sanctuary and of the mountains towering over it. Leave the car and walk for 20min to the beautiful **Lago di Santa Anna**★, lying below the Lausfer and Arène Grosse peaks. Walk along the shore to the end of the lake for the best view of it. The lake is the starting point of longer hikes.

★**Vallon de Chastillon** – *17km/10.6mi. D 97 leads from Isola 2000 down to the village of Isola at the confluence of the Guerche and Tinée rivers.* The road runs down the steep Vallon de Chastillon then widens as it leaves the high-pasture area. Many waterfalls cascade down the rock face. Isola's Romanesque bell-tower can be seen from afar.

Isola – *See Vallée de la TINÉE.*

Route de l'IZOARD★★

Michelin map 77 folds 18 and 19 or 244 fold 43
Local map see Le BRIANÇONNAIS

The Col de l'Izoard links the Briançonnais and Queyras regions. The summits on either side of the pass look quite different: covered with grass on the Briançonnais side, they appear rocky and barren on the Queyras side.

FROM BRIANÇON TO CHÂTEAU-QUEYRAS

38km/23.6mi – about 1hr 45min
The Col d'Izoard is usually obstructed by snow from October to June.

★★**Briançon** – *See BRIANÇON – 1hr 30min.*
Between Briançon and Cervières, the itinerary follows the cliff road through the Gorges de la Cerveyrette.

Cervières – This village, damaged during the Second World War, has nevertheless retained a few traditional houses and a 15C church.
From Cervières, a 10km/6.2mi-long road, partly surfaced, runs through the lovely **Vallée de la Cerveyrette**.
Large stone-and-wood chalets covered with larch shingles, form a succession of hamlets scattered over pastures and woodland.
Drive out of Cervières, stop the car and turn round to see the top of the Barre des Écrins (alt 4 102m/13 458ft) through the lower Cerveyrette Valley.

As the road winds up towards the pass along the River Izoard, the Pic de Rochebrune, one of the familiar silhouettes of the Briançonnais' landscapes, appears on the left.

Refuge Napoléon – It was erected in 1858, with funds bequeathed by Napoleon *(see ROUTE NAPOLÉON)*.

★★**Col d'Izoard** – Alt 2 360m/7 743ft. This is the highest point of the Route des Grandes Alpes south of the Col du Galibier. There is a memorial dedicated to Alpine forces who contributed to the construction of many mountain roads. A small **museum** ⊙, situated at the pass itself, is devoted to the Tour de France cycling race which goes across the Col d'Izoard.

Go up (15min return on foot) to the viewing panels overlooking the road. The superb **panorama** includes, to the north, the Briançonnais

Casse Déserte

mountains with Mont Thabor in the background, and, to the south, the heights of the Queyras region, the Pic des Houerts, Pic de la Font Sancre and Chambeyron Massif.

★★**Casse Déserte** – The road goes through a strange desolate landscape: jagged rocks, gullied slopes and screes. Two plaques commemorate two heroes of the Tour de France: the Italian Fausto Coppi, who won the race in 1952 and the Frenchman Louison Bobet who won it in 1953, 54 and 55.

Arvieux – *See Le QUEYRAS.*
The site of Château-Queyras comes into view as soon as the road reaches the narrow Guil Valley.

★**Château-Queyras** – *See CHÂTEAU-QUEYRAS.*

The sentries guarding the Casse Déserte

The ruiniform spires, towering over the Col de l'Izoard road, are due to a local geological phenomenon causing layers of ground limestone and gypsum to be bonded into a yellowish conglomerate, known as *cargneule*. The hardest blocks of this conglomerate are less eroded than the rest and form groups of "needles" such as those of the Casse Déserte whose name refers to the scree-covered slopes also characteristic of the area.

Lacs de LAFFREY ★
Michelin map 77 folds 5 and 15 or 244 fold 39

The Laffrey lakes, stretching from north to south along the Route Napoléon *(see ROUTE NAPOLÉON)*, include: the Lac Mort, the Grand Lac de Laffrey, the largest of the four (3km long), the Lac de Petichet (meaning "small") and the Lac de Pierre-Châtel. Two more itineraries, running parallel, the Corniche du Drac and Vallée de la Morte, are also described here.

★PLATEAU DE LA MATHEYSINE
① From La Mure to the Lacs de Laffrey

La Mure – This lively market town, situated on the southern edge of the Plateau de la Matheysine, owes its prosperity to the nearby coal mines. La Mure is the starting point of the mountain railway line running to St-Georges-de-Commiers *(see La Mure Mountain Railway)*.

Musée Matheysin ⊙ – Situated near the covered market, inside a historic building, this museum deals with local history, including mining (the last mine closed down in 1996), by means of many reconstructions.

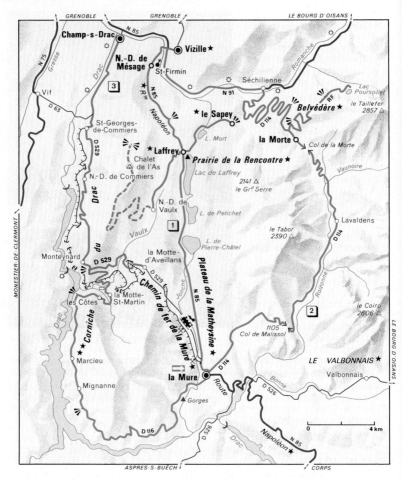

The road to Laffrey runs along the plateau not far from the former mining complex of Le Villaret, then along the lakes, sometimes hidden by vegetation, with the heights of the Chartreuse Massif barring the horizon ahead.

The austere Plateau de la Matheysine, extending from north to south, is windswept and exposed to the full harshness of winter, in spite of its relatively low altitude (below 1 000m/3 281ft); the lakes are often iced over during the winter months. The 45th parallel, drawn at an equal distance from the North Pole and the Equator, goes across the southern shore of the Lac de Pierre-Châtel.

From Laffrey, it is possible to go on an easy hike *(about 2hr)* to the **Montagne de Beauregard**, via the village of Notre-Dame-de-Vaux. Park the car near the Chalet de l'As and continue on foot to the top of the ridge which offers a splendid **view** of the plateau, the lakes and the Drac Valley.

★**Le Sapey** – The narrow road skirts the Lac Mort which supplies a power station in the Romanche Valley. From the end of the road, one can climb to the Chapelle du Sapey *(15min return on foot)* which offers a clear view of the Chamrousse-Belledonne and Taillefer massifs.

★★ROUTE DE LA MORTE

② From La Mure to Vizille *45km/28mi – about 2hr*

La Mure – *See Plateau de la Matheysine on previous page.*

Between La Mure and the Col de Malissol (alt 1 105m/3 625ft) the road offers views of the Obiou and the eastern escarpments of the Vercors Massif. From the Col de Malissol to the Col de la Morte, it runs along the narrow valley of the Roizonne.

La Morte – Lying at the foot of the Grand Serre and Taillefer summits, La Morte (alt 1 348m/4 423ft) offers beautiful ski runs. In summer, it is the starting point of the ascent of the Taillefer.

The forest road leading to the Lac Poursollet *(6km/3.7mi)* affords fine views of the Romanche Valley.

★**Viewpoint over the Vallée de la Romanche** – *Next to the first bend on the way down north of the Col de la Morte.* There are bird's-eye views of the Romanche Valley 1 000m/3 281ft below.

Road N 91 leads to Vizille.

★**Vizille** – *See VIZILLE.*

Drive on to Grenoble along D 5 via Eybens, which is the last section of the Route Napoléon (see ROUTE NAPOLÉON).

★★CORNICHE DU DRAC

③ From Champ-sur-Drac to La Mure *45km/28mi – about 2hr*

Between Champ-sur-Drac and Monteynard, the road rises gradually and offers views of the deep Drac Valley and of the extensive works carried out to harness the river at Notre-Dame de Commiers and Monteynard. On leaving Monteynard, stop the car at the intersection of the road leading to La Motte-St-Martin to admire the splendid view of the artificial lake below.

Continue along D 529 to La Motte-d'Aveillans.

Mine-Image ⓥ – This horizontal gallery, situated on one of the former mining sites, recreates the environment of miners and shows the evolution of mining technology. The site was mined until 1956 by means of horizontal galleries.

One of the "seven wonders of Dauphiné", known as the **Pierre Percée**, stands just outside La Motte, along D 529 to La Mure, then left at the signpost marked "Pierre Percée". A path starting from the parking area leads to the ridge *(45min)*. According to legend, the natural arch, 3m/10ft high, represents the devil turned into stone!

Return to La Motte-d'Aveillans and turn left onto D 116.

Beyond Les Côtes, the cliff road affords striking **views★★★** of the escarpments plunging into the River Drac, of the power station at Avignonet, of the Monteynard Dam and artificial lake and of the heights of the Vercors Massif.

The panorama unfolding beyond Mignanne includes the Obiou (highest summit of the Dévoluy mountains, alt 2 790m/9 154ft), the Petit Chaillol slightly east of it and, further east still, the highest snow-capped peaks of the Écrins Massif.

The road overlooks the Gorges de la Jonche just before reaching La Mure.

★LA MURE MOUNTAIN RAILWAY ⓥ

This railway line was built in 1888 over a distance of 30km/18.6mi to transport coal from the mining site of La Mure to St-Georges-de-Commiers linked to the national network. At the time, it was a daring technical achievement: the line negotiated a difference in height of 560m/1 837ft by means of 12 curved viaducts and 18 tunnels, also curved. At the beginning of the century, the La Mure Railway became the first railway in the world to be powered by high-voltage direct electric current.

The line is now only used as a tourist attraction. From St-Georges, the railway rises gradually to the highest point of the line at the Festinière Tunnel (924m/3 032ft). There are some spectacular sections, over the Gorges du Drac, across the Vaulx Viaduct (170m/186yd over nine arches) and La Lousse viaducts.

Chemin de fer de la Mure

La Mure Mountain Railway

Route de la MADELEINE ★

Michelin map 89 folds 6, 16 and 17 or 244 folds 30 and 31

Opened in 1969, this road links the Maurienne (N 6) and Tarentaise (N 90) valleys across moderately high mountains.

FROM LA CHAMBRE TO MOÛTIERS *53km/33mi – about 2hr*

The Col de la Madeleine is blocked by snow from November to early June.

Road D 213 rises from La Chambre *(11km/6.8mi northwest of St-Jean-de-Maurienne)* in a series of hairpin bends and offers views of the Allevard and Grandes Rousses massifs through the Glandon Pass.

St-François-Longchamp – This winter sports complex spreads between St-François (1 450m/4 757ft) and Longchamp (1 610m/5 285ft) on the east side of the Bugeon Valley, beneath the Cheval Noir Summit.

★**Col de la Madeleine** – Alt 2 000m/6 562ft. Covered with pastures, this wide gap between the Gros Villan and Cheval Noir (alt 2 832m/9 291ft) Summits offers a remarkable view of the Mont-Blanc Massif to the northeast and of the Grandes Rousses and Écrins massifs to the south *(viewing tables)*.

Between Celliers and Pas de Briançon, the cliff road clings to the western slopes of the Celliers Valley dotted with villages, the Beaufortain mountains barring the horizon down-river.

Drive to La Léchère via Notre-Dame-de-Briançon along D 97.

✣ **La Léchère-les-Bains** – Lying deep down in the lower Tarentaise Valley, La Léchère is the newest Alpine spa resort, specialising in the treatment of vascular diseases, gynecological complaints and rheumatism. The springs were discovered when a landslide occurred in 1869.

Follow the twisting road on the right, which rises to St-Oyen.

Doucy – The 17C Baroque church is furnished in similar style: note the carved-wood polychrome retable over the **high altar** and the Rosary retable.

Continue along the road to Villaret (D 95^B).

This road, running along the ridge separating the Morel and Eau Rousse valleys, offers fine views of the Vanoise, Mont Jovet, part of Courchevel and the ski slopes of Méribel-les-Allues.

Drive to Valmorel via le Meillet.

❄**Valmorel** – *See VALMOREL.*

Follow the Morel Valley (D 95) down to Aigueblanche.

Barrage des Échelles d'Annibal – Built across a narrow passage of the Basse-Tarentaise Valley, this dam diverts part of the flow of the River Isère to the power station at Randens on the Arc, through an 11.5km/7mi tunnel. The diversion was inaugurated in 1956.

Moûtiers – *See MOÛTIERS.*

MANE ★

Population 1 135
Michelin map 81 fold 15 or 245 fold 19 – Local map see Pays de FORCALQUIER

Built on an isolated rocky knoll standing in the centre of a plain, this village nestles round its medieval citadel. The local stone, quarried near Porchères, was used in the construction of many buildings, including the Priory of Notre-Dame-de-Salagon and Sauvan Castle.

SIGHTS

Église St-André ⊙ – The 16C church has a Florentine doorway decorated with palm leaves. Inside, the Gothic chancel contains a fine marble altar.
Follow the paved street on the left of the church; the old Renaissance houses have carved lintels over the doors.

Citadel *(not open to the public)* – These are the best-preserved 12C fortifications in Haute-Provence; the two walls wind round the hillock overlooking the village. From the top there is a fine **view** of the Plateau du Vaucluse, the Luberon, the Observatoire St-Michel and the Durance Valley.

EXCURSIONS

Drystone huts – These circular constructions, half-hidden by the dense vegetation, can be seen to the north and east of Mane. They were built in the 18C and 19C with stones taken out of the cultivated fields, both as shelters from the burning sun and as tool sheds. Inside, the roof is in the shape of a corbelled dome, as that of an igloo. There is a narrow window, a fireplace and a cupboard all made of stone. The height of these huts varies from 3-7m/10-23ft and their circumference from 10-30m/33-98ft.

Hikers are asked not to pick up stones, even loose ones, not to climb onto walls or light fires beneath them *(the heat would split the stones)*.

Road N 100 south on Mane is lined with several monuments which bear witness to the rich historical background of the village.

Drystone hut

⭐**Notre-Dame de Salagon** ⊙ – The church dates from the 12C and has retained its Romanesque structure and decoration in spite of alterations. The priory buildings were rebuilt in the late 15C and later used as a farm. In 1981, the priory was turned into an ethnological museum of the Haute-Provence region and extensive restoration work was undertaken. The west front of the church is decorated with a deeply inset rose window and a doorway, similar to that of the Ganagobie Monastery *(see Monastère de GANAGOBIE)*. Inside, the capitals and engaged columns denote a definite Provençal influence. Gallo-Roman finds have been discovered in the chancel together with evidence of an earlier church dating from the 6C. Note the mullioned windows and stair turret of the priory buildings.

Medieval bridge across the Laye – *On the right of N 100; follow the signposting to the Auberge de la Laye.*
The highest arch of this cutwater bridge is Romanesque.

⭐**Château de Sauvan** ⊙ – This classical edifice, dating from the early 18C, is shaded by ancient trees. A typical Mediterranean landscape, reminiscent of Tuscany, unfolds from the terrace. In 1793, the lady of the manor, who bore a striking resemblance to Queen Marie-Antoinette, offered to take her place in the Conciergerie; Marie-Antoinette refused her generous sacrifice and the countess fled the country. However, the lords of Sauvan Castle were well liked in the area and the castle was not destroyed during the Revolution. Neglected for many years, the castle was eventually restored in 1981.
Particularly noteworthy is the hall separated by pilasters with Ionic capitals from the imposing stone staircase overlooked by the first-floor gallery.
The fine reception rooms contain a rich collection of 17C, 18C and 19C furniture. French-style gardens adorned with fountains surround the castle.

Tour de Porchères – *At the end of a path on the right of the road, just beyond the Château de Sauvan.*
This massive rectangular keep, in Romanesque style, dates from the 12C; note the long voussoirs forming the arched doorway.

MANOSQUE ⭐

Population 19 107
Michelin map 81 fold 15, 114 folds 4 and 5 or 245 folds 32 and 33
Local map see Vallée de la Moyenne DURANCE

Nestling among foothills on the edge of the Luberon Mountain, a stone's throw from the River Durance, this peaceful little town has only recently expanded owing to its position along the rich agricultural Durance Valley and the proximity of the Cadarache Nuclear Centre.
This modernisation has altered the rural setting of Manosque, celebrated by the native born novelist, **Jean Giono** (1895-1970): "At the foot of the hill was the town like a tortoise shell in the grass".

According to a local legend, King François I, on a visit to Manosque, was welcomed at the Porte Saunerie by the beautiful Péronne de Voland, who offered him the town keys on a velvet cushion. The king courted her and, not knowing how to turn him down, the consul's daughter exposed her face to sulphur fumes in order to spoil her looks. Since then, the town has been known as "the bashful Manosque".

★OLD TOWN *1hr*

Wide boulevards have replaced the ramparts which once enclosed the old town; the typically Provençal streets are narrow and lined with tall houses concealing secluded gardens, patios, beautiful cellars and galleries. The streets are linked by covered passages and extremely narrow alleyways known as *androns*.

★Porte Saunerie – This 12C gate, which formed part of the original town walls, owes its name to nearby salt warehouses *(now gone)*. Note the twinned openings supported on slender columns and the machicolated side turrets.

Rue Grande (10) – This lively picturesque high street offers a wealth of old doorways, fine stairwells, courtyards and balconies. **No 14** was the workshop where Giono's father used to mend shoes and where his mother ironed clothes. Note the wrought-iron balconies of the 16C-17C house at **No 23**. Beyond the Église St-Sauveur, have a look at the doorways of **nos 31, 39** and **42**.

Église St-Sauveur ⊘ – The plain façade overlooks a square decorated with a fountain. Beyond the Gothic doorway, lies the Romanesque nave, which was given a pointed vault in the 17C. The transepts are barrel vaulted and the crossing is surmounted by a dome on squinches. The apse is covered with ribbed oven vaulting. The fine organ case, in carved gilt wood, dates from 1625.
The square bell-tower is surmounted by a famous wrought-iron **campanile**, made in 1725 by a blacksmith from Rians.

Place de l'Hôtel-de-Ville (13) – A **colourful market** livens up the square three times a week. The **town hall** (H), with its elegant 17C façade and beautiful staircase, is one of the finest buildings in Manosque.

Église Notre-Dame-de-Romigier ⊘ – The church has a Renaissance doorway, but the nave was remodelled in the 17C and the aisles were added. The altar is a splendid 4C or 5C **sarcophagus★** in Carrara marble. According to legend, the **statue of the Virgin Mary**, in a sitting position, was discovered at the end of the 10C under a bramble bush, where it had been hidden when the Sarracens invaded Provence in the 9C; it was later placed inside the church. Before the statue was restored, its face, neck and hands were darker.

Porte Soubeyran – The 12C gate, remodelled in the 14C like the Porte Saunerie, was later decorated with a lovely stone balustrade and a tower surmounted by a graceful onion-shaped dome in wrought iron.
Turn back, then left into rue Soubeyran.

Place des Observantins (19) – A former monastery has been turned into the music and dance conservatory. The square is decorated with a lovely old fountain. The library and municipal archives are housed in the **Hôtel d'Herbès** (E), which has a fine 17C staircase inside.
Return to the Porte Saunerie via rue Jean-Jacques-Rousseau, rue des Ormeaux, past place des Ormeaux and along rue de la Saunerie, admiring some lovely doors on the way.

★★Fondation Carzou ⊘ (M) – Jean Carzou, a French painter of Armenian descent, born in 1907, departed from Abstract painting and evolved his own intricate style, full of fantasy, against a monochrome background, to depict modern cities, Venice and Provence.

MANOSQUE

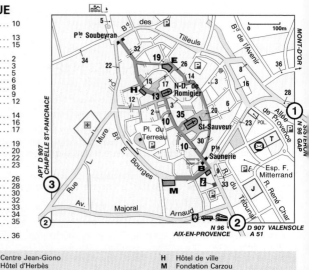

B	Centre Jean-Giono	H	Hôtel de ville
E	Hôtel d'Herbès	M	Fondation Carzou

He decorated the former Couvent de la Présentation with murals adapted from a group of paintings on the theme of *The Apocalypse*. The interesting neo-Classical church, built in 1840, has a single nave surmounted by a dome on pendentives, a coffered vault, capitals decorated with acanthus leaves and a frieze running round the nave.

The Apocalypse – It took the artist seven years to complete this amazing fresco. Each decorated panel illustrates one of Carzou's favourite themes. The unity of the work is emphasized by the blue-green backgrounds.

Start with the left-hand side of the nave. In the left wing of the chancel the artist depicts destructions and massacres accomplished by Man, in the apse he illustrates lust; the right side of the church is devoted to women's accomplishments. Most of the **stained-glass windows** ★ were also designed by Carzou; the four knights of the Apocalypse symbolize the great genocides which have occurred in the history of mankind. The left wing announces the reconstruction of the world through love and work. Note the reference to Millet's *Angelus* in the corner of the left wall. The *Tree-woman* symbolizes the earth's revival; note that, in spite of the disasters brought about by Man, the sky remains blue for there is hope in the future. The lovers clasped in each other's arms represent the universality of Love. Eve appears triumphant whereas Adam, who faces her, is less sure of himself.

The Tree-Woman, Fondation Carzou

Fondation Carzou, Manosque

Centre Jean-Giono ⊘ (**B**) – This fine Provençal house, dating from the 18C, houses a museum devoted to the life and works of Jean Giono.

On the ground floor (note the beautiful ceilings), Giono's life, written works and films are presented with the help of documents. The library contains manuscripts of his works and a collection of translations from all over the world. Most of the films to which he contributed, as well as interviews and television programmes, can be seen in the video library.

EXCURSIONS

Chapelle St-Pancrace (also known as Chapelle de Toutes Aures) – *2km/1.2mi southwest. Leave Manosque by* ③ *on the town plan and follow the signposted road.* Near this chapel, at the top of the hill, there is an extended **view** ★ (almost 380°) of the Luberon, Manosque and the Préalpes de Digne beyond the Durance Valley and Valensole Plateau.

Mont d'Or – *1.5km/0.9mi northeast. Starting from the rue Dauphine, climb up the montée des Vraies-Richesses then follow a no-through road on the right to the last house on the right, known as Le Paraïs.*

Le Paraïs ⊘ – *The house is still inhabited by the Giono family and discretion is therefore highly appreciated.* This is the house where Giono wrote most of his works from 1930 onwards. He acquired the property in 1968. The tour goes through his library and his last study decorated with a bunch of flowers painted by Giono himself. His study is on the next floor; note the cast of his right hand and other mementoes. The roofs of the old town can be seen from the window.

Mont d'Or Summit – The **view** ★ gradually extends to embrace the old town and its roofs, "overlapping like the plates of an armour" as Giono once said, the Durance Valley, the Luberon and, in the distance, the Ste-Victoire and Ste-Baume mountains.

The large tarred slabs which can be seen from the Sentier des Roches mark the area where crude oil and natural gas are being stored beneath the forest. Some 30 wells have been drilled to reach a vast layer of rock salt. Water is pumped in to dissolve the salt which is then recovered and gradually replaced by oil and gas brought in by pipeline from the Étang de Berre. When the operation in progress is completed, 10 million m³/353 million cu ft of oil and gas will be stored on the site.

Forêt de Pélicier – *10km/6.2mi along D 5; 3hr. Drive out of Manosque along boulevard Martin-Bret; leave the car at the pass.*
The forest was created last century as part of a plan of reafforestation of mountain areas and therefore consists mainly of Austrian pines, which are very hardy trees. From the Col de la Mort d'Imbert, follow the path on the right which skirts a former tile factory; turn left 400m/437yd further on and follow another path which goes through gypsum quarries, known as **gipières**, then round Escourteja Hill. Climb up to "Les Deux-Moulins" where an old building houses the Centre de Découverte de l'Espace Pastoral (Centre for the Discovery of Rural Environment). The tour continues along a forest road to the Sentier des Roches aménagées. At the intersection of three tracks, you will find a map of the forest. Return to the Col de la Mort d'Imbert along the signposted track.

La MAURIENNE

Michelin map 74 folds 16, 17 and 19, 77 folds 7, 8 and 9
or 244 folds 30, 31, 32 and 33

The valley of the River Arc, known as La Maurienne, is one of the longest intra-Alpine valleys (118km/73mi), deeply enclosed all the way. There is a striking contrast between the beautiful natural environment and the major industrial complexes lining the valley, although the upper Maurienne has been spared intensive industrialization and still retains its traditional character.

Tourism and industry – The Maurienne lies on an important route between France and Italy across the Col du Mont-Cenis and, since 1980, via the Fréjus Tunnel, so that international traffic can now get through all year round by road and rail.
Between Avrieux, up-river of Modane, and Aiguebelle, near the confluence of the Arc and Isère rivers, the course of the middle and lower-Maurienne Valley is dotted with some 10 factories (aluminium, steel and chemicals), using the energy produced by about 20 power stations.
One of the most important hydroelectric projects carried out in the area was the building of the underground power station at Randens (1954), supplied with water diverted from the River Isère at Les Échelles d'Annibal *(see Route de la MADELEINE).*

Busy river – The vast works undertaken to harness the Arc were completed by the building of a dam which led to the creation of a huge reservoir of 320 million m³/259 200acft, at the foot of Mont Cenis, which supplies the power station at Villarodin-Bourget built lower down in the valley, near Avrieux.

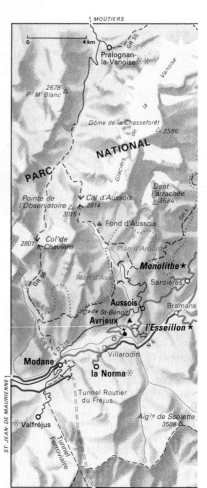

Three more power stations, situated between Modane and St-Jean-de-Maurienne, regulate the course of the Arc. One of the most daring achievements of the harnessing programme was the building of a 19km/11.8mi-long tunnel going through the Belledonne Massif and intended to divert part of the flow of the Arc to the Isère Valley on the other side of the mountains.

★HAUTE-MAURIENNE

From Bonneval-sur-Arc to Modane

56km/34.8mi – about 2hr not including the tour of the chapels decorated with murals in Bessans and Lanslevillard, the detour up the Route du Mont-Cenis and the recommended hikes. Possibility of taking a ski-bus part of the way.

Road D 902 may be blocked by snow from Bonneval-sur-Arc to Bessans.

★Bonneval-sur-Arc – *See BONNEVAL-SUR-ARC.*

There are many religious monuments left between Bonneval and Lanslebourg: Stations of the Cross, oratories and chapels erected by local people or by pilgrims who had safely travelled over the border passes.

Turn left past Notre-Dame-des-Grâces towards the Refuge d'Avérole.

★★Vallée d'Avérole – *See BESSANS.*

Return to D 902.

✳Bessans – *See BESSANS.*

The Col de **la Madeleine** between Bessans and Lanslevillard, with its piles of rocks scattered among larches, marks a transition in the landscape: downstream, the slopes appear more rounded, the vegetation is darker and the view extends further towards the **Dent Parrachée** (alt 12 087ft), the most southern peak of the Vanoise Massif, and, behind it, to the jagged Rateau d'Aussois.

Lanslevillard – *See VAL CENIS.*

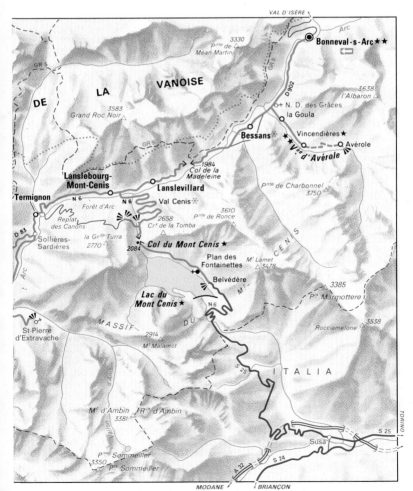

Lanslebourg-Mont-Cenis – *See VAL CENIS.*

★**Route du Mont-Cenis** – *16km/9.9mi from Lanslebourg – about 45min – see Route du MONT-CENIS.*

Termignon – The present **church** ⊙ dates from the second half of the 17C; the pine retable over the high altar is the work of Claude and Jean Rey; the other two are by Sébastien Rosaz. From Termignon, a winding road *(D 83)* leads to Bellecombe (alt 2 310m/7 579ft). Park the car and continue on foot to the **Col de la Vanoise** ★★★ *(6hr 30min return)* or stop at the **Plan du Lac** Refuge *(1hr 30min return)*; from the viewing table near the refuge, there is a splendid **panorama** ★★ of the Dent Parrachée, Dôme de Chasseforêt, Vanoise glaciers, Grande Casse and Grande Motte summits... The path then goes past the Entre-Deux-Eaux refuge through a pastoral landscape dotted with traditional chalets, where ibexes and chamois roam freely, to the Col de la Vanoise affording splendid **views** of the Grande Casse.

The main interest of the Sollières-Villarodin section lies in the detour to **St-Pierre-d'Extravache** *(in Bramans, 8km/5mi beyond Sollières, turn onto D 100)*. The 10C church, which is said to be the oldest church in Savoie, has retained a well-preserved chancel and bell-tower.

Return to Sollières and follow D 83.

The road rises among pastures and pine woods to the ledge where the pointed steeple of Sardières can be seen from afar, with the Ambin and Thabor summits in the distance.

Go into Sardières and follow the path leading to the monolith.

★**Monolithe de Sardières** – This 83m/272ft-high needle stands isolated on the southern edge of the Parc national de la Vanoise. It was first climbed in 1957.

Aussois – *See AUSSOIS.*

In Aussois, turn left in front of the church.

★**L'Esseillon Fortifications** – Between Aussois and Avrieux, l'Esseillon is a rocky knoll crowned by impressive fortifications built by the Sards during the early 19C to repell a possible French invasion. There are five forts situated at different altitudes so that they could defend one another. The highest, Fort Marie-Christine, overlooking Aussois, has been restored and now serves as a gateway into the Parc national de la Vanoise; it is also the starting point of many hikes. Opposite, on the south bank of the Arc, Fort Marie-Thérèse is linked to the complex by the impressive Pont du Diable *(see La Norma below)*.

The cliff road runs across the St-Benoît Stream (fine waterfall facing a chapel) and dips into the Avrieux Basin.

Take a small road on the left leading to Avrieux.

Avrieux – The **church** ⊙ is said to have been founded in the 12C by two English families connected with Thomas Becket to whom it is dedicated. The façade is decorated with 17C frescoes depicting the seven virtues and the seven capital sins and the fine interior **decoration** ★ is Baroque. On the west wall, there is a diptych, dating from 1626, which retraces the life of St Thomas Becket; note also the 16C stone stoup and several polychrome wooden statues.

The **Souffleries de Modane-Avrieux**, the most important of their kind in Europe, were designed to try out and experiment on aeroplanes, helicopters, missiles, rockets and space shuttles before test flights are carried out. It all began when the elements of a huge wind tunnel, discovered in Austria by the Allies in 1945, were brought back to this site where the nearby power station supplied the hydroelectricity necessary to produce wind acceleration inside the tunnel.

Just beyond Villarodin, turn left onto D 214 for La Norma.

※**La Norma** – This picturesque little resort, founded in 1971, occupies a favourable position on top of a plateau (alt 1 350m/4 429ft) overlooking the upper Maurienne Valley, 6km/3.7mi from Modane.

The **skiing area**, which extends over 700ha/1 730 acres facing north-northwest, offers good snow cover and there are 17 ski-lifts for 60km/36mi of ski runs of varying levels of difficulty between 1 350-2 750m/4 429-9 022ft. The steep slopes are at the top, alongside the Norma 2 Drag-lift and the Clot Chair-lift. In addition, there are exceptional **panoramas** ★★ of the Thabor and Vanoise Massifs.

It is possible to combine a **gondola ride** ★ to **Le Mélezet** (alt 1 990m/6 529ft, *via Le Mélezet Gondola* ⊙), offering views of the snow-capped Péclet-Polset, of the Aiguille de Doran, the Rateau d'Aussois and Dent Parrachée, with a pleasant **walk** ★ down to the resort via **La Repose** and Chapelle Ste-Anne *(in winter beware of skiers)*.

Via ferrata du Diable – This rock-climbing course located near the Pont du Diable includes three one-way itineraries of varying difficulty and length *(3-6hr)*. The easiest is the section linking Fort Marie-Thérèse to the Pont du Diable. Information is available from the "Maison de la Norma" *(see Practical information)*.

Return to N 6 and turn left towards Modane.

Modane – *See MODANE.*

MEGÈVE ✱✱✱

Population 4 750
Michelin map 89 fold 7 or 244 fold 20
Local map see Massif des ARAVIS

Inaugurated soon after the First World War, Megève remains one of the major French ski resorts thanks to its accommodation potential and fashionable atmosphere.

The native town of **Émile Allais**, who was the 1937 downhill, slalom and combination world champion and initiated the "French skiing method", prides itself on its nucleus of unconditional admirers. Situated at an altitude of 1 113m/3 652ft, the resort is sought after in summer for its bracing climate, nearby forest, numerous possibilities of mountain hikes and drives and wide choice of sporting activities (tennis, swimming, skating etc). Megève is also a children's health and holiday resort.

Skiing area – Sunny and safe, it is appreciated more by amateurs of "relaxed skiing" than by keen experienced skiers. There are many ski-lifts but snow cover is not guaranteed owing to the low altitude. The skiing area, which extends over the slopes of the Mont d'Arbois, Rochebrune and the Aravis, is linked by gondola or shuttle to the other resorts of the Mont-Blanc Massif. In addition, Megève has one of the most important ski schools in the world.

SIGHTS

Musée du Haut Val d'Arly ⊘ – *173 rue St-François*. The museum houses collections of traditional objects displayed in reconstructed authentic settings. Several themes are dealt with: domestic life, agricultural tools, milk processing, textiles and winter sports.

Le Calvaire (BY) – This is the replica of the Stations of the Cross in Jerusalem, lined with 15 oratories and chapels decorated with paintings and sculptures *(unfortunately in poor condition)* made by local craftsmen between 1844 and 1864. From the lower chapel, there is a pleasant view of the upper Val d'Arly.

Plane trips ⊘ – These trips over the valleys of the Mont-Blanc Massif, start from the local mountain airport, Côte 2000.

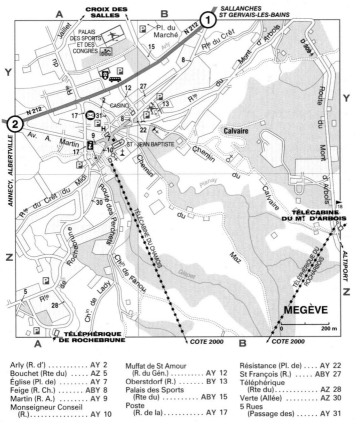

MEGÈVE

VIEWPOINTS ACCESSIBLE BY GONDOLA

★★**Mont d'Arbois** ⊙ (**BZ**) – Alt 1 833m/6 014ft. *Access by gondola from the Plateau du Mont d'Arbois or by the Princesse Gondola from the Petit-Bois crossroads.*

Splendid **panoramic view** of the Aravis and Fiz mountains as well as Mont Blanc. It is possible to walk in 20min to the upper station of the cable-car which goes back down to St-Gervais.

★★**Croix des Salles** ⊙ (**AY**) – Alt 1 705m/5 594ft. *About 1hr 30min return, including 6min ride in the Jaillet Gondola and 45min return on foot.*
Having reached the upper station, continue on foot to the cross through pastures and woodland. **View** of the Fiz range and Mont-Blanc Massif.

★**Rochebrune Super-Megève** ⊙ (**AZ**) – Alt 1 754m/5 755ft. *About 1hr return, including a 5min cable-car ride.*
View of the Val d'Arly, the Aravis mountains and Mont Blanc.

HIKES

A map on sale at the tourist office will enable you to take full advantage of the possibilities the area has to offer.

★★★**Mont Joly** – Alt 2 525m/8 284ft. *4hr 30min return on foot from Mont d'Arbois via a well-marked path. Mountain boots are recommended, particularly for the last part of the itinerary.*
The exceptional **panorama**★★★ unfolding from the summit *(viewing table)*, includes the Mont-Blanc Massif, the Vanoise, the Beaufortain, the Écrins, the Grandes Rousses, the Belledonne range, the Chartreuse and the Aravis.

★★**Mont de Vorès** – Alt 2 067m/6 781ft. *5hr 30min on foot. Difference in height: 800m/2 625ft. This itinerary is not difficult but requires stamina. Board the cable-car preferably before 10am. If it is not working, it is possible to make a similar round tour from Leutaz.*
The path rises to l'Alpette and the Col de Véry on the way to Mont de Vorès. Splendid **view** of the Mont-Blanc Massif to the east, with the Col du Joly and Lac de la Girotte in the foreground, and the Aravis mountains to the west. The path then follows the mountain ridge to Crêt du Midi which offers a remarkable **view** of Megève on the right and Le Planay on the left. Walk down to Les Fontanettes then up again to Rochebrune *(hard-going walk lasting 1hr)* along a fairly steep path.

MÉRIBEL✱✱✱

Michelin map 89 fold 7 or 244 fold 31 – local map see Massif de la VANOISE

Méribel is an attractive ski resort situated in the Allues Valley, at the heart of the **Trois Vallées**✱✱✱ skiing area *(see Massif de la VANOISE)*, the largest in the world.
British skiing enthusiasts were the first to realise the touristic potential of the area. After the annexation of Austria by Germany in 1938, they stopped going to Austrian resorts and turned to the French Alps in their search for places suitable for skiing. Lord Lindsay discovered the Allues Valley with its 13 old hamlets and founded Méribel. After the war, regulations concerning architectural styles were laid down: all residential buildings must be chalets with ridged roofs and wood or stone façades. This concern about blending the resort's architecture with the landscape, combined with the area's potential, has resulted in Méribel being one of the finest French ski resorts welcoming regular international visitors who appreciate the refined atmosphere of this exceptional resort.

THE RESORTS

Skiing area – It is excellent for competent skiers: a network of gondolas provides fast and comfortable links with Courchevel, Les Ménuires and Val Thorens. The recently equipped areas of Mont Vallon, Mont de la Chambre, Roc des Trois Marches and Roc de Fer offer some of the finest ski slopes in Europe. The fact that they face north-south and west makes it possible for skiers to remain in the sun all day.
It is for these reasons that Méribel was chosen as the main Olympic site of the Albertville Games in February 1992. All the women's Alpine skiing events were held on the difficult Roc de Fer run and hockey matches took place in the new ice-skating rink. The cross-country skiing area is not very extensive but delightful: there are 33km of well-covered tracks round the Altiport and Plan du Tueda, in a fine woodland setting (spruce and Arolla pine), at an altitude of 1 700m/5 577ft.

Non-skiers can enjoy the superb landscapes of the Trois Vallées area. Various paths criss-cross the forest or skirt the ski runs and special **pedestrian passes** give hikers access to gondolas and chair-lifts in Méribel and Courchevel. In summer, Méribel is a sought-after **hiking base**, since nearly a quarter of the surrounding area, covering 8 500ha/21 004 acres, is situated inside the Parc national de la Vanoise.

Méribel – The numerous chalet-apartments are dotted around the forest between 1 450-1 600m/4 757-5 249ft. The only drawback is that, apart from La Chaudanne, there is no real resort centre. The road continues to the mountain airport, where golf is played in summer. Themed flights are available in all seasons: the Trois Vallées, the Olympic sites and Mont Blanc.

Méribel-Mottaret – This resort, between 1 700-1 800m/5 577-5 906ft, on the edge of the Parc national de la Vanoise, offers a compromise between modern comfort and traditional architecture. It is the centre of the Trois Vallées area.

MAIN SUMMITS

★★★**La Saulire** ⊘ – Access from Méribel by the Burgin Saulire gondola or from Mottaret by the Pas du Lac gondola. Splendid **panorama** *(see COURCHEVEL).*

★★**Mont du Vallon** – Alt 2 952m/9 685ft. *From Mottaret, walk to Plan des Mains alt 2 150m/7 054ft. Allow 1hr 15min in summer.* In winter, the only access is via the Plattières gondola *(second section, skiers only).* Continue to the summit by the Mont Vallon gondola. On arrival, go to the panel marked "Réserve de Tueda": superb close-up **view**★★★ of the Allues Valley's conservation area, including the Aiguille du Borgne and the Gébroulaz Glacier to the south and, further away, the rocky mass of the Pointe de l'Échelle; the Aiguille and Col du Fruit can be seen in the foreground to the north, backed by Mont Pourri and Mont Blanc in the distance; the Vanoise glaciers and the Grande Casse bar the horizon to the east. Turn back and take a path leading towards the Lacs du Borgne: fine view of the Vallée des Belleville with the Aiguille d'Arves and Grandes Rousses Massif in the distance.

★★**Roc des Trois Marches** – Alt 2 704m/8 871ft. *In winter, access from Mottaret by the Plattières gondola (three sections).* Beautiful **circular view**, including the Vanoise glaciers and the Meije.

★★**Tougnète** ⊘ – Alt 2 410m/7 907ft. *Access from Méribel by gondola.* On the way up, there is a view of Méribel and the villages dotted around the valley, with Mont Blanc and the Beaufortain in the background. From the upper station, the view extends over the whole Vallée des Belleville.
Skiers can also enjoy the various panoramas unfolding from the **Roc de Fer**★★, **Pas de Cherferie**★★, **Mont de la Challe**★, **Mont de la Chambre**★★ and **Col de la Loze**★★.

Y. Bontoux

Tuéda nature reserve with the Aiguille du Fruit in the background

HIKES

★**Plan de Tuéda** – *As you reach Mottaret, follow signs for Le Chatelet and park your car at the end of the road.*
The **Réserve naturelle de Tuéda** was created in 1990 for the preservation of one of the last large forests of Arolla pines in Savoie. These trees, which sometimes reach 600 years of age, are sought after for making furniture and musical instruments and have therefore been considerably reduced in numbers. The Tuéda Forest surrounds a lovely lake overlooked by the jagged silhouette of the Aiguille du Fruit and by Mont Vallon. A nature trail, lined with many flower species, offers hikers the possibility of discovering this exceptional and fragile environment.

★★**Col de Chanrouge** – Alt 2 531m/8 304ft. *Start from Plan de Tuéda. On the way up, allow 2hr to the Refuge du Saut then 1hr 15min to the pass. On the way down, allow 2hr.* From the pass, there is a fine **view** of the Courchevel Valley, of the skiing area of La Plagne (overlooked by the Sommet de Bellecôte) and of the Mont-Blanc Massif.

MODANE

Population 4 250
Michelin map 89 fold 8 or 244 fold 32 – Local map see La MAURIENNE

This border town at the entrance of the middle-Maurienne Valley, beneath the southern heights of the Vanoise Massif, controls the access to the Fréjus tunnels linking France and Italy. There are three ski resorts nearby: **Valfréjus**, **Arrondaz 2000** and **La Norma**.

Tunnel ferroviaire du Fréjus – This rail tunnel (1857-1872) was the first of the great Alpine tunnels (the area of the section is 57m^2/68.17sq yd) to be built; **Germain Sommeiller** (1815-1871) was the local engineer who devised the pneumatic drills used to dig the 13 657m/8.5mi-long tunnel.

TUNNEL ROUTIER DU FRÉJUS

Inaugurated in July 1980, the 12 870m/8mi-long road tunnel is shorter than the Arlberg Tunnel (Austrian) and the St-Gothard Tunnel (Swiss), but longer than the Mont-Blanc Tunnel. This Franco-Italian project was designed to ease road traffic when the Col du Mont Cenis is blocked by snow.
It rises slightly towards Italy as it passes beneath the Fréjus Massif. The 85m^2/101.66sq yd section allows a dual carriageway through, with parking areas and refuges dotted along the way; 54 video-cameras are spaced every 200m/218.7yd. The ventilation system pumps 1 530m3/54 032cu ft of fresh air per second; at each end of the tunnel there are four zones of progressive lighting for visual comfort. Toll-booths are on the French side.
Journey time: about 20min. Recommended speed: 70kph/43.5mph. Overtaking and stopping (except in an emergency) are forbidden. The tunnel is not accessible to vehicles with an engine capacity below 50cc and to pedestrians.
The charge payable is indicated in the current Michelin Red Guide France.

FOURNEAUX

Church ⊘ – A street crosses the railway line and rises to this interesting modern chalet-style church. Inside, the lean-to roof makes the church look spacious.

EXCURSIONS

★**Sentier nature de l'Orgère** – *From N 6 at Le Freney, turn right onto D 106, which rises steeply to the Orgère refuge (parking) over a distance of 13km/8mi.*
This nature trail *(2km/1.2mi)* winds round the Orgère Vale across meadows, woodland and pastures. The first part is lined with information panels about the specific environment. Ask the warden of the Maison du Parc for a leaflet giving details about the trail.

★★★**Hikes to the Col de Chavière** – *Departure from the Orgère refuge: 3hr up (including 2hr to the Lac de Partie); 2hr down. Difference in height: about 900m/2 953ft. Mountain boots recommended (snow to the end of July). Take a pair of binoculars to observe the fauna.*
The path climbs to the ruins of the Chalets de l'Estiva: **view**★★ from left to right of Longe Côte, La Norma, Modane and Valfréjus. When the path starts going down, the Col de Chavière comes into view flanked by the snow-capped **Péclet-Polset** and high cliffs. Chamois and ibexes roam about the area. Beyond the Lac de Partie, the path rises steeply to the pass (2 801m/9 190ft): splendid view of the Pralognan Valley and Mont Blanc in the distance.

✳**Valfréjus** – Alt 1 500m/4 921ft. *8km/5mi southwest.* The main attractions of this small ski resort, created in 1983, are its tasteful architecture and the nearby forest planted with spruces, larches and Arolla pines.

The **skiing area** enjoys adequate snow cover in its upper part facing north; there are 12 ski-lifts and some 20 ski runs.

In summer, Valfréjus is the starting point of hikes to the Pointe du Fréjus and Thabor Massif.

★★**Punta Bagna** ⊙ – Alt 2 750m/9 022ft. The summit is only accessible by gondola in wintertime; in summer, only the first section operates.

The **panorama**★★ is superb. The Italian Alps are visible straight ahead, beyond the Col du Fréjus; from the terrace of the restaurant, it is possible to see the northern summits of the Écrins Massif (Grande Ruine, Pic Gaspard, Meije and Rateau) to the southwest and the Valfréjus skiing area with the Vanoise Massif in the background to the north.

MOLINES-EN-QUEYRAS ★

Population 336
Michelin map 77 fold 19 or 244 fold 44 – Local map see Le QUEYRAS

This is a peaceful resort situated at the confluence of the Aigue Agnelle and Aigue Blanche valleys. The picturesque old houses are surmounted by large barns with canopies, where crops continue to ripen after the harvest.

In summer, Molines is popular with nature lovers for the many hiking possibilities it offers. There are few hotels but accommodation is available in private homes in the old village and surrounding hamlets.

In winter, Molines offers skiing in a lovely woodland setting; the small skiing area is linked to that of St-Véran *(see ST-VÉRAN)*. The ski-lifts are situated 1km/0.6mi from the village, on the road to St-Véran, at an altitude of 1 740m/5 709ft.

★**Église de St-Romain de Molines** – This church, in typical regional style, stands between La Rua and Molines *(see Le QUEYRAS: Route de St-Véran)*.

EXCURSIONS

★★**Route de St-Véran (Aigue Blanche Valley)** – See Le QUEYRAS.

★★**Route du Col Agnel (Aigue Agnelle Valley)** – *15km to the Col Agnel – about 30min. Road closed in winter.*

Drive to Pierre Grosse, which owes its name to the **erratic blocks** scattered over the surrounding pastures, then on to Fontgillarde, the valley's highest hamlet (1 997m/6 552ft). Beyond Fontgillarde, the road offers a fine **view** of the Pic de Château Renard, towering above the trees. A plaque, fixed to a rock on the right-hand side of the road, reminds passers-by that Hannibal's and Caesar's armies went through here on their way across the Alps.

The road continues to rise through a high-mountain landscape, offering **views** of the snow-covered Pelvoux Massif to the northwest. It finally reaches the Agnel Refuge and, 2km/1.2mi further on, the Agnel Pass on the Italian border. Walk up to the **viewing table** (alt 2 744m/9 003ft): splendid **panorama**★★ of the Pain de Sucre and Mont Viso to the east, the Grand Queyras and Pointe des Sagnes to the northwest, with the Pic de Rochebrune further away and the Meije and Pelvoux in the distance.

★★★**Hike to the Pain de Sucre** – Alt 3 208m/10 525ft. *Leave the car on the roadside between the refuge and the Col Agnel. 1hr 45min to the top, 1hr 15min down. Difference in height: 600m/1 968ft. This itinerary is suitable for experienced hikers equipped with mountain boots; dry weather essential.*

The **Col Vieux**★ (2 806m/9 206ft) is easily reached in 30min; another 15min climb takes you to a ledge; carry straight on to a path which winds up to the Pain de Sucre *(very steep climb, caution is recommended)*. The magnificent **panorama**★★★, one of the finest in the Alps, includes Mont Viso and the Italian Alps to the east, the Brec and Aiguille de Chambeyron to the south, the Oisans Massif to the west. To the north, the view extends as far as Mont Blanc in clear weather. Go down along a marked path starting near the cross and leading back to the Col Vieux.

To plan a special itinerary :
– consult the Map of touring programmes which indicates the recommended
  routes, the tourist regions, the principal towns and main sights.
– read the descriptions in the Sights section which include Excursions
  from the main tourist centres.
Michelin Maps *nos 70, 74, 77, 81, 84, 88, 89, 243, 244 and 245*
indicate scenic routes,
interesting sights, viewpoints, rivers, forests...

Massif du MONT-BLANC ★★★

Michelin map 89 Fold 4 or 244 folds 10, 21 and 22 – Local map see pp 238-239

The Mont-Blanc Massif surpasses in height all other European mountains, its highest peak reaching 4 807m/15 771ft, yet it owes its fame essentially to the wonderful variety of scenery offered by its domes, needles and glaciers. Motorists can enjoy an excellent overall view by driving up the Chamonix Valley, through which flows the Arve, or delight in the pastoral landscapes of the Val Montjoie (Bon Nant Valley).

The long "Round Tour of Mont Blanc" *(320km/199mi)*, via the Grand and Petit St Bernard passes, is highly recommended; on the other hand, the round tour of Mont Blanc on foot, is a long and fascinating walk suitable for experienced hikers. It is also possible to fly over the massif, starting from Megève or Sallanches airport.

THE FIRST ASCENT OF MONT BLANC

In the mid 18C, it became fashionable for wealthy young men on a grand tour of Europe to stop in Chamonix, where they were shown the Mer de Glace by local guides. In 1760, a young scientist from Geneva, **Horace Bénédict de Saussure** offered a reward to whoever reached the summit of Mont Blanc first. A few local people attempted the climb but were all defeated by ignorance, fear and lack of equipment.

In 1776, **Jacques Balmat** showed that one could spend a night at very high altitude and survive. **Michel-Gabriel Paccard**, a local doctor, found his experience interesting and the two of them took up Saussure's challenge: they left on 7 August 1786 and reached the summit the next day, completely exhausted.

The following year, it was Saussure's turn to make the ascent accompanied by 18 guides laden with scientific equipment.

Many more attempts followed, some of them made by women such as Marie Paradis in 1809 and Henriette d'Angeville in 1838.

Saussure and his team climbing Mont Blanc

D. Rigault/Conservatoire d'Art et d'Histoire, Annecy

GEOGRAPHICAL NOTES

Mont Blanc... – Like the rest of the Alpine range, Mont Blanc has two different aspects. On the French side, it appears like a "gentle giant" impressively flanked by snow-covered domes underlined by a few rocky escarpments (Aiguille du Goûter and Aiguilles de Bionnassay) whereas on the Italian side, it offers a grim dark wall bristling with needles (Aiguille Noire du Peutérey); the ascent from this side requires a lot of mountaineering skill but endurance is more important if you want to climb Mont Blanc from Chamonix or St-Gervais.

...and its satellites – The Chamonix Valley owes its fame to the **"needles"**, carved out of a kind of greenish coarse granite, known as *protogine*. Along the rock face of these splendid walls, mountaineers can find the same hand and footholds year after year, for several decades. The most famous peaks are the Grépon, the Aiguille de Blaitière and the Aiguille du Dru. Three huge **glaciers** are sought after by summer visitors: the **Mer de Glace**, the longest (14km/8.7mi from the head of the Géant Glacier) and most popular, owing to the famous Montenvers scenery; the Glacier des **Bossons** (7km/4.3mi), the most picturesque, thrusting through the forest; the Glacier d'**Argentière** (11km/6.8mi), the most impressive, beneath the imposing north face of the Aiguille Verte. The size of these glaciers has changed considerably since the last Ice Age.

On the other side of the Arve Valley, the Aiguilles Rouges, which are the training ground of rock-climbers, offer some remarkable viewpoints such as the Brévent.

South of Mont Blanc, the snow-covered Dômes de Miage form the typical background of the Val Montjoie.

TUNNEL DU MONT BLANC

The Col du Géant (alt 3 365m/11 040ft), which is the lowest pass across the range, could not play an important economic role owing to its high altitude. France and Italy therefore decided to finance the building of the 11.6km/7mi-long Mont-Blanc Tunnel, which took place between 1959 and 1965. Chamonix is now only 20km/12.4mi from Courmayeur. The thickness of the layer of rock covering the tunnel reaches 2 480m/ 8 136ft below the Aiguille du Midi. The 7m/23ft-wide roadway is lined with pavements all along and with lay-bys and refuges every 300m/328yd. The ventilation system supplies fresh air at a rate of 900m³/31 783cu ft per second.

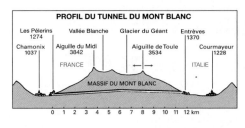

PROFIL DU TUNNEL DU MONT BLANC

Les Pélerins 1274 — Vallée Blanche — Glacier du Géant — Entrèves 1370

Chamonix 1037 — Aiguille du Midi 3842 — Aiguille de Toule 3534 — Courmayeur 1228

FRANCE — ITALIE

MASSIF DU MONT BLANC

0 1 2 3 4 5 6 7 8 9 10 11 12 km

Journey time: 25min. Recommended speed: 80kph/49.7mph. Overtaking and stopping (except in an emergency) are forbidden. Customs and police offices are on the Italian side. Toll-booths at either exit (for charges, see the current Michelin Red Guide France). No access for motor vehicles under 50cc and pedestrians.

★★★ROUTE DE CHAMONIX

☐ From St-Gervais-les-Bains to Vallorcine

41km/25.5mi – about 2hr – local map see pp 238-239

Le Fayet – *See ST-GERVAIS-LES-BAINS.*

Beyond Le Fayet and past the modern power station at Passy, the road rises above the Chedde Plain, within sight of the long viaduct, carrying the Autoroute Blanche to Chamonix, and of the splendid Chaîne des Fiz to the north, then makes its way through the Défilé du Châtelard and a tunnel to the Servoz Basin.

At Servoz Station, turn left towards D 13.

★**Gorges de la Diosaz** ⊘ – On its way to join the River Arve, the Diosaz flows through a famous gorge with a **succession of waterfalls★★**, particularly abundant in July and August.

The entrance of the gorge can be reached by car (1km/0.6mi) from Servoz village.
The itinerary follows a path and overhanging galleries to several waterfalls including the Cascade des Danses, the Cascade de Barme-Rousse and the triple Cascade de l'Aigle, the most impressive of them all. The galleries continue to the natural bridge formed by a rock, fallen in the 16C and stuck inside a fissure from which springs the Cascade du Soufflet.

The road then follows the narrow wooded *cluse* (transverse valley) through which the Arve flows out of the Chamonix Valley. The railway line crosses the valley over the Pont Ste-Marie (height: 52m/171ft), which marks the beginning of a succession of superb landscapes.

Turn right onto D 213.

☆**Les Houches** – *See Les HOUCHES.*

Continue along D 213 which joins N 205.

A regal representation of Christ stands halfway down the wooded northern bank of the Arve. The road runs close to the lower end of the Bossons Glacier and the view embraces the superb Aiguilles de Chamonix with Mont Blanc towering above, to the left of the Dôme du Goûter.

MASSIF DU MONT-BLANC

The principal summits in the Alps

Mont Blanc (France)	4 807 m/15 771 ft
Monte Rosa (Italia)	4 638 m/15 217 ft
Weisshorn (Suisse)	4 512 m/14 803 ft
Cervin/Matterhorn (Suisse-Italie)	4 482 m/14 705 ft
Grandes Jorasses (France)	4 208 m/13 806 ft
Jungfrau (Suisse)	4 168 m/13 675 ft
Aiguille Verte (France)	4 122 m/13 524 ft
Barre des Écrins (France)	4 102 m/13 458 ft

The principal passes in the French Alps

Col du Géant (Haute-Savoie)	3 369 m/11 053 ft
Col de la Bonnette (Alpes-H.-Pr.)	2 802 m/ 9 193 ft
Col de l'Iseran (Savoie)	2 761 m/ 9 059 ft
Col d'Agnel (Hautes-Alpes)	2 744 m/ 9 003 ft
Col du Galibier (Savoie)	2 645 m/ 8 678 ft
Col du Fréjus (Savoie)	2 542 m/ 8 340 ft
Col de la Vanoise (Savoie)	2 527 m/ 8 291 ft

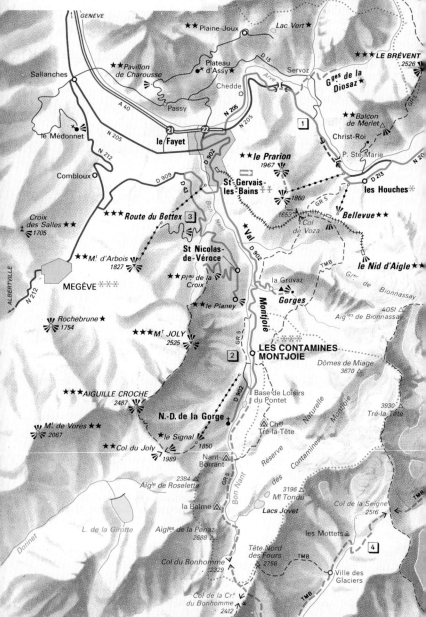

Massif du MONT-BLANC

✽✽✽ **Chamonix and excursions** – *See CHAMONIX-MONT-BLANC.*

Just beyond Chamonix, the slender spire of the Aiguille du Dru standing next to the Aiguille Verte forms a striking picture. At Les Tines, the road leaves the Chamonix Valley to enter the Argentière Basin.

Beyond Les Tines, turn right onto the road leading to Le Lavancher.

The road rises rapidly to **Le Lavancher** situated on a spur separating the Argentière and Chamonix basins. *Turn right before the Beausoleil Hotel.*

There are contrasting **views**★★ of the Chamonix Valley and its glaciers down-river and of the rocky peaks framing Argentière up-river, with the Glacier d'Argentière in the foreground beneath the Aiguille du Chardonnet.

✽✽✽ **Argentière** – *See ARGENTIÈRE.*

As you leave Argentière, turn right towards Le Tour: the landscape becomes more austere and the Glacier du Tour comes into view.
From **Trélechamp**, there is a fine **vista**★★ of the high summits of the Mont-Blanc Massif; looking down-river, one can admire the Aiguille du Tour backing the glacier of the same name, the Glacier d'Argentière, the Aiguille Verte with the Aiguille du Dru next to it, the four Aiguilles de Chamonix and Mont Blanc.

N 506 *(blocked by snow from December to April)* continues past Trélechamp through scrubland covered with alpenrose and juniper bushes to the **Col des Montets** (alt 1 461m/4 793ft) overlooked by the Aiguilles Rouges.

★★ **Réserve naturelle des Aiguilles Rouges** – *See ARGENTIÈRE.*

The road follows the wooded valley of the River Eau Noire, offering views of the Swiss Alps.

Vallorcine – *Drive past the station on the right and turn left towards Le Mollard. Turn round at the entrance of the hamlet.*
The Vallorcine Church stands out against the impressive rock face of the Aiguille de Mesure at the northern extremity of the Aiguilles Rouges and Mont-Blanc massifs *(in order to prolong this excursion to Martigny across the Forclaz Pass, see Michelin Green Guide Switzerland).*

Race to the top of the Aiguille Verte (alt 4 122m/13 523ft)
This vertiginous peak towering above the Mer de Glace was first climbed in June 1865 by the British mountaineer Edward Whymper (who went on to conquer the Cervin), accompanied by two Swiss guides. Two guides from the Chamonix Valley, Croz and Ducroz, who did not wish to be outdone, climbed the Aiguille Verte a month later, this time by a new route, with a team of Swiss and British mountaineers.

★**VAL MONTJOIE**

② **From St-Gervais to Notre-Dame de la Gorge**
16km/10mi – about 45min – local map see p 238

♨♨ **St-Gervais-les-Bains** – *See ST-GERVAIS-LES-BAINS.*
Leave St-Gervais by ② on the town map, D 902 towards Les Contamines.

Beyond Bionnay, a wooded narrow passage opens the way into the Contamines Basin in its picturesque mountain setting.

Gorges de la Gruvaz ⊙ – *On the left, 1.5km/0.9mi from D 902. Caution: the first section includes several footbridges, the second a steep slippery path. Leave the car after La Gruvaz, in front of the entrance of the gorge.*
The path starts by going through the woods, within sight of the stream; once above the tree line, it climbs up the schist slopes of the south side; look back to admire the gorge with St-Nicolas-de-Véroce in the distance. The path leads to a **viewpoint**★: upstream, the gorge forms a perfect V carved out of schist with the tumultuous stream cascading down from the Miage Glacier.

✽✽✽ **Les Contamines-Montjoie** – *See Les CONTAMINES-MONTJOIE.*
Continue along D 902 to the end of the road.

Notre-Dame-de-la-Gorge – A pilgrimage to the Virgin Mary *(15 August and 8 September)* takes place in this sanctuary, erected at the heart of a wooded valley. The interior decoration of the chapel is one of the finest examples of Baroque art in Haute-Savoie. The high altar (1707) and its **retable** adorned with twisted columns forms the main part of this harmonious ensemble.
Stay on the west bank of the Bon Nant and take a walk through the woods. This place is the starting point of many excursions and the GR footpath which goes round Mont Blanc passes through here.

★★VAL MONTJOIE CLIFF-ROAD

③ From St-Gervais-les-Bains to the Plateau de la Croix (via St-Nicolas-de-Véroce)

15km/9.3mi – about 45min – local map see p 238

This cliff-road overlooking the Bon Nant Valley, known as Val Montjoie, offers clear views of the Mont-Blanc Massif.

✚✚ **St-Gervais-les-Bains** – *See ST-GERVAIS-LES-BAINS.*

Leave St-Gervais by ③ on the town plan, towards Megève, then turn onto the first road on the left.

Soon after Robinson, there are fine panoramic views of, from left to right, the cliffs of the Aiguille du Goûter, the Dôme and Aiguille de Bionnassay framing the Bionnassay Glacier and, behind, the snow-capped Dômes de Miage and the Aiguille de la Bérangère. The **Val Montjoie** has retained an interesting group of churches and chapels whose Baroque interior decoration is in striking contrast with the relatively plain façades.

St-Nicolas-de-Véroce – The village occupies a splendid high **position★★** facing the Mont-Blanc Massif.

The 18C **church** has retained its original Baroque **altarpiece** situated inside the chancel decorated with paintings illustrating scenes from the life of St Nicholas. The **church treasury** ⊘ is displayed in a room of the presbytery: monstrances adorned with gems, reliquaries, crucifixes (one of them decorated with the rare motif of the "brass serpent" from the Old Testament) and precious objects are exhibited next to less refined works which are the expression of popular faith (statue of Notre-Dame-des-Ermites).

Continue towards Le Planey.

From the last bend before Le Planey, there is a **panoramic view★★** of the whole Val Montjoie and its mountain frame (Mont Tondu, Arête des Fours, Aiguille de la Penaz and Aiguille de Roselette).

Return to St-Nicolas and take the road to the Plateau de la Croix.

Plateau de la Croix – *Leave the car near the chalet called "l'Étape" and walk to the base of the cross.* The **view★★** extends to Mont Blanc, the Aiguilles de Bionnassay, the Massif de Miage, the Chaîne des Fiz and Aiguilles de Chamonix.

★★★④ SHORT ROUND TOUR OF MONT BLANC ON FOOT

You need identification papers to cross the border. Information about this hike is included in the topo-guide of the Tour du Mont Blanc GR path published by the Fédération Française de la Randonnée Pédestre (see Practical information).
Local map see p 238. Starting from Les Contamines-Montjoie, follow D 902 for 2km/1.2mi, then GR 5 and TMB paths and S 26⁰ (4.5km/2.8mi between Courmayeur and La Palud); a cable-car ride completes this itinerary.

This four-day tour is suitable for determined hikers with stamina and a predilection for mountain hiking.
Minimum equipment: mountain boots with non-slippery soles, spare warm clothing, rainwear, sunglasses.

Suggested programme:

1st day – Les Contamines-Montjoie – Col du Bonhomme – Les Chapieux.

2nd day – Les Chapieux – Ville des glaciers – Col de la Seigne – Refuge Elisabetta.

3rd day – Refuge Elisabetta – Checrouit Cliff-path – Courmayeur.

4th day – Courmayeur – La Palud – Cable-car ride across the range to Chamonix.

Start very early in the morning. The full round tour of the Mont-Blanc Massif takes 10 to 12 days including resting periods and excursions. It is only suitable for very experienced hikers with adequate equipment.

⑤ ACROSS THE MONT-BLANC MASSIF *local map see p 239*

It is possible to go on an unforgettable one-day excursion from Chamonix by combining cable-car rides across the massif with a bus ride through the tunnel. *It is recommended to take as much time as possible (rapid changes in altitude can be tiring) and to inquire about the weather forecast before going.*

The journey from Chamonix is broken up into several sections:

Chamonix – Plan de l'Aiguille – Difference in height: 1 300m/4 265ft – 9min cable-car ride.

Plan de l'Aiguille – Piton Nord de l'Aiguille du Midi – Difference in height: 1 500m/4 921ft – 8min cable-car ride. See *CHAMONIX-MONT-BLANC.*

Climb to the Piton Central of the Aiguille du Midi – Difference in height: 65m/213ft – 35 seconds by lift. Terrace with panoramic view.

B. Langlade

The Vallée Blanche from the Aiguille du Midi

Aiguille du Midi – Pointe Helbronner – Difference in height: 1 300m/4 265ft – 35min gondola ride above the Glacier du Géant and the Vallée Blanche *(summer skiing)*, offering one of the finest Alpine panoramas.

Pointe Helbronner – Refuge Torino – Difference in height: 100m/328ft – 3min cable-car ride. Terrace with panoramic view on the Pointe Helbronner.

Refuge Torino – La Palud – Difference in height: 2 000m/6 562ft – 15min cable-car ride in two sections.

La Palud – Chamonix via the tunnel – Bus journey. *Information from the bus station in Chamonix and Courmayeur.*

MONTBRUN-LES-BAINS ★

Population 467
Michelin map 81 fold 4 or 245 fold 18 – southeast of Buis-les-Baronnies

Situated at the confluence of the rivers Anary and Toulourenc, Montbrun-les-Bains comprises the old village, clinging to the south-facing hillside beneath the castle ruins, and the new district spread in the green valley below.
Distilling lavender, processing aromatic plants and manufacturing crates are the main activities. In summer, the holiday village and the recently reopened baths liven up the area.

Calvinist stronghold – In the 16C, Montbrun became a Protestant stronghold under the leadership of **Charles Dupuy-Montbrun**, the lord of Montbrun Castle, who fought ceaselessly during the Wars of Religion, gaining control of the whole Baronnies region, until he was eventually captured, tried in Grenoble and executed.

Spa resort – Already known to the Romans, the sulphur waters are excellent for the treatment of rheumatism, bronchitis, skin diseases and ear, nose and throat complaints.

In the late 19C, Montbrun was a sought-after spa town with baths resembling those of Baden-Baden. However, the First World War put an end to this thriving activity which was only resumed much later, in 1987.

SIGHTS

Place du Beffroi – The square gets its name from the 14C machicolated **Tour de l'Horloge**, which was one of the four fortified town gates. The old village high street begins here. From the terrace there is an extended **view** of the Anary Valley and the hilltop village of Reilhannette standing out against the white silhouette of Mont Ventoux.

Church ⊙ – The plain exterior, which is partly 12C, offers a striking contrast with the rich 17C interior decoration, recently restored. The walls of the nave are covered with wood-panelling imitating pink and grey marble. Note in particular the superb **altarpiece★** by a member of the famous Bernus family. Four twisted columns decorated with plant motifs form a decorative frame round recesses containing statues of St Benedict and St Lawrence; the centre is occupied by a painting representing the Virgin Mary with Child. The balustrade extending above is adorned with flame-shaped pots in gilt wood.

The embrasures of the windows have retained some older murals, including a scene depicting the Flight into Egypt.

Castle – A few ruins and four round towers overlooking the village are all that remain of the mighty castle, which could accommodate more than 200 men with their horses. Built in the 14C, it was dismantled by Catholic troops during the Wars of Religion and partly rebuilt by Charles Dupuy-Montbrun in 1564; this explains the Renaissance ornamentation of the main doorway.

Montbrun-les-Bains

EXCURSION

Haute vallée du Toulourenc

38km/23.6mi round tour – about 1hr 30min

Leave from the top of the village and join D 159.

The road goes through a fertile valley with many orchards.

★**Gorges du Toulourenc** – Squeezing its way between the Montagne de l'Ubac and the Montagne du Buc along a deep gorge overlooked by the cliff-road, the impetuous Toulourenc River rushes over rocks.

As the road leaves the gorge, the imposing Château d'Aulan suddenly appears on top of a rocky spur.

Château d'Aulan ⊙ – The original 12C castle was destroyed and the present castle was completely rebuilt in the 19C by the Suarez d'Aulan family who still own it. Inside, there is a fine collection of furniture and mementoes of the owners. Note a fine *Adoration of the Magi* by Leonard Bramer (17C Flemish School).

Next to the castle, the **church** ⊘ has retained its 12C east end in spite of being remodelled in the 17C. It contains a beautiful 18C Baroque altar.

Beyond Aulan, the road runs through arid landscapes dotted with lavender fields.

Turn right onto D 546.

The road now follows the Charuis Valley as far as Mévouillon.

Mévouillon – The village is named after a local family who owned the whole Baronnies region. A so-called "impregnable" fortress, which stood on a ridge on the left-hand side of the road, was at the centre of bitter fighting during the Wars of Religion and has now completely disappeared.
The National Hang-gliding Centre of the Baronnies region is situated in Mévouillon, in a place known as Le Col.

Continue along D 546 then turn right onto D 542.

The road follows the Méouge Valley.

Séderon – The Montagne de Bergiès (1 367m/4 485ft) towers above this peaceful mountain village.

Turn towards Montbrun-les-Bains at the intersection with D 546.

When you reach the Col de Macuègne (alt 1 968m/3 504ft), turn left towards Ferrassières and stop 50m/55yd further on to admire the fine **views** of the gullied slopes of the Montagne d'Albion and Mont Ventoux.

Return to the pass.

On its way to Montbrun, the road runs down the Anary Valley, dotted with picturesque peaks.

Route du MONT-CENIS ★

Michelin map 89 fold 7 or 244 fold 32

A major international road linking France and Italy goes through the vast Mont-Cenis Basin now occupied by a huge artificial lake *(see below/overleaf)*. Climbing above the Haute-Maurienne Valley, it offers clear views of the Vanoise Massif.

A dreaded pass – Before the 19C, travellers had to climb up to the pass on the French side along a mule track and, from all accounts, it was worse on the way down as everyone (except, it seems, English travellers!) found the sledge ride organised by local monks positively hair raising.
Napoleon I ordered the construction of the present road (1803-1811) with a carefully planned gradient averaging 8%.

FROM LANSLEBOURG TO THE MONT-CENIS LAKE

16km/10mi – about 45min – local map see La MAURIENNE
The Col du Mont-Cenis is usually blocked by snow from December to April.

Lanslebourg – *See VAL CENIS.*
Drive south out of Lanslebourg along N 6 towards Italy.

The road rises through a conifer forest, including fine larches, then continues beyond the tree line.

Leave the car in a bend to the left (8km/5mi from Lanslebourg, ski-lift arrival point).

Beautiful **view**★ of the Vanoise glaciers leaning against the Dent Parrachée and of the Haute-Maurienne extending towards Bessans through the narrowing of the Col de **la Madeleine** *(see La MAURIENNE)*, with ski slopes in the foreground below.
Stop just before the pass near a small monument; walk along the road leading to the **Replat des Canons**; 1km/0.6mi further on, there is a striking **view**★★ of the Dent Parrachée and Bessans village.

★**Col du Mont-Cenis** – Alt 2 083m/6 834ft. The pass used to mark the border between France and Italy, which is now a few kilometres further south. The view embraces the green Mont-Cenis Basin, an ideal place for amateur botanists, framed by Mont Lamet and Pointe de Clairy, the artificial lake and to the south, through the opening of the Petit-Mont-Cenis Pass, the high summits of the Aiguille de Scolette (alt 3 508m/11 509ft) and Pointe Sommeiller.

The road skirts the lake past **Plan des Fontainettes**, where there is a busy transport café; the **"Salle historique du Mont-Cenis"** ⊘ can be seen beneath the **chapel** of the priory built above the old hospice, which was flooded by the lake: it shows the Mont-Cenis area before and after the building of the dam. Small Alpine garden nearby.

★**Lac du Mont-Cenis** – From the EDF viewpoint *(parking)*, there is a general **view**★ of the lake and the **dam**. The latter is slightly larger (1 485 000m³/ 52 442 775cu ft) and much longer at the top (1 400m/1 531yd) but lower (maximum 120m/394ft) and narrower at the base (460m/1 509ft) than the Serre-Ponçon Dam in the southern Alps. It consists of a riprap dyke with earth in the centre to ensure watertightness.

The lake has a maximum capacity of 320 million m³/259 424acft, the major part being at the disposal of the French power station of Villarodin and about one sixth being diverted to the Venàus power station in Italy.

MONT-DAUPHIN ★

Population 73
Michelin map 77 fold 18 or 245 fold 9

Mont-Dauphin (alt 1 030m/3 379ft) is a mighty citadel situated on top of a promontory overlooking the Durance Valley.

HISTORICAL NOTES

When the duke of Savoie's troops seized the towns of Gap, Embrun and Guillestre in 1692, King Louis XIV of France asked Vauban, his military engineer, to build fortifications along the border. Mont-Dauphin was one of the strategic places where Vauban chose to build a fortified town from which one could guard the Queyras region, the Durance Valley and the road leading south across the Col de Vars. When the army deserted Mont-Dauphin in 1980, efforts were made to attract a civilian population, in particular craftsmen, for whom the **Caserne Campana** ⊘ was turned into workshops.

TOUR OF THE TOWN ⊘ *1hr*

Go through the Porte de Briançon which can be reached by turning off N 94 onto D 37.

Moat – There is an interesting **view** of the moat from the bridge joining the gate and the guardhouse; note the scarp and counterscarp, the bastions and the lunette which communicates with the outside through an underground passage.

The Town – The **Porte de Briançon** leads to place Vauban. The **Pavillon des Officiers** on the right houses the Tourist Information Centre. The high street, known as rue Catinat, starts from the square. Another pavilion, adjacent to the gate, used to be occupied by high-ranking officers. These edifices are built of pink marble from Guillestre, which looks lovely in the sunshine.

Mont-Dauphin

Powder magazine – Only an earth mound and a few air pipes can be seen from the outside. The building looks fine from the inside: the upper room is covered with pointed vaulting and the lower room with a solid larch framework. Ventilation is provided by a gallery going all the way round. Exhibitions are held here in summer.

Arsenal – Built in the mid 18C, it comprised two wings set at right angles. One of them was destroyed by a bomb dropped in 1940 by an Italian bomber. The other building, decorated with elegant bull's-eyes, houses an exhibition entitled **Vauban dans les Alpes** ⊙.

Church – The only remaining part of the church designed by Vauban is the chancel, which explains the building's strange proportions. The wide openings let in a fair amount of light. There is a portrait of St Louis (Louis IX), to whom the church is dedicated, but, oddly enough, he looks like Louis XIV!

Plantation – Several tree species were planted as an experiment on this vast area of spare ground.

Caserne Rochambeau – On the outside, these large barracks form a defence wall overlooking the Porte d'Embrun and the ramparts above the gorge of the River Guil. Inside, the remarkable 260m/853ft-long wooden **framework**★, in the style of Philibert Delorme, dates from 1820. King Henri II's famous architect, Philibert Delorme (1512-1570) designed a framework consisting of a succession of wooden arches held together by wooden dowels, which could easily be dismantled.

EXCURSIONS

Le Cros – *6km/3.7mi along D 37; leave by the Porte de Briançon, go through Eygliers and continue to Le Cros. Tricky road.* This itinerary offers interesting **views**★ of Mont-Dauphin and the surrounding area: on one side, the citadel overlooks the Gorges du Guil and, on the other side, Vauban's fortifications defend the access to the town. Beyond Le Cros, there is a fine **view** of the Gorges du Guil.

Réotier – *6km/3.7mi via the Porte d'Embrun along the ramp leading directly to N 94. Follow D 37 across the Durance.*
The road runs past an artificial lake. Take an unsurfaced road signposted **Fontaine pétrifiante du Réotier**. The water, high in mineral content, has formed strange concretions including a stalactite looking like a gargoyle.

MONTGENÈVRE ✳ ✳

Population 518
Michelin map 77 fold 18 or 244 fold 43 – Local map see Le BRIANÇONNAIS

This small border town between France and Italy was the birthplace of French skiing.

THE RESORT

Skiing area – Montgenèvre is an important ski resort which forms part of the Franco-Italian Voie Lactée together with other resorts such as Clavière, Cesana, Sansicario, Sestrières and Sauze-d'Oulx (representing a total of 350km/218mi of ski runs and 100 ski-lifts). The Montgenèvre skiing area offers 60km/37mi of pistes with good snow cover and 34 ski-lifts, suitable for skiers of all levels. Experienced skiers like the Chalvet, Rocher de l'Alpet and Rhodos black runs, whereas beginners ski down the long green run of Le Lac (Les Anges area) and intermediate skiers prefer the beautiful Souréou run.

The resort is expanding lengthwise along the flat section of the Col de Montgenèvre (alt 1 850m/6 070ft). The pass, which is open all year round, is on a busy commercial and touristic route. The obelisk situated near the French customs office is a reminder that the road was made suitable for wheeled vehicles in 1807.

VIEWPOINTS ACCESSIBLE BY GONDOLA

★★**Le Chalvet** – *In winter, access by the Chalvet gondola and chair-lift (alt 2 577m/8 455ft); in summer access on foot: 4hr 15min return. Walk up to the viewing table (make sure with the ski patrol that there are no avalanche hazards).*
Splendid **panorama**★★ of the Oisans region to the west, including the Bans, the Pointe de Sélé, the Pelvoux, the Barre des Écrins, the Agneaux, the Grande Ruine, the Rateau, the Pic Gaspard and the Meije. The Thabor and Aiguilles d'Arves can be seen to the north whereas, to the south, the view embraces the Montgenèvre skiing area overlooked by the Janus and Chenaillet summits, with the Pic de la Font Sancte, Pic de Rochebrune and Mont Viso in the background. The Italian Alps seem very close to the east.

Les Chalmettes Gondola – Alt 2 200m/7 218ft. **View** of the Chalvet and Chaberton to the north, of Les Anges and Janus to the south.

★★**Les Anges and Le Querelay** – Alt 2 400m/7 874ft. *In winter, access to skiers via Les Anges Drag-lift or the Observatoire Chair-lift; in summer, access on foot.* Superb **panorama** of the Écrins, the Serre-Chevalier skiing area, the Grand Peygu, the Col d'Izoard and the Pic de Rochebrune.

MONTMAUR

Population 311
Michelin map 77 fold 15 or 245 fold 7

This former medieval "barony" marks the transition between the Bochaine and Dévoluy regions. The ruins of the 11C stronghold overlook the village. The nearby 18C manor was the birthplace of Ponson du Terrail (1829-1871), a writer of romantic novels full of extraordinary adventures.

CASTLE ⊘

The present castle dates from the 14C. Extended in the 16C and decorated in Renaissance style, it was more imposing than it is now, its two upper storeys having been destroyed in a fire. It looks quite austere from the outside, with its two round towers, mullioned windows and lovely 17C embossed doorway but the interior ornamentation is its main attraction. The four reception rooms are decorated with richly carved monumental fireplaces, French-style ceilings with ornamental beams, frescoes and friezes representing scenes based on war or morality. Doors carved with symbols, stucco work and *trompe-l'œil* add to the charm of the building.
During the Second World War, the castle was occupied by a Résistance network.

★★HIKE TO THE PIC DE BURE

4hr 30min from Les Sauvas

From Montmaur, drive along D 320 towards the Col de Gaspardon (5km/3mi). Leave the car in the parking area near the Maison Forestière des Sauvas (alt 1 320m/4 331ft). A wide stony path rises to the north towards the cliffs of the Bure Mountain, on the west bank of the stream. After an hour's walk, you will reach the Roc des Hirondelles; a path, marked in blue, leads across a small pass to the Plateau de Bure *(3hr 30min altogether)*. Continue eastwards for 45min to reach the summit of the Pic de Bure (alt 2 709m/8 888ft) which offers, in clear weather, one of the finest **panoramas**★★★ of the Alps, extending from the foothills of Mont Blanc in the northeast to the Cévennes *(to the right of Mont Ventoux)* and the Italian massifs.
Return by the same route.

EXCURSION

Lac du Sautet via the Col du Festre *36km/22.4mi along D 937*

The road follows the east bank of the River Béoux through a desolate landscape then crosses over to the west bank at the Défilé de Potrachon, offering a fine view on the right of the western edge of the Plateau de Bure.

La Cluse – This small village, situated at an altitude of 1 272m/4 173ft, is the starting point of many hikes to the various summits of the Aurouze Mountain, particularly the **Pic de Bure** (alt 2 709m/8 888ft). Other itineraries lead to the Lauteret and Recours passes.

Col du Festre – Alt 1 441m/4 728ft. It offers a fine overall **view** of the Aurouze Massif and is the starting point of excursions westwards to the top of the Crête des Aiguilles. Beyond the pass, leave D 17 on the right, which leads to the resort of Superdévoluy *(see SUPERDÉVOLUY)*, and follow D 937 down to Agnières-en-Dévoluy overlooked by the Roc d'Aurouze. The road then runs along the narrow, sinuous valley of the Ribière.

Turn left onto D 217 and follow the cliff-road overlooking the mountain stream through picturesque hilltop villages: Grand-Villard, Truchière, Villard-Joli, offering interesting excursions to the surrounding heights.

St-Disdier – *See Le DÉVOLUY.*

Beyond St-Disdier, the **Défilé de la Souloise** is the gateway to the greener landscapes of the Drac Valley and Lac du Sautet.

★★Lac et Barrage du Sautet – *See Barrage et lac du SAUTET.*

MORZINE ★★

Population 2 967
Michelin map 89 fold 3 or 244 fold 9 – Local map see Le CHABLAIS

The Morzine-Montriond conurbation lies at an altitude of 980m/3 215ft, inside a vast Alpine coomb flanked by the Pointe de Ressachaux and the Pointe de Nyon. Owing to its prime position at the intersection of six picturesque roads, running through densely wooded valleys towards high-pasture areas, Morzine has, since the 1930s, been the main tourist town and excursion base of the Haut-Chablais region.

THE RESORT

Skiing area – Its gentle slopes and beautiful landscapes make it the ideal skiing area for those who prefer a more relaxed style of skiing. Itineraries leading from Super-Morzine to Avoriaz are particularly enjoyable. Beginners can also have a go down the "Choucas" green run (from the summit of the Ran Folly). Experienced skiers are mainly drawn to Les Creux and L'Aigle runs or to **Avoriaz**★★, at the heart of the **Portes du Soleil**★★ **Skiing Area**. Cross-country skiers can practice along 97km/60mi of fairly easy tracks spread over five areas.

MAIN VIEWPOINTS

★Le Pléney ⊙ – *1hr return. Access by cable-car then on foot.* From the upper cable-car station, walk alongside the Belvédère Chair-lift to a small mound crowned by a viewing table (alt 1 554m/5 098ft) offering a **panoramic view** of Avoriaz and the Dents Blanches to the east, of the Mont-Blanc Massif to the southeast, of the Aravis range to the south and of the Pointe de Marcelly, Mont Chéry and Roc d'Enfer to the west. In clear weather, Lake Geneva is visible through the Dranse Valley.

★Pointe de Nyon ⊙ – *Access by cable-car and chair-lift.* Impressive view of the rocky barrier of the Dents Blanches and of Mont Blanc on one side, of Lake Geneva and of the Morzine Valley on the other.

★★Chamossière Chair-lift – Alt 2 000m/6 562ft. *In winter, access is limited to skiers; in summer, access is on foot.* From the viewing table, splendid **panorama**★★ of the Dents du Midi, Dents Blanches, Buet, Aiguille du Midi, Mont Blanc and Aravis range.

DRIVES

★★Round tour via the Lac de Montriond, Avoriaz and Super-Morzine – *20km/12.4mi – about 2hr. From Morzine, follow the road to Montriond (east bank of the Dranse). Turn right towards the lake immediately after Montriond Church.*

★Lac de Montriond – Alt 1 049m/3 442ft. Framed by steep escarpments, the area surrounding the lake is well shaded and criss-crossed by footpaths.

Cascade d'Ardent – Stop by the viewpoint on the right-hand side of D 228. The waterfall, which is superb during the spring thaw, drops below from a height of 30m/98ft.

The road then climbs up in a series of hairpin bends to a ledge gullied by a succession of waterfalls. The Roc d'Enfer is visible downstream. Beyond the village of Les Lindarets, the road rises along the wooded slopes of the Joux Verte, within sight of the Mont de Grange to the north.

A road leaves the **Col de la Joux Verte** on the left towards Avoriaz.

★★**Avoriaz and Avoriaz to Morzine** – *See AVORIAZ.*

★★From Morzine to Samoëns via the Col de Joux Plane – *20km/12.4mi – about 1hr. Local map see Le FAUCIGNY.*

The narrow road *(D 354)*, which is passable in summer, rises very quickly above the Morzine Valley, between Le Pléney on the right and the Pointe de Nyon on the left, meandering across high pastures and some lovely wooded sections. It goes right round the Ran Folly and over the pass of the same name (alt 1 650m/5 413ft) before reaching the Plateau de Joux Plane.

★★**Col de Joux Plane** – Alt 1 698m/5 571ft. The road runs between a small lake and a restaurant. From the restaurant, there is a remarkable **view** of Mont Blanc to the southeast, extending south to the Platé Massif and the resort of Flaine.

The road continues beyond the path on the left, which ends at the Col de Joux Plane, and runs down towards Samoëns offering bird's-eye **views★** of the Eméru Coomb on the left and the Giffre Valley on the right.

★★**Samoëns** – *See SAMOËNS.*

MOUSTIERS-STE-MARIE★★

Population 580
Michelin map 81 fold 17, 114 folds 7 and 8 or 245 fold 34
Local map see Grand Canyon du VERDON

Moustiers nestles beneath a large gap in the limestone cliffs towering over the town; a 227m/745ft-long chain stretching across this amazing **setting★★** holds a star suspended over Notre-Dame-de-Beauvoir. It was fixed into the rock in fulfillment of a wish made by a knight who came back from the crusades after being kept a prisoner for a long time.

Moustiers owes its name to a monastery founded in the 5C, but it owes its fame to the manufacture of glazed ceramics which reached its peak in the 17C and 18C, disappeared at the end of the 19C and was revived in the 20C.

Built near the downstream exit of the Grand Canyon du Verdon *(see Grand Canyon du VERDON)*, close to the Lac de Ste-Croix *(see Lac de STE-CROIX)*, the town is a highly popular centre for excursions. Those who choose to stay in Moustiers can enjoy the outdoor leisure park at the extremity of the Lac de Ste-Croix. The traditional Fête de la Nativité de Notre-Dame, which takes place every year on 8 September, is the highlight of a week of feasting, dancing and rejoicing *(see Calendar of events)*.

Moustiers earthenware – *(See also Introduction: Handicraft).* According to tradition, an Italian monk brought with him the secret formula used by Pierre I Clérissy in 1679 to manufacture the first Moustiers glazed ceramics decorated with light blue motifs, including hunting and mythological scenes, arabesques and draperies.

In 1738, high-temperature polychrome decoration was imported from Spain by Joseph Olérys: small objects of daily life, decorated with birds, flowers and sometimes supernatural characters known as *grotesques*, became extremely popular. After 1770, the

Moustiers faience decorated by J Olérys

Ferrat and Féraud brothers introduced Chinese, exotic and sometimes topical motifs. By the end of the 18C, twelve workshops manufactured the famous Moustiers ceramics. A century later they had all closed down. However, the revival of Moustiers earthenware, prompted by Marcel Provence in 1925, has met with great success.

SIGHTS

★**Church** – Its warm-coloured massive bell-tower, characteristic of the Lombard Romanesque style, comprises three storeys with twinned openings and blind arcading resting on pillars or slender columns. The Romanesque chancel was replaced in the 14C by a Gothic chancel which forms an angle with the 12C nave. The base of the straight east end is decorated with twinned arcading opening onto rounded arches. Note the beautifully carved 16C and 18C stalls in the chancel and, in the nave, a 16C painting depicting Moustiers at that time, without the famous star. The room situated beneath the tower houses a collection of holy objects.

★**Musée de la Faïence** ⊘ – The earthenware museum is situated near the church, beneath the presbytery, in a vast medieval crypt. The displays are centred round the ceramic-makers who made Moustiers ceramics famous: the Clérissy family (1679-1783) who initiated the blue motifs on a white background; the Olérys family who introduced the polychrome motifs in 1738; the Fouque and Pelloquin family (1749-1783) who used a yellow background; the Ferrat brothers (1761-1794) who were strongly influenced by the technique and decoration of Strasbourg ceramics.

★**Chapelle Notre-Dame-de-Beauvoir** – *1hr return on foot*
The chapel, which has been a place of pilgrimage since medieval times, stands on a ledge overlooking the town. The wide stepped path leading to it offers glimpses of the village and of the Notre-Dame Gorge. it is lined with 14 Stations of the Cross decorated with ceramic scenes by Simone Garnier. At the end of the path, there is an enclosed terrace dating from the Middle Ages, planted with Mediterranean trees; from there, the **view** embraces the rooftops of Moustiers, the Maire Valley and the straight edge of the Valensole Plateau. The first chapel was probably built on this site in the 5C, then rebuilt in the 12C and remodelled in the 16C. Protected by an overhanging roof covered with glazed tiles, the Romanesque porch is surmounted by a bell-tower of the same period. The carved wooden door dates from the Renaissance.
Inside, the first two bays of the nave are Romanesque, the others are Gothic; the ribs of the Gothic apse rest on engaged columns.
The Baroque altarpiece enhances the beauty of the statue of Notre-Dame-de-Beauvoir.

EXCURSIONS

★★★**Grand Canyon du Verdon** – *154km/96mi round tour – 1 day – see Grand Canyon du VERDON.*

★★**Lac de Ste-Croix** – *70km/43.5mi round tour starting from Moustiers – about 3hr – see Lac de STE-CROIX.*

MOÛTIERS

Population 4 295
Michelin map 89 fold 6 or 244 fold 31 – Local map see Massif de la VANOISE

Moûtiers, which lies deep inside a basin, at the confluence of the Dorons and Isère rivers, used to be the capital of the Tarentaise region and a major religious centre whose feudal lords boasted the title of "princes of the Holy Roman Empire".

SIGHTS

Cathédrale St-Pierre – This is the most typical building in Moûtiers. The edifice dates mostly from the 15C (porch). Inside, note the wooden bishop's throne, dating from the same period, and, on the left of the nave, a Romanesque statue of the Virgin Mary, reminiscent of a 13C Burgundian statue; a large and expressive representation of the Entombment (16C), decorating the north transept, is also noteworthy.

Espace baroque Tarentaise ⊘ – Housed on the ground floor of the former archbishop's residence, this museum illustrates Baroque art in the Tarentaise area and explains its historic and religious origins. An audiovisual presentation completes the display of *objets d'art* from the various chapels dotted about the valley.

Musée de l'Académie de la Val d'Isère ⊘ – This small museum, situated on the first floor of the archbishop's residence, displays collections illustrating the history of the Tarentaise region from prehistoric times (Bronze-Age jewellery, Roman pottery, medieval books and documents).
The 17C archbishop's drawing-room, decorated with paintings on wood panelling, and the 18C chapel are nearby.

Detail of the Entombment in the Cathédrale St-Pierre

EXCURSION

✤ **Brides-les-Bains** – *6km/3.7mi south*. Brides-les-Bains, whose treatment of obesity and circulatory complaints can be associated to that of the nearby town of Salins-les-Thermes, has the accommodation and sports facilities usually found in similar spa resorts. It is also a lively tourist centre lying deep in the lower valley of the Doron de Bozel.

Situated 4km/2.5mi northeast of Brides, **Salins-les-Bains**✤ offers stimulating salty waters, recommended in the treatment of gynecological diseases, anemia, complaints affecting the lymph glands, rickets in children and fractured bones.
The large open-air swimming pool, which can rightfully claim to provide sea bathing in the mountains, is very popular.

Gorges du NAN★

Michelin map 77 fold 4 or 244 fold 27 – east of St-Marcellin

The gorge, through which flows the Nan, a mountain stream coming down from the western foothills of the Vercors, is followed from a great height by a small picturesque cliff-road. This offers motorists, travelling along the east bank of the River Isère, the possibility of adding a spectacular detour to their itinerary.

FROM COGNIN-LES-GORGES TO MALLEVAL

9km/5.6mi – about 30min

Road D 22 rises in a series of hairpin bends along the escarpment overlooking the Nan Valley. Stop between the second and third tunnels, along the most impressive section of the route, on the edge of a precipice with a drop of 200m/656ft. A second, less vertiginous narrow, leads to the cool and verdant upper valley. The road continues upwards through meadows to Malleval. The village, which was burnt down in 1944, has been rebuilt.
A new road, built in 1983, prolongs D 22, giving access to the Coulmes Forest and Vercors Plateau (in summer only).

L'OISANS★★★

Michelin map 77 folds 6, 7, 16 and 17 or 244 folds 29, 40 and 41
Local map see p 253

The high Écrins Massif, bounded by the valleys of the rivers Romanche, Durance and Drac, occupies the major part of the Oisans region; with its 10km²/4sq mi of glaciers and its summits reaching or exceeding 4 000m/13 000ft, it comes next after the Mont-Blanc Massif as the favourite training ground of mountaineers. The most splendid landscapes are to be found along the Romanche and Vénéon valleys, which make up the geographic entity of the Oisans region and form part of the **Parc national des Écrins**.
The region includes three other typical areas: the U-shaped **upper valleys of the Romanche and Vénéon rivers** *(see below)*, the enclosed **Bourg-d'Oisans Basin** and the **industrial corridor of the lower Romanche Valley**.
Rural economy is still influenced by the past isolation of the country and continues to combine cattle-farming with the production of basic crops (wheat, rye and potatoes).

Massif des Écrins – Its summits form a huge horseshoe round the Vénéon Valley.
The **Barre des Écrins** is the highest point of the massif (alt 4 102m/13 458ft); its icy solitude is so well concealed that the motorist only catches rare and fleeting glimpses of its peak, first climbed in 1864 by the British mountaineer **Edward Whymper**.
Long regarded as the highest point in the French Alps – Mont Blanc having become French only after the annexation of Savoie – **Mont Pelvoux** was first climbed in 1828 by Captain Durand who soon acknowledged that the Barre des Écrins was higher.
The "glorious" **Meije** has three summits, the most distinctive being the Grand Pic de la Meije (alt 3 983m/13 068ft) whose sharp silhouette looks very striking when seen from La Grave. It was first climbed in 1877 – after 17 unsuccessful attempts – by a Frenchman accompanied by two local guides *(see Practical information)*.

★★★① VALLÉE DU VÉNÉON

From Le Bourg-d'Oisans to La Bérarde

31km/19.3mi – about 1hr 30min – local map see p 253

The road follows the deep, austere Vénéon Valley offering occasional glimpses of the high summits; we therefore strongly advise you to go on the hikes suggested below, bearing in mind that some of them are meant for experienced hikers.
Along the main part of the journey, the road to La Bérarde clings to the steep slope of the U-shaped valley, rising sharply in places or going through tunnels to overcome the obstructions, known as "bolts", left behind by the glaciers.
The last section beyond Champhorent is closed from November to May.

Le Bourg-d'Oisans – *See Le BOURG-D'OISANS.*

From Le Bourg-d'Oisans, drive eastwards along N 91 towards Briançon.

The road to La Bérarde *(D 530)*, branching off from N 91 at Les Clapiers, enters the wide lower Vénéon Valley in striking contrast with the narrow gorge through which flows the Romanche; this is explained by the fact that, during the Ice Age, the Vénéon Glacier was more important than the Romanche Glacier. The small depression of the Lac Lauvitel appears straight ahead, overlooked by the Tête de la Muraillette.

★★ **Lac Lauvitel** – *2.5km/1.5mi from D 530 then 3hr return on foot. At Les Ougiers, turn right towards La Danchère and leave the car on the roadside.*
Beyond La Danchère, take the left fork via Les Selles; this nature trail is lined with markers providing explanations on geology, local fauna and flora, which are detailed in a book on sale in information centres throughout the Parc national des Écrins.
The path follows the natural dyke formed by successive landslides, which contains the Lac Lauvitel (60m/197ft deep in parts) set in a wild landscape.
Follow the La Rousse path back to La Danchère.

Venosc – *Turn left off D 530 to a parking area.* Walk up to the village which has thriving handicraft activities.
A paved street leads to the church with its onion-shaped steeple, which houses a fine altarpiece (17C Italian School).

Slate-quarry workers
In the 19C, slate quarrying in the Vénéon Valley was one of the main resources of the Oisans region. The splitting of the layers of slate into thin plates was left to experienced local workers. After 1918, this task was performed on an industrial scale as much slate was needed in northern France for the rebuilding of houses destroyed during the First World War. Production went on until the Second World War. Nowadays, the mining site has been entirely reafforested.

Le Bourg-d'Arud – The village nestles inside a charming verdant basin.

The road tackles the first glacial obstruction, a jumble of huge boulders, by means of the steepest climb along the way. It then runs through the Plan du Lac Basin, with the Vénéon meandering below, towards St-Christophe-en-Oisans, past the **Cascade de Lanchâtra** on the right and across the Torrent du Diable.

★ **St-Christophe-en-Oisans** – Although it includes 15 hamlets, this vast *commune*, one of the largest in France, barely has 30 inhabitants in winter, several of which are professional guides from generation to generation. The **church** shows up against the Barre des Écrins; in the cemetery, young mountaineers killed in the Écrins Massif are buried next to local guides.

★★ **From Champhorent to the Refuge de la Lavey** – Alt 1 797m/5 896ft. *3hr 30min return on foot (1hr 45min to reach the refuge); easy hike. Difference in height: 380m/1 247ft. Leave the car just outside Champhorent, in the parking area laid out below D 530, just before the Parc national des Écrins panel.*

The path leads rapidly down to the Vénéon, within sight of the **Cascade de la Lavey** at the confluence of the Vénéon and Lavey rivers; it then goes over the humpback bridge and meanders up to a couple of chalets before following the glacial valley of the Lavey, offering a lovely view of Champhorent and of the road to La Bérarde. Markers signal the entrance of the Parc national des Écrins and the view extends towards the **Glacier du Fond** on the left and the **Glaciers des Sellettes** on the right. The path goes through a scree-covered area and the sparse vegetation is essentially represented by tufts of Alpine sea holly and columbine. A picturesque stone bridge leads over to the west bank of the Muande *(close the gate behind you)*; water comes cascading down the opposite slope and the vegetation becomes sparser until the glacial hollow of the Lavey and its refuge come into view with the **Glacier d'Entre-Pierroux** and **Glacier du Lac** towering right above and the **Pic d'Olan** barring the horizon to the south; there are colonies of marmots in the area.

Return to Champhorent along the same route.

Beyond Champhorent, there is an overall view of the Lavey Valley and the glacial cirque at the end of it before the road goes through a small tunnel into a desolate gorge followed by the greener Combe des Étages. The Dôme de Neige des Écrins (alt 4 012m/13 163ft) looms ahead in the distance.

La Bérarde – This former shepherds village is the ideal starting point of mountaineering expeditions in the Écrins Massif and a lively place in summer.

★★HIKES STARTING FROM LA BÉRARDE

These itineraries are suitable for moderately experienced hikers equipped with non-slip shoes.

★★Tête de la Maye Alt 2 517m/8 255ft

North of La Bérarde. 4hr return (2hr 30min on the way up); suitable for hikers familiar with steep terrain and not liable to feel dizzy. Difference in height: 800m/2 625ft.

The path starts before the bridge over the Étançons, winds its way across fields hemmed in by stone walls then runs along rows of Arolla pines used as avalanche barriers. Bear left at the intersection with the path to Le Châtelleret; caution is required through the few difficult sections ahead in spite of metal steps and safety cables.

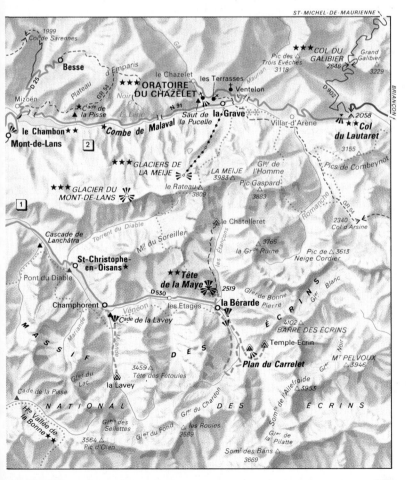

From the viewing table at the summit, there is an overall view of the Écrins Massif and of the peaks surrounding the Vénéon Valley: note in particular, from left to right the **Grand Pic de la Meije** (3 983m/13 068ft), the **Glacier des Étançons**, the **Dôme des Écrins** (4 000m/13 123ft) and the **Glacier de la Bonne Pierre**.

It is possible to walk back along the east bank of the stream; at the intersection, bear left towards a bridge, then right to a footbridge and down to La Bérarde.

★★Plan du Carrelet Alt 2 000m/6 562ft – Return via Le Chardon

South of La Bérarde. 2hr return; easy hike. Difference in height: 300m/984ft.

Take the footpath starting beyond the Maison du Parc and following the east bank of the Vénéon. From the park's information panels, there is a fine view of the **Meije** and **Tête de la Maye** overlooking La Bérarde. The U-shaped valley widens at the confluence of the Vénéon and Chardon. From the Plan du Carrelet refuge, the Chardon and Pilatte glaciers appear to bar the horizon to the south.

Retrace your steps, cross the stream and follow the path towards the Chardon Glacier. You then have to go over two footbridges in order to come back along the west bank of the Vénéon. Cross again as you reach the parking in La Bérarde.

★★★ ② VALLÉE DE LA ROMANCHE

From Le Bourg-d'Oisans to the Col du Lautaret *57km/35.4mi – about 2hr – Local map see p 253.*

This itinerary, combined with those of the Croix de Fer (see Route de la CROIX DE FER) and of the Galibier (see Route du GALIBIER), completes the unforgettable round tour of the Alps' great passes ("Circuit des grands cols").

The Col du Lautaret is now open throughout the winter but can be closed for a few hours in case of important snowfalls or poor visibility; watch out for information panels in Le Bourg-d'Oisans, Le Péage-de-Vizille and Champagnier or listen to the recorded information *(see Admission times and charges)*. The Briançon road leaves the Bourg-d'Oisans Basin and runs through wild gorges; beyond La Grave, the valley widens, offering lovely views of the summits and glaciers of the Meije.

Le Bourg-d'Oisans – See Le BOURG-D'OISANS.

From Le Bourg-d'Oisans, drive along N 91.

At first, the road runs southeast to the confluence of the Vénéon and Romanche rivers then turns eastwards, leaving the wide Vénéon Valley to the south.

Rampe des Commères – In the days of stagecoaches, tongue-wagging was the favourite pastime of travellers who had to step down and walk up this steep section, hence the name given to the place!

★**Gorges de l'Infernet** – Fine **viewpoint**★ over this wild gorge in a tight bend, near a ruined oratory.

The green Freney Basin offers a pleasant contrast.

At the Chambon Dam, take the road to Les Deux-Alpes.

Mont-de-Lans – This hilltop mountain village has retained a few old houses.

Musée des Arts et Traditions populaires ⊙ – Daily life in the Oisans region during the 19C illustrated by folk songs and stories; permanent exhibition devoted to local pedlars.

Climb up to the church and follow a narrow ridge to a high-voltage pylon for a fine **view**★ of the Chambon Lake and Gorges de l'Infernet.

★★**Barrage du Chambon** – The dam was built across a narrowing of the Romanche Valley in order to regulate the river flow and supply hydroelectric power stations. This gravity dam *(see Introduction: Hydroelectric power)* is 294m/965ft long at the top, 70m/230ft thick at the base, and 90m/295ft high (137m/450ft including the foundations). The reservoir, which covers an area of 125ha/309 acres, contains 54 million m^3/43 778cft. Three hamlets were flooded when the dam was built.

Return to the Chambon Lake and follow D25 on the opposite slope.

Beyond Mizoën, the cliff-road climbs up the deep ravine through which flows the Ferrand, affording close-up views of the Grandes Rousses.

Besse – This high **mountain village** (alt 1 550m/5 085ft) is characteristic of the area: the houses lining its narrow twisting lanes have wooden balconies and heavy roof structures, which used to be covered with *lauzes* (thick slabs of schist).

Return to the Chambon Dam and continue along N 91.

★**Combe de Malaval** – The tumultuous flow of the Romanche is almost level with the road all the way through this long gorge, past two impressive waterfalls on the north bank, the **Cascade de la Pisse**★ and **Cascade du Saut de la Pucelle**.

Spotting birds of prey

- **Eagles** have square-cut dark wings and fly very high and their size makes it easy to identify them.
- **Sparrow hawks** are small, grey, with rounded wings and rather long tails; they fly faster than all the others.
- **Buzzards** and **kites** are similar in size; the former have grey underbellies and their cry sounds like miawing; the latter are completely black with split tails.
- **Bearded vultures** have a wide wing span; they fly up cliff faces in search of dead birds. There are a few couples in the Alps.
- **Griffon vultures** are being reintroduced into the Parc naturel régional du Vercors. In the southern part of the Alpine massifs (Vercors, Tirèves), **short-toed eagles** can easily be spotted owing to their white colour and slow flight. These protected migrating birds eat a lot of adders.

The Meije and its glaciers come into view as one approaches La Grave.

✳ ✳ **La Grave and excursion** – *See La GRAVE.*

Upstream from Villar-d'Arène, the road leaves the Romanche Valley which veers southeast along the Val d'Arsine; at the end of this glacial valley, the Pic des Agneaux (alt 3 663m/12 018ft) and the Pic de Neige Cordier (alt 3 613m/11 854ft) can be seen towering above the cirque of the Glacier d'Arsine. Nearer the Col du Lautaret, the jagged peaks of the Combeynot Massif appear in the foreground.

P. Tetrel/EXPLORER

Meije Massif from the Col du Lautaret

★★ **Col du Lautaret** ⊘ – In spite of its relatively high altitude (2 057m/6 749ft), the Col du Lautaret is the busiest pass of the Dauphiné Alps and the road is now kept clear of snow throughout most of the winter. In summer, wild flowers (narcissi, anemones, lilies, gentians, alpenroses and even edelweiss) growing over vast expanses brighten up the rather austere lanscape.
Take the path leading to the Alpine garden.
From the viewing table situated on top of a knoll, there is a striking **view★★** of the Meije Massif surrounded by glaciers (Glacier de l'Homme).

★ **Jardin alpin** ⊘ – This famous garden, created at the beginning of the century contains several rockeries and 2 000 species of wild and medicinal plants from all over the world. A research laboratory welcomes scientists and students.
The **Refuge Napoléon** is an information and exhibition centre devoted to the local fauna, flora and geology.

ORCIÈRES-MERLETTE ✳

Michelin map 77 fold 17 or 245 fold 8 – Local map see Le CHAMPSAUR

Orcières-Merlette occupies a promontory overlooking the village of Orcières *(see Le CHAMPSAUR)* at the heart of the Champsaur Valley, between the Oisans and Dévoluy regions, in an austere high-mountain setting. Created in 1962 at an altitude of 1860m/6 102ft, it has become one of the best equipped ski resorts of the Hautes-Alpes.

THE RESORT

In spite of being spread on several levels, it retains a certain architectural unity as buildings are linked by a network of covered stairs.

The **skiing area**, spread over three distinct areas (Drouvet, Lac des Estaris and Méollion), is well adapted to average skiers with a difference in height of 800m/2 625ft and 46 runs, but not really suitable for beginners (no real green run) or for advanced skiers (too restricted).
The **cross-country skiing area** includes two 5km/3mi itineraries on the Roches Rousses and Jujal plateaux (alt 2 200m/7 218ft, accessible by chair-lift) and 25km of tracks at the bottom of the valley (alt 1 450m/4 757ft). When snow cover conditions are good, cross-country skiers can ski along 100km of tracks linking the valleys.

Orcières-Merlette is a family resort enjoying 300 days of sunshine a year and offering a wide choice of après-ski activities. The **Palais des sports** has a swimming-pool, ice-skating rink, fitness club and bowling alley.

There is an outdoor leisure centre along the Drac for summer holidaying and the **Parc national des Écrins** offers numerous hikes.

HIKES

★★**Drouvet** ⊙ – Alt 2 655m/8 711ft. *Gondola ride in two sections.*
Panoramic view★★ of the southern peaks of the Écrins Massif to the north, the Vieux Chaillol and Gap region to the west, the resort of Merlette in the foreground to the south, the Pic de la Font Sancte in the distance to the east.

★**Lac des Estaris** – Alt 2 558m/8 392ft. *1hr on foot from the Drouvet Summit along a stony path. Mountain boots recommended.*
Beautiful mountain lake. The journey back to Merlette takes 1hr 30min without stopping. There are several lakes along the way.
Experienced hikers can continue from the Lac des Estaris to the Col de Prelles or Col de Freissinières *(45min climb in each case).*

★★**Col de Prelles** – Alt 2 808m/9 213ft. Fine **view**★★ of the Pelvoux Massif and Ailefroide summits.

★**Col de Freissinières** – Alt 2 782m/9 127ft. View restricted by nearby summits: Crête du Martinet and Pointes de Rougnoux to the north, Roc Diolon to the east.

PEISEY-NANCROIX ✳

Population 521
Michelin map 89 fold 6 or 244 fold 32 – Local map see Massif de la VANOISE

The villages of Peisey and Nancroix, linked to form one resort overlooking the upper Isère Valley, are fine mountaineering and skiing centres.

Local traditions are very much alive in the area: the *"frontière"*, a headdress worn by women from the Tarentaise region, can be seen on Sundays and feast days.

Branching off N 90, the road leading to Peisey-Nancroix goes up the wooded **Vallée du Ponturin**★; to the northwest, view of the Roignais summits, the isolated Pierre Menta and the rocky barrier of the Grande Parei.

THE RESORT

Skiing area – The resort comprises several villages, each having its own speciality: cross-country skiing in Nancroix with 40km/25mi of tracks, Alpine skiing in Plan Peisey (alt 1 600m/5 249ft) at the foot of the Aiguille Grive. Vallandry is more recent and boasts an architecture which blends well with the landscape.
Peisy-Nancroix is directly linked to Les Arcs, La Plagne, the Espaces Killy and the Trois Vallées by an area pass. Several snow-cannons ensure adequate snow cover.

Peisey – This resort overlooking the Isère Valley is typical of the area. The church with its slender steeple makes a lovely picture against the Bellecôte or Roignais massifs.

Nancroix – As one reaches this village of the upper Ponturin Valley, the Aliet Peak can be seen soaring above the last foothills of the Bellecôte Massif.

Beyond Les Lanches, the road ends at the Rosuel refuge, one of the gateways to the Parc national de la Vanoise on the edge of the desolate **Cirque de la Gura★** gullied by cascading water, with Mont Pourri towering above.

HIKE

★★Lac de la Plagne

Start from Rosuel – 2hr 30min on the way up. Difference in height: 650m/2 133ft. Follow footpath GR 5 for a while but remain on the west bank of the stream then walk down to the lake in 1hr 45min along the east bank of the Ponturin. From there, it is possible to rejoin GR 5 which leads to the Col du Palet (about 4hr return).

La PLAGNE ★★

Michelin map 74 fold 18 or 244 fold 31 – Local map see Massif de la VANOISE

The **Grande Plagne** ★★, which covers an area of 10 000ha/24 711 acres, is one of the most extended skiing areas in France, with gentle slopes and marvellous landscapes embracing the Mont-Blanc, Beaufortain and Vanoise massifs.

THE RESORTS

Skiing area – The 1992 Olympic **bobsleigh** competitions were staged in La Plagne. The artificially frozen run, built for the occasion, is unique in France (overall view near the intersection with the Plagne-Bellecôte road): 1 500m/0.9mi; 19 bends. Possibility to enjoy taxi-bob, skeleton and bob-rafting. Above 2 000m/6 562ft, the quality of the snow is exceptional and ideal for amateurs of moderately difficult runs (mainly blue runs). Experienced skiers can find a few suitable runs when snow cover is generous. Summer skiing takes place on the Glacier de la Chiaupe and Glacier de Bellecôte.

Created in 1961, La Plagne now includes six high villages and four lower ones. The high villages, situated at altitudes around 2 000m/6 562ft, enjoy good snow cover from December to May; being centrally located, they offer easy access to the whole skiing area.

Plagne Bellecôte, **Plagne Centre** and Aime 2000 have a more urban atmosphere than Plagne 1800, Plagne Villages and above all **Belle Plagne** which blend harmoniously with the landscape.

Snow conditions are not so good in the lower villages, situated at altitudes ranging from 1 250-1 450m/4 101-4 757ft, but they have other advantages. **Champagny-en-Vanoise** ★★ and, to a lesser extent, **Montchavin** have the charm of authentic Savoyard villages and offer superb views of the Vanoise Massif.

Hikers can climb up to **Mont Jovet★★**, which offers a beautiful view of the Alps *(a guidebook of the area's hiking itineraries is published by the tourist office).*

VIEWPOINTS ACCESSIBLE BY GONDOLA

★★**La Grande Rochette** ⊙ – Alt 2 508m/8 228ft. *Access by gondola from Plagne Centre. From the upper station, climb to the viewing table on the summit.* The splendid **panorama** includes the main summits of the Vanoise Massif (Mont Pourri, Bellecôte, Grande Motte, Grande Casse, Grand Bec...) and extends to the Oisans (Meije), the Aiguilles d'Arves, the Étendard, Belledonne, Beaufortain and Mont-Blanc massifs.
The high villages of La Plagne can be seen below to the north and Courchevel to the southwest.

★★**Bellecôte** ⊙ – *Access from Plagne-Bellecôte.* The exceptionally long gondola ride (6.5km/4mi) leads to Belle-Plagne and then to the **Roche de Mio** (2 739m/8 986ft). Climb to the summit *(viewing table)* in 5min to enjoy the splendid **panorama★★**. The Sommet de Bellecôte (3 416m/11 207ft) and its glaciers can be seen in the foreground, with the Grande Motte, the Grande Casse, Péclet-Polset and the Trois Vallées further away to the south. Mont Pourri appears quite close to the northeast with Mont Blanc and the Grandes Jorasses in the distance.
Take the gondola leading to the **Col** and **Glacier de la Chiaupe** (alt 2 994m/9 823ft): beautiful **view** of the Vanoise.
In summer and autumn, skiers can admire a broader landscape by taking the ski-lift up to the pass. In winter, on the other hand, the Traversée Chair-lift gives access to the most interesting area for advanced skiers. A magnificent off-piste itinerary, with a difference in height of 2 000m/6 562ft, leads down to Montchavin *(take a guide with you).*

PLATEAU D'ASSY ★

Michelin map 89 fold 4 or 244 fold 20

This well-known health resort is spread over several terraces backing on to the Fiz range, at altitudes ranging from 1 000-1 500m/3 281-4 921ft; from this prime position, there is a magnificent **panorama**★★ of the Mont-Blanc Massif *(see also Bassin de SALLANCHES)*.

★ÉGLISE NOTRE-DAME-DE-TOUTE-GRÂCE

The church is a good example of the contemporary revival of religious art. It was built between 1937 and 1945 by Novarina who took his inspiration from the region's traditional domestic architecture; the result is a stocky edifice, adapted to Alpine climatic conditions and in harmony with traditional architecture, which is surmounted by a 29m/95ft-high campanile.

Famous contemporary artists contributed to the exterior and interior **decoration**★★: Fernand Léger made the mosaic which brightens up the façade, Lurçat decorated the chancel with a huge tapestry on the theme of the Woman triumphing over the Dragon of the Apocalypse. Bazaine designed the stained-glass windows lighting up the gallery, Rouault designed those situated at the back of the façade, notably in the side chapel on the north side.

A bronze crucifix by Germaine Richier stands in front of the high altar.

Bonnard, Matisse, Braque, Chagall and Lipchitz are also represented.

Walk round the building and go through the east-end doorway down to the crypt decorated with stained glass by Marguerite Huré and a representation of the Last Supper by Kijno.

PONT-EN-ROYANS ★

Population 879
Michelin map 77 fold 3 or 244 fold 38 – Local map see Le VERCORS

Picturesquely situated at the exit of the long gorge of the River Bourne, this village has a definite southern atmosphere.

VIEWPOINTS

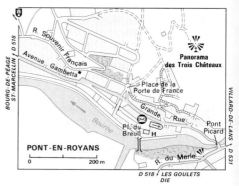

★★**The site** – *At the Pont Picard, take the steps leading to the embankment along the Bourne; from there it is possible to reach the medieval district.* In spite of being partly destroyed during the Wars of Religion, the medieval district has retained a number of tall old houses clinging to the rock, overlooking the Bourne or dipping their narrow façades into the stream and forming a charming picture which once captured Stendhal's imagination.

★**Trois Châteaux** – *1hr return on foot. Steep paths going across screes, start with a series of steps from place de la Porte-de-France.* From the belvedere, there is a fine **view** of the Royans region and Isère Valley.

EXCURSIONS

★★**Round tour via Presles** *32km/20mi – about 1hr 30min*

From Pont-en-Royans, drive along D 531 towards Villard-de-Lans and turn left onto D 292 immediately after the Pont Rouillard over the Bourne. The road climbs up the sunburnt slopes within sight of the escarpments overlooking the river. From the wide bend known as the "Croix de Toutes Aures" (do not look for the cross!), the view extends from the rolling hills of the Royans region to the impressive gorge of the River Bourne overlooked by the Grand Veymont.

After a series of hairpin bends, the road finally reaches the Presles Plateau. It continues to rise beyond Presles through the Coulmes Forest to a small hamlet called Le Fas, where the view embraces a long stretch of the lower Isère Valley, including the imposing aqueduct of St-Nazaire-en-Royans.

The road then winds steeply down to St-Pierre-de-Chérennes across green fields, offering more picturesque views.

Walnuts from Grenoble

Walnuts from Grenoble have, since 1938, been protected by a label guaranteeing their origin and quality *(appellation d'origine contrôlée)*. Three different kinds are grown in the region:
– the *mayette*, a large walnut with a thin shell and a refined taste;
– the *parisienne*, a round walnut with a brown shell, rich in oil;
– the *franquette*, an oblong walnut with a rough shell, which is the most sought-after by confectioners and the most widely cultivated.
The producing area straddles three *départements;* however, 75% of the annual production (around 10 000t) come from just four *communes:* Pont-en-Royans, St-Marcellin, Vinay and Tullins.
The September harvest is followed by the washing, drying and conditioning process (there are two sizes: over 30mm/1.2in and between 20mm/0.8in and 30mm/1.2in).
This energy-giving fruit can be eaten fresh, within two weeks of the harvest, or dried, in salads, in cakes and in confectionery (stuffed walnuts are a Grenoble speciality traditionally eaten during the Christmas period).

D 31 reaches N 532. Turn left almost immediately towards Beauvoir-en-Royans.

Château de Beauvoir – The picturesque ruins of the 13C castle stand on top of an isolated hill overlooking the village; a square tower, a gate and ivy-covered walls are all that remains of the former residence of the "dauphins" *(see Introduction: Historical notes)*. However the site is pleasant and affords a fine view of the meandering River Isère.

Return to N 532 and, in St-Romans, take D 518 leading back to Pont-en-Royans.

St-Nazaire-en-Royans *9km/5.6mi west along D 531*

As one approaches St-Nazaire-en-Royans along D 531, old houses huddled on the bank of the River Isère appear framed by the arches of an imposing **aqueduct** carrying water from the Bourne into the Valence Plain.
The **Pont St-Hilaire-St-Nazaire** is an elegant single-arched bridge with a 110m/361ft span built across the confluence of the Isère and Bourne rivers, now flooded by the more recent building of a dam.
Situated on the shore of the lake, beneath the aqueduct, the **Grotte de Thaïs** ⊘ is a natural cave resulting from the chemical action of the water of an underground river; the deeply carved rock is, in some places, coloured in bright red and grey. Inhabited in prehistoric times (about 13 000 years ago) the cave has yielded a wealth of tools and engraved bones.
There are **paddle-boat trips** ⊘ on the artificial lake (220ha/494 acres), starting from the village of La Sône and going through an important bird sanctuary known as the **Roselière de Creux**.
The **Jardin des Fontaines pétrifiantes** ⊘ is a green open space with 500 different species of plants and flowers, laid round the petrifying springs at La Sône.

PRALOGNAN-LA-VANOISE
Population 667
Michelin map 89 fold 7 or 244 fold 32 – Local map see Massif de la VANOISE

This health and ski resort is the best starting point of fine hikes and mountaineering expeditions in the Parc national de la Vanoise. *(see Massif de la VANOISE).* The curling matches of the 1992 Olympic Games, based in Albertville, were held in Pralognan's new ice rink.

THE RESORT

The sunny **skiing area** is interesting but relatively small compared to those of the nearby Tarentaise resorts. However, there are remarkable possibilities of cross-country skiing.

In summer, Pralognan, which attracts thousands of hikers and mountaineers, is one of the liveliest resorts in Savoie. The first climbing attempts date from the late 19C; in 1860, the British mountaineer William Matthews and the Frenchman Michel Croz hewed their way up one of the peaks of the Grande Casse – now called Pointe Matthews – by carving no fewer than 1 100 steps (800 of them with an axe).

The eastern part of the Pralognan Basin is undoubtedly the most picturesque with the cirques of the Grand Marchet and Petit Marchet in the foreground, backed by the Glaciers de la Vanoise.

Lac Blanc and Mont Parraché

HIKES

★**La Chollière** – *1.5km/0.9mi along a mountain road, then 30min on foot. Start from the Hôtel La Vanoise, cross the Doron and follow the road which winds up La Chollière Hill. Leave the car above the chalets.* A handsome group of mountains can be seen in the background behind the hamlet: the Pointes de la Glière, the Grande Casse (alt 3 855m/12 648ft, the highest peak of the Vanoise Massif). The surrounding pastures are famous for their wealth of wild flora: narcissi and gentians in June, Alpine sea holly, known as the "Queen of the Alps", in August *(see Introduction: Vegetation)*.

★**Mont Bochor** ⊙ – *About 3hr return on foot or 6min by cable-car.* From the upper station, walk up to the summit (alt 2 023m/6 637ft, viewing table) for a bird's-eye view of the Pralognan Basin and the Doran de Chavière Valley, closed upstream by the Péclet-Polset Massif and lined on the left by the huge Vanoise glaciers.

A 1.4km/0.9mi-long **nature trail** enables visitors to become familiar with this typical mountain environment. Information panels detail the geological and ecological wealth of the site.

★★★**Col de la Vanoise** – *Alt 2 517m/8 258ft. Start from Mont Bochor. If the cable-car does not operate, start from the Fontanettes parking area. 3hr up, 2hr 30min down to Pralognan.*

Inexperienced hikers can come down via the Barmettes refuge and Fontanettes parking area. Trained hikers, on the other hand, can, in fine weather conditions only, enjoy a splendid hike via the Arcellin cirque and ravine. From the Barmettes refuge, the path rises steeply to the Lac des Vaches before reaching the pass; view of the Grande Casse Glacier and Pointe de la Réchasse. On the way down, there is a fine view of the Lauzière Massif with the Sommet de la Saulire, Dent de la Portetta and Aiguille du Fruit in the foreground. Martagon lily, columbine and houseleek are some of the wild-flower species which can be see along the route.

★★**Petit Mont Blanc** – *Alt 2 677m/8 783ft. Start from Les Prioux. 3hr up via the Col du Môme; 2hr down.*

For a description of the **panorama★★** *, see COURCHEVEL.*

★★**Cirque de Génépy** – *Start from the Pont de la Pêche. Go up via Montaimont, return via Ritord: 5hr including 2hr of steep climbing. Difference in height: about 700m/2 297ft. Owing to snow, this excursion can be tricky until mid-July.*

Views of the Génépy Glacier, the Aiguille de Polset and the Gébroulaz Glacier. On the way down, the view extends towards Mont Blanc and the Grand Bec. Beaufort cheese is made and sold in the village of Ritord.

★★**Lac Blanc** – *Start from the Pont de la Pêche. Long and arduous climb; 3hr 15min up, 2hr 30min down.* Situated below the Péclet-Polset refuge, the Lac Blanc is one of the loveliest lakes in the Vanoise Massif. Walk along the right side of it and climb towards the Col du Soufre. View of the Aiguille de Polset, the Gébroulaz Glacier, the Col de Chavière, the Pointe de l'Échelle and the Génépy Glacier.

★★★**Round tour of the Vanoise Glaciers** – 3-day trip *(see Massif de la VANOISE)*.

We strongly advise holiday-makers to attend slide shows organised by the Association des Chasseurs d'Images de Pralognan, which are a useful introduction to the local fauna and flora as well as to hikes and mountain excursions in the surrounding area.

PRA-LOUP ✳

Situated in a dense larch forest, on the edge of a plateau (alt 1 630m/5 347ft) overlooking the Ubaye Valley, Pra-Loup is one of the main and most attractive ski resorts in the Alpes-de-Haute-Provence.
The access road offers fine views of the Barcelonnette Basin and surrounding summits. The entrance to the resort is guarded by the statue of a "howling wolf". A natural ice rink marks the centre of Pra-Loup which continues to expand.

THE RESORT

Its architecture, going back to the 1960s, is not very harmonious and the resort essentially owes its fame to the quality of its environment, to the long hours of sunshine it enjoys and to its facilities.

Skiing area – Linked with that of La Foux d'Allos (see VAL D'ALLOS), it forms a vast area known as the Espace Lumière: 54 ski-lifts and 230km/143mi of runs. However, the link with La Foux is generally only suitable for experienced skiers. Pra-Loup's own skiing area, which numbers 33 ski-lifts and has a maximum altitude of 2 500m/8 202ft, has moderately steep snow fields ideal for intermediate skiers. A fair number of snow-cannons ensures adequate snow cover down to the lowest part of the resort.

In summer, Pra-Loup offers a wide choice of activities (swimming, white-water sports, paragliding...) as well as fine rambles along marked trails.

EXCURSIONS

Costebelle – Alt 2 120m/6 955ft.

The gondola rises above the ski runs, offering a fine overall view of the resort. Further on, it affords views of the Ubaye Valley, of Barcelonnette and of the upper station, including the unmistakable silhouettes of the Pain de Sucre and Chapeau de Gendarme. *The Costebelle Gondola ⊙ operates every other summer, alternating with the Dalle en Pente Gondola. The two rides are similar.*

✳ Hike to the Col des Thuiles

This itinerary is suitable for strong experienced hikers (5hr) and requires a good sense of direction. The ascent to the pass, alongside the ski-lifts, is arduous but the walk down through the Gimette Valley is quite pleasant.
Take the Costebelle Gondola. Go down to the right to join the Bergeries Ski-lift. A marked stony path leads to the ski-lifts of Le Lac – note the lovely green setting of the lake – *a total of 45min on foot from the gondola.* Continue alongside the ski-lifts then leave the path as it veers to the right and crosses the 12 ski-lifts; a

View of the Grande Séolane from the Col des Thuiles

narrow path on the left leads to the ridge on which stand several posts. On the other side, the path running along the mountain slope offers a fine **view★** of Les Agneliers, the Gorges du Bachelard, the Cimet and Chapeau de Gendarme, eventually reaching the Col des Thuiles beneath the Grande Séolane.

On the way down through the **Vallon de la Gimette★★**, the pastoral landscape is charming. Follow the markings closely; 100m/110yd beyond the Cabane de Gimette, turn sharply to the right along a path lined with rare wild flowers (martagon lily), which overlooks the hamlet of Clos Meyrat.

The last section of the itinerary is not very clearly marked. Turn right at the first three intersections, eventually following the direction of the Col des Thuiles. Shortly afterwards, as the path goes down steeply, watch out for a panel fixed to a tree; 10m/11yd further on, take a narrow path to the right *(blue markings on a stone at the intersection and on a tree just beyond)*. Continue straight ahead at the next intersection and cross the Langail to return to the resort in 30min.

PUGET-THÉNIERS ★

Population 1 703
Michelin map 115 folds 13 and 14 or 245 fold 23
Local map see CLUES DE HAUTE-PROVENCE

This small town nestling beneath a rocky spur crowned with the ruins of a castle, at the confluence of the Var and Roudoule rivers, has a lively southern atmosphere in summer and is the starting point of excursions to the nearby mountains.

SIGHTS

★**Old town** – It is mainly concentrated on the west bank of the Roudoule and includes Place A Conil and its lovely fountain as well as many old houses which have retained beautiful doorways and signs carved in stone.

Church – Built in the 13C by the Knights Templars, this Romanesque church was remodelled and richly decorated in the 17C (chancel vaulting and church furniture). It contains many works of art *(time switch at the entrance on the left)*.

Note the amazing **calvary carved in wood★** consisting of three tiers representing the Crucifixion, the Entombment and the Resurrection. The faces of the different characters are very expressive and the representation of the thieves' bodies, tied to their crosses, and of Christ, carried by his disciples bending beneath the weight, is most realistic.

The high altar **retable of Notre-Dame-de-Secours★**, placed above a polychrome statue of the Virgin Mary carved out of an olive tree trunk, dates from 1525 and is believed to be the work of Antoine Rouzen. Note the beautiful representations of the Virgin Mary and of St James.

★**"L'Action enchaînée"** – This statue by Maillol depicting a naked woman with a full rounded shape, is dedicated to the memory of **Louis-Auguste Blanqui** (1805-1881), the revolutionary who spent more than 36 years in prison. The statue stands on a charming square planted with very old plane trees on the edge of N 202.

Scenic railway between Puget-Théniers and Annot ⊘ – The Nice to Digne railway line, built from 1890 to 1911, continues to offer a daily service between the two towns. A steam-powered scenic railway runs during the season on the Puget-Théniers-Annot section *(see Practical information)*.

EXCURSION

Pays de la Roudoule *45km/28mi round tour – about 3hr*

The area lying north of Puget-Théniers forms a succession of unusual landscapes which include the Gorges de la Roudoule and several picturesque villages.

The **Écomusée du Pays de la Roudoule** was created for the preservation and development of the area's traditional life (agricultural activities, rural architecture) and cultural heritage.

From Puget-Théniers, drive along D 16.

The road rises above Puget and offers a lovely view of the old town before entering the Gorges de la Roudoule.

Turn right onto D 116 towards Puget-Rostang.

The road follows the Mairole Valley and goes through a strange landscape darkened by the presence of black marl, known as *"les robines"*.

Puget-Rostang – This hilltop village is overlooked by the square tower of a restored castle. The **Écomusée du Pays de la Roudoule** ⊘ organises exhibitions.

From Puget-Rostang, a twisting road leads to **Auvare** *(13km/8mi return)*, clinging to the rock, which used to be a refuge for all kinds of fugitives.

Return to D 16 and continue along the Gorges de la Roudoule.

*Pont de St-Léger – This bridge occupies an amazing site. The Roman bridge can be seen below with the paved Roman way at either end.

Continue towards Léouvé and turn right onto D 416 to La Croix-sur-Roudoule.

La Croix-sur-Roudoule – Perched high and backing onto the rock in a picturesque **setting***, this village is still guarded by an old fortified gate. The small Romanesque **church**, which has a wall-belfry with twin openings, houses two panels from an altarpiece by

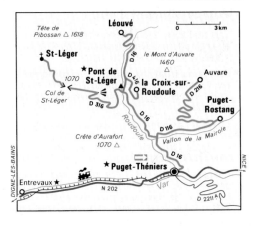

François Bréa representing St John the Baptist on the right of the altar and St Michael on the left.

From the top of the village, there is an interesting **view** of the upper Roudoule Valley.

Return to D 16 and turn right.

Léouvé – The Léouvé Cirque is carved out of red sandstone; copper was mined here from 1861 to 1929 and the high chimneys of the foundry works can still be seen.

Return to the Pont de St-Léger and cross over.

The road rises to the Col de St-Léger, unfolding a totally different landscape to that of the Gorges de la Roudoule. The village of St-léger lies in verdant surroundings framed by mountains.

St-Léger – The small Romanesque church is surmounted by an arcaded pinnacle.

Turn back towards Puget-Théniers.

Just before the Pont de St-Léger, there is a fine **view** of the Roman bridge and of the Roman way, as well as of the village of La Croix-sur-Roudoule.

PUY-ST-VINCENT✳

Population 235
Michelin map 77 fold 17 or 244 fold 42 – Local map see La VALLOUISE

The creation of a fast-expanding ski resort greatly contributed to the development of this village situated in the splendid Vallouise Valley.

Puy-St-Vincent is also a sought-after summer resort close to the Parc national des Écrins, which offers many possibilities of hikes and mountain excursions. The Combe de Narreyoux, a lovely pastoral conservation area, offers additional possibilities of fine walks. Other summer activities include mountain biking and white water sports on the rivers Durance and Gyr.

Birdwatching

With a pair of ordinary binoculars, neutral-coloured clothes, which can blend with the surroundings, a calm behaviour and a lot a patience (keep watch for at least 30min), hikers should succeed in detecting and enjoying the presence of the rock thrush, the rock bunting or the shrike. These birds are more likely to be found on south-facing slopes, between April and late July, shortly after sunrise or three hours or so before sunset.

THE RESORT

The forested **skiing area**, well known for the quality of its snow cover, due to its northern aspect and its location near the Écrins Massif, lies at altitudes ranging from 1 400m/4 593ft to 2 700m/8 858ft. It comprises 26 runs suitable for all levels of skiing; international competitions, such as the ladies' downhill of the world championship, have been held along the steepest runs. There are 30km/18.6mi of cross-country tracks, in particular on the Tournoux Plateau at an altitude of 1 800m/5 906ft.

In addition, it is possible to practise cross-country skiing in the lower Vallouise Valley and Alpine skiing in the Pelvoux *(see la VALLOUISE)*.

The resort's facilities are spread over two centres lying at different altitudes.

Puy-St-Vincent 1400

This traditional and peaceful village comprises the main resort's hotels. It is linked by chair-lift to Puy-St-Vincent 1600. The houses of the Hameau des Prés have attractive larch-wood upper parts.

★**Panorama from the church** – Go round the Église des Prés for a lovely view of the Vallouise, framed by mountains: The Pelvoux, Glacier Blanc and Pic de Clouzis to the northwest, the Sommet des Bans to the west, the Pic de Peyre-Eyraute to the east.

Chapelle St-Romain – Park the car near l'Aiglière and walk up through the meadow to the chapel, dating from the 16C, which is used for exhibitions. There is a splendid **panorama**★ of Vallouise, overlooked by the Pelvoux, Condamine and Montbrison summits.

Chapelle St-Vincent – Follow the road to Puy-St-Vincent 1600 and park the car on the right, at the intersection of the Narreyoux Valley road. Walk up to the chapel. Inside there are some remarkable 15C **frescoes**★: the apostles are represented in the apse, scenes from the Gospel on the right-hand side and the life of St Francis of Saragossa on the left-hand side.

Puy-St-Vincent 1600

The modern resort, situated above the old village and sheltered from the wind by Mont Pelvoux, faces the ski runs on two levels; in winter and summer, a gondola gives access to the upper part of the skiing area, just below the Pendine (2 749m/9 019ft).

*Some hotels have their own tennis court, swimming pool, private beach or garden. Consult the current edition of the annual **Michelin Red Guide France**.*

Le QUEYRAS★★

Michelin map 77 folds 18 and 19 or 244 folds 43 and 44 and 245 folds 9 and 10
Local map see p 267

Partly situated across the Italian border, the Queyras region is an isolated bastion accessible all year round through the Combe du Queyras and in summer via the Col d'Izoard and the Col Agnel (on the Italian border). This geographical, historical and human entity, centred round the Guil Valley is one of the most authentic areas of the southern Alps. Several tributary valleys, including the St-Véran Valley, converge towards the Guil Valley which, as one follows it downstream, is in turn imposing, charming, restful and austere.

Unusual relief – The Queyras region is divided into two distinct areas: the Haut-Queyras to the east, consisting of folded sedimentary schist mixed with volcanic porphyry which resulted in jagged summits and shiny mica-schist ridges overlooking rounded glacial valleys; the limestone Bas-Queyras to the west, offering impressive austere landscapes such as those of the Casse déserte near the Col d'Izoard or the Combe du Queyras *(see CHÂTEAU-QUEYRAS: Espace géologique).*

Sunny climate – The Queyras region has one of the sunniest climates in France tempered by a certain coolness in the air which makes a stay in the area most enjoyable both in summer and winter. Snow cover is excellent for six months of the year, the flora displays a great variety of Mediterranean and Alpine species (2 000 in all) and the fauna includes usual mountain species (chamois, black grouse...) and rarer species such as the black salamander.

Astragalus centralpinus

Moufflons

Twelve Corsican moufflons were introduced into the Queyras Massif in 1973. In 1995 they numbered 300 head spread around the Parc naturel régional du Queyras. Moufflons are wild sheep with short-haired coats which turn from russet in summer to dark brown in winter. Males can weigh as much as 50kg/110lb and have splendid horns, which grow during their first year and, by the third year, curve right round to their neck.

In winter, moufflons in search of food go near the villages where they are usually given hay to eat; it then becomes easy to observe them closely, although it is preferable to remain at a distance of at least 50m/55yd and observe them with binoculars for fear of frightening them away, thus putting their survival at risk.

Historical notes – Inhabited since prehistoric times, the Queyras region was torn by the Wars of Religion when an army of Huguenots, under the command of Lesdiguières, seized Fort Queyras in 1587. After the revocation of the Edict of Nantes in 1685, many Protestant families emigrated to Switzerland and Germany.

During the 19C, the Queyras region remained unaffected by industrialization; however, the first surfaced road was built between Guillestre and Château-Queyras in 1856.

Arts and crafts – The Queyras region is particularly rich in folk art: objects made by peasants during the long winter evenings spent in their traditional houses *(see Introduction: Handicraft)*. Pieces of **furniture** made of larch wood or Arolla pine are particularly famous (there are fine collections in the Musée Dauphinois in Grenoble, in the Musée départemental in Gap and in the Musée des Arts et Traditions populaires in Paris); they include box beds, wedding chests, spinning-wheels, cots, decorated with geometric motifs carved with a knife.

This tradition has been perpetuated until today with the help of the Traditional Craftsmen's Union. There is a permanent display of their work in the **Maison de l'Artisanat** in Ville-Vieille *(see Practical information)*.

There are many sundials in this exceptionally sunny region (300 days of sunshine a year). They were the work of travelling artists, often natives of Italy, and are decorated with mottos which express popular wisdom *(see Introduction: Traditional architecture and Practical information)*.

Croix de la Passion, which depict Christ's Passion, are another characteristic feature of the region; there are several of them in St-Véran and Ceillac.

There are also numerous wooden **fountains**, with a rectangular basin and a circular bowl, which are fine examples of the skill of craftsmen from the Queyras region.

Croix de la Passion

Usually standing in front of churches, sometimes inside, these *croix de la Passion* represent the various symbols of Christ's Passion:
– the cock standing at the top is a reminder of Christ's words to Peter: "this night, before the cock crows, thou shalt deny me thrice" (Matthew XXVI, 34);
– the hand suggests Pontius Pilate's gesture at Jesus's trial;
– the coins symbolize the price of Judas's betrayal;
– the arms, placed on either side of the central axis, represent those used for the Crucifixion;
– in some cases, a crown has been added as a reminder of Jesus's Crown of Thorns.

Economic revival – By the mid 20C, isolation and depopulation had considerably slowed down the region's economy so that, in the 1960s, it was decided to modernize traditional agriculture, to develop handicraft and above all tourism. The **Parc naturel régional du Queyras** was created in 1977 and accommodation possibilities and skiing facilities increased rapidly in St-Véran, Abriès and Ceillac; the region is particularly well-adapted to cross-country skiing, ski-trekking and hiking.

★★COMBE DU QUEYRAS

① From Guillestre to Château-Queyras

17km/10.6mi – about 1hr local map p 267

Guillestre – *See GUILLESTRE.*

From Guillestre, drive along D 902.

Viewing table at Pied-la-Viste – It is located on top of a mound above the road. The imposing Pelvoux-Écrins Summits can be seen through the gap of the Durance Valley and Vallouise Depression.

Between Pied-la-Viste and Maison du Roy, the valley becomes narrower and the road goes through several tunnels.

Maison du Roy – According to tradition, King Louis XIII stopped at this inn on his way to Italy in 1629. A painting hanging inside is said to be a gift from the king.
D 60, which goes up the Ceillac Valley (see CEILLAC-EN-QUEYRAS), branches off here. Continue along D 902.

The road enters the **Combe du Queyras★★★**, a long steep gorge. The narrowest part lies between La Chapelue and L'Ange Gardien, where there is barely room for the cliff-road above the limpid and abundant flow of the river. Beyond the Rocher de l'Ange Gardien, the road offers a fine view of the splendid setting of Château-Queyras with its fort crowning the rocky knoll.

★Château-Queyras – *See CHÂTEAU-QUEYRAS.*

★★ST-VÉRAN ROAD

② From Château-Queyras to St-Véran
15km/9.3mi – about 30min local map below

★Château-Queyras – *See CHÂTEAU-QUEYRAS.*
From Château-Queyras, drive east along D 947.

Ville-Vieille – This village, administratively linked to Château-Queyras, forms part of **Château-Ville-Vieille**. A nature trail on the left just below the village, called **Sentier écologique des Astragales**, offers a pleasant 1hr 30min walk with views of the valley and of the Bric Bouchet Summit. Rare plant species can be seen along the way, in particular specimens of milk-vetch, pheasant's eye and Ethiopian sage. The path leads to **Pierre Fiche**, probably a prehistoric standing stone, which stood 7m/23ft high before it was broken. *A booklet containing explanations about the trail is on sale in the Maison de l'artisanat.*

Maison de l'artisanat ⊙ – Situated on the left-hand side of D 947 towards St-Véran, near the intersection with D 5, this handicraft centre houses exhibitions of fine furniture made by local craftsmen and sells regional specialities.
Follow D 5.

Note the **church** doorway, with its arching resting on carved heads, and the lovely sundial decorating the bell tower.
The road rises along the north-facing slope covered with larches, offering a fine downstream view of the Guil Valley. Beyond a hairpin bend, it enters the Aigue Blanche Valley overlooked by the densely forested slopes of the Sommet Bucher. At the exit of the Prats Ravine, note the **demoiselle coiffée** *(see Demoiselles coiffées de THÉUS)*, a strange rock formation showing above the larches on the opposite slope. The end of the Aigue Blanche Valley is barred by the Tête de Longet.

La Rua – Go through the village *(narrow street)* and admire the typical architecture of the St-Véran area including a few traditional *mayes* (barns entirely built with beams roughly joined together and covered with laths).

★Église St-Romain-de-Molines – Situated below the village to the right, this isolated church, rebuilt in the 15C, comprises a massive nave and an amazing campanile, next to a tiny enclosed cemetery. Inside, there is a wealth of Baroque decoration; note the imposing altarpiece, framed by twisted columns adorned with vine leaves and surmounted by a broken pediment. The chancel vaulting, restored in the 19C, is decorated with stucco work.

★Molines-en-Queyras – *See MOLINES-EN-QUEYRAS.*

The road continues to rise through a lovely pastoral landscape and the houses of St-Véran suddenly appear, scattered over the sunny slope of the valley.

★★St-Véran – *See ST-VÉRAN.*

HAUT-QUEYRAS

③ From Château-Queyras to the Monte Viso Belvedere

30km/18.6mi – about 1hr – local map below

This itinerary takes you through the most open and most pleasant part of the Guil Valley, between Château-Queyras and Abriès, and offers splendid views of Monte Viso.

★**Château-Queyras** – *See CHÂTEAU-QUEYRAS.*

From Château-Queyras, follow D 947 towards Abriès.

The road runs up the Guil Valley, densely forested with larches and pines on the north-facing side. There is a clear **view** ahead towards the heights lining the Italian border with the Bric Bouchet (alt 3 216m/10 551ft) soaring above.

★**Aiguilles** – Lying in pleasant surroundings and enjoying an exceptionally fine climate, Aiguilles is the liveliest resort of the Queyras region. The nearby larch woods are charming and, in winter, the sun shines generously on the ski runs.

"American" residences – A large number of local inhabitants emigrated to South America at the beginning of the 19C; most of them came back at the end of the century, having made their fortune across the Atlantic *(see BARCELONNETTE).* They had sumptuous houses built in a style which was fashionable in large urban areas at the time. The best examples are: the town hall, the Château Margnat (on D 947) and above all the luxurious Villa Challe. Note also the amazing "Maison Eiffel", improperly linked with the name of Gustave Eiffel, built entirely of metal for the 1898 Bordeaux Exhibition.

The **Maison du Queyras** holds exhibitions about the region and displays furniture made by local craftsmen.

Beyond Aiguilles, note the contrast between the barren south-facing slope and the densely forested north-facing slope.

Abriès – *See ABRIÈS.*

Continue along D 947.

The Guil Valley changes direction and the landscape becomes more austere.

L'Échalp – This is the last village in the valley and the starting point of excursions to the Monte Viso belvederes. The hike to the **Chalets de la Médille★** *(1hr 30min return on foot),* affords a fine view of Monte Viso; take the first bridge over the Guil upstream of L'Échalp and follow the path which rises towards the Plateau de la Médille, a charming meadow surrounded by larches.

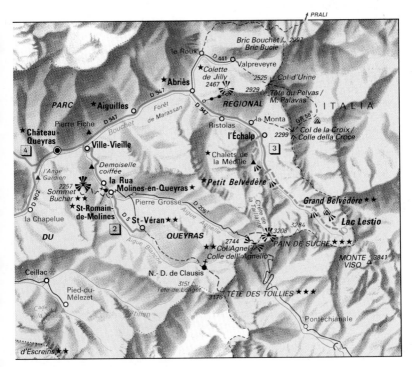

Le QUEYRAS

Mont Viso

The road continues up the Guil Valley, which becomes narrower, passing near a huge rock, known as "**la Roche écroulée**" ⊘ used for rock-climbing practice. The road is closed to traffic at the point where it crosses the Guil.
Leave the car in the parking area and continue on foot, in order to get a close-up view of the rocky ridge of Monte Viso. Amateurs of mountain hiking can make a round tour via the Grand Belvédère, the Lac Lestio and the Refuge du Viso. A shorter and easier itinerary leads to the Petit Belvédère and the Pré Michel Nature trail. For other hiking possibilities, see ABRIÈS.

★**Petit Belvédère du mont Viso and sentier écologique du Pré Michel** – *45min on foot and 1hr on the site. Obtain the booklet describing the nature trail, on sale in the Information centre, near the parking area.*
In addition to the view of Monte Viso, it is possible to admire a great variety of plant and flower species (from late June to early August): martagon lily, delphinium, fritillary...

★★**Hike to the Grand Belvédère, the Lac Lestio and the Refuge du Viso** – *5hr 30min return. Difference in height: about 700m/2 297ft. This round tour is varied and pleasant but does not offer outstanding panoramas.*
You will reach the Grand Belvédère after 1hr 45min walk along a landscaped path (explanatory tables) running parallel to the road. From there the **view**★ extends to **Monte Viso** (alt 3 841m/12 602ft) across the Italian border, which seems to bar the upper end of the Guil Valley.

After climbing for a while, take a path on the right which follows the stream. This easy itinerary is recognisable by the yellow markings along the way; after joining the path leading to the refuge and crossing the stream, one reaches the **Lac Lestio** (2 510m/8 235ft).

Retrace your steps and follow the path identified by red and blue markings, which leads to the refuge: **view**★ of Monte Viso; go back along the road to the Grand Belvédère and the parking area.

The Tour du Procureur

Several villages in the Haut-Queyras region have a characteristic campanile built of larch logs and crowned with a bell, known as the Tour du Procureur. Dating from the early Middle Ages, it is all that remains of the original village building. The sound of the bell called the villagers to a meeting where decisions concerning the community were taken: baking day in the village oven, harvest time, sharing of communal duties and help for widows. The set of rules governing community work was called the "Ruido".
During the 19C, the tower was used for a different purpose in valleys where Protestants had returned: it was used as an ecumenical bell tower. During the extensive flooding which occurred in 1957, the temporary absence of modern means of communication gave it back its original function.

ARVIEUX VALLEY

④ From Château-Queyras to Brunissard
10km/6.2mi – about 1hr local map p 267

This valley is also on the Route de l'Izoard itinerary *(see Route de l'IZOARD).*

★Château-Queyras – *See CHÂTEAU-QUEYRAS.*
2km beyond Château-Queyras, turn right onto D 902 towards the Col d'Izoard.

Arvieux – This village and the surrounding hamlets are interesting for their traditional architecture represented by arcaded houses covered with larch shingles. Owing to its pleasant climate, Arvieux has become a lively summer resort and winter sports centre.
The 16C **church** has retained an 11C porch and doorway; note the naïve-style carvings decorating the capitals.

La Chalp – Situated above Arvieux, this village has been a toy-making centre since the 1920s; the wooden toys are decorated by hand *(see Introduction: Handicraft).*

Brunissard – An interesting wooden **campanile** overlooks the village oven.

RIEZ

Population 1 707
Michelin map 81 fold 16, 114 fold 7 or 245 fold 34

This lively ancient town, overlooked by Mont St-Maxime, lies at the confluence of the Auvestre and Colostre rivers. Riez, which was an important religious and economic regional centre in the past, nowadays specializes in the lavender, honey and wheat trade and has a small earthenware and *santons* industry.

SIGHTS

★Baptistère ⊙ – This is one of the few Merovingian buildings still standing in France. It probably dates from the 5C but its cupola was rebuilt in the 12C. The square edifice comprises an octagonal room with four radiating chapels. Eight granite columns with marble Corinthian capitals form a circle round the christening font which has almost entirely disappeared. The room is surmounted by a cupola.
A museum displays finds excavated on the site: altars, Roman inscriptions, sarcophagi, mosaics etc.

Part of the Gallo-Roman town and the foundations of a cathedral dating from the 5C have been excavated opposite the baptistery.

Roman columns – Four beautiful granite columns, surmounted by white-marble Corinthian capitals and supporting an architrave, stand 6m/20ft high in a meadow. It is all that remains of a temple probably dedicated to Apollo at the end of the 1C.

★Old town – Start from place Javelly or place du Quinconce, shaded by plane trees, and enter the old town through the 13C **Porte Aiguière**. The Grand-Rue running through the old town is lined with splendidly decorated houses:

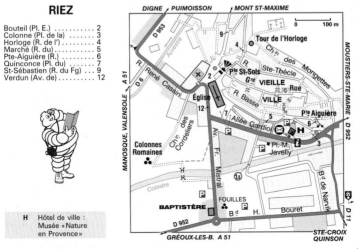

corbelled house (no 1), 16C **Hôtel de Mazan** (no 12) with fine stucco work in the staircase *(restoration work in progress)*, lovely façade decorated with twin windows (no 25), windows surrounded by moulded friezes (no 27).

As you reach the 14C **Porte St-Sols**, turn right towards rue St-Thècle; a tiny square on the left offers an interesting view of what remains of the town walls and of the **Tour de l'Horloge**.

Go back to the church past the Porte St-Sols.

Church – Rebuilt during the 19C, it has retained the bell tower and apsidal chapels of the 15C cathedral.

The town hall is housed in the former bishop's palace.

Musée "Nature en Provence" ⊙ (**H**) – Situated beneath the town hall, this museum illustrates the geological history of Provence from the Primary Era until today; it contains 3 000 specimens of minerals, rocks and fossils spanning 600 million years.

Maison de l'abeille et du miel ⊙ – *2km/1.2mi norhteast on the Puimoisson road.* A bee-keeper and lavender-grower presents an exhibition about bee-keeping: the life of a bee (5 weeks in summer), what goes on inside a beehive (which houses as many as 50 000 working bees), the honey harvest (about 12kg/26lb per beehive) and the conditioning of honey to be sold. *Tasting and sale on the premises.*

The black gold of the Haute-Provence region

There are two kinds of truffle, known as **rabasse** in Provençal dialect.

The white truffle, picked in the spring, has very little culinary value; it is used to train truffle hounds.

The black truffle, rarer and tastier, is gathered in December; it is used to enhance the taste of dishes and sauces.

Truffles, which are burried beneath oak and hazzlenut trees, are the signs of a disease in these trees. Nowadays, the harvest takes place in fields containing trees which favour the growth of these sought-after mushrooms.

Montagnac, near Riez, is a producing centre famous in the Haute-Provence region.

EXCURSION

Mont St-Maxime – *2km/1.2mi northeast along rue du Faubourg-St-Sébastien.* This 636m/2 087ft-high hill is a familiar landmark in the Riez area.

Chapelle St-Maxime – The chapel has retained its Romanesque apse: the ambulatory is lined with six beautiful Corinthian columns, taken from a much older edifice.

★**Panorama** – From the shaded terrace in front of the chapel, the **view** extends over part of Riez, the Valensole Plateau, the Préalpes de Castellane, the Plans de Canjuers, the hills of the Haut-Var area, the Luberon and the Montagne de Lure.

Michelin Maps (scale 1: 200 000),
which are revised regularly provide much useful motoring information.
Keep current Michelin Maps in the car at all times.

Domaine de RIPAILLE ★

Michelin map 89 fold 2 or 244 fold 9 – 2km/1.2mi north of Thonon

This monastery-castle comprises a group of imposing buildings in typical Savoyard style, set in the midst of fine vineyards.

The duke who became a monk – At the beginning of the 14C, the wife of the count of Savoie, Amédée VI, turned the modest hunting lodge into a stately home. Duke Amédée VIII extended it considerably and offered accommodation to a whole community of Augustine monks. When he abdicated in favour of his son Louis, he had the 7-towered castle built for himself and his suite of six gentlemen. In 1439, he became Pope Felix V at the time of the Great Schism but gave up the papacy after 10 years and returned to Ripaille as a monk.

Fondation Ripaille – The castle has, since 1976, been the headquarters of the Fondation Ripaille whose aim is to promote a research centre concerned with ecology, geology and the development of natural resources.

TOUR ⊘ *about 1hr for the castle and the monastery*

A classical doorway leads to the main courtyard: the castle is on the right – four out of the seven towers are still standing – the monastery buildings are on the left; between 1619 and the Revolution, they were occupied by Carthusian monks, hence the name of *chartreuse* by which they are known today.

Castle – The interior was restored at the end of the 19C and decorated in neo-Gothic and modern styles. There are exhibitions about the castle's history.

Chartreuse – The winepress and 17C kitchens can be visited.

Forest and arboretum ⊘ – *The visit of the arboretum is not included in the tour of the castle. Leave the grounds and take the first road on the left.*
The Ripaille Forest, which was the hunting ground of the dukes of Savoie, covers an area of 53ha/131 acres. Marked paths lead to the favourite haunts of roe-deer and to the arboretum whose trees were planted between 1930 and 1934 (firs, thujas, red oaks from America, black walnuts etc).

La ROCHE-SUR-FORON ★

Population 7 116
Michelin map 74 fold 6 or 244 fold 8

This ancient city, overlooking the lower Arve Valley, is an important crossroads and the venue of two international events, the Foire de Haute-Savoie-Mont-Blanc, and the Salon du décolletage (metal-parts fair). Lively markets take place regularly and the national school of the dairy and meat industry is based in the town.
In 1885, La Roche-sur-Foron was the first European town to enjoy electric lighting. In the park of the castle, a plaque acknowledges this event.

★★OLD TOWN *1hr 30min*

The tour of the medieval town offers the opportunity to admire many houses with ogee-arched mullioned windows. This charming district is being carefully restored. Several houses and public buildings have been repainted with bright colours, in typical Sard style.
The Plain-Château District is accessible from place St-Jean.
Follow rue des Fours on the left of the church to reach the Tower.
Go through the Porte Falquet into the school yard. The entrance to the Tower is at the end, on the right.

Tower ⊘ – It is all that remains of the counts of Geneva's castle built on a rocky spur which gave its name to the town.
On the way down, take **rue du Plain-Château** (on the right), and admire the carved façades of the 17C houses; note in particular the **Maison des Chevaliers** (1565).
Turn right at the end of the street towards the Château de l'Échelle.
Retrace your steps and walk down rue du Cretet beyond the porte St-Martin. There are a couple of interesting houses in rue du Silence, in particular no 30. Walk round the church and into rue des Halles; a stone bench dating from 1558 has three grain measures, for 20, 40 and 80l/4.4, 8.8 and 17.6gal.

Église St-Jean-Baptiste – The arms of the counts of Geneva can be seen above the doorway of this 12C church surmounted by an onion-shaped steeple dating from the 19C. The chancel and the apse are Romanesque, the apsidal chapels are Gothic. The stained-glass windows date from the 1978 restoration.

In rue Perrine, note the **Maison Boniface** (no 79) in Renaissance style and the emblazoned lintels inside the courtyard. The picturesque *halle aux grains* (corn exchange), known as "la Grenette", is near the town hall.
Walk onto the Pont-Neuf in order to admire the fine overall view of the Foron overlooked by terraced gardens.

Every year
the Michelin Red Guide France
revises its selection of stars for cuisine (good cooking)
mentioning the culinary specialities and local beers and wines;
and proposes a choice of simpler restaurants offering
well-prepared meals often regional specialities
at a moderate price.
It is well worth buying the current edition.

ROUTE DES GRANDES ALPES★★★

Michelin maps 70, 74, 77, 81, 89, 115, or 244, 245
Local map see p 273 – Michelin Green Guides French Alps and French Riviera

The Route des Grandes Alpes is the most renowned of the great routes crossing the French Alps. It links Lake Geneva with the Riviera via a road which follows the line of the peaks, often running alongside the border, and is only fully open at the height of summer.

The Alps were formed during the Tertiary Era, when the Italo-African and Eurasian plates collided, folding the area situated between them and forcing it up: this resulted in the long curved line of mountain ranges stretching from Nice to Vienna. The Grandes Alpes include the central massifs and the intra-Alpine zone.

The former belonged to a very ancient Hercynian range worn down by erosion, covered with sediment during the Secondary Era and forced up again to high altitudes during the Tertiary Era; it is a sparsely populated region of high rounded summits, needle-shaped peaks reaching up to clear skies, of sunny landscapes and larch forests.

The intra-Alpine zone lies along the axis of the upthrust of the range: its sedimentary rocks, often crystallized and folded under their own pressure and heat to form huge layers through which the glaciers and great rivers of the Quarternary Era carved large sunny valleys enjoying a mild climate.

Water from the Alpine valleys is drained by the rivers Isère and Drac into a large depression lying at the foot of the high Alps: this is the Alpine trench *(sillon alpin)* which makes communications easier. The Durance Valley plays a comparable role in the southern Alps.

The Préalpes, a vast area of foothills, open out to the south; their most striking feature is the ruggedness of their limestone surfaces which are either tabular or folded.

Two-day itinerary

It is possible to go from Thonon to Menton in two days, by spending a night in Briançon; this, however, is a tiring trip which entails making sacrifices. For instance, it involves leaving out most of the excursions which make the trip worthwhile, such as Chamonix with the Aiguille du Midi and the Vallée Blanche, or La Grave with the panoramic viewpoint at Le Chazelet...and only allows for carefully timed stops.

Five-day itinerary

– Thonon – Beaufort: *146km/91mi – allow 5hr 30min (tours included)*
– Beaufort – Val d'Isère: *71km/44mi – allow 3hr (tours included)*
– Val d'Isère – Briançon: *180km/111mi – allow 7hr 30min (tours included)*
– Briançon – Barcelonnette: *133km/83mi – allow 6hr 30min (tours included)*
– Barcelonnette – Menton: *206km/128mi – allow 7hr (tours included)*

FROM THONON TO THE COL DU LAUTARET *347km/216mi*

Follow D 902 from Thonon to Cluses.

⧻⧻ **Thonon** – *See THONON-LES-BAINS.*

The damp forested gorge of the Dranse de Morzine leads into the **Chablais★★**, a pastoral region of the northern Préalpes and the grazing area of the famous Abondance breed of cattle. The site of the **Gorges du Pont du Diable★★** *(see Le CHABLAIS)*, through which the Dranse has carved its way, with its impressive piles of huge blocks eroded into all kinds of shapes, is the highlight of this section of the route.

※※**Morzine** – *See MORZINE.* Note the hamlets scattered along the verdant coombs, the spruce forests and the chalets with their balconies splendidly decorated with openwork. After reaching the upper station of the Pléney cable-car, go to the viewing tables to admire the superb panorama of Mont Blanc and Lake Geneva.

※**Les Gets** – *See Le FAUCIGNY: Les Gets.*

From Tanninges, the road enters the **Faucigny★★** region, an area drained by the River Giffre, with landscapes shaped by glacial moraines through limestone folds. Spruce forests and pastures are the main natural resources.

Cluses – *See CLUSES.*

South of Cluses, the road enters the central massifs of the high Alps; the Bassin de Sallanches to the southeast is overlooked by the limestone cliffs of the Désert de Platé and offers views of Mont Blanc and the surrounding summits.

From Cluses, follow D 4 across the Col de la Colombière (see Massif des ARAVIS).

Grandes Alpes	Central massifs		Boundary between the Northern and Southern Alps
	Sedimentary zone		
Préalpes			District boundary
Sub-Alpine furrow			Route des Grandes Alpes, with alternative
Principal massifs			Route Napoléon

La Clusaz – *See La CLUSAZ.*

D 909 from La Clusaz to Flumet is one of the most famous routes in the French Alps. Try to reach the Col des Aravis in the afternoon to enjoy one of the finest views of the Mont-Blanc Massif. From the pass, the road runs through the Gorges de l'Arondine to Flumet *(see Massif des ARAVIS: Route des Aravis).*

From Flumet, it is possible to drive up the Val d'Arly to **Chamonix-Mont-Blanc** via Megève and Les Houches *(61km/38mi).*

Take D 218⁸ towards the Col des Saisies, via Notre-Dame-de-Bellecombe.

There are glimpses to the right of the Aravis Massif and of the Gorges de l'Arly. The Col des Saisies (1 633m/5 358ft), overlooked by the Signal de Bisanne (1 939m/6 362ft), offers a fine viewpoint of the Beaufortain Region.
Beyond Hauteluce, the road runs down to Beaufort.

Beaufort – *See BEAUFORT.*

Between Beaufort and Bourg-St-Maurice, the road goes through **Arèches** and the charming hamlet of **Boudin★**, then runs across the top of the Barrage de Roselend and along the **Cormet de Roselend** depression *(see Le BEAUFORTAIN)*.

Bourg-St-Maurice – *See BOURG-ST-MAURICE.*

From Bourg-St-Maurice to Val d'Isère, D 902 rises in a series of hairpin bends and enters the Haute-Tarentaise Region, within sight of the Mont Pourri Glaciers to the right. From **Le Monal** *(small road to the left leading to Chenal)*, splendid **view★★** of these heights.

Before reaching Tignes, fine view of the dam and the Lac du Chevril. *For the next section of the route to Bonneval-sur-Arc, see Route de l'ISERAN.*

Beyond Val d'Isère, the road starts climbing to the Col de l'Iseran, the highest pass along the Route des Grandes Alpes (2 770m/9 088ft), and enters the Parc national de la Vanoise. In clear weather, it is worthwhile for experienced hikers, who do not suffer from vertigo, to climb up to the **Pointe des Lessières★★★** and enjoy the magnificent panoramic view.

★★Bonneval-sur-Arc – *See BONNEVAL-SUR-ARC.*

From Bonneval-sur-Arc to Modane – *56km/34.8mi along D 902 and N 6. See La MAURIENNE.*

Continue along the Arc Valley to St-Michel-de-Maurienne (17km/10.6mi). Turn left towards the Col du Galibier via Valloire and continue to the Col du Lauraret, see Route du GALIBIER.

★★★Col du Galibier – Alt 2 646m/8 681ft. *See Route du GALIBIER.*

At the **Col du Lautaret** (2 057m/6 749ft), turn right towards La Grave then left just before the second tunnel towards Le Chazelet to enjoy the lovely panorama of the Meije Massif.

★★★Oratoire du Chazelet – *See La GRAVE.*

Return to the Col du Lautaret.

Beyond the pass, the road runs down the Guisanne Valley to Briançon.

ALTERNATIVE ROUTES

There are two possibilities in the northern part of the route:
– From St-Jean-de-Sixt through Les Bauges via Annecy *(127km/79mi):* Annecy to Sévrier (along N 508), Pont-de-Lescheraines, St-Pierre-d'Albigny, Albertville (via N 90) and Beaufort (along D 925);
– From St-Michel-de-Maurienne via the Col du Glandon and Col de la Croix de Fer to the Col du Lautaret *(120km/75mi):* St-Jean-de-Maurienne to the Col du Glandon (along D 926), Rochetaillée (by D 526) and the Col du Lauraret (along N 91).

Route du Col du Galibier

FROM THE COL DU LAUTARET TO THE VALLÉE DE LA TINÉE

Follow N 91 to Briançon, then N 94 to Guillestre.

South of the Col du Lautaret, the road enters the southern Alps. Oaks, ash trees and beeches can be seen along the Guisanne Valley, landscapes become brighter, valleys open out. This is the intra-Alpine zone.

★★**Briançon** – *See BRIANÇON.*

The road winds its way along the Durance Valley. Layers of marine sediment, shifted from east to west during the formation of the Alps, formed what is known as the **"nappes briançonnaises"** (consisting of schist and flysch).
The River Durance has dug its way through thick layers of limestone, flowing through a striking gorge (at l'Argentière-la-Bessée) before widening as it reaches the Guillestre Basin.

★**Mont-Dauphin** – *See MONT-DAUPHIN.*

Guillestre – This village, whose church has a beautiful porch or **réal★**, lies at the exit of the **Combe du Queyras★★**, an impressive canyon through which flows the Guil.
An alternative route links Guillestre and Barcelonnette via Embrun (see Alternative route via the Lac de Serre-Ponçon).
At the intersection with D 902, it is also possible to turn left towards Château-Queyras (see CHÂTEAU-QUEYRAS), eventually reaching St-Véran (15km/9mi east). In Ville-Vieille, turn right towards St-Véran along the Aigue Blanche Valley.
St-Véran★★ *(see ST-VÉRAN)*, the highest village in Europe, found an original way to adapt to severe mountain-life conditions by building wooden chalets over a schist base. There are also interesting *croix de la Passion* in the area.
Return to Guillestre by the same route and continue along D 902 towards Vars.

Col de Vars – Alt 2 111m/6 926ft. The pass is the gateway to the Ubaye Valley in an arid landscape of meagre pastures dotted with blocks of sandstone and tiny pools. South of the pass, hamlets scattered across the south-facing slopes live on cattle-farming and handicraft. The upper Ubaye Valley, carved out of black schist, is obstructed by alluvial fans where mountain streams deposit sediment. Note the strange rock formation of the Colonnes coiffées on the left, just before Les Prats. The slender octagonal steeple in the village of **St-Paul** signals the beginning of the Haute Ubaye region.

★**Barcelonnette** – *See BARCELONNETTE.*

The narrow road runs along the bottom of the wild **Gorges du Bachelard★** then winds round the Mont Pelat Massif (3 053m/10 016ft), the main summit of the southern Alps.

★★**Col de la Cayolle** – Alt 2 327m/7 635ft. The pass separates three distinct areas: the Ubaye to the northwest, the upper Verdon to the southwest and the upper Var to the east and south, offering fine views of the heights and plateaux of the Haute-Provence region.
There are numerous possibilities of hikes starting from the pass towards the Lac d'Allos and Lac des Garets (see Route de la CAYOLLE).

★★**Upper Var Valley** – The road follows the upper Var Valley lined with schist mountains until **St-Martin-d'Entraunes**, where it leaves the high Alps and enters the southern Préalpes. At Guillaumes, ignore the road on the right, which runs through the **Gorges de Daluis★★** *(see Haute-Vallée du VAR)*, carved out of red porphyry, and turn left towards Beuil. The road rises regularly to the Col de Valberg, affording varied views of the valley: the forested north-facing slope offers a striking contrast with the south-facing slope covered with vineyards and orchards. Beuil lies at the beginning of the **Gorges du Cians** *(see Gorges du CIANS)*, running south to join the River Var. On the way down to Roubion from the **Col de la Couillole** (alt 1 678m/5 505ft), the road offers interesting views of the Vionène and Tinée valleys. The beauty of the wild landscape is enhanced by the contrasting colours of the rocks. Beyond **Roubion★**, perched on top of a rocky spur, at an altitude of 1 300m/4 265ft, the scenery is marked by red schist and waterfalls. **Roure★** *(4km/2.5mi along a tiny road on the left)* is another fine village with characteristic architectural features: houses have red-schist bases and are covered with *lauzes* (heavy slabs of schist).
At the end of the village, there is a bird's-eye view of the Gorges de la Tinée to the left. The road winds its way alongside the Vionène, to its confluence with the River Tinée in St-Sauveur-sur-Tinée.

St-Sauveur-sur-Tinée – *See Vallée de la TINÉE.*

The road follows the lower Tinée Valley for 4km/2.5mi before veering to the left towards St-Martin-Vésubie along the Valdeblore Valley. *(For the rest of the itinerary, see Michelin Green Guide French Riviera.)*

ALTERNATIVE ROUTE VIA THE LAC DE SERRE-PONÇON

From Guillestre, it is possible to reach Barcelonnette via Savines-le-Lac and the Lac de Serre-Ponçon (27km/17mi detour).

★**Embrun** – *24km/15mi southwest of Guillestre. See EMBRUN.*

Beyond Embrun, the road crosses over to the south bank of the Durance then skirts the Serre-Ponçon Lake. With its 3 000ha/7 413 acres, this is one of the largest reservoirs in Europe. As you come out of Savines-le-Lac, there is a splendid **view**★ of the Dévoluy Massif.

Further on, on the left-hand side of D 954, there is a group of Demoiselles coiffées, rock formations characteristic of Alpine relief *(see Demoiselles coiffées de THÉUS)*. The road then winds round the rocky promontory of Sauze-le-Lac marking the confluence of the rivers Durance and Ubaye.

★**Barcelonnette** – *See BARCELONNETTE.*

Great passes of the southern Alps

– Col du Lautaret
– Col de Vars
– Col d'Allos
– Col de la Cayolle
– Col de la Lombarde
– Col d'Izoard
– Col Agnel
– Col de la Bonette

ROUTE NAPOLÉON ★

Michelin maps 77 and 81 or 244 and 245

The Route Napoléon – Napoleon's road – follows the Emperor's route on his return from Elba, from the point where he landed in Golfe Juan to his arrival in Grenoble. The new road was opened in 1932. The commemorative plaques and monuments bear the flying eagle symbol inspired by Napoleon's remark: "The eagle will fly from steeple to steeple until he reaches the towers of Notre-Dame".

FLIGHT OF THE EAGLE

After landing at Golfe Juan on 1 March 1815, Napoleon and his troops, preceded by an advance guard, made a brief overnight stop at Cannes. Wishing to avoid the Rhône area, which he knew to be hostile, Napoleon made for Grasse to get to the valley of the Durance by way of the Alps. Beyond Grasse, the little column had a difficult time along mule tracks. It halted at St-Vallier, Escragnolles and Séranon, from which, after a night's rest, it reached Castellane on 3 March; by the afternoon, it arrived in Barrême. The next day (4 March), the party lunched at Digne. That evening, Napoleon halted at the Château de Malijai, impatiently awaiting news from Sisteron, where the fort commanded the narrow passage of the Durance.

Sisteron was not guarded. Napoleon lunched there (5 March) and, as he left the town, support for his cause was already growing. Travelling along a coach road once more, he arrived in Gap that night and received an enthusiastic welcome. He slept in Corps the next day. On 7 March he reached La Mure, only to find troops from Grenoble facing him at Laffrey. This is the place where the famous episode, which turned events in his favour, took place and is commemorated by a monument. It happened in the Prairie de la Rencontre, situated near the Grand Lac de Laffrey; in the afternoon, the

---

Napoleon's journey across the Alps

"He disembarked at Golfe Juan, several hours before nightfall, and set up a bivouac. As the moon rose, between one and two o'clock in the morning, he broke camp and went on to Grasse. There, the Emperor expected to find a road which he had ordered to be built when he was Emperor, but he discovered that his orders were never carried out. He was therefore obliged to follow a difficult route in deep snow, which meant that he had to leave his coach and two cannons in Grasse with the town guard.

... The Emperor moved like lightning. He felt that victory depended on his willpower and that France would rally to him if he reached Grenoble. There were a hundred leagues to go and we made it in five days, from 2 to 7 March, but on such roads and in such weather..."

Las Cases *(Mémorial)*

Emperor found the road to Grenoble blocked by a battalion which greatly out-numbered his own escort; he took a calculated risk, went forward and, opening his grey coat, said to the troops: "Soldiers, I am your Emperor! If anyone among you wishes to kill his general, here I am!" In spite of being ordered to fire by a young officer, the soldiers rallied to Napoleon shouting: "Long live the Emperor!" and marched with him to Grenoble. That same evening, he entered the town triumphantly.

"Refuges Napoléon" – As a sign of gratitude for the enthusiastic welcome he received in Gap, Napoleon bequeathed to the Hautes-Alpes *département* a sum of money intended for the construction of refuges at the top of passes particularly exposed in winter. This sum, which was only accepted in 1854, was used to build refuges at the Col de Manse, Col du Lauraret, Col d'Izoard, Col de Vars, Col du Noyer, Col Agnel and Col de la Croix *(the last two are now in ruins and the refuge of the Col du Noyer has been replaced by a hotel).*

The first part of the itinerary from Golfe Juan to the Col de Valferrière is described in the Michelin Green Guide French Riviera. The route from the Col de Valferrière to Grenoble is described below.

FROM THE COL DE VALFERRIÈRE TO CORPS

210km/130mi – allow 1 day

Beyond the pass, the road goes through the **Clue de Séranon**. Napoleon spent the night (2 to 3 March) in the village of **Séranon** hidden in the midst of a pine forest. Further on, on the way down from the Col de Luens, the road affords views of Castellane nestling at the foot of its "rock", crowned by Notre-Dame du Roc.

★**Castellane** – *See CASTELLANE.*

Between Castellane and Châteauredon, the road follows the Vallée d'Asse through a series of gorges and *"clues"* which reveal interesting strata.
On the way up to the Col des Lèques (alt 1 148m/3 766ft), lovely **views** of Castellane, the Lac de Castillon and the Préalpes de Provence.

★**Clue de Taulanne** – This opening cut through sheer rock leads from the Verdon Valley to the Asse Valley.

6km/3.7mi further on, cross the Asse to enter Senez.

Senez – This ancient Gallo-Roman town was one of the oldest and poorest bishoprics in France. It came into the limelight in the 18C, when Bishop **Jean Soanen** refused to condemn Jansenism and was removed from office.

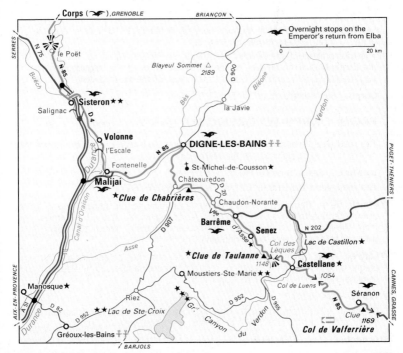

277

The **former cathedral** ⊙ dates from the early 13C. The east end is decorated with arcading in Lombard style, resting on slender engaged columns. A Gothic doorway gives access to the nave in typical Provençal Romanesque style. Inside, note the 17C stalls, altarpiece and lectern, as well as the 18C antiphonary.

Return to N 85 and continue towards Digne-les-Bains.

Barrême – The station houses an exhibition concerning one stage of the Cretaceous geological period, particularly well represented in the area.
Napoleon spent the night of 3 March 1815 here *(plaque on a house along N 85)*.

The Préalpes de Digne start beyond Chaudon-Norante. Napoleon went to Digne along the route followed by D 20. However, carry on along N 85.

★**Clue de Chabrières** – The gorge is framed by tall limestone cliffs.

‡‡ **Digne-les-Bains** – *See DIGNE-LES-BAINS.*

Leave Digne-les-Bains by ③ on the town plan.

The road *(N 85)* continues along the Bléone Valley, between the Plateau de Valensole and the Préalpes de Digne. The imposing Château de Fontenelle stands on the right-hand side of the road, just before Malijai.

Malijai – Napoleon spent the night of 4 to 5 March in the elegant 18C **castle** ⊙, famous for its stuccoed interior decoration.

Beyond Malijai, the view embraces the Durance Valley and extends towards the bluish mass of the Montagne de Lure. The road skirts the Canal d'Oraison until it reaches L'Escale and the impressive dam across the river.

Leave the bridge to your left and drive north along D 24.

Volonne – This village, clinging to a rocky spur picturesquely crowned by two old towers, is surrounded by lovely orchards. The ruined **Église St-Martin** is a fine specimen of early Romanesque style (11C); the nave flanked by side aisles is open to the sky.

Shortly after the Salignac Dam across the Durance, there is a splendid overall **view**★ of Sisteron and its remarkable setting.

★★**Sisteron** – *See SISTERON.*

The road *(N 85)* follows an EDF (French Electricity Board) feeder canal part of the way to Gap. Stop at the viewing table situated at the exit of the village of Le Poët *(off the road)* and admire the **panorama** of the Gapençais and Embrunais heights and of the Écrins summits. After La Saulce, the road veers northwards.

★**Gap** – *See GAP.*

Beyond Gap, N 85 rises sharply to the **Col Bayard** (alt 1 248m/4 094ft, viewing table) and comes down again into the open valley of the upper Drac *(see Le CHAMPSAUR)*; fine overall view from the outskirts of Laye.

Les Baraques – Napoleon stopped here on 6 March 1815 and refused the offer made by local farmers to join his troops.

The escarpments of the Dévoluy (Montagne de Féraud) lie ahead, the Pic d'Olan in the Écrins Massif can be seen to the northeast, through the **Valgaudemar** Valley *(see Le VALGAUDEMAR)*, and the Obiou to the west of the **Lac du Sautet**.

Corps – *See Barrage et Lac du SAUTET.*

FROM CORPS TO GRENOBLE 63km/39mi – allow half a day

The road *(N 85)* winds its way above the Drac Valley, then crosses the Bonne Valley before running straight across the Matheysine Plateau.

La Mure – *See Lacs de LAFFREY.*

The road skirts the Lacs de Laffrey *(see Lacs de LAFFREY)*.

★**Prairie de la Rencontre** – Two monuments, bearing the imperial eagle symbol, draw attention to the access road. Napoleon's equestrian statue by Frémiet, visible from the road, is a reminder of the famous "meeting" which took place in this pleasant setting of lakes and mountains.

★**Laffrey** – This holiday resort is particularly sought after by anglers and bathers. A plaque on the wall of the cemetery recalls the speech addressed by Napoleon to the soldiers sent from Grenoble to stop him.

★**Vizille** – *See VIZILLE.*

Napoleon went from Vizille to Grenoble along the route now followed by D 5, which offers, on the way down to Eybens, an overall view of Grenoble.

★★**Grenoble** – *See GRENOBLE.*

ROUTE DES PRINCES D'ORANGE

Michelin map 81 folds 3, 4, 5 and 12 or 245 folds 17, 18 and 19

This scenic route links Orange in the Rhône Valley and Eyguians in the Hautes-Alpes via the Ouvèze and the Céans valleys, over a distance of 109km/68mi.

The ancient Gallo-Roman way was probably used by Hannibal in 218 BC when he marched across the Alps with 60 000 men. Between the 14C and 18C, this road linked the Orange Principality and the Orpierre Barony, both belonging to the house of Orange-Nassau, whose descendants are still reigning in the Netherlands.

The route between Entrechaux and Eyguians is described below. Orange and Vaison-la-Romaine are described in the Michelin Greeen Guide Provence.

FROM ENTRECHAUX TO EYGUIANS

78km/49mi – allow 3hr – Local map see Les BARONNIES.

Entrechaux – This village is overlooked by the ruins of its castle, which include a 20m/66ft-high keep.

Drive northeast along D 13.

Mollans-sur-Ouvèze – This small "border" town is the gateway to the Baronnies region. The bridge across the Ouvèze links the *basse ville*, with its elegant 18C fountain surmounted by a dolphin and its 18C covered wash-house, and the *haute ville* with its belfry crowning an old round tower; opposite stands a small chapel projecting over the Ouvèze. From there, a walk through the narrow streets of the "high town" leads to the church and a large square keep, which is all that remains of the castle.

Pierrelongue – Perched on a rocky knoll overlooking the village, the **church**, built at the end of the 19C, looks totally out of place in this attractive setting.

Buis-les-Baronnies – *See BUIS-LES-BARONNIES.*

D 546 runs through the picturesque **Gorges d'Ubrieux** carved out by the Ouvèze.

St-Auban-sur-l'Ouvèze – Built on a rocky promontory at the confluence of the rivers Ouvèze and Charuis, this old village has retained part of its former defences. From place Péquin, at the top of the village, there is a fine view of the surrounding area dotted with many farms. There is a wide choice of hikes in and around a beautiful chestnut grove. The area's economic life is centred round medicinal (lime, sage and camomile) as well as aromatic plants.

Beyond St-Auban, follow D 65 via the Col de Perty.

The road goes through Montguers (note the charming isolated chapel on the plateau) then rises in a series of hairpin bends through a wild landscape, offering **views** of the whole Baronnies area.

★★**Col de Perty** – Alt 1 303m/4 275ft. A path to the right leads to the viewing table *(10min return on foot)*. Splendid panorama of the Durance Valley and the southern Alps to the east, of the Ouvèze Valley and the Mont Ventoux Massif to the west. The road continues along the Céans Valley.

Orpierre – *See Les BARONNIES.*

How to recognize a good olive oil

The essential characteristic of virgin olive oil is its extraction by a mechanical process from the first cold pressing without being refined. Six further operations are necessary before the oil is ready to be marketed; grading *(calibrage)* and washing in cold water *(lavage)*, crushing *(broyage)* in a traditional mill, after which the resulting paste is pressed on fibre mats *(scourtins)*. The oil thus obtained is purified by centrifuge (or by natural settling and decanting if the traditional process is followed throughout).

Regulations define several categories of oil which must be mentioned on the label:

- Extra-virgin oil *(huile vierge extra)* which is easily digested, has most flavour and a very low acidity level (less than 1%),
- Virgin oil *(huile vierge)* which also has a very good flavour but can have double the acidity level of extra-virgin oil,
- Olive oil *(huile d'olive)* which has an acceptable taste for local cooking but a fairly high acidity level (about 3%),
- Refined oil *(huile d'olive lampante)* which is mixed with virgin oil as its acidity level (nearly 4%) makes it unsuitable for consumption.

Beyond Orpierre and several gorges, the Céans Valley suddenly widens as the river joins the Buëch and the Blaisance.

Lagrand – Of the important monastery which flourished here in medieval times, only the **church** ⊘ remains; this well-preserved Romanesque building has a large nave, covered with broken barrel vaulting, ending with a pentagonal apse set within a rectangular east end. Inside, the only decorations are floral motifs carved on the capitals. Note the gilt-wood tabernacle in a recess on the right-hand side.
The west doorway has been heavily restored. The south side used to open onto the cloister and the monastery buildings. Note the funeral recesses near the base.
The town hall at the entrance of the old village is a fine 18C building characteristic of Provençal country houses of that period.

Eyguians – It is here that the Route des Princes d'Orange reaches the Buëch Valley.

ST-DALMAS-LE-SELVAGE ★

Population 114
Michelin map 81 fold 9 or 245 fold 23

St-Dalmas, situated at the top of the upper Tinée Valley, is the highest village of the Alpes-Maritimes *département*. The tall steeple of the village church stands out against the splendid wild setting of the Jalorgues Valley.

SIGHTS

Church ⊘ – The Lombard-style steeple rises into the sky next to the 17C church, built in neo-Romanesque style and covered with larch shingles.
The west front is decorated with *trompe-l'œil* paintings; one of these depicts St Dalmas, a 3C martyr who preached the gospel in the Alps. Inside, fine 16C altarpiece and several interesting paintings.

St-Dalmas-le-Selvage

Village – The narrow streets are lined with stocky houses built of dark schist, covered with shingles and adorned with many sundials.
The small **Chapelle des Pénitents** contains fine specimens of church furniture; a *croix de la Passion* stands in front of the chapel *(see Le QUEYRAS)*.

EXCURSION

★**Col de la Moutière** – *12km northwest along a narrow road*. The road offers bird's-eye views of the village and goes through a splendid larch wood, known as the Bois de Sestrière. Beyond the refuge of the same name, the road enters the central zone of the Parc national du Mercantour. Colonies of marmots can be observed near the pass situated below the Cime de la Bonette.

ST-ÉTIENNE-DE-TINÉE★

Population 1783
Michelin map 81 fold 9, 115 fold 4 or 245 folds 23 and 24

This charming Alpine town, rebuilt after the devastating fire which occurred in 1929, lies on the banks of a tumultuous river, in a pleasant **setting**★ of pastures and terrace cultivation against a beautiful mountain background.

In summer, St-Étienne-de-Tinée is the ideal starting point of very interesting hikes, in particular from the Route de la Bonette. In winter, it offers a small **skiing area** – highest point: **Cime de la Berchia**, alt 2 274m/7 461ft – linked to that of Auron by cable-car and chair-lift.

SIGHTS

Church – The most striking feature is the 4-tiered **steeple**★ in Lombard Romanesque style, surmounted by a tall octagonal stone spire surrounded by four gargoyled pinnacles; the date inscribed on the base of the steeple is 1492. Inside, the high altar, in gilt wood, bears the mark of the Spanish influence; note, on the left, some carved wood panels depicting scenes of Christ's life surrounding a statue of the Virgin Mary with Child.

Chapelle St-Sébastien ⊘ – Well-preserved frescoes by Baleison and Canavesio include the creation of Adam and Eve on the vaulting, Jesus between the two thieves on the back wall and scenes from the life of St Sebastian on the right.

Chapelle St-Michel ⊘ – Small museum and lovely 17C altarpiece.

Chapelle des Trinitaires ⊘ – The chapel, which belonged to the former monastery (now a college), is decorated with 17C frescoes and two paintings depicting the life of the monks who used to buy back Christians detained on the Barbary Coast. Fine carved-wood panels.

Two small museums illustrate aspects of traditional life: the **Musée des Traditions** ⊘, housed in the former village oven, explains the process of making rye bread and the **Musée du Lait** ⊘ displays the equipment used in cheese-making.

Chapelle St-Maur ⊘ – *2km along the road to Auron*. It was decorated in the 15C with piituresque frescoes depicting the legends of St Maur and St Sebastian.

HIKES

There are numerous possibilities starting from St-Étienne-de-Tinée or Auron. A wide choice of itineraries is available from the tourist office in both resorts.

Starting from Le Pra

★★★**Hike to the Lacs de Vens** – *Leave the car in Le Pra, on the road to La Bonette (10km/6.2mi north of St-Étienne-de-Tinée). 6hr on foot via the Col de Fer. Difference in height: about 1 100m/3 609ft. Easy but long and taxing itinerary; one of the finest hikes in the French Alps.*

The path goes through a larch forest to reach the Plateau de Morgon *(after 1hr)* then past waymark no 33 to the Tortisse forest lodges. From there it is possible to go straight to the Refuge de Vens, but the detour via the **Col de Fer** (alt 2 584m/8 478ft) is recommended to experienced hikers for the **view**★ it offers.

Lacs de Vens

Well-equipped hikers, who do not suffer from vertigo, can climb up to the Cime de Fer (alt 2 700m/8 858ft; *add 35min return on foot*). The splendid **panorama**★★ includes the Mont Vallonnet and the Lacs de Vens in the foreground, the road to the Col de Larche and the Tête de Moïse Summit further north.

From the Col de Fer, the path leads to the Refuge and **Lacs de Vens**★★. The reflection of the mountains and of the sky in the clear waters of the lakes enhances the beauty of the landscape. Skirt the first lake and part of the second then turn right beyond a pile of huge rocks. The path divides several times: keep left every time in order to reach the top of a ridge; on the other side there is a splendid **view**★ of the Cime de la Bonette and Crête de la Blanche.

Go up the path, running just below, to waymark 23 and turn towards Le Pra. The path runs along the mountain slope in a splendid **setting** then down to the Tortisse forest lodges. From there, retrace your steps to Le Pra.

★★**Hike to the Refuge de Rabuons** – *This extension of the previous hike includes a night in the Refuge des Lacs de Vens. About 5hr on foot. Marked itinerary.*
The main purpose in combining these hikes is to link the two highest mountain refuges in the Parc national du Mercantour along a route which overlooks the Tinée Valley and offers a succession of superb panoramic views. Walk along the right side of the middle and lower lakes, cross a footbridge then climb up to the Crête des Babarottes. On the way down, follow part of the "Chemin de l'énergie" to the Lac de Rabuons and the refuge of the same name.
The **"Chemin de l'énergie"** was built in the 1930s at high altitude, through very uneven terrain with retaining walls and tunnels, in order to supply a power station in St-Étienne-de-Tinée which was never completed.

★★**Mont Ténibre** – Alt 3 031m/9 944ft. *Owing to the considerable difference in height (nearly 2 000m/6 562ft), this high-mountain excursion implies a night in the Refuge de Rabuons. About 8hr.*
If this hike does not call for any knowledge of mountaineering techniques, it certainly requires a lot of stamina. The itinerary is quite popular in summer. From the summit – the highest point of the upper Tinée Valley – the magnificent **panorama**★★★ extends, in clear weather, from the Oisans to the Argentera.

Starting from the Camp des Fourches

★★**Hike to the Pas de la Cavale** – Alt 2 671m/8 763ft. *Leave the car at the Camp des Fourches, on the road to La Bonette (see Route de la BONETTE) and walk to the Col des Fourches (5min). Mountain boots recommended. 3hr 30min return on foot. Difference in height: about 750m/2 461ft.*
Walk down a narrow path, marked in white and red, to an old shack just below the Salso Moreno Cirque. The austere yet splendid landscape is very interesting from a geological point of view: sink-holes have resulted from the action of water and snow erosion. Colonies of marmots inhabit the area.

From waymark 37 onwards, the stony, slippery path climbs steadily to the Pas de la Cavale framed by the Rocher des 3 Évêques and the Tête Carrée. The **view**★★ embraces the Lacs d'Agnel, the heights lining the Italian border and the Auron Skiing area to the south, the Vallon du Lauzanier and the Brec de Chambeyron to the north. The Lac de Derrière la Croix lies just below.

Alpine flora protection
Picking endangered species of Alpine flora is strictly regulated inside nature parks and reserves:

– *cyclamen*
– *Alpine sea holly*
– *martagon lily*
– *edelweiss*

Walkers, campers, smokers...
please be careful!

Fire is the worst threat to woodland.

ATTENTION au FEU

ST-GERVAIS-LES-BAINS✠✠

Population 5 124

Michelin map 89 fold 4 or 244 fold 20 – Local map see Massif du MONT-BLANC

St-Gervais-les-Bains occupies one of the most open sites in the Alps, at the meeting point of the Autoroute Blanche and of the Val Montjoie widening out into the Sallanches Basin. Launched more than a century ago thanks to its hot springs, the spa town is now regarded as the main health resort in the Mont-Blanc Massif and is sometimes called St-Gervais-Mont-Blanc. This important holiday resort welcomes many children and is the starting point of many drives and cable-car rides offering out-standing views of the Mont-Blanc Massif.

Mountaineers traditionally start the ascent of Mont Blanc from St-Gervais, via the Tramway du Mont-Blanc, Tête Rousse and the Aiguille du Goûter.

Finally, owing to its position at the centre of the network of cable-cars and mountain railways linking Mégève to the Chamonix Valley via the Mont d'Arbois, the Col de Voza and Bellevue, the town, together with its high-altitude satellites of Le Bettex, Voza-Prarion and St-Nicolas-de-Véroce, has become an important skiing resort.

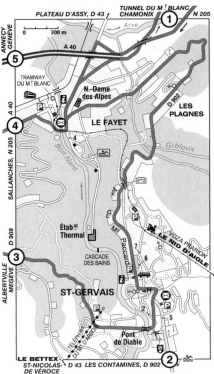

**ST-GERVAIS-
LES-BAINS
LE FAYET**

Comtesse (R.)	2
Gontard (Av.)	4
Miage (Av. du)	5
Mont-Blanc (R. et jardin du)	6
Mont-Lachat (R. du)	7

ST-GERVAIS

The town nestles round its church, on the last gentle slopes of the Val Montjoie above the wooded gorge through which flows the River Bon Nant.

Pont du Diable – This bridge spans the wooded gorge of the Bon Nant. Up-river, there is a clear view of the Mont Joly, Mont Tondu and Dômes de Miage framing the Val Montjoie; down-river, the view extends to the escarpments of the Chaîne des Fiz (Pointe and Désert de Platé).

LE FAYET

This is the spa district. The **Établissement thermal** is situated at the exit of the Bon Nant Gorge, inside a park enhanced by a lovely waterfall. The waters are used for the treatment of skin diseases and respiratory complaints.

Église Notre-Dame-des-Alpes – Designed in 1938 by Nova-rina, it is a good example of religious art at that time.

EXCURSIONS

★★★**Le Bettex** – *8km/5mi along D 909 to Mégève, then left along D 43 to Le Bettex. It is also possible to reach Le Bettex from St-Gervais by the Mont d'Arbois cable-car ⊙.*

Extremely varied views of the Mont-Blanc, Fiz and Aravis massifs.

It is possible to continue by cable-car up to the **Mont d'Arbois★★★** (alt 1 827m/5 994ft, viewing table) for an even finer **panoramic view**.

St-Nicolas-de-Véroce and excursions – *12km/7.5mi along D 909 to Mégève, then left along D 43. See Massif du MONT-BLANC.*

Col de Voza – Alt 1 653m/5 423ft. *Journey from Le Fayet or St-Gervais-Ville aboard the Tramway du Mont-Blanc ⊙.*

The electric tramway on its way to the Nid d'Aigle *(see below)* stops at the Col de Voza; the journey halfway up the mountainside, above the Bionnassay Valley, affords splendid **views★★** of the Mont-Blanc Massif.

★★**Le Nid d'Aigle (Glacier de Bionnassay)** – Alt 2 286m/7 828ft. *Allow 3hr return by the Tramway du Mont-Blanc (see above).* This journey provides a good introduction to high-mountain landscapes through the discovery of the wild setting of the Bionnas-say Glacier *(from the upper station, 1hr return on foot to the moraine)* stretched out at the foot of the Aiguilles de Bionnassay *(spectacular avalanches)* and of the Aiguille du Goûter. **View** of the massifs surrounding the Bassin de Sallanches.

ST-JEAN-DE-MAURIENNE

Population 9 439
Michelin map 89 fold 17 or 244 fold 30

The historic capital of the Maurienne region, situated at the confluence of the rivers Arc and Arvan, owes its development to its role as diocesan town until 1966.

SIGHTS

Cathédrale St-Jean-Baptiste ⊙ – An isolated square tower (11C-12C), which was the bell-tower of the Église Notre-Dame and was partly dismantled during the Révolution, stands in front of the cathedral.
The cathedral, dating from the 11C and 15C, was built over a **crypt** ⊙ excavated in 1958; it is preceded by a peristyle built in 1771, beneath which stands a mausoleum dedicated to Humbert "White Hands", the founder of the House of Savoie. The interior, partly restored, contains some splendid 15C church furniture and two frescoes: one of them, on the north side, illustrates the Annunciation, the other, on the south side, depicts the Entombment.

★**Ciborium** – This delicate Flamboyant masterpiece, carved in alabaster, is situated on the left-hand side of the apse. Three of St John the Baptist's fingers used to be kept in the central recess (they are now in the vestry). These relics were brought back from a pilgrimage by St Thècle in the 6C.

★**Stalls** – This superb piece of woodwork was carved between 1483 and 1498 by Pierre Mochet from Geneva. It was restored in 1969. There are 43 high stalls and 39 low ones. The high backs are decorated with low-relief carvings depicting various saints whereas the backrests and misericords show a freer inspiration. There are two stalls under a baldaquin, near the high altar; the one on the right is the bishop's seat and the other is intended for the president of France who is an honorary canon of the cathedral.

Cloister – Situated on the north side of the church, the well-preserved 15C cloister has retained its original alabaster arches. A flight of steps in the south gallery leads to the crypt.

Musée Opinel ⊙ – The museum illustrates the history of the famous knife from Savoie *(see CHAMBÉRY: Useful tips)* produced by the Opinel dynasty of cutlers, who were natives of St-Jean-de-Maurienne. There is a reconstruction of the workshop of the founder of the dynasty, Daniel Opinel and a video film explains modern manufacturing methods.

EXCURSION

★**Round tour via La Toussuire** *36km/22.4mi – allow 1hr 30min*

From St-Jean, drive along D 926 then turn right towards La Toussuire.

The road rises above the St-Jean-de-Maurienne Basin offering bird's-eye views of the valley below.

★**Fontcouverte** – This ancient hilltop village commands a panoramic view of the surrounding area.

Le Corbier – The skiing area is linked to that of the neighbouring resorts of La Toussuire and St-Sorlin-d'Arves.

La Toussuire – This ski resort was created in a setting of vast barren slopes.
On the way down to St-Jean-de-Maurienne, the road goes through **La Rochette**; note the isolated rock which gave its name to the hamlet.

ST-MICHEL-L'OBSERVATOIRE ★

Population 844
Michelin map 81 fold 15 or 245 fold 19

This pleasant old village built on a hillside is famous for its observatory whose cupolas shine beneath the clearest skies in France.

THE VILLAGE *30min*

It has retained part of its fortifications, its old houses with their beautiful doorways, several fountains, two interesting churches and some chapels.

Église haute – Narrow streets lead to this church crowning the hill, which was built of white stone in the 12C by the Benedictine monks of St-André in Villeneuve-lès-Avignon and extended in the 14C and 16C. The adjacent bell-tower, although dating from the 16C, is also in Romanesque style. Inside, the 12C barrel-vaulted nave is surmounted by a dome on squinches. The chancel arches rest on lovely twisted columns with Corinthian capitals. A 14C frescoe painted above the triumphal arch depicts Christ in Glory between the holy women and several angels. Note the splendid Romanesque stoup in carved marble.

From the terrace, there is a fine **view** of the area around Forcalquier, of the Montagne de Lure and of the Luberon.

Église basse – Situated at the heart of the village, St Peter's Church was built in the 13C and 14C by the counts of Anjou who ruled over Provence at the time.
The pediment of the doorway is framed by a pointed archivolt. In the apse, there is a beautiful 15C wooden crucifix.

Chapelle St-Paul – *1km/0.6mi south along D 105.* Note the massive columns surmounted by Corinthian capitals, which belonged to a 12C priory.

★OBSERVATOIRE DE HAUTE-PROVENCE ⊙

North of the village along D 305.

The location of the observatory in St-Michel was justified by the quality of the air in the Forcalquier region. There are 14 cupolas containing astronomical instruments (among the largest in Europe), laboratories, workshops and living quarters. Many astronomers from France and other countries work here.
One of the telescopes, which has a diameter of 1.93m/6.5ft, was built with the latest electronic refinements. Spectrographs analyse light from the stars, thus establishing their chemical components, their temperature and their radial speed. A team of geophysicists is studying the upper strata of the atmosphere by means of laser sounding.
The **view★** extends to the Luberon, the Préalpes de Grasse, the Prélapes de Digne and the Montagne de Lure, with Forcalquier in the foreground.
From the entrance of the observatory, a path on the right leads to the interesting 11C **Chapelle St-Jean-des-Fuzils**.

ST-PIERRE-DE-CHARTREUSE ✳

Population 660

Michelin map 77 fold 5 or 244 fold 28 – Local map see Massif de la CHARTREUSE

This medium-altitude health resort is sought after in summer and winter by those who enjoy the peaceful setting and the beautiful forested landscapes of the Chartreuse Massif.

THE RESORT

Skiing area – Situated at altitudes ranging from 900m/2 953ft and 1 800m/5 906ft, on the slopes of La Scia, it offers a variety of ski runs but snow cover is unreliable owing to the relatively low altitude and the Col de Porte (alt 1 326m/4 350ft), where snow cover is better, is a welcome alternative.

In summer, St-Pierre-de-Chartreuse is a popular touring and hiking base with 270km/168mi of marked paths. The ascent of the **Dent de Crolles** or of **Mont Granier** is ideal for experienced hikers who do not suffer from vertigo.

★**Terrasse de la Mairie** – Fine **view** of the elegant silhouette of Chamechaude (alt 2 082m/6 831ft) and of the rocky summit of La Pinea across the Col de Porte.

EXCURSION

St-Hugues-de-Chartreuse – *4km south.* The 19C **church** ⊙ looks quite ordinary from the ouside, but, inside, the **sacred art decoration★** in contemporary style is amazing; paintings, sculptures, stained glass, holy objects are signed by a single artist, Jean-Marie Pirot Arcabas, who worked from 1953 to 1986.
Red and gold are the main colours. The works are displayed in three tiers representing different periods. The early red and black paintings on canvas are rather austere whereas those of the upper tier, painted 20 years later, are glitter rather like gilt icons. The predella, completed in 1986 is a mixture of abstract and realist art illustrating the artist's vision of the world. The artist donated the whole of his work to the Isère *département* in 1984.

HIKES

★★**Grand Som** – Alt 2 026m/6 647ft. *Difference in height: 1 175m/3 855ft. Taxing hike: 4hr ascent. The main interest of this itinerary lies in the panoramic view enjoyed from the summit.*
From St-Pierre, drive west along D 520[B] for 3km/2mi; leave the car in the parking reserved for hikers of La Correrie (see Massif de la Chartreuse).
Walk 300m/328yd back along the road and take the road on the right leading to the monastery. Walk alongside it and turn right past a house on the left. The path leads to a calvary; climb to the top of the meadow on the edge of the forest. There is a fine **view** of the monastery.
Return to the road and follow the direction of the Grand Som via the Col de la Ruchère. After walking for 30min and reaching two chapels, take the path *(marked in orange)* on the right; 15min later, turn right again onto a signposted path and shortly after that turn left into a steep path leading to the Habert de Bovinan

Refuge *(45min)*. Continue until you reach the foot of the Grand Som then take the path on the right marked with arrows painted on the rock. At the next intersection, take the stony path used by sheep. From the cross at the summit, there is a magnificent **panorama**★★★ of the whole Chartreuse Massif and a bird's-eye view of the monastery. Mont Blanc and the Belledonne range can be seen in the distance.

★★**Belvédère des Sangles** – *2km/1.2mi then 2hr 30min return on foot. Drive to La Diat and follow the road to St-Laurent-du-Pont. Leave the car beyond the bridge on the Guiers Mort, then cross back and take the Valombré Forest road.*
It leads to the lovely **Prairie de Valombré** which offers the nicest **view**★ of the Grande Chartreuse Monastery, framed by the escarpments of the Grand Som on the right and the forested ridges of the Aliénard on the left.
The road ends at a roundabout. From there, a path climbs up to the **belvedere** overlooking the wooded gorge of the Guiers Mort.

★**Perquelin** – *3km/2mi east.* The path ends in the upper valley of the River Guiers Mort, beneath the escarpments of the Dent de Crolles.

★**La Scia** – *1hr 30min return, including 45min ride on Les Essarts gondola and La Scia chair-lift* ⊙.
It is easy to climb from the upper station of the second section of the gondola to the summit of La Scia (alt 1 782m/5 846ft) which offers a fine **panorama** of the Chartreuse, with the Taillefer, the Obiou and the Vercors to the south, the Dent du Chat and the Grand Colombier to the north.

ST-VÉRAN★★

Population 255
Michelin map 77 fold 19 or 244 fold 43 and 245 fold 10
Local map see Le QUEYRAS

St-Véran, lying at altitudes ranging from 1 990m/6 529ft to 2 040m/6 693ft, is the highest village in Europe. It owes its name to a 6C archbishop who is the hero of a local legend *(see below)*. The houses are built on a gentle slope covered with pastures, which rises to 2 990m/9 810ft at its highest point, the **Pic de Châteaurenard**. St-Véran also includes two hamlets, La Chalp and Le Raux, where several craftsmen are busy carving pieces of furniture.
In summer, the main assets of St-Véran are the quality of its environment and the interesting hikes it offers. In winter, the resort's fairly easy and very sunny skiing area is linked to that of Molines-en-Queyras.

St Véran and the dragon – St Véran fought and wounded a dragon terrorizing the area in the 6C. While the beast was flying off to Provence, 12 drops of blood dripped from its wounds. These later symbolized each of the places where shepherds, moving livestock from the Luberon to summer pastures in the Queyras, used to stop.

St-Véran

THE VILLAGE

★★**Old village** – Built entirely of wood and stone, the village has a characteristic architectural style. Chalets, facing south and spread over a distance of 1km/0.6mi, have long galleries in front of their barns, where cereals go on maturing after the harvest. Each of St-Véran's six districts has its own wooden fountain, *croix de la Passion* and communal oven. Many houses are decorated with elaborate sundials.

THE BEST WAY TO ENJOY YOUR STAY

Traffic banned in summer, except for temporary residents who must obtain a disc from the tourist office. There are several parking areas at the entrance of the village.
There are three distinct hamlets: La Chalp, Le Raux and Le Travers, the last one forming the village centre.
From June to the end of August, the road to the Chapelle Notre-Dame de Clausis is only open to the shuttle service vehicles *(charge)* and to ramblers.
The Italian border being quite close, hikers may wish to cross it and should therefore make sure they carry their identity papers at all times.

At the bottom of the village, on the left as you go in, note the workshop of one of the most famous woodcarvers in the Queyras region. The road climbs up to the village square surrounded by the church, the town hall and the Tourist office.

Church – Situated at the centre of the cemetery, it dates from the 17C. The porch is supported by two columns resting on lions, which belonged to an earlier edifice. Inside, note the stone stoup, the 18C pulpit and the 17C altarpiece carved by Italian artists. The east-end wall is decorated with a sundial.

★**Musée du Soum** ⊙ – *On the right as you go in through the western parking area.* The name means "the end" (of one of the districts); built in 1641, it is the oldest house in the village.
The museum illustrates traditional life in St-Véran through a succession of rooms furnished in local style. It has become a symbol of Haut-Queyras houses, in spite of its typically local features: outside pen for the household's pig, inside courtyard floored with logs and intended for cattle and on the ground floor, "shepherd's room" intended for seasonal workers usually from Piedmont.
In the living room, note the box bed (1842) used by several members of the family, the fireplace – the kitchen would normally be the only room to have a chimney – and the hay rack which is a reminder that humans and cattle cohabitated in winter. Upstairs, the joiner's and the lapidary's workshops have been reconstructed.

Musée de l'Habitat ancien ⊙ – The interior of a house has been preserved exactly as it was at the beginning of the century. It illustrates the daily life of the villagers at that time.

EXCURSIONS

★★**Route de St-Véran** – *See Le Queyras.*

★★★**Drive to the Col Agnel and hike to the Pain de Sucre** – *Allow a minimum of 4hr.* Follow the 4km/2.5mi-long **Route des Amoureux**★ starting in St-Véran and offering views of the northern side of the Guil Valley overlooked by the Pic de Rochebrune. The road leads to Pierre Grosse. Turn right twice towards the Col Agnel *(for the rest of the itinerary, see MOLINES-EN-QUEYRAS).*

HIKES

Chapelle Notre-Dame de Clausis – Alt 2 390m/7 841ft. *Road banned to motor vehicles. Access by shuttle (charge; journey: 20min then 15min on foot as the last section of the road is not suitable for wheeled vehicles) or on foot (3hr return). We advise you to choose the first option.*
The road runs along disused marble quarries and copper mines. Colonies of marmots live in the area. The chapel, where a Franco-Italian pilgrimage takes place on 16 July, stands in the centre of a vast cirque within sight of the surrounding summits soaring to 3 000m/9 843ft.

★★★**Tête des Toillies round tour** – *Splendid but taxing hike offering varied scenery: allow 5hr 30min for the walk and at least 1hr 30min for the breaks. Difference in height: 1 050m/3 445ft. Leave early in the morning, catching the shuttle to Notre-Dame de Clausis no later than 10am.*

The return of the ibex to the Queyras Region

The ibex gradually disappeared from the Alps during the 17C. At the beginning of the 19C, there were fewer than 100 head in the Grand Paradisio Massif on the Italian side. The reintroduction of the ibex within the Parc naturel régional du Queyras took place in 1995 when 12 ibexes were transferred from the Parc national de la Vanoise. Transmitters tied to the animals make it possible to locate them. The Parc régional du Queyras aims to draw the attention of hikers who can be of great help in locating ibexes.

Leave the road on the last bend before the chapel and follow a path straight ahead, which leads to the Lac du Blanchet and to the refuge of the same name. Turn right before the refuge *(yellow markings)* towards the **Col de la Noire** (alt 2 955m/9 695ft) affording **views**★ of the impressive rocky summit of the Tête des Toillies and of nearby peaks.

The path runs down quickly to the **Lac de la Noire**; walk past the lake for another 10min and turn left then immediately head for to the bottom of the valley. Shortly afterwards, there is a tricky passage through the rocks then the path runs along the mountainside to the Lac du Longet and disappears. Join another path leading to the **Col du Longet**, set in a wild landscape of screes dotted with lakes; **view** of Monte Viso.

Walk down for 10min and turn left towards the **Col Blanchet** *(inscription on a rock)*. Allow 45min to climb up to the pass through pastures: striking **panorama**★★ of the Tête des Toillies soaring up to the sky, of the Pelvoux, Pic de Rochebrune, Monte Viso and the Italian Alps.

Allow 1hr 15min to return to the shuttle.

★★**Col St-Véran and Pic de Caramantran** – *Take the shuttle to the Chapelle Notre-Dame de Clausis. Continue on foot for 5min then, just before a bridge, take GR 58 (panel). Difference in height: about 700m/2 297ft.*

It takes 1hr 30min to get to the pass: **view**★ of Monte Viso and Lake Castello on the Italian side. Follow the ridge line on the left, which leads in 30min to the Pic de Caramantran (alt 3 021m/9 911ft): superb **panorama**★★ of the surrounding peaks on both sides of the border.

Follow a path running between the two peaks of the Caramantran to the **Col de Chamoussière**★ offering a fine view of the Pain de Sucre, and return to the shuttle in 1hr 15min along the path marked in white and red.

★★**Crête de Curlet** – *Drive down to Le Cros then turn left to the Pont du Moulin (parking area). Allow 3hr return on foot. Difference in height: 550m/1 804ft.*

Follow GR 58 to the Col des Estronques; as it veers to the right, continue straight on towards the Crête de Curlet through a larch and pine forest. Follow the yellow-marked path in preference to the main path.

After 1hr, turn left onto a steep path, past a small cairn, to the Croix de la Marron: splendid **view**★ of St-Véran, Molines and the surrounding area.

Follow the **ridge line** within sight of the border summits (Caramantran and Les Toillies) then go down to the right through pastures to the bottom of the valley. A marked path leads to Lamaron and the forest beyond, eventually joining up with the original path.

The Caramantran
Caramantran is a character of the Provençal Carnival, traditionally burnt on Ash Wednesday; it is also the name of the festivities taking place at the end of the carnival. In other regions, this traditional character was stoned or thrown into the sea, as in Marseille for instance.

Lac de STE-CROIX★★

Michelin map 81 fold 17, 84 fold 6, 114 folds 7 and 8 or 245 fold 34

When the dam was built in 1975, a 2 200ha/5 436-acre lake filled the Ste-Croix-du-Verdon Basin covered with orchards and fields. The turquoise-coloured lake, into which flows the green River Verdon as it comes out of the famous canyon, is framed by the desolate heights of the Plateau de Valensole and Plan de Canjuers. Its shores have been turned into pleasant beaches and its vast expanse is ideal for the practice of water sports.

TOUR OF THE LAKE (starting from Moustiers)

70km/44mi – about 3hr

★★**Moustiers-Ste-Marie** – *See MOUSTIERS-STE-MARIE.*
From Moustiers, drive towards Riez then turn left towards Ste-Croix.

The road rises in a series of hairpin bends, offering interesting views of Moustiers and its remarkable setting, then runs along the top of the plateau as the lake comes into view.

Ste-Croix – This old hilltop village, which gave its name to the lake, is today almost level with the water. There is a beach along the shore.

The road goes down to the lake.

Barrage de Ste-Croix – The reservoir created by the dam contains 767 million m³/ 621 807acft of water supplying a power station which produces 162 million kWh per year.

Beyond the dam, turn right onto D 71.
The road runs through the Gorges de Baudinard.

Beyond Baudinard, turn left onto the path leading to the chapel. It is preferable to walk (allow 1hr return).

★**View from Notre-Dame de Baudinard** – A small belvedere has been set up on the roof of the chapel; the **view** extends over the Lac de Ste-Croix, the Plateau de Valensole, Plan de Canjuers and, beyond, towards the Alpine summits.

Return to the lake and continue eastwards.

Bauduen – This Provençal village, formerly situated on high ground, is now on the edge of the lake. The setting is nevertheless remarkable. Old houses, with lovely rounded doorways decorated with hollyhock, line the picturesque streets climbing towards the church which stands out against the rocks overlooking the village. The lake shores are equipped for the practice of water sports.

The scenic road planned between Bauduen and Les Salles will avoid the detour via St-Andrieux, along D 49 and D 957.

Les Salles-sur-Verdon – The old village of Les Salles is now lying 40m/131ft below the surface of the lake. A few architectural features (doors, tiles), as well as the church steeple and the village fountain were saved and used again when the new village developed on the shores of the lake.

Continue along D 957 to Moustiers past the leisure park.

Anglers, please abide by the national regulations concerning the minimum size allowed depending on the catch. Throw back into the water fish whose size is smaller than 40cm/16in for a pike or 23cm/10in for a trout.

Lac de Ste-Croix

*The chapter on **Practical information** at the end of the guide lists :*
– local or national organisations providing additional information;
– events of interest to the tourist
– admission times and charges.

STE-FOY-TARENTAISE

Population 643
Michelin map 89 fold 6 or 244 fold 21 – Local map see Massif de la VANOISE

Built on high ground overlooking the east bank of the River Isère, between Bourg-St-Maurice and Val-d'Isère, and surrounded by traditional villages and hamlets, Ste-Foy-Tarentaise is the ideal starting point of pleasant excursions in the area.

HIKES

★★**La Sassière** – *10km/6.2mi then 2hr return on foot. Leave Ste-Foy-Tarentaise towards the Col de l'Iseran and turn onto the first road on the left.*
After driving for 2km/1.2mi, you will come within sight of **Le Miroir**, a large hamlet whose chalets, climbing up the south-facing slope, have wooden balconies.
The road continues to rise, eventually reaching the high-pasture area where houses are built of stone with small openings and flat roofs covered with *lauzes* (heavy slabs of schist) in order to withstand bitter winter conditions.
Leave the car at the end of the road and continue on foot.

The path rises among clusters of alpenrose. As you approach the Chapelle de la Sassière, the Rutor Glacier, situated across the Italian border and overlooking a pastoral landscape, suddenly comes into **view**★★.

Le Monal

★★**Viewpoint from Le Monal** – *8km/5mi then 1hr return on foot. Drive south along D 902 then turn left to Chenal. Leave the car there and continue on foot.*
From the hamlet, there is a remarkable **view** of the Mont Pourri and its glaciers, in particular the waterfalls coming down from the Glacier de la Gurra and the village of La Gurraz below.

Notre-Dame de la SALETTE★

Michelin map 77 fold 16 or 244 fold 40 – 15km/9.3mi north of Corps

The basilica stands in a remote high-pasture area, at an altitude of 1 770m/5 807ft. It is a place of pilgrimage to the Virgin Mary, particularly famous for the beauty of its natural and austere **setting**★.

The weeping Virgin – On 19 September 1846, Mary appeared to two young shepherds, a boy aged 11 and a girl aged 14, in the form of a woman weeping. She spoke to them at length, in French and in local dialect, then climbed up a steep path and disappeared in a halo of light.
Five years later, in 1851, at the end of a thorough investigation, the Church acknowledged the testimony of the two children and accepted the message of reconciliation brought by the "Beautiful Lady". A basilica was built and today the sanctuary welcomes between 150 000 and 200 000 pilgrims a year.

FROM CORPS TO NOTRE-DAME DE LA SALETTE

15km/9.3mi – about 1hr

Corps – *See Barrage et Lac du SAUTET.*

Between Corps and the village of La Salette, the road follows the deep and green valley of the Sezia, past a cemetery containing the graves of the Canadian victims of the air crash which happened on 13 November 1950.

The road rises rapidly from the village to Notre-Dame de la Salette within sight of the imposing Obiou Peak (2 793m/9 163ft).

Vast parking areas are available at the Col de l'Homme and near the basilica.

★**Notre-Dame de la Salette** – It is the venue of many pilgrimages.
The most important takes place on 19 September, on the anniversary of the apparition of the Virgin Mary. The main events are:
9am and 2pm: audiovisual presentation of the apparition.
10 45am: mass inside the basilica.
3pm: pilgrims' meetings.
6pm: rosary and meditation.
8 30pm: torchlight procession.
It is possible to spend the night in the hostel ⊙.
Behind the basilica, walk round a mound surmounted by a cross to enjoy a panoramic **view**★ of the Oisans, Dévoluy and Beaumont regions.

★★**Mont Gargas** – Alt 2 207m/7 241ft. *2hr return on foot. Climb northwards along marked paths to the Col de l'Éterpat then follow the ridge line to the left.* Vast **panorama** of the Obiou and of the heights south of the Oisans.

Le SALÈVE ★

Michelin map 89 folds 15 and 16 or 244 folds 7 and 8

The tiered cliffs of the Mont Salève (highest point: Grand Piton, 1 380m/4 528ft), towering above Geneva from the French side of the border, are one of the favourite haunts of Swiss tourists. The area is particularly sought after by rock-climbers who have adopted the name of one of the most tricky sections, **varappe**, as a general term meaning rock-climbing.
A road following the ridge line offers, all along the way, splendid views of the Arve Valley and the Faucigny heights to the east with the Mont-Blanc Massif in the distance, and of Geneva and its lake to the west with the Jura mountains in the background.

★★LE SALÈVE CABLE-CAR ⊙

Departure from the Pas de l'Échelle, 500m/547yd south of the customs post of Veyrier. The cable-car leads to a ridge from which there is a breathtaking **view**★ of Geneva, Lake Geneva and the Jura mountains. Climb above the station to a bend marked by a panel for a view of Mont Blanc.
It is also possible to follow D 41 *(30min)* up to the Treize-Arbres Hotel.

FROM CRUSEILLES TO ANNEMASSE

34km/21mi – about 1hr 45min

The itinerary goes through the free zone (see Practical information) in two places: Les Lirons and Bas-Mornex. Road D 41 is closed to tourist traffic in winter between Les Avenières and the Col de la Croisette. This drive is particularly attractive in the late-afternoon light.

Cruseilles – Situated on the lower slopes of the Salève, overlooking the deep and narrow valley of the Usses, the village has retained a specimen (Maison de Fésigny, near the church) of the opulent 14C-15C residences typical of the area.
The **Parc des Dronières**, a vast outdoor leisure centre built round a 6ha/15-acre expanse of water, lies 1.5km/0.9mi east of the village.

The road rises through the forest on the slopes of the Plan de Salève, offering **glimpses**★★ of the Bornes depression linking Annecy and the Arve Valley against a mountain background formed by the Faucigny, the Bargy, the Jallouvre and the Pointe Percée, with the snow-capped Mont Blanc in the distance.
Between Petit Pommier and the Col de la Croisette, the cliff road affords bird's-eye views of Geneva and the pointed end of the lake.
Further north, there are closer views of Lake Geneva as far as the opposite shore and the Swiss town of Lausanne.

Grande Gorge – Geneva and the meandering Arve River can be seen through this break. A parapet runs along the edge of the road at this point.

★★**Les Treize-Arbres Viewing table** – *15min return on foot along a path starting from the parking of the hotel-restaurant.* From there, the **panoramic view** embraces a long succession of summits from the Dents du Midi to Mont Blanc. The rocky ridge is one of the favourite sites of paragliders.

Monnetier-Mornex – This important holiday resort stretches its long line of villas right down to the Viaison Valley.

Annemasse – Important border town and economic centre influenced by the proximity of Geneva.

SALLANCHES

Population 12 767
Michelin map 89 fold 6 or 244 fold 20 – Local map see Le FAUCIGNY

Situated at the entrance of the long transverse valley of the Arve, Sallanches offers a superb **view**★★ of Mont Blanc, particularly spectacular at sunset. In place Charles-Albert, a viewing table gives details of the panorama.
Sallanches is an important centre of medium-altitude excursions and tourist facilities include a leisure and sports complex known as **Mont-Blanc-Plage**, on the shores of the **Lacs de Cavettaz** *(2km/1.2mi).*

SIGHTS

Church – This imposing edifice is decorated in Italian style. The christening chapel on the left as you go in, houses a small Flamboyant ciborium and, inside a glass case, a collection of silver religious objects, including a 15C monstrance.

Château des Rubins – Introduction to nature in mountainous areas ⊙ – This 17C castle displays, on two levels, an instructive presentation of ecosystems in mountainous areas. The food chain in forested areas is explained on the first floor, whereas the second floor is devoted to animal life in high-pasture areas (hibernation of marmots) and man's activities conditioned by the rhythm of the seasons. Specific lake ecosystems and the role of water are also illustrated as are the ways in which life adapts to high altitude and relief.

Plane trips ⊙ – *Cross the Arve and turn left after the bridge to reach the airfield.*
The AMS Company organizes round trips over the Mont-Blanc Massif all year round.

Bassin de SALLANCHES★★

Michelin map 89 fold 4 or 244 folds 9 and 20

In spite of the omnipresence of Mont Blanc, towering some 4 000m/13 000ft above Sallanches, the tiered escarpments forming an amphitheatre to the north also draw the attention of visitors. The basin is framed by the Pointe Percée (alt 2 752m/9 029ft), the highest summit of the Aravis range, to the west and by the **Chaîne des Fiz** which extends its strange rocky heights to the east; the strangest of these is no doubt the **Désert de Platé**, a desolate and deeply fissured limestone plateau covering an area of 15km²/6sq mi.
The Sallanches Depression lies at the intersection of tourist routes converging towards the Chamonix Valley.

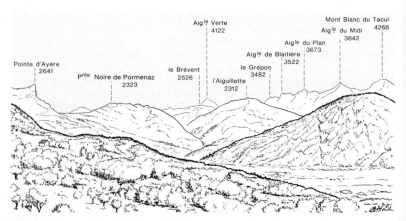

★THE OLD SERVOZ ROAD

13km from Sallanches – allow 30min

This itinerary follows the old Sallanches to Chamonix road, described by generations of travellers – particularly during the Romantic period – thrilled to be getting close to Mont Blanc.

Sallanches – *See SALLANCHES.*

From Sallanches, D 13 crosses the motorway and then the River Arve, 150m/164yd upstream of the old humpback bridge of **St-Martin**, painted and photographed many times over the past 100 years.

The road then climbs up the last slopes of the Plateau d'Assy and, between Passy and Servoz, it overlooks the narrow industrial Chedde Plain and the gorge through which the railway enters the Servoz Basin. Ahead is the narrow wooded valley of the Diosaz. Just beyond the hamlet of Joux, the imposing **Viaduc des Egratz** comes into view: this materpiece of modern engineering, carrying the Chamonix motorway, is 2 277m/2 490yd long and some of its pillars are 68m/223ft high.

The road then goes through a wood, crosses a stream, offers glimpses of the Arve Valley towards the glaciers of the Dôme du Goûter and enters the verdant Servoz Basin.

Servoz – The village lies at the heart of a wooded basin beneath the cliffs of the Fiz mountains and the scree-covered slopes of the Pas du Dérochoir.

★**Gorges de la Diosaz** – *See Massif du MONT-BLANC.*

★★FROM PASSY TO PLAINE-JOUX VIA PLATEAU D'ASSY

12km/7.5mi along D 43 – allow 1hr 30min

The road, branching off the Servoz road in Passy, rises onto wooded south-facing ledges, well sheltered from the wind and dotted with health establishments and family holiday homes. During the climb, the view gets gradually broader, embracing the Mont-Blanc Massif and the Chaîne des Fiz.

★★**Pavillon de Charousse** – *500m/547yd southwest of Bay. Leave the car in front of the Relais de Charousse and take the path on the left of the chapel leading to the wooded mound on which the house stands.*

Remarkable **panorama** *(see p 293).*

It is possible to walk along the edge of the escarpment, on the right of the house, to admire the view of Sallanches and the Aravis Massif.

As the road reaches Plateau d'Assy, the Aiguille Verte can be seen pointing behind the Brévent.

★**Plateau d'Assy** – *See PLATEAU D'ASSY.*

The road then goes through a forested area before reaching Plaine-Joux.

★★**Plaine-Joux** – A chalet at the centre of this small skiing resort houses the Information Centre of the **Réserve naturelle de Passy** covering 2 000ha/4 942 acres.

Beyond Plaine-Joux, the road reaches an open area of high pastures offering close-up **views** of the cliffs of the Fiz range and of the scree-covered Pas du Dérochoir.

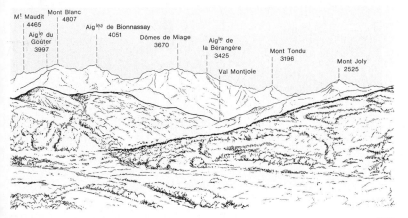

★**Lac Vert** – The lake, surrounded by firs and overlooked by the escarpments of the Fiz mountains, is of a dark green colour *(you can walk round in 15min)*.

Most ski resorts are also pleasant summer resorts offering a wide choice of outdoor activities: hiking, rock-climbing, hang-gliding, tennis, mountain biking, even summer skiing..., as well as other leisure activities such as the discovery of a region's architectural heritage, an introduction to botany, a course in photography or birdwatching.

★★★FROM SALLANCHES TO ST-GERVAIS VIA COMBLOUX

18km/11.2mi – allow 45min

The roads running along the mountainside offer splendid and varied overall views of the Mont-Blanc Massif and of the escarpments forming an amphitheatre to the north of the basin.

From Sallanches, drive south along N 212 towards Albertville.

The approach to Combloux affords broad views of the Aravis range, the Fiz mountains and the southern part of the Mont-Blanc Massif.

✳**Combloux** – *See COMBLOUX.*

3km/1.9mi north of Megève, turn left towards Chamonix.

On the way down to St-Gervais, there are views of the *cluse* (transverse valley) of the Arve, downstream of Sallanches, framed by the Aravis and Fiz mountains, with the Pointe de Marcelly and the Roc d'Enfer straight ahead.

D 909 reaches St-Gervais.

♯♯ **St-Gervais-les-Bains** – *See ST-GERVAIS-LES-BAINS.*

★★ROUND TOUR VIA CORDON *11km/6.8mi – allow 1hr*

Sallanches – *See SALLANCHES.*

From Sallanches, drive west along D 113 towards Cordon.

The road winds its way along the ridge separating the gorges of the Rivers Sallanche and Frasse, as Mont Blanc comes into sight.

Cordon – This charming village, backed by the Aravis mountains, occupies an attractive **position**★ facing the prestigious Mont-Blanc Massif, amid orchards of cherry and walnut trees. In winter, the resort offers possibilities of Alpine and cross-country skiing, as well as sledge rides. The 18C church is a fine example of Savoyard Baroque style, including interesting paintings and a rich central **altarpiece** with twisted columns.

As you leave Cordon, follow the road to Combloux then turn left towards Nant Cruy. Drive through the village.

The gilt onion-shaped steeple of Cordon's church can be seen above the orchards.

The road runs down to an intersection (2km/1.2mi); turn right to the Chapelle du Médonnet (600m/656yd).

Chapelle du Médonnet – The east end of this unassuming little chapel faces a magnificent **panorama**★★ which includes, from left to right, the Pointe d'Areu, the Chaîne des Fiz, the Aiguilles Rouges and the Mont-Blanc Massif from the Aiguille Verte to the Aiguille de la Bérangère.

Turn round to go back to Sallanches then right towards N 212.

P. Jacques/FOC

Cordon

SAMOËNS ✶✶

Population 2 148
Michelin map 89 fold 3 or 244 folds 9 and 10 – Local map see Le FAUCIGNY

Samoëns lies at the bottom of a wide glacial valley through which flows the River Giffre. Each its nine satellite hamlets, scattered over the forested slopes, has a chapel surmounted by a graceful onion-shaped steeple. In spite of its considerable expansion, Samoëns has retained a wealth of traditional stone houses built by its famous stone-masons.

This tourist centre of the Haut-Faucigny is the ideal starting point of untaxing hikes and splendid mountain excursions. Summer activities include mountaineering, canoeing and rafting on the Giffre, swimming, tennis as well as paragliding and hang-gliding which have become a local speciality. In winter, the resort is linked by gondola and lifts to the skiing area of the Grand Massif.

Stonemasons of Samoëns – Stone-cutting has been a local speciality since 1659, when the village's stonemasons and builders founded a brotherhood. They were called to work all over France, taking part in Vauban's military projects or building canals, and even went abroad, to Poland and Louisiana. The brotherhood also did benevolent work, looking after the sick, training the young; it had its own drawing school and a large library. It was revived in 1979 when an association was created to preserve the architectural heritage of Samoëns and organise guided tours.

The good "Samaritan" – Louise Jaÿ was born in 1838 in le Villard, one of the local hamlets; at the age of 15, she went to Paris to work as a sales girl and met Ernest Cognacq with whom she founded "la Samaritaine" department store. Having acquired a large fortune, the couple, who had no children, devoted the last years of their life to charitable work. In Samoëns, Louise Cognacq-Jaÿ created an Alpine garden, had a house built for the doctor and paid for the restoration of the church.

SIGHTS

★**Place du Gros Tilleul** – Located at the centre of the village, the square owes its name to the lime tree planted here in 1438.

La Grenette, a 16C covered market, restored in the 18C, stands on the south side; note the strange "bulges" on the central pillars: the arms of Samoëns were to be carved on these pillars, but the mason did not complete his work following a disagreement with the municipality over his contract. A lovely fountain (**E**) stands in the centre of the square and the north side is lined with the Château de la Tour and the church.

Church – The church was rebuilt in the 16C and 17C; at the foot of the 12C bell tower, a graceful canopy covered with copper scales shelters a 16C doorway with older features including two lions supporting twisted columns.

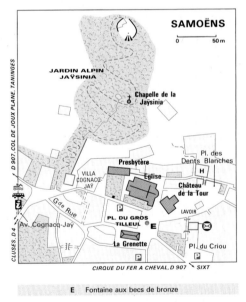

E   Fontaine aux becs de bronze

The stained-glass windows on the left, dating from 1982, depict the four patron saints of the stonemasons' brotherhood.
The baptistery chapel is in Flamboyant Gothic style. The stoup was carved in 1844 out of a single block of marble.
The sundial decorating the front of the **presbytery** indicates the time in 12 large cities of the world.

Maison de la Jaÿsinia – Situated at the garden entrance, it contains documents relating the story of the village's benefactress.

295

Chapelle de la Jaÿsinia, Samoëns

⋆**Jardin botanique alpin Jaÿsinia** ⊘ – These botanical gardens, complete with pools and waterfalls and covering an area of 3ha/7.5 acres, were created in 1906 by Louise Cognacq-Jaÿ on sloping ground ovelooking the village; they contain more than 5 000 species of mountain plants from the main temperate areas of the world. Walking past the **Chapelle de la Jaÿsinia**, one reaches the terrace and its ruined castle offering an extended view of Samoëns and the surrounding mountains.

What more could you want to restore your strength at the end of a tiring hike than the local "soupe châtrée". This nourishing soup is made with slices of bread soaked in onion sauce, covered with Tomme de Savoie (the local cheese) and browned under the grill. Wooden spoons are best to deal with the melted cheese.

EXCURSIONS

Les Vallons – *2km/1.2mi along D 907 towards Sixt, then a road on the left.* This hamlet is interesting for its lovely stone fountains and its chapel.

⋆⋆**La Rosière (view)** – *6km. Leave Samoëns along D 907 towards Sixt; turn left almost immediately towards Les Allamands, left again 750m/0.5mi further on and sharp right 1km/0.6mi after that.* From la Rosière, there is a particularly fine view of Mont Blanc framed by the forested Rochers du Criou and the rock face of the Pointe de Sales.

⋆⋆**Col de Joux Plane** – *10km/6.2mi via Chantemerle and D 354. See MORZINE.*

⋆⋆**Cirque du Fer à Cheval** – *13km/8mi east. See Le FAUCIGNY.*

Barrage et lac du SAUTET ★★

Michelin map 77 folds 15 and 16 or 244 fold 40 – Local map see Le DÉVOLUY

The Sautet Dam was built across the downstream end of the canyon (200m/656ft deep and only 7m/23ft wide in places) through which flows the Drac, thus creating a picturesque reservoir and enhancing the charm of the area.

SIGHTS

⋆⋆**Barrage** – This elegant arch dam, 126m/413ft high, has created a reservoir of 115 million m³/93 231acft. The hydroelectric power station, situated downstream, was partly built underground.

⋆**Pont du Sautet** – Road D 537 crosses the River Drac over this bridge, a daring piece of engineering with a single reinforced-concrete arch spanning 86m/282ft.

⋆**Lac** – The flooded valley of the Souloise, a tributary of the Drac, forms the most picturesque of the two arms of the lake, overlooked by the imposing Obiou Summit.

ROUND TOUR OF THE LAKE (starting from Corps)

35km/22mi – allow 2hr

Corps – Overlooking the Lac du Sautet, the capital of the **Beaumont** region (middle Drac Valley between Corps and the confluence of the Bonne) is a lively summer resort along the famous Route Napoléon *(see ROUTE NAPOLÉON)* and a convenient meeting place for pilgrims on their way to Notre-Dame de la Salette.

Follow N 85 south towards Gap and, as you leave Corps, turn right past the Total petrol station. Walk the last 91m/100yd, as it is impossible to turn round further on. The small **Chapelle St Roch** ⊘, overlooking the lake, has some interesting modern stained-glass windows.

Rejoin N 85.

This road overlooks the lake. At Le Motty, turn right towards Ambel along D 217 which rises above the south bank of the lake and soon offers views of the Obiou, the Vercors Massif, Corps and the heights of Notre-Dame de la Salette *(beware of falling rocks).*

Beyond Ambel, the road runs above the lower Souloise Valley which forms the other arm of the lake; the Grand-Ferrand soars straight ahead. The road then runs down to the bottom of the valley; from the bridge over the Souloise, there is a view of the Petites Gillardes, resurgent springs which are dry during certain periods.

1km/0.6mi beyond the bridge, turn right onto D 537.

Past Pellafol, there is a fine view on the right of the promontory crowned by the village of Ambel; the road then goes over the Sautet Bridge and leads back to Corps.

SERRE-CHEVALIER ✳✳✳

Michelin map 77 folds 7, 17 and 18 or 244 fold 42
Local map see Le BRIANÇONNAIS

Situated in the Guisane Valley, between the Col du Lautaret and Briançon, Serre-Chevalier is the largest and most northern winter sports complex in the southern Alps. The resort, sheltered by the surrounding mountains, enjoys a microclimate characterised by 300 days of sunshine a year.

Facilities and accommodation are spread over four main sites (Le Monêtier, Villeneuve, Chantemerle and Briançon) but there are, in fact, 13 villages and hamlets on either side of the road leading to the Col du Lautaret.

THE RESORT

Skiing area – Created in 1941, the resort is now equipped with 70 lifts giving access to 250km/155mi of north-facing ski runs, suitable for skiers of all levels of competency but particularly well-suited to amateurs of snowboarding and surfing. The first-section runs go through a larch forest and are equipped with snow-cannon. The second section is more exposed and snow cover is adequate until mid-April. The Serre-Chevalier Summit, rapidly accessible from Chantemerle and Villeneuve, is at the heart of the skiing area. Briançon, to the southeast, is linked to the complex at an altitude of 2 500m/8 202ft by the Prorel lifts. At the other end of the complex, Le Monêtier offers the wildest and most appealing section, suitable for good skiers. The Yret (alt 2 800m/9 186ft) and Cibouit chairlifts give access to remarkable off-piste runs affording lovely scenery. The fine Cucumelle red run leads down to Villeneuve. In addition, there are 45km/28mi of cross-country skiing tracks at the bottom of the valley, from Le Lauzet to Villeneuve and from Chantemerle to Briançon.

In summer, the valley offers a wide range of activities: mountain biking, canoeing on the Guisane, riding tours, paragliding and hang-gliding. It is also the starting point of medium-altitude hikes (Parc national des Écrins, Cerces Massif) and excursions to the Oisans Massif (the Rateau, the Meije and the Dôme des Écrins).

The valley's 13 villages are grouped into three municipalities: Saint-Chaffrey, La Salle-les-Alpes and Monêtier-les-Bains. Traditional stone houses, nestling round 13C and 15C churches, stand next to modern buildings housing shops, hotels and apartments. Yet each resort retains its own character and activities within the vast skiing area known as the "**Grand Serre-Che**".

Monêtier-les-Bains, also called **Serre-Chevalier 1500**, owes its name to a monastery and its hot springs, already famous in Roman times. Today, Monêtier is a spa and ski resort with reasonable access to the "Grand Serre-Che" ski runs and adequate snowmaking equipment. Its appeal lies in its traditional architecture, including a 15C **church** ⊘ with Lombard arcading, and its peaceful atmosphere.

The ski runs are at least 5min by car from the village.

Villeneuve (Serre-Chevalier 1400) and **Chantemerle** (Serre-Chevalier 1350) – These modern functional resorts lack charm but offer direct access to the ski runs and a choice of après-ski activities (swimming, skating, fitness club, riding, ice-driving).

Briançon *(see BRIANÇON)*, now linked to the skiing area by the **Téléphérique du Prorel** ⊙, is known as **Serre-Chevalier 1200** and has an impressive number of snow-cannon. Night-skiing is another possibility.

The old hamlets are less functional but more picturesque and more restful.

La Salle-les-Alpes is particularly interesting for its religious architecture. The **Église St-Marcellin** has a Romanesque bell tower (13C-14C), surmounted by a spire and four pyramidions from an earlier edifice, an elegant 16C canopied south porch and a late Gothic nave with quadripartite vaulting. The chancel altarpiece, dating from the 17C, is framed by Baroque ornamentation including twisted columns and recesses. The lectern and pulpit are the work of local artists.

The **Chapelle St-Barthélemy** ⊙, standing on a platform overlooking the Guisane Valley, is decorated with murals depicting various saints and scenes from the life and martyrdom of St Bartholomew.

St Chaffrey, which was the starting point of the skiing complex, has an interesting bridge which can be raised in case of flooding. The 11C **Chapelle St-Arnoult** ⊙, situated on high ground behind the church, contains fine frescoes.

Le Bez, overlooking Villeneuve, is another hamlet worth exploring.

HIKES

Starting from Chantemerle

★★Sommet de Serre-Chevalier – Alt 2 483m/8 146ft. *Access from Chantemerle by a two-section cable-car ⊙.* From the upper station, climb to the viewing table: splendid **panorama★★★** of the Oisans Massif to the west, the Aiguilles d'Arves and Pic du Galibier to the northwest, the Vanoise to the north and the Queyras to the east.

★★Hike round the Eychauda Summit – *5hr on foot on fairly level ground. Get a 1:25 000 map; the hike starts in Chantemerle and ends in Le Monêtier; return to Chantemerle by coach (information from the Tourist office).*

Take the cable-car to the top of Serre-Chevalier. From the viewing table, go down towards the Col de Serre-Chevalier and follow tracks leading to the path going round the Eychauda and walk up to the **Col de la Pisse** (alt 2 501m/8 205ft).

The path runs along the mountainside, offering lovely **views★★** of the Eychauda Lake and the Pelvoux Massif *(a few tricky sections)*, and finally reaches the **Col de l'Eychauda**, overlooking the Col du Lautaret road. A large path leads down to a mountain restaurant. Go to the left, leave the path and take another one to the right *(GR 54, marked in white and red, sometimes in yellow)*. It follows the stream, crosses it and enters a pleasant larch forest.

Towards the end of the hike, continue straight on past a chapel and follow a small road going down to the left. When you reach a square with a playground, turn right, cross a small bridge and walk up the rue de la Grande-Turière. As you join the Route Nationale, the coach stop is on your right, just before the post office.

Hiking in Les Écrins

Starting from Le Bez

Botanical trail – *Start from the road to Fréjus. About 2hr untaxing round tour.* Leave the car near the starting point. There are explanatory panels along the way.

From Le Bez to Le Monêtier – *Start from the rock-climbing school; 4hr return on foot; untaxing hike.* Walk towards Fréjus then take the path rising to the Clos de la Salette above the rock-climbing site; at the intersection, turn right to Le Monêtier. The viewpoint offers a panorama of the Guisane Valley. The path runs down to a stream and into the Monêtier Valley.

Starting from Le Casset

★**Lac de la Douche and Col d'Arsine** – *Starting from the village: 1hr 45min return on foot to the lake and 5hr return to the Col d'Arsine along GR 54. Difference in height: 800m/2 625ft. Very easy hike to the lake; walking shoes necessary beyond.* Walk through Le Casset and across the bridge on the Guisane. The path runs through a larch wood offering views of the Casset Glacier before reaching the **Lac de la Douche**. Beyond the lake, the landscape becomes more arid and the path skirts a series of small lakes on its way to the pass (alt 2 340m/7 677ft). *Retrace your steps.*

Starting from Le Lauzet

★★**Lac du Combeynot** – *5hr return along a path marked in blue. It is forbidden to take dogs inside the central zone of the Parc national des Écrins.* Start from Les Boussardes, 200m/219yd south of Le Lauzet. On the way up to the lake, hikers are likely to meet chamois *(keep to the path and do not disturb them)*. The splendid glacial lake (alt 2 555m/8 383ft) is 16m/52ft deep.

★**Via ferrata de l'Aiguillette du Lauzet** – These high limestone cliffs are the favourite haunt of rock-climbers from the Briançon area. Via ferrata climbing has become very popular in the last few years and the parking area near the starting point of the different courses is very congested *(see Practical information)*.

Starting from the Col du Lautaret

This hike takes at least 7hr; it is imperative to be picked up by car from Le Casset.

★**Réserve naturelle du Combeynot** – *Start from the Refuge Napoléon at the Col du Lautaret. Not recommended in rainy weather, after a snowfall, and for persons who suffer from vertigo.* Walk across N 91, then due west along the marked Sentier des Crevasses. The path goes through the nature reserve and round the west side of the Pic du Combeynot before joining GR 54 at the Col d'Arsine. On the way up to the Refuge de l'Alpe du Villard *(food available)*, there are fine views of the Romanche Valley and numerous opportunities to observe high-altitude flora and birdlife. Continue to the Col d'Arsine and enjoy the splendid panorama of the glacial valleys, the Pic de Neige Cordier (3 613m/11 854ft) and the Arsine Glacier. The path then runs down to the lovely Lac de la Douche and back to the Guisane along the Petit Tabuc Valley.

Barrage et lac de SERRE-PONÇON ★★

Michelin map 77 folds 17 and 18, 81 fold 7 or 245 folds 8 and 9

The River Durance comes down from the Montgenèvre, flows through the Briançonnais region and is joined by two tributaries, the Queyras and the Ubaye. This typical mountain stream has a reduced flow in winter. It was therefore decided in 1955 to compensate for this irregular flow by building a dam.

SIGHTS

★★**The dam** – It was the first time an earth dam with a waterproof core of clay was built on such a scale in France, by applying a technique widely used in the USA. The dyke, made up of alluvial material from the river bed, is 600m/1969ft long at the top, 650m/2 133ft wide at the base and 123m/404ft high. The clay core has a volume of 2 million m³/1 621acft against a total volume of 14 million m³/11 350acft. A mixture of clay and concrete is used to prevent seepage.

Power station ⊙ – Imbedded in the rock of the south bank, the power station can produce 720 million kWh per year. In order to regulate the flow of the Durance downstream of the dam, a reservoir covering 100ha/247 acres was created on the site where the alluvial soil was removed.
The latest works completing the harnessing of the river have increased the production of electricity to a total of 6 billion kWh per year.

Barrage et lac de SERRE-PONÇON

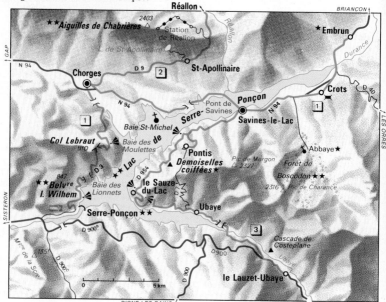

★★The lake – Created in 1960, the lake, covering an area of 3 000ha/7 413 acres *(more than the Lac d'Annecy)*, is one of the largest reservoirs in Europe *(20km long, 3km wide at its widest; capacity: 1 270 million m3/1 029 589acft)*.

The curved shape of the lake, its indented shores and the promontory marking the confluence of the Durance and the Ubaye have made it easier for this vast expanse of water to blend with the natural scenery and to offer at the same time a variety of water sports.

EXCURSIONS

1 From the lower dam to Embrun *39km/24mi – allow 1hr 30min*

Road D 3 to Chorges follows the downstream reservoir before rising sharply within sight of the riprap embankment of the dam.

★★Belvédère Ivan-Wilhem – This viewpoint (alt 847m/2 779ft), built along the axis of the ridge line of the dam and named after the engineer who designed the dam, offers a fine overall view.

Beyond the tunnel, the road veers away from the lake.

Col Lebraut – Alt 1 110m/3 642ft. From the pass, there is a view of the Gap Basin to the west and of the lake to the east. Further on *(1.2km/0.7mi)*, the **panorama★** extends to the whole northeast arm of the lake.

Chorges – From its prosperous past, the village has retained a few old houses, a lovely 16C fountain and a hilltop church with a rounded 12C porch; to the right stands an imposing pink-marble stela, known as "Nero's stone", which might be the pedestal of a Roman statue. Also noteworthy is the 14C bell-tower with its two tiers of windows and its narrow-stone bond.

From Chorges, the Savines road runs east towards the lake; note, on the right, a chapel standing on a tiny island in the **Baie St-Michel**. Further on, N 94 runs across the lake over the **Pont de Savines**, practically level with the water.

Savines-le-Lac – The village, which disappeared beneath the surface of the lake, was rebuilt here. **Boat trips** ⊙ are organised.

Beyond Savines, a road branching off to the right leads to the Boscodon Abbey and Forest *(see Abbaye de BOSCODON)*.

Crots – Lying on the edge of the lake, this ancient village and its 14C church are overlooked by the 13C **Château de Picomtal** ⊙, extended in the 16C.

Just before Embrun, the road crosses the Durance near the expanse of water reserved for sailing and water sports.

★Embrun – See EMBRUN.

② Vallée de Réallon *18km/11mi – allow 1hr*

Two alternative access roads: D 41 north from the Pont de Savines or D 9 from Chorges; choose the second one in preference.

From Chorges, D 9 offers lovely views on its way to **St-Apollinaire**, a picturesque village overlooking the Serre-Ponçon Lake. The pastoral Lac de St-Apollinaire can be reached along a road on the left. This route sometimes forms part of the Monte-Carlo Rally.

Réallon – The church spire soars above the village which has retained its Alpine atmosphere and is now a pleasant family ski resort. It has also been a famous archeological site since the discovery last century of Bronze-Age precious objects, including a set of jewellery exhibited in the Gap Museum. The **Église St-Pléaide**, built on a narrow ledge, has an interesting 13C bell-tower topped by two rows of rounded twinned windows.

Fort Carré – *About 1hr on foot. Walk towards the waterfall above the village.* Follow the stream to an oak and pine forest; the path reaches a plateau crowned with the ruins of the 15C fort. Fine view of the Aiguilles de Chabrières.

★★**Aiguilles de Chabrières** – *5hr hike to be attempted in clear weather only.* The itinerary goes across a deeply gullied limestone plateau to the ridge of the Aiguilles de Chabrières. Bad visibility can be dangerous. From the resort, follow the path with yellow markings, known as the "Tour des Aiguilles-Serre-du-Mouton" *(Detailed topo-guides are available at the tourist office).*

③ From Savines-le-Lac to Le Lauzet-Ubaye
25km/15.5mi – allow 1hr

Savines-le-Lac – *See drive* ①.

From Savines, D 954 winds along the indented shore of the lake; the view becomes gradually broader, embracing the wild southern part of the lake *(on a bend to the left; parking facilities).*

A small road, branching off to the left, leads to Pontis.

Pontis – The old school houses a **museum** ⊘ illustrating 19C schooling conditions.

Turn back towards D 954.

★**Demoiselles coiffées de Pontis** – *For more details about these strange rock formations, see Demoiselles coiffées de THÉUS.* There are 12 of them here. It is possible to get quite close along a stony path *(30min return on foot).*

Le Sauze-du-Lac – The village is picturesquely situated on top of a promontory overlooking the lake, at the confluence of the Durance and Ubaye rivers.

The road winds rapidly down, offering a clear **view** of the Ubaye arm of the lake. On the opposite shore, the scenery is wild and the shoreline deeply indented.

Demoiselles coiffées de Pontis

Ubaye – The church and the cemetery are all that remains of the flooded village.

The road runs through two tunnels *(single lane)* then across a bridge at the extremity of the lake. The **Cascade de Costeplane** flows through a deep gorge near the intersection of D 954 and D 900.

Continue along D 900 towards Barcelonnette.

Le Lauzet-Ubaye – The village lies next to a small lake (*lauzet* in local dialect). A Roman bridge spans the river near the modern one *(15min return on foot).*

For a description of the lower-Ubaye itinerary from Le Lauzet-Ubaye to Barcelonnette, see L'UBAYE.

For an insight into Alpine flora, read the chapter on "Vegetation" in the Introduction.

SEYNE

Population 1 222
Michelin map 81 fold 7 or 245 fold 8

The strategic position of this small town along the valley of the River Blanche, close to the Durance, explains why, in the 17C, Vauban ordered fortifications to be built. In the 19C, part of the local population emigrated to Mexico and returned later.

Today, Seyne is a sunny summer and winter resort (with an annexe at Grand-Puy), but horse and mule breeding are still traditional activities and a mule show and horse fair take place every year *(see Practical information).*

Mules from Seyne

The mule show (second Saturday in August) and the mule and horse fair (St Matthew's day, 21 September) testify to a strong tradition which brought fame and prosperity to the town. The mule is a remarkable beast of burden, used in the past in mountain areas for farming and for carrying munitions and food to isolated mountain troops *(chasseurs alpins)*. Young mules, which are the sterile offspring of a male donkey and a female horse, were cared for and trained by specialists until the age of two. They were then sent, depending on demand, either to the nearby Drôme *département* or to Spain or even to Algeria. This activity remained vital until the 1950s, but the introduction of tractors and the progress made by artificial-insemination techniques caused it to decline rapidly. However, the development of tourism and pony-trekking in rural areas has recently given it a new lease of life.

SIGHTS

Church ⊙ – This fine example of Romanesque architecture in mountain areas has features in common with Notre-Dame-du-Bourg in Digne. The attractive pink and blue 13C edifice has two elegant Gothic doorways and a large rose-window. The nave, surmounted by a broken barrel vault, contains a beautiful 17C set of stalls, pulpit and retable as well as a large single-block christening font.

Citadel ⊙ – *Restoration work in progress.* Commissioned by Vauban in 1693, the citadel includes the 12C watch tower. There are summer exhibitions about the history of the fortress and mule-breeding in Seyne.

EXCURSION

St-Jean-Montclar – *12km/7.5mi north along D 900.*
This family ski resort, backed by the Dormillouse Massif, is situated on a plateau which is the starting point of the ski runs. The skiing area is linked to that of **Le Lauzet**, situated on the north side of the Dormillouse Massif, via the Brèche runs.
The summit of **Dormillouse** (alt 2 505m/8 218ft) is accessible by chair-lift to the Plateau de la Chau and then by a forest road *(45min on foot)*. From the 17C fort, there is a fine **view★** of the Ubaye Valley. The cliff below the fort is used for paragliding.
The village of **Montclar** has retained a 17C castle framed by two round towers *(not open to the public)* and the 13C Chapelle St-Léger.

*To choose a hotel, a restaurant or a campsite
consult the current edition of the annual **Michelin Red Guide France**
and the annual **Michelin Guide Camping Caravaning France**.*

SISTERON★★

Population 6 594
Michelin map 81 fold 6 or 245 fold 20
Local maps see p 304, Vallée de la Moyenne DURANCE and ROUTE NAPOLÉON

Sisteron is situated along a transverse section *(cluse)* of the Durance Valley which marks the transition between Dauphiné and Provence. Arriving from the south along D 4, one enjoys a remarkable view of the highly original **setting★★**: the town climbing up the steep side of a hillock crowned by a citadel facing the impressive Rocher de la Baume whose almost vertical strata seem to rise from the river bed. Tall narrow houses, covered with tiles, nestle behind the ruined 14C walls. A tunnel, going through the hillock beneath the citadel and intended for through traffic, has enabled the town to retain its ancient character.

Going back to Roman times – During the Roman occupation, Sisteron, known as Segustero, was a major stopover along the **Domitian Way** linking Italy and the Rhone Delta. It later became a bishopric and a stronghold guarding the northern border of Provence, before being ceded to the king of France in 1483. The citadel was built during the Wars of Religion (late 16C). Napoleon, returning from the island of Elba in 1815 *(see ROUTE NAPOLÉON)*, had lunch in Sisteron before marching on to Grenoble. The town was partly destroyed by bombing during the Second World War.

Sisteron today – The harnessing of the Durance, completed in 1977, includes the underground power station at Sisteron, supplied by pressure pipeline, and the Salignac Dam with its 118ha/292-acre reservoir.
The town's economic activities are centred round the production of lamb meat and the food-processing industry. A trade fair takes place in the summer and Sisteron is linked by motorway *(A 51)* to the lower Durance Valley and Marseille.
A theatre and dance festival, **Les Nuits de la Citadelle**, takes place in the open-air theatre below the citadel. Chamber music concerts are given in the Église St-Dominique and the cathedral.

★THE CITADEL ⊙ *1hr*

The Porte charretière (**Y**) *leading into the citadel is accessible by car and on foot. In summer, a small tourist train provides a shuttle service between the town hall and the citadel.*
There is nothing left of the 11C castle. The keep and the watchpath are late 12C. New defences, designed by Vauban in 1692, were added to the powerful 16C fortifications. The citadel, damaged by bombing in 1944, was tastefully restored.

Follow the arrows.
A succession of steps and terraces, offering views of the town and the Durance Valley, lead to the watchpath. Walk on and pass below the keep to reach the terrace *(viewing table)* and enjoy the bird's-eye **view★** of the lower part of town, the reservoir and the mountains barring the horizon to the north.

The Rocher de la Baume seen from the citadel

SISTERON

D   Tour de l'Horloge

The 15C **chapel**, partly rebuilt, is an exhibition centre.
Walk to the north side of the citadel, to the "**Guérite du Diable**" offering an impressive
view★ of the Rocher de Baume.
On the way out, one goes through the open-air theatre where the festival takes
place. The citadel museum includes a room devoted to Napoleon's "Return from
Elba" and an exhibition featuring horse-drawn vehicles.

ADDITIONAL SIGHTS

★**Église Notre-Dame** ⊘ (**Z**) – The former cathedral, built between 1160 and 1220,
is a fine example of Provençal Romanesque art. Its elegant doorway in Lombard
style has alternate black and white voussoirs prolonged by half-rounded arches
leaning against strong buttresses. The main pediment is also flanked by two half
pediments; jambs and slender columns are decorated with carvings and capitals
forming a continuous frieze representing a bestiary.
With its three naves, Notre-Dame is one of the largest churches in Provence. The
square bell-tower is surmounted by a spire in the shape of a pyramid.
A slightly pointed barrel vault, supported by massive square pillars, rests over the
dark nave flanked by narrow aisles. The floor is paved with terracotta and stone.
Over the high altar, a large retable provides a frame for a painting by Mignard:
Concert given by the Angels for the Holy Family. Side chapels on the south side
contain paintings by Van Loo, Parrocel, Coypel and Natoire.

Towers – Sisteron has retained five towers dating from 1370, which formed part
of the town's fortifications: four of them stand just south of Notre-Dame, the fifth
is located at the foot of the citadel.

★**Old Sisteron** – *Follow the arrows, starting on the left of Notre-Dame; guided tours
of the old town are organised in summer by the Tourist Information Centre.* The old
town lies between rue Droite and the Durance; narrow streets running down to the
river are lined with tall houses sometimes linked by vaulted passages known as
andrônes. Note the elegant carved doorways (16C, 17C and 18C) along the way.
Walk along **rue Deleuze** (**YZ 9**) to the **Tour de l'Horloge**★ (**Y D**) surmounted by a
magnificent wrought-iron campanile bearing Sisteron's motto: "Tuta montibus et
fluviis" (Safe between its mountains and its rivers). The **Longue andrône** (**Y 18**), a
narrow arcaded passageway, branches off rue Mercerie. Continue along **rue du
Glissoir** (**Y 14**) *(slippery in winter)*, which has retained a 13C Romanesque façade
(no 5). Beyond the square, the rue Basse-des-Remparts leads to **rue Font-Chaude**
(**Y 12**) then through a covered passageway up to **rue Saunerie** (**Y**); Napoleon had
lunch at no 64.

Église St-Dominique ⊙ (Y) – Situated on the opposite bank of the Durance, below the Rocher de la Baume, this former monastery church has retained a Lombard bell-tower. Concerts and literary evenings take place in summer.

Pieds et paquets are a traditional speciality of Sisteron, combining stuffed mutton tripe, cooked with lard and seasoned with herbs and peppar, with grilled mutton trotters.

EXCURSIONS

① **Prieuré de Vilhosc** *10km/6mi east along D 4 towards Volonne*

Drive 5km/3mi then turn left onto D 217; 4km/2.5mi further on, cross the Riou de Jabron and follow the signposted road on the right.

The 3-naved **crypt** ⊙ of an ancient monastery, located near the river, beneath farm buildings, is a rare example of 11C early Romanesque art.
Continue along D 217 for 5km/3mi to reach the single-arched **Pont de la Reine Jeanne** spanning the Vançon in a picturesque wooded setting.

★ ② **Haute vallée du Vançon** *92km/57mi round tour – allow 3hr*

Cross the bridge over the Durance and drive northeast along D 951 then D 3.

The road rises, offering interesting **views**★ of Sisteron and of the Buëch Valley in the foreground, with the Montagne de Lure to the southwest. Beyond the pass, there are bird's-eye views of the Riou de Jabron as it comes out of the Défilé de Pierre Écrite and flows towards the Durance.

Défilé de Pierre Écrite – The rock face of this deep gorge, on the left of the road near a small bridge, bears a Roman inscription celebrating CP Dardanus, a prefect of Gaul converted to Christianism, who opened this way in the 5C AD. Beyond St-Geniez on the right, Notre-Dame de Dromon can be seen at the foot of the Rocher de Dromon.

Notre-Dame de Dromon ⊙ – *Leave the car near a farm and continue on foot (15min return).* This plain 11C chapel was a place of pilgrimage until the 19C. The vaulting dates from the 17C. The tiny crypt beneath the building, which has alabaster columns and capitals, is a fine example of early Romanesque art.

Continue along D 3.

The road overlooks the wooded upper Vançon Valley and the view extends through the Durance Valley to the Luberon and the Montagne Ste-Victoire.
The road, which narrows considerably beyond Authon, goes over the **Col de Fontbelle** (alt 1 304m/4 278ft) and through Mélan Forest.

At Le Planas, follow the small road to Thoard.

Thoard – This old picturesque village has retained part of its medieval walls and a Romanesque keep which is now the bell-tower.

From Thoard, continue along D 17 to reach N 85 and follow the Route Napoléon (see ROUTE NAPOLÉON) back to Sisteron.

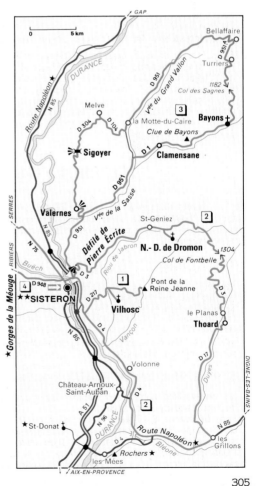

③ Vallée de la Sasse *85km/53mi round tour – allow 3hr*

From Sisteron, drive north along D 951.

The Sasse Valley, lying northeast of Sisteron, is an area modelled by erosion into a succession of ravines and gorges.
The road follows the river closely, past the villages of Châteaufort and Nibles.
Turn right onto D 1.

Clamensane – This village is perched on a rocky spur.

The landscape becomes gradually wilder and austere. Beyond the **Clue de Bayons**, the road enters an open basin.

Bayons – A large and beautiful abbey **church** overlooks the village square. Built in the 12C and 13C, it is a harmonious mixture of Romanesque and Gothic art: the nave is surmounted by a broken barrel vault and the chancel has a pointed vault with a remarkable pendant figuring an Agnus Dei. The archivolt of the 14C porch is framed by lancet arcades.

Beyond Bayons, D 1 veers due north towards Turriers.

The road rises in a series of steep hairpin bends to the Col des Sagnes, in a setting of gullied mountain slopes, before running down to Turriers and Bellaffaire (18C castle).

Beyond Bellaffaire, turn left onto D 951.

The road follows the **Grand Vallon** Valley, famous for its orchards (apple, pear and peach trees).

Beyond La Motte, turn right onto D 104 to Melve then left onto D 304.

Sigoyer – From the partly restored 15C castle, the **view★** extends to the Durance and, beyond, to the Baronnies and the Montagne de Lure.

The road runs down to Valernes through lavender fields.

Valernes – This hilltop village, which has retained part of its fortifications, offers a good view of the Sasse Valley.

Return to Sisteron along D 951.

★④ Gorges de la Méouge *90km/56km round tour – allow 4hr*

From Sisteron, drive northeast on D 948 towards Ribiers; continue to Le Plan along the Buëch Valley then turn left onto D 942. The road winds through the gorge along the north bank of the tumultuous Méouge, a tributary of the Buëch. Several sections of the river are suitable for canoeing, particularly in the spring.
It is possible to return to Sisteron via the north side of the Montagne de Chabre. Continue to La Calandre, turn right towards the Col St-Jean and Laborel then follow the Céans Valley to Orpierre *(see Les BARONNIES)* and Eyguiers.

Return to Sisteron along N 75.

SUPERDÉVOLUY ✴

Michelin map 77 folds 15 and 16, 189 fold 20 or 245 fold 7

This ski resort, situated at an altitude of 1 500m/4 921ft; is interesting from an architectural point of view: all the buildings are grouped to form a 2-tiered ensemble extending along the slopes of the Montagne d'Aurouze with rows of wooden balconies all facing southwest.

THE RESORT

The **skiing area**, linked to that of **La Joue-du-Loup**, includes a variety of ski runs down the northern slopes of the Sommarel and the Pic Ponçon. The link with La Joue skiing area is accessible to intermediate skiers. Advanced skiers on the other hand like the Pierra, Sommarel and Mur red runs. There is a choice of mountain restaurants. Cross-country skiers have access to 50km/31mi of marked tracks.

In summer, the resort is the starting point of mountain-climbing excursions to the surrounding summits and passes.

ST-ÉTIENNE-EN-DÉVOLUY *4km/2.5mi northeast*

It's an excellent winter and summer excursion base. Sheep-farming is still an important activity in the area.
From St-Étienne, D 17 leads to L'enclus. From the village, a private cable-car gives access to the IRAM (Institue of microwave radio astronomy) observatory situated on the **Plateau de Bure** (alt 2 563m/8 409ft). Set up in 1990, the observatory offers astronomers the possibility of observing the sky by using microwaves. From the cable-car station, there is a fine overall **view** of the Montagne de Barges and the Pic de Bure.

TALLARD

Population 1 185
Michelin map 81 fold 6 or 245 fold 7

Tallard lies in the middle Durance Valley, surrounded by orchards and vineyards, which produce a highly rated white wine.

SIGHTS

Church – It was erected in the 12C and partially rebuilt in the 17C. The main doorway (dated 1549 on the lintel) is the most interesting feature: it is decorated with Renaissance medallions depicting women, children and soldiers. Inside, the 17C pulpit and the christening font supported by lions are particularly noteworthy. An Armenian pilgrimage takes place every year in September.

Castle ⊙ – Its dismantled towers stand on a rock spur overlooking the Durance. Built in the 14C and 16C, it was taken time and again by both sides during the Wars of Religion and seriously damaged by the duke of Savoie's troops in 1692. The castle, which has been extensively repaired, is the venue of a summer festival of music.

Chapel – The Flamboyant style is represented here by an elegant doorway surmounted by a pinnacle and finial standing between flame-like windows. Inside, note the beautiful keystones, carved capitals and fireplaces.

Main building – Dating from the Renaissance, it has a rounded doorway surmounted by the arms of the Clermont-Tonnerre Family (who once owned the castle) and beautiful windows decorated with twisted mullions.

EXCURSIONS

★Round tour via Urtis *22km/13.7mi – about 1hr*

From Tallard, drive east across the Durance and turn left almost immediately.

The road rises above the river.

4km/2.5mi further on, turn right towards D 854 leading to Venterol.

A bend to the left *(cross)* offers a fine **view**★ of the Durance. Just beyond Venterol, there is an extended **view**★ of a large section of the Durance Valley. Soon after Les Marmets, the road runs rapidly down to the river and, 2.5km/1.5mi beyond Urtis, the view embraces a small reservoir along the Durance.

Turn right at the intersection with the road to Curbans to rejoin the Tallard road within sight of the castle.

Ventavon *18km/11mi southwest*

From Tallard, drive along D 942 towards Sisteron. The new route followed by N 85, linking the Durance and Buëch valleys, starts at La Saulce. Immediately after Valenty, turn right onto D 21 towards Laragne-Montéglin.

Built on the site of a ruined 11C fortress, Ventavon is a typical Provençal hilltop village (in spite of the modern belfry adjacent to the church), with a wealth of old houses and a small 15C castle flanked by round towers. From the top of the belfry *(58 steps, viewing table)*, there is a beautiful **panorama**★ of the pink-tiled roofs and the castle with the Durance Valley and surrounding summits beyond.

TALLOIRES ★★★

Population 1 287
Michelin map 89 fold 14 or 244 fold 19 – local map see Lac d'ANNECY

Talloires, lying on the eastern shore of the "Petit lac" d'Annecy, is one of the most opulent resorts in the Alps.
Until the Revolution, the village prospered round its Benedictine abbey, founded in the 9C. The present buildings, dating from the 17C and 18C, have been turned into a hotel.
The famous chemist, Claude-Louis **Berthollet** is a native of Talloires *(see Introduction: Famous natives of the Alps)*.

★★THE SETTING

The resort lies in beautiful surroundings: the harbour nestles inside a harmoniously rounded bay, sheltered by the cliffs of the Roc de Chère opposite the wooded promontory of the Duingt Castle, with the Montagne d'Entrevernes in the background.

Route de TAMIÉ

Michelin map 89 fold 15 or 244 fold 19

The Tamié gap, which creates an opening between the Bauges and the small isolated massif of the Dent de Cons, provides a scenic link between the Lac d'Annecy region and the Combe de Savoie-Tarentaise area.

FROM FAVERGES TO ALBERTVILLE *39km/24km – allow 1hr 30min*

Faverges – *See Lac d'ANNECY.*

From Faverges, drive south along the Col de Tamié road.

The road follows the green valley of the Nant de Tamié, framed by the wooded foothills of the Sambuy and Dent de Cons Mountains.

In Seythenex, turn right towards Le Vargnoz.

Montagne de la Sambuy – The Seythenex Chair-lift ⊘ leads to the Favre refuge (alt 1 820m/5 971ft) affording a fine **view** of the Belledonne range to the souh, the Aravis Massif and Lac d'Annecy to the north, the Mont-Blanc Massif to the north-east and the Vanoise glaciers to the southeast. The **panorama★** is even more extended from the Petite Sambuy (2 107m/6 913ft).

5km before the Col de Tamié, the abbey buildings come into sight.

Abbaye de Tamié – *1km/0.6mi detour.* The Church alone is open to the public. Founded in 1132, the abbey was rebuilt in the 17C and restored in 1861 by Cistercian monks who make a tasty cheese called "Tamié". An audiovisual show depicts life in the monastery.

At the Col de Tamié, turn left onto D 104 towards Albertville then left again at the Col de la Ramaz to the Plateau des Teppes.

★Plateau des Teppes – The road rises to La Ramaz, offering fine views of the Abbaye de Tamié. Leave the car on the second bend and follow a path on the right *(15min return on foot)*. Beyond the wood, climb to the top of a hillock which offers a charming **view★** of the Albertville Basin.

Return to the Col de la Ramaz.

Beyond the pass, there is a lovely view of the Albertville Basin, at the confluence of the rivers Isère and Arly marking the beginning of the Combe de Savoie *(see COMBE DE SAVOIE)*. The snow-capped Mont Blanc is visible through the Doron de Beaufort Valley.

The road winds its way towards Albertville, through vineyards and orchards.

Albertville – *See ALBERTVILLE.*

La TARENTAISE★★

Michelin map 89 folds 5 and 6 or 244 folds 21 and 31

The sinuous course of the upper Isère Valley is the geographical entity of the Tarentaise region. The long and narrow passages of the Haute and Basse Tarentaise provide a contrast with the more open Moyenne Tarentaise stretching from Moûtiers to Bourg-St-Maurice. This pastoral and wooded middle Tarentaise is the natural environment of fawn-coloured **Tarine cows**, one of the most carefully preserved mountain breeds in France which, owing to their high milk yield, have spread to areas outside the Alps, particularly in the southern part of the country.

The Moûtiers area is the only industrialised part of the region, although hydroelectric power is produced in other areas such as Tignes *(see TIGNES)*.

"Frontière" country – The "frontière", which is one of the symbols of traditional life in Savoie and particularly in the Tarentaise region, is a black-velvet headdress decorated with a golden braid, seemingly worn by women since the 16C.

★MOYENNE TARENTAISE

From Moûtiers to Bourg-St-Maurice

41km/25.5mi – allow 2hr – local map see Massif de la VANOISE

Beyond Aime, the itinerary leaves N 90 and follows secondary roads along the cultivated south-facing slope of the valley, within sight of the wooded slope across the river, backed by the tall silhouette of Mont Pourri (alt 3 779m/12 398ft).

Moûtiers – *See MOÛTIERS.*

The **Chapelle St-Jacques** stands on a rocky spur at the entrance of the Étroit du Siaix Gorge, in front of the village of St-Marcel.

Étroit du Siaix – It is recommended to stop 50m/55yd before the tunnel *(beware of falling rock)* in order to appreciate the depth of this gorge, which is the narrowest passage of the whole Isère Valley.

On the way to Aime, the valley is blocked by two successive glacial obstructions; beyond the first of these lies the small **Centron Basin**, within sight of the Mont-Pourri Summit and glaciers.

Aime – There have been settlements on this site since prehistoric times. Today, Aime is a thriving little town, specialising in the making of Beaufort cheese, with its own ski resort at La Plagne *(see La PLAGNE)*.

Ancienne basilique St-Martin ⊘ – This 11C edifice with its massive bell-tower is the best example of early Romanesque architecture in Savoie. The chancel and the apse are decorated with 12C and 14C frescoes – partly restored in the 19C – which illustrate scenes of the Old and New Testament. Excavations have revealed traces of two previous edifices; the older of these, which may have been Roman, was used by the first Christians. The 11C **crypt**, with its plain square capitals, supports the chancel.

Musée Pierre-Borrione ⊘ – Housed in a former 14C chapel, this small museum displays Gallo-Roman and Merovingian finds (coins, skeletons, sarcophagi), including the moving 5C tomb of the "Child with a bird".

There is also a collection of minerals and fossils found in the area and other parts of France.

Leave N 90 and turn left onto D 218 towards Tessens.

Between Aime and Granier, the road rises above the valley in successive hairpin bends, offering views of the Siaix Gorge downstream and of the Aime Basin. Beyond Valezan, the view extends over the other bank of the Isère, along the Ponturin Valley to the Bellecôte Massif (highest point: 3 416m/11 207ft).

Beyond Montgirod, Bourg-St-Maurice gradually comes into view, backed by the Col du Petit-St-Bernard flanked on the left by the jagged silhouette of the Roc de Belleface.

Bourg-St-Maurice – *See BOURG-ST-MAURICE.*

★HAUTE TARENTAISE

From Bourg-St-Maurice to Tignes

32km/20mi – allow 1hr – local map see Massif de la VANOISE

Bourg-St-Maurice – *See BOURG-ST-MAURICE.*

The road rises in a series of hairpin bends to Ste-Foy-Tarentaise *(see STE-FOY-TARENTAISE)* with the Pointe Foglietta barring the horizon straight ahead.

Upstream of Ste-Foy, the wild wooded valley widens slightly between La Raie and the Pont de la Balme. Water can be seen cascading down the opposite slope from the Mont Pourri glaciers (the view is particularly interesting from Le Monal). Towards the end of the drive, the huge fresco of a giant decorating the Barrage de Tignes seems to bar the end of the valley.

★★★**Tignes** – *See TIGNES.*

Demoiselles coiffées de THÉUS ★

Michelin map 81 fold 6 or 245 fold 8

This geological phenomenon occurring in the upper valley of the Valauria, a tributary of the Durance, offers one of the strangest sights in the southern Alps.

Access – *8km/5mi along the Théus road branching off the main road (from Tallard to the Serre-Ponçon Dam) east of Remollon.*

Demoiselles coiffées – The road goes through **Théus**, whose houses are picturesquely spread over a hilltop, then rises steeply *(18% gradient in places; difficult bends)*. Leave the car near the **"Salle de bal"** (ballroom), where there is a great concentration of these rock formations.

The **"Demoiselles coiffées"** (capped maidens), sometimes called "cheminées de fées" (fairies' chimneys), are columns of soft material – in this case morainic debris – preserved from erosion by rocky caps, which help to compress the soft material underneath and make it longer-lasting. However, the column quickly disappears once its cap has toppled over.

It is possible to continue *(4.5km/2.8mi)* to the **Mont Colombis** Television relay (alt 1 733m/5 686ft) for a panoramic **view** of the Serre-Ponçon Lake.

There are other examples of this strange phenomenon near Pontis, on the eastern shore of the Serre-Ponçon Lake, on the right of the road to St-Véran as you leave Château-Ville-Vieille and on the right of the road to the Col de Vars as you leave St-Paul.

THÔNES ★

Population 4 619
Michelin map 89 fold 14 or 244 fold 19
Local map see Massif des ARAVIS

Nestling round its church, below the cliffs of the Roche de Thônes, at the confluence of the rivers Fier and Nom, this market town is the ideal starting point of mountain excursions. The Forêt du Mont is the favourite haunt of ramblers and the slopes of Mont Lachat attract amateur botanists looking for edelweiss.

Every year, on the Sunday closest to 14 July, the local fire-brigade marches through the town with its picturesque equipment dating from 1836!

Musée du Pays de Thônes/J. Dubost

17C wooden beehive, Musée de Thônes

SIGHTS

Church ⊘ – The 17C church stands on the main square lined with old arcaded houses. The elegant onion-shaped steeple surmounted by a slender spire (42m/138ft), and the interior decoration are in typical Baroque style. Note the high-altar retable (1721), the carved figurines of the 17C altarpiece to the left of the chancel and the woodwork including 18C stalls.

Musée du pays de Thônes ⊘ – The first floor is devoted to local history and the second floor to local arts and crafts; exhibits include a 15C Pietà.

Écomusée du bois ⊘ – *3km/1/9mi west of the town centre.* Until the beginning of the 20C, there were many water-mills and sawmills along the Mainant Valley. The Étouvières Sawmill has found a new lease of life by housing an *écomusée* devoted to timber work in the Thônes region.

THONON-LES-BAINS ✚✚

Conurbation 53 078
Michelin map 89 fold 12 or 244 folds 8 and 9 – Local map see Le CHABLAIS

Thonon is the historic capital of the Chablais region as well as a health and spa resort overlooking Lake Geneva. The season lasts from 15 May to 15 September.

THE SPA TOWN

Thonon is a pleasant and lively spa resort, which specialises in the treatment of kidney and bladder diseases.

The lake shore – The **Rives** district, situated near the harbour where the ships sailing across the lake have their moorings, has retained a few picturesque fishermen's cottages brightened up by colourful climbers. On the way to Ripaille, there is a well-appointed beach. From Rives, Thonon can be reached either by car, along the avenue du Général-Leclerc and avenue de Corzent (magnificent private estates among chestnut groves), or by a picturesque **funicular** ⊘ or even by walking up several inclines, preferably through the gardens laid out beneath the Château de Sonnaz.

★★VIEWPOINTS

Several viewpoints line the way from the boulevard de la Corniche to the Jardin Anglais.

Place du Château (BY) – This was the site of the dukes of Savoie's castle destroyed by the French in 1589. In the centre of the square stands the statue of **Général Dessaix** (1764-1834), a native of Thonon, who fought courageously for the reunion of France and Savoie and was made a general by Napoleon.

From the terraces, there is an open **view★** of the Swiss side of Lake Geneva from Nyon to Lausanne. Below, the Rives district clusters round the brownish roofs of the Rives-Montjoux Castle and the Ripaille Castle can be seen to the right. The Vaudois Alps and Jura mountains form the panoramic background.

Jardin du château de Sonnaz and Jardin Paul-Jacquier (BY) – This is a pleasant area for relaxation. Situated at the end of the vast open space of the Jardin Paul-Jacquier, the ancient Chapelle St-Bon, adjacent to a 13C tower (part of the town's fortifications), attracts water-colourists.

The Maison des arts et loisirs, designed by Novarina, was completed in 1966.

OTHER SIGHTS

Musée du Chablais ⊙ (**AY M**) – Housed in the 17C Château de Sonnaz, this regional folk museum illustrates local history; a room is devoted to the lakeside-village period and to local Gallo-Roman finds.

Église St-Hippolyte ⊙ (**AY**) – St François de Sales preached in this church and the local population renounced Protestantism within its walls. This edifice illustrates different styles; the interior decoration, dating from the 17C, includes stucco work as well as painted cartouches and medallions over the nave **vaulting★**.
Note, on the right-hand side of the first nave, a 13C stoup bearing the arms of Savoie. The pulpit dates from the 16C and the organ loft from 1672.
The three-naved Romanesque **crypt** (12C) was partly rebuilt in the 17C.

Basilique St-François-de-Sales ⊙ (**ABY**) – The neo-Gothic basilica communicates with St-Hippolyte. It contains the last work painted by Maurice Denis, one of the founders of the Nabis movement: two large frescoes entitled **Chemin de Croix** (1943), depicting Christ dying on the cross and his apparition to the holy women after his resurrection. The christening font dates from the 13C.

Monastère de la Visitation (**BY N**) – It was erected in the 17C and recently restored. The chapel is surmounted by Gothic ribbed vaulting.

Hôtel-Dieu (**ABZ**) – Occupying the site of the former Minimes Convent, founded in 1636, the edifice is centred round a cloister whose upper part is decorated in Baroque style.

Foyer Don-Bosco (**AZ K**) – The small modern chapel of this institution is decorated with ceramics.

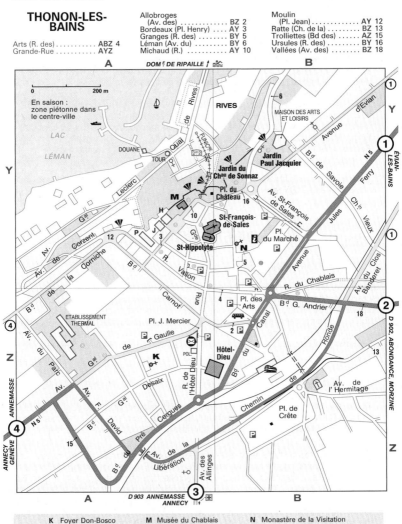

K Foyer Don-Bosco   M Musée du Chablais   N Monastère de la Visitation

EXCURSIONS *in addition, see the excursions starting from Évian-les-Bains.*

★**Domaine de Ripaille** – *7km/4.3mi round tour. Go down to Rives and follow the quai de Ripaille to the end then turn left into the avenue leading to the Château de Ripaille (see Domaine de RIPAILLE).*

Return to the road and the intersection to reach Vongy.

Vongy – **Notre-Dame-du-Léman** is a graceful modern church with a large roof supported by transverse gables and surmounted by a slender spire. The apse is adorned with a large mosaic depicting the Virgin Mary surrounded by local saints.

Return to Thonon along N 5.

★**Round tour via Bellevaux** – *68km/42mi round tour – allow 2hr 30min – local map see Le CHABLAIS. Leave Thonon by ② on the town plan and turn right towards Bellevaux (D 26).*
The road overlooks the Gorges de la Dranse and runs through the charming Bellevaux Valley. Note the charasteristic silhouette of the Dent d'Oche to the east.

Bellevaux – The village lies on the west bank of the Brevon, in the charming verdant **valley**★ of the same name. The church, surmounted by a copper onion-shaped steeple, contains some elegant woodwork and has retained a 14C chapel.

Turn right past the cemetery, cross the Brevon and take the forest road on the left.

The road rises very steeply above the Bellevaux Valley.

Chalets de Buchille – Fine view of the Mont d'Hermone to the northwest.

Return to Bellevaux and continue towards Jambaz. Follow the itinerary St-Jeoire to Thonon via the Col de Jambaz, Col de Terramont and Col du Cou.

Château des Allinges – *7km/4.3mi south, leaving Thonon by ③ on the town plan and following D 12. Take the first road on the right as you enter Macheron.*
The hilltop was originally crowned by two castles belonging to rival feudal lords until 1355 when they both came into the possession of the count of Savoie. In 1594, St François de Sales made it his headquarters when he preached in the area. Walk through the two fortified gates to the east platform offering an open view of the Bas-Chablais Region and the Dent d'Oche.
The restored **chapel** ⊙ has retained its oven-vaulted apse decorated with a Romanesque fresco (late 10C) showing a clear Byzantine influence (rich colours and hieratic figures); it represents Christ in Glory, surrounded by the Evangelists, the Virgin Mary on the left and St John on the right.
Before leaving, walk to the west platform affording an extended **view**★ of Lake Geneva, Thonon and the Jura mountains.

★★**Yvoire** – *16km/10mi west, leaving Thonon by ④ on the town plan and driving along N 5 and D 25 (see YVOIRE).*

THORENS-GLIÈRES ★

Population 2 077
Michelin map 89 fold 16 or 244 fold 19

This small town lies in the Bornes depression, on the banks of the River Fillière, a tributary of the Fier, at the point where the narrow valley opens out. It is the birthplace of St François de Sales who was christened in the parish church *(see ANNECY)*. Nothing remains of François de Sales' native castle, but the Chapelle de Sales standing on the site, along the Usillon road, has become a place of pilgrimage *(Sunday following 15 August)*. A folk festival takes place in Thorens on the same day.

★CHÂTEAU DE THORENS ⊙

The castle stands in an attractive setting, within sight of the Vallon de la Fillière and the Parmelan Mountain. The foundations date from the 11C, the round keep – unusual in Savoie – from the 13C and the whole edifice was remodelled in the 19C.

Interior – The tour starts with the vaulted basement (guardroom and prison cells). The ground-floor rooms contain mementoes of St François de Sales, 16C tapestries from Brussels, a wealth of furniture and a collection of paintings; note in particular: *St Stephen* by Marco d'Oggiono, 16C Lombard School, *Portrait of the Infanta Isabella* by Van Dyck and *Portrait of the Marquise de Grollier* by Madame Vigée-Lebrun. Two rooms are devoted to Count Cavour, who achieved Italian unity (he was related to the Sales family).

PLATEAU DES GLIÈRES

14km/8.7mi east along a forest road.

During the Second World War, the high-pasture area of the Plateau des Glières was chosen by Resistance leaders as the site of one of their fortified camps. It was unsuccessfully attacked in February 1944 by Vichy security forces. A second attempt in March was equally unsuccessful. The Germans then sent 12 000 soldiers and the 465 besieged men were forced to retreat in spite of putting up a fierce resistance. There were heavy losses on both sides and the surrounding towns and villages suffered bitter repression.

However, the Resistance became gradually stronger, regained possession of the plateau and eventually liberated the Haute-Savoie *département* with the help of other resistance groups in the area.

The surfaced road ends at the **Col des Glières** (alt 1 440m/4 724ft), where a panel explains the sequence of the military operations which took place in 1944. The **memorial**, standing slightly below on the right, symbolises the V for Victory together with renewed hope and life. There is a chapel inside.

The resistant fighters killed in 1944 are buried in the "Nécropole nationale des Glières" *(see Massif des ARAVIS).*

A trail called "Nature et Paysages des Glières" (nature and landscapes of the Glières region) offers a marked itinerary which includes the main historic sites *(1hr 30min).*

TIGNES ✳✳✳

Population 1 998
Michelin map 89 fold 6 or 244 fold 32 – Local map see Massif de la VANOISE

The old village, flooded as a result of the building of the dam *(see Excursions: Barrage de Tignes)*, was replaced by a ski resort which developed 6km/3.7mi higher up in a lovely **setting**✳✳, near a lake.

Lac de Tignes – This small natural lake lies at the centre of a treeless high-pasture basin backed by the snowfields of the **Grande Motte** sloping down to the Rochers de la Grande Balme. The setting of La **Grande Sassière** across the river is very similar. The summit of La Tovière to the east, facing Val d'Isère, is accessible by gondola. The Col du Palet and Col de la Tourne to the west give access to the Parc national de la Vanoise. In summer, the lake offers a variety of water sports and there is an 18-hole golf course nearby.

Tignes

THE RESORT

Situated at an altitude of 2 100m/6 890ft, Tignes has gradually expanded into several districts spread around the lake: Tignes-le-Lac, Le Lavachet and Val Claret further south.

Skiing area – It is linked to that of Val d'Isère to form the famous **Espace Killy** ✷ ✷ ✷ *(see Massif de la VANOISE)*, one of the largest and most beautiful skiing areas in the world, in a barren high-mountain setting. Snow cover is excellent and available all year round (summer skiing on the Grande Motte Glacier). Some 100 snow-cannons make it possible for skiers to ski down to the resort from October to May. Slopes are generally less steep than in Val d'Isère but some ski runs are however suitable for advanced skiers (Le Vallon de la Sache, Les Pâquerettes and La Ves). In addition, it is possible to practice mogul skiing and experience non-pisted powder runs.

The world championships of artistic and acrobatic skiing take place every year in Tignes. The events include mogul skiing as well as ballet and jumping in the Lognan Olympic stadium.

VIEWPOINTS

★★★**La Grande Motte** – This glacier is famous for its scenery and for its summer skiing. An underground **rack-railway** ⊙, starting from Val Claret, leads over a distance of 3 400m/2.2mi to a panoramic platform offering an overall view of the glacier. From there, a huge cable-car *(capacity: 125)* takes skiers up to 3 450m/11 319ft, near the Grande Motte Summit (3 656m/11 995ft). The splendid **panorama★★** includes Tignes, its lake and the Lac de Chevril to the north, overlooked by the Mont Pourri and Dôme de la Sache with Mont Blanc and the Grandes Jorasses in the distance. The Grande Sassière and Tsanteleina summits can be seen to the northeast, along the Italian border.

★★**La Tovière** – Alt 2 696m/8 845ft. *Access from Tignes-le-Lac by the Aéro-Ski gondola in winter.* **Panorama** of the Espace Killy from the Grande-Motte to Belle-varde.

HIKES

Tignes is the ideal starting point of **hikes** in the Parc national de la Vanoise.

★★★**Col du Palet and Col de la Tourne** – *Allow 1 day. Difference in height: 750m/2461ft minimum. Experienced hikers can extend the itinerary if they wish: Col de la Grassaz or Lac de la Plagne are two splendid detours which can be included in the following tour.* Start from Tignes-le-Lac; 1hr 30min to the Col du Palet (alt 2 653m/8 704ft); interesting flora; from the pass, 30min to the **Pointe du Chardonnet★★★** (2 870m/9 416ft) *(for hikers not suffering from vertigo; mountain boots essential):* exceptional panoramic view of the Tarentaise region; less adventurous hikers can aim for the **Col de la Croix des Frêtes★★**, 10min further on from the Col du Palet. Walk down to the Lac du Grataleu then up again to the **Col de la Tourne★★** (2 656m/8 714ft), offering splendid views of the Espace Killy. On the way down, note the superb **Aiguille Percée** on the left.

★★**Refuge de la Martin** – Alt 2 154m/7 067ft. *5hr return from Tignes-le-Lac or Les Boisses.* This untaxing hike offers lovely views of the Lac du Chevril, the surrounding summits and Mont Blanc in the distance.

EXCURSIONS

Barrage de Tignes *6km/3.7mi northeast along D 87*

The downstream side of this arch dam, inaugurated in 1953, is decorated with a huge fresco covering 12 000m² depicting a **"giant"** (fine view from D 902 and the village of Les Brévières). Its total height is 180m/591ft including the foundations and its total volume is 630 000m³/22 248 450cu ft. The reservoir, known as the **Lac du Chevril★**, holds 230 million m³/186 461acft.

Hydroelectric complex – The total height of the chute is 1 000m/3 281ft. The water supplies the **Brévières** Power station (yearly production: 154 million kWh), before travelling along a 15km/9mi-long tunnel to the **Malgovert** Power station (yearly production: 750 million kWh).

In addition, the Chevril Power station is partly supplied by the reservoir of La Sassière situated at an altitude of 2 460m/8 071ft.

A **viewpoint** situated on the roof of the Chevril Power station, just off D 902, offers an overall **view★** of the dam and its reservoir.

Les Boisses – Alt 1 810m/5 938ft. The new village was built on a rocky spur overlooking the dam; the **church** ⊙ was modelled on the old parish church flooded when the dam was built; it contains the ornaments saved at the time, including 17C and 18C retables carved by Italian artists from the Val Sesia region.

★★Réserve naturelle de la Grande Sassière

From the Tignes Dam, follow the road to Val d'Isère. Immediately beyond the Giettaz Tunnel, turn left towards the Barrage du Saut (6km/3.7mi), situated at an altitude of 2 300m/7 546ft (parking).

The nature reserve covering 2 230ha/5 511 acres, was created in 1973 and the beauty of the environment has been totally preserved in spite of important investments in hydroelectric projects. Overlooked by the **Grande Sassière** (3 747m/12 293ft) and **Tsanteleina** (3 605m/11 827ft) summits, it extends to the Glacier de Rhême-Golette on the Italian border. The observation of the rich flora and fauna (marmots, ibexes, chamois...) is a great attraction.

★★**Lac de la Sassière** – Alt 2 460m/8 071ft. *1hr 45min return on foot from Le Saut; go up along a path following the stream and return by the EDF road.* This untaxing hike offers the possibility of enjoying high-mountain scenery.

★★**Glacier de Rhême-Golette** – Alt about 3 000m/9 843ft. *1hr 30min steep climb from the Lac de la Sassière; it is dangerous to go onto the glacier.* Beautiful scenery with the Grande Casse and Grande Motte in the distance.

Vallée de la TINÉE★★

Michelin map 89 folds 9, 10 and 20, 115 folds 4, 5, 15 and 16 or 245 folds 23 and 24

The River Tinée flows southwards from the Col de la Bonette to its confluence with the Var. Gorges and open basins alternate along this green valley covered with forests of chestnuts, firs and larches.
Hilltop villages line the way on both sides of the river.

FROM THE PONT DE LA MESCLA TO AURON

143km/89mi – allow 1 day

This itinerary is lengthened by detours to hilltop villages.
From Pont de la Mescla, drive along D 2205.

★**Gorges de la Mescla** – The road runs along the bottom of the gorge, beneath overhanging rocks.

At Pont de la Lune, turn right onto D 32.

La Tour – This isolated village, perched on a rocky spur above the Tinée Valley, has retained its medieval character and boasts a charming square, lined with arcades, a shaded fountain and *trompe-l'œil* façades.
The Romanesque-Gothic **church** ⊘ is decorated with three beautiful Renaissance retables and two 15C stoups.
Several 16C water-powered oil-mills are still in working order.
The **Chapelle des Pénitents Blancs** ⊘ stands along D 32 at the northeast end of the village. The side walls are covered with frescoes by Brevesi and Nadale, dating from 1491, depicting 20 scenes from the Passion. Older frescoes, painted on the east-end wall, illustrate the Last Judgement.

Return to D 2205 and drive north to Pons-de-Clans then turn left into D 56.

The road winds its way to Bairols in a series of spectacular hairpin bends, amid olive trees, oaks and chestnuts.

Bairols – This hilltop village (alt 830m/2 723ft) has been tastefully restored. It offers bird's-eye views of the valley below. The old flour-mill has been turned into a restaurant and the oil-mill into a bar.

Rejoin D 2205 and turn immediateley right onto D 55 to Clans.

Clans – This pleasant village, overlooking the steep Clans Valley on one side and the Tinée on the other, is surrounded by a large forest of spruces, larches and firs and framed by mountains. From its medieval past, it has retained many fountains.
The Romanesque **church** ⊘ has been turned into a Baroque edifice: the beautiful doorway, dating from 1702, is preceded by a portico. The interior decoration is rather elaborate; the chancel contains two panels of a retable from the Nice School on either side of a Virgin with Child; in the side chapel on the left of the chancel, there is a Baroque altarpiece in 17 parts; 11C **frescoes** representing hunting scenes have been discovered behind the high altar, together with a 15C Christ in Glory. The organ case was made in 1792 by **Honoré Grinda** from Nice.

Chapelle St-Antoine ⊘ – *It stands 500m/547yd from the village, on the left of the Pont-de-Clans road.* The small rustic chapel has a wall-belfry and a large porch. The interior is extensively decorated with 15C **frescoes** depicting scenes from the life of St Anthony.

Chapelle St-Michel ⊘ – *Situated at the top of the village: walk along the left-hand side of the church to the end of the surfaced road.*

The flat east end is adorned with 16C **frescoes;** St Michael can be seen in the centre, weighing souls. From the terrace, the **view** embraces Clans, the Tinée Valley with Bairols and the Pointe des Quatre Cantons across the river.

Return to D 2205 once more and, a little further on, turn left to Ilonse.

Ilonse – Ilonse lies in a beautiful mountain setting, at an altitude of 1 210m/3 970ft. From the viewing table at the top of the village, several hilltop villages can be seen standing out against dark forest patches.

Back to D 2205; continue towards St-Sauveur-sur-Tinée.

The Valdeblore road on the right links the Tinée and Vesubie Valleys. Red schists add colour to the landscape.

St-Sauveur-sur-Tinée – Situated at the confluence of the rivers Tinée and Vionène, this village is a maze of twisting lanes lined with tall canopied buildings. It houses an information centre of the **Parc national du Mercantour** *(see Introduction: Nature parks and reserves).*

The 15C **church** has a Romanesque bell-tower decorated with gargoyles. Inside, the rich ornaments include the **Retable Notre-Dame** (1483) by Guillaume Planeta.

Beyond St-Sauveur, D 30 winds its way westwards along the Vionène *(see Route de la VIONÈNE)* and across the Col de la Couillole, linking the Tinée and Cians valleys. D 2205 follows the Tinée through the dark and barren corridor of the **Gorges de Valabres**, between the Mont Gravières on one side and the Cime des Lauses and Mont St-Sauveur on the other.

Isola – The lovely Romanesque bell-tower of the church, destroyed by a spate of the Guerche, stands at the entrance of the village. The rounded twinned windows with carved capitals are typical of the Lombard influence.

The road on the left leads to the **Cascade de Louch★**; the water falls from a "hanging" valley, 100m/328ft above the Tinée.

To reach Isola 2000✷✷ *(see ISOLA 2000), turn right into D 97 and follow the Vallon de Chastillon.*

The road runs close to the Italian border lined with snow-capped peaks. Mountain streams come rushing down the slopes on both sides of the River Tinée and the valley widens within sight of St-Étienne-de-Tinée.

✷**Auron** – *See AURON.*

★**St-Étienne-de-Tinée** – *See ST-ÉTIENNE-DE-TINÉE.*

Beyond St-Étienne-de-Tinée, the road rises above the Tinée Valley, towards the Col de la Bonette *(see Route de la BONETTE).*

Route de TOURNEFORT★

Michelin map 81 fold 20, 115 fold 15 or 245 fold 24

This picturesque road links the rivers Var and Tinée across the foothills of the Pointe des Quatre-Cantons, some 10km/6mi upstream of their confluence. The artistic heritage of Villars-sur-Var adds another attraction to this interesting route.

FROM THE VAR TO THE TINÉE *15km/9.3mi – about 1hr*

Drive 11km/6.8mi west of Pont de la Mescla along N 202 and turn right onto D 26.

The road rises above the Var Valley towards Villars.

Villars-sur-Var – Villars lies at the heart of a wine-growing area surrounded by high mountains. From its medieval past, the village has retained part of its fortifications and a richly decorated church standing on a square shaded by ancient plane trees. The large **high-altar retable★** is made up of 10 panels painted by an unknown artist; the central panel represents a splendid **Entombment★★**. The polychrome woodwork bears the arms of the Grimaldi, a powerful family bitterly opposed to the dukes of Savoie

St Lucy (detail) from the high-altar retable, Villars-sur-Var

P. et G. Leclerc

from the 14C to the 17C. The **Annunciation altarpiece** (Nice School c 1520), located on the left of the chancel, is also remarkable. In addition, the church contains some fine statues and a painting by Veronese entitled *Martyrdom of St Bartholomew*.

From Villars, it is possible to make an interesting detour *(14km/8.7mi northwest along D 226)* to the isolated hilltop village of **Thiéry**★ overlooking the Gorges du Cians **(viewpoint)**, which has retained its narrow streets and covered alleyways.

Road D 26 winds its way along the forested slopes of Mont Falourde, offering glimpses of the Chapelle de la Madone d'Utelle across the River Tinée.

Massoins – From this mountain village, there is a fine **view** of the Var Valley.

The small hilltop village of Tournefort suddenly appears round a bend.

2km/1.2mi further on, turn right onto a small road.

Tournefort – The village clings to a steep rock spur. Near the chapel, the **view**★ embraces the Var and Tinée valleys framed by mountains, the Madone d'Utelle and the hilltop village of La Tour *(see Vallée de la TINÉE)*.

Return to D 26 and follow it down to the Tinée Valley.

The road runs through a forested area, within sight of magnificent cliffs barring the horizon, and reaches the River Tinée at Pont-de-Clans *(see Vallée de la TINÉE)*.

Route de TOUTES AURES ★

Michelin map 81 fold 18 or 245 folds 22 and 23

This road is a section of the "winter Alpine route" *(N 202)* linking the upper valleys of the rivers Verdon and Var.

FROM ST-JULIEN-DU-VERDON TO ENTREVAUX

30km/18.6mi – allow 1hr

St-Julien-du-Verdon – This ancient village partially disappeared when the Barrage de Castillon was built. There is a water sports park on the lakeside.

From St-Julien, drive along N 202.

Mountain streams, which are subject to fearsome spates, have cut across mountain crests, carving deep wild gorges known as *"clues"*.

★**Clue de Vergons** – The road rises as it goes through the gorge, offering fine views of the lake and the lovely setting of St-Julien-du-Verdon.

The Romanesque **Chapelle Notre-Dame de Valvert** stands on the roadside just beyond Vergons.

Col de Toutes Aures – Alt 1 124m/3 688ft. Tilted rock strata – sometimes almost vertical – form a striking contrast with the forested slopes.

★**Clue de Rouaine** – The road runs between impressive cliffs.

Beyond Les Scaffarels, where one can see the famous Grès d'Annot *(see ANNOT)*, the Coulomp Valley is deep and narrow, except where the river joins the Var (Pont de Gueydan). The road then follows the Var Valley and the typically southern character of the arid landscape is enhanced by the Mediterranean sun.

★**Entrevaux** – See ENTREVAUX.

Château du TOUVET ★

Michelin map 89 fold 19 or 144 fold 29

The castle is built on the slopes of the Chartreuse Massif, facing the Belledonne range across the Grésivaudan depression; the present edifice, dating from the 15C, was originally surrounded by a fortified wall, but only two round towers marking the entrance are still standing.

The castle was extensively remodelled in the 18C: the courtyard was enclosed, a main staircase was built inside and the gardens were adorned with a remarkable **water stairway**★ in the Italian style.

TOUR OF THE CASTLE ⊘ *40min*

The richly decorated interior has retained some interesting furniture.

The gallery, adorned with Italian stucco work, houses many archives including letters signed by Henri VIII of England and François I of France. This is explained by the fact that the owner of the castle was ambassador at the English court.

The music room contains two harpsichords; one of them, made by Jan Couchet in 1652, is exquisitely decorated.

In the drawing room, there are a few pieces of furniture from the famous Hache workshop in Grenoble and the walls of the dining room are decorated with leather from Cordoba.

Le TRIÈVES ★

Michelin map 77 folds 14 and 15 or 244 folds 39 and 40

The rivers Drac and Ebron have carved deep trenches through the green Trièves depression enclosed by the Vercors and Devoluy massifs and overlooked by N 75, the winter Alpine road leading to the Col de la Croix Haute.

Dauphiné's Mount Olympus – **Mont Aiguille** (alt 2 086m/6 844ft) is an isolated table mountain forming a kind of bastion guarding the approaches of the Vercors Massif. The conquest of Mont Aiguille was the first mountaineering expedition to take place in France. It was achieved in 1492 at the request of King Charles VIII who had heard tales of supernatural manifestations on top of the mountain. When the party got to the top, they found a charming meadow dotted with wild flowers and a flock of chamois roaming freely.

★COL DE LA CROIX HAUTE

1 From Monestier to the Col de la Croix Haute

36km/22.4mi – about 1hr 30min

Monestier-de-Clermont – The surrounding woods offer numerous possibilities of shaded walks and the nearby village of Avignonet to the northeast is an excellent belvedere overlooking the Drac, the Monteynard dam and its reservoir *(water sports)*.

The road leading to the Col de la Croix Haute affords a vast panorama of mountains, with the splendid escarpments of the Mont Aiguille in the foreground on the right.

Col de la Croix Haute – It offers a landscape of pastures and dark fir forests, characteristic of northern Alpine scenery.

UPPER GRESSE VALLEY

2 Round tour starting from Monestier *61km/38mi – about 2hr*

Monestier-de-Clermont – *See Col de la Croix Haute above.*

From Monestier-de-Clermont, drive northwest along D 8.

The road goes through St-Guillaume, a typical village of the Trièves region, with its stocky houses covered with steep tiled roofs. It then rises above the Gresse Valley to Miribel-Lanchâtre (lovely views) and runs down again to St-Barthélemy.

Turn left onto D8^8.

The village of Ruthière with Mont Aiguille in the background

J.-M. Blache/DIAF

318

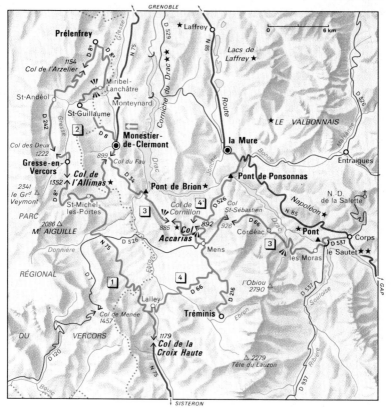

Prélenfrey – This small summer resort lies at the heart of a vale beneath the escarpments of the Vercors Massif (Arêtes du Gerbier).

Continue along D 8^B to the Col de l'Arzelier.

The road rises to the **Col de l'Arzelier** (skiing area), then runs down to Château-Bernard, offering more fine views of the Vercors.

Follow D 242 towards St-Andéol.

The pastoral landscapes of the Trièves are backed by the impressive cliffs of the Vercors, including the Grand Veymont (alt 2 341m/7 680ft), the massif's highest peak.

D 242 goes over the Col des Deux to join the road leading to Gresse-en-Vercors.

Gresse-en-Vercors – Note the strange local means of transport known as *trinque-balles*, vaguely looking like sledges. The Maison du Parc naturel régional du Vercors is in the village centre.

★**Col de l'Allimas** – From the pass, there is a striking view of the Mont Aiguille, followed by fine views of the Trièves on the way down to St-Michel-les-Portes.

Return to Monestier along N 75 towards Grenoble.

★ACROSS THE TRIÈVES

③ From Monestier-de-Clermont to Corps
46km/28.6mi – about 1hr 30min

Monestier-de-Clermont – *See Col de la Croix Haute opposite.*

From Monestier, drive south along N 75 then turn left onto D 34.

From the Col du Fau to Mens, the road winds its way through the Trièves Basin, within sight of the Mont Aiguille, the Obiou and the Grand Ferrand.

★**Pont de Brion** – This suspension bridge, looking surprisingly light, spans the sombre gorge of the Ébron. It used to be 126m/413ft above the river bed, but since the building of the Monteynard Dam on the Drac, downstream, the level of the Ébron has been raised by 60m/197ft.

319

Near the Col de Cornillon, there is a clear view, on the left, of the Corniche du Drac and the reservoir of the Monteynard Dam.

Beyond Mens, drive northeastwards along D 66.

The road skirts the Obiou Massif before running along the terrace-cultivations of the left bank of the Drac, offering a wide panorama extending north as far as the summits of the Chartreuse.

The road turns left at Les Moras and crosses the Drac, affording lovely views of the Lac du Sautet.

★★**Barrage et lac du Sautet and Corps** – *See Barrage et lac du SAUTET.*

④ From La Mure to the Col de la Croix Haute

65km/40mi – allow 2hr

La Mure – *See Lacs de LAFFREY.*

Between La Mure and the Pont de Ponsonnas, the snow-capped southern peaks of the Écrins Massif can be seen through the Valbonnais Corridor.

Pont de Ponsonnas – This bridge spans the gorge of the Drac 100m/328ft above the river bed.

★**Col Accarias** – Alt 892m/2 927ft. Extended **view**★ of the Trièves enclosed by the Obiou, the Grand Ferrand and the Tête du Lauzon.

From Mens, drive south along D 66, then turn left onto D 216.

Tréminis – Tréminis lies in the upper Ébron Valley, covered with fir forests and overlooked by the limestone escarpments of the Dévoluy. This **site**★ is one of most attractive of the whole area and the resort is a pleasant place to spend a summer holiday.

Return to D 66 and continue towards Lalley.

Col de la Croix Haute – *See Col de la Croix Haute p 318.*

L'UBAYE★

Michelin map 77 folds 18 and 19, 81 folds 8 and 9 or 245 folds 9 and 10

The valley of the River Ubaye, a tributary of the Durance, forms the most northern region of the Provençal Alps. It is an area of deeply gullied marly slopes, of huge alluvial fans covered with scrub, but also of fine conifer forests and rocky peaks, conveying an impression of spaciousness to travellers used to the deep valleys of the northern Alps.

The Ubaye Region remained isolated during the long winter months until 1883, when the road linking Barcelonnette to the Durance Valley *(D 900)* was completed.

The Barcelonnette Basin, lying at the intersection of the international Gap-Cuneo Route *(D 900-S 21)* and the Route des Grandes Alpes *(D 902)* from the Col de Vars to the Col de la Cayolle, forms the central part of the region.

LOWER UBAYE VALLEY

① From Le Lauzet-Ubaye to Barcelonnette

21km/13mi along D 900 – about 30min – local map see opposite

The road which follows the River Ubaye to Barcelonnette was opened in 1883, replacing a narrow path through a 23km/14mi-long gorge.

Le Lauzet-Ubaye – *See Barrage et Lac de SERRE-PONÇON.*

The road skirts the south bank of the Ubaye flowing between wooded slopes, within sight of the snow-capped summits of the Petite and Grande Séolane. Between Le Lauzet and Le Martinet, several viewpoints offer the possibility of observing the numerous rafters and canoeists.

Le Martinet – As you drive through the village, look right up the Grand Riou Valley sloping down from the Montagne de la Blanche. Before the bridge, a road runs down to an important water sports park.

The landscape becomes more open beyond Les Thuiles and the view embraces the Barcelonnette Basin at the heart of the valley. To the right, the ski resort of **Pra-Loup** ✲ *(see PRA-LOUP)* can be seen clinging to the steep slopes of the Péguieu. On its way to Barcelonnette, the road runs between the tributary valleys of the Riou Bourdoux *(see BARCELONNETTE)* and of the Bachelard.

★**Barcelonnette** – *See BARCELONNETTE.*

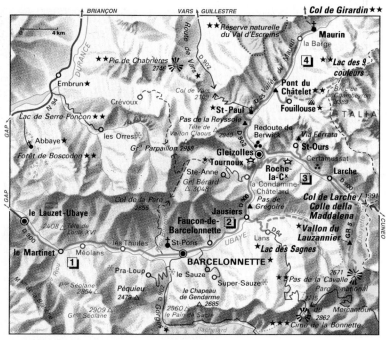

BARCELONNETTE BASIN

2 From Barcelonnette to Les Gleizolles

15km/9.3mi – about 1hr – local map see above

★Barcelonnette – *See BARCELONNETTE.*

The road *(D 900)* runs across the Barcelonnette Basin where crops alternate with scree.

Faucon-de-Barcelonnette – This ancient village going back to Roman times is said to owe its name to the numerous birds of prey (falcons) inhabiting the area.

An elegant 12C campanile overlooks the village. Note the carved cover of a Gallo-Roman sarcophagus on the right of the church doorway.

The characteristic silhouettes of the Pain de Sucre and Chapeau de Gendarme summits can be seen on the horizon to the south.

Jausiers – The Arnaud Brothers who pioneered the mass emigration of the local population to Mexico in 1805 *(see BARCELONNETTE)*, were natives of this village which has been twinned with Arnaudville in Louisiana since 1995.

Several buildings testify to the success of the emigrants in the New World: Villa Morélia, Villa Manon and above all the **Château des Magnans** *(along the Route de la Bonette)*, a neo-Gothic folly built at the beginning of the 20C by a Swiss architect.

The 18C **church** has a beautiful doorway in carved wood and an interesting 17C Baroque ornamentation, in particular the amazing "altar of the dead" decorated with sculptures representing human skulls and bones. The barrel vault of the nave is made of blocks of tufa.

Beyond Jausiers, wooded basins alternate with deep gorges. The strategic importance of the narrow **Pas de Grégoire** and **Pas de la Reyssole** *(see upper Ubaye Valley)* was at the origin of the construction of the Fort de Tournoux.

A road, branching off D 900 at La Condamine, leads to the small ski resort of **Ste-Anne**.

★Fort de Tournoux ⊙ – *Turn left before the bridge over the Ubaye, 1km beyond La Condamine-Châtelard, leave the car on the open space. Follow the twisting track which goes up to the middle fort. This is only possible on days when there are guided tours. Walking shoes recommended.*

These extensive fortifications, straddling a ridge line at the confluence of the Ubaye and Ubayette valleys, are a real feat of engineering: there is a difference in height of 700m/2 297ft between the barracks along the river and the upper fort. The main part was built from 1843 to 1865 and the different batteries are linked by underground passages and steps (including a flight of 808 steps). Other batteries were added later on the heights surrounding the fort. The tour includes the middle fort with its monumental machicolated gate, several other buildings and the inclines giving access to the upper fort; from the upper batteries, there is a splendid **view★** of the two valleys.

Fort de Roche-la-Croix ⊙
– 7km/4.3mi along a forest road branching off D 900 to the right, just before the intersection with D 902.
This fort, built between 1931 and 1940, formed part of the Maginot line of defence in the Alps; it was meant to be completely autonomous, like a submarine. The tour illustrates the fighting which took place here in 1940 and 1945. Other fortifications along the Ubayette Valley may be open to the public during the season *(inquire at the tourist office in Barcelonnette).*

Fort de Tournoux

Hike

★Lac des Sagnes – *Start from Jausiers. Leave the car in the hamlet of Lans, along the Route de la Bonette. 3hr untaxing hike.*
Walk northwards; go past a wooden cross, round some ruins and up a slope, crossing a mountain stream on the way. On the opposite slope can be seen the rock spur known as Côtes d'Abriès. The path leads to the bottom of the Grand Bois wooded vale.
The lake is situated within the Parc national du Mercantour where strict regulations are enforced: dogs on a leash, no mountain biking beyond the lake etc.

Mountain bike tour

★Parpaillon round tour – There is a difference in height of almost 1 000m/3 281ft over a distance of 30km/18.6mi. Start from Ste-Anne towards the Chapelle Ste-Anne and the Pont Bérard.
This cycle tour is interesting on two accounts: it satisfies sports enthusiasts and offers them the opportunity of discovering the Parpaillon military road, built by the *chasseurs alpins* (mountain troops) at the end of the 19C to link the upper Ubaye Valley and the Embrun region from La Condamine to Crévoux and then Embrun.

Medal for bravery

Passes of the upper Ubaye Valley were, until relatively recently, the only means of communication between Provence, Dauphiné and Piedmont. Today, their interest is purely touristic. A diploma of the seven passes of the Ubaye is attributed by the Maison de la Vallée and the Barcelonnette tourist office. The passes are:

Col de Vars,
Col de Larche,
Col de Restefond-la-Bonette,
Col de la Cayolle,
Col d'Allos,
Col St-Jean,
Col de Pontis.
Cyclists are asked to buy a notebook which must be stamped each time they go over a pass; there are no time penalties.
Such an achievement is rewarded with a diploma and a medal.

★UBAYETTE

③ From Les Gleizolles to the Col de Larche (on the Italian border)

11km6.8mi – about 30min – local map see p 321

The road *(D 900)* follows the Ubayette Valley lined with villages destroyed in 1944 and rebuilt after the war.

St-Ours – A narrow twisting road, branching off D 900, leads to this isolated hamlet, famous for its fortifications. On the north side of the Rochers de St-Ours, a path gives access to the base of the **Via ferrata de St-Ours** offering rock-climbers two different courses, *l'Ourson* and *l'Aiguille de Luce (see Practical information)*.

Tour of the fortifications – *3km/1.9mi round tour starting from the village.* The fort of **St-Ours-Haut** ⊙ forms the central part of the fortifications. It was used together with the Roche-la-Croix Fort to block the Col de Larche.

Larche – This is the last French village on the way to the Italian border, beyond which lies the lovely Lago della Magdalena.

★**Hike to the Lac du Lauzanier** – *In Larche, turn right after the border post and leave the car in the Pont Rouge parking area (alt 1 907m/6 257ft), 6km/3.7mi further. 2hr walk to the Lac de Lauzanier along GR 5-56.*
A great number of sheep spend the summer in this area of the Parc national du Mercantour; the grass is dense and the path is lined with typical high-pasture huts. The lake (alt 2 284m/7 493ft) fills one of the finest glacial depressions in this part of the Alps. The small chapel used to be a place of pilgrimage.
Experienced hikers can continue to the **Pas de la Cavalle**★★ *(see ST-ÉTIENNE-DE-TINÉE). Allow at least 2hr return.*

★★UPPER UBAYE VALLEY

④ From Les Gleizolles to Maurin

28km/17.4mi – about 3hr – local map see p 321

The Briançon road *(D 902)*, follows the upper Ubaye Valley. The **Redoute de Berwick** on the right formed part of fortifications built at the beginning of the 18C in anticipation of the union of the Ubaye region with France. The road and the river then go through the corridor formed by the **Pas de la Reyssole**.

St-Paul – This pleasant village is the starting point of numerous excursions. The **church**★ dates from the early Middle Ages but the chancel was rebuilt in the 15C and the vault in the 16C, at the end of the Wars of Religion. The doorway is surmounted by a three-lobed rose-window. Note the partly Romanesque octagonal bell-tower with twinned openings, surmounted by a pyramid and four pyramidions. Inside, there is a 17C rood-beam and some fine woodwork.
A picturesque fair of local produce takes place every year on 13 August.

Musée Albert-Manuel (barn of the former Maison Arnaud) ⊙ – This former barn houses an annexe of the Musée de la Vallée de Barcelonnette devoted to agriculture; it displays tools and machinery from the Ubaye region and illustrates traditional techniques.

From St-Paul, continue along D 25 and the River Ubaye.

The road goes through a succession of small hamlets overlooked by the slender steeples of their remarkably well-restored churches, in particular the façades, often decorated with frescoes.

★★**Pont du Châtelet** – This site is famous throughout the region; the single-arched bridge, built in 1880, spans the gorge 100m/328ft above the stream.

Turn right towards Fouillouse.

★**Fouillouse** – This high-mountain hamlet (alt 1 907m/6 257ft) lies on the edge of a desolate glacial cirque overlooked by the Brec de Chambeyron (alt 3 389m/11 119ft). The houses occupy the south-facing slope; note the charming 16C Église St-Jean-Baptiste. Food is available at the inn-café.

Église de Maurin – The church stands on an isolated site, surrounded by the old cemetery. An inscription in Provençal tells how an avalanche destroyed the previous 12C church in 1531. This explains why the present edifice, although built in the 16C, has a Romanesque appearance.

★Hike to the Lac des Neuf couleurs

6hr return starting from Fouillouse. Leave the car at the entrance of the village. It is possible to make it a two-day trip by booking a night in the Refuge du Chambeyron. It may be necessary to go across névés and it is therefore essential to wear mountain boots.

Go through the village and take a path on the left winding its way through a pine wood to a ledge. After climbing for 2hr, hikers will reach the **Refuge du Chambeyron** and **Refuge Jean-Coste** overlooking Lac Premier. The superb high-mountain landscape is framed by the Aiguille de Chambeyron (3 412m/11 194ft) to the north and the Brec de Chambeyron (3 389m/11 119ft) to the east.

The path runs northeast to Lac Long. From the top of a mound on the left there is a fine view of Lac Noir. Continue along the path which goes past the Lac de l'Étoile before reaching the magnificent **Lac des Neuf couleurs★★** (2 834m/9 298ft). It is possible to continue climbing for another hour to the **Col de la Gypière** (2 927m/9 603ft), in clear weather only; hikers must be used to walking across steep screes.

Return to the Ubaye Valley.

The road rises towards Maurin through a gorge and suddenly affords a magnificent view of the valley framed by steep rocky slopes. The desolate Alpine landscape is enhanced by the Mediterranean light. The road goes through several hamlets whose houses are covered with *lauzes* (heavy slabs of schist). From La Barge and Maljasset, hikers can reach the **Col Girardin** in 3hr *(see CEILLAC-EN-QUEYRAS)*. The Église de Maurin comes into view beyond Maljasset.

VAL D'ALLOS★★

Population 709
Michelin map 81 fold 8 or 245 fold 22

Situated in the upper Verdon Valley, on the edge of the Parc national du Mercantour, the Val d'Allos includes Allos village and two nearby ski resorts, Le Seignus and La Foux-d'Allos. Owing to its sunny climate, its beautiful landscape, overlooked by the Trois Évêchés, the Grande Séolane and the Mont Pelat, and its important facilities the Val d'Allos has become one of the most sought-after resorts in the southern Alps.

THE RESORTS

Allos – Alt 1 400m/4 593ft. This old village whose past is linked to that of Barcelonnette, is the starting point of many excursions including the popular hike to the Lac d'Allos.

In summer, the outdoor leisure park, set in green surroundings round a large expanse of water, offers swimming with water chutes, canoeing, tennis...

Skiing area – Cross-country skiers have 25km/15.5mi of marked tracks at their disposal near the village, which is linked by gondola to Le Seignus and the ski runs.

The 13C **Église Notre-Dame-de-Valvert** ⊙ is an interesting example of Provençal Romanesque art; note in particular its harmonious proportions, its elegant east end with Lombard arcading and its larch roof.

Le Seignus – Alt 1 500m/4 921ft. This long-established family resort inaugurated the first ski-lift of the upper Verdon region in 1936.

Skiing area – Situated just above Allos village, Le Seignus offers a limited but varied skiing area; 12 skilifts and some 20 runs (including the Valcibière red run) between 1 500-2 400m/4 921-7 874ft. The first section is equipped with snow-cannon.

★**Le Gros Tapy** – 2 371m/7 779ft. *Allow 1hr 30min return including 1hr chair-lift ride and 15min walk.*

The **panorama★** embraces the Grande Séolane, the Val d'Allos and part of the Parc national du Mercantour (Mont Pelat).

★★**La Foux d'Allos** – Alt 1 708m/5 604ft. La Foux is an important modern resort, situated between Allos and the Col d'Allos, whose wooden houses decorated with small balconies blend well with the surroundings.

Skiing area – Situated inside a glacial cirque, overlooked by the Trois Évêchés Massif, the skiing area is spread over five slopes, which catch the sun in turn, and linked to that of Pra-Loup *(see PRA-LOUP)* to form the **Espace Lumière**, one of the largest skiing areas in France with a total of 230km/143mi of runs. The snowfields around La Foux are ideal for advanced skiers, particularly the runs starting from the upper station of the Observatoire Gondola and the Pouret Chair-lift. Snow-making guarantees resort-level snow until late in the season.

★**Observatoire Gondola** – Alt 2 600m/8 530ft. View of the Tête de l'Estrop, the Préalpes de Digne, the Grande Séolane and the Mont Pelat.

Nature Trail – *Park the car near the tennis courts and the Pont de Labrau Chair-lift as you go into the resort (on the Allos side).* This hike enables visitors to get to know the area surrounding La Foux-d'Allos and its history.

Lac d'Allos

HIKES INSIDE THE PARC DU MERCANTOUR

★★Lac d'Allos – *This excursion attracts many tourists from mid-July to mid-August. Leave very early. Drive east along D 226 for 13km/8mi; twisting road, narrow and steep from Allos onwards. From the end of the road (parking), allow 1hr return on foot and 30min to read the panels and admire the landscape.*
Situated at the heart of the Parc national du Mercantour, the 60ha/148 acre **lake**, which has a maximum depth of 50m/164ft, is the largest natural lake in Europe at that altitude (2 230m/7 316ft). The lake and the surronding jagged peaks form a splendid barren landscape. The azure-coloured expanse of water is supplied by melting snow and numerous springs. Another glacial lake situated below has been replaced by a bog. This and other phenomena concerning Alpine geology and flora are explained on panels dotted along the **nature trail** linking the parking and the lake. Experienced hikers can combine this excursion to the Lac d'Allos with one of the two hikes mentioned below.

★★★Hike to the Mont Pelat – Alt 3 050m/10 007ft. *3hr on the way up and and 1hr 45min on the way down. Difference in height: 925m/3 035ft. Leave the car in the same parking as for the previous excursion. The yellow and green-marked path is untaxing but it is steep and stony towards the end and mountain boots are recommended.*
From the summit, the magnificent **panoramic view★★** of the roads leading to the Col d'Allos, Col de la Cayolle and Col de la Bonette and of the surrounding summits extends in clear weather to the Mont Blanc, Mont Viso and Mont Ventoux. A recently discovered underground glacier runs beneath the surface of the Mont Pelat. Ten ibexes, fitted with transmitters, were reintroduced into the Mont Pelat Massif in 1994. This is just one of several projects designed to encourage the survival of this species in the Mercantour (upper Var, upper Verdon and upper Ubaye valleys).

★★Hike to the Col de la Petite Cayolle and the Pas du Lausson – *6hr round trip. Difference in height: 620m/2034ft. Park the car in the same parking area as for the Lac d'Allos excursion. For a description of the main viewpoints, see Route de la CAYOLLE.*

VALBERG ☀

Michelin map 115 fold 4 or 245 folds 23 and 24

Valberg, lying amid larch forests and green pastures, is a sunny summer and winter resort created in 1935 at an altitude of 1 669m/5 476ft. It is only 80km/50mi away from the Mediterranean coast and is the starting point of round tours of the 'Gorges du Cians and Gorges du Daluis as well as hikes to Mont Mounier (alt 2 817m/9 242ft).

THE RESORT

Skiing area – In spite of being less than an hour's drive from the coast, the resort offers adequate snow cover. The skiing area, linked to that of Beuil *(see BEUIL)*, includes some 50 runs between 1 500m/4 921ft and 2 066m/6 778ft, offering opportunities to practise ski-jumping, speed skiing and snowboarding as well as night-skiing. There are about 40km/25mi of tracks available for cross-country skiers.

Chapelle Notre-Dame-des-Neiges – This high-mountain church is very plain outside. The **interior**★, however, is more elaborate; the coffered ceiling is a fine example of modern religious art.

Croix de Valberg – *45min return on foot. Pleasant hike.* Start from the Col du Sapet road and continue along a steep path. The cross, which is made with wooden skis, is lit at night. Standing at the foot of the cross, one embraces a vast **panorama**★★ from the Grand Coyer to Mont Pelat, and from Mont Mounier to the Mercantour.

EXCURSION

★Route de Guillaumes par Péone *14.5km/9mi along D 29*

The road runs down to Péone in a series of hairpin bends, offering views of the line of peaks extending between the Grand Coyer and the Col de la Cayolle.

Péone – The tall houses of this ancient village nestle at the foot of dolomitic peaks which are one of the natural attractions of the area. Several Catalan families settled in the village during the 13C and the inhabitants continue to be called "Catalans". Strolling through the maze of narrow streets and stepped lanes, one discovers a wealth of beautiful doorways, windows and *trompe-l'œil* façades, the amazing place Thomas-Guérin with its sundial and carved doorways, the Chapelle des Pénitents Blancs and the church.

Beyond Péone, the road follows the Tuébi Valley, deep and narrow at first, but gradually widening as the mountain stream rushes towards the Var. Note the strange ruin-like rock formations dotted along the way.

Guillaumes – *See Haute vallée du VAR.*

It is a duty to protect the environment:
Nature lovers do not just abide by regulations in preservation areas such as the Parc du Mercantour and Parc des Écrins, where species like the marta-gon lily are protected; they also abstain from picking rare plants anywhere and if they do pick other flowers, they make sure they do not pull up the roots.

Le VALBONNAIS ★

Michelin map 77 folds 5, 6, 15 and 16 or 244 folds 39, 40 and 41

The lower valley of the River Bonne, a tributary of the Drac, is known as the **Valbonnais**, whereas its upper valley, upstream of Entraigues, is called **Valjouffrey**. This is a region of deep valleys and wild landscapes characteristic of the Dauphiné mountains. The Bonne Valley leads nowhere, but the valley of its tributary, the Malsanne, allows a scenic road through to the Bourg-d'Oisans region via the Col d'Ornon.

FROM LA MURE TO LE DÉSERT *55km/34mi – about 1hr 30min*

La Mure – *See Lacs de LAFFREY.*

Between La Mure and Le Pont Haut, N 85 offers panoramic views, south towards the imposing Obiou and east towards the snow-capped peaks of the Écrins Massif (Roche de la Muzelle, Pic d'Olan).

Pont-Haut – Capped columns (or "capped maidens" or even "fairies' chimneys" as they are sometimes called) are forming in the nearby ravines.
At Pont-Haut, turn onto D 526.

Valbonnais – Together with Entraigues, Valbonnais is the region's trading centre. As you leave, note the small lake below on the right.

Entraigues – This unassuming village is pleasantly situated on a sunny ledge overlooking the confluence of the rivers Bonne and Malsanne.
From Entraigues, follow D 117 towards Valjouffrey. At the Pont de la Chapelle, turn left onto D 117ᴬ and follow the Valsenestre road.

★**Valsenestre** – The road rises above the **Gorges du Béranger**★, then runs along the wooded slopes (larches and firs). Many waterfalls can be seen on the way. Valsenestre, situated at the entrance of a vast glacial cirque, is the starting point of numerous mountain excursions.
Return to D 117.

★★**Haute-Vallée de la Bonne** – *3hr return on foot. Parking compulsory at the entrance of Le Désert-en-Valjouffrey.*
This untaxing itinerary follows the bottom of the galcial valley carved through the crystalline massif.

Le Désert-en-Valjouffrey (1 267m/4 157ft) is the last village along the upper Bonne Valley; barns still line the main street, testifying to the strong rural traditions.

Beyond the hamlet, the U-shaped valley can be seen clearly; it is blocked by an impressive rock wall reaching over 3 000m/9 843ft. On the left, the alluvial fan of a side valley is cultivated thanks to the patient stone-extracting done by the farmers. The dark-grey Aiguille des Marmes (3 046m/9 993ft) soars above the area. On the right, the Bonne flows at the centre of a vast stony river bed. Beyond the park's gate, the landscape becomes wilder *(read the regulations attentively)*; trees are more and more meagre owing to the altitude. Heather and juniper grow of the south-facing slope whereas the shadier north-facing slope is dotted with alpenrose. The path goes across a scree before reaching the **Cascade de la Pisse★** on the left.

Walk over the footbridge then across a small pine wood: the trees owe their twisted trunks to the fact that they had to adapt to severe conditions. The meagre pastures give way to bare rock within sight of the imposing Pic d'Olan (3 564m/11 693ft) overlooking the Font-Turbat glacial cirque.

Return to Le Désert along the same path.

VAL CENIS ✳

Michelin map 77 fold 9 or 244 fold 32 – Local map see La MAURIENNE

In 1967, the *communes* of Lanslevillard and Lanslebourg united under the name of Val Cenis, a winter resort which occupies a central position in the Haute-Maurienne region and is the ideal starting point of many excursions. It is overlooked all round by high summits: the Dent Parrachée (3 684m/12 087ft) to the west, the Grand Roc Noir to the north and the Pointe de Ronce (3 610m/11 844ft) to the southeast.

THE RESORT

Skiing area – It extends over 500ha/1 236 acres, at altitudes ranging from 1 400m/4 593ft to 2 800m/9 186ft, and a weekly pass giving access to most of the ski resorts in the Maurienne region is available. Europe's longest green run, l'**Escargot**, comes down from the Col du Mont-Cenis *(10km/6.2mi)*; there are also several more difficult runs such as Jacquot, Le Lac and l'Arcelle. The north-facing aspect and the wind which frequently blows from Italy, guarantee adequate snow cover but the weather is often cold and changeable.

Lanslebourg-Mont-Cenis – A garrison was stationed in this border town and a monument was erected to Flambeau, the army dog who, between 1928 and 1938, helped to carry the mail from the barracks up to the Sollières Fort (2 780m/9 121ft).

The **Espace baroque Maurienne** ⊙ is one of the starting points of the themed tour **"Les Chemins du baroque"** *(see Practical information).*

Lanslevillard – The church and its high steeple, camped on a promontory, tower over the village.

Chapelle St-Sébastien ⊙ – *Leave the car near the parish church and continue on foot beyond the school.* The chapel, which looks very plain from the outside, was built in the 15C by a local man following a vow he made during an epidemic of plague. The **murals★**, distempered on all the walls, have retained their fresh colours and are still extremely vivid: the martyrdom of St Sebastian on the right, the life of Jesus Christ elsewhere. Costumes and backgrounds are 15C.

The Renaissance coffered ceiling is remarkable.

VIEWPOINTS

★Vieux Moulin Gondola ⊙ – Alt 2 100m/6 890ft. View of the Dent Parrachée, the Vanoise glaciers and the Arc Valley. Mountain restaurant.

★★Col de la Met – Alt 2 800m/9 186ft. *Access to skiers in winter by chair-lift and to hikers in summer.* Splendid view of the Italian Alps to the south, of the Mont-Cenis Dam and Lake to the southwest, of the Vanoise Massif to the north.

*Constantly revised **Michelin Maps** at a scale of 1:200 000, indicate:*
– difficult or dangerous roads, steep gradients
– car and passenger ferries
– bridges with height and weight restrictions.
*Keep current **Michelin Maps** in the car at all times.*

Plateau de VALENSOLE

Michelin map 81 folds 15 and 16, 114 folds 5 and 6 or 245 folds 21, 33 and 34

This region extends from the middle Durance Valley to the first escarpments of the Préalpes de Digne and Préalpes de Castellane, and from the River Bléone to the lower Verdon. It is a vast plateau sloping from east to west and towering 200-300m/656-984ft above the River Durance. The Asse Valley splits it into two: the north includes arid wooded areas and a few inhabited valleys; the south is flatter and more open with vast fields of cereals and *lavandin* (cultivated lavender) dotted with traditional almond trees. The best time to drive across the plateau is in March, when the almond trees are in bloom, or in July when the scent of the *lavandin* flowers fills the air.

ROUND TOUR STARTING FROM VALENSOLE

89km/55mi – allow 5hr

Valensole – This large village, spread over a gently sloping hill, is the birthplace of Admiral de Villeneuve (1763-1806), who lost the battle of Trafalgar. The church and its massive tower overlook the village; the flat Gothic apse is lit by six lancet windows. The stalls in the chancel date from the 16C.

From Valensole, drive northeast along D 8.

The road skirts the edge of the Valensole Plateau and runs through fields of cereals and *lavandin*, offering interesting **views** of the Asse Valley.

Turn right onto D 953 towards Puimoisson then left to St-Jurs.

St-Jurs – From the church overlooking this ancient hilltop village, the **view**★ extends over the Valensole Plateau and the southern Alps.

Return to D 953.

Lavender and almond trees at Puimoisson

Puimoisson – In the 12C, Puimoisson belonged to the Knights of the Hospital of St John at Jerusalem. The 15C church stands on a vast square planted with nettle trees.

Continue along D 953.

Riez – *See RIEZ.*

Drive southeast along D 952.

The road follows the Colostre Valley which abounds in lavender distilleries.

Allemagne-en-Provence – *See GRÉOUX-LES-BAINS: Excursions.*

Continue along D 952 through fields of *lavandin* and tulips alternating with vineyards.

★**St-Martin-de-Brômes** – Note the date and various inscriptions over the doors of the village's old Romanesque or classical houses. The Romanesque **church** ⊙, dating from the 11C, has a lovely rustic east end and a steeple surmounted by a stone

The "transhumance" of bees

Between early June and mid-July, a feverish activity invades the Plateau de Valensole as beehives are set up everywhere, in time for the flowering of aromatic plants. The season starts in spring with the flowering of rosemary and reaches its climax at the end of June when the lavender fields are in bloom.

At that time, some 250 000 beehives are set up on the plateau; they belong to 500 beekeepers from the nearby *départements* and even from abroad, who rent the land from the farmers. The transport of beehives is strictly regulated. Lorries can only operate at night for obvious security reasons but also for reasons concerning the specific behaviour of bees who all get together inside the beehive after dusk.

pyramid. Inside, note the carved corbels and, behind the altar, an interesting polychrome tabernacle. The 14C **Tour templière** ⊘, once part of the castle, houses a Roman grave found in 1972, dating from the early 4C AD.

Drive southeast along D 82 to Esparron.

Esparron-de-Verdon – The old village built on either side of a ravine is overlooked by the Château des Castellane. Today, Esparron is a small resort for sailing and fishing enthusiasts on the shore of the Gréoux artificial lake.

Go back along the same road and turn left towards Gréoux after 6km/3.7mi.

Barrage de Gréoux – It is 260m/853ft thick at the base, 67m/220ft high and 220m/722ft long. The reservoir holds 85 million m³/68 910cuft of water from the River Verdon, which supply the power station at Vinon (producing 130 million kWh) and the Canal de Provence.

The road reaches the lower Verdon Valley and leads to Gréoux.

‡‡ **Gréoux-les-Bains** – *See GRÉOUX-LES-BAINS.*

Return to Valensole along D 8 which follows the Ravin de Laval.

Le VALGAUDEMAR ★★

Michelin map 77 folds 16 and 17 or 244 folds 40 and 41

The Séveraisse, a clear mountain stream, penetrates deeper than any other tributary of the upper Drac into the Écrins Massif; this is the reason why the Valgaudemar Valley is a sought-after mountaineering area.

The scenery changes dramatically at Villar-Loubière: downstream, the deep smiling valley is covered with pastures separated by rows of poplars and dotted with picturesque villages lost amid clusters of trees, whereas upstream, the landscape becomes oppressive as the river runs between scree-covered south-facing slopes and densely forested north-facing slopes.

FROM N 85 TO THE GIOBERNEY CHALET HOTEL

27km/16.8mi – allow 1hr 30min

Leave N 85 3km/1.9mi north of Chauffayer (between Gap and Corps), turning right onto D 16.

This narrow twisting road, which follows the left bank of the Séveraisse and goes through several villages, is nicely shaded. The elegant pyramid of the Pic d'Olan (alt 3 564m/11 693ft) looms ahead.

Cross the Séveraisse at l'Ubac and turn left towards St-Firmin.

The Church of **St-Maurice-en-Valgaudemar**, standing next to a huge lime tree, forms a charming picture.

Turn back and continue towards Villar-Loubière.

Villar-Loubière – The village clinging to the rockside forms a picturesque setting with the heights of the Écrins Massif in the background: Pic de Bonvoisin, Glacier des Aupillous, Pic des Aupillous and Sommet des Bans (3 669m/12 037ft).

Les Andrieux – The Aiguille du Midi des Andrieux towering above this hamlet screens it from the sun for 100 days every year.

La Chapelle-en-Valgaude-mar – This mountaineering centre is ideally located beneath the Pic d'Olan. From there, it is easy to walk *(1hr return)* to **Les Portes**, which has retained a few lovely old houses; fine view of the Pic d'Olan on the left and of the Cime du Vallon. Beyond the hamlet, a path leads down to the bridge spanning the **"Oulles du Diable"★**, a series of potholes carved by erosion, where the River Navette whirls round with a thundering noise.

Upstream of La Chapelle-en-Valgaudemar, D 480 offers views of several waterfalls gushing down from the slopes or from the glaciers; beyond the Cascade de Combefroide, the road enters the wildest part of the valley and climbs along the northern slope.

★Cascade du Casset – This fine waterfall can be seen on the left, at the intersection with the road leading to Le Bourg.

Les Oulles du Diable

B. Bodin/FOC

Chalet-hôtel du Gioberney – It lies inside a wild and austere glacial **cirque★★**, brightened up by waterfalls including the famous **"Voile de la Mariée"★**, which owes its name to its long frothy train.
The *chalet-hôtel* (alt 1 700m/5 577ft) is the starting point of many excursions into the Écrins Massif.

★Lac du Lauzon – *2hr 30min return on foot; start upstream of the Chalet-hôtel du Gioberney, on the left.* From the lake (alt 2 200m/7 218ft) there is a splendid **view★★** of the glacial cirque which closes off the Valgaudemar Valley: the Bans, Pigeonnier and Rouies massifs.

The high-pasture lookout

Marmots, who live in colonies above 1 000m/3281ft, have evolved an elaborate warning system: one single strident cry announces the presence of a golden eagle or a bird of prey, whereas a series of cries warns of the arrival of a land predator such as a fox or a dog.
Marmots lead a strictly regulated family life. The colony, which forms the social unit, includes several families living in communicating burrows. Marmots find their way along the galleries (up to 10m/yd long) by means of their vibrissae acting as a radar. During their six-month hibernation period, their body temperature falls to 4°C/39.2°F and they lose half their weight. During this time, they are only awake for short periods to allow their body to eliminate its waste. At the end of the mating season, which lasts from mid-April to the mid-May, three to four baby marmots are born to every couple.
The species is protected throughout the Alpine nature parks and reserves, where marmots are relatively friendly towards hikers. In spite of the size of the colonies, many marmots have been taken from one Alpine massif to another in order to even out their numbers. The southern part of the Parc national des Écrins, in particular the Valgaudemar region, is known to shelter large colonies.

---

*The towns and sights described in this guide
are indicated in black lettering on the local maps and town plans.*

VAL D'ISÈRE ✳✳✳

Population 1 703
Michelin map 74 fold 19 or 244 fold 32
Local maps see Route de l'ISERAŃ and Massif de la VANOISE

Val d'Isère is one of the most prestigious Alpine ski resorts, located in the deep valley of the upper Isère River, at an altitude of 1 850m/6 070, beneath the imposing Rocher de Bellevarde, Tête du Solaise and Grande Sassière summits. Beside the resort centre, Val d'Isère includes Le Fornet to the east and La Daille to the north.

Among the numerous champions who won medals in Val d'Isère, two achieved the outstanding record of winning a gold medal in each of the three events (downhill, special slalom and giant slalom): **Toni Sailer** in 1956 and **Jean-Claude Killy** in 1968.

THE RESORT

Skiing area – This family resort owes its success to its abundant snow cover and to its extensive snow fields particularly suitable for experienced skiers who try their skill on the Face de Bellevarde, "S" de Solaise and Tunnel runs... Possibilities of practising cross-country skiing are equally good, owing to the presence, in a 10km/6mi radius, of some 30 passes and summits soaring to 3 000m/9 843ft.

The first ski-lift was built in 1934 and the École Nationale du Ski Français was created in 1935. Later on, the **Route de l'Iseran**★★★ and then the Solaise and Bellevarde cable-cars proved a great asset. The **Critérium de la Première Neige**, held on the Oreiller Killy run, has been marking the beginning of the international Alpine skiing season since 1955. The skiing area is now linked to that of Tignes under the name of **Espace Killy** ✳✳✳ *(see Massif de la VANOISE)* and the men's Alpine events of the 1992 Olympic Games were held along the spectacular **Bellevarde** slopes.

In summer, Val d'Isère is also a lively holiday resort with summer skiing on the Grand Pissaillas Glacier and International Four-wheel-drive Vehicles Show.

Val-d'Isère

VIEWPOINTS ACCESSIBLE BY CABLE-CAR

★★★**Rocher de Bellevarde** ⊙ – Alt 2 826m/9 272ft. *1hr return, including a 7min cable-car ride or 4min 30s by Funival starting from La Daille.*
From the upper station, steep flights of steps lead to the viewing table in 5min. The splendid **panoramic view**★★★ includes Val d'Isère 1 000m/3 281ft below, over-looked by the Grande Sassière, the Tsanteleina and the Glacier des Sources de l'Isère. Note the Lac du Chevril to the north with Mont Blanc in the distance and the main summits of the Vanoise Massif to the west and south.

★★**Tête du Solaise** ⊙ – Alt 2 551m/8 369ft. *45min return, including a 6min cable-car ride.* During the journey and from the platform of the café situated on the summit, the magnificent view embraces the Isère Valley, Val d'Isère and the Lac du Chevril (the Bellevarde Olympic run can be seen opposite) as well as the Grande Sassière, Mont Pourri, Grande Motte and Pointe de la Sana.

★**Col de l'Iseran** – *Access by the Fornet Cable-car and the Vallon de l'Iseran gondola in winter.*

In summer it is preferable to drive up to the pass along the impressive Route de l'Iseran *(see Route de l'ISERAN)*.

From the pass, skiers can go up to the Grand Pissaillas Glacier (3 300m/10 827ft) where they can enjoy superb **views**★★ of the Haute-Maurienne and Haute-Tarentaise.

HIKES

The best itineraries are in the Parc national de la Vanoise, a few kilometres/miles from Val d'Isère.

★★**Refuge de Prariond and Col de la Galise** – *Park the car by the Pont St-Charles on the way to the Col de l'Iseran. 1hr on foot up to the refuge then 2hr to the pass. Difference in height: 900m/2 953ft. 2hr on the way down.*

The steep path goes through the Gorges du Malpasset, where ibexes roam freely, to the foot of the Glacier des Sources de l'Isère. Beyond the refuge it becomes steeper until it reaches the Col de la Galise (alt 2 990m/9 810ft).

★★**Col des Fours** – *Taxing hike requiring a lot of stamina. From the centre of Val-d'Isère, drive south to Le Manchet (3km/1.9mi, parking area). 1hr 30min on foot up to the Fonds des Fours Refuge then 1hr to the pass. Difference in height: 1 100m.3 609ft. 2hr on the way down. It is recommended to wear a windcheater and warm clothing.*

From the refuge, **view**★ of the Grande Sassière, the Mont-Blanc Massif, the Dôme de la Sache and Bellevarde. The path then veers to the left and climbs to the pass (3 000m/9 843ft): splendid **view**★★ of a lake surrounded by the Glacier de la Jave and of the Maurienne and Tarentaise mountains. Chamois are frequently seen in the area.

La VALLOUISE ★★

Michelin map 77 folds 17 and 18 or 244 fold 42 – Local map see p 335

The valley of an important tributary of the Durance, which penetrates deep into the Écrins Massif, was named Vallouise in the 15C after Louis XI, who was king of France at the time. The verdant landscapes are reminiscent of Savoie but the luminous sky is characteristic of the southern Alps. Large villages and spacious stone-built houses, typical of the Briançonnais region *(see Introduction)*, add to the charm of the area. The ski resort of Puy-St-Vincent *(see PUY-ST-VINCENT)* has contributed to the development of tourism.

THE VAUDOIS

Not to be confused with the Swiss from the Vaud County, these Vaudois were members of a sect founded in the 12C by a rich merchant from Lyon, **Pierre Valdo** who believed that salvation depended on the renunciation of all worldly possessions and put his beliefs into practice. The Vaudois cult consisted in praying and reading the holy scriptures. As this new religion, which was a forerunner of the Reformation, spread throughout the Lyon region, the Church became worried and the pope excommunicated Pierre Valdo in 1184.

The Vaudois scattered and took refuge in nearby regions, settling in remote valleys where they were forgotten for two centuries. In 1401, St Vincent Ferrier, the most famous preacher of that time, tried to convert them and persecutions started again, leading eventually to real crusades against them in 1488 and in 1545.

The final blow came in the 17C, after the Revocation of the Edict of Nantes: 8 000 soldiers were sent to clear the Vallouise, Valgaudemar and Champsaur valleys and the Vaudois took refuge over the border in the valleys of the Piedmont region.

The Glacier Blanc and the Refuge du Glacier Blanc

FROM L'ARGENTIÈRE-LA-BESSÉE
TO THE PRÉ DE MADAME CARLE *38km – allow 3hr*

L'Argentière-la-Bessée – *See L'ARGENTIÈRE-LA-BESSÉE.*

From L'Argentière, drive along D 994ᴱ which follows the Vallouise Valley.

The road crosses the Durance and the Gyronde near their confluence. Note on the right, below a pipeline carrying water from the Gyronde to the power station at Argentière, the ruins of some 14C fortifications improperly called **Mur des Vaudois**.

As you drive through La Batie, the twin peaks of Mont Pelvoux come into view with, further south, the Sommet des Bans and the Pic des Aupillous.

Turn right towards Les Vigneaux.

Les Vigneaux – The outside wall of the 15C **church**, to the right of the traditional *réal* (porch), typical of the Embrun region, is decorated with **murals** on the theme of vices and their punishments.

At Pont des Vigneaux, follow the road leading to Puy-St-Vincent.

The cliff-road rises through a larch forest, opposite the beautifully coloured escarpments of the Tête d'Aval and Tête d'Amont.

The view becomes more open and the Glacier Blanc can be seen overlooked by the Pic de Neige Cordier.

✳**Puy-St-Vincent** – *See PUY-ST-VINCENT.*

From Puy-St-Vincent, drive down to Vallouise.

The **Maison du Parc national des Écrins** ⊙ stands on the left, near the intersection with D 994ᴱ. It houses exhibitions about the flora, fauna and geology of the area and also about traditional architecture inside the park. Various shows and activities are designed to make children aware of the environment. A nature trail *(30min walk)* offers an introduction to the natural environment.

★**Vallouise** – This picturesque village has retained a wealth of architecture, including large houses whose arcades are supported by columns sometimes decorated with sundials.

P. Francou

The 15C-16C **church** ★ is an example of Lombard style in the Alps. The elegant porch *(réal)* rests on red-marble columns; beneath the porch, the tympanum is adorned with a mural depicting the Adoration of the Magi. Note the splendid wrought-iron **lock** ★ on the carved door.

The interior is characteristic of the Embrunais region: quadripartite vaulting over the nave and broken barrel vaulting over the aisles.

The chapel on the right of the entrance is covered with frescoes and houses a 15C polychrome Pietà carved in wood. Note the 17C altarpiece and tabernacle in the chancel and the stone stoup with its 16C carved-wood cover bearing the arms of France and Dauphiné.

The treasury beneath the bell-tower houses local religious objects.

Situated next to the church, the 16C **Chapelle des Pénitents** has a façade decorated with murals.

Continue along D 994ᵀ running close to the Gyr. Beyond Le Poët-en-Pelvoux, turn right towards Les Choulières.

The road rises in a series of hairpin bends and offers **close-up views** ★★ of the Grande Sagne, the twin peaks of the Pelvoux, the Pic Sans Nom and L'Ailefroide.

Turn back at Les Choulières and rejoin D 994ᵀ.

Ailefroide – This hamlet, which seems crushed by the Pelvoux foothills, makes an ideal mountaineering base.

D 204ᵀ follows the bottom of the valley which becomes wilder as it gains altitude; larches become rarer. The jagged Pic de Clouzis soars quite near on the right.

★★**Pré de Madame Carle** – This basin previously filled by a lake and planted with larches is today nothing more than a stony field named after a former owner.

This kind of **landscape** ★★ is characteristic of the Dauphiné mountains.

HIKES THROUGH THE VALLOUISE

The Vallouise offers numerous possibilities of hikes along 50 paths totalling 250km/155mi and it is also a superb mountaineering area. It is one of the rare valleys of the southern Alps to afford views of snow-capped high mountains and many glaciers all year round. It is also fascinating from a geological point of view and its varied flora and fauna (chamois) are an added attraction.

★★**Glacier Blanc** – *Fine hike, very popular in summer; 4hr return on foot. Difference in height: 676m/2 218ft to the refuge. Start from the Pré de Madame Carle, waymarked path. Average difficulty.*

The path crosses the mountain stream and climbs up the lateral moraine of the glacier, then, leaving on the left the path leading to the Glacier Noir, it winds its way to the Glacier Blanc, once linked to the Glacier Noir but now receding. Continue to the refuge; difficult sections are fitted with metal ladders. Standing on a ledge on the right, the former Refuge Tuckett (alt 2 438m/7 999ft) has been turned into a mountaineering museum. In July 1862, the British mountaineer Francis Tuckett and his French guides, set up camp here before attempting the ascent of the Barre des Écrins. From the refuge, there is a fine **view** ★★ of the glacier and the north side of the Mont Pelvoux.

★★**Glacier Noir** – *Start from the Pré de Madame Carle (parking area); 1hr 45min up a steep path; 1hr 15min on the way down. Narrow path not suitable for people prone to vertigo. Mountain boots essential.*

Follow the same itinerary as for the Glacier Blanc but turn left towards the Glacier Noir and walk alongside it. It is covered with a thick layer of stones. The Pic Coolidge stands straight ahead with the Ailefroide and **Pelvoux** on the left.

★**Refuge des Bans** – *Alt 2 076m/6 811. From Vallouise, drive west along D 504 and park the car at the end of the road (Entre-les-Aigues, alt 1 615m/5 299ft). This hike requires a certain amount of endurance: 2hr on the way up and 1hr 30min on the way down. Difference in height: 540m/1 772ft.*

The Sommet des Bans is already visible from the parking area. There is a great variety of wild flowers along the path which runs close to the mountain stream then climbs a rocky escarpment to reach the refuge: **view** ★ of the Glacier des Bruyères, the Pic and Glacier de Bonvoisin...

★★**Circuit du Fournet** – *Start from the Refuge des Bans: 1hr 30min up and 1hr down. Difference in height: 470m/1 542ft. The path is marked with white arrows and cairns. Make a note of intersections on the way up as indications are less visible on the way down. Some handrail-assisted passages.*

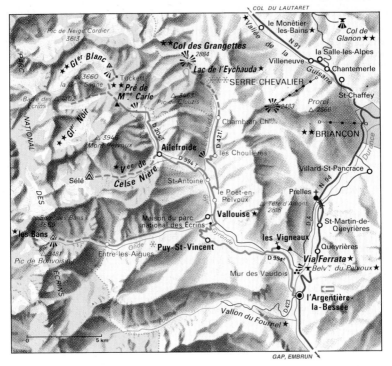

GAP, EMBRUN

Stop by the viewing table situated on a grassy mound: to the west, **view**★★ of Les Bans (alt 3 669m/12037ft) and Pic des Aupillous; to the east, the view extends across the Italian border to Monte Viso. *Retrace your steps.*

★**Lac de l'Eychauda** – Alt 2 514m/8 248ft. *From Vallouise, drive along D 994^T along the Gyr Valley towards Ailefroide, then turn right to Les Choulières.*
The narrow road rises in successive hairpin bends, offering **close-up views**★ of the Grande Sagne, the Pelvoux, the Pic Sans Nom and the Ailefroide. Go to the end of the road (Chalets de Chambran) and park the car (alt 1 720m/5 643ft). Sheep graze on the high pastures framed by soaring peaks. *Continue on foot: 2hr 30min to the lake; 1hr 45min on the way down.*
The ascent is very tiring and monotonous, but the beauty of the lake makes up for it. Walk along the right side of the lake towards the Col des Grangettes to get a good view of the Glacier de Séguret Foran, which feeds the lake.

★★**Col des Grangettes** – Alt 2 884m/9 462ft. *45min climb from the Lac de l'Eychauda. Steep stony path suitable for experienced hikers equipped with non-slip shoes.*
Splendid **panorama**★★: the Guisanne Valley in the foreground, backed by Mont Thabor, the Col du Lautaret and Col du Galibier.

★**Vallée de Celse Nière or Vallon du Sélé** – *4hr 30min return on foot from Ailefroide. Easy hike during the first hour. Walking shoes essential.*
Start from the Celse Nière parking and follow the signposting for the Refuge du Sélé. The path rises along the north bank of the stream, through larch and birch woods. Panels remind visitors of the presence long ago of disciples of Pierre Valdo. The path continues towards the rocky ridge which closes off the valley; a powerful waterfall is fed by melting water from the Sélé Glacier. Chamois can be seen perched on rocky ledges.

Respect the life of the countryside
Drive carefully on country roads
Protect wildlife, plants and trees

VALMOREL ✷

Valmorel is one of the most attractive modern resorts in the Alps, situated at an altitude of 1 400m/4 593ft, at the upper end of the verdant Morel Valley, and surrounded by mountains. Fine old hamlets (Doucy, Les Avanchers) are dotted along the valley renowned for its Beaufort cheese; tourism is expanding rapidly.

THE RESORT

Traffic-free village centre

Skiing area — There is a wide choice of runs for skiers of all levels of proficiency. Experienced skiers prefer the area around St-François-Longchamp via the Madeleine Chair-lift and around the Massif de la Lauzière. The Morel Drag-lift makes it possible to avoid the resort centre and go directly to the Gollet and Mottet skiing areas. Snow-cannons more than make up for insufficient snow cover. It is possible to practise night-skiing on the Planchamp runs and there is a recently opened snowboarding stadium. The Valmorel skiing area is linked to that of **St-François-Longchamp** to form the Grand Domaine *(area pass available)*.

Valmorel is made up of several hamlets which blend well with the surrounding landscape; modern chalets, built with traditional materials (wood, *lauzes*), have large balconies. In the village centre, pedestrian streets and squares are lined with shops and cafés decorated with *trompe-l'œil* paintings.

In summer, there is a wide choice of outdoor activities and excursions.

✶✶✶**Crève-Tête** — Alt 2 341m/7 680ft. *Take the Pierrafort gondola.* From the upper station (1 830m/6 004ft), it is easy to reach the **Col du Golet** which offers a fine view. The path to the summit is steeper, but the panorama is really superb: on one side, the Valmorel Valley framed by the Cheval Noir and the Grand Pic de la Lauzière with the Belledonne range in the distance; on the opposite side, the Trois Vallées area with many famous resorts and, to the left, the Sommet de Bellecôte, Mont Pourri, the Isère Valley and Mont Blanc on the horizon.

Michelin Maps (scale 1: 200 000) which are revised regularly, indicate:
- *golf courses, sports stadiums, racecourses, swimming pools, beaches, airfields,*
- *scenic routes, public and long-distance footpaths, viewpoints,*
- *forest parks, interesting sights...*

The perfect complement to the **Michelin Green Guides** *for planning holidays and leisure time.*

Keep current **Michelin Maps** *in the car at all times.*

Michelin map 74 folds 17, 18 and 19, 77 folds 7, 8 and 9 or
244 folds 20, 21, 31, 32 and 33 – Local map pp 338 and 339

The Massif de la Vanoise, covering a third of the total area of the Savoie *département*, extends between the Isère Valley in the north and the Arc Valley in the south and is adjacent to the Gran Paradiso Park across the Italian border. Its magnificent landscapes, its rich fauna and flora have fascinated mountaineers and hikers since the 19C; it seemed therefore quite natural that the first French national park should be created in this area (1963). One of its goals being the preservation of the last ibexes in the Alps, this animal was chosen as the first emblem of the park.

Lac Blanc and the Col de Soufre

CONSERVATION AREAS

The peripheral zone (1 450km²/560sq mi) – It offers an impressive number of first-class accommodation and sports facilities. The Tarentaise region alone includes some of the largest and most prestigious winter sports resorts as well as picturesque hamlets and villages and a remarkable architectural heritage.

The central zone (530km²/205sq mi) – It is accessible to hikers; however, its exceptional environment is protected by strict regulations *(see also Introduction: Nature parks and reserves)*.
The Vanoise is essentially a high-mountain area: 107 summits above 3 000m/9 843ft and glaciers covering an area of 88km²/34sq mi.
The name Vanoise refers to the huge ice cap extending from the Col de la Vanoise to the Col d'Aussois. The most famous summits are: the Mont Pourri (3 779m/12 398ft) and the Sommet de Bellecôte (3 416m/11 207ft) in the north; the Aiguille de la Grande Sassière (3 747m/12 293ft) in the northeast; the Grande Casse (3 855m/12 648ft) and the Grande Motte (3 656m/11 995ft) in the centre; the Pointe de la Sana (3 456m/11 339ft) and the Pointe de Méan Martin (3 330m/10 925ft) in the east, and finally the Massif de Péclet-Polset (3 562m/11 686ft) and the Dent Parrachée (3 684m/12 087ft) in the south.
Below 2 000m/6 562ft, there are some beautiful forests with a variety of species: spruce, larch and Arolla pine and an exceptionally rich flora including some very rare arctic species such as the buttercup and the catchfly.
The fauna has considerably expanded since the creation of the park; hikers are likely to meet marmots on their way, but the observation of rarer species, such as the ptarmigan, rock partridge, black grouse and golden eagle, requires a great deal of patience and a fair knowledge of animal life in mountain areas.
Owing to its extensive network of waymarked footpaths, the Vanoise is today one of the favourite haunts of hikers in France. In addition to the tourist offices situated in the peripheral zone, there are five information centres known as *"portes du Parc"* at Orgère (near Modane), at Fort Marie-Christine (Aussois), at Plan du Lac (above Termignon), at Rosuel (Peisey-Nancroix) and at le Bois (Champagny-le-Haut).

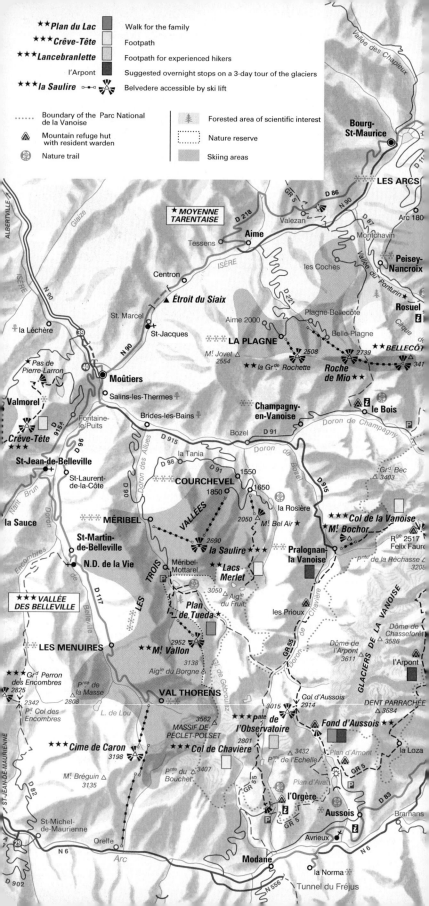

Massif de la VANOISE

★★DRIVES

★★ **La Tarentaise** *(see La TARENTAISE)*
★★ **Route du Petit Saint-Bernard** *(see BOURG-ST-MAURICE: Excursions)*
★★★ **Route de l'Iseran** *(see Route de l'ISERAN)*
★ **La Haute-Maurienne** *(see La MAURIENNE)*
★ **Route du Mont-Cenis** *(see Route du MONT-CENIS)*
★★★ **Vallée des Belleville** *(see La Vallée des BELLEVILLE)*

Fine roads running along the Arc and Isère valleys make it possible to drive right round the park. However, it is not possible to explore the centre of the massif by car; the best scenery is available to skiers in winter and hikers in summer.

★★★HIKES

For more information, please refer to:

– the map entitled "Massif et Parc national de la Vanoise" (Didier & Richard, Grenoble) on a scale of 1:50 000;
– the topo-guide of GR 5 and GR 55 footpaths (see Practical information);
– "L'Estive", a periodical detailing the activities of the Parc national de la Vanoise.

Main viewpoints accessible by lift

★★★ **Cime de Caron** – *See La vallée des BELLEVILLE: Val-Thorens*
★★★ **Bellevarde** – *See VAL D'ISÈRE*
★★★ **Aiguille Rouge** – *See Les ARCS*
★★★ **La Grande Motte** – *See TIGNES*
★★★ **La Saulire** – *See COURCHEVEL or MÉRIBEL*
★★ **Mont du Vallon** – *See MÉRIBEL*
★★ **Bellecôte Gondola** – *See La PLAGNE*

Hiking possibilities in the Vanoise are infinite. First-time visitors can stay in Pralognan, Champagny, Peisey-Nancroix or Bonneval-sur-Arc. Ski resorts are also excellent hiking bases: Pralognan, Tignes, St-Martin-de-Belleville (Les Ménuires), Méribel or Courchevel.

There are fine hiking trails in the peripheral zone as well as in the central zone. The best hikes described in this guide are listed below and graded according to their level of difficulty *(see Practical information for advice as mountain areas can be dangerous)*. The best time for hiking is from 4 July to 15 August. Later on, the flora is less interesting and at the end of June there is still a fair amount of snow which makes itineraries above 2 000m/6 562ft a bit tricky. On the other hand, at the beginning and at the end of summer, the area offers the great advantage of being less crowded.

■ Family rambles

These short and easy itineraries are accessible to children but it is advisable to be properly equipped all the same.

★★ **Lac de la Sassière** *(see TIGNES)*
★★ **Le Monal** *(see STE-FOY-TARENTAISE)*
★★ **Refuge de Prariond** *(see VAL D'ISÈRE)*
★★ **Plan du Lac** *(see La MAURIENNE)*
★★ **Refuge d'Avérole** *(see BESSANS)*
★★ **Fond d'Aussois** *(see AUSSOIS)*
★ **Chalets de la Duis** *(see BONNEVAL-SUR-ARC)*
★ **Plan de Tueda** *(see MÉRIBEL)*

☐ Hikes

These itineraries require stamina and physical fitness but are not technically difficult.

★★★ **Col de la Vanoise** *(see PRALOGNAN and La MAURIENNE)*
★★★ **Col du Palet and Col de la Tourne** *(see TIGNES)*
★★★ **Col de Chavière** *(see MODANE)*
★★★ **Crève-Tête** *(see VALMOREL or La vallée des BELLEVILLE)*
★★ **Lac de la Plagne** *(see PEISEY-NANCROIX)*
★★ **Refuge du Carro** *(see BONNEVAL-SUR-ARC)*
★★ **Refuge des Évettes** *(see BONNEVAL-SUR-ARC)*
★★ **Lacs Merlet** *(see COURCHEVEL)*
★★ **Col des Fours** *(see VAL D'ISÈRE)*

▌ Itineraries for experienced hikers

These itineraries require stamina and include difficult sections (extremely steep or vertiginous paths...). They do not, however, require any knowledge of rock-climbing or mountaineering techniques *(non-slip mountain boots essential)*.

★★★ **Pointe du Chardonnet** *(see TIGNES)*

★★★ **Pointe de l'Observatoire** *(see AUSSOIS)*

★★★ **Pointe des Lessières** *(see Route de l'ISERAN)*

★★★ **Lancebranlette** *(see BOURG-ST-MAURICE)*

▌ Three-day round tour of the Vanoise Glaciers

This itinerary is suitable for experienced hikers in top form. Before leaving, it is essential to book overnight stays in refuges (ask at the Pralognan tourist office) and to inquire about the weather forecast over several days. Leave very early in the morning in order to reach the refuge before 7pm (reservations are cancelled after that time). See the advice on hiking given in the Practical information.

First day: Pralognan – **Mont Bochor**★ (by cable-car) – **Col de la Vanoise**★★★ – Refuge de l'Arpont.

Second day: Refuge de l'Arpont – La Loza – La Turra – **Refuge du Fond d'Aussois**★★★.

Third day: Refuge du Fond d'Aussois – Col d'Aussois – **Pointe de l'Observatoire**★★★ – Les Prioux – Pralognan.

SKIING AREA

The peripheral zone of the Vanoise Massif includes an exceptionally fine skiing area with three major assets: its size, the quality of its equipment and of its snow cover. The Maurienne Valley specialises in charming family resorts, whereas the Tarentaise has, since the 1930s, acquired an impressive number of winter sports resorts. The high quality of these resorts was officially acknowledged when the 1992 Winter Olympics were held there. The Espace Olympique Pass gives access to the following areas: Les Trois Vallées, L'Espace Killy, L'Espace La Plagne-les-Arcs, Pralognan, Ste-Foy-Tarentaise, La Rosière, Valmorel and Les Saisies.

Espace Killy ★★★ – This skiing area, linking that of **Tignes** ★★★, and **Val d'Isère** ★★★, has gained international fame because of its size (100km²/39sq mi), its high-quality snow cover (all year skiing on the Grande Motte Glacier) and its superb high-mountain scenery. There are some 100 ski-lifts and 300km/186mi of runs.
Val d'Isère is particularly suitable for advanced skiers whereas Tignes has easier runs and skiers are able to ski right down to the resort.

USEFUL TIPS

Given the size of the skiing area, it is advisable to acquire the skier's guide to the Trois Vallées from one of the tourist offices, to make up some suitable itineraries and eventually ask for advice at the resort. Marking is excellent and, in general, the area is open from Christmas to the beginning of May. It is recommended to ski along less crowded runs (if conditions were bad, they would be closed). Be aware of the time and of bad weather conditions so that you may be sure to return to your base in good time.

In addition to the two main skiing areas of the Trois Vallées and the Espace Killy, the Tarentaise offers a choice of first-class resorts such as **La Plagne** ★★ and **Les Arcs (Peisey-Nancroix)** ★★★.
There are also smaller resorts which are interesting from a sightseeing point of view and enjoy very good snow cover conditions such as **La Rosière** ★ and **Valmorel** ★.

★★★ **Les Trois Vallées** – This skiing area, covering 400km²/154sq mi and extending over the **St-Bon Valley (Courchevel** ★★★, **La Tania)**, the **Allues Valley (Méribel** ★★★) and the **Belleville Valley** ★★★ (**St-Martin-de-Belleville** ★, **Les Ménuires** ★★ and **Val-Thorens** ★★★), is the largest skiing area in the Alps: 210 ski-lifts including 37 gondolas and cable-cars, 300 runs and itineraries totalling 700km/435mi. These are extremely varied: there are large pisted runs for all levels of proficiency, technical pistes – among the most difficult in the Alps – and numerous possibilities of off-piste skiing in conservation areas as well as 110km/68mi of cross-country skiing tracks.

Massif de la VANOISE

The Trois Vallées owe their success to the efficient links operating between resorts, to their high-quality snow cover from the end of November to mid-May and to the opportunities they offer visitors of discovering the diversity of mountain landscapes and life. Some resorts are modern and functional (Les Ménuires, Val-Thorens), others are more traditional (St-Martin-de-Belleville, Méribel). Courchevel has luxury districts and a fashionable atmosphere whereas Les Ménuires boasts a young sporting atmosphere. However, skiers appreciate above all else the quality of the area's natural environment from the Val-Thorens glaciers to the fine forests at Méribel and Courchevel.

Haute vallée du VAR★★

Michelin map 81 folds 9 and 19, 115 folds 2, 3, 13 and 14 or 245 fold 23

Road D 2202 follows the upper Var Valley through some deep narrow passages. It is one of the main routes leading from the Alps to the Nice region.

FROM ENTRAUNES TO PUGET-THÉNIERS

51km/32mi – allow 3hr

Entraunes – This village lies in a pleasant setting at the confluence of the rivers Var and Bourdoux, below the Col de la Cayolle. The church has a strange asymmetrical bell-tower.
The **Chapelle St-Sébastien** ⊙, situated at the northern end of the village, is worth a visit: frescoes by Andrea de Cella, dating from 1516, cover the wall of the apse, forming a kind of Renaissance altarpiece (St Sebastian's martyrdom surmounted by the Crucifixion).

The road runs through an austere mountain landscape; beyond a tunnel, the valley opens out into the St-Martin Basin.

St-Martin-d'Entraunes – The verdant setting of this village perched on a morainic mound offers a contrast with the mostly arid landscapes of the upper Var Valley. The Provençal Romanesque **church** ⊙ has a blind façade and a Gothic side porch bearing the emblem of the Knights Templars. The sundial bears the inscription: "The sun guides me, your pastor shows you the way". Inside, there is a fine altarpiece, known as the **Retable de la Vierge de Miséricorde**, by François Bréa, dating from 1555.

3.5km/2.2mi beyond Villeneuve-d'Entraunes, turn left onto D 74 which rises above the Barlatte Valley.

Châteauneuf-d'Entraunes – The village lies in a desolate landscape, above the upper Var Valley. The church houses an altarpiece in Primitive style (1524), reminiscent of François Bréa's work.

Return to D 2202 and turn left.

Guillaumes – This old fortified village, situated at the confluence of the rivers Var and Tuébi, is today a summer resort overlooked by the ruined castle (fine view). Shortly after Guillaumes, the valley narrows into a gorge.

★★**Gorges de Daluis** – This deep, austere gorge, through which flows the River Var, is quite impressive. The cliff road between Guillaumes and Daluis winds its way along the west bank of the upper Var, high above the clear green water of the river. In the narrowest parts, tunnels had to be dug through the rock, in order to ease the traffic. It is in those places that the road affords the finest **views**★★ of the red-schist gorge dotted with fresh greenery.
A rock in the shape of a female bust seems to guard the downstream entrance of the gorge.

Between Daluis and Entrevaux, the road follows the river which veers left at Pont de Gueydan. The valley narrows once more near Entrevaux.

★**Entrevaux** – *See ENTREVAUX.*

On the way to Puget-Théniers along N 202, there is a lovely view of the **setting**★★ of Entrevaux.

★**Puget-Théniers** – *See PUGET-THÉNIERS.*

*The annual **Michelin Guide Camping Caravaning France** offers a selection of campsites and up-to-date information on their location, setting, facilities and services.*

VARS ✳ ✳

Population 941
Michelin map 77 fold 18 or 245 folds 9 and 10

Situated between Guillestre and Barcelonnette, Vars is one of the main winter and summer resorts of the southern Alps, sought after for its sunny climate, the quality of its facilities and the beauty of its natural environment.

THE RESORT

Accommodation is spread over three traditional hamlets (Ste-Marie, St-Marcellin and Ste-Catherine) and a modern resort (Les Claux) at altitudes ranging from 1 600-1 800m/5 249-5 906ft. **Ste-Marie-de-Vars** and **Les Claux** alone offer direct access to the ski runs.

Skiing area – It is linked to that of Risoul under the name of "Forêt Blanche" and is constantly expanding; at present, it includes 56 ski-lifts, 170km of runs with adequate snow cover. It is ideal for intermediate skiers who love beautiful scenery. The Speed-skiing World Championships are held here. Several fine runs start from the Pic de Chabrières and advanced skiers can enjoy the "Olympic" run above Ste-Marie and the "Mur du Grand Ubac" near Les Claux. Off-piste skiing can be practised in the Risoul area and there are 25km/16mi of marked cross-country skiing tracks.

In summer, Vars is an excellent hiking base. In addition to skiing and rambling, the resort offers a wide choice of summer and winter activities: skating, snow mobiling, swimming, riding, mountain biking, paragliding, squash, fitness courses...

EXCURSIONS

✳✳Pic de Chabrières – *In winter: access via the Chabrières Gondola ⊙, the Crévoux and Chabrières Chair-lifts. In summer: access via the Chabrières gondola, then on foot (3hr 30min return).*
The upper station of the Chabrières gondola is situated at the foot of the speed-record trial run; view of the villages and surrounding summits.
The **Pic de Chabrières** (alt 2 727m/8 947ft) offers a magnificent **panorama✳✳** of the "Forêt Blanche" backed by the Pic de la Font Sancte, the Queyras Massif, the snow-capped Pelvoux and the peaks surrounding the Serre-Ponçon Lake, which is visible from the **Col de Crévoux✳**.

✳✳Réserve naturelle du Val d'Escreins ⊙ – *From Vars, drive down towards Guillestre along D 902; turn right onto a small road following the Val d'Escreins.*
The Rif-Bel Valley, which is inaccessible during eight months of the year, has been a nature reserve (2 500ha/3 707 acres) since 1964 and was later joined to the Parc naturel régional du Queyras.
At the end of the valley, the forested slopes give way to barren summits, including the **Pic de la Font Sancte** (alt 3 387m/11 112ft). The name, meaning "holy fountain", comes, according to tradition, from a spring, discovered by a young shepherdess, which became a place of pilgrimage in times of drought. The climb to the summit is only suitable for experienced hikers who are rewarded with one of the finest panoramas in the Alps.
The reserve, open to visitors in summer, offers 37km/23mi of marked footpaths linking this valley to that of Ceillac in the north and Maurin in the east. Accommodation is available during the season at the Basse Rua refuge.

Nature trail – *40min walk.* The fairly steep path offers the possibility of observing the main species of Alpine trees (larches, firs, spruces, pines...) and a few flower species (mountain centaury, large gentian, orchis...).

✳✳Hike to the Tête de Paneyron – Alt 2 787m/9 144ft. *Leave the car at the Col de Vars. 3hr 30min return on foot. Difference in height: 677m/2 221ft. It is advisable to wear mountain boots.*
Walk down towards Barcelonnette for a few minutes and turn left onto a wide path leading to a shepherd's house in 20min; on the right, slightly above, you will see some cairns showing you the way. After a 10min walk across pastures, you will find a real path which climbs very steeply as it nears the summit. Beautiful **panorama✳✳** of the skiing area from the Pointe de l'Eyssina to the Val d'Escreins and of the road to the Col de Vars, from Guillestre to the Ubaye River.
Turn back.

St-Marcellin-de-Vars – This ancient hamlet has retained its mountain-village atmosphere. The church, rebuilt in the 18C, has a beautiful doorway and a set of lions which once supported the columns of the porch.

✳Walk to the castle – *Leave the car in one of St-Marcellin's parking areas. Allow 1hr 30min return on foot (steep path).*
Walk along the right side of the church. The path is marked in yellow. After the first bend to the left, carry straight on *(ignore the house up on the right)*. The path crosses a small road. Continue to the summit where you will find explanations about the ruined castle and enjoy an extended **view✳** of the various hamlets around Vars, of Guillestre and of Mont-Dauphin.

Route de VARS ★

Michelin map 77 fold 18 or 245 folds 9 and 10

The road leading to the Col de Vars links the Embrun-Queyras region with the Ubaye Valley. Motorists driving from the south discover the first snow-capped peaks of the Écrins Massif.

FROM GUILLESTRE TO ST-PAUL 27km/17mi – allow 1hr

The Col de Vars may be blocked by snow from December to April.

Guillestre – *See GUILLESTRE.*

From Guillestre, drive south along D 902.

Between Guillestre and Peyre-Haute, there are views of the fortified city of Mont-Dauphin *(see MONT-DAUPHIN)* perched on its promontory, of the Durance Valley upstream of Embrun and of the Guil Valley. The road rises up to a rocky ridge separating the Rif-Bel (Val d'Escreins) and Chagne valleys.

Peyre-Haute Viewing table – *15min return on foot; 100m upstream of Peyre-Haute (panel), climb onto the mound on the left.* The **view★** includes, from left to right, the Ailefroide, the Pic sans Nom, the Pelvoux, and the Pic de Neige Cordier with the Glacier Blanc coming down from it.

The next few bends offer views of the snow-capped summits of the Écrins Massif.

The Val d'Escreins road branches off on the left.

★★**Val d'Escreins** – *See VARS: Excursions.*

The road goes through the hamlets which make up the resort of Vars.

★★**Vars** – *See VARS.*

From Vars to the pass, the road runs along the foot of the slopes, equipped with ski-lifts between Ste-Marie and the Refuge Napoléon.

Col de Vars – Alt 2 111m/6 926ft. Meagre pastures dotted with blocks of sandstone; monument commemorating the renovation of the road by Alpine troops.

On the way down to Melezen, the pastoral landscape remains austere. The truncated summit of the Brec de Chambeyron (alt 3 390m/11 122ft), preceded by a long ridge, can be seen to the east.

Between Melezen and St-Paul, there is an interesting group of "colonnes coiffées" (capped columns) on the roadside. It is possible to park the car before the small bridge and walk close to them *(see Demoiselles coiffées de THÉUS).*

St-Paul – *See L'UBAYE.*

VASSIEUX-EN-VERCORS

Population 283
Michelin map 77 fold 13 or 244 fold 38 – Local map see Le VERCORS

During the Second World War, tragic events took place in this village lying in a valley of south Vercors. In 1944, while fierce fighting was going on in the region, the Resistance built an airfield for the Allies near Vassieux; unfortunately this was used by German gliders filled with commandos, who killed the population and burnt the village. Vassieux was entirely rebuilt and a monument, surmounted by a recumbent figure by Gilioli, was erected to the "Martyrs of the Vercors, 1944"; a commemorative plaque on the town hall square bears the names of the 74 civilian victims.

The Resistance members who took part in the events of 1944 came from various walks of life: dismissed member of parliament, writer, officers, photographer, priest-…they all contributed to the heroic effort which led to the liberation of the region.

SIGHTS

Church – Built after the war, the edifice is decorated with a fresco by Jean Aujame *(the Assumption)* and bears a touching commemorative plaque.

Musée de la Résistance du Vercors ⊙ – Founded by a former member of the Resistance, it deals with the events which took place in the Region in 1944, as well as the Nazi camps and the Liberation.

EXCURSIONS

Cimetière national du Vercors – *1km/0.6mi north along D 76.*
The cemetery contains the graves of 193 Resistance fighters and civilian victims who died during the operations of July 1944. View of the Memorial.

★**Mémorial du Vercors (Col de la Chau)** ⊙ – *3km/1.9mi from Vassieux; from the cemetery, take D 76 on the left. Parking area at the pass.*

The memorial stands out like the prow of a ship against the dense Forêt de Lente. Built by a group of architects from Grenoble at an altitude of 1 305m/4 282ft, it is covered with junipers and pines which grow naturally in the Vercors Massif. The intentionally plain building contains a succession of rooms devoted, with the help of audiovisual means, to mementoes of the Vercors Resistance Movement and to national events which took place at the time. There are reconstructions and dioramas about collaboration with the Germans, questioning by the Milice (French paramilitary organisation created by the Vichy Government), the role of women in the Resistance movements... Recorded individual accounts are available and contemporary films recall the "République du Vercors" which lasted until 23 July 1944.

On the way out, the names of 840 civilian victims are inscribed in recesses along a large wall. From the terrace, the view embraces the Vassieux Valley.

There are plans to link the main fighting sites, the villages and the cemeteries involved in the events of July 1944 by a historic trail called "**Parcours du Site National Historique de la Résistance**".

★**Atelier préhistorique de taille de silex** ⊘ – *3km/1.9mi south along D 615 (signposts).* Excavations made in 1969 revealed a concentration of flints over an area of $100m^2$/120sq yd, which proved the existence 4 000 years ago of a flint-cutting workshop. This is the third of its kind discovered in Europe; this one specialized in making knife and dagger blades, which were exported throughout Europe. A building now protects the site. There are flint-cutting demonstrations, an audiovisual show, displays, explanatory panels and the reconstruction of prehistoric dwellings.

Flint-cutting technique

Flint blades are made out of a rough piece of rock in four successive stages:
– rough-hewing the nodule with the help of another rock
– smoothing the surface with a hard round stone (pebble)
– flattening one of the extremities
– flaking the blade off the main block: a delicate operation which requires a sure hand to prevent the nodule from splitting. One blow on the end of the block with a piece of hard wood is sufficient.

Le VERCORS ★★★

Michelin map 77 folds 3, 4, 12 to 14 or 244 folds 27, 28, 37, 38 and 39
Local map pp 352 and 353

The Vercors, which has the densest network of roads of all the mountain areas in the Dauphiné region, is a high, massive limestone plateau, covered with beech and conifer forests; daring cliff roads follow the many deep gorges (Combe Laval, Grands Goulets) carved by the tributaries of the lower Isère, particularly the Bourne.

A potholer's paradise – The "crust" of the Vercors Plateau consists of a gently undulating layer of limestone from the Cretaceous period, up to 300m/984ft thick in places, which forms impressive cliffs in the gorges and along the edge of the massif. Water flows freely through these calcareous rocks, streams disappear into sink-holes known as *scialets*, similar to the *chourums* of the Dévoluy region, and reappear as resurgent springs. The most striking example of this phenomenon is the underground **Vernaison**; identified in the depths of the Luire Cave, it reappears in the Bournillon Cave, 20km/12mi further on, which makes it one of the major underground rivers in France.

The exploration of the **Gouffre Berger**, which opens on the Sornin Plateau (west of Sassenage), led the Spéléo-club de la Seine down to – 1 141m/3 743ft.

Regional differences – The Vercors includes two geographical entities separated by the Bourne Valley. The **"Montagnes de Lans"** north of the River Bourne, a cattle-farming area with its own breed, known as the Villard-de-Lans breed, is economically more developed. South of it lies the **"real" Vercors**, on either side of the Ver-naison Valley. It is a densely forested area, which remained isolated until the Grands Goulets road was built. Its natural outlet is the **Royans Region** on the western edge of the massif.

Stronghold of the Resistance Movement

The strategic advantage of the Vercors Massif, i.e. easily controlled access, became apparent to the local resistance movements as early as 1942 and several defensive camps were established from 1943 onwards.

Two amateur mountaineers, the writer Jean Prévost and the architect Pierre Dalloz drew up a plan with General Delestraint, head of the Secret Army, to establish an allied bridgehead in the Vercors support by the air force. It was the famous **"plan Montagnards"**.

In March 1944, there were two Resistance groups in the Vercors, totalling 400 men. After D-day, there were 4 000 volunteers under the command of professional soldiers. On 3 July, the "République du Vercors" was proclaimed and the Allies dropped light armament and material. The area was soon surrounded by two German Alpine divisions numbering 15 000 men and, on 21 July, German gliders used the airfield intended for allied planes to drop special commandos and SS troops. After three days of fierce fighting, the outnumbered resistants retreated towards the Forêt de Lente while the St-Martin Hospital was evacuated south to the Grotte de la Luire; however all its staff and patients were either killed or deported to Ravensbrück a few days later and reprisals continued until 19 August.

Memorials in the Vercors Massif:

– The Cour des fusillés (execution courtyard) in La Chapelle-en-Vercors
– The Mémorial du Vercors at the Col de la Chau (inaugurated in 1994)
– The Grotte de la Luire
– Malleval Village
– The cemetery in St-Nizier-du-Moucherotte
– The ruins in Valchevrière
– The cemetery and monument to the victims of Vassieux-en-Vercors

Remarkable ecosystem – Forests, which cover more than half the total area of the Vercors Massif, offer great variety: beeches and firs are gradually replaced by pines in the south of the region. There are more than 1 800 plant species including some very rare species which are protected: lady's slipper, martagon lily and forest tulip.

The Vercors is one of the rare areas where the six species of wild hoofed animals living in France can be found: chamois, deer, roe-deer, wild boars, moufflons and ibexes (reintroduced in1989, these now number 100 head).

Birds of prey are also well represented: golden eagles, peregrines, eagle owls, Bonelli's eagles (in the south) and a few bearded vultures. Since 1994, griffon vultures have gradually been reintroduced in the Parc naturel régional du Vercors.

★① GORGES DE MÉAUDRE AND GORGES D'ENGINS

88km/55mi round tour – allow 5hr – local map see p 353

From Villard-de-Lans to Grenoble

✳**Villard-de-Lans** – *See drive* ②: *Grands Goulets.*

From Villard, drive west along D 531.

The road follows the River Bourne. At Les Jarrands, turn right onto D 106 which goes up the **Gorges de Méaudre** through pastoral scenery.

Beyond Méaudre, bear left onto D 106ᶜ.

✳**Autrans** – This resort is sought after for cross-country skiing.

Col de la Croix Perrin – Alt 1 220m/4 003ft. The pass is a vast clearing between slopes clad with splendid forests of firs. In Jaume, D 106 veers to the right, goes through **Lans-en-Vercors** then rises above the Furon Valley, offering bird's-eye views of the picturesque Gorges d'Engins and Gorges du Bruyant.

St-Nizier-du-Moucherotte – This village, burnt down by the Germans in 1944 and subsequently rebuilt, occupies a splendid open site on the plateau; it is one of the favourite winter and summer resorts of the population of Grenoble. A path, starting from the Bel-Ombrage Hotel leads to a **viewpoint★★** offering extended views of the Chartreuse, Mont-Blanc, Belledonne and Écrins Massifs. The church, which was extensively restored, houses some interesting modern works of art.

Mémorial du Vercors – This cemetery, containing the graves of 96 members of the Resistance, is situated on the first line of defence attacked by the Germans in July 1944.

Sommet du Moucherotte – Start from the parking at the top of the Olympic ski-jump and follow GR 91 *(2hr on foot)*. The vast panorama★★★ unfolding from the summit includes Mont Blanc when the weather is clear and, at night, the view of Grenoble is enchanting.

The heyday of the Moucherotte Summit

For 10 years, the Hôtel Ermitage, built in 1955 on the Moucherotte Summit, was a fashionable venue sought after by a show biz crowd which included Roger Vadim and Brigitte Bardot. However, the establishment, which was only accessible by cable-car from Grenoble when the weather permitted, ran into financial difficulties and closed down five years after the Grenoble Olympic Games of 1968. Plans for its renovation are being considered.

On the way down to Grenoble, there are views of the Grenoble Basin where the Isère and Drac rivers meet.

Tour Sans Venin – *15min return on foot.* One of the Seven Wonders of Dauphiné. According to legend, a crusader brought back some soil from the Holy Land and, by spreading it round his castle, rid the area of all venomous snakes. From the foot of the ruined tower, the **view★** extends south to the Dévoluy.

★★**Grenoble** – *See GRENOBLE.*

From Grenoble to Villard-de-Lans

★★**Grenoble** – *See GRENOBLE.*

From Grenoble, drive northwest to Sassenage along D 532.

Sassenage – This little town lies only 6km/3.7mi west of Grenoble, at the beginning of one of the sceninc routes through the Vercors Massif; the church contains the grave of **François de Bonne de Lesdiguières**, the last Constable of France.

A pleasant walk along the banks of the Furon leads to **Les Cuves** ⊙, a couple of caves situated one above the other and linked by a waterfall. The tour offers the possibility to explore a vast underground maze of galleries full of stalactites, stalagmites and fossils.

The 17C **castle** ⊙ stands in a landscaped park *(open to the public)*, at the foot of a rocky knoll crowned by the ruins of the feudal castle.

Beyond Sassenage, D 531 rises rapidly, offering fine **views★** of the Chartreuse Massif and the Belledonne range further away.

★**Gorges d'Engins** – The smooth rock walls of this deep trench frame the verdant valley of the Furon.

Gorges du Bruyant – A convenient footpath, linking D 531 and D 106, leads to the bottom of the gorge *(1hr return)*.

From Jaume to Villard-de-Lans, the road follows the Lans Valley, whose gentle slopes are clad with dense forests of firs, within sight of the peaks marking the eastern edge of the Vercors. Note the stepped gables of traditional houses.

★★★② GRANDS GOULETS

From Villard-de-Lans to Pont-en-Royans

36km/22.4mi – allow 2hr – local map see p 353

※**Villard-de-Lans** – The tourist capital of the Vercors region has the best facilities of all the resorts in the Dauphiné Préalpes. Its dry, sunny climate, its pure atmosphere, its sheltered position are ideal for children and holidaymakers in general enjoy the many outdoor activities available: paragliding, potholing, canyoning and ballooning.

The **Cote 2000** ⊙ (spot height 2000, 6 562ft) can be reached by gondola *(4.5km/2.8mi southeast of Villard)* and then on foot *(1hr return for the gondola ride and the walk)*. Blocked to the east and south by the nearby Moucherolle and Gerbier summits, the view embraces the undulating plateaux of the Montagnes de Lans and Vercors to the north and west.

A small scenic road, lined with the Stations of the Cross dedicated to the victims of the fighting which took place in 1944, leads to the **Calvaire de Valchevrière ★** *(8km/5mi west along D 215C)* erected on the last position held on 23 and 24 July 1944 by members of the Resistance. The deep **Gorges de la Bourne** *(see drive* ③*)* can be seen below. Continue to the Chalets de Chalimont, then right along a forest road *(by car or on foot – 1hr return – depending on the weather)* to the **Brèche de Chalimont ★**, a narrow ridge offering extended views of the whole area.

The likely return of the bear

Since it was last seen near St-Martin-en-Vercors in 1938, the European brown bear has completely disappeared from the French Alps. This animal, which lives in forests, is particularly discreet and can sense human presence several hundred yards away. Occasionally carniverous, it is fond of plants and looks for them in remote and steep wooded areas. The Haut-Vercors region, which is totally desolate in winter and has no permanent settlements, offers the ideal conditions for the return of the bear, which is represented by statues in many villages. However, the Parc naturel régional du Vercors Authorities, who have drawn plans for this possible return, are first looking for the support and active involvement of the local population, particularly farmers.

Drive along D 531 towards Pont-en-Royans.

Beyond Les Jarrands, the road runs beside the stream through a deep gorge.

At the Pont de la Goule Noire, bear left along D 103.

La Goule Noire – This important resurgent spring is visible downstream of the Pont de la Goule Noire, level with the river bed.

The cliff-road rises above the south bank of the Bourne, offering lovely views of cliffs known as the Rochers du Rang, then continues through the St-Martin-en-Vercors Valley; beyond St-Julien, there are clear views of the upper Vernaison Valley.

St-Martin-en-Vercors – This was the French headquarters during the 1944 fighting. The last bear was seen here in 1937.

Caverne de l'ours ⊙ – Situated at the entrance of St-Martin, this exhibition illustrates the ties which have always existed between men and bears, with the help of reconstructions and the display of stuffed animals.

Beyond Les Barraques, D 518 enters the Grands Goulets.

Parking facilities at the entrance of Les Barraques.

★★★**Grands Goulets** – *Extreme care is required as you drive through the Grands Goulets. Parking areas for one or two cars are on the right-hand side of the road driving towards Les Barraques. The tunnels are not designed for large vehicles.*

This deep narrow gorge is the most impressive natural sight of the Vercors region. Before driving through, walk as far as the second bridge over the Vernaison *(15min return)*. Daylight barely reaches the road through the thick vegetation and when you suddenly enter the gorge on a blazing summer's day, the effect is striking. Near the last tunnels, the cliff-road clings to the rock face above the river bed (numerous waterfalls). Downstream, the ravine opens out; look back after the last tunnel to appreciate the depth of the gorge. The road continues high above the valley; arid slopes, overlooked by rocky escarpments high in colour, contribute to the southern atmosphere which pervades the scenery.

★**Petits Goulets** – The sharp-edged rocky slabs plunging almost vertically into the river are remarkable.

Beyond Ste-Eulalie, the smiling Royans countryside offers a strong contrast with the last *cluse* (gorge) of the Bourne, looking like a natural gateway.

★**Pont-en-Royans** – *See PONT-EN-ROYANS.*

★★ 3 GORGES DE LA BOURNE

From Pont-en-Royans to Villard-de-Lans

24km/15mi – allow 1hr 30min – local map see p 353

This gorge, lined with thick layers of coloured limestone, gets deeper and deeper as one follows the river upstream.

★**Pont-en-Royans** – *See PONT-EN-ROYANS.*

The road enters the gorge immediately then follows the river, often reduced to a small stream in summer. The valley widens slightly before Choranche then becomes narrow again and the road leaves the river bed to rise along the steep north bank, with many waterfalls cascading down the cliffside in rainy weather.

Grotte du Bournillon – *1km/0.6mi south of D 531, then 1hr return on foot. Follow the private road leading to the power station, cross the courtyard of the plant and turn right; the path giving access to the cave starts on the left, on the other side of a bridge over the Bournillon (parking allowed, but beware of falling rocks).* Continue left along the base of the escarpments to reach the huge **porch**★ (100m/328ft high) of the cave. Walk as far as the footbridge to appreciate the size of this enormous arch.

Grottes de Choranche

R. Delon/Grottes de Choranche

★★**Grottes de Choranche** – *2.5km/1.5mi from D 531 across the Bourne (parking); continue on foot to the Grotte de Coufin.*

There are seven caves in all at the foot of tall cliffs overlooking the village of Choranche. Two of them are open to the public.

The **Grotte de Coufin** ⊙ is the most spectacular cave in the Vercors Massif. Discovered in 1875, it includes a vast chamber where thousands of snow-white stalactites, 1-3m/3-10ft long, are reflected in the water of a lake. The tour continues along a winding gallery where light effects create a supernatural atmosphere. The visit ends with an audiovisual show. An aquarium contains an olm, a blind cave-dwelling salamander with external gills. Outside, there is an exhibition about prehistoric men who lived in the area and a **nature trail** *(allow 1hr)* offers a very pleasant and interesting walk.

The **Grotte du Gournier** contains a beautiful lake, 50m/164ft long and 8m/26ft deep. To explore this cave you need proper equipment and an experienced guide. This underground network consists in a succession of waterfalls with a considerable difference in height *(for information about potholing, see Practical information).*

The road then runs through the basin of La Balme, at the confluence of the Rencurel and Bourne Valleys *(see Route des Écouges below)* then enters the Goule Noire Gorge. Note the large Calvaire de Valchevrière standing on the opposite bank. After the Pont de la Goule Noire, the gorge, barely wide enough for the river and the road, finally opens out into the spacious Lans Valley.

★**Villard-de-Lans** – *See drive* 2.

★★ 4 ROUTE DES ÉCOUGES

From La Balme-de-Rencurel to N 532

21km/13mi – allow 1hr – local map see p 353

This itinerary includes one of the most vertiginous sections in the Vercors region, similar to Combe Laval.

From La Balme, drive north along D 35.

The road runs up the Rencurel Valley up to the Col de Romeyère (alt 1 074m/3 524ft), where a forest road leads to the vast Coulmes Forest. The valley itself is densely forested and uninhabited. At Pont Chabert-d'Hières, the Drevenne leaves this wide coomb and veers left through a spectacular **gorge★** towards the Isère Valley. There are bird's-eye **views★★** of the Isère Valley and the hills of the Bas-Dauphiné; the road can be seen going over a bridge, 200m/656ft below.

Bridge over the Drevenne – Get out of the car to admire the **waterfall** dropping from a height of 50m/164ft.

Just beyond St-Gervais, the road joins N 532 along the east bank of the Isère.

★★ 5 COL DE ROUSSET

From Les Barraques-en-Vercors to the Col de Rousset

24km/15mi – allow 1hr 30min – local map see p 353

From Les Barraques-en-Vercors, drive south along D 518.

La Chapelle-en-Vercors – This tourist centre located near the Forêt de Lente was bombed and burnt down in July 1944. Two plaques in a farmyard (Ferme Albert), one of the rare places which was not destroyed, honour the memory of 16 inhabitants of the village who were shot.

From La Chapelle, drive along D 178 for 4km/2.5mi then follow the signposting for La Draye Blanche.

★Grotte de la Draye Blanche ⊙ – Although this is one of the most ancient caves in the Vercors region, it was only opened to the public in 1970 and is now directly accessible from the parking area via a tunnel. The tour includes a vast chamber, 100m/110yd long, in which calcite comes in different colours, white, ochre or blue-grey. A stalagmite, 12m/40ft high and 2m/6.5ft thick, looks like a petrified waterfall.

Return to La Chapelle-en-Vercors and follow D 518 south.

Grotte de la Luire ⊙ – *0.5km/0.3mi off D 518 on the left and 15min return on foot; allow 30min more to see the Decombaz Chamber.* The cave is interesting from a geological and historic point of view. In July 1944, the Nazis killed or deported the wounded and the staff of the hospital of the Resistance movement set up inside the cave.

The **Decombaz Chamber** is 60m/197ft high under a natural vault; deep inside it, there is a chasm which led potholers 470m/1 542ft down to what is thought to be the underground Vernaison. During periods of exceptional spates, the water of the river rises up the chasm and overflows into the cave.

Continue south along D 518 to the Col de Rousset Station and go through the tunnel.

★★Col de Rousset – Alt 1 141m/3 743ft. *Leave the car at the tunnel exit and walk to a viewpoint.* The Col de Rousset marks the climatic limit between the northern and southern Alps: the green landscapes of the Vercors on the northside, the arid Bassin de Die on the southside.

The ski runs of the recent **Col de Rousset** ski resort are on the slopes of the Montagne de Beurre, near the pass. In summer, a new fun vehicle takes advantage of the available slopes: the **"trottinherbe"**, a cross between a mountain bike and a scooter.

From the viewing table, situated on the edge of the plateau, an impressive **panorama★★** unfolds: the Grande Moucherolle to the north, the Grand Veymont to the east (in the foreground) and the heights of the Diois to the south with Mont Ventoux on the horizon.

★★RÉSERVE NATURELLE DES HAUTS-PLATEAUX

This desolate area, covering 16 600ha/41 020 acres and situated at altitudes ranging from 1 200m/3 846ft to 2 300m/7 546ft, was declared a nature reserve in 1985 in order to safeguard the balance which existed between traditional activities (foresters and shepherds) and natural ecosystems. No road goes through it and there are no permanent dwellings.

The area consists of karst-like limestone plateaux, dotted with fissures and sink-holes into which surface water disappears, and includes the two highest summits of the Vercors Massif, the Grand Veymont (2 341m/7 680ft) and the Mont Aiguille (2 086m/6 844ft); it is edged by impressive cliffs on the east and west sides.

The main species of fauna are the black grouse, the blue hare and the chamois. The last Alpine bear was spotted in this area in 1938. Cave-dwellers, on the other hand, are plentiful, in particular bats of which there are many species.

Hikes

Many marked footpaths such as GR 91 and 93 criss-cross the high plateaux, but in the absence of access roads, hikes are inevitably lengthened and often imply camping overnight. Specialised topo-guides are available at tourist offices.

From Rousset to the Col des Escondus – *The excursion described below is relatively easy and should only take half a day; start from Rousset, where you can leave the car. Difference in height: 400m/1 312ft.*

Aim for the Chapelle St-Alexis, cross a stream then walk south along its east bank to the end of the Combe Male and then to the Col des Escondus at the intersection of GR 93. Impressive views of the hamlet of La Grange and the Montagne de Beurre. Follow the path going north through the woods to the Chalet des Ours *(it is also possible to go west to the Col de Rousset across high pastures)*. Take the path running behind the chalet towards the Combe Male and follow it back to your starting point.

BEFORE GOING

- Water is rare on the Vercors plateaux: an extra supply is never superfluous.
- Do not go off marked paths, even when going across open spaces.
- Sheepfolds which look deserted always belong to shepherds; if you want to stop for a break or to take cover, make sure you do not leave anything behind.
- When a flock or herd approaches, avoid being noisy or gesticulating and make a wide detour round it.
- Camping and fires are forbidden and dogs are not allowed inside the reserve's perimeter.

★★**Grand Veymont** – *Allow 1 day – difference in height: 1 000m/3 281ft – Altitude at the starting point: 1 350m/4 429ft.*

From La Chapelle-en-Vercors, drive along D 518 towards the Col de Rousset; 1km/0.6mi before Rousset, turn left onto a narrow forest road signposted "Route forestière de la Coche". Follow it to the vast parking area of the Maison Forestière de la Coche (9km/5.6mi). Leave the car there.

Continue on foot to the Maison Forestière de Pré Grandu. Walk east along the marked path running across the plateau. The rocky wall of the Grand Veymont bars the horizon straight ahead. On the way down through the central depression, aim for the **Nouvelle Jasse de la Chau**, where you can get a fresh supply of water.

Behind the information panel, a path climbs towards the **Pas de la Ville**, the last stage before the summit, exposed to high winds. A path on the right of the iron cross leads up to the summit but it is worth walking a few extra metres/yards east beyond the pass for some wonderful bird's-eye views of the Trièves Valley.

The climb to the summit along the scree-covered slope requires particular care. Several cairns mark the summit (2 341m/7 680ft); the impressive **panorama**★★★ includes the major part of the Alps from Mont Blanc in the northeast to the Pelvoux and the Meije facing the Grand Veymont, with the solitary Mont Ventoux in the south. But the most striking silhouette is undoubtedly that of the Mont Aiguille (2 086m/6 844ft) in the foreground.

The way down to the south is very steep. At the foot of the ridge, take the path on the right which runs west to the Pas de Chattons and joins GR 91 just before La Grande Cabane. Continue westwards and turn right at the intersection. The path runs north for 5km/3mi to meet the large path leading to the Maison Forestière du Pré Grandu.

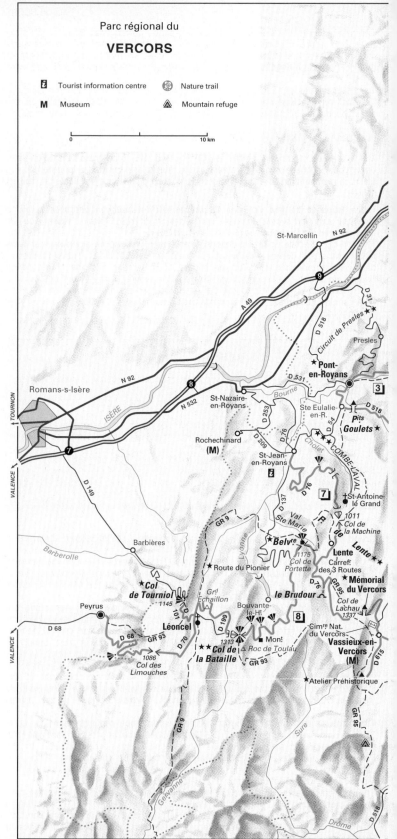

Parc régional du
VERCORS

🛈 Tourist information centre	⊛ Nature trail
M Museum	⛺ Mountain refuge

0 _____ 10 km

St-Marcellin

N 92

⑨

Circuit de Presles

D 518

D 31

Presles

★ Pont-en-Royans

③

A 49

Romans-s-Isère

N 92

⑧

N 532

ISÈRE

Bourne

St-Nazaire-en-Royans

D 531

Ste Eulalie-en-R.

D 518

pits

Goulets ★

TOURNON

St-Jean-en-Royans

D 253

D 209

Rochechinard

(M)

D 76

Cholet

COMBE-LAVAL

D 137

VALENCE

D 149

7

★ St-Antoine-le Grand

D 76

▽ 1011

Col de la Machine

Barberolle

GR 9

Val Ste Marie

Lyonne

★ Belvre

R

de

Lente

Lente ★ ★

Barbières

1175

Col de Portette

Carref. des 3 Routes

★ Mémorial du Vercors

★ Route du Pionier

le Brudour ⛺

GR 95

★ Col de Tourniol

Grd Echaillon

1145

101

D

Bouvante-le-Ht

Col de Lachau

1337

⛺

Peyrus

D 68

Léoncel

D 199

⑧

Cim.re Nat. du Vercors

D 68

GR 93

D 76

1313

Mon!

Vassieux-en-Vercors

(M)

D 615

VALENCE

1086

Col des Limouches

★ ★ Col de la Bataille

△ Roc de Toulau

GR 93

★ Atelier Préhistorique

GR 9

GR 95

Sure

⛺

Gervanne

D 518

Drôme

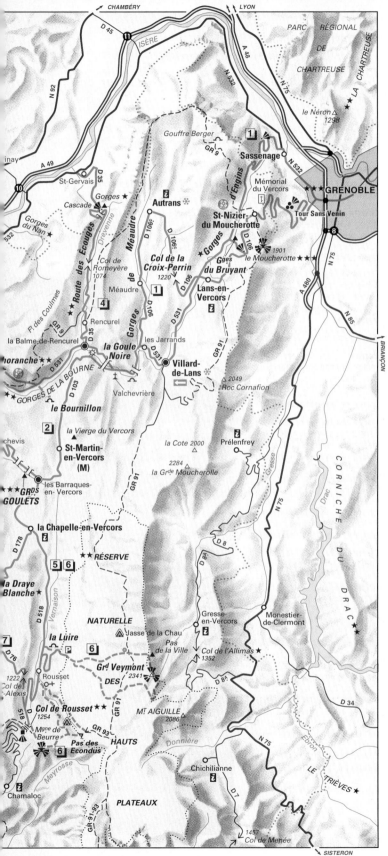

CHAMBÉRY

LYON

PARC   RÉGIONAL
DE
CHARTREUSE

D 45

11

ISÈRE

A 48

N 532

LA CHARTREUSE

N 92

le Néron △
1298

★★★

inay

A 49

D 35

St-Gervais

Gouffre Berger

GR 9

Sassenage

1

N 532

Gorges ★

Cascade

Autrans ❋

Col de
Romeyère
1074

Méaudre

4

Rencurel

la Balme-de-Rencurel

D 35

les Jarrands

la Goule
Noire

horanche ★★

D 103

Valchevrière

le Bournillon

2

la Vierge du Vercors

chevis

St-Martin-
en-Vercors
(M)

★★ GR^DS
GOULETS

les Barraques-
en- Vercors

la Chapelle-en-Vercors

D 178

5 6

★★ RÉSERVE

la Draye
Blanche ★

D 518

Vernaison

NATURELLE

7

D 76

la Luire

P

6

1222
Col de
-Alexis

Rousset

Grd Veymont
2341

DES

513

M^ne de
Beurre

❋ 6

Col de Rousset ★★
1254

Pas des
Econdus

GR 93

HAUTS

Meyrosse

Chamaloc

7

PLATEAUX

D 106^c

D 106^c

D 1066

Col de la
Croix-Perrin
1220

1

Méaudre

Gorges

D 531

D 106

de

Méaudre

D 106

Drevenne

Route des Écouges

Gorges

de

GR 9

Ft des Coulmes

D 531

GORGES DE LA BOURNE

Gouffre Berger

d'Engins

Mémorial
du Vercors

St-Nizier-
du Moucherotte

Gorges

D 106

le Moucherotte ★★★
1901

Gües
du Bruyant

Lans-en-
Vercors

i

GR 91

Villard-
de-Lans ❋

△ 2049
Roc Cornafion

la Cote 2000
△

2284
la Gr^de Moucherolle
△

Prélenfrey

i

Tour Sans Venin

★★★ GRENOBLE

8

N 75

A 480

N 85

BRIANÇON

Gresse

N 75

Drac

CORNICHE   DU   DRAC ★★

GR 91

D 8

D 8A

D 8A

Jasse de la Chau

Pas
de la Ville

Gresse-
en-Vercors

i

Col de l'Allimas ★
1352

Monestier-
de-Clermont

D 84

MT AIGUILLE
2086 △

Donnière

GR 91 · 93

1457
Col de Menée

D 7

Chichilianne

i

N 75

Ebron

LE   TRIÈVES ★

D 34

SISTERON

353

★★★ 6 COMBE LAVAL

41km/25.5mi – allow 3hr – local map see p 353

From the Col de Rousset to the Carrefour des 3 Routes

From the Col de Rousset, drive north and bear left onto D 76 to Vassieux.

The road rises gently through a wooded area above the upper Vernaison Valley. The Col de St-Alexis gives access to the Vassieux Coomb in an austere landscape of meagre pastures. Just before Vassieux, you will see, on the roadside, pieces of German gliders dating from the Second World War.

Vassieux-en-Vercors – *See VASSIEUX-EN-VERCORS.*

The road continues towards the Col de la Chau where there is an important **Mémorial du Vercors★** *(see VASSIEUX-EN-VERCORS).*

Grotte du Brudour – *From the bridge across the Brudour, 30min return on foot along a very pleasant path.* It leads to a cave where a resurgent spring can be seen. It is possible to follow the left-hand gallery to a chamber containing a small lake *(30min return).* The Brudour itself soon disappears into many sink-holes to reappear under the name of Cholet below the cirque of the Combe Laval.

From the Carrefour des 3 Routes to St-Jean-en-Royans

Continue along D 76.

Lente – Forestry personnel make up the population of this village.

The road goes through the forest to a vast clearing.

★★**Forêt de Lente** – The forest consists essentially of firs and beeches. Timber was used in the 19C by the navy and the coal industry and, in 1897, a road was built through the Combe Laval to convey cart loads of timber to St-Jean-en-Royans; the journey took a day and a half at the time!

★★★**Combe Laval** – The spine-chilling journey starts from the **Col de la Machine**. The road, hewn out of the rock face, literally hangs above the gorge of the upper Cholet from a height of 600m/1 968ft. *Take a few steps along the road at the most vertiginous spots.* Note the Cascalde du Cholet, a resurgent spring of the Brudour. After going through several tunnels, the road suddenly overlooks the whole Royans region, offering bird's-eye **views★★** of this deeply burrowed area and of the Bas-Dauphiné plateaux (Chambaran Forest).

To the north, are the deep furrows dug through the mountain by the Bourne and Vernaison rivers. To the west, the view extends to the Cévennes mountains.

B. Bodin/FOC

Combe Laval

St-Jean-en-Royans – Lying below the cliffs of the Vercors Plateau, this small town is the starting point of magnificent excursions. The chancel of the **church** ⊙ is decorated with fine 18C woodwork from a former Carthusian monastery. There is an interesting **viewpoint** on top of the **Toura** Hill accessible via the cemetery lane.

Situated 5km/3mi west along D 209, **Rochechinard** is overlooked by the ruins of an 11C-12C **castle**; its small country church and its presbytery form a lovely picture with the cliffs of the Combe Laval in the background; the **Musée de la Mémoire** ⊙ contains a collection of tools and regional costumes as well as reconstructions of traditional interiors.

There is a fine excursion to be made south of St-Jean *(17km/10.6mi on D 131 and D 331)* along a cliff road known as the **Route du Pionnier★**, which overlooks the Lyonne Valley. *It is possible to make it a round tour by returning via the Combe Laval (see above) or via the Col de la Bataille (see drive* ⑦*).*

★ ⑦ COL DE LA BATAILLE

From Peyrus to the Carrefour des 3 Routes
45km/28mi – allow 2hr – local map p 353

From Peyrus, drive along D 68.

The road rises in a series of wide hairpin bends above a wooded vale. About half a mile before it reaches the plateau, there is an extended view of the Valence Plain with the Cevennes in the background. The Col des Limouches gives access to the Léoncel Vale whose meagre pastures, dotted with box and juniper bushes, denote a Mediterranean influence.

Léoncel – From its Cistercian abbey founded in 1137, the village has retained a vast Romanesque **abbey church★** dating from the late 12C, surmounted by a stocky square bell-tower topped by a pyramid. The oven-vaulted apse and apsidal chapels are typical of Provençal Romanesque art. The crossing is crowned by a dome on squinches. The quadripartite vaulting of the nave, on the other hand, already bears the mark of Gothic art.

From Léoncel, follow D 101 to the Col de Tourniol.

★**Col de Tourniol** – The view extends beyond the Vercors foothills across the Valence Basin.

Return to Léoncel.

The road climbs up the eastern slope of the Léoncel Vale and reaches the densely forested plateau.

Col de la Bataille – *The road is closed from 15 November to 15 May.* A tunnel gives access to the pass (alt 1 313m/4 308ft) overlooked by the Roc de Toulau.
The **panorama** is impressive. From the pass to Malatra *(2km/1.2mi)*, the **cliff-road★★** winds it way above the Bouvante Cirque and its small lake; there are three viewpoints along this section, before the road veers north towards the Col de la Portette.

★**Belvédère de la Portette** – *15min on foot return from the Col de la Portette. Leave the car in the last bend and follow the stony path which starts behind a forest marker; bear right 200m/219yd further on. From the belvedere, the* **view** *plunges over the Val Ste-Marie, with the Royans Region and Isère Valley beyond; note the huge modern bridge of St-Hilaire-St-Nazaire.*

From the pass, it is only a short distance to the Carrefour des 3 Routes.

*Walkers, campers, smokers...
please be careful!*

Fire is the worst threat to woodland.

Michelin map 81 folds 17 and 18, 84 folds 6 and 7, 114 folds 7, 8, 9 and 10 or 245 folds 34 and 35

The River Verdon, a tributary of the Durance, has carved magnificent gorges through the limestone plateaux of the Haute-Provence region, the most spectacular being the Grand Canyon which extends over a distance of 21km/13mi from Rougon to Aiguines. The sight of this vast furrow lined with sheer walls in wild unspoilt surroundings is unique in Europe; as Jean Giono would say: "Here, it is more than remote, it is elsewhere…"

The reason why this gorge is so deep may be explained by the fact that when the Alpine area folded during the Tertiary tectonic upheaval, the huge layers of limestone deposits rose slowly and the existing river bed sank deeper and deeper. The Verdon subsequently widened and modelled the sinuous corridor through which it now flows. Intense erosion carved huge caves in the cliffside and water penetrating through the thickness of the plateau created a vast network of underground caves and galleries.

The width of the gorge varies from 6 to 100m/20 to 328ft at water level and from 200 to 1 500m/656 to 4 921ft at the top of the cliffs. Its depth varies from 250 to 700m/820 to 2 297ft.

Exploration and development of tourism – EA Martel (1859-1938), the initiator of potholing, was the first to explore the 21km/13mi-long gorge *(see CASTELLANE: Explorers of the Verdon Canyon)*. In 1928, part of the canyon was equipped to receive visitors…on foot; the main viewpoints were signposted. In 1947, the cliff road *(D 71)*, known as the Corniche Sublime, was hewn out of the rock, thus opening the way to motorists. The north bank road, on the other hand, was only completed in 1973.

Motorists arriving from Draguignan may find D 955 exceptionally closed as it goes through the Canjuers Firing Range.

In 1997 the Parc naturel régional du Verdon was inaugurated to safeguard the outstanding natural site of the Grand Canyon du Verdon.

★★★CORNICHE SUBLIME *81km/50.3mi – half a day*

This itinerary is almost perfect from a tourist's point of view: the road turns and twists to reach the most impressive viewpoints; the bird's-eye views of the canyon are amazing.

From Castellane to the Balcons de la Mescla

★**Castellane** – *See CASTELLANE.*

Leave Castellane by ② on the town plan and drive along D 952.

The road follows the north bank of the Verdon meandering beneath impressive escarpments. The rocky ridge of the Cadières de Brandis can be seen of the right.

★**Porte de St-Jean** – Beyond this narrow passage cut through limestone heights, the river takes a wide turn to the left and flows southwards.

★**Clue de Chasteuil** – This long transverse gorge is lined with vertical rock strata.

In Pont-de-Soleils, turn left into D 955.

The road leaves the Verdon to follow the green Jabron Valley. On the right, the hilltop village of **Trigance** is overlooked by an imposing medieval castle remodelled in the 16C, now turned into a hotel.

Comps-sur-Artuby – This ancient village, which once belonged to the Knights Templars and later to the Knights Hospitallers, nestles at the foot of a rock crowned by the 13C **Église St-André** ⊙; the nave, surmounted by a pointed vault, ends with an oven-vaulted apse. Note the christening font.

From the church, there are fine views of the Artuby Gorge and the entrance of several caves.

From Comps, drive west along D 71.

A bend in the road affords a wide **view**★ of the arid Préalpes de Castellane and Préalpes de Digne.

★★★**Balcons de la Mescla** – *On the right side of the road and on either side of the Balcons Café.* From these belvederes, there are bird's-eye views of the Mescla 250m/820ft below, the name given to the confluence of the Verdon and its tributary the Artuby. The Verdon takes a sharp bend round a narrow promontory and the view embraces the upstream part of the gorge, 400 to 500m/1 312 to 1 640ft deep. The upper belvedere offers the most impressive view.

The road then runs towards the Artuby.

From the Balcons de la Mescla to Moustiers-Ste-Marie

The road may be blocked by snow from December to March.

★**Pont de l'Artuby** – This remarkable piece of engineering in reinforced concrete comprises a single arch with a 110m/361ft span thrown across the Artuby Canyon lined with vertical cliffs. This is the favourite haunt of amateurs of bungee jumping. Parking area at the other end of the bridge.

The road goes round the Pilon du Fayet to reach the Verdon Canyon.

Tunnels de Fayet – Between the two tunnels and immediately beyond there is a breathtaking **view★★★** of the curve of the canyon near the Étroit des Cavaliers.

★**Falaise des Cavaliers** – The road follows the edge of the cliff where there are two viewpoints. Turn right towards the Restaurant des Cavaliers. From the terrace, there is a striking **view** of the 300m/984ft-high cliff.

Over the next 3km/1.9mi, the road runs 250 to 400m/820 to 1 312ft above the gorge; it is one of the most impressive sections of the whole itinerary.

★**Falaise de Baucher** – Lovely view of the Pré Baucher Basin upstream.

Pas de l'Imbut – Bird's-eye view of the Verdon overlooked by huge sheer cliffs; the river disappears 400m/1 312ft below under a pile of fallen rocks.

Falaise des Cavaliers, Gorges du Verdon

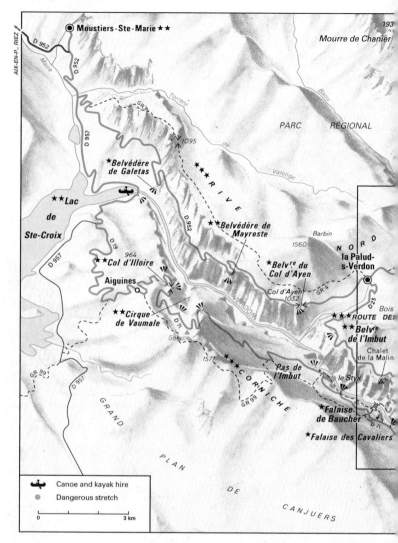

Further on, the road leaves the edge of the cliffs and one loses sight of the gorge for a while.

★★Cirque de Vaumale – The road enters the cirque after a sharp bend to the left and the view then embraces the downstream section of the gorge. The road reaches its highest point at an altitude of 1 204m/3 950ft. The gorge backed by the heights of the opposite bank forms a superb landscape.

As it comes out of the cirque, the road leaves the gorge once more and winds its way westwards, offering **views★** of the Lac de Ste-Croix and, further away, of the Luberon, the Montagne de Lure and the Ventoux beyond the Durance Valley.

★★Col d'Illoire – The road comes out of the gorge for good. Stop and admire the the Grand Canyon once more.

The **view★** now embraces the flat expanse of the Plateau de Valensole, with a line of bluish heights on the horizon.

Aiguines – This village, overlooking the vast expanse of the Lac de Ste-Croix, has retained its old-world charm: twisting lanes, old houses and a 17C castle with four corner towers. Aiguines was famous for the work of its wood-turners who used boxwood from the nearby forests.

Musée des Tourneurs ⊘ – The museum presents the various species of wood used by turners and illustrates their work; it contains lathes and a collection of objects made this way: bottle cases, powder boxes, potato-masher, handles... A video show is devoted to the speciality of Aiguines: **nail-studded boules** for playing *pétanque*! Beyond Aiguines, the road winds down to the Lac de Ste-Croix.

Turn right into D 957.

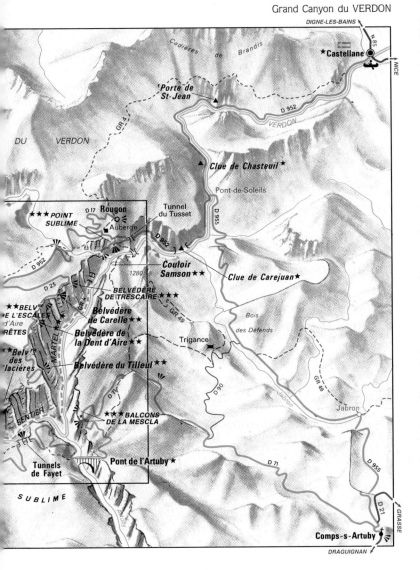

Grand Canyon du VERDON

★★Lac de Ste-Croix – *See Lac de STE-CROIX.*

There is a fine **view★** of the entrance of the canyon from the bridge across the Verdon; the road then follows the Maïre Valley and skirts the outdoor leisure park of Moustiers-Ste-Marie.

★★Moustiers-Ste-Marie – *See MOUSTIERS-STE-MARIE.*

Showing consideration for nature:
The beauty of this itinerary through the canyon depends also on its tidiness.
Do not leave any rubbish (bottles, plastic bags, cans, papers etc) anywhere;
take it along with you.

The gold of the River Verdon

For a long time, the bottom of the gorge and the river bed provided the local population with their main means of support: boxwood and wild honey.
It required a great deal of skill and courage to reach the virtually inaccessible sites, where box and honey could be found. Honey gatherers moved about on a plank held by a hemp rope whereas box cutters climbed up and down a succession of long poles fitted with bars; The most daring among them worked their way along the cliffs by driving spikes into the rock; they were the forerunners of today's rock-climbers whose demonstrations up and down the Falaise de l'Escalès draw the admiration of onlookers.

NORTH BANK *73km/45mi – allow half a day*

The direct road *(D 952)* from Moustiers to Castellane only runs close to the Grand Canyon at each end. However, the "Route des Crêtes" *(D 23)* offers an unforgettable round tour from La Palud-sur-Verdon via a number of viewpoints.

From Moustiers-Ste-Marie to La Palud-sur-Verdon

★★Moustiers-Ste-Marie – *See MOUSTIERS-STE-MARIE.*

On the way down the Maïre Valley, the scenery is unmistakenly Provençal with its lavender fields and twisted olive trees. The view embraces the edge of the Plateau de Valensole, overlooking the vast turquoise expanse of the Lac de Ste-Croix, and takes in Aiguines and its castle as well.

★Belvédère de Galetas – This viewpoint marks the entrance of the gorge. View of the gateway of the Grand Canyon and of the Lac de Ste-Croix in a picturesque landscape of ochre-coloured cliffs.

The road enters the Cirque de Mayreste and rises rapidly.

★★Belvédère de Mayreste – *15min on foot return along a marked stony path.* First overall upstream view of the deep furrow.

★Belvédère du col d'Ayen – *15min on foot return.* Interesting upstream view of the twisted course of the canyon; however, the bottom remains out of sight.

The road veers away from the Verdon towards the cultivated area surrounding La Palud-sur-Verdon.

La Palud-sur-Verdon – This family resort is the ideal starting point of hikes through the canyon and a good base for rock-climbers.
A 12C Romanesque bell-tower is all that remains of the original church. The 18C castle and its four corner towers overlook the village.

***Route des Crêtes (round tour starting from La Palud-sur-Verdon)

A succession of belvederes line this itinerary; they are sometimes situated so high above the gorge that it feels as if one were looking at an aerial view. The main belvederes are listed below.

From La Palud, continue along D 952 towards Castellane then turn right into D 23.

The road rises through lavender fields and woodland areas.

★★★Belvédère de Trescaïre – Looking upstream, the Verdon is seen to flow through a jumble of fallen rocks and disappear under the vault of the Baulme aux Pigeons Cave, in the Samson Corridor. During the fine season, this is one of the favourite haunts of rock-climbers.

★★Belvédère de Carelle – Bird's-eye view of the river meandering deep down in the gorge. To the left is the Auberge du Point Sublime and, above it, the hilltop village of Rougon. It is one of the main free-climbing sites in the Grand Canyon.

★★★Belvédère de l'Escalès – It is situated on top of the sheer cliffs below which runs the Sentier Martel. In summer, numerous rock-climbers add to the interest of the site.

★★Belvédère de la Dent d'Aire – Alt 1 300m/4 265ft. The golden cliffs of the Dent d'Aire and of the Barre de l'Escalès can be seen towering on the left; straight ahead is the narrow corridor of the Baumes-Frères.

★★Belvédère du Tilleul – The confluence of the Verdon and Artuby, known as "La Mescla", lies ahead with the single-arched Pont de l'Artuby behind. The Verdon changes course to the northwest.

★★Belvédère des Glacières – Impressive view of the Mescla and its enormous promontory, of the Verdon and Plan de Canjuers. When the weather is clear, it is possible to see the Mediterranean Sea.

The road runs past the Chalet de la Maline, which is the starting point of the hike through the Grand Canyon *(see Sentier Martel).*

★★Belvédère de l'Imbut – The Verdon disappears under a pile of fallen rocks and the Sentier Vidal and Sentier de l'Imbut can be seen running along the opposite bank. The **view** embraces the mighty cliffs of the Baou Béni. Upstream, the narrowing of the **"Passage du Styx"** affords glimpses of the Pré Baucher.

The road veers away from the Verdon to return to La Palud-sur-Verdon.

From La Palud-sur-Verdon to Castellane

The picturesque hilltop village of Rougon suddenly appears ahead, slightly to the left, and the road runs within sight of the gorge once more.

★★**Point Sublime** – *15min return on foot. Leave the car in the parking area, near the Auberge du Point Sublime.* Follow the signposted path on the right across the deeply fissured Plateau des Lauves to the belvedere towering 180m/590ft above the confluence of the Verdon and its tributary the Baou. Splendid **view**★★★ of the entrance of the Grand Canyon and of the Samson Corridor.

Return to the car and follow D 17 to Rougon.

Rougon – Alt 960m/3 150ft. This "eyrie", overlooked by medieval ruins, affords a fine **view**★ of the entrance of the Grand Canyon from the slope above the parking. *Access to the ruins can be tricky and requires special care.*

Return to D 952 and follow it towards Castellane.

USEFUL TIPS FOR A SUCCESSFUL TRIP

Duration – Allow 2hr extra as a safety precaution, to make sure you will return before nightfall. Stick to the times indicated for each section of the itinerary so as not to be caught by surprise. Follow the itinerary in the direction that is recommended (usually the easiest) to avoid encountering awkward crossings and having to make too great an effort to come out of the gorge.

Equipment – Take some food and 2l/4 pints of water (the river water is not suitable for drinking), one or two torches, additional clothing (the tunnels and a few places are quite cool) and mountain boots.

Strictly prohibited – Camping on unauthorized sites, lighting a fire, digging up fossils. Hikers are also asked to refrain from taking shortcuts (it tends to increase the gullying of slopes), crossing the river except via bridges and footbridges and picking flowers (they wane rapidly anyway) as many species are protected.

Domestic animals – Dogs should not be taken along the Sentier Vidal as they would find the 240 steps along the Sentier Martel difficult to tackle.

Children – Going into the gorge with children under 10 is not recommended; the Sentier Vidal is too difficult for them.

Variation of the water level – Water released by the Chaudanne or Castillon plants can cause a sudden rise in the level of the Verdon; the flow of the river is liable to increase from 10 to $100m^3$/353 to 3 531cu ft per second. The EDF recorded information only lists forecast rates of flow; it is therefore essential, when stopping for any length of time, to choose a few rocks at water level as markers and watch them carefully. Releases from the dams are usually preceded by warning releases intended for informed hikers.
The Sentier de l'Imbut, which is only suitable for experienced hikers, is accessible under special conditions *(see hike* ④*)*.

Recorded information – Weather forecast in St-Auban: ☎ 04 92 64 90 60. Rate of flow of the Verdon: ☎ 04 92 83 62 68.

Taxis – A taxi service operates between the Auberge du Point Sublime, La Palud-sur-Verdon and the Chalet de la Maline. It enables hikers to return to where they left their car.

Maps and topo-guides – In addition to the local maps included in this chapter, it would be useful to buy the Moustiers-Ste-Marie local map (1:50 000) and the Grand Canyon du Verdon map by A Monier. "Le guide du Verdon", by JF Bettus, is on sale in La Palud-sur-Verdon; another useful guide is "Randonnées pédestres dans le pays du Verdon", published by Édisud.

Exploration of the bottom of the gorge – It can be done mostly on foot, swimming being necessary in places, but in general it is closer to canyoning (see Practical information). Whatever the conditions and the length of the exploration planned, it is a sporting feat which entails danger and requires a thorough knowledge of the techniques of white-water sports.

Rock-climbing sites – The main one is the Belvédère de Carelle where it is easy to film rock-climbers at work; there is also the Belvédère de Trescaïre and the Falaise de l'Escalès.

★★Couloir Samson – *Just before the Tunnel du Tusset, a dead-end road branching off to the right leads to the confluence of the Verdon and the Baou (parking facilities); it meets the path running along the river from the Chalet de la Maline.*

From this spot, the narrowing of the Grand Canyon downtream looks wild and impressive as huge rocks lie across the river bed.

Beyond the tunnel, the cliff road runs down towards the river.

★Clue de Carejuan – The limestone strata are strangely coloured. The water cascades over fallen rocks and its clear green colour is temporarily disturbed.

After the heavy spates, which occurred in the Autumn of 1994, the banks of the stream had to be consolidated.

For the section of the itinerary from Pont-de-Soleils to Castellane, see the drive entitled Corniche Sublime.

★★★HIKES THROUGH THE GRAND CANYON

★★★① Sentier Martel

Between the Chalet de la Maline and the Point Sublime, GR 4, known as the Sentier Martel, offers tourists who do not mind a tiring day's hike an unforgettable close contact with the Grand Canyon.

From the Chalet de la Maline to the Point Sublime

5hr hike, not counting resting time, along a difficult itinerary – local map opposite – torch essential – GR 4 is marked in white and red.

From the steps going down to the river, there are fine views of the Pas de l'Estellié.

Ignore the path branching off to the right towards the Estellié Footbridge; it leads to the Restaurant des Cavaliers and the Corniche Sublime.

At the Pré d'Issane, the path runs close to the river and follows it through the Étroit des Cavaliers with sheer cliffs towering 300m/984ft above. The gorge widens and the path reaches the Talus de Guègues, a scree framed by steep slopes.

The Canyon du Verdon from the Sentier Martel

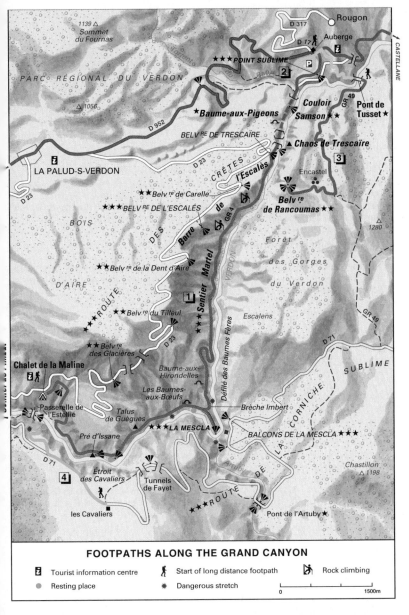

FOOTPATHS ALONG THE GRAND CANYON

🛈 Tourist information centre	🚶 Start of long distance footpath	🧗 Rock climbing
● Resting place	✳ Dangerous stretch	0 ⸺ 1500m

Continue upstream past the vast Baumes-aux-Bœufs Cave and take the second path to the right leading to **La Mescla★★★**, where the flow of the Verdon mixes with that of the Artuby. There is a splendid view upstream of the Défilé des Baumes-Frères.

Retrace your steps to the intersection and turn right.

The path winds its way up to the Brèche Imbert (steps): superb view of the Baumes-Frères and the Barre de l'Escalès. The canyon, overlooked by very high cliffs (400 to 500m/1 312 to 1 640ft), becomes wider then suddenly narrower. The Chaos de Trescaïre, on the right, is an extraordinary jumble of fallen rocks. The hilltop village of Rougon can be seen in the distance. Next come two tunnels; inside the second, metal steps lead to the **Baume-aux-Pigeons★**, a vast cave, 30m/98ft high, situated at the foot of a 350m/1 148ft-high cliff. From the bottom of the stairs, it is possible to see, on the opposite bank, the huge blocks which fell when the roof caved in. This cave and the caved-in roof indicate that in the past, the Verdon partly flowed underground. From the last opening, there is a view of the **Couloir Samson**, a very narrow corridor with smooth vertical sides. Beyond the tunnel, the path goes over the footbridge across the Baou and climbs to the parking area. The hike ends at the **Belvédère du Point Sublime★★★** *(see North Bank)*.

Walk to the inn where you can call a taxi.

Édouard-Alfred Martel's guide

Isidore Blanc, a schoolteacher in Rougon, was EA Martel's guide when he explored the entire Grand Canyon *(see Castellane)*, but he was above all the initiator of tourism in the area; he adapted the existing paths to make them suitable for hikers and in 1920 he founded the first guide service in the Verdon. He drew from his expeditions throughout the area the inspiration to write poems which delighted his pupils. A monument, situated near the Point Sublime, is dedicated to his memory and quotes one of his poems in Provençal.

You can join D 952 from the Auberge du Point Sublime by taking shortcuts.

If you wish to go to La Palud-sur-Verdon without going past the Point Sublime, take the path on the left just before the footbridge over the Baou; it goes up along the south bank of the stream and joins D 952 4km/2.5mi from La Palud-sur-Verdon. This shortens the hike by 3km/1.9mi.

2 Starting from the Point Sublime

★**"Sentier de découverte des Lézards"** – This well-marked nature trail starts from the Plateau des Lauves. A small explanatory boolet is available at the Auberge du Point Sublime or at the Tourist office in La Palud-sur-Verdon.
Another itinerary leads to the Pont de Tusset along GR 49 *(local map see p 363)*. These round tours usually last between 1hr and 3hr 30min.

3 East bank starting from the Point Sublime

★★**Belvédère de Rancoumas** – *3hr 30min return; local map p 363. It is possible to start from the Point Sublime parking area and to walk south, following GR 49 markings, or to drive towards the Couloir Samson (D 23^B) and park the car on the last bend before the straight line leading to the dead-end parking area. 2km/1.2mi before reaching the parking, take GR 49 on the left, marked in white and red; it leads through an oak forest down to the* **Pont de Tusset★***, dating from the early 17C.*
The path starts rising through a forest of pines, maples and beeches, then joins a wide track. Leave the marked path and follow the track on the right; it runs across a stream before reaching the ruins of Encastel. Go up to the edge of the cliff.
The natural Belvédère de Rancoumas offers a striking **panorama★★** of the whole Falaise de l'Escalès with the Sentier Martel running below. The **Mourre de Chanier** (alt 1 930m/6 332ft), the highest summit of the Verdon Region, soars in the distance to the northwest.
Return along the same itinerary.

★★ 4 Sentier de l'Imbut

3km/1.9mi. Local map see p 363. It is advisable to tackle this difficult itinerary after having spent a day along the Sentier Martel.
– The path must be followed in one direction only, i.e. exit via the Vidal steps.
– Do not take domestic animals or children under ten on this hike.
– Do not undertake this hike when the forecast rate of flow reaches 40m³/1 413cu ft per second.
– It is possible to be accompanied by a qualified guide (tourist offices in the area have lists of guides).
– It is possible to cross the Verdon over the Estellié Footbridge and follow the Sentier Martel to the Chalet de la Maline.
Start from the Auberge des Cavaliers, 2.5km/1.5mi to the Estellié Footbridge including 340m/372yd downwards. The itinerary runs entirely on the south bank, along a cliff path equipped with handrails in several places.
This is the most secluded and impressive part of the canyon where one can see huge beech trees, caves, groves of hazelnut trees, potholes...Beyond the Vidal steps, the itinerary follows the long Styx Corridor and reaches the Imbut Beach, where the path ends. This is the place where the water disappears down a sump. Great caution is required if you wish to go over the jumble of rocks forming the "Chaos de l'Imbut".
The return journey up the steep Vidal steps requires a constant effort to negotiate the difference in height of 400m/1 312ft; the steps are often 50cm/20in apart and the only help comes from a steel handrail.

Haute vallée du VERDON★

Michelin map 81 folds 8 and 18 or 245 fold 22

Upstream of the Lac de Castillon, the Verdon Valley gradually loses its wild appearance. The vegetation is typically Alpine, with forests of beeches, pines and larches covering the lower slopes. The cool climate and luminous sky are attractive features of this pleasant area.

FROM COLMARS TO THE LAC DE CASTILLON

36km – allow 45min

★**Colmars** – *See COLMARS.*

From Colmars, drive south along D 908. Before going into Beauvezer, turn left towards Villars-Heyssier and drive as far as the parking area.

★**Gorges de St-Pierre** – *1hr 30min on foot return.* A marked path leads to the gorge carved by a tributary of the Verdon. The path rises along the steep sides, offering impressive views of the grey schist and white and ochre limestone lining the gorge.

Beauvezer – Small summer resort in a pleasant verdant setting.

The road follows the bottom of the valley, overlooked in the east by the imposing Grand Coyer (2 693m/8 835ft).

Beyond the Pont de Villaron, D 955 runs between arid mountains where lavender alternates with wood patches. The river then flows through a long and narrow transverse valley which opens out into the small basin of St-André-des-Alpes.

St-André-des-Alpes – This village lies at the confluence of the Issole and Verdon rivers and at the crossroads of several tourist routes, in a pleasant setting of orchards and lavender fields. It is a fine base for excursions in the surrounding area.

Downstream of St-André, the Lac de Castillon lies at the centre of a scrubland area.

Lac de Castillon – *See Lacs de CASTILLON ET CHAUDANNE.*

Route de la VIONÈNE★

Michelin map 81 folds 9, 10 and 20, 115 folds 4 and 5 or 245 fold 24

The Vionène Valley provides a useful link, via the Col de la Couillole, between the Tinée and Cians rivers running parallel towards the River Var in the south. From Beuil, it is then possible to drive down the Gorges du Cians *(see Gorges du CIANS)* or to continue westwards to the upper Var Valley *(see Haute vallée du VAR)*.

FROM ST-SAUVEUR-SUR-TINÉE TO BEUIL

35km/22mi – allow 2hr

The wild beauty of the scenery is enhanced by the contrasting colours of the rocks.

St-Sauveur-sur-Tinée – *See ST-SAUVEUR-SUR-TINÉE.*

From St-Sauveur-sur-Tinée, drive west along D 30.

The road rises above the Tinée Valley and the village of St-Sauveur in a series of tight hairpin bends, through a landscape of red schist and patchy forest.

4km/2.5mi further on, turn right into D 130.

The small twisting road climbing up towards Roure offers bird's-eye **views** of the Gorges de la Tinée.

★**Roure** – Lying at the heart of a beautiful mountain setting, this ancient village has retained a wealth of interesting 17C and 18C domestic architecture. The houses are partly built of red schist and their roofs are covered with red-schist slabs *(lauzes)*. Some of them still have walls made of roughly hewn larch trunks.
The **church** contains some fine works of art: the 16C **St-Laurent altarpiece★**, richly coloured in green and red against a gold background, is framed by twisted columns and surmounted by a representation of the Entombment. Another altarpiece, in the first side chapel on the north side, was painted in François Bréa's style.
The **Chapelle St-Bernard-et-St-Sébastien** ⊘ is decorated with naïve frescoes by Andrea de Cella depicting the life of St Bernard of Menthon and of St Sebastian, famous for his healing powers against plague and cholera. The friezes separating the panels date from the Renaissance.

Return to D 30.

The road runs through the verdant Vionène Valley then crosses the tumultuous stream and continues through a **landscape★** where red schist provides the predominant colour. Note the lovely waterfall on the right before the first tunnel.

Beyond the tunnels, the village of Roubion appears, perched high up on a ridge, and the view extends over the Vionène Valley and the village of Roure, with the Tinée Valley in the background.

Roubion – This village, perched on top of a red-schist ridge, at an altitude of 1 300m/4 265ft, forms a striking picture. It has retained part of its 12C fortifications, some old houses, a belfry carved out of rock and the 18C Fontaine du Mouton on the village square.

The church dates from the 18C, apart from the crenellated Romanesque bell-tower. The interior decoration is interesting: particularly noteworthy are a 15C Virgin in one of the south-side chapels and a 15C Crucifixion in the chapel on the left of the chancel.

The **Chapelle St-Sébastien** ⊙, situated below the village, is a rustic 16C building decorated with murals: 12 panels relating the legend of St Sebastian with captions in old Provençal. Outside, there is a representation of St Michael slaying the dragon.

Continue to the Col de la Couillole.

The climb to the pass offers fine **views** of Roubion and of the Vionène and Tinée Valleys.

Col de la Couillole – Alt 1 678m/5 505ft. Extended view on either side of the pass. This is the popular rendezvous of fans of the Monte-Carlo Rally. The road winds down from the pass, within sight of the Gorges du Cians and the village of Beuil, amid spruce and larch woods.

⋆**Beuil** – *See BEUIL.*

VIZILLE ⋆

Population 7 094
Michelin map 77 fold 5 or 244 fold 39 – Local map see Lacs de LAFFREY

This small industrial town has retained one of the major historic buildings of the Dauphiné region, the castle of the Duc de Lesdiguières.

Constable of France – François de Bonne de **Lesdiguières** (1543-1627) was one of the most colourful characters of his time. A staunch supporter of the Reformation, he was made governor of Dauphiné by King Henri IV and exercised his authority with vigour and such cunning that he was nicknamed the "fox". He became duke, peer of the realm and marshall of France but his ambition was not yet satisfied. In 1622 he finally became the last constable of France, not, however, before he renounced the Protestant faith.

In 1602 he supervised the building of the Château de Vizille to which his son-in-law added the monumental staircase leading down to the park. In 1780, the castle was bought by a wealthy financier from Grenoble who lent it to the États du Dauphiné for their historic meeting in 1788 *(see below)*. Later on and until 1972, it was one of the national estates at the disposal of the French President.

Château de Vizille

The Assemblée de Vizille – The major event in the history of this little town took place on 21 July 1788, one year before the French Revolution began. The meeting of the regional assembly, including members of the nobility, of the clergy and of the middle and lower classes, which was banned in Grenoble, took place instead in the Château de Vizille. Discussions went on from 8am to 3am the next morning and the resolution finally voted by the assembly protested against the suppression of Parliament by Louis XVI, called for a meeting of all the regional assemblies and demanded individual freedom for all French citizens. For having expressed wishes that the whole nation adopted a year later, Vizille can rightly be called the "cradle" of the French Revolution.

★CHÂTEAU ⊘ 1hr

The asymmetric silhouette of the castle, deprived of its east wing by a fire in 1865 and flanked by a round and a square tower, looks quite original. One of the entrances is decorated with a bronze low relief by Jacob Richier, depicting Lesdiguières on horseback. The austere main façade overlooks the Romanche whereas the more elegant Renaissance façade overlooks the park.

Interior – It is divided into two parts: the **Musée de la Révolution française** and the old castle.

The museum is arranged on three floors; the ground floor contains French and English earthenware, an authentic model of the Bastille and some large paintings stored there by the Musée du Louvre and the Château de Versailles. The first floor is devoted to themed temporary exhibitions and the second floor houses a collection of portraits and furniture.

The historic part of the old castle comprises several reception rooms including the Grand Salon des tapisseries (17C tapestries, portraits of Lesdiguières) and the Salon Lesdiguières (Louis XIII furniture), the terrace (lovely view of the park with the Mont Thabor in the distance) and the library (Louis XIV panelling).

Park – In the vast park (100ha/247 acres), extending south of the château, deer, moufflons, herons... roam freely and huge trouts can be seen swimming in the lake.

Jardin du Roi – *Access during the fine season*. Medieval ruins crown the rocky promontory overlooking the old town, north of the present castle.

EXCURSION

Notre-Dame de Mésage – *2.6km/1.6mi south along N 85*. The church stands on the right of the main road; note its fine Romanesque stone bell tower.

Slightly further on, the 11C Chapelle St-Firmin or Chapelle des Templiers has an elegant east end.

Les VOIRONS ★

Michelin map 89 fold 15 or 244 fold 8

This mountain, like its neighbour the Salève *(see Le SALÈVE)*, forms part of the landscape surrounding the Swiss town of Geneva. Unlike the Salève, however, the Voirons are densely forested and attract ramblers who can enjoy glimpses of the Mont-Blanc Massif through the fir trees. The northwest side of the mountain gently slopes down to a pleasant countryside dotted with peaceful holiday resorts like **St-Cergues** between Annemasse and Thonon.

FROM BONS TO THE GRAND SIGNAL

15km/9.3mi – allow 1hr 45min

From Bons, drive southeast along D 20 towards Boëge.

The road rises gently through the woods, offering lovely glimpses of the Bas-Chablais and Lake Geneva.

From the Col de Saxel, D 50 follows the ridge line to the right; the view gradually extends to the east beyond the Chaîne du Reposoir to the Dents du Midi, the Mont Buet and the snow-capped Mont Blanc.

Leave the car at the end of the road, in the parking area situated just before the monastery.

★**Grand Signal** – *1hr return on foot. From the parking, follow the road signposted "voie sans issue" which rises through the woods; 50yd beyond the woods, follow the forest track climbing on the left through a meadow, signposted "les crêtes". It soon joins up with the path running along the ridge line; turn right onto it. Turn left and back slightly before the monastery building towards the ridge line; follow it to the right in order to reach the summit of the Grand Signal (1 480m/4 856). surmounted by a cross.*

There is a clear **view** to the east and southeast as far as Mont Blanc.

YVOIRE ★★

Population 432
Michelin map 89 fold 12 or 244 fold 8

Situated on the shores of Lake Geneva, Yvoire occupies a splendid position at the tip of the promontory which separates the "Petit Lac" and the "Grand Lac".

Flowers abound in this picturesque village which has retained its medieval character. Its restaurants are renowned for their fish specialities and in summer the marina is kept busy by keen yachtsmen from Switzerland and Savoie.

★MEDIEVAL VILLAGE

Yvoire has retained part of its 14C fortifications, including two gateways, the **castle** *(not open to the public)* with its massive square keep flanked by turrets and a few old houses.

Leave the car outside the fortifications, in the paying car park, on the right coming from Thonon.

Take a stroll through the lively streets lined with workshops; now and then a lovely square decorated with flowers offers views of the lake.

The **Église St-Pancrace** adds the finishing touch to this attractive picture; the chancel dates from the 14C but the building was only completed at the end of the 17C.

From the end of the pier, where ships sailing round the lake have their moorings *(see Évian: Boat trips)*, there are views of the Swiss shore backed by the Jura mountains. Day excursions are organised along the opposite shore *(see Practical information)*.

★**Jardin des Cinq Sens** ⊘ – *Rue du Lac.* The former kitchen garden of the castle has been turned into the reconstruction of a medieval enclosed garden where monks used to grow vegetables and herbs. Such places later became leisure gardens.

From the Alpine garden, there is a fine view of the castle. Next comes the **Labyrinthe végétal**, which suggests an original discovery of nature on the theme of the five senses: the Jardin du goût (taste) with its strawberries, raspberries and apple trees, the Jardin des textures (touch) with its subtle variety of foliage, the Jardin des couleurs (sight) with its harmonious range of colours changing with the seasons (geraniums, roses, bluebells) and the Jardin des senteurs (smell) with its lilies, honeysuckle and daphnes; at the centre of the garden, an aviary, full of pheasants and turtledoves, symbolises the sense of hearing.

Vivarium ⊘ – *Rue de l'Église.* This observation centre, housed in a medieval building, contains more than 50 different species of reptiles from the five continents: green mambas, rare snakes, lizzards, batrachians and crocodiles.

EXCURSION

★**Excenevex** – *3km/1.9mi southeast along D 25.*

This charming lakeside resort, sheltering inside the Golfe de Coudrée, is famous for having the most extensive beach on the French side of Lake Geneva. The coast is lined with luxury holiday villas.

Gold leaf used for bookbinding, picture-framing and wrought-iron work, has been made here since 1939 *(not open to the public)*. Some of the gold leaf manufactured in Excenevex was used for the restoration of numerous monuments, including Versailles, and for regilding the wrought-iron gates and railings of the Place Stanislas in Nancy.

Michelin on the Net: www.michelin-travel.com.
Our route planning sevice covers all of Europe - twenty-one countries and one million kilometres of highways and byways - enabling you to plot many different itineraries from wherever you are.
The itinerary options allow you to choose a preferred route - for example, quickest, shortest, or Michelin recommended.
The network is updated three times weekly, integrating ongoing road works, detours, new motorways, and snowbound mountain passes.
The description of the itinerary includes the distances and travelling times between towns, selected hotels and restaurants.

Practical
Information

Canyoning

P. Bodin/FOC

Planning your trip

French tourist offices

For information, brochures, maps and assistance in planning a trip to France, travellers should apply to the official tourist office in their own country.

Australia - New Zealand

BNP Building, 12 Castlereagh Street, Sydney, New South Wales 2000, ☎ (61) 2-231-5244; Fax (61) 2-221-8682

Canada

30 St Patrick's Street, Suite 700, Toronto, ONT M5T 3A3, ☎ (416) 593 4723

1981 Avenue McGill College, Suite 490, Montreal, PQ H3A 2W9, ☎ (514) 288 4264; Fax (514) 845 4868

Eire

38 Lower Abbey Street, Dublin 1, ☎ (1) 703 4046; Fax (1) 874 7324

United Kingdom

179 Piccadilly, London W1, ☎ (0891) 244 123; Fax (0171) 493 6594

United States

France On Call Hotline: Dial 900-990-0040 (US $0.50/min) for information on hotels, restaurants and transportation.

East Coast: 444 Madison Avenue, New York, NY 10022, ☎ (212) 838-7800; Fax (212) 838-7855

Mid West: 676 North Michigan Avenue, Suite 3360, Chicago, IL 60611 ☎ (312) 751-7800; Fax (312) 337-6339

West Coast: 9454 Wilshire Boulevard, Suite 715, Beverly Hills, CA 90212 ☎ (310) 271-2693; Fax (310) 276-2835

Cyberspace

www.info.france-usa.org

The French Embassy's Web site provides basic information (geography, population, history), a new digest and business-related information. It offers special pages for children and pages devoted to culture, language study and travel and you can reach other selected sites (regions, cities and ministries) with a hypertext link.

www.fr-holidaystore.co.uk

The new French Travel Centre in London has gone on-line with this service, providing information on all of the regions of France, including updated special travel offers and details on available accommodation.

Local tourist offices

In addition to the French tourist offices abroad, listed above, visitors may wish to contact local offices for more precise information, to receive brochures and maps. Below, the addresses are given for each local tourist office by *département*. The index lists the *département* after each town and the *départements* are delimited on the Principal sights map in the introduction.

Address enquiries to the Comité régional de tourisme (CRT):

Departmental Tourist Offices - Fédération Nationale des Comités Départmentaux de Tourisme, 2 rue Linois, 75015 Paris. ☎ 01 45 75 62 16.

Alpes-de-Haute-Provence: Comité départemental du tourisme et des loisirs, 19, rue du Docteur-Honnorat, BP 170, 04005 Digne-les-Bains Cedex, ☎ 04 92 31 57 29.

Côte-d'Azur: Comité régional du tourisme Côte-d'Azur, 55, promenade des Anglais, BP 1602, 06011 Nice Cedex 1, ☎ 04 93 37 78 78.

Drôme: Comité départemental du tourisme, 31, avenue du Président-Herriot. Valence ☎ 08 36 68 02 04

Hautes-Alpes: Comité départemental du tourisme, 5ter, rue Capitaine-de-Bresson, 05000 Gap, ☎ 92 53 62 00.

Haute-Savoie: Agence touristique départemental Haute-Savoie Mont-Blanc, 56, rue Sommeiller, BP 348, 74012 Annecy, ☎ 04 50 51 32 31.

Isère: Comité départemental du tourisme, Maison du tourisme, 14, rue de la République, BP 227, 38019 Grenoble, ☎ 04 76 54 34 36.

Savoie: Agence touristique départemental de la Savoie, 24, bd de la Colonne, 73000 Chambéry, ☎ 04 79 85 12 45.

Var: Comité départemental du tourisme, 5, avenue Vauban, BP5147, 83000 Toulon, ☏ 04 94 09 00 69.

Tourist offices - Further information can be obtained from the *Syndicats d'initiative*, as the tourist offices in most large towns are called. The addresses and telephone numbers are listed after the symbol 🖪 in the Admission times and charges.

Tourism for the Disabled – Some of the sights described in this guide are accessible to handicapped people and are indicated in the Admission times and charges section by the symbol ♿. Useful information on transport, holiday-making and sports associations for the disabled is available from the Comité National Français de Liaison pour la Réadaptation des Handicapés (CNRH), 236 bis, rue de Tolbiac, 75013 Paris. Call their international information number ☏ 01 53 80 66 44 or write to request a catalogue of publications or in France use the Minitel service **3614 HANDITEL** (1.01F/min - includes a message board, in French). If you are a member of a sports club and would like to practise your sport in France, or meet with others who do, ask the CNRH for information on clubs in the Fedération Française du Sport Adapté (FFSA), ☏ 01 48 72 80 72. For information on museum access for the disabled contact La Direction, Les Musées de France, Service Accueil des Publics Spécifiques, 6, rue des Pyramides, 75041 Paris Cedex 1, ☏ 01 40 15 35 88.

The Michelin Red Guide France and the Michelin Camping Caravaning France indicate hotels and campsites with facilities suitable for physically handicapped people.

Formalities

Passport - Visitors entering France must be in possession of a valid national passport. Citizens of any of the European Union countries need only a national identity card. In case of loss or theft report to the embassy or consulate and the local police.

Visa - No entry visa is required for US and Canadian citizens whose stay in France does not exceed 3 months. Australian and New Zealand citizens should apply for a visa at the nearest French consulate. Citizens of other countries should check visa requirements with the French consulate or a travel agent.

US citizens should obtain the booklet *Your Trip Abroad* (US $1.25) which provides useful information on visa requirements, customs regulations, medical, care etc for international travellers. Apply to the Superintendent of Documents, PO Box 371954, Pittsburgh, PA 15250-7954. ☏ (202) 783-3238.

Customs - Apply to the customs office in your country for a leaflet on customs regulations and the full range of duty-free allowances. The US Customs Service, PO Box 7407, Washington DC 20044, ☏ (202) 927-5580 offers a publication *Know Before You Go* for US citizens. There are no customs formalities for holiday-makers bringing their caravans into France for a stay of less than 6 months. No customs document is necessary for pleasure boats and outboard motors for a stay of less than 6 months but the registration certificate should be kept on board.

Americans can bring home, tax-free, up to US $400 worth of goods; Canadians up to CND $300; Australians up to AUS $400 and New Zealanders up to NZ $ 700. Member citizens of the European Union are not restricted in regard to purchasing goods for private use, but the recommended allowances for alcoholic beverages and tobacco are as follows:

Spirits (whisky, gin vodka, etc)	10 litres	Cigarettes	800
Fortified wines (vermouth, port, etc)	20 litres	Cigarillos	400
Wine not more than 60° sparkling)	90 litres	Cigars	200
Beer	110 litres	Smoking tobacco	1kg

Embassies and consulates

Australia	Embassy	4, rue Jean-Rey, 75015 Paris; ☏ 01 40 59 33 00; Fax 01 40 59 33 10
Canada	Embassy	35, avenue Montaigne, 75008 Paris; ☏ 01.44 43 29 00; Fax 01 44 43 29 99
Eire	Embassy	4, rue Rude, 75016 Paris; ☏ 01 44 17 67 00; Fax 01 45 00 84 17
New Zealand	Embassy	7 ter, rue Léonard-de-Vinci, 75016 Paris; ☏ 01 45 00 24 11; Fax 01 45 01 26 39
UK	Embassy	35, rue du Faubourg-St-Honoré, 75008 Paris; ☏ 01 42 66 91 42; Fax 01 42 66 95 90
	Consulate	16, rue d'Anjou, 75008 Paris; ☏ 01 42 66 06 68 (visas)
USA	Embassy	2, avenue Gabriel, 75008 Paris; ☏ 01 43 12 22 22; Fax 01 42 66 97 83
	Consulate	2 , rue St-Florentin, 75001 Paris; ☏ 01 42 96 14 88.

Getting there

By air

Choose between scheduled flights on national airlines (Air France, British Airways and Swissair) or commercial and package-tour flights with rail or coach link-ups or Fly-Drive schemes to one of the key gateway airports (Geneva, Lyon-Satolas and Chambéry). Contact airlines and travel agents for information. There are daily flights from Paris to Grenoble (1hr), Chambery/Aix-les-Bains (1hr 10min) and Annecy (1hr 15min).

By rail

There are two options by rail for those who appreciate short transfers and want to avoid weather delays and ski-luggage supplements, the Eurostar Ski Train and the Snow Train operated by Rail Europe. The **Eurostar Ski Train** from London (Waterloo International Station) and Ashford Kent to Bourg-St-Maurice via Moutiers takes eight hours, departing and returning every Saturday between mid-December and the end of April. The Moutiers stop serves Val Thorens, Meribel, Courchevel, Les Menuires and La Plagne whereas those heading for Tignes, Val d'Isère and Les Arcs should continue to Bourg-St-Maurice. Details from Eurostar UK ☎ 0345 303030. The **Snow Train**, chartered by various ski companies runs both a daytime and night service with a motorail facility. Rail Europe ☎ 0990 300003.

French Railways (SNCF) and British companies operate a daily service via the Channel Tunnel on Eurostar taking 3 hours between London (Waterloo International Station), ☎ 0345 881 881 and Paris (Gare du Nord).

The French National Railway (SNCF) operates an extensive network of lines including many high-speed passenger trains (TGV) and rail services throughout France. Fast inter-city service from Paris (Gare de Lyon) to Annecy, Chambery and Grenoble.

There are rail passes offering unlimited travel and group travel tickets offering savings for parties. **Eurodomino Rover** tickets for unlimited rail travel over 3, 5 or 10 days are available in the UK, along with other kinds of tickets, information and bookings, from French Railways in the French Travel Centre at 179 Piccadilly, London WIV OBA, 24hr brochure hotline ☎ (0181) 880 8161, bookings ☎ (0171) 203 7000 and from travel agencies. **Eurailpass, Flexipass** and **Saverpass** are options available in the US for travel in Europe and must be purchased in the US from Rail Europe Inc, ☎ (800) 438-7245.

The French railways SNCF operates a telephone information, reservation and prepayment service in English from 7am to 10pm (French time). In France call ☎ 08 36 35 35 39. From outside France ☎ 33 8 36 35 35 39. Ask about discount rates if you are over 60, a student or travelling with your family.

Tickets bought in France must be validated (composter) by using the orange automatic date-stamping machines at the platform entrance. Baggage trolleys (10F coin required - refundable) are available at mainline stations.

A good investment is the **Thomas Cook European Rail timetable**, which gives all the train schedules throughout France and Europe as well as useful information on travelling by train (US ☎ 1 800 367 7984).

By sea

There are numerous **cross-Channel services** (passenger and car ferries, hovercraft, SeaCat) from the United Kingdom and Eire. For details contact travel agencies or:

P&O Stena Line, Channel House, Channel View Road, Dover CT17 9TJ; ☎ (0990) 980 980

Hoverspeed, International Hoverport, Marine Parade, Dover, Kent CT17 9TG; ☎ (01304) 240-241

Brittany Ferries, Millbay Docks, Plymouth, Devon PL1 3EW; ☎ (0990) 360 360

Sally Line, Argyle Centre, York Street, Ramsgate, Kent CT11 9AS; ☎ (0800) 636 465

Irish Ferries, 50 West Norland Street, Dublin 2; ☎ (353) 1-6-610-511

Le Shuttle-Eurotunnel, ☎ (0990) 353-535

To choose the most suitable route between your port of arrival and your destination use the Michelin Tourist and Motoring Atlas France, Michelin map 911 (which gives travel times and mileages) or Michelin maps from the 1:200,000 series (with the yellow cover).

By coach

Scheduled coach services are operated from London to Paris and to towns such as Grenoble, Chambery, Annecy and Chamonix:

Eurolines (London), 52 Grosvenor Gardens, Victoria, London SWIW OAU. ☎ 0171 730 8235.

Eurolines (Paris), 28 avenue du Général-de-Gaulle, 93541 Bagnolet; ☎ 01 49 72 51 51.

The **Snowcoach** vehicles leave London every Friday at 5.30pm and arrive in Méribel, Valloire or St Gervais by 10am the next morning. ☎ 01727 833141.

Cyberspace

www.sncf.fr/voy/indexe.htm
Visit the English version of the SNCF site

www.eurostar.com
Eurostar's home page

Motoring in France

Documents - Nationals of the European Union countries require a valid national **driving licence**; nationals of non-EU countries require an **international driving licence** (obtainable in the US from the American Automobile Club; US $10 for members, US $22 for non-members). For the vehicle it is necessary to have the **registration papers** (log-book) and a **nationality plate** of the approved size.

Insurance - Insurance cover is compulsory and although an international insurance certificate (green card) is no longer a legal requirement in France for vehicles registered in Great Britain, it is internationally recognised by the police and other authorities. Most British insurance policies give the minimum third party cover required in France (check with your insurance company) - but be warned that this amounts to less than it would in the UK. Certain UK motoring organisations (AA, RAC) offer special accident insurance and breakdown service schemes for members, and the AA also has a scheme for non-members. Motorists should contact their own insurance company to enquire about special policies for foreign travel.

Members of the American Automobile Club should obtain the free brochure *Offices To Serve You Abroad*.

Highway code - Traffic drives on the right. The minimum driving age is 18 years old. It is compulsory for front-seat passengers to wear **seat belts** where they are fitted. Children under the age of ten should not travel in the front of the car.must travel on the back seat. Full or dipped headlights must be switched on in poor visibility and at night; use sidelights only when the vehicle is stationary. Headlight beams should be adjusted for driving on the right. It is illegal to drive with faulty lights in France, so it is advisable to take a spare set of bulbs with you.

In the case of a **breakdown** a red warning triangle or hazard warning lights are obligatory. Drivers should watch out for unfamiliar road signs and take great care on the road. In built-up areas **priority** must be ceded to vehicles coming **from the right**. However, traffic on main roads outside built-up areas (indicated by a yellow diamond sign) and on roundabouts has priority. Vehicles must come to a complete stop at stop signs and when the lights turn red at road junctions (where they may filter to the right only if indicated by a flashing amber arrow).

The regulations on **drinking** and **driving** (maximum permissable blood alcohol content: 0.05%) and **speeding** are strictly enforced - usually by an on-the-spot fine and/or confiscation of the vehicle.

Speed limits

Although liable to modification **speed limits** are as follows:
– toll motorways 130kph/80mph (110kph/68mph when raining);
– dual carriage roads and motorways without tolls 110kph/68mph (100kph/62mph when raining);
– other roads 90kph/56mph (80kph/50mph when raining) and in towns 50kph/31mph;
– outside lane on motorways during daylight, on level ground and with good visibility – minimum speed limit of 80kph/50mph).

Parking regulations - In town there are zones where parking is either restricted or subject to a fee; tickets should be obtained from the ticket machines *(horodateurs* - small change necessary) and displayed inside the windscreen on the driver's side); failure to display may result in a heavy fine (and, in extreme cases, removal of the offending vehicle).

In some towns, there are "blue" parking zones *(zone bleue)* marked by a blue line on the pavement or a blue signpost with a P and a small square underneath. In this particular motorists should display a cardboard disc which can be adjusted to display time of arrival and which allows a stay of up to 1hr 30min (2hr 30min over lunch time) free. Discs are available in supermarkets or petrol stations (ask for a *disque de stationnement*); they are sometimes given away free.

Route planning - The French road network is excellent and includes many motorways, mostly toll-roads *(autoroute à péage)*. The roads are very busy during the holiday period (particularly weekends in July and August), and to avoid traffic congestion it is advisable to follow the recommended secondary routes (signposted as *Bison Futé* *itinéraires bis).* The motorway network includes rest areas *(aires)* every 10-15km/5-10mi and petrol stations, usually with restaurant and shopping complexes attached, about every 40km/25mi, so that long-distance drivers have no excuse not to stop for a rest every now and then.

For 24-hour road traffic information in France: dial 0156 96 33 33 or consult Minitel 3615 Code Route (1.29F/min).

Tolls - In France, most motorway sections are subject to a toll *(péage)*. This can be expensive especially if you take the motorway all the way. Tolls can be paid in cash or with a credit card (Visa, Mastercard).

Car rental - There are car rental agencies at airports, air terminals, railway stations and in all large towns throughout France. European cars usually have manual transmission but automatic cars are available on request (advance reservation recommended). It is relatively expensive to hire a car in France; Americans in particular will notice the difference and should consider booking a car from home before leaving or taking advantage of Fly-Drive schemes. Those who rent a car before leaving home should make sure that they inform the car hire company that they intend to take the car to France, so that their hire contract includes insurance for the car while on French soil. Some credit cards have car rental insurance included. Generally speaking most car rental firms will not rent to those under 21 and make an extra charge for those aged between 21 and 25. Check this out before leaving.

Central reservation in France:

Avis: ☎01 46 10 60 60	Europcar: ☎01 30 43 82 82
Budget: ☎01 46 86 65 65	Hertz: ☎01 47 88 51 51
Eurodollar: ☎01 49 58 44 44	

Petrol

In France four different types of petrol (US gas) are available:

sans plomb 95 - unleaded 95 octane   *sans plomb 98* - unleaded 98 octane
super - super leaded   *diesel/gazole* - diesel

Petrol is more expensive in France compared to the US and the UK. The French Tourist Office issues a map showing the location of cheaper petrol stations within a mile or so of motorway exits, usually in a hypermarket complex (send an SAE).

Minitel - France Telecom operates a system offering directory enquiries (free of charge up to 3min), travel and entertainment reservations, and other services (cost varies between 0.375-5.57F/min). These small, computer-like terminals can be found in some post offices, hotels and France Telecom agencies and in many French homes. **3614 PAGES E** is the code for directory assistance in English (turn on the unit, dial 3614, hit the "connexion" button when you get the tone, type in "PAGES E", and follow the instructions on screen). For route planning, use Michelin services **3615 MICHELIN** (tourist and route information) and **3617 MICHELIN** (information sent by **fax**).

Route planning with Michelin on the Net: www.michelin-travel.com

Our route planning service covers all of Europe - twenty-one countries and one million kilometres of highways and byways - enabling you to plot many different itineraries from wherever you are.

The itinerary options allow you to choose a preferred route - for example, quickest, shortest or Michelin recommended.

The network is updated three times weekly, integrating ongoing road works, detours, new motorways and snowbound mountain passes.

The description of the itinerary includes the distances and travelling times between towns, selected hotels and restaurants.

Michelin Maps (scale 1:200 000) which are revised regularly,
– highlight towns cited in the Michelin Red Guide France for their hotels
* or restaurants;*
– indicate which towns in the Red Guide are accompanied by a town plan.
Michelin makes it so easy to choose where to stay and to find the right route.
Keep current Michelin Maps in the car at all times.

Accommodation

The **Places to Stay** map in the Introduction indicates recommended places for overnight stops, spas, winter and seaside resorts; it can be used in conjunction with the **Michelin Red Guide France** which lists a selection of hotels and restaurants.

Loisirs Accueil is a booking service which has offices in most French *départements*. For information contact Réservation Loisirs Accueil, 280, boulevard St-Germain, 75007 Paris, ☎ 01 44 11 10 44.

The **Accueil de France** tourist offices, which are open all year, make hotel bookings for a small fee for personal (non-business) callers only. The head office is in Paris (127, avenue des Champs-Elysées, ☎ 01 49 52 53 54 for information only) and there are offices in many large towns and resorts.

The **Logis et Auberges de France** brochure (a selection of inns) is available from the French Government Tourist Office.

Relais et Châteaux, 9, avenue Marceau, 75016 Paris, ☎ 01 47 42 20 92; hotel accommodation in châteaux and manor houses around France.

Rural accommodation

Contact the Maison des Gîtes de France, 59, rue St-Lazare, 75009 Paris; ☎ 01 49 70 75 75, Fax 01 42 81 28 53, or 178 Piccadilly, London W1V OAL; ☎ (0891) 244 123, for a list of addresses of self-catering accommodation, usually in a local style cottage or apartment where you will be able to make yourself at home.

Useful publications on farm accommodation (bed & breakfasts, camping etc) include *Bienvenue à la ferme* (published by Editions Solar) and *Vacances et weekends à la ferme* (Editions Balland).

Gîtes et Refuges, France et Frontières by A and S Mouraret (published by La Cadole, 74, rue Albert-Perdreaux, 78140 Vélizy; ☎ 01 34 65 10 40) is a useful handbook in French aimed at ramblers, mountaineers, climbers, skiiers, canoeists and cross-country cyclists.

Gîtes de France also publishes a booklet on bed and breakfast accommodation *(chambres d'hôtes)*.

Bed and breakfast

Gîtes de France *(see above)* publishes a booklet on bed and breakfast accommodation *(chambres d'hôtes)* which includes a room and breakfast at a reasonable price.

You can also contact an association that provides addresses of this type of accommodation throughout the region:

Bed & Breakfast (France), International reservations centre, PO Box 66, Henley-on-Thames, Oxon RG9 1XS, ☎ (01491) 578 803, Fax (01491) 410 806.

Youth Hostels - There are two main youth hostel associations *(auberges de jeunesse)* in France:

Ligue Française pour les Auberges de Jeunesse, 38, boulevard Raspail, 75007 Paris, ☎ 01 45 48 69 84, Fax 01 45 44 57 47 and

Fédération Unie des Auberges de Jeunesse, 27, rue Pajol, 75018 Paris, ☎ 01 44 89 87 27, Fax 01 44 89 87 10, Minitel 3615 code FUJA (1.01F/min).

Holders of an International Youth Hostel Federation card should apply for a list from the International Federation or from the French Youth Hostels Association to book a bed.

Hostelling International / American Youth Hostel Association in the USA (☎ 202-783-6161) publishes the *International Hostel Guide for Europe* (US $13.95) - also available to non-members.

Camping

There are numerous officially graded sites with varying standards of facilities throughout the region. The **Michelin Guide Camping Caravaning France** lists a selection of camp sites. An International Camping Carnet for caravans is useful but not compulsory; it may be obtained from the motoring organisations or the Camping and Caravaning Club (Greenfields House, Westwook Way, Coventry CV4 8JH, ☎ 01203 694 995).

The annual **Michelin Red Guide France** *offers an up-to-date selection of hotels and restaurants serving carefully prepared food at reasonable prices.*

General information

Electricity - The electric current in France is 220 volts. Circular two pin plugs are the rule. Adapters should be bought before you leave home; they are on sale in most airports.

Medical treatment - First aid, medical advice and chemists' night service rota are available from chemists/drugstores (*pharmacie* - identified by the green cross sign).
It is advisable to take out comprehensive insurance cover as the recipient of medical treatment in French hospitals or clinics must pay the bil. Nationals of non-EU countries should check with their insurance companies about policy limitations. Reimbursement can then be negotiated with the insurance company according to the policy held.
All prescription drugs should be clearly labelled; it is recommended that you carry a copy of the prescription.
American Express offers its members a service, "Global Assist", for any medical, legal or personal emergency - call collect from anywhere ☎ 01 47 16 25 29.
British and Irish citizens should apply to the Department of Health and Social Security for **Form E 111**, which entitles the holder to urgent treatment for accident or unexpected illness in EU countries. A refund of part of the cost of treatment can be obtained on application in person or by post to the local Social Security Offices (*Caisse Primaire d'Assurance Maladie*).

Tipping - Since a service charge is automatically included in the prices of meals and accommodation in France, it is not necessary to tip in restaurants and hotels. However, taxi drivers, bellboys, doormen, filling station attendants or anybody who has been of assistance are usually tipped at the customer's discretion. French people do give an extra tip in restaurants and cafés (at least 50 centimes for a drink and several francs for a meal).

Currency - There are no restrictions on the amount of currency visitors can take into France. Visitors wishing to export currency in foreign banknotes in excess of the given allocation from France should complete a currency declaration form on a arrival.

Notes and coins - *See illustration on page 380.* The unit of currency in France is the French franc (F), subdivided into 100 centimes. French coins come in the following values: 5, 10, 20 and 50 centimes (all gold-coloured, except the 50-centime coin which is silver); 1, 2, 5, 10 and 20 francs (all silver, except the 10- and 20-franc coins which are silver with a gold band). French banknotes are issued to the values of 50, 100, 200 and 500 (the old 20-franc note is being phased out).

Banks and currency exchange - Banks are generally open from 9am to 4.30pm (smaller branches may close for lunch) and are closed on Mondays or Saturdays (except if market day). Some branches open for limited transactions on Saturdays. Banks close early on the day before a bank holiday.

A passport is necessary as identification when cashing cheques (travellers' or ordinary) in banks. Commission charges vary and hotels usually charge more than banks for cashing cheques for non-residents.
By far the most convenient way of obtaining French currency is the 24hr **cash dispenser** or ATM (*distributeur automatique de billets* in French), found outside many banks and post offices and easily recognisable by the CB (Carte Bleue) logo. Most accept foreign credit cards (don't forget your PIN) and some even give instructions in English. Note that American Express cards can only be used in dispensers operated by the Crédit Lyonnais bank or by American Express. Foreign currency can also be exchanged in major banks, post offices, hotels or private change offices found in main cities and near popular tourist attractions.

Credit cards - American Express, Visa, Mastercard/ Eurocard and Diners Club are widely accepted in shops, hotels and restaurants and petrol stations. If your card is stolen, call the appropriate 24hr hotline:
    American Express ☎ 01 47 77 70 00
    Visa ☎ 01 42 77 11 90
    Mastercard/Eurocard ☎ 01 45 67 84 84
    Diners Club ☎ 01 47 62 75 50

You should also report any loss or theft to the local police who will issue you with a certificate (useful proof to show the credit card company).

Post - Main post offices open Monday to Friday from 8am to 7pm and Saturdays from 8am to noon. Smaller branch post offices generally close at lunchtime between noon and 2pm, and finish for the day at 4pm. Stamps are also sold in newsagents and cafés that sell cigarettes *(tabac)*. Stamp collectors should ask for *timbres de collection* in any post office (there is often a *philatélie* counter).

Postage via airmail:
    UK - letter (20g) 3F
    North America - letter (20g) 4.40F
    Australia and NZ - letter (20g) 5.20F.

Public holidays - The following are days when museums and other monuments may be closed or vary their hours of admission:

1 January	New Year's Day (Jour de l'An)
	Easter Sunday and Monday (Pâques)
1 May	May Day
8 May	V E Day
	Ascension Day
	Whit Sunday and Monday (Pentecôte)
14July	France's National Day (Bastille Day)
15 August	Assumption
1 November	All Saints' Day (Toussaint)
11 November	Armistice Day
25 December	Christmas Day (Noël)

In general, national museums and art galleries are closed on Tuesdays whereas municipal museums are closed on Mondays.

In addition to the usual **school holidays** at Christmas and in the spring and summer, there are long mid-term breaks (10 days to a fortnight) in February and late October/early November.

Time - France is one hour ahead of Greenwich Mean Time (GMT);

When it is **noon in France**, it is

    3am in Los Angeles
    6am in New York
    11am in Dublin
    11am in London
    7pm in Perth
    9pm in Sydney
    11pm in Auckland

In France, time is generally given using the 24hr-clock and "am" and "pm" are not used.

Shopping - Department stores and chain stores are open Monday to Saturday from 9am to 6.30-7.30pm. Smaller, more specialised shops may close during the lunch hour. Food stores (grocers, wine merchants and bakeries) are open from 7am to 6.30-7.30pm, and some open on Sunday mornings. Many food stores close between noon and 2pm and on Mondays. Hypermarkets usually open until 9-10pm.

Local radios - These usually give frequent updates on traffic, local demonstrations, etc. as well as information on local cultural events. Motorway traffic information is available on FM 107.7.

Michelin Green Guides for North America:

California
Canada
Chicago
Florida
New England
New York City
Quebec
San Francisco
Washington

Telephoning

Public telephones - Most public phones in France use pre-paid phone cards *(télécartes)*. Some telephone booths accept credit cards (Visa, Mastercard/Eurocard: minimum monthly charge 20F). *Télécartes* (50 or 120 units) can be bought in post offices, branches of France Telecom, cafés that sell cigarettes *(tabacs)* and newsagents, and can be used to make calls in France and abroad. Calls can be received at phone boxes where the blue bell sign is shown.

National calls - French telephone numbers have 10 digits. In Paris and the Paris region numbers begin with 01; 02 in northwest France; 03 in northeast France; 04 in southeast France and Corsica; 05 in southwest France.

International calls - To call France from abroad, dial the country code (33) + 9-digit number (omit the initial zero). When calling abroad from France, dial 00; folllowed by the country code, followed by the area code and number of your correspondent.
To use your personal calling card dial:

AT&T: 0-800 99 00 11	**Sprint:** 0-800 99 00 87
MCI: 0-800 99 00 19	**Canada Direct:** 0-800 99 00 16

International dialling codes:

Australia: 61	Eire: 353	United Kingdom: 44
Canada: 1	New Zealand: 64	United States: 1

Emergency numbers:

Police: 17	Fire (Pompiers): 18	Ambulance (SAMU): 15.

Telephone rates from a public phone are about 3F/min from France to the UK, and about 4.50F/min from France to the US and Canada. Cheap rates with 50% extra time are available from private telephones to the UK on weekdays between 9.30pm and 8am, from 2pm on Saturdays and all day on Sundays and holidays. Cheap rates to the US and Canada are from 2am to noon all week, and to Australia between 9.30pm and 8am Monday to Saturday and all day Sunday.

Toll-free numbers in France begin with 0 800.

Minitel – France Telecom operates a system offering directory enquiries (free of charge up to 3min), travel and entertainment reservations, and other service (cost varies between 0.37F-5.75F/min). These small computer-like terminals can be found in some post offices, hotels and France Telecom agencies and in many French homes. **3614 PAGES E** is the code for directory assistance in English (turn on the unit, dial 3614, hit the "connexion" button when you get the tone, type in "PAGES E", and follow the instructions on the screen). For route planning, use Michelin services **3615 MICHELIN** (tourist and route information) and **3617 MICHELIN** (information sent by fax).

Cellular phones - In France, these have numbers beginning with 06. Two-watt (lighter, shorter reach) and eight-watt models are on the market, using the Itinéris (France Telecom) or SFR network. Cell phone rentals (delivery or airport pickup provided):

Ellinas Phone Rental	☎ 01 47 20 70 00
Euro Exaphone	☎ 01 44 09 77 78
Rent a Cell Express	☎ 01 53 93 78 00

Conversion tables

Weights and measures

1 kilogram (kg)	2.2 pounds (lb)	2.2 pounds
1 metric ton (tn)	1.1 tons	1.1 tons

to convert kilograms to pounds, multiply by 2.2

1 litre (l)	2.1 pints (pt)	1.8 pints
1 litre	0.3 gallon (gal)	0.2 gallon

to convert litres to gallons, multiply by 0.26 (US) or 0.22 (UK)

1 hectare (ha)	2.5 acres	2.5 acres
1 square kilometre (km²)	0.4 square miles (sq mi)	0.4 square miles

to convert hectares to acres, multiply by 2.4

1 centimetre (cm)	0.4 inches (in)	0.4 inches
1 metre (m)	3.3 feet (ft) - 39.4 inches - 1.1 yards (yd)	
1 kilometre (km)	0.6 miles (mi)	0.6 miles

to convert metres to feet, multiply by 3.28 . kilometres to miles, multiply by 0.6

Clothing

Women

	EU	US	UK
	35	4	2½
	36	5	3½
	37	6	4½
Shoes	38	7	5½
	39	8	6½
	40	9	7½
	41	10	8½
	36	4	8
	38	6	10
Dresses & Suits	40	8	12
	42	12	14
	44	14	16
	46	16	18
	36	08	30
	38	10	32
Blouses & sweaters	40	12	14
	42	14	36
	44	16	38
	46	18	40

Men

EU	US	UK	
40	7½	7	
41	8½	8	
42	9½	9	
43	10½	10	Shoes
44	11½	11	
45	12½	12	
46	13½	13	
46	36	36	
48	38	38	
50	40	40	Suits
52	42	42	
54	44	44	
56	46	48	
37	14½	14,5	
38	15	15	
39	15½	15½	Shirts
40	15¾	15¾	
41	16	16	
42	16½	16½	

Sizes often vary depending on the designer. These equivalents are given for guidance only.

Speed

kph	10	30	50	70	80	90	100	110	120	130
mph	6	19	31	43	50	56	62	68	75	81

Temperature

Celsius (°C)	0°	5°	10°	15°	20°	25°	30°	40°	60°	80°	100°
Fahrenheit (°F)	32°	41°	50°	59°	68°	77°	86°	104°	140°	176°	212°

To convert Celsius into Fahrenheit, multiply °C by 9, divide by 5, and add 32.
To convert Fahrenheit into Celsius, subtract 32 from °F, multiply by 5, and divide by 9.

Notes and coins

500 Francs featuring scientists Pierre and Marie Curie (1858-1906), (1867-1934)

200 Francs featuring engineer Gustave Eiffel (1832-1923)

100 Francs featuring painter Paul Cézanne (1839-1906)

50 Francs featuring pilot and writer Antoine de Saint-Exupéry (1900-1944)

20 Francs

10 Francs

5 Francs

2 Francs

1 Franc

50 Centimes

20 Centimes

10 Centimes

5 Centimes

Weather - For any outdoor activity on sea or land, it is useful to have reliable weather forecasts. For general weather reports, dial 08 36 68 02 followed by the number of the *département*.

      Alpes de Haute Provence ☎ 04
      Alpes Maritimes ☎ 06
      Drôme ☎ 26
      Haute-de-Savoie ☎ 74
      Hautes-Alpes ☎ 05
      Isère ☎ 38
      Savoie ☎ 73
      Var ☎ 83
      Vaucluse ☎ 06

The Minitel services 36 15 METEO, 36 15 CIEL and 36 17 METPLUS give weather forecasts for the next 10 days. See also the chapter on Safety on the mountains.

Heritage trails - All over France, since 1975, *routes historiques* have been designated by the Caisse nationale des Monuments historiques et des Sites (62 rue St-Antoine, 75004 Paris, ☎ 01 44 61 21 50. These itineraries are described in leaflets available from the CNMHS. The French Alps' heritage trails are: Route Stendhal; Route des ducs de Savoie, Route historique des Dauphins and Route Historique Jean-Jacques Rousseau.

Tourist Pass: 100 sights for 280F

This pass gives unrestricted access to more than one hundred historic buildings managed by the Caisse Nationale des Monuments Historiques et des Sites (CNMHS). It is valid for one year throughout France as of the date of purchase. It is available in some of the historic buildings and from the CNMHS directly or by mail from the Service du droit d'entrée, 62, rue St-Antoine, 75004 Paris, ☎ 01 44 61 21 50 or 51.

*The current edition of the annual **Michelin Red Guide France***
offers a selection of pleasant and quiet hotels in convenient locations.
Their amenities are included (swimming pools, tennis courts,
private beaches and gardens...)
as well as their dates of annual closure.
The selection also includes establishments which offer excellent cuisine:
carefully prepared meals at reasonable prices, Michelin stars for good cooking.
*The current annual **Michelin Camping Caravaning France** lists the facilities*
offered by many campsites (shops, bars, restaurants, laundries, games rooms, tennis
courts, miniature golf courses, playgrounds, swimming pools...)

Sports and recreation

SAFETY ON THE MOUNTAINS

Mountain areas are potentially dangerous, even for the most experienced enthusiasts. Avalanches, falling rocks, bad weather, fog, treacherous terrain and snow fields, icy water, loss of one's bearings, wrong assessment of distances are the dangers threatening mountaineers, skiers and hikers.

Driving in mountain areas

Unaccustomed drivers may be overawed by the experience and it is essential to take certain precautions. Cars must be in good working order (brakes and tyres particularly) and drivers must abide rigorously to the highway code. For instance, horns must be sounded on twisting roads with reduced visibility and along narrow roads, cars going downhill must give way to those climbing. When climbing continuously, it is advisable to watch the oil and cooling liquid levels. In addition, it is recommended to avoid driving in bad weather, getting caught by nightfall, stopping beneath a cliff (falling rocks are frequent) or leaving the car unattended in an isolated spot (danger of theft).

Tricky scenic roads – Michelin maps nos 70, 74, 77, 81, 89, 243, 244 and 245 on a scale of 1:200 000 mention very narrow roads (where passing is difficult or impossible), unusually steep ones, difficult or dangerous sections, tunnels, the altitude of major passes...

Snow cover – Maps nos 916, 919 and 989 on a scale of 1:1 000 000 mention major roads regularly blocked by snow with their probable closing date or their clearing within 48 hours. Access roads to resorts are normally cleared daily.

A few words of advice

Advice given to off-piste skiers also applies to hikers and mountaineers. However, a prolonged stay above 3 000m/9 842ft calls for special precautions. Atmospheric pressure is one third lower and the heart beats faster to compensate for the lack of oxygen. It takes roughly a week to get used to it as the production of red cells in the blood is intensified so that as much oxygen can be carried as at lower altitudes.

The main dangers are the following: **Mountain sickness** or hypoxaemia (symptoms: digestive problems, breathing difficulty, headache) which can normally be treated with appropriate medicine that tourists are advised to take with them; the more serious cases (pulmonary oedema) have to be treated in hospital. **Hypothermia** is also a danger in high-mountain areas for people caught by a sudden change in the weather such as fog, for instance, which always brings a cold snap. **Frostbite** is less obvious as symptoms appear progressively: loss of feeling in the hands and feet, numbness and paleness of the skin. The danger lies in the wrong treatment being applied on the spot: never try to warm up the affected part of the body, by whatever means, unless you can continue until the doctor arrives, as a new attack of frostbite on a partially rewarmed limb would cause even more damage.

Accidents can be avoided or their consequences lessened by following these simple rules; it is also recommended never to go hiking or mountaineering on your own, and to let someone know of your planned itinerary and when you intend to return.

Weather forecast

Up-to-date recorded information about regional weather is available to hikers (for telephone numbers, see Tourist information). In addition, more specific information can be obtained:
– Five-day forecast in high-mountain areas: ☎ 08 36 68 04 04;
– Risk of avalanche: ☎ 08 36 68 10 20.

Avalanche-risk scale

1 – **Low**: snow cover is stable and there are only rare avalanches on very steep slopes.

2 – **Limited**: snow cover is again stable but avalanches may be started in specific areas by an excessive number of skiers or hikers.

3 – **Likely**: snow cover is moderately stable and avalanches may be started in many places by isolated persons; avalanches are also likely to start naturally as for 4 on the scale.

4 – **Very likely**: snow cover is fairly unstable on all steep slopes and avalanches are very likely to occur as skiers or hikers go by, or even spontaneously.

5 – **Extremely likely**: snow cover is very unstable following a heavy snow fall and major avalanches will occur even on gentle slopes.

Avalanches – Whether they happen naturally or are started by passing skiers, they represent a permanent danger which must not be dismissed lightly. **Bulletins Neige et Avalanche** (BNA), posted in every resort and hiking base, warn of the risks that must be taken into consideration by anyone planning an excursion. A new more precise scale of potential risks has been devised for the benefit of those who practise off-piste skiing, cross-country skiing or snowshoeing.

This is only a general guideline which needs to be supplemented with more precise information concerning the planned itinerary. In addition, it is recommended to be fairly flexible and evaluate the risks incurred in each case.

Warning signs and flags for the benefit of skiers

 1 – NO We do not need any help.

 *3 – Risk of avalanche in all areas.*

 2 – YES We are calling for help.

 4 – Risk of avalanche in certain areas.

Lightning – Violent gusts of wind are the warning signs of an imminent thunder storm which brings with it the danger of being struck by lightning. Avoid walking along ridges, taking shelter beneath overhanging rocks or isolated trees, at the entrance of caves or hollows in the rock and near metallic fences. Do not carry large metallic objects such as an ice-axe and crampons. Do not huddle under a metallic-framed shelter. Stand more than 15metres/yards from any high point (rock or tree) and adopt a crouching position, keeping your hands and any bare parts of your body away from the surface of the rock. Before lightning strikes, the atmosphere often becomes electrified and a sound like that made by a swarm of bees can be heard. Finally, remember that a car provides a safe shelter during a storm as it makes an excellent Faraday cage.

Assistance – Contact the **gendarmerie** who will get their own rescue service to deal with the problem or will call on the local rescue teams.

Who pays for it? – The cost can be very high according to the means used during the rescue (helicopter...) and the person rescued or his family are normally expected to pay. It is therefore advisable to take out insurance so as to cover such risks.

Warning signs in nature parks

Mountain environments are fragile particularly when they have to cope with thousands of visitors. Their safeguard therefore depends on people abiding by a few regulations which are listed below.

 – **No dogs** (except on marked footpaths). Dogs bark and run after animals who often panick and harm themselves. Introducing a dog in the central zone of a national park can cost its owner a fine of 600F.

– **No camping**. Tents crush plants and grass which, eventually, stop growing altogether. However a bivouac for one night, more than one hour's walk from the entrance of a national park is tolerated.

 – **No dumping**. Rubbish must be removed; think of taking a bag for this purpose.

– **Do not pick** flowers or other plants, do not collect insects or minerals. They form part of the scenery.

 – **No fires**. The damage they cause can be catastrophic (gas rings are allowed).

– **Do not wander off footpaths** in order to preserve flowers and meadows and prevent unnecessary erosion. Shortcuts harm the vegetation and accelerate the erosion process.

SKIING

The Alpine Mountains are the ideal area for the practice of winter sports. New ways of getting across snowfields have been experimented and existing techniques perfected in this privileged environment.

Downhill skiing

This is the most popular form of skiing, available in all the Alpine resorts. The French champion, Émile Allais devised its present form in 1931.

Cross-country or Nordic skiing

This type of skiing is ideal on fairly level terrain; skis are long and narrow, boots are low and fixed at the point only. Since 1968, cross-country skiing forms part of the Olympic events. There are marked tracks of various lengths in most resorts.

In addition, most resorts provide specially marked areas for cross-country skiers in the lower part of ski slopes. This form of skiing can be practised at any age, each skier going at his own pace. The Vercors region is particularly suitable for cross-country skiing, with special markings, mountain refuges and shelters. Information is available from the Parc naturel régional du Vercors.

Some resorts offer the possibility of trying **skijörring** which consists in being pulled by sledge dogs while cross-country skiing.

Ski touring

This form of skiing is suitable for experienced skiers with lots of stamina as it combines the technique of cross-country skiing for uphill sections and that of off-piste skiing for downhill sections. It is recommended to be accompanied by a qualified guide and special equipment is necessary: skis fitted with seal skins for climbing. There are several famous itineraries across the Alps: the **Grande Traversée des Alpes** (GTA) which follows footpath GR 5 from Lake Geneva to the Mediterranean, the **Chamonix-Zermatt**, the **Dômes de la Vanoise**, the **Haut-Beaufortain** and other itineraries in the Haute-Provence region. For more information, contact CIMES GTA, 14 rue de la République, 38000 Grenoble ☎ 04 76 42 45 90 or Minitel **3615 CIMES.**

Off-piste skiing

It is intended for very experienced skiers who ski outside marked runs at their own risk. The presence and advice of a guide or instructor with a comprehensive knowledge of dangerous areas is highly recommended. In some resorts, there are off-piste areas which are unmarked but patrolled.

Off-piste deep powder experience

Monoskiing

This requires a great sense of balance as both feet are on the same ski. It is essentially practised off-piste.

Snowboarding

This increasingly popular sport, now an Olympic event in its own right, is practised without sticks on steep slopes, with snowboarders usually enjoying going over snow mounds.

Mogul skiing

This acrobatic form of skiing has also become an Olympic event; it consists of skiing down very bumpy runs and a good way of getting used to off-piste skiing.

Special training courses are organised in all the resorts to introduce amateurs to these various forms of "skiing".

Sledge racing and touring

Since this type of racing was first organised in France in 1979, its popularity has grown. Four different breeds of dogs are used: huskies from Siberia (the fastest), malamutes from Alaska (the strongest), Eskimo dogs from Greenland and samoyeds with their characteristic white coat. These breeds are better suited either for touring or racing and are trained accordingly.

The **musher** (driver) usually stands at the back of the sledge but he can also be on cross-country skis and let himself be pulled by the team: this is called skijörring. It is possible to get training along short distances in many resorts.

Dog sledging

The skiers' ten commandments

1 – Respect: do not endanger others.

2 – Control: adapt your speed and your skiing to snow conditions and the amount of traffic.

3 – Choice of route: a skier is responsible for the safety of other skiers below him.

4 – Overtaking: it can take place in any direction, but always leave plenty of space

5 – Entering a marked run and starting: make sure there is no danger for you and others.

6 – Stopping: do not stop along narrow sections with reduced visibility; if you fall, clear the way as soon as possible.

7 – Walking along pistes: keep to the side of the run when walking up or down.

8 – Signs and markings: obey signs and markings posted at the starting point of ski-lifts.

9 – Assistance: if you witness an accident, contact the rescue service.

10 – All those involved in an accident should make themselves known to the rescue personnel.

WINTER SPORTS RESORTS

See map pages 10-13 and the table of resorts overleaf. All the resorts mentioned offer accommodation listed in the Michelin Red Guide France.

The Alps boast a great variety of resorts. Beside internationally famous resorts such as Tignes, Val d'Isère, Courchevel, Chamonix, there are a great number of more modest ones which have retained their village character and attract a family clientele. Skiing resorts have changed over the past decades as skiing itself developed. The first ones evolved from existing traditional villages or small towns, such as Morzine or Megève; the second generation of resorts, Val d'Isère, L'Alpe-d'Huez, Les Deux-Alpes, moved to high pastures in search of good skiing slopes. The post-war period saw the blossoming of planned resorts like Courchevel, Chamrousse, Tignes and the latest resorts, Les Arcs, Avoriaz, Les Ménuires, Val-Thorens and Flaine, all of which were designed by a single property developer.

Ski-lifts reach higher and higher, extending the resorts' skiing areas which are often linked. In some cases (L'Alpe-d'Huez, Val d'Isère, Tignes, Les Deux-Alpes, Val-Thorens), they reach so high that the snow cover holds throughout the summer making all year skiing possible.

RESORTS	Lowest resort altitude	Highest resort altitude	Linked to	Mountain airport	Cable-cars and gondolas	Chair-lifts and draglifts	Km of runs	Km of marked pistes	Ice rink	Heated swimming pool
L'Alpe-d'Huez	1 500	3 350	OI	●	14	72	220	50	✓	✓
Arèches-Beaufort	1 050	2 150				12	22	42		
Les Arcs	1 200	3 226	HT		4	77	150	15	✓	✓
Argentière	1 252	3 275	SK		5	14	187	18		
Auris-en-Oisans	1 600	3 350	OI			15	45	40		
Auron	1 600	2 450			3	25	60	4	✓	✓
Aussois	1 500	2 750	HM			11	45	15		
Àutrans	1 050	1 710				15	30	160		✓
Avoriaz	1 100	2 466	PS		2	28	150	40		
Bernex	1 000	1 900				15	50	35		✓
Bessans	1 750	2 220	HM			4	5	80		
Beuil-les-Launes	1 600	2 000	VB			10	90	25		
Bonneval-sur-Arc	1 800	3 000	HM			10	21			
Les Carroz-d'Arâches	1 140	2 480			8	71	250	78		
Ceillac-en-Queyras	1 650	2 480				8	20	60		
Chamonix	1 035	3 795	SK		12	34	150	40	✓	✓
Chamrousse	1 400	2 253			1	25	70	55		✓
La Chapelle-d'Abondance	1 020	2 000	PS		1	11	45	35		
Châtel-Super Châtel	1 200	2 100	PS		2	48	65	30		
La Clusaz	1 100	2 600		●	5	51	120	60	✓	
Combloux	1 000	1 853	SK		1	24	50	15		
Les Contamines-Montjoie	1 164	2 500	SK		3	22	100	25	✓	
Le Corbier	1 450	2 450				24	24	25		
Cordon	850	1 600	SK			6	11	12		
Courchevel	1 300	2 707	TV	●	10	56	180	50	✓	✓
Crest-Voland	1 230	2 000	EC			33	48	80		
Les Deux-Alpes	1 300	3 560	OI		8	56	196	20	✓	✓
Flaine	1 600	2 500		●	2	29	150	14	✓	✓
Flumet	1 000	2 030				13	60	25		
La Foux-d'Allos	1 800	2 600			4	49	170	4	✓	
Le Gets	1 172	2 002	PS		5	51	130	50		
Le Grand-Bornand	1 000	2 100			2	38	20	65		
La Grave-Villar-d'Arène	1 450	3 550			2	8	36	30		
Les Houches	1 008	1 960	SK		2	15	50	35		
Isola 2000	2 000	2 610			1	25	120	12	✓	✓
Les Karellis	1 600	2 500				17	45	30		
Lans-en-Vercors	1 400	1 807				16	24	90		
Megève	1 113	2 350	SK	●	9	74	150	60	✓	✓
Les Ménuires	1 400	2 850	TV		6	44	120	26		✓
Méribel-les-Allues	1 400	2 910	TV	●	16	34	120	25	✓	✓
Montgenèvre	1 860	2 680	VL		2	23	60	28	✓	✓
Morzine	1 000	2 460	PS		14	60	65	70	✓	
La Norma	1 350	2 750	HM			16	65	6	✓	
Notre-Dame-de-Bellecombe	1 150	2 030				17	70	8	✓	
Orcières-Merlette	1 850	2 650			2	28	80	97	✓	
Les Orres	1 550	2 770				23	62	40	✓	✓
Peisey-Nancroix	1 600	2 400	HT		1	15	62	40		
Pelvoux	1 250	2 300				6	15	20		
La Plagne	1 250	2 250	HT		9	103	210	96	✓	✓
Pralognan	1 410	2 360			1	13	35	25		
Pra-Loup	1 600	2 500			3	30	110	8	✓	
Puy-sur-Arly	1 036	1 900				14	50	20		
Puy-St-Vincent	1 400	2 700			1	14	40	35		

Risoul 1850	1 850	2 750	FB		1	20	650	70	⛷
La Rosière	1 850	2 400			1	34	135	20	
St-Étienne-les-Orgues/ Montagne de Lure	1 600	1 700				6	10	5	
St-François-Longchamp	1 415	2 550				17	65		◹
St-Gervais-les-Bains	850	2 350	SK		3	70	220	30	⛷
St-Jean-Monclar/Le Lauzet	1 300	2 500				19	50	30	⛷
St-Jeoire-les-Brasses	900	1 500				17	52	40	◹
St-Pierre-de-Chartreuse	900	1 800			2	13	17	55	
St-Sorlin-d'Arves	1 550	2 600				17	95	20	
St-Véran/Molines	1 850	2 800				15	40	35	
Ste-Anne-La-Condamine	1 830	2 420				6	15		
Les Saisies	1 600	1 950	EC			36	70	100	
Samoëns	800	2 480			4	42	150	70	
Le Sappey-en-Chartreuse	1 000	1 700				11	15	40	
Le Sauze/Super-Sauze	1 400	2 450				24	65	10	⛷ ◹
Serre-Chevalier (complex)	1 200	2 800			9	67	20	45	3 ◹
Superdévoluy/ La Joue-du-Loup	1 455	2 510				33	105	44	
La Tania	1 350	2 280	TV		1	3	180	65	
Termignon	1 300	2 500	HM			2	30	40	
Thollon	1 000	2 000			1	16	55	25	
Tignes	1 550	3 460	EK		9	44	150	19	⛷
La Toussuire	1 800	2 400				18	40	17	
Val d'Allos	1 400	2 425			1	11	22	15	
Valberg	1 400	2 025				27	90	50	
Val Cenis	1 400	2 800	HM		1	22	80	40	
Val Fréjus	1 550	2 550			2	11	52	40	
Val d'Isère	1 850	3 260	EK		16	88	300	18	⛷ ◹
Valloire	1 430	2 550		•	1	32	150	30	⛷ ◹
Valmorel	1 400	2 400			2	28	105	25	
Val-Thorens	2 300	3 200	TV		4	30	120		⛷ ◹
Vars	1 650	2 750			2	51	95	30	⛷ ◹
Villards-de-Lans	1 050	2 170			2	35	120	120	⛷

Key to linked resorts

BE = Beuil	EC = Espace Cristal
EK= Espace Killy	FB = Forêt Blanche
HM = Haute-Maurienne	HT = Haute-Tarnetaise
OI= Oisans - Les Grandes Rousses	PS = Porte du Soleil
SK = Ski-pass Mont-Blanc	TV = Trois-Vallées
VB = Valberg	VL = Voie Lactée (linked with Italy)

Insurance and ski passes

The Carte Neige issued by the Fédération française de ski provides the holder with a comprehensive insurance and assistance on Alpine and cross-country ski runs. It is possible to acquire it by joining a club affiliated to the FFS. For more information, contact the headquarters of the Fédération française de ski, 50 avenue des Marquisats, 74000 Annecy, ☎ 04 50 51 40 34 or Minitel **3615 CARTE NEIGE**. This service also gives the timetable of cross-country skiing races and lists special passes available in some resorts. Wherever skiing areas are too vast, passes covering part of the area are available; this is particularly convenient for beginners.

Ski passes giving access to vast skiing areas *(see table below)* enable holders to use several skiing areas often linked by gondola.

Summer skiing resorts

Five resorts offer summer skiing as well as more traditional summer activities:
– **L'Alpe-d'Huez** – July to mid August on the Sarennes Glacier (3 000m/9 842ft).
– **Les Deux-Alpes** – mid June to early September on the Mont-de-Lans Glacier (3 420m/11 220ft).
– **La Plagne** – July to August on the Bellecôte Glacier (3 416m/11 207ft).
– **Tignes** – July to August on the Grande Motte Glacier (3 430m/11 253ft).
– **Val-Thorens** – July to August on the Péclet Glacier (3 400m/11 155ft).

ON THE MOUNTAIN

Hiking

Hiking is the best way to explore mountain areas and discover the finest scenery. Footpaths are extensively described in this guide and three types of hikes are identified. **Rambles** are, in principle, suitable for anyone, including children. **Day hikes** require more stamina and some prior training for a walking time exceeding 4hr and a difference in height of 700m/2 297ft. A few more demanding **itineraries for experienced hikers** are also described (including extremely steep or vertiginous sections which do not however require any specialised mountaineering knowledge) where panoramas are exceptional. Before leaving, it is highly recommended to get the latest weather forecast and make sure that the length of the hike is compatible with the time of departure. In mountain areas, the estimated length of an excursion is calculated according to the difference in height: 300m/984ft per hour going up and 500m/1 640ft going down, excluding stops.

Leave early in the morning if you can so that all the climbing can be done during the cool hours of the day and you stand a better chance of observing the fauna.

Whatever the type of hike, you should carry with you a map on a scale of 1:25 000 or 1:50 000, 1 or 2 litres of water per person, energy-building food, waterproof clothing, a pullover, sunglasses, a sun cream and a first-aid kit. You should also wear mountain boots and carry a pair of binoculars to spot distant peaks and observe the fauna (avoid wearing brightly coloured clothes, moving too abruptly and being too noisy for fear of frightening the animals away).

Mountain-refuge bookings – Refuges are now equipped with radio-telephones (numbers available at tourist offices) and booking is now compulsory during the summer season. Hikers arriving without a booking should not therefore count on finding a bed for the night.

Long-distance footpaths (GR) – Many footpaths marked in red and white run through the Alps. Topo-guides give detailed itineraries, accommodation information (refuges and lodges), and useful advice (also Minitel **3615 RANDO**).

GR 5 goes across the Alps from Lake Geneva to Nice, following the high Alps and crossing other footpaths on its way.

The **TMB** (Tour du Mont Blanc) goes round the massif, entering Switzerland and Italy. Allow eight days.

GR 55 runs through the Parc national de la Vanoise.

GR 54 goes round the Parc national des Écrins and the Oisans region.

GR 58 enables hikers to explore the Queyras region (numerous refuges and lodges).

GR 56 goes through the Ubaye region.

Other footpaths run through the Préalpes.

GR 96 goes through the Chablais, the Aravis and the Bauges massifs.

GR 9, 91, 93 and 95 criss-cross the Vercors.

GR 93 continues across the Dévoluy and GR 94 runs through the Buëch, Bochaine and Baronnies regions.

GR 6 "Alpes-Océan" links the Ubaye and Forcalquier Regions via Sisteron.

GR 4 "Méditerranée-Océan" goes right through Haute-Provence via Entrevaux, Castellane and Moustiers-Ste-Marie.

In addition, there are numerous local footpaths offering interesting hikes or linking main itineraries.

Useful addresses – Topo-guides are published by the Fédération française de la randonnée pédestre, Comité national des sentiers de Grande Randonnée, 64 rue de Gergovie, 75014 Paris, ☎ 01 45 45 31 02.

A very comprehensive hiking guide is published by the Comité régional de tourisme Rhône-Alpes, 104 route de Paris, 69260 Charbonnières-les-Bains, ☎ 04 72 59 21 59.

In the Alps, contact CIMES, 14 rue de la République, 38000 Grenoble, ☎ 04 76 42 45 90; Association randonnée en Savoie, 4 rue du Château, 73000 Chambéry, ☎ 04 79 75 02 01; ADRI, 19 rue du Docteur-Honnorat, 04000 Digne-les-Bains, ☎ 04 92 31 07 01 (Haute-Provence region); Comité départemental de randonnée pédestre des Hautes-Alpes, 7 rue du Four-Neuf, 05000 Gap, ☎ 04 92 53 65 11.

Mountaineering

The Alps are one of the major mountaineering regions of the world.

Climbing fever – Until the 18C, mineral and crystal seekers, botanists, hunters and smugglers were the only ones to venture up the high peaks without, however, attempting to reach the fearsome summits. In 1741, two Englishmen, Windham and Pococke explored the Chamonix Valley, drawing attention to Mont Blanc *(see Massif du MONT-BLANC)*. The golden age of mountaineering began in the mid 19C with Whymper, Mummery and Coolidge and some local guides including Gaspard (father and son), not forgetting some ladies like Miss Straton who climbed to the top of Mont Blanc during the winter of 1877.

In the early 20C, mountaineers attempted more and more "winter" ascents by routes thought to be inaccessible.

Techniques and equipment have greatly improved over the past decades and moutaineering has become a popular sport practised nowadays by an increasing number of enthusiasts who look for ever greater difficulties, essentially in the Mont-Blanc, Écrins and Vanoise massifs, using nearby resorts as their base: Chamonix, St-Gervais-les-Bains, Pralognan-la-Vanoise, Bourg-d'Oisans (La Bérarde) and La Grave are the main starting points of mountaineering expeditions.

Guides usually belong to a *"compagnie"*, the most famous being that of Chamonix founded in 1823.

Useful addresses – Club alpin français, 24 rue de Laumière, 75019 Paris; for information, telephone ☎ 01 53 72 87 13.

Fédération française de la montagne et de l'escalade, 10 quai de la Marne, 75019 Paris, ☎ 01 40 18 75 50.

Rock-climbing – Rock-climbing schools offer beginners the possibility to learn basic techniques with qualified instructors (half-day, day or progressive courses). Information is available at tourist offices and guides offices. The main rock-climbing areas are listed below.

– Maurienne region – **Aussois,** where several international competitions have been held, has some ten sites for all levels; apply to the guides office.

– Vercors – The **Presles** Cliffs offer a variety of itineraries; information available at the guides office in Pont-en-Royans, ☎ 04 76 36 10 92.

– Briançonnais – Some ten sites for all levels; apply to the guides office in Briançon and l'Argentière-la-Bessée. For special beginners' courses apply to the guides office, 05240 La Salle-les-Alpes, ☎ 04 92 24 75 90.

– Vallouise region – Courses of varying difficulty (some suitable for children); apply to the Guides office in Vallouise and Ailefroide, ☎ 04 92 23 32 02.

– Les Baronnies – Information and a list of guides is available at the Tourist office in Orpierre.

– Alpes-de-Haute-Provence – This area has a choice of sites suitable for beginners accompanied by instructors. **Annot**: contact Association "Vive les gestes", ☎ 04 92 83 35 17; **Chabrières**: contact the Club alpin in Digne, centre Desmichel, ☎ 04 92 32 32 98; Méolans: contact the Club alpin in Barcelonnette, ☎ 04 92 81 28 23; Quinson: contact Association "Roc et falaise" at the town hall.

– Gorges du Verdon – La Palud-sur-Verdon: contact the regional rock-climbing centre at the town hall or at the Tourist office in season; Castellane: contact Verdon-Accueil, ☎ 04 92 83 67 36.

Via ferrata – *Via ferrata* climbing, which is a cross between mountaineering and hiking has become increasingly popular in the past few years.

These rock-climbing courses fitted with metal rungs and cables originated in the Dolomites during the First World War, at the initiative of the Italian army and only discovered by the public in the 1950s. The first *via ferrata* courses were set up in the Briançonnais region at the beginning of the 1980s. A few well-equipped courses are mentioned in this guide. Basic equipment includes a harness, a helmet and two ropes (preferably with a fall absorber) to secure oneself to the cable which runs the whole length of the course. It is imperative that inexperienced climbers should be accompanied by a guide or join a group. Below are some useful contacts:

– **Presles**: 200m/656ft-high cliff; contact the guides office in Pont-en-Royans, ☎ 04 76 36 10 92.

– **St-Christophe-en-Oisans**: easy course; contact the guides office in La Bérarde.

– **St-Jean-de-Maurienne** (Mont Vernier and Croix des Têtes): contact the Guides office in St-Jean-de-Maurienne, 76 rue Joseph-Perret, ☎ 04 79 59 90 80.

– **Aussois**: Via ferrata du Diable; contact the guides office, ☎ 04 79 20 32 48.

– **Valloire**: Via ferrata de Poingt-Ravier (1 644m/5 394ft) and Via ferrata du Rocher St-Pierre; contact the guides office in Valloire, ☎ 04 79 83 35 03.
– **Val d'Isère**: Via ferrata des Plates de la Daille (excellent equipment).
– **Chamonix**: the Balcon de la Mer de Glace course is one of the most thrilling but is only suitable for experienced climbers.
There are other *via ferrata* courses in Courchevel and La Norma.
– **Briançon**: the Croix de Toulouse *via ferrata* offers superb views of the old town and the surrounding fortifications; contact the guides office, ☎ 04 92 20 15 73.
– **L'Argentière-la-Bessée**: the *via ferrata* at **Les Vigneaux** is the most popular in the area; it is moderately difficult and offers impressive bird's-eye views; contact "Azimut" guides ☎ 04 92 23 04 51.
– **Freissinières**, near L'Argentière-la-Bessée, is the oldest *via ferrata* in France; moderately difficult.
– **L'Aiguillette du Lauzet** in the Guisane Valley offers views of the Écrins Massif; contact the guides office in Serre-Chevalier, ☎ 04 92 24 75 90.
– **St-Ours**: Via ferrata de l'Aiguille de Luce; a leaflet is available at the Tourist office in Barcelonnette; contact the guides office of the Ubaye region, place des Sept-Portes, Barcelonnette, ☎ 04 92 81 04 71.

Ruisseling – This winter sport could be described as ice-climbing since those who practise it use rock-climbing techniques and equipment to climb up frozen waterfalls and mountain streams. Contact the guides office in Aussois and Val Cenis.

Cycling and mountain biking

The Route des cols (Galibier, Croix de Fer, Iseran Lautaret, Izoard etc) was made famous by the Tour de France and in summer many cycle and mountain bike races take place throughout the region, in particular in the area around Vars: "Six jours de Vars", French mountain bike championship...
IGN maps with cycling itineraries are available and many lodges *(gîtes d'étape)* offer budget accommodation. Tourist offices have lists of establishments providing a rental service.
Mountain biking is extremely popular as it can be practised almost anywhere, in particular along forest roads, mule tracks, cross-country skiing tracks and even downhill runs (in Montgenèvre and the Queyras Massif for instance). Some areas offer a choice of marked itineraries (Aussois, Bourg-St-Maurice, Parc naturel régional du Vercors). Mountain biking itineraries are available locally from the Maisons (information centres) du Parc régional du Vercors, from ADRI, 19 rue du Docteur-Honnorat, 04000 Digne-les-Bains, ☎ 04 92 31 07 01, and from the regional centres of the **Fédération française de cyclisme**, 5 rue de Rome, 93561 Rosny-sous-Bois cedex, ☎ 01 49 35 69 45.

WHITE-WATER SPORTS

White-water sports are increasingly popular, particularly in the Alps which offer a dense network of rivers and streams, pleasant summer temperatures and many outdoor leisure parks where it is possible to discover and practise these activities for which special equipment is available.
In every area, the Comité départemental de tourisme *(see Tourist information)* has a list of the various organisations providing group activities. Below is a selection.
Haute-Savoie – In Thonon, Les Dranses, AN Rafting, ☎ 04 50 71 89 15; in Samoëns, Haut Giffre Rafting, ☎ 04 50 34 45 26; in Passy, Eldorado Rafting, ☎ 04 50 78 18 76.
Isère – Vénéon Eaux Vives, 38250 St-Christophe-en-Oisans, ☎ 04 76 80 23 99; Oisans Eaux Vives, Bois de Gauthier, 38520 Bourg-d'Oisans, ☎ 04 76 80 02 83.
Savoie – In Bourg-St-Maurice, international white-water sports centre, ☎ 04 79 07 33 20; in Mâcot-la-Plagne, AN Rafting, ☎ 04 79 09 72 79.
Hautes-Alpes – In Briançon, H²O Loisirs, Central Parc, ☎ 04 92 20 38 98; in Château-Queyras, AN Rafting, ☎ 04 92 46 80 05; in Les Vigneaux, Base de loisirs d'eau vive ☎ 04 92 23 11 94.
Alpes-de-Haute-Provence – In Le Martinet, Base de loisirs d'eau vive, AN Rafting, ☎ 04 92 85 54 40; in Méolans, Base de Rioclar, ☎ 04 92 81 90 26; in Entrevaux, Base Sport et Nature, ☎ 04 93 05 42 45.
For general information, contact: Association Alpes-de-Haute-Provence Eau Vive, Hôtel du département, 13 rue DR Romieu, BP 216, 04003 Digne-les-Bains, ☎ 04 92 32 25 32.

Rafting

This is the easiest of all the white-water sports. It consists in going down impetuous rivers in groups of six to eight persons, aboard inflatable rubber rafts manoeuvred with paddles and controlled from the rear by an instructor/cox. The technique is simple and team spirit is the key to success. Isothermal and shockproof equipment is provided by the club organising the trip. The level of difficulty is graded from I to VI (easy to virtually impossible). Beginners and amateurs who have not acquired a solid technique are advised not to attempt any difficulty rated above III. Remember to book in advance.

White-water rafting on the Haute-Isère

The Alps are the ideal area for the practice of rafting, preferably during the thaw (April to June) and in summer along rivers which maintain a constant flow. Among the rivers particularly suitable for rafting are the upper Isère (between Bourg-St-Maurice and Centron, grade III), the Doron de Bozel in the Vanoise region (between Brides-les-Bains and Moûtiers, grades IV and V), the Giffre, the Dranses de Savoie and the Rabioux, a tributary of the Durance.

Canoeing and kayaking

Canoes (of Canadian origin) are manoeuvred with a simple paddle. They are ideal for family trips along rivers.

In kayaks (of Eskimo origin) on the other hand, paddlers use a double-bladed paddle. There are canoeing-kayaking schools in white-water sports centres throughout the Alps and touring takes place on the lakes and the lower course of most rivers: the Giffre, Chéran, Arly, Doron de Bozel, Guiers Vif and Guiers Mort, Isère, Ubaye, Verdon, Clarée, Guisane, Gyronde, Biaisse, Durance, Guil, Buëch, Méouge, Drac, Souloise and Severaisse.

The Fédération française de canoë-kayak, 87 quai de la Marne, 94344 Joinville-le-Pont cedex, ☎ 01 45 11 08 50 (also on Minitel **3615 CANOPLUS**), publishes an annual guide called *Vacances en canoë-kayak* as well as maps of suitable rivers.

Hydrospeed

Those who wish to practise swimming down mountain streams must first know how to swim with flippers and be in top physical condition. Swimmers wear a wet suit and a helmet and rest over a very tough streamlined float, the hydrospeed.

First rafting experience

On their arrival at the club, beginners have to testify that they can swim before being given a wet suit; they are then introduced to the **barreur** (instructor/cox) who briefs them. The six **rafteurs** (clients) then get hold of the dinghy by the **ligne de vie** (rope fitted round the raft) and carry it to the water. Once the foot-clips are secure, the **olive** (handle) of the paddle firmly in hand and the rhythm set, the instructor starts giving his orders. He must remain extremely vigilant in order to negotiate the rapids and overcome any difficulty, otherwise his crew may experience a **crêpe** (the raft turns over) or even a **cravate** (the raft wraps itself round a rock)! As the raft gets close to a **contre-courant** (a sheltered creek), the instructor tells the **jumper** (person sitting in front) to jump into the water, get hold of the **boute** (front rope) and pull the raft out of the water. During the welcome break which follows, the instructor comments on the way the crew has handled the raft until then and offers suggestions. Depending on the level of the current and on that of the participants, the instructor may treat his crew to a spectacular **pop-corn** (the instructor alone remains on board, the others being ejected) which is usually the climax of a first rafting experience.

Canyoning

A good knowledge of potholing, diving and rock-climbing techniques is necessary to rope down or jump down tumultuous mountain streams and to follow their course through narrow gorges (*clues*) and down steep waterfalls. The magic appeal of this sport lies in the variety of the terrain, in the sunlight playing on the foaming water, or in the contrast between the dense vegetation and the bare rocks heated by the sun. Summer is the best period to practise canyoning: the water temperature is bearable and the flow of the streams is moderate. However, the weather forecast plays a crucial role when it comes to deciding whether to go canyoning or not for, a storm upriver can make it dangerous to go through a gorge and cause bowls to fill up with alluvial sediments. In any case, it is preferable to leave early in the morning (storms often occur during the afternoon) to allow oneself time to solve unforeseen minor problems. There are two basic techniques: **tobogganing** which consists in sliding over smooth rocks on one's back with folded arms and **jumping** from an average height of 8 to 10m/26 to 33ft into a bowl (it is imperative to sound the depth of the bowl before jumping). A beginners' course does not exceed 2km/1.2mi and is supervised by instructors. Later on it is essential to go canyoning with a qualified instructor, who can evaluate the state of a stream and has a good knowledge of local weather conditions, and to respect the environment.

The main canyoning areas are the Vallée d'Abondance in Haute-Savoie, La Norma and Val Fréjus ("Indiana Jones" course) in the Haute-Maurienne, the Canyon des Écouges and Gorges du Furon in the Vercors, the Ubaye Valley between Les Thuiles and Le Lauzet, in particular the Ravin de Sauze, the upper Var and Cians valleys, and, of course, the Verdon (Ravin du Four near Beauvezer).

Useful terms

These will help you to understand the information on panels posted near canyoning itineraries:

- **Bassin**: basin filled with water, deep enough to swim in; if no distance is indicated, it is inferior to 10m/6.2mi.
- **Chenal**: area where the water flows along a large "gutter" requiring a special technique to tackle it; a small gutter is called a **goulotte**.
- **Durée parcours amont** (or **aval**): the estimated time to complete the course upstream (or downstream) allows time to gain access + time to go through the canyon (upstream or downstream of the panels) + time to return on foot to the starting point.
- **Escalier de géant**: a succession of rocky ledges forming a flight of steps several metres high.
- **Échappatoire**: exit making it possible to shorten the course.
- **Longueur de nage**: indicates the total distance that has to be swum.
- **Marmite**: hollow filled with water in which it is possible to jump (after checking the depth).
- **Vasque**: shallow bowl.

CAVING AND POTHOLING

This activity requires thorough training if participants wish to explore caves left in their natural state. However, several sites are accessible to amateurs on the condition that they are accompanied by instructors from potholing clubs.

The necessary equipment is sophisticated: reinforced suit, rock-climbing equipment (fines ropes for roping down), inflatable dinghy, helmet, waterproof bag, carbide and halogen lamps. The main risk comes from sudden spates which are difficult to forecast as they can be caused by storms occurring miles away. Particular care should be taken in the Vercors Massif where it is essential to be accompanied by a qualified guide with a perfect knowledge of the waterways network.

Fédération française de spéléologie, 130 rue St-Maur, 75011 Paris, ☎ 01 43 57 56 54.

Vercors Massif — This is one of the best areas for potholing: there are more than 1 500 caves or entrances marking the beginning of itineraries, often situated along hiking itineraries. It is therefore essential to remain cautious particularly when attempting an unplanned exploration.

The following sites offer the opportunity to spend a day discovering underground exploration: the Goule Blanche and Goule Noire, the Grotte de Bournillon, the Scialet de Malaterre (near Villard-de-Lans), the Trou qui souffle (dry cave) near Méaudre, the Grotte de la Cheminée and the Scialets d'Herbouvilly.

The **Grotte du Gournier** (above the Grotte de Choranche), is particularly interesting for beginners who practise various techniques under supervision while progressing horizontally through a fossil cave. Only experienced potholers may venture beyond the fossil gallery. The whole network covers a distance of 18km/11.2mi.

To discover potholing in the Vercors Massif, contact the Maison de l'aventure, 26420 La Chapelle-en-Vercors, ☎ 04 75 48 22 38 and Dimension 4, 38000 Villard-de-Lans, ☎ 04 76 95 00 81.

Savoie – There are more than 2 000 caves listed in the area; the temperature inside these caves remains constant throughout the year, around 4°C/39°F. The highest chasms are situated in the Vanoise Massif, at Pralognan and Tignes (3 000m/9 842m) whereas the Gouffre Jean-Bernard in Haute-Savoie holds the depth record (– 1 600m/5 249ft).

The most extensive Alpine chasm (58km/36mi) is situated under the Alpette, in the **Chartreuse Massif.**

RIDING

There are many riding centres throughout the Alps and numerous touring itineraries of varying length (one day or several days). In every *département*, there are special itineraries with orange markings. In addition, tours for beginners and experienced riders are organised by the *associations régionales de tourisme équestre* (ARTE).
In Savoie: Equisabaudia, M Cominazzi, 73200 Mercury, ☎ 04 79 32 40 05.
In Isère: Isère Cheval Vert, Maison du Tourisme, 14 rue de la République, 38000 Grenoble, ☎ 04 76 42 85 88.
For experienced riders wishing to organise their own tours, there are *relais d'étapes équestres* (riding lodges) looked after by the FRETE (Fédération des relais d'étapes de tourisme équestre), same address as the Fédération de tourisme équestre *(see below)*.

Useful addresses

The Fédération de tourisme équestre, 170 quai de Stalingrad, 92130 Issy-les-Moulineaux, ☎ 01 40 93 01 77, publishes a yearly brochure called *Tourisme et loisirs équestres en France.*
Délégation nationale au tourisme équestre (DNTE), 30 avenue d'Iéna, 75116 Paris, ☎ 01 53 67 44 44 (free call within France: 08 00 02 59 10).
A list of riding centres and registered guides is available from:
Isère – Association Rhône-Alpes pour le tourisme équestre (ARATE), Maison du tourisme, BP 227, 14 rue de la République, 38019 Grenoble, ☎ 04 76 44 56 18.
Haute-Savoie – Comité départemental de tourisme équestre (CDTE), Mme Jackie Simonotti, 97a avenue de Genève, 74000 Annecy, ☎ 04 50 69 84 08.
Savoie – CDTE, M Paul Michelland, RN 6, 73220 Aiguebelle, ☎ 04 79 36 20 45.
Drôme – CDTE, M Jean-Luc Delhomme, 7 rue Godifrais, 26200 Dieulefit, ☎ 0475 90 63 52.
Hautes-Alpes – CDTE, M Pavie, 05000 Gap, ☎ 04 92 53 16 00.
Alpes-de-Haute-Provence – CDTE, M Barbier, Ferme du Petit St-Martin, 04000 Gaubert, ☎ 04 92 31 27 50; ADRI in Digne-les-Bains *(see "Hiking")*.
Alpes-Maritimes – Association régionale du tourisme équestre en PACA, 19 boulevard Victor-Hugo, 06130 Grasse, ☎ 04 92 42 62 98.
Comité départemental de la randonnée équestre, M Desprey, La Jumenterie, 06460 St-Vallier-de-Thiey.

Hiking with a pack donkey – It is possible to hire a pack donkey for a day or a week. The animal can carry a 40kg/88lb pack and follow hikers at a pace of 4kph/2.5mph, whatever the terrain.
Fédération nationale "Âne et randonnées", Broissieux, 73340 Bellecombe-en-Bauges, ☎ 04 79 63 84 01.
For information about organised tours in the Massif de la Chartreuse, ☎ 04 78 87 73 76, Lachal, 38950 St-Martin-le-Vinoux.
Many farms provide the animals, the equipment and the necessary information for a successful tour; below are some useful addresses.
Thorens-Glières: Compostel'Ane, ☎ 04 50 22 83 96; **Les Carroz:** ☎ 04 50 90 02 74; **St-Sigismond:** ☎ 04 50 34 83 72; **St-Martin** (Vercors): ☎ 04 75 45 53 17; **Tinée Valley:** Itinérance, hameau de Villeplane, 06470 Guillaumes, ☎ 04 93 05 56 01.

ANGLING

Trout is the prize catch in mountain areas; it can be caught with live insects or larvae (in mountain streams with steep banks) or with artificial flies and a rod and reel in wider streams and mountain lakes. It is essential to abide by the national and local regulations and to get a permit. The opening of the fishing season differs according to the type of fish and stream. The most common fish found in Alpine streams and lakes are trout, salmon, char, pike, carp and perch.
Special regulations apply to fishing in some of the large lakes.
Lac du Bourget – White-fish angling along the shore is only allowed near harbours (Aix-les-Bains, St-Innocent) but it is possible to hire a boat and get a special permit to fish for trout and char with a dragnet.
Tarentaise region – Upstream of Albertville, angling for trout is the norm and it is still possible to select a quiet spot along the River Isère. Lower down, barbels and chars can be caught as well.

Lac de Serre-Ponçon – Special regulations apply; contact local angling associations in Savines, Chorges or Embrun.
Lac de Ste-Croix-du-Verdon – Closed to anglers from the beginning of September.

IN THE AIR

The Alps are the ideal region for the practice of various forms of gliding.
Fédération française de vol libre, 4 rue de Suisse, 06000 Nice, ☎ 04 93 88 62 89.
Fédération française de planeur ultra-léger motorisé, 96bis rue Marc-Sangnier, 94700 Maisons-Alfort, ☎ 01 49 81 74 43.

Paragliding – This summer sport, which began in Haute-Savoie in 1978, does not require any special training and has now spread to winter sports resorts where participants are equipped with skis. Many summer resorts with easy access to nearby summits offer various possibilities of practising this popular sport and of joining training courses: Les Saisies, Signal de Bisanne, L'Alpe-d'Huez are among the best but **Chamonix** is still one of the main paragliding centres: particularly favourable conditions enabled a team of paragliders to cover a distance of 160km/99mi. There is restricted access to the slopes of Mont Blanc in July and August (École de parapente de Chamonix, 79 rue Whymper, ☎ 04 50 53 50 14). The **Vercors** is also one of the favourite areas of paragliding enthusiasts. Two remarkable sites are worth mentioning: the Cornafion, near Villard-de-Lans

Paragliding

(500m/1 640ft flights, access forbidden in May and June for the protection of the fauna); and the Moucherotte (landing in Lans-en-Vercors). For all-level courses, contact: Dimension 4 in Villard-de-Lans, ☎ 04 76 95 00 81 and Fun Fly in Lans-en-Vercors.
The Haute-Provence is also an ideal area for practising paragliding. The national centre is located in Saint-Auban-sur-Durance and there are many schools in the area: École de parapente du Queyras, 05350 Château-Ville-Vieille, ☎ 04 92 46 77 51; École de parapente Espace Soleil, 05700 La Queyra, ☎ 04 92 67 06 82.
In order to avoid accidents and disappointments, it is recommended to register with a recognised school. A list is available from the Fédération française de vol libre (*see above*, also on Minitel: **3615 FFVL**). Courses, usually lasting a week, are followed by some 20 flights monitored from the ground by an instructor.
A brochure entitled **Parapente**, is published by the Comité régional de tourisme.

Hang-gliding – This "older" sport requires greater technical knowledge and training.

Ballooning – A few resorts organise balloon flights: Les Saisies, Corrençon and Villard-de-Lans, Sisteron and the Embrun region.

Something different...

Visitors willing to "take their time" have the opportunity to travel in a way that will help them to discover the wealth of a region and its traditional life.

THEMED ITINERARIES

Chemins du Baroque – Some 60 churches and chapels in the Tarentaise and Maurienne regions were selected for their characteristic Baroque style. It is recommended to start in Moûtiers or Lanslebourg. There are guided tours in some places and day tours are organised.

The **Fondation pour l'action culturelle internationale en montagne** (Facim), Hôtel du département, 73018 Chambéry cedex, ☎ 04 79 96 74 19, proposes 19 half-day hikes and drives with commentary as well as 13 tours without commentary.

Two **Espaces baroque** offer information and displays about the various sites:
Espace baroque Maurienne, Lanslebourg, ☎ 04 79 05 90 42.
Espace baroque Tarentaise, Moûtiers, ☎ 04 79 24 33 44.

Route Stendhal – A marked itinerary called **Route historique Stendhal** makes it possible to discover places where the writer spent his childhood and those which inspired him. In Grenoble: the flat where he was born, the Café de la Table Ronde, one of the oldest cafés in France, where he would quite often be seen, the Maison Stendhal (which belonged to his grandfather, Dr Gagnon), the Musée Stendhal and the municipal library where his works are kept. For detailed information, contact the tourist office in Grenoble.

Route des ducs de Savoie – This itinerary includes several prestigious "châteaux" having belonged to the House of Savoie: Ripaille, Thorens-Glières, Menthon, Clermont, Annecy, Chambéry, as well as the Abbaye royale de Hautecombe.
The Caisse nationale des monuments historiques et des sites (CNMHS) publishes a brochure listing the castles and residences with their opening times.

In Vauban's footsteps – The comprehensive defence system designed by Vauban, during Louis XIV's reign is an exceptional ensemble of military architecture and now some of these former strategic sites can be visited: citadels in Mont-Dauphin and Briançon, the castle in Château-Queyras, the citadel in Seyne-les-Alpes and the two forts in Colmars-les-Alpes are the finest examples of Vauban's work.
Later military fortifications can also be visited: 18C works are centred round Briançon whereas 19C defences are situated further afield. A fort by Maginot, known as Janus, can be visited by appointment. For detailed information, contact the tourist office in Briançon.
The upper Ubaye Valley also boasts several defence works: Fort de Tournoux, Fort de Roche-Lacroix, St-Ours Fortifications... Visits are organised by the tourist office in Barcelonnette.

Route des campaniles – Wrought-iron campaniles form part of the Haute-Provence scenery (see illustration in the Introduction).
There are several possibilities of 100km/62mi-long itineraries in the Digne, Forcalquier and Manosque regions. The most remarkable campaniles are in Les Mées, Lurs, St-Michel-l'Observatoire, Manosque, Allemagne-en-Provence and Estoublon. For detailed information, contact the Comité départemental du Tourisme.

Routes des cadrans solaires – There are detailed itineraries and brochures concerning sundials in three areas of the Hautes-Alpes region.
The **Briançonnais** offers a variety of mostly 18C or contemporary sundials; there are 20 of them in Briançon alone as well as very original ones in the villages of Prelles, Puy-St-Vincent, Les Alberts, Val-des-Prés, Plampinet, La Salle-les-Alpes and Névache.

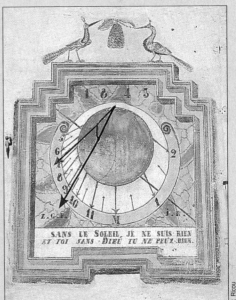

Sundial in Val-des-Prés

The **Vallouise** Valley has a choice of sundials mainly by Zarbula.

In the Queyras, sundials are often decorated with exotic birds; they were designed by Zarbula or other artists influenced by him.

There are also interesting sundials in the **Bochaine**, to the west and in the **Ubaye** Valley to the south; contact the Maison de la Vallée in Barcelonnette.

How to tell the time by looking at a painted sundial

A sundial consists of a panel, usually facing south, and of a metal rod representing the Earth's axis. Its length must not prolong the shadow beyond the panel at the time of the summer solstice and be sufficient for the shadow to be visible at the time of the winter solstice. Reading the time on a sundial is relatively easy but the conversion into legal time is rather involved and requires three adjustments to take into account: the longitude which results in a 20 to 30min difference with Paris; real time (solar time) and average time (24-hour day) corresponding to the variation in the Earth's rotating speed (in summer, it can vary from + 3min to − 6min); and finally, the difference between summer and winter time.

Nature trails – Many excursions on the theme of nature are organised by the UNCPIE, head office, 2 rue de Washington, 75008 Paris, ☎ 01 45 63 63 67.

In the Parc national du Mercantour, hikes are organised every Thursday in summer to enable visitors to observe ibexes, marmots and birds; information from the Maison du parc in Valberg, ☎ 04 92 02 58 23.

The Réserve géologique de Haute-Provence in Digne also organises weekly themed hikes in summer. Information on the spot, ☎ 04 92 31 51 31.

Route des fruits et des vins – This itinerary stretching from the shores of the Serre-Ponçon Lake to Sisteron is dotted with tasting breaks *(dégustation)* in various wine and fruit cooperatives, according to the season: Chorges, Espinasses, Tallard, Plaine de Theüs, Laragne etc. Information from the Comité départemental du tourisme in Gap.

Routes de l'olivier – Olive trees, which are the symbol of Provence, are the main theme of several tours in the Drôme and Bouches-du-Rhône *départements*, which take in the main olive groves and olive-oil producers. There are informative panels about local production. Some local restaurants make a point of including a local produce in their menus. There is an itinerary in the Baronnies region and another one on the Plateau de Valensole.

For more information, contact the Comité économique de l'olivier, 22 rue Henri-Pontier, 13626 Aix-en-Provence cedex 1, ☎ 04 42 23 01 92.

CRUISING IN THE ALPS

Several large lakes situated in shallow valleys, such as the Lac du Bourget, Lac d'Annecy, Lac Léman (Lake Geneva) and Lac d'Aiguebelette offer a wide range of outdoor activities (sailing, water-skiing, diving, wind-surfing etc). The mildness of the climate is underlined by the presence of vineyards and olive groves.

Lake Geneva cruises – There are 41 landing-stages round the lake, along the French and Swiss shores. During the season, from May to September, there are numerous possibilities of boat trips: daily direct link Évian-Lausanne (35min), daily 3hr cruises round the Haut-Lac, complete tour of the lake (10hr); *(see Admission times and charges)*.

In July and August, there is a regular service (20min) between **Yvoire** and **Nyon** in Switzerland several times a day and at night. In June and September, times are different. Information from the Compagnie générale de navigation sur le Lac Léman in Nyon and the tourist office in Yvoire.

Several clubs offer **yachting** facilities: Société nautique du Léman, port de Rives, 74200 Thonon-les-Bains, ☎ 04 50 71 07 29 and Cercle de la voile d'Évian, port des Mouettes, 74500 Évian-les-Bains, ☎ 04 50 75 06 46.

There is a colourful gathering of yachts on the lake in mid-June, called the Bol d'or de Genève.

Lac du Bourget – The largest natural lake in France also offers a variety of water-based activities. Cruises starting from the Grand Port in Aix-les-Bains, from Portout-Chanaz or from Le Bourget-du-Lac include a choice of trips from 1hr tour of the lake to a day trip to the Savière Canal and the River Rhône. Contact the tourist office in Aix-les-Bains and the Compagnie des bateaux du lac du Bourget, Grand Port, 73100 Aix-les-Bains, ☎ 04 79 88 92 09.

The lake is exposed to high winds and sailing conditions, which are similar to those encountered at sea and ideal for the practice of funboards. There are also several sailing clubs in Aix-les-Bains and Le Bourget-du-Lac.

Lac d'Annecy – The superb scenery is the major attraction of the lake. There is a tour of the lake starting from the Thiou pier in Annecy and cruises are organised by the Compagnie des bateaux d'Annecy, 2 place aux Bois, 74000 Annecy, ☎ 04 50 51 08 40.

The best period to sail on the lake is from March to early November. Sailing courses are organised by various clubs including: Base nautique des Marquisats in Annecy, ☎ 04 50 45 48 39; Cercle de la voile in Sévrier, ☎ 04 50 52 40 04.

Sailing takes place on other lakes such as the **Lac d'Aiguebelette**, **Lac du Monteynard** (on the edge of the Parc régional du Vercors) and on the **Lacs de Laffrey**.

TOURIST TRAINS

Circuit touristique du Léman – The Rive-Bleue-Express follows the shores of Lake Geneva from Évian, over a distance of some 20km/12mi, to Le Bouveret in Switzerland. The steam trains run from late June to September some weekdays and every weekend. Information from the tourist office in Évian; tickets can be bought at the railway stations in Évian and Le Bouvet.

From Vallorcine to Émosson – This is an extension to the Émosson Dam of the international railway line from Chamonix to Martigny via Vallorcine. The trip offers beautiful views of the north face of Mont Blanc. From Châtelard-Village, a funicular in three sections climbs to 1 961m/6 434ft in 13min. The first section is the steepest in Europe with a gradient of 87%. There is a daily service from mid-June to mid-September. Return fare: 33SF; it is possible to buy a one-way ticket and come down on foot in 2hr 30min. Information from the tourist office in Chamonix and the railway station in Martigny (Switzerland), ☎ 00 41 26 68 12 36.

Montenvers railway

Chemin de fer de la Mure – The 30km/19mi itinerary of this former mining railway between St-Georges-de-Commiers and La Mure includes an impressive number of engineering works and offers exceptional views of the Gorges du Drac. Today, it is powered by electric engines dating from the 1930s *(see Lacs de LAFFREY)*.

Chemin de fer de la Provence – The famous Train des Pignes links Nice and Digne-les-Bains over a distance of 150km/93mi via Puget-Théniers, Entrevaux, Annot and St-André-les-Alpes.
The line, built between 1890 and 1911, includes some 60 engineering works: metal bridges, viaducts, tunnels... The magnificent landscapes are dotted with hilltop villages. Steam trains run on the section between Puget-Théniers and Annot in season. The line allows access all year round to the Lac de Castillon, the Gorges du Verdon and skiing resorts of the Alpes-Maritimes region.
Information from Gare du Sud, 4 bis rue Alfred-Binet, 06000 Nice, ☎ 04 93 82 10 17; Gare des CP, avenue P.-Semard 04000 Digne-les-Bains, ☎ 04 92 31 01 58.

INDUSTRIAL SITES

These offer an insight into traditional and contemporary techniques.

Caves de la Chartreuse – 10 boulevard Kofler, 38500 Voiron, ☎ 04 76 05 81 77 *(see Massif de la CHARTREUSE).*

Eaux minérales d'Évian – *See ÉVIAN-LES-BAINS.*

Musée Opinel – *See ST-JEAN-DE-MAURIENNE.*

Barrage de Monteynard – 38650 Monestier-en-Clermont, ☎ 04 76 34 06 22.

Hydrelec – 38114 Allemont *(see Route de la CROIX DE FER).*

La Mine-Image – 38770 La Motte d'Aveillans *(see Lacs de LAFFREY).*

Centrale hydroélectrique de La Bâthie (beneath the Roselend Dam) – 73540 La Bâthie, ☎ 04 79 31 06 60.

COURSES

Various courses in the field of sport, culture, art, nature, technical skills and crafts are organised in the main resorts: billiards in Pralognan, martial arts in Valloire, archery in Les Houches, astronomy in Méribel and in the southern Alps (contact Plein Air Nature, 42 boulevard Victor-Hugo, 04000 Digne-les-Bains, ☎ 04 92 31 51 09); bird-watching and fauna observation in Val d'Isère, ☎ 04 79 06 00 03; decorative painting on wood in the Chartreuse region (information from the Comité départemental du tourisme in Grenoble). The above list is not exhaustive.

Ice-driving is becoming increasingly popular; specialised schools, open from mid-December to late March, teach the basic techniques for safe driving on ice. It is sometimes possible to get tuition in one's own car. There are different levels. Below is a list of resorts where there are ice-driving schools:
L'Alpe-d'Huez, Chamrousse, Flaine, Val d'Isère, Serre-Chevalier, Isola 2000, Val d'Allos and Vars. Addresses are available at tourist offices.

CRAFTS AND GASTRONOMY

Woodcarving and painting – The **Queyras** is undoubtedly the most famous of Alpine regions for the skill of its woodcarvers. The Maison de l'Artisanat, 05350 Ville-Vieille, ☎ 04 92 46 75 06 has a fine selection of wooden objects as well as other handicraft samples. Arvieux, on the other hand is famous for its traditional toys, on sale at a local cooperative: L'Alpin chez soi, 05350 Arvieux, ☎ 04 92 46 73 86.

Wood painting is the speciality of the **Chartreuse** region, in the area of Entremont-le-Vieux.

A Queyras speciality

Objects and furniture made by craftsmen from the Queyras region are not usually painted or varnished (but sometimes stained) and have to meet with five criteria to be granted the Queyras seal of origin:
– the article must be made in the region by a local craftsman;
– it must be entirely made of solid pine;
– it must be decorated with traditional carved motifs from the Queyras region;
– the parts must be joined with pegs, dovetailed and all be hand-made;
– at least 20% of the surface of the object or piece of furniture must be carved.

Salt box from Queyras

F.X. Emery/Musée Départemental, Gap

Opinel, the famous knife from Savoie – At the end of the 19C, a toolmaker from a village close to St-Jean-de-Maurienne, began making pocket knives in his spare time. He met with such success that he launched into the manufacture of knives in a big way and in 1890 he put the finishing touch to his famous knife and offered it to his clientele in 12 sizes; at first these knives were sold on local markets and fairs, but their fame gradually spread to Italy and Switzerland. In 1905, a seal was added as a mark of authenticity. Today the knives are still manufactured in Cognin near Chambéry: the tempered-steel blade is held by a beech handle and pivoting safety ring. It is listed in the Modern Art Museum in New York as an industrial object of permanent usefulness. There is an Opinel Museum in St-Jean-de-Maurienne.

© Opinel

Earthenware and santons – These are the speciality of the **Haute-Provence** region. **Faïences de Moustiers** are world famous but there are other earthenware workshops in Barcelonnette, Reillanne and St-Michel-l'Observatoire. Fine pottery is manufactured in the nearby towns of Forcalquier and Castellane. **Santons** (human and animal figures which make up a Provençal Christmas crib) are handmade and painted in Riez, Gréoux-les-Bains, Champtercier, Volx and Manosque.

Gastronomy – Cheese and wine in the north and olive oil and honey in the south are the main Alpine specialities.

Cheeses – Below are the addresses of some places where it is possible to watch cheese being made:
– Cave coopérative du val d'Aillon (Tomme des Bauges).
– Cave coopérative du Beaufort, ☎ 04 79 07 08 28 (Beaufort cheese).
– St-François-de-Longchamp: it is possible to watch Beaufort being made in high-pasture chalets at the Col de la Madeleine.

Wines – Two itineraries offer the opportunity of discovering and tasting wines from Savoie: the "red itinerary" starts from Chambéry and goes through the Combe de Savoie via Apremont, Montmélian and Challes-les-Eaux; the "blue itinerary" skirts the shores of the Lac du Bourget. Below are some useful addresses:
– Coopératives des vins de Savoie in Ruffieux, ☎ 04 79 54 51 08.
– Coopératives viticoles de Cruet, ☎ 04 79 84 28 52.
– Comité interprofessionnel des vins de Savoie, 3 rue du Château, 73000 Chambéry, ☎ 04 79 33 44 16, has a list of cooperatives where tasting is available.

The French shores of Lake Geneva produce a white wine called Roussette de Savoie which is very palatable served with fried fish; several local inns have it on their menu, particularly in Excevenex, Port de Séchex, Corzent, Amphion-les-Bains...

Olive oil – The production is concentrated in the Alpes-de-Haute-Provence *département*; the Moulin de l'Olivette, place de l'Olivette in Manosque, ☎ 04 92 72 00 99, produces and sells high-quality olive oil and suggests ways of using it. There are other mills in Oraison (Moulin Paschetta) and Peyrus (Moulin Mardaric).

Honey – The Haute-Provence region produces large quantities of honey from a whole variety of plants; lavender honey comes essentially from the Alpes-de-Haute-Provence *département*. There are two official seals of origin, namely "miel de lavande" and "miel toutes fleurs de Provence". The Maison du miel et de l'abeille in Riez *(for the address, see Admission times and charges)* offers an introduction to bee-keeping. Several bee-keepers in the area sell their production in towns like Castellane, Château-Queyras, Molines-en-Queyras and St-Véran (Maison du miel, ☎ 04 92 45 82 47).

Calendar of events

Mid-December to early May

L'Alpe-d'Huez . . . . Organ concerts

3rd week in January

Avoriaz . . . . Film Festival

March

Chamrousse . . . . Comic Film Festival

Mid-April to early May

Orcières-Merlette . . . . Jazz Festival

Digne-les-Bains . . . . Film Festival

Gréoux-les-Bains . . . . Spring Music Festival

End of May

Évian . . . . Music Festival (Rencontres Musicales d'Évian)

Weekend after Whitsun

Moustiers-Ste-Marie . . . . . . "Faïence" Festival

July to early September

Chambéry . . . . Rousseau Evening at Les Charmettes

July

Aix-les-Bains . . . . Light Opera Festival (Estivades d'opérette)

Château-Arnoux . . . . Jazz and Pop Music Festival

Digne-les-Bains . . . . Jazz Festival

Grenoble . . . . Short Film Festival

Manosque . . . . Jean Giono Festival

Weekend of 14 July

Les Arcs . . . . International Haute-Tarentaise Folklore Festival

Bourg-St-Maurice . . . . Edelweiss Festival

16 July

St-Véran . . . . Pilgrimage to the Chapelle Notre-Dame-de-Clausis

2nd fortnight in July

Digne-les-Bains . . . . Music Festival (Sonates d'été)

Château de Tallard . . . . "Son et lumière": a thousand years of history

26 July

Ceillac . . . . Pilgrimage to the Lac Ste-Anne

End of July

Le Bourget-du-Lac . . . . Lake Festival

July and August

L'Alpe-d'Huez . . . . Organ concerts

Combloux . . . . Musical evenings (Heures musicales)

Courchevel . . . . Baroque Music Festival

Gréoux-les-Bains . . . . Theatre Festival in the courtyard of the castle

Notre-Dame-des-Neiges . . . Organ concerts

Mont-Dauphin . . . . Historic Show with light effects

St-André-de-Rosans . . . . "Son et lumière" Historic Show

Simiane-la-Rotonde . . . . Ancient Music Festival (Les riches heures musicales)

End of July and early August

Allos . . . . Music in Notre-Dame-de-Valvert

Digne-les-Bains . . . . Summer Film Festival (Cinéma d'été)

Sisteron . . . . Night Shows at the Citadel (Nuits de la Citadelle)

Early August

L'Alpe-d'Huez . . . . Feast of Notre-Dame-des-Neiges

Digne-les-Bains . . . . Lavender Festival, Procession of floats (corso)

Forcalquier . . . . Singing Festival (Festival Les Voix)

Manosque . . . . Luberon International Festival

Seyne . . . . Mule Show

1st Saturday in August
Annecy . . . . Lake Festival with musical fireworks display

1st weekend in August
Entrevaux . . . . Entrevaux in the Middle Ages

1st week in August
Megève . . . . Jazz Festival

15 August
Chamonix . . . . Guides Festival (Blessing of ice axes and ropes)
La Grave. . . . . Mass and Blessing of the Mountain – Guides Festival
Peisey-Nancroix . . . . Costume and Mountain Festival
St-Martin-de-Belleville . . . . Pilgrimage to Notre-Dame-de-Vie

16 August
Pont de Cervières . . . . Dance of the Swords "Bacchu Ber"

Mid-August
Château de Clermont . . . . . "Son et lumière"

Sunday after 15 August
Thorens-Glières . . . . Procession of floats with singing and dancing

3rd weekend in August
Aix-les-Bains. . . . . Flower Festival

1st Sunday in September
Notre-Dame-de-Belleville . . Pilgrimage to Notre-Dame-de-Vie

1st week in September
Moustiers-Ste-Marie . . . . . . Feast of "Diane"

Early October
Digne-les-Bains . . . . International Accordion Festival

Mid-October
Chambéry . . . . Cartoon Festival

November
Isola . . . . Chestnut Festival

1st fortnight in November
Château-Arnoux . . . . Art Festival

Late November early December
Autrans . . . . International Film Festival on the theme of "ice and snow"

Late December
Château-Arnoux . . . . Crib
Forcalquier . . . . International Balloon Show *(Montgolfiades)*

Sporting events

Early January to mid-August
Avoriaz. . . . . Alpine skiing Wolrd Championships, Paragliding Open Championship

Late January to mid-July
Châtel. . . . . Vasilopette (cross-country race), Paragliding Championship

Winter season
Courchevel. . . . . Several ski shows

Early January
Champagny-en-Vanoise. . . . Sledge-dog racing

Mid-January
Haute-Maurienne . . . . Alpirod (European dog-sledge racing)

Last Sunday in January
Autrans . . . . "Foulée blanche" (cross-country skiing across the Vercors Plateau)

Late January
Chamonix . . . . Alberg-Kandahar (downhill race)

Early March
Megève . . . . Dog-sledge racing
Valloire . . . . Snowboard Jumping Competition

Traditional festivals and specialist fairs

Lumber-jacks' competition

Further reading

History

First Lady of Versailles: Mary Adelaide of Savoy, Dauphine of France - Lucy Norton

Princesse of Versailles: The Life of Marie Adelaide of Savoy - Charles Elliott

The Eagles of Savoy: The House of Savoy in Thirteenth Century Europe - Eugene L Cox

Victor Amadeus II: Absolutism in the Savoyard State, 1675-1730 - Geoffrey Symcox

Tears of Glory: The Betrayal of Vercors, 1944 - Michael Pearson

Mountaineering and skiing

Mont Blanc: Discovery and Conquest of the Giant of the Alps - Stefano Ardito

The Mont Blanc Massif: The 100 Finest Routes - Gaston Rebuffat

Savage Snows: The Story of Mont Blanc - Walt Unsworth

High Level Route, Chamonix, Zermatt, Saas: Ski Mountaineering in the Mont Blanc Range and Pennine Alps - Eric Roberts

The Alpine 4000m Peaks by the Classic Routes: A Guide for Mountaineers - Richard Goedeke, translated by Hill Neate

The Summits of Samivel - Samivel

A History of Mountain Climbing - Roger Frison-Roche

Films and the French Alps

Most of the recommended films are in English but a few of the better known French ones have been included. Local locations and settings are given.

The Eagle with the Two Heads (1948) - Jean Cocteau; Vizille

La Bride sue le Cou (1961) - Roger Vadim; St-Nizier-du-Moucherotte

Murmur of the Heart (1971) - Louis Malle; Aix-les-Bains

Allons z'enfants (1980) - Yves Boisset; Curial district in Chambéry

The Woman Next Door (1981) - François Truffaut; Grenoble

Louis: Enfant Roi (1993) - Roger Planchon; Baroque chapel in the Musée Dauphinois in Grenoble

Les Marmottes (1993) - Elie Chouraqui; Chamonix

Le Parfum d'Yvonne (1994) Patrice Leconte; a passionate liaison in a luxury hotel in Evian on the banks of Lake Geneva

Rien ne vas plus (1997) - Claude Chabrol; Aix-les-Bains

Admission times and charges

As admission times and charges are liable to alteration, the information printed below is for guidance only. Where it has not been possible to obtain up-to-date information, details from the previous edition of the guide are printed in italics.

⊙ – Every sight for which times and charges are listed below is indicated by the symbol ⊙ after the title in the Sights Section of the guide.

Order – The sights are listed below in the same order as in the Sights Section of the guide.

Dates – Dates given are inclusive. The term weekends means Saturdays and Sundays; the term holidays means public holidays.

Last admission – Ticket offices usually shut 30min before closing time; only exceptions are mentioned below.

Charge – The charge given is for an individual adult. Concessionary rates may be available for families, children, students, senior citizens and the unemployed. In some cases admission is free on certain days. Many places offer special rates for group bookings and some have special days for group visits. Large parties should apply in advance.

Guided tours – Where there are regular, organised lecture tours of towns or their historic districts (usually during the tourist season), this is indicated below.
Most tours are conducted by French-speaking guides but in some cases, the term "guided tours" may cover group-visiting with recorded commentaries. Some of the larger and more frequented sights may offer guided tours in other languages.
The symbol 🄰 indicates that a tour is given by a lecturer from the Historic Monuments Association (Caisse Nationale des Monuments Historiques et des Sites); enquire at the ticket office or book stall.

Churches and chapels – They are usually closed from noon to 2pm and do not admit visitors during services. Times are indicated if the interior is of special interest and if the church or chapel has unusual opening times. Visitors to chapels are often accompanied by the person who keeps the key; a donation is welcome.

& **Facilities for disabled visitors** – As the range of possible facilities is great (for impaired mobility, sight and hearing), visitors are advised to telephone in advance to check what is available.

🄱 **Tourist offices** – The addresses and telephone numbers are given for local tourist offices, which provide information on local market days, early closing days, local religious holidays etc. In some small towns, you will need to apply to the "Mairie" (town hall) for information.

A

ABONDANCE
🄱 74360 ☎ 04 50 73 02 90

Abbey cloisters – Open July and August, daily except Sundays and holidays, 10am to midday and 2pm to 6pm (5pm from 20 December to March, closed Sunday afternoons), 10F; guided tours (30min), 10am and 2pm, 20F. ☎ 04 50 73 02 90.

Abbey church – Open daily except Sunday mornings and during services, 10am to midday and 2pm to 6pm.

Museum of Religious Art – Guided tours (30min) June to August, daily except Sunday mornings and holidays, 10am to midday and 2pm to 6pm. No charge. ☎ 04 50 73 02 90.

ABRIÈS
🄱 05460 ☎ 04 92 46 72 26

Jilly Chair-lift – In summer, operates July and August, daily 9am to 12.30pm and 1.30pm to 4.30pm. 26F return (enquire about the transport of mountain bikes). ☎ 04 92 46 78 08.

AIX-LES-BAINS
🄱 place Maurice-Mollard – 73100 ☎ 04 79 35 05 92

Guided tour of the town – Organised by the association "Au fil de l'eau". Apply to the tourist office.

Musée Faure – Open daily except Tuesdays, 9.30am to midday and 1.30pm to 6pm (open 2pm at weekends). 20F. ☎ 04 79 61 06 57.

Thermes nationaux – Guided tour (1hr) May to 15 October daily 3pm, 16 October to April Wednesday 3pm. Closed 1 May, 14 July, 15 August and 25 December to 15 January. 20F. ☎ 04 79 35 38 50.

Musée d'Archéologie et de Préhistoire – Same as the tourist office. Open May to September weekdays 8.45am to midday and 2pm to 7pm, Sundays and holidays 9.30am to 12.30pm and 2pm to 6pm; September to April 8.45am to midday and 2pm to 6pm. No charge. ☎ 04 79 35 05 92.

Boat trips – Regular sailings between Aix-les-Bains and Le Bourget-du-Lac several times a week. 52F return.
– Simple tour of the lake: 2hr. 70F.
– Extensive tour of the lake: 3hr. 80F.
– Guided trip to the Rhône River via the Savière Canal: 4hr. 95F.
– Boat trip and tour of the Abbaye de Hautecombe: daily except Tuesdays. 2hr 15min. 52F return.
Apply to Bateaux du Lac du Bourget et du Haut-Rhône, Grand Port, 73100 Aix-les-Bains, ☎ 04 79 88 92 09.

Aquarium – Open July to 15 September, daily 10am to midday and 2pm to 8pm (closes 6pm in September); May and June 2pm to 6pm; February to April weekends 2pm to 6pm. 24F. ☎ 04 79 61 08 22.

L'ALBANAIS

Rumilly – **Guided tour of the town** in July and August; apply to the tourist office, ☎ 04 50 64 58 32.
Chapelle Notre-Dame-de-l'Aumône – Open 2pm to 6pm. 10F. Apply to the tourist office.
Musée de l'Albanais – Open July to 15 September 10am to noon and 3pm to 7pm; June 9am to 11am and 2pm to 6pm; closed Tuesdays. 10F. ☎ 04 50 64 58 32.

Alby-sur-Chéran – **Guided tour of the town** in July and August; apply to Maison du pays d'Alby, ☎ 04 50 68 11 99.
Musée de la Cordonnerie – Only visited as part of the guided tour of the town; apply to Maison du pays d'Alby.
Canoe trips through the Gorges du Chéran – During the season, bookings from Société Kokopelly, ☎ 04 50 68 21 96.

Gruffy: Musée de la Nature – *Open mid-March to mid-November, Tuesdays to Sundays 2pm to 6pm. 20F.* ☎ *04 50 77 58 60.*

Marcellaz-Albanais: Musée l'Art de l'enfance – Open April to October, Mondays, Wednesdays, Thursdays and Sundays 2pm to 8pm. 26F (children 13F). ☎ 04 50 69 73 74.

Château de Clermont – *Open May to October 2pm to 6pm; mid-June to mid-September 11am to 9pm with lunch break. Admission charge not available.* ☎ *04 50 69 63 15.*

Vaulx: Jardins secrets – Open July to 14 September, daily 1.30pm to 7pm; 15 September to 2 November and Easter to June, weekends and holidays only. 30F. ☎ 04 50 60 53 18.

ALBERTVILLE
🖪 11 rue Pargoud – 73200 ☎ 04 79 32 04 22

Guided tour of the town 🅰 – Apply to the tourist office.

Maison des 16es Jeux olympiques – Open July and August, daily except Sunday mornings 9am to 7pm; September to June, daily except Sundays 9am to noon and 2pm to 6pm. 15F. ☎ 04 79 37 75 71.

Conflans
🖪 11 rue Pargoud, Albertville – 73200 ☎ 04 79 32 04 22

Guided tour of the town 🅰 – Apply to the tourist office in Albertville.

Château Manuel de Locatel – Guided tour (45min) daily in July and August, every hour from 3pm to 5pm, Sundays and holidays from 15 May to June, at 2.30pm and 4.30pm. 10F. ☎ 04 79 32 29 93.

Maison Rouge – Open June to September, daily 10am to noon and 2pm to 7pm; October to 3 November, daily except Tuesdays 2pm to 7pm; April and May, weekends 10am to noon and 2pm to 7pm; closed the rest of the year. 15F. ☎ 04 79 32 57 42.

ALLEVARD
🖪 place de la Résistance – 38580 ☎ 04 76 45 10 11

Chartreuse de St-Hugon – Guided tour (30min) May to September Sundays and holidays at 3pm, 4pm and 5pm. ☎ 04 79 65 64 62.

L'ALPE-D'HUEZ
🖪 place Paganon – 38750 ☎ 04 76 80 35 41

Notre-Dame-des-Neiges – Concerts take place on Thursdays at 6.15pm in winter and 8.45pm in summer.

Musée d'Huez et de l'Oisans – Open July, August and December to April, 10am to noon and 3pm to 7pm. 12F. ☎ 04 76 80 32 97.

Pic du Lac Blanc Gondola and Cable-car – Operate December to April, July and August, all day; journey time: 20min. 79F in summer. ☎ 04 76 80 30 30.

La Grande Sure Chair-lift – Operates December to April. Foot passengers: 30F return. ☎ 04 76 80 30 30.

ANNECY

Guided tour of the town 🅰 – Apply to the tourist office.

Palais de l'Isle – Same opening times as the Musée-Château. 20F

Musée-Château – Open June to September, daily 10am to 6pm; closed holidays. 30F. ☎ 04 50 33 87 31.

Observatoire régional des lacs alpins – Same times and charges as the Musée-Château. Combined ticket.

Conservatoire d'Art et d'Histoire de la Haute-Savoie – Open July to September, daily 9am to noon and 2pm to 6pm; closed Sunday mornings from October to June and 1 January, 1 May. ☎ 04 50 51 02 33.

Basilique de la Visitation – Chimes ringing July and August, Saturdays at 4pm.

Basilique St-Joseph-des-Fins – Open daily. For guided tour apply to the presbytery ☎ 04 50 57 03 12.

Lake cruises – April to September several 1hr trips. Boats calling in every port from May onwards: 68F. Cruise with a stop in Doussard: 71F. Night cruises including dinner on board during the season. For timetables and reservations ☎ 04 50 51 08 40.

Excursion

Gorges du Fier – Open daily, mid-June to mid-September 9am to 7pm, mid-March to mid-October 9am to noon and 2pm to 6pm. 24F. ☎ 04 50 46 23 07.

Château de Montrottier – Guide tour (1hr) mid March to mid October 9.30am to noon and 2pm to 6pm; closed Tuesdays except June to August. 28F. ☎ 04 50 46 23 02.

Lac d'ANNECY

Sévrier: Écomusée du costume savoyard – Open June to September 10am to noon and 2.30pm to 6.30pm; May afternoons only; closed Sundays and holidays. 20F. ☎ 04 50 52 41 05.

Musée de la Cloche – Open 10am to noon and 2.30pm to 5.30pm (6.30pm June to August); closed Sunday mornings, Mondays, 1 January, 1 May and 25 December. 23F. Guided tour (1hr 30min) of the foundry June to September Friday, Saturday and Sunday afternoons. 33F (including tour of the museum). ☎ 04 50 52 47 11.

Seythenex: Grotte and Cascade – Guided tour (40min) June to September 10am to 12.30pm and 2pm to 5.30pm; July and August 9.30am to 6pm; closed October to April. 32F. ☎ 04 50 44 55 97.

Viuz: Musée archéologique – Open 2.30pm to 4.30pm weekdays, daily in July and August. 14F. ☎ 04 50 32 45 99.

Menthon-St-Bernard: Château de Menthon – Guided tour (1hr) July and August daily noon to 6pm; May to September Thursdays and weekends 2pm to 6pm. 25F. ☎ 04 50 60 12 05.

Massif des ARAVIS

Cimetière des Glières: Musée de la Résistance – Open mid-June to mid-September 10am to noon and 2pm to 7pm. No charge. ☎ 04 50 57 13 84.

Entremont: Church – *open daily April to October;* **treasury** – *telephone in advance* ☎ *04 50 03 52 18.*

Ugine: Musée d'Arts et Traditions Populaires du Val d'Arly – Guided tour (1hr) mid-June to mid-September, daily except Tuesdays 2pm to 6pm. 20F. ☎ 04 79 37 56 33.

Les ARCS

"Arc-en-ciel" Funicular – Operates from 8.30am to 7.30pm (7min), July and August every half hour; in winter mid-December to April. 55F return. ☎ 04 79 41 55 18.

Aiguille Rouge Cable-car – Operates daily except Tuesdays, Thursdays and Saturdays July and August 9.45am to 4.30pm, 30F; in winter mid-December to April. ☎ 04 79 41 55 18.

Télécabine le Transarc – Operates July and August, daily 9.15am to 4.45pm (6min). 55F return.

Télésiège de la Cachette – Operates July to mid-September daily 9.15am to 5.30pm (6min). 30F

ARGENTIÈRE

Lognan and Grands Montets Cable-cars – Operate December to mid-May and July to early September; 1st section: 6min, 2nd section: 7min. Both sections: 134F return; Lognan-Les Grands Montets: 83F return. ☎ 04 50 54 00 71.

Col de Balme Gondola – Operates 9am to 4pm (20min) December to mid-April and mid-June to mid-September. 65F return. ☎ 04 50 54 00 58.

Réserve naturelle des Aiguilles Rouges: Chalet d'accueil – Open June to mid-September daily 9.30am to 12.30pm and 1.30pm to 7pm (6pm in September). No charge. ☎ 04 50 54 02 24 (in summer).

L'ARGENTIÈRE-LA-BESSÉE

05120 ☎ 04 92 23 03 11

Chapelle St-Jean – Guided tour in July and August, apply to the town hall's cultural department ☎ 04 92 23 04 48.

Musée des mines d'argent – Open mid-June to mid-September, daily 9.30am to noon and 2pm to 6pm. 10F. ☎ 04 92 23 02 94.

Church – Same as Chapelle St-Jean *(see above)*.

Anciennes mines d'argent – Guided tour (2hr) mid-June to mid-September, daily by appointment ☎ 04 92 23 02 94. Walking shoes recommended; open to children over 12. 40F, 25F (child).

Réserve biologique des Deslioures – Guided tours organised by the Office National des Forêts (ONF) mid-July to mid-August (flowering season of the Alpine sea holly). Apply to the local tourist offices ☎ 04 92 23 02 94.

AURON

Immeuble Annapurna – 06660 ☎ 04 93 23 02 66

Chapelle St-Érige – Open all year 9am to noon and 2.30pm to 6pm. Leave identity papers at the tourist office to obtain the key. ☎ 04 93 23 02 66.

Las Donnas Cable-car – Operates June, July and August every hour from 9am to 4pm. In winter according to the demand. Foot passengers: 29F return. ☎ 04 93 23 02 66.

AVORIAZ

74110 ☎ 04 50 74 02 11

Télésiège du Choucas – Operates July and August, daily (on the way up only). 40F ☎ 04 50 74 02 15.

B

BARCELONNETTE

place Frédéric-Mistral – 04400 ☎ 04 92 81 04 71

Musée de la Vallée – Open July to early September, daily 10am to noon and 2.30pm to 7pm; September to June, Wednesdays, Thursdays and Saturdays 3pm to 6pm; closed 1 January and 25 December. 18F. ☎ 04 92 81 27 15.

Maison du Parc national du Mercantour – Open mid-June to mid-September 3pm to 6pm; July and August 10am to noon and 3pm to 7pm; closed Fridays. ☎ 04 92 81 21 31.
Themed hikes – July and August; apply to the Bureau du Parc.

Excursion

Le Sauze: **Cable-car to Super-Sauze** – *Operates July to August and mid-December to mid-May 9am to 4.45pm. 32F return.* ☎ 04 92 81 05 35.

BARGÈME

Church – *Guided tour July and August at 11am, 3.30pm, 4.30pm and 5.30pm.* ☎ 04 94 76 81 25.

Les BAUGES

Château de Miolans – Open June to September, daily except Sunday mornings 10.30am to 1pm and 2.30pm to 7.30pm; April and May, Sunday and holidays 2.30pm to 6.30pm. 25F. ☎ 04 79 28 57 04.

Le BEAUFORTAIN

Hauteluce: **Écomusée** – Open daily during school holidays 4pm to 7pm; Saturday 10am to noon and 2pm to 7pm. No charge. ☎ 04 79 38 81 67.

Château de Miolans

La vallée des BELLEVILLE

Val-Thorens:

Caron Cable-car – Operates July and August, Mondays, Tuesdays, Wednesdays and Thursdays (4min). 52F return. ☎ 04 79 00 07 08.

Péclet Funitel – *Operates July to the end of winter. Passengers on foot: 48F return.* ☎ *04 79 00 07 08.*

BESSANS

Church and Chapelle St-Antoine – The chapel is closed for restoration. For more information telephone ☎ 04 79 05 96 52.

BEUIL
🛈 place Jean-Robion – 06470 ☎ 04 93 02 32 58

Chapelle des Pénitents Blancs – Guided tour 10am to noon. If closed, apply to the presbytery ☎ 04 93 05 50 19.

The village of Serres in Le Bochaine

BONNEVAL-SUR-ARC
🛈 73480 ☎ 04 79 05 95 95

Fromagerie – From the shop, open weekdays 9am to noon and 2pm to 6pm, it is possible to see the workshop and watch the cheese-making process. ☎ 04 79 05 93 10.

Abbaye de BOSCODON

Abbey – Open 9.30am to 5pm (10am to 6pm in summer). No visits during services and on Sunday mornings. Guided tour (1hr 30min) several times a day in July and August. 15F. ☎ 04 92 43 14 45.

Le BOURG-D'OISANS
🛈 quai Girard – 38520 ☎ 04 76 80 03 25

Musée des Minéraux et de la Faune des Alpes – ♿ Open July and August 11am to 7pm; September to June 2pm to 6pm; closed mid-November to mid-December. 25F. ☎ 04 76 80 27 54.

Lac du BOURGET

Abbaye royale de Hautecombe: **Church** – Audio-guided tour (30min) daily except Tuesdays 10am to 11.30am and 2pm to 5pm; Sundays 10.30am to noon and 2pm to 5pm; donation welcome. ☎ 04 79 54 58 80.

Le Bourget-du-Lac: **Château-Prieuré** – Guided tour (1hr 30min) July to mid-September at 4.30pm. 20F. ☎ 04 79 25 01 43.

BOURG-ST-MAURICE
🛈 place de la Gare – 73700 ☎ 04 79 07 04 92

Musée des minéraux et faune de l'Alpe – Open July and August, daily except Sunday and Monday mornings 10am to noon and 3pm to 7pm. 20F. Out of season: telephone ☎ 04 79 07 12 74.

Excursions

Chapelle de Vulmix – Guided tour July and August, apply to the tourist office in Bourg-St-Maurice.

Hauteville-Gondon: **Musée du Costume** – Open daily except Tuesdays 2pm to 6pm; when closed, apply to the tourist office. 10F. ☎ 04 79 07 09 01.

BRIANÇON

Guided tour of the town 🅰 – Apply to the Service du patrimoine, Porte Pignerol ☎ 04 92 20 29 49.

Porte Pignerol – Temporary exhibitions in July and August ☎ 04 92 20 29 49.

Church – Part of the guided tour of the Ville haute. Admission charge. ☎ 04 92 20 29 49.

Chapelle des Récollets – Closed for restoration. Enquire at the Service du patrimoine *(see above)*.

Fort du château – Guided tour (45min) of the upper part of the fort July and August, 9am to 12.30pm and 1.30pm to 6pm; closed September to June. 22F. No guided tour and no charge on Sundays. ☎ 04 92 20 29 49.

Excursions

Fort des Salettes – Open July and August, 10am to noon and 2.30pm to 6pm. Admission charge ☎ 04 92 20 29 49.

Téléphérique du Prorel – In summer, operates mid-June to early September, 9am to 4.30pm. 1 section: 20F (24F return); 2 sections: 40F (48F return); monthly pass for 2 sections: 80F (enquire about special conditions). With mountain bike or hang-glider: 48F for 2 sections. ☎ 04 92 25 55 00.

Puy-Chalvin: Chapelle Ste-Lucie – Closed for restoration. Enquire at the town hall in Puy-St-André ☎ 04 92 20 24 26.

Le BRIANÇONNAIS

Pamplinet: Église St-Sébastien and Chapelle Notre-Dame-des-Grâces – June to September apply to M or Mme Caramello ☎ 04 92 20 27 50.

Névache: Church – Open June to September 10.30am to 6pm. ☎ 04 92 21 19 17.
Musée d'art religieux – Open June to September, 10.30am to 6pm; October to May, Sundays only. ☎ 04 92 21 19 17.

Villard-St-Pancrace: Chapelle des Pénitents and Chapelle St-Pancrace – Ask for the keys at the presbytery, 1 rue des Pénitents, ☎ 04 92 21 07 05.

Prelles: Chapelle St-Jacques – Ask for the key at the Bortino Bar next door.

BUIS-LES-BARONNIES

Church – Open 8am to noon. For a guided tour, apply several days in advance (except Tuesdays) to M Pierre Varlet, ☎ 04 75 28 07 51.

Maison des Arômes – Open 9am to noon and 3pm to 6pm; closed Sundays and Mondays. 20F. ☎ 04 75 28 04 59.

C

CASTELLANE

Ethnological Museum – *Open June to September. 10F. Apply to the tourist office* ☎ *04 92 83 71 80.*

Église St-Victor – Open July and August, Tuesdays, Thursdays and Saturdays 3pm to 6.30pm; September to June, leave identity papers at the tourist office and get the key.

Lacs de CASTILLON ET CHAUDANNE

Barrage de Chaudanne – Guided tour July to September Wednesday afternoons. ☎ 04 92 83 63 60.

CEILLAC-EN-QUEYRAS

Église St-Sébastien – Usually open; if closed, apply to Mme Imbert.

Chapelle des Pénitents – Open July to 25 August 4pm to 6.30pm. ☎ 04 92 45 05 74.

Le CHABLAIS

Gorges du Pont du Diable – *Guided tour (45min) May to September 9am to 6.30pm. 22F.* ☎ *04 50 72 10 39.*

Châtel: Super-Châtel Gondola – Operates December to April, July and August 9am to 5.30pm (20min); 2 sections. 42F return (there are day passes for hikers and paragliders). ☎ 04 50 73 34 24.

CHAMBÉRY

24 boulevard de la Colonne – 73000 ☎ 04 79 33 42 47

Guided tour of the town A – Apply to the tourist office. Departure from the "bureau des guides", place du Château.

Small train – Operates mid-April to October 10am to noon and 2pm to 7pm. 30F. ☎ 04 79 33 42 47.

Musée savoisien – Open daily except Tuesdays 10am to noon and 2pm to 6pm; closed holidays. 20F (guided tour: 30F). Possibility of combined ticket (see Les Charmettes). ☎ 04 79 33 44 48.

Cathédrale métropolitaine – Guided tour organised by the tourist office. ☎ 04 79 85 12 45.
Treasury – Open May to August 3pm to 6pm. No charge. ☎ 04 79 33 23 91.

Château – Guided tour (1hr) May to September, daily at 2.30pm; 3.30pm, 4.30pm and 5.30pm as well in July and August. Meeting point: Tour de la Trésorerie. 25F. ☎ 04 79 33 42 47.

Peal of 70 bells – Guided tour May to September at 11.30am. 30F. Bookings from the tourist office.

Musée des Beaux-Arts – Open daily except Tuesdays 10am to noon and 2pm to 6pm; closed holidays. 20F (guided tour: 30F). ☎ 04 79 33 75 03.

Église St-Pierre-de-Lémenc – Open Saturdays 5pm to 6pm and Sundays 9.30am to 10.30am. ☎ 04 79 39 35 53.

Excursion

Les Charmettes – Open 10am to noon and 2pm to 6pm (4.30pm October to March); closed Tuesdays and holidays. Combined ticket with the Musée savoisien and Musée des Beaux-Arts: 20F. ☎ 04 79 33 39 44.

CHAMONIX-MONT-BLANC

place Triangle de l'Amitié – 74400 ☎ 04 50 53 00 24

Musée Alpin – ♿ Open 2pm to 7pm (3pm from 20 December to early May); closed 25 December. 20F. ☎ 04 50 53 25 93.

Excursions

Aiguille du Midi – **Cable-car** in 2 sections; departure every 30min; operates 8am to 3.45pm (6am to 5pm in July and August); closed mid-November to 10 December. Return journey with stop to admire the view: 1hr 30min. 180F (190F in July and August). ☎ 04 50 53 30 80.
Lift to Piton Central – Operates 8am to 4.30pm (6.30am to 5.30pm in July and August); closed mid-November to 10 December. No charge except in July and August (13F). ☎ 04 50 53 30 80.
Vallée Blanche – The gondola linking the Aiguille du Midi and the Pointe Helbronner operates, weather permitting, from 8am to 4.30pm in July and August, 9am to 3pm from mid-April to mid-September. Return journey with stop: 3hr. 260F (280F in July and August); half price for under-12-year-olds. ☎ 04 50 53 30 80.

Le Brévent – The gondola (10min) and cable-car (10min) operate all year except in May and from October to mid-November. 78F return. ☎ 04 50 53 13 18.

La Flégère – In summer, the cable-car (13min) operates from mid-June to mid-August 8am to 12.30pm and 1.30pm to 4.30pm (no lunchtime interruption in July and August). Return fare in summer: 78F. ☎ 04 50 53 18 58.
L'Index – The gondola (7min) follows the same timetable as the cable-car. 39F return; combined return fare for the cable-car and the gondola rides: 75F. ☎ 04 50 53 18 58.

Mer de Glace via the Montenvers – The **rack-railway** (20min) operates from May to October. 61F return; from mid-May to September, combined ticket (rack-railway, gondola and ice cave): 82F. ☎ 04 50 53 12 54;
Musée alpin – Open July to mid-September 11am to 5pm. 5F. ☎ 04 50 53 25 93.
Ice cave – Open June to September, daily 9am to 4.30pm. 15F (combined ticket available, see rack-railway above).
Gondola to the cave – Operates June to September 9.30am to 4.30pm. 13F (combined ticket available, see rack-railway above).
Rock-crystal Gallery – Open mid-June to September 9am to 5pm. Admission charge included in the rack-railway combined ticket. ☎ 04 50 53 12 54.

CHAMPAGNY-EN-VANOISE

73830 ☎ 04 79 55 06 55

Church – Open daily in summer; Wednesday at 5.30 in winter.

Télécabine de Champagny – Operates July and August, daily except Saturdays. 38F. ☎ 04 79 55 06 55.

Le CHAMPSAUR

Prapic: **Museum** – Open mid-June to early September 9am to 6pm. 15F. ☎ 04 92 55 62 58.

Massif de CHAMROUSSE

Chamrousse: **Croix de Chamrousse** – The cable-car (6min) operates from early June to early September, 8am to 12.30pm and 1.30 to 5pm and from early December to April 9am to 5pm. 37F return. ☎ 04 76 89 91 08.

Massif de la CHARTREUSE

La Correrie: **Musée Cartusien** – Open April to October 10am to noon and 2pm to 6pm; May to September 9.30am to noon and 2pm to 6.30pm. 12F. ☎ 04 76 88 60 45.

Voiron: **Chartreuse Cellars** – Guided tour (45min) daily 8.30am to 11.30am and 2pm to 6.30pm; November to Easter, closed weekends and holidays. No charge. ☎ 04 75 05 81 77.

Les Échelles: **Tour of the caves** – Departure from the Auberge du Tunnel; guided tour (1hr) June to September 10am to 6pm; October to May weekends 10am to 6pm. The tour is cancelled in bad weather conditions. 15F, 10F (child). ☎ 04 79 65 75 08.

CHÂTEAU-QUEYRAS

Fort Queyras – Open June to August 9am to 7pm; May and September 10am to 6pm. 30F. ☎ 04 92 46 83 73.

Espace géologique – Open mid-June to mid-September daily 10.30am to noon and 2.30pm to 6pm. 20F. ☎ 04 92 45 06 23.

Fort Queyras, Château-Queyras

Gorges du CIANS

Lieuche: **Church** – If the church is closed, apply to Mme Daniel Augusta. ☎ 04 93 05 01 65.

CLUES DE HAUTE-PROVENCE

Notre-Dame d'Entrevignes – To visit the chapel, apply to the town hall in Sigale. ☎ 04 93 05 83 52.

COLMARS   🛈 1 place Joseph-Girieud – 04370 ☎ 04 92 83 41 92

Church – Open May to September. October to April, the Chapelle St-Martin alone is open. ☎ 04 92 83 47 65.

Fort de Savoie – Guided tour (1hr 30min) July and August at 10am. 20F. September to June, apply to the tourist office. ☎ 04 92 83 43 21.

Les CONTAMINES-MONTJOIE   🛈 place de la Mairie – 74170 ☎ 04 50 47 01 58.

Le Signal – The Gorge and Signal Gondolas operate July and August daily 8.45am to 5pm; combined journey: 20min. 56F return. ☎ 04 50 47 02 05.

COURCHEVEL   🛈 La Croisette – 73120 ☎ 04 79 08 00 29

La Saulire – The Verdon Gondola and Saulire Cable-car operate early July to August Tuesdays and Thursdays 9.30am to 5pm. Combined journey: 18min. Foot-passenger fare: 44F in summer. ☎ 04 79 08 04 09.

411

COURCHEVEL

Télécabine des Chenus – Operates daily, except Saturdays, during July and August. 20F.

Mont Bel-Air – The Télécabine d'Arondiaz operates Wednesdays and Sundays from 9am to 12.30pm and 1.45pm to 5pm between mid-July and 20 August. 28F.

Route de la CROIX DE FER

Hydrelec – Open mid-June to mid-September daily except Tuesdays 10am to 6pm; other times, weekends 2pm to 6pm; school holidays daily except Tuesdays 2pm to 6pm; closed 1 January, 1 May and 25 December. No charge. ☎ 04 76 80 78 00.

D

Les DEUX-ALPES

Viewpoints

Glacier du Mont-de-Lans and Grotte de glace – The Jandri-Express Cable-car and the Dôme-Express funicular operate mid-June to early September and late November to late April. 7.30am to 5.30pm. 105F return (117F including admission to the ice cave). ☎ 04 76 79 75 00.

Croisière Blanche – Excursion by tracked minibus (45min). Booking necessary; apply to the "Service des pistes des Deux-Alpes 3200". 140F including the cable-car journey, the tour of the ice cave and the minibus excursion (excursion alone: 40F). ☎ 04 76 79 75 00.

DIE
☒ Quartier St-Pierre – 26150 ☎ 04 75 22 03 03

Chapelle St-Nicolas – Can be visited when the town hall is open, 9am to noon and 1.30pm to 4pm; closed weekends and holidays. ☎ 04 75 22 06 19.

Museum – Open July and August 3.30pm to 6.30pm; June and September, Tuesdays and Fridays only; closed Sundays and holidays. 20F. ☎ 04 75 22 00 69.

Excursion

Abbaye de Valcroissant – Private property. Guided tour June to September, apply to the tourist office. 20F. ☎ 04 75 22 12 70.

DIGNE-LES-BAINS
☒ Rond-Point du 11 Novembre – 04000 ☎ 04 92 36 62 62

Guided tour of the town – Apply to the tourist office.

Musée de Digne – Closed for refurbishing; opening planned in 2000. ☎ 04 92 31 45 29.

Musée d'art religieux – Open July to September 10am to 6pm. No charge. ☎ 04 92 31 34 61.

Musée de la Seconde Guerre mondiale – Open July to September 2pm to 6pm; October to June Wednesdays 2pm to 5pm. No charge. ☎ 04 92 31 28 95.

Jardin botanique des Cordeliers – Open April to September 9am to noon and 4pm to 6pm (7pm in summer); closed Mondays, Sundays and holidays. ☎ 04 92 31 42 73.

Ancienne cathédrale Notre-Dame-du-Bourg – Open every afternoon. Enquire at the tourist office.

Fondation Alexandra-David-Neel – Guided tour (45min) early July to late September at 10.30am, 2pm, 3.30pm and 5pm; October to June at 10.30am, 2pm and 4pm. No charge. ☎ 04 92 31 32 38.

Centre and Musée de Géologie – Open all year weekdays 9am to noon and 2pm to 5.30pm (4.30pm on Fridays); April to October weekends as well, same times; closed from 24 December to 3 January. 25F. ☎ 04 92 36 70 70.

E

EMBRUN
☒ place Général-Dosse – 05200 ☎ 04 92 43 72 72

Guided tour of the town – Apply to the tourist office.

Small train – Operates July and August at 10.15am and 5pm. Departure from the lakeside. Several formulae from 30F upwards. Enquire at the tourist office.

Cathédrale Notre-Dame-du-Réal – Closed on Wednesdays during term time and during services.

Treasury – Guided tour (45min) July and August, Mondays and Wednesdays at 4pm, Tuesdays and Thursdays at 11am. September to June by appointment. 25F. ☎ 04 92 43 72 72.

Maison des Chanonges –

Tour Brune – Open mid-June to mid-September, daily 10.30am to 12.30pm and 3pm to 7.30pm; open also during winter school holidays. 20F. ☎ 04 92 43 23 31.

Chapelles des Cordeliers – The first and second chapels are the only ones open to visitors, Mondays to Saturdays 9am to noon and 2pm to 6.30pm (7pm in July and August); also Sunday and holiday mornings in July and August. ☎ 04 92 43 72 72.

ENTREVAUX
🛈 Porte Royale – 04320 ☎ 04 93 05 46 73

Guided tour of the town – July and August; apply to the tourist office.

Cathedral – Open daily in July and August; guided tour optional; September to June, apply to the tourist office.

Musée de la Moto – *Open daily June to late September. No charge.* ☎ *04 93 05 46 73.*

Citadel – Open all year. Access via automatic gate: insert a 10F coin.

Moulin à huile et à farine – Guided tour (30min) daily in July and August; September to June by appointment. 20F. ☎ 04 93 05 46 73.

Route de l'ÉPINE

St-Geoire-en-Valdaine: **Château de Longpra** – Open mid-June to mid-September, weekends 2.30pm to 6pm. Admission charge not available.

Aoste: **Musée archéologique** – Closed for refurbishing; opening planned for spring 1999.

ÉVIAN-LES-BAINS
🛈 1 place d'Allinges – 74500 ☎ 04 50 75 04 26

Exhibition and information centre about Évian water – Open mid-June to mid-September 10.30am to 12.30pm and 3pm to 7pm; early May to late September 2pm to 6.30pm. No charge. ☎ 04 50 26 80 29.

Bottling factory – Guided tour (1hr 30min) by appointment (except Tuesdays and weekends) at 9am, 10.30am, 2pm and 3.30pm; closed 15 December to 5 January. Apply in writing to Service des Visites, Eaux Minérales d'Évian, 22 avenue des Sources, 74503 Évian-les-Bains or telephone ☎ 04 50 26 80 80. Transport: 10F.

Boat trips – *"Tour Grand-Lac" (5hr): daily in July and August; Sundays in June and September. Departure from Évian: 9.50am. 148F.*
– "Tour du Haut-Lac" (3hr): daily June to September. Departure from Évian: 2.50pm. 148F.
– Night cruise with orchestra (3hr 40min): Saturdays in July and August. Departure from Évian: 7pm. 86F.
Information from the Compagnie Générale de Navigation, ☎ *04 50 70 73 20 or* ☎ *04 50 75 27 53.*

F

Le FAUCIGNY

Les Gets: **Musée de la Musique Mécanique** – Open January to October 2pm to 5pm; July and August 10am to noon and 2.30pm to 7.30pm; closed in November. 38F. ☎ 04 50 79 85 75.

Mont Chéry – The gondola (10min) operates 10am to 5.40pm in July, August and from December to late April. Passengers on foot are only allowed access in summer. 23F return. ☎ 04 50 75 80 99.
The chair-lift operates from early July to early September 10.15am to 5pm. 12F one way.

Cluses: **Musée de l'Horlogerie et du Décolletage** – Open July and August, daily 10am to noon and 2pm to 6pm; September to June closed 3.30pm and weekends. ☎ 04 50 89 13 02.

Mieussy: **Church** – Guided tour (30min) July and August; apply to the tourist office. ☎ 04 50 43 02 72.

Sixt-Fer-à-Cheval: **Maison de la réserve naturelle** – Open July and August 10am to noon and 2pm to 6pm; September to June 4.30pm to 6pm; closed Mondays, 1 May and November. No charge. ☎ 04 50 34 91 90.

Cirque du Fer-à-Cheval: **Chalet de la réserve** – Open July and August 10am to noon and 2pm to 6pm; September to June 4.30pm to 6pm. Closed Mondays, 1 May and November. No charge. ☎ 04 50 34 91 90.

FESSY

Musée d'Art et de Folklore régional – Open early May to November 2pm to 6.30pm. 20F. December to April by appointment. ☏ 04 50 36 31 93.

FLAINE
🛈 galerie des Marchands – 74300 ☏ 04 50 90 80 01

Téléphérique des Grandes Platières – Operates late June to August 10am to noon and 2pm to 5pm. 65F return. ☏ 04 50 90 80 01.

FORCALQUIER
🛈 place du Bourget – 04300 ☏ 04 92 75 10 02

Guided tour of the town – All year round on Saturdays. Apply to the tourist office.

Couvent des Cordeliers – Guided tour (1hr) July to mid-September, daily at 11am, 2.30pm, 3.30pm, 4.30pm and 5.30pm; closed Tuesdays; May and June, mid-September to October, Sundays and holidays only at 2.30pm and 4pm. 15F. ☏ 04 92 75 02 38.

Museum – Open July and August 10am to noon and 3pm to 6pm; September to June open Wednesdays at 3pm. 10F. ☏ 04 92 75 10 02.

Excursion

St-Étienne-les-Orgues: Church – Open mornings; if closed, apply to M. le Curé. ☏ 04 92 76 03 07.

Notre-Dame de Lure – *Open mid-July to mid-August; other times apply to M. le Curé of St-Étienne-les-Orgues.* ☏ 04 92 73 22 04.

Pays de FORCALQUIER

Montfuron: Windmill – *Guided tour (30min) by appointment; apply to the town hall.* 10F. ☏ 04 92 76 41 65.

Vachères: Musée communal – Visit by appointment; apply to the town hall. ☏ 04 92 75 62 15.

Simiane-la-Rotonde: Rotonde – Open mid-June to mid-September 3pm to 7pm; closed Sunday mornings; early April to late September, 3pm to 5.30pm; closed Tuesdays. 10F. ☏ 04 92 75 90 14.

G

Route du GALIBIER

Valloire: Church – Guided tour Mondays to Saturdays at 5pm and 6pm; Sundays at 9.30am and 10.30am. Apply to the presbytery. ☏ 04 79 59 03 96.

Monastère de GANAGOBIE

Open 3pm to 5pm except Mondays. ☏ 04 92 68 00 04.

GAP
🛈 12 rue Faure du Serre – 05000 ☏ 04 92 51 57 03

Guided tour of the town – July and August, apply to the tourist office.

Musée départemental – ⚃ Open July to mid-September 10am to noon and 2.30pm to 6.30pm; mid-September to June 2pm to 5pm (except Tuesdays); closed 1 January, 1 May, 1 November and 25 December. 20F. ☏ 04 92 51 01 58.

La GRAVE
🛈 05320 – ☏ 04 76 79 90 05

Church – Open daily June to September; October to May apply to the presbytery after 3pm. ☏ 04 76 79 91 29.

Chapelle des Pénitents – Guided tour in summer. ☏ 04 76 79 91 29.

Téléphérique des glaciers de la Meije – Operates late December to early May and mid-June to early September; 2 sections (alt 3 200m/10 499ft): 35min. Foot passengers : 98F return. ☏ 04 76 79 91 09.

Grotte de glace – Open July and August 9am to 5pm. 15F.

GRENOBLE
🛈 14 rue de la République – 38000 ☏ 04 76 42 41 41

Guided tour of the town 🅰 – Apply to the tourist office.

Musée de Grenoble – ⚃ Open daily except Tuesdays 11am to 5pm (10pm on Wednesdays); closed 1 January, 1 May and 25 December. 25F ☏ 04 76 63 44 44.

Cable-car to the Fort de la Bastille – Operates (7min) daily 10am (11am on Mondays) to 6pm (midnight April to October; 7.30pm Sundays in September and October); closed 8 to 19 January. 33F return. ☏ 04 76 44 33 65.

Maison Stendhal – *Open 10am to noon and 2pm to 6pm; closed Sundays, Mondays and 1-15 September.* 10F. ☎ 04 76 42 02 62.

Palais de Justice – For information about tours, telephone ☎ 04 76 44 78 68.

Musée Stendhal – Open 9am to noon and 2pm to 6pm; closed Sundays and Mondays. 10F. ☎ 04 76 46 01 56.

Musée de l'Ancien Évêché – Patrimoines de l'Isère – Opening planned for June 1998. Open daily except Tuesdays 10am to 6pm. Charge not yet available. ☎ 04 76 03 15 25.

Musée Dauphinois – Open daily except Tuesdays 10am to 6pm (7pm in summer); closed 1 January, 1 May and 25 December. 20F; free on Wednesday afternoons. ☎ 04 76 85 19 01.

Église-musée St-Laurent – Open daily except Tuesdays 9am to noon and 2pm to 6pm; closed 1 January, 1 May and 25 December. 20F. ☎ 04 76 44 78 68.

Musée de la Résistance et de la Déportation – &. Open daily except Tuesdays 9am to noon and 2pm to 6pm; closed 1 January, 1 May and 25 December. 15F. ☎ 04 76 42 38 53.

Musée des Troupes de montagne – Open Mondays, Wednesdays and Fridays 2pm to 5pm. No charge. ☎ 04 76 76 22 12.

Musée des Rêves mécaniques – Open 2pm to 6.30pm. 30F. ☎ 04 76 43 33 33.

Musée d'Histoire naturelle – Open daily except Tuesdays 9.30am to noon and 1.30pm to 5.30pm, Sundays and holidays 2pm to 6pm; closed 1 January, 1 May and 25 December. 15F. ☎ 04 76 44 05 35.

Musée Hébert – Open April to October, daily except Tuesdays 2pm to 6pm; closed 1 May, Whit Monday, 14 July, 15 August, 25 December and January to March. No charge. ☎ 04 76 44 66 55.

Centre national d'art contemporain – Open daily except Mondays noon to 7pm during exhibitions; closed August. 15F. ☎ 04 76 21 95 84.

Excursions

Réserve naturelle du Luitel – Open all year (free). The best time to observe the flora is June to September. Guided tour (1hr 30min) June to early September, daily 9am to 6pm; departure from the Chalet de la réserve. 40F. ☎ 04 76 86 39 76.

Lancey: Musée de la houille blanche – Open Tuesdays and Saturdays 2pm to 5pm; other days by appointment. 10F. ☎ 04 76 45 66 81.

GRÉOUX-LES-BAINS   🛈 avenue des Marronniers – 04800 ☎ 04 92 78 01 08

Guided tour of the town – Every Wednesday; apply to the tourist office.

Crèche de Haute-Provence – *Open daily 9am to noon and 3pm to 7pm (6pm out of season); closed Mondays out of season, January and February.* 25F. ☎ 04 92 77 61 08.

Excursion

Allemagne-en-Provence: Castle – Guided tour (1hr) July to mid-September, Wednesdays to Fridays at 5pm; closed Mondays and Tuesdays; April to June and mid-September to October weekends only. 30F. ☎ 04 92 77 46 78.

Le GRÉSIVAUDAN

St-Hilaire-du-Touvet: Rack-railway – Operates (20min) April to mid-December weekends and holidays 10am to 6pm; June to mid-September daily 10am to 7pm; departure every hour. 58F return (child: 35F). ☎ 04 76 08 32 31 or ☎ 04 78 08 33 99.

Laval: Church – *Apply to M or Mme Chalaye.* ☎ 04 76 71 48 60.

Château-Bayard: Musée Bayard – Guided tour (45min) July and August, daily 2pm to 6pm; mid-May to June weekends and holidays 3pm to 6pm; closed October to mid-May. 12F. ☎ 04 76 97 11 65.

GUILLESTRE   🛈 place Salva – 05600 ☎ 04 92 45 04 37

Church – Open Easter to 1 November. Guided tour summer evenings; information from the tourist office.

H

Les HOUCHES
74310 – ☎ 04 50 55 50 62

Le Prarion – In summer the gondola operates (12min) July to mid-September 9am to 12.30pm and 1.30pm to 5.45pm. 70F return. Possibility of going down by mountain bike. ☎ 04 50 54 42 65.

Bellevue – the cable-car operates (4min) December to April and mid-June to mid-September. 68F return. ☎ 04 50 54 40 32.

Parc du Balcon de Merlet – Open May to September 10am to 6pm; July and August 9am to 8pm. No picnics. 22F (under-12-year-olds: 16F). ☎ 04 50 53 47 89.

I

ISOLA 2000
Immeuble le Palvos – 06420 ☎ 04 93 23 15 15

Tête de Pélévos – The gondola operates July and August daily 9am to 11.45am and 3pm to 4.30pm. 34F return (child: 18F). ☎ 04 93 23 15 15.

Route de l'IZOARD

Col d'Izoard: Museum – Open July and August, daily 10am to 6pm. ☎ 04 92 45 06 23.

L

Lacs de LAFFREY

La Mure: Musée Matheysin – Open daily except Tuesdays 1pm to 6.30pm during school holidays. 15F. ☎ 04 76 30 98 15.

La Motte-d'Aveillans: Mine-Image – Guided tour (1hr) June to mid-September 10am to 5pm every hour. 27F. ☎ 04 76 30 68 74.

La Mure Mountain Railway – Operates mid-April to mid-October weekends only; mid-May to mid-September daily; departure 4 times a day from St-Georges-de-Commiers Station; 1hr 50min one way. 80F one way, 97F return (child: 69F). Timetable available from the station. ☎ 04 76 72 57 11.

M

MANE

Église St-André – Closed Sunday afternoons.

Excursions

Notre-Dame de Salagon – Open July to September, daily 10am to noon and 2pm to 7pm; April to June, afternoons only 2pm to 6pm; October to 11November, weekends 2pm to 6pm; closed the rest of the year. 28F. ☎ 04 92 75 19 93.

Château de Sauvan – Guided tour (1hr) July and August daily except Saturdays at 3.30pm; September to June Sundays and holidays only, same time; closed 1 January and 25 December. 30F. ☎ 04 92 75 05 64.

MANOSQUE
place Dr-Joubert – 04100 ☎ 04 92 72 16 00

Guided tour of the town – Thursdays; apply to the tourist office.

Église St-Sauveur – Closed Sunday afternoons.

Église Notre-Dame-de-Romigier – Open Mondays to Saturdays 10am to 5pm; information from the tourist office.

Fondation Carzou – Open 10am to 12.30pm and 3pm to 7pm (2.30pm to 6.30pm from October to April); guided tour (30min) optional; closed Tuesdays and 23 December to 5 January. 25F. ☎ 04 92 87 40 49.

Centre Jean-Giono – Open Tuesdays to Saturdays 9am to noon and 2pm to 6pm; closed Sundays, Mondays and holidays. 20F. ☎ 04 92 70 54 54.

Le Paraïs – Guided tour (1hr 30min) by appointment, Fridays except holidays 2.30pm to 4pm. No charge. ☎ 04 92 87 73 03.

La MAURIENNE

Termignon: Church – Apply to the presbytery. ☎ 04 79 20 50 06.

Avrieux: Church – Apply to the town hall ☎ 04 79 20 33 16.

La Norma: Le Mélezet – In winter, the gondola operates (7min) from mid-December to late April. 28F. ☎ 04 79 20 31 46.

MEGÈVE

rue de la Poste – 74120 ☎ 04 50 21 27 28

Musée du Haut Val d'Arly – Open mid-June to mid-September, daily except Tuesdays 2pm to 7pm; closed 6.30pm mid-December to 27 April. 20F. ☎ 04 50 91 81 00.

Plane trips – From the Côte 2000 Airfield: the "Aérocime" Company suggests several options (price per person): Vallée de Megève (10min) 120F; Vallée de Chamonix (20min) 240F; Vallée Blanche and Mer de Glace (30min) 360F; Massif du Mont-Blanc (40min) 480F. To make a booking for a minimum of two persons, telephone ☎ 04 50 21 33 67.

Viewpoints

Mont d'Arbois – The **gondola** operates (13min) mid-June to mid-September and mid-December to mid-April. Summer fare: 43F return; winter: 57F return. ☎ 04 50 21 22 07. The **Princesse Gondola** operates (15min) mid-December to mid-April. 64F return. ☎ 04 50 93 00 83.

Croix des Salles – The Jaillet Gondola operates (6min) late June to early September, daily 9.15am to 1pm and 2pm to 6pm; without lunchtime interruption from mid-December to mid-April. 45F return. ☎ 04 50 21 01 50.

Rochebrune Super-Megève – The cable-car operates (5min) 26 June to 10 September and mid-December to March. Summer fare: 29F one way. ☎ 04 50 21 01 51.

MÉRIBEL

La Saulire – The Burgin Gondola operates from Méribel Wednesdays from 12 July to 23 August. The Pas du Lac Gondola operates from Mottaret Tuesdays and Thursdays from 11 July to 1 September; journey time: 20min. Summer fare (2 sections): 58F return. ☎ 04 79 08 65 32.

Tougnète – The gondola operates from 6 July to 31 August, Mondays, Wednesdays, Thursdays and Fridays. 2 sections: 45F. ☎ 04 79 08 63 32.

MODANE

place du Replaton – 73500 ☎ 04 79 05 22 35

Fourneaux: Church – Apply to the presbytery, ☎ 04 79 05 05 93.

Excursion

Valfréjus: Punta Bagna – The gondola operates in summer, July and August Tuesdays and Thursdays 9am to 11am. One way only: 31F (child: 21F). ☎ 04 79 05 32 71.

Massif du MONT-BLANC

Gorges de la Diosaz – Open mid-June to 10 October 8am to 6.30pm, mid-May to mid-June and 11 to 30 September 9.30am to 5.30pm. 22F. ☎ 04 50 47 21 13.

Gorges de la Gruvaz – Open mid-June to September 9am to 7pm. 10F (child: 5F). ☎ 04 50 93 45 75.

St-Nicolas-de-Véroce: Church treasury – Open June and July, Tuesdays, Thursdays and weekends 3.30pm to 6pm. No charge.

MONTBRUN-LES-BAINS

L'Autin – 26570 ☎ 04 75 28 82 49

Church – Key available at the Boutique du Beffroi, a hairdresser's, place du Beffroi. ☎ 04 75 28 62 18.

Excursion

Aulan: Château – Guided tour (45min) July and August daily 10am to noon and 2pm to 6.30pm; out of season by appointment. 20F. ☎ 04 75 28 80 00.

Church – Apply to the castle. ☎ 04 75 28 80 00.

Route du MONT-CENIS

Salle Historique du Mont-Cenis – Open July and August 10am to 12.30pm and 2pm to 6pm; closed when the pass is closed. 10F. ☎ 04 79 05 23 66.

MONT-DAUPHIN

quartier des Artisans d'Art – 05600 ☎ 04 92 45 17 80

Caserne Campana – Handicraft centre open 10am to 12.30pm and 2.30pm to 7pm in summer; otherwise 10.30am to noon and 3pm to 5.30pm.

Guided tour of the walled town (2hr) – July and August daily at 3pm; during school holidays Wednesdays at 3pm. Information from the tourist office. 10F. ☎ 04 92 45 17 80.

"Vauban dans les Alpes" Exhibition – Information from the tourist office.

MONTMAUR

Castle – Guided tour (45min) July and August 3pm to 5pm. 25F. ☎ 04 92 58 11 42.

MORZINE

place de la Crusaz – 74110 ☎ 04 50 79 03 45

Le Pléney – The cable-car operates (6min) 29 June to 31 August and December to April. 42F return. ☎ 04 50 79 00 38.

Pointe de Nyon – The cable-car and chair-lift operate mid-July to 22 August and mid-December to mid-April. 49F return (ticket combined with the Pléney Cable-car). ☎ 04 50 79 13 23.

▪ 04360 – ☎ 04 92 74 67 84

Musée de la Faïence – Open April to October 9am to noon and 2pm to 6pm (7pm in July and August); closed Tuesdays and 1 May. 10F. ☎ 04 92 74 61 64.

MOÛTIERS
▪ place St-Pierre – 73600 ☎ 04 79 24 04 23

Espace baroque Tarentaise – Open daily except Sunday afternoons 9am to noon and 2pm to 6.30pm; closed Sundays from mid-June to mid-September. 15F. ☎ 04 79 24 33 44.

Musée de l'Académie de la Val d'Isère – Guided tour (45min) mid-June to mid-September, daily except Sundays 3pm to 5pm; otherwise by appointment only. 10F. ☎ 04 79 24 04 23.

O

L'OISANS

Mont-de-Lans: Musée des Arts et Traditions populaires – Open July and August 10am to noon and 2pm to 7pm; June, September and winter school holidays 2pm to 6pm. 12F. ☎ 04 76 80 23 97.

Col du Lautaret: Recorded information – Dial ☎04 92 24 44 44 for weather conditions.
Jardin alpin – Open 25 June to 5 September, daily 10am to 6.30pm. 23F. ☎ 04 92 24 41 62.

ORCIÈRES-MERLETTE
▪ 05170 – ☎ 04 92 55 89 89

Drouvet – The gondola operates 26 June to 2 September daily 9am to 5pm. 45F (child: 35F). ☎ 04 92 55 89 89.

P

La PLAGNE
▪ 73210 – ☎ 04 79 09 79 79

La Grande Rochette – The gondola operates (10min) July and August daily except Saturdays 9.15am to 5.30pm; mid-December to April 9am to 4pm. Summer fare: 39F. ☎ 04 79 09 67 00.

Bellecôte – The gondola operates mid-December to April, July and August daily. Journey time: 30min to the Roche de Mio and 40min to the Glacier de la Chiaupe. Total fare: 70F. ☎ 04 79 09 67 00.

PONT-EN-ROYANS

Excursions

St-Nazaire-en-Royans: Grotte de Thaïs – Guided tour (45min) July and August daily 10am to noon and 2pm to 5pm; April, May and October Sundays and holidays; June, September and October weekdays 2pm to 5pm; closed November to late March. 28F. ☎ 04 78 48 45 76.
Paddle-boat trips – July and August daily at 10.30am, 2pm, 3.30pm and 5pm; April to June, September and October Sundays and holidays; do not operate from 1 November to Easter. 48F (child: 32F). ☎ 04 76 64 43 42.
Jardin des Fontaines pétrifiantes – Open June to August 9.30am to 6.30pm (5.30pm in April, May and October); closed November to March. No dogs allowed. 25F. ☎ 04 76 64 43 42.

PRALOGNAN-LA-VANOISE
▪ 73710 – ☎ 04 79 08 71 68

Mont Bochor – The **cable-car** operates (3min) from early June to mid-September and mid-December to early May; frequency: every 20min in summer. Summer fare: 27F one way, 35F return; with mountain bike: 37F one way. ☎ 04 79 08 70 07.

PRA-LOUP
▪ maison de Pra-Loup – Uvernet-Fours – 04400 ☎ 04 92 84 10 04

Costebelle Gondola – Operates mid-December to Easter, July and August 9am to 5pm. Foot passengers: 20F. ☎ 04 92 84 11 54.

PUGET-THÉNIERS
▪ gare des C.P. – 06260 ☎ 04 93 05 02 81

Scenic railway – Timetable and fares: apply to the Direction des Chemins de fer de Provence in Nice, ☎ 04 93 82 10 17 or at the local station, ☎ 04 93 05 00 46.

Excursion

Puget-Rostang: Écomusée du Pays de la Roudoule – Open May to September 10am to noon and 2pm to 7pm; closed Mondays and November to February; other times by appointment. 30F. ☎ 04 93 05 07 38.

Q

Le QUEYRAS

Ville-Vieille: Maison de l'artisanat – Open July and August, daily 10am to 7pm; June and September, closed for lunch noon to 3pm; otherwise afternoons 2pm to 6pm; closed 1 January and 25 December. ☎ 04 94 46 80 29.

La Roche écroulée (rock-climbing) – Information centre open mid-June to mid-September daily 10am to noon and 3pm to 6pm. ☎ 04 92 45 06 23.

R

RIEZ
🛈 place des Quinconces – 04500 ☎ 04 92 77 82 80

Baptistère – Guided tour (30min) July to September 10am to noon and 3pm to 5pm; closed Sundays and Mondays. 25F. ☎ 04 92 77 82 80.

Musée "Nature en Provence" – Open all year 9am to noon and 2pm to 5pm; July and August no lunch break; closed Mondays and weekends out of season. 25F.

Maison de l'abeille et du miel – Guided tour (1hr) 10.30am to noon and 2.30pm to 6.30pm. No charge. ☎ 04 92 77 84 15.

Domaine de RIPAILLE

Castle and monastery – Guided tour (1hr) July and August at 10.30am and every hour from 2.30pm to 5.30pm; April to June and September at 10.30am, 2.30pm and 4.30pm; February, March and November 3pm and 4.30pm; closed mid-November to mid-February. 25F. ☎ 04 50 26 64 44.

Arboretum – Open May to September 10am to 7pm; otherwise 10am to 4pm; closed Mondays (except in July and August) and 20 November to 20 December. Itinerary marked with red arrows: 2hr; itinerary marked with blue arrows: 1hr. Admission charge: July to mid-September 7.50F, otherwise 4F. ☎ 04 50 26 28 22.

La ROCHE-SUR-FORON
🛈 place Andrevedan – 74800 ☎ 04 50 03 31 38

Guided tour of the town – Mid-June to mid-September, every afternoon. Apply to the tourist office.

Tower – Open mid-June to mid-September 10am to noon and 2pm to 6.30pm. 10F. ☎ 04 50 03 36 68.

ROUTE NAPOLÉON

Senez: Former cathedral – Open to visitors 8am to 7pm in summer, 10am to 4pm in winter. ☎ 04 92 34 21 04.

Malijai: Castle – Open same times as the town hall: weekdays 9am to noon and 3pm to 6pm. ☎ 04 92 34 01 12.

ROUTE DES PRINCES D'ORANGE

Lagrand: Church – Apply to the town hall, ☎ 04 92 66 25 35 or to Mme Coussy, ☎ 04 92 66 23 10.

S

ST-DALMAS-LE-SELVAGE

Church – Apply to the town hall, ☎ 04 93 02 41 01.

ST-ÉTIENNE-DE-TINÉE
🛈 06660 – ☎ 04 93 02 41 96

Chapelles St-Sébastien, St-Michel and des Trinitaires – Guided tour July and August by appointment the day before (minimum 2 persons); departure from the tourist office. Charge not available. ☎ 04 93 23 02 66.

Chapelle St-Maur – Same times as the other chapels.

Musée des Traditions – Tour by appointment in July and August, daily during opening hours of the tourist office.

Musée du Lait – Tour by appointment in July and August; apply to the tourist office.

ST-GERVAIS-LES-BAINS
🅸 115 avenue du Mont-Paccard – 74170 ☎ 04 50 47 76 08

Mont d'Arbois Cable-car – Operates (17min) late June to mid-September and mid-December to mid-April. Summer fare: 43F return. ☎ 04 50 93 17 30.

Tramway du Mont-Blanc – **To the Col de Voza**: operates (2hr return) all year except mid-April to early June. 86F.
To the Nid d'Aigle: operates (2hr 30min return) late June to mid-September. 129F. For timetable, telephone ☎ 04 50 47 51 83.

ST-JEAN-DE-MAURIENNE
🅸 Ancien Évêché – 73300 ☎ 04 79 64 03 12

Cathédrale St-Jean-Baptiste – Guided tour of the cathedral, cloister and crypt in July and August except Sundays and holidays; apply to the tourist office.
Crypt – Guided tour (1hr) at 10am and 11am, weekends at 2pm, 3pm, 4pm and 5pm; other times apply to the tourist office.

Musée Opinel – Open Mondays to Saturdays 9am to noon and 2pm to 7pm. No charge. ☎ 04 79 64 04 78.

ST-MICHEL-L'OBSERVATOIRE

Observatoire de Haute-Provence – Guided tour (1hr) April to September Wednesdays 2pm to 4pm; otherwise Wednesdays at 3pm; closed holidays. 15F. ☎ 04 92 70 64 00.

ST-PIERRE-DE-CHARTREUSE

Excursions

St-Hugues-de-Chartreuse: **Church** – If closed, telephone ☎ 04 76 88 65 90.

La Scia: **Les Essarts Gondola and La Scia Chair-lift** – Operate (15min) July, August and mid-December to mid-April. 39F. ☎ 04 76 88 62 08.

ST-VÉRAN
🅸 05 490 – ☎ 04 92 45 82 21

Musée du Soum – Open 10am to 6.30pm. 20F. ☎ 04 92 45 86 42.

Musée de l'Habitat ancien – Guided tour in July and August. ☎ 04 92 45 84 77. If closed, apply to the tourist office.

Notre-Dame de la SALETTE

Hostel – Open all year except November. Bookings in writing or by telephone: Service Réception, Sanctuaire de la Salette, 38970 La Salette. ☎ 04 76 30 03 65.

Le SALÈVE

Le Salève Cable-car – Operates (4min) all year except in bad weather conditions, April to October daily 9.30am to 5.30pm (8pm May to September); mid-December to March weekends only. 58F return; family fare (2 adults and 1 child): 116F. ☎ 04 50 39 86 86.

Fountain in St-Véran

SALLANCHES
🅸 31 quai de l'Hôtel-de-Ville – 74700 ☎ 04 50 58 04 25

Château des Rubins – Open daily except Sunday mornings and Mondays 9am to noon and 2pm to 6pm. 20F. ☎ 04 50 58 32 13.

Plane trips – The "AMS – Mont-Blanc Aviation" Company organises various tourist flights: Circuit de Warens (10min): 160F; Vallée de Chamonix (25min): 290F; Massif du Mont-Blanc (35min): 440F; Cœur du Massif to the Swiss border (50min to 1hr): 590F. For bookings (minimum 2 persons) telephone ☎ 04 50 58 05 99.

SAMOËNS
🅸 gare routière – 74340 ☎ 04 50 34 40 28

Guided tour of the town 🅰 – Apply to the tourist office.

Jardin botanique alpin Jaÿsinia – Open May to September 8.30am to noon and 1.30pm to 7.30pm; closes at 5.30pm October to April. No charge; guided tour optional: 25F. ☎ 04 50 34 49 86.

Barrage et lac du SAUTET

Corps: **Chapelle St-Roch** — Usually closed. Open July and August Wednesday for service.

SERRE-CHEVALIER
🛈 La Salle-les-Alpes – 05240 ☎ 04 92 24 71 88

Monêtier-les-Bains: **Church** — Apply to the tourist Office in Monêtier. ☎ 04 92 24 41 98.

Briançon: **Téléphérique du Prorel** — See BRIANÇON.

La Salle-les-Alpes: **Chapelle St-Barthélemy** — No longer open; apply to the town hall.

St-Chaffrey: **Chapelle St-Arnoult** — Closed for restoration.

Sommet de Serre-Chevalier — The cable-car operates (2 sections: 17min) from Chantemerle mid-June to 11 September, weekends and Wednesdays 9am to 4.15pm; daily in July and August. 44F return in summer; pass available in winter. Combined ticket with the Téléphérique du Prorel in Briançon. ☎ 04 92 25 55 00.

Barrage et lac de SERRE-PONÇON

Power station — Guided tour (1hr) June to September at 2pm and 4pm; closed weekends and holidays; October to May apply to EDF-GEH Haute-Durance, 16 avenue Jean-Jaurès 05000 Gap. ☎ 04 92 52 28 50. Under tens are not allowed inside the power station.

Excursions

Savines-le-Lac: **Boat trips** — The Société des Bateaux Carline organises cruises with running commentary June to September daily at 10am, 2.30pm and 4.15pm. Cruising time: 1hr 30min. 59F (child: 48F). March to May and October to mid-December bookings only. ☎ 04 92 44 26 88.

Crots: **Château de Picomtal** — Open July and August Tuesdays 2pm to 5pm. 25F. ☎ 04 92 43 12 03.

Pontis: **Museum** — Open July to mid-September daily 3pm to 7pm; by appointment in winter; apply to the town hall one week before. 6F. ☎ 04 92 44 26 94.

SEYNE
🛈 place d'Armes – 04140 ☎ 04 92 35 11 00

Church — Open July and August 10am to 6pm; if closed, apply to the town hall. ☎ 04 92 35 00 42.

Citadel — Open July and August 10am to noon and 2pm to 4.30pm. 10F. Guided tour (30min) optional. Out of season, apply to the town hall for appointment. ☎ 04 92 35 00 42.

SISTERON
🛈 04200 – ☎ 04 92 61 12 03

Citadel — Open 22 March to mid-November daily 9am to 7pm. 20F. ☎ 04 92 61 27 57.

Église Notre-Dame — Open weekdays 2.30pm to 5.30pm.

Église St-Dominique — Usually closed; apply to the museum.

Excursions

Prieuré de Vilhosc: **Crypt** — Apply to M. Giovale's farm. ☎ 04 92 61 26 70.

Notre-Dame-de-Dromon — Open July and August Tuesdays, Thursdays and weekends 2pm to 6pm; apply to the town hall in St-Geniez.

T

TALLARD

Castle — Closed for restoration.

TALLOIRES
🛈 place de la Mairie – 74290 ☎ 04 50 60 70 64

Guided tour of the town — In July and August; apply to the tourist office.

Route de TAMIÉ

Montagne de la Sambuy — The Seythenex Chair-lift operates (20min) mid-December to mid-April, daily 9am to 5pm; June and September Sundays and holidays only; July and August, daily 10am to 6pm (7pm Sundays and holidays from 14 July). 38F return. ☎ 04 50 44 51 94.

La TARENTAISE

Aime: **Ancienne basilique St-Martin** — Open July and August daily except Sunday afternoons and holidays 9am to noon and 2pm to 6pm; at other times, apply to the tourist office for the key. 10F.

Musée Pierre-Borrione — Guided tour (30min) July and August, daily except Tuesdays 9am to noon and 2pm to 6pm. 10F. ☎ 04 79 09 74 38.

THÔNES

Church – Guided tour Tuesdays in July and August. Apply to the tourist office.

Musée du pays de Thônes – Open daily except Tuesdays and Sundays 9am to noon and 1.30pm to 5.30pm; low season closed Thursday and Friday afternoons; July and August 10am to noon and 3pm to 7pm. 13F. ☎ 04 50 02 96 92.

Écomusée du bois – Guided tour July and August daily except Wednesdays and Saturdays at 11am, 3pm and 4pm. 16F. ☎ 04 50 02 00 26.

THONON-LES-BAINS

Funicular – Operates (2min) July and August 8am to midnight; June and September 8am to 10pm; otherwise 8am to noon and 1.30pm to 6.30pm. 10F return. ☎ 04 50 71 21 54.

Musée du Chablais – Open July to mid-September daily except Sundays and Mondays 10am to noon and 3pm to 6pm. 10F. ☎ 04 50 70 26 96.

Église St-Hippolyte – Open daily mid-June to mid-September; at other times apply to the presbytery. ☎ 04 50 71 03 20.

Basilique St-François-de-Sales – *Closed Sunday afternoons.*

Excursion

Château des Allinges: **Chapel** – Usually open. Guided tour mid-June to mid-September; apply to the town hall. ☎ 04 50 71 21 18.

THORENS-GLIÈRES

Château de Thorens – Guided tour (45min) July to 10 September 10am to noon and 2pm to 6pm; April to June and 11 September to October weekends only 2pm to 6pm. 28F. ☎ 04 50 22 42 02.

TIGNES

La Grande Motte Rack-railway – Operates all year 7.15am (9.15am in winter) to 4.45pm; closed for 2 weeks mid May-to mid-June. Summer fare: 78F return. ☎ 04 79 06 34 66.

Excursion

Les Boisses: **Church** – Open during services only.

Vallée de la TINÉE

La Tour: **Church** – Apply to Mme Roblès, Grand'Place, La Tour, ☎ 04 93 02 06 01.
Chapelle des Pénitents Blancs – Apply to the town hall ☎ 04 93 02 05 27 or to Mme Roblès, Grand'Place, La Tour, ☎ 04 93 02 06 01.

Clans: **Church** – *Apply to Mlle Marinette Roux,* ☎ *04 93 02 90 08.*
Chapelle St-Antoine and Chapelle St-Michel – *Same as for the church above.*

Château du TOUVET

Guided tour (40min) July and August daily except Saturdays 2pm to 6pm; Easter to 1 November Sundays and holidays only. 30F. ☎ 04 76 08 42 27.

U

L'UBAYE

Fort de Tournoux – Guided tour (1hr 30min) July and August Tuesdays, Thursdays and Saturdays at 10am and 2.30pm; departure from the Fort Moyen; walking shoes essential. Booking the day before from the tourist office or the Maison de la Vallée in Barcelonnette. 30F. ☎ 04 92 81 03 68.

Fort de Roche-la-Croix – Guided tour (1hr 30min) July and August Mondays and Fridays at 10am and 2.30pm. Booking the day before from the tourist office or the Maison de la Vallée. 30F. ☎ 04 92 81 03 68.

St-Ours: **Fort de St-Ours-Haut** – Guided tour by appointment, 7 July to 31 August Wednesdays and Sundays; 1 to 15 September Sundays only. Two possibilities: 2hr guided tour: 30F or half-day guided walk: 60F. Bookings from the Maison de la Vallée, 4 avenue des Trois-Frères-Arnaud, 04400 Barcelonnette, ☎ 04 92 81 42 69.

St-Paul: **Musée Albert-Manuel** – Open early July to August, daily 3pm to 7pm; other times by appointment (telephone one week before). 18F. ☎ 04 92 84 32 36.

V

VAL D'ALLOS

Allos: **Église Notre-Dame-de-Valvert** – Usually closed. The key is available at the Magasin "Neige, Glace et Sport", Grande Rue (ask for M Caire).

VAL CENIS

Lanslebourg-Mont-Cenis: **Espace baroque Maurienne** – Open July and August daily except Sundays 2pm to 7pm; mid-June to mid-September daily except Sundays and Mondays 3pm to 6pm. 15F. ☎ 04 79 05 90 42.

Lanslevillard: **Chapelle St-Sébastien** – Guided tour in July and August; other times apply to the presbytery. ☎ 04 79 05 90 85.

Vieux Moulin Gondola – Operates on Wednesdays and Thursdays between mid-july and mid-August. 35F.

Plateau de VALENSOLE

St-Martin-de-Brômes: **Church** – Apply to the town hall Mondays to Fridays. ☎ 04 92 78 02 02.
Tour templière – Open May to mid-September 3pm to 6pm; closed Sundays and Mondays. 10F. ☎ 04 92 78 02 02.

VAL D'ISÈRE   🛈 73150 – ☎ 04 79 06 10 83

Viewpoints

Rocher de Bellevarde – The **cable-car** operates (6min) December to early May and late June to August every hour from 9.30am to 4.30pm. Foot-passenger fare: 65F return. ☎ 04 79 06 00 35.
The **Funival** operates (4min) December to mid-May and in August during the Four-wheel-drive Vehicles Show. Foot-passenger summer fare: 55F return. ☎ 04 79 06 00 35.

Tête du Solaise – The **cable-car** operates (5min) December to early May and late June to August every hour from 9am to 4pm. 65F return. ☎ 04 79 06 00 35.

La VALLOUISE

Vallouise: **Maison du Parc national des Écrins** – Open in summer mornings and afternoons; low season, closed weekends and holidays. ☎ 04 92 23 32 31.

Haute-vallée du VAR

Entraunes: **Chapelle St-Sébastien** – Apply to the town hall. ☎ 04 93 05 51 26.

St-Martin-d'Entraunes: **Church** – Apply to Mme Liautaud opposite the church.

VARS   🛈 05560 – ☎ 04 92 46 51 31

Excursions

Chabrières Gondola – Operates (10min) in summer from 10am to 6pm; closed May, June, September and October. Summer return fare: 26F. ☎ 04 92 46 51 04.

Réserve naturelle du Val d'Escreins – Open late June to mid-September from sunrise to sunset. Dogs must be kept on a leash; picking flowers is forbidden. Admission and parking charge: 15F (Dormobile: 20F). ☎ 04 92 46 51 31.

VASSIEUX-EN-VERCORS   🛈 hôtel de ville – 26420 ☎ 04 75 48 27 40

Musée de la Résistance du Vercors – Open April to 1 November 9am to noon and 2pm to 6pm. No charge. ☎ 04 75 48 28 46.

Excursions

Mémorial du Vercors (Col de la Chau) – ⅋ Open April to September daily 10am to 6pm; October to 12 November and 24 December to March 10am to 5pm; closed 13 November to 23 December. 25F. ☎ 04 75 48 26 00.

Atelier préhistorique de taille de silex – Open April to September daily except Tuesdays 10am to 6pm (5pm October to March). 25F. ☎ 04 75 48 27 81.

Le VERCORS

Sassenage: **Les Cuves** – Guided tour (1hr) April to October 10am to 6pm. 27F. ☎ 04 76 27 55 37.
Castle – Park open all year. Castle open July to mid-September daily except Mondays 10.30am to 6pm. ☎ 04 76 27 54 44.

Villard-de-Lans: **Côte 2000** – The gondola operates (12min) 5 July to 9 September 9.30am to 6.30pm. 38F return. ☎ 04 76 94 50 50.

Le VERCORS

St-Martin-en-Vercors: **Caverne de l'ours** – Open 9am to noon and 2pm to 7pm; winter school holidays 2pm to 6.30pm. 28F. ☎ 04 75 45 53 96.

Grottes de Choranche: **Grotte de Coufin** – ♿ Guided tour (1hr) July and August several times a day between 9am and 6.30pm; April to October 9.30am to noon and 1.30pm to 6pm; other times 10am to 5pm every hour. 38F. ☎ 04 76 36 09 88.

Grotte de la Draye Blanche – Guided tour (45min) April to October daily 9am to 6.30pm; Christmas, February and spring school holidays 10am to 4pm. 26F. ☎ 04 75 48 24 96.

Grotte de la Luire – Guided tour (30min) April to September 10am to noon and 2pm to 5.30pm; July and August 9am to 6.30pm. 26F. ☎ 04 75 48 25 83.

St-Jean-en-Royans: **Church** – Open daily except Mondays.

Rochechinard: **Musée de la Mémoire** – Guided tour (1hr 30min) June to September Sunday afternoons; July and August daily; closed Mondays. 17F. ☎ 04 75 48 62 53.

Grand Canyon du VERDON

Taxi service: **La Palud-sur-Verdon**. ☎ 04 92 77 38 20 or 04 92 83 65 34.
Point Sublime. ☎ 04 92 83 65 38.

Comps-sur-Artuby: **Église St-André** – Key available at the Grand Hôtel Bain (leave identity papers).

Aiguines: **Musée des Tourneurs** – Open mid-June to mid-September 10am to noon and 2pm to 6pm; closed Tuesdays. 10F. ☎ 04 94 70 21 64.

Route de la VIONÈNE

Chapelle St-Bernard-et-St-Sébastien – Apply to the town hall Tuesdays to Saturdays ☎ 04 93 02 00 70 or to "Le Robur" Inn on Sundays ☎ 04 93 02 03 57.

Roubion: **Chapelle St-Sébastien** – Key available at the town hall in Roubion on Tuesdays and Fridays (leave identity papers); when the town hall is closed, telephone ☎ 04 93 02 10 30.

VIZILLE   🅱 38220 – ☎ 04 76 68 15 16

Castle – Open April to September 9.30am to noon and 2pm to 6pm, closed Tuesdays; October to March 10am to noon and 2pm to 5pm, closed Mondays, Tuesdays and holidays. 15F. ☎ 04 76 68 07 35.

Y

YVOIRE   🅱 place de la Mairie – 74140 ☎ 04 50 72 80 21

Jardin des Cinq Sens – Open mid-May to mid-September 10am to 7pm; mid-April to mid-May 11am to 6pm; mid-September to mid-October 1pm to 5pm. 37F. ☎ 04 50 72 88 80.

Vivarium – Open Easter to September daily except Mondays 10am to 12.30pm and 2pm to 8pm; October to Easter 2pm to 5.30pm; closed November. 28F. ☎ 04 50 72 82 28.

Useful French words and phrases

ARCHITECTURAL TERMS
See the ABC of Architecture in the Introduction

SIGHTS

abbey	abbaye	market	marché
belfry	beffroi	monastery	monastère
bridge	pont	museum	musée
castle	château	park	parc
cemetery	cimetière	port/harbour	port
chapel	chapelle	quay	quai
church	église	ramparts	remparts
cloisters	cloître	statue	statue
convent	couvent	street	rue
courtyard	cour	tower	tour
covered market	halle	square	place
fountain	fontaine	television relay	relais de
garden	jardin	station	télévision
gateway	porte	town hall	mairie
house	maison	windmill	moulin
lock (canal)	écluse		

NATURAL SITES

beach	plage	pass	col
beacon	signal	river	rivière
cave	grotte	source	spring
chasm	gouffre	stream	ruisseau
coast, hillside	côte	swallow-hole	aven
dam	barrage	valley	vallée
forest	forêt	waterfall	cascade
lake	lac	viewpoint	belvédère
scenic road	corniche		

ON THE ROAD

car park	parking	petrol/gas station	station essence
driving licence	permis de conduire	right	droite
east	Est	south	Sud
garage (for repairs)	garage	toll	péage
left	gauche	traffic lights	feu tricolore
motorway/highway	autoroute	tyre	pneu
north	Nord	west	Ouest
parking meter	horodateur	wheel clamp	sabot
petrol/gas	essence	zebra crossing	passage clouté

TIME

today	aujourd'hui	week	semaine
tomorrow	demain	Monday	lundi
yesterday	hier	Tuesday	mardi
		Wednesday	mercredi
autunm/fall	automne	Thursday	jeudi
winter	hiver	Friday	vendredi
spring	printemps	Saturday	samedi
summer	été	Sunday	dimanche

NUMBERS

0	zéro	10	dix	20	vingt
1	un	11	onze	30	trente
2	deux	12	douze	40	quarante
3	trois	13	treize	50	cinquante
4	quatre	14	quatorze	60	soixante
5	cinq	15	quinze	70	soixante-dix
6	six	16	seize	80	quatre-vingts
7	sept	17	dix-sept	90	quatre-vingt-dix
8	huit	18	dix-huit	100	cent
9	neuf	19	dix-neuf	1000	mille

SHOPPING

bank	banque	fishmonger's	poissonnerie
baker's	boulangerie	grocer's	épicerie
big	grand	newsagent, bookshop	librairie
butcher's	boucherie	open	ouvert
chemist's	pharmacie	post office	poste
closed	fermé	push	pousser
cough mixture	sirop pour la toux	pull	tirer
cough sweets	cachets pour la gorge	shop	magasin
entrance	entrée	small	petit
exit	sortie	stamps	timbres

FOOD AND DRINK

beef	bœuf	lamb	agneau
beer	bière	lunch	déjeuner
butter	beurre	lettuce salad	salade
bread	pain	meat	viande
breakfast	petit-déjeuner	mineral water	eau minérale
cheese	fromage	mixed salad	salade composée
chicken	poulet	orange juice	jus d'orange
dessert	dessert	plate	assiette
dinner	dîner	pork	porc
fish	poisson	restaurant	restaurant
fork	fourchette	red wine	vin rouge
fruit	fruits	salt	sel
sugar	sucre	spoon	cuillère
glass	verre	vegetables	légumes
ice cream	glace	water	de l'eau
ice cubes	glaçons	white wine	vin blanc
ham	jambon	yoghurt	yaourt
knife	couteau		

PERSONAL DOCUMENTS AND TRAVEL

airport	aéroport	railway station	gare
credit card	carte de crédit	shuttle	navette
customs	douane	suitcase	valice
passport	passeport	train/plane ticket	billet de train/d'avion
platform	voie	wallet	portefeuille

CLOTHING

coat	manteau	socks	chaussettes
jumper	pull	stockings	bas
raincoat	imperméable	suit	costume
shirt	chemise	tights	collants
shoes	chaussures	trousers	pantalons

USEFUL PHRASES

goodbye	au revoir	yes/no	oui/non
hello/good morning	bonjour	I am sorry	pardon
how	comment	why	pourquoi
excuse me	excusez-moi	when	quand
thank you	merci	please	s'il vous plaît

Do you speak English?	Parlez-vous anglais?
I don't understand	Je ne comprend pas
Talk slowly	Parlez lentement
Where's...?	Où est...?
When does the ... leave?	A quelle heure part...?
When does the ... arrive?	A quelle heure arrive...?
When does the museum open?	A quelle heure ouvre le musée?
When is the show?	A quelle heure est la représentation?
When is breakfast served?	A quelle heure sert-on le petit-déjeuner?
What does it cost?	Combien cela coûte?
Where can I buy a newspaper in English?	Où puis-je acheter un journal en anglais?
Where is the nearest petrol/gas station?	Où se trouve la station essence la plus proche?
Where can I change traveller's cheques?	Où puis-je échanger des traveller's cheques?
Where are the toilets?	Où sont les toilettes?
Do you accept credit cards?	Acceptez-vous les cartes de crédit?

Index

B

433

Notes

MANUFACTURE FRANÇAISE DES PNEUMATIQUES MICHELIN

Société en commandite par actions au capital de 2 000 000 000 de francs

Place des Carmes-Déchaux - 63 Clermont-Ferrand (France)

R.C.S. Clermont-Fd B 855 200 507

© Michelin et Cie, Propriétaires-Éditeurs 1998

Dépôt légal Juillet 1998 – ISBN 2-06-130101-0 – ISSN 0763-1383

Printed in the EU 06-98/1

Illustration de la couverture par Bernard DUMAS

Travel with Michelin

Maps, Plans & Atlases

With Michelin's cartographic expertise you are guaranteed easy-to-read, comprehensive travel and tourist information. And you can also be confident that you'll have detailed and accurate mapping, updated annually to make this collection the best travel companion for any motorist.

Red Guides

Each of these 12 titles, revised annually, offer a range of carefully selected hotels and restaurants rated according to comfort; From the friendly farmhouse to the luxury hotel, there is something to suit everyone.
Titles: Benelux, Deutschland, España/Portugal, Europe, France, Great Britain & Ireland, Ireland, Italia, London, Paris, Portugal, Suisse.

Green Guides

With over 160 titles covering Europe and North America, Michelin Green Guides offer independent travellers a cultural insight into a city, region or country, with all the information you need to enjoy your visit.
Each guide includes recommended main sights with detailed descriptions and colour photographs, accurate plans, suggested routes and essential practical information.

In Your Pocket Guides

These handy pocket-sized guides are designed for short breaks and are available to destinations all over the world. Drawing on Michelin's acclaimed expertise in this field, they offer essential cultural and practical information in an easy-to-read, colourfully illustrated format, to help the reader make the most of any visit.
Titles available in English, 'In Your Pocket'' and French, "Escapade".

Michelin Route planner on the Internet

With Michelin's new website all you have to do is type in your start and finish points and your route is planned for you in a matter of seconds, with travel time, distances, road numbers, and tolls, for any destination in Europe
http://www.michelin-travel.com

Michelin Green

Atlantic Coast
From the Loire to the Pyrenees

Auvergne
Rhône Valley

Brittany

Burgundy
Jura

Châteaux
of the Loire

Dordogne
Périgord-Quercy

Northern France
and the Paris Region

Flanders, Picardy
and
the Paris region

French Riviera
Côte d'Azur

Normandy

Paris

Provence

Pyrenees
Languedoc
Tarn Gorges

California

Canada

Chicago

Florida

New England

New York
City

Quebec

San Francisco

Washington DC